This scholarly and eminently readable book integrates techniques and examines the capacity of various approaches that put human beings at the center of their own self-care. I applaud Dr Michael Mayer for his monumental work, which hopefully foreshadows the shape of body-mind approaches for years to come.

– Bessel van der Kolk, MD
Medical Director, The Trauma Center, Boston University School of Medicine
Professor of Medicine, Boston University School of Medicine
Past Associate Professor of Psychiatry, Harvard University

BODYMIND HEALING PSYCHOTHERAPY is a unique addition to the literature on psychological therapy and healing. The procedures described in Michael Mayer's splendid book are truly integrative. Not only to they embrace mind and body, East and West, and "physical" and "mental" sicknesses, they coordinate external therapy with internal healing. The result is a process that goes deeply into the human psyche, one that seeks for lasting change rather than a superficial removal of symptoms. The latter approach may be a "quick fix," but a temporary one, something that will not satisfy Dr. Mayer or the readers who work their way through his book.

– Stanley Krippner, PhD
Professor of Psychology, Saybrook Graduate School

The most characteristic and self-renewing quality of any organism is its energy, and any true healing of the human organism requires both patient and practitioner to attend to the implications of that fact. Michael Mayer's conviction that energy is what joins body to mind informs his determination as a psychotherapist to redeem that junction, and he offers tools that really work to enhance and enliven it. There is wise caring in this search for contemporary ways to achieve the sublime goal of both Eastern and Western traditions of therapeutic practice: a healthy mind in a healthy body.

– John Beebe, M.D. Jungian analyst, author of *Integrity in Depth*.
Past President of the C. G. Jung Institute of San Francisco.

The most comprehensive study of the therapy scene – and more – that exists. Dr. Mayer has done a brilliant job integrating all aspects of all schools of thought as well as techniques of mind/body healing."

– Jane Goldberg, Ph.D. Psychoanalyst,
Author of *The Dark Side of Love*

The past decade has seen a creative explosion in the integration of ancient healing practices with modern psychotherapy. Michael Mayer provides an ambitious and welcome map for psychotherapists and other healers wishing to embark upon the life-changing journey of adapting these traditions into their own practices.

– David Feinstein, Ph.D.
Author of The Mythic Path and Energy Psychology Interactive

Around 1970, we in the West began our encounter with Eastern thought and traditions. The profound significance of this expansion of our worldview is now becoming evident thanks in part to people like Dr. Mayer, a psychologist who has deeply and critically explored the Eastern path to mastery and healing. Now, drawing on his 30 years of Tai Chi and Qigong practice, his explorations of ancient healing in China and Greece, his familiarity with Jung and Gendlin, and his grasp of new integrative therapies like energy psychology, Dr. Mayer provides us with a contemporary and practical integration of these paths. Bodymind Healing Psychotherapy should be read and studied by everyone who is interested in activating our untapped human potential for healing.

– Larry Stoler, MSSA, Ph.D.
President, The Association for Comprehensive Energy Psychology

Michael Mayer's practical synthesis and deep knowledge of Qigong and Tai Chi movement forms has greatly impressed me during my years administering the Esalen Institute Movement Arts Program. Michael traces the roots of these practices back to their origins and presents a very usable as well as spiritual approach to these ancient and very valuable systems. He stands out among the many teachers I've met and practiced with and has provided me with insights available from no other teacher.

– Rick Cannon, Esalen Institute,
Coordinator, Movement Arts Program

And last, but certainly not least, my Sifu Fong Ha,
Internationally-Renowned Master of Tai Chi Chuan and Yi Chuan Qigong says,

In the nineteen seventies Dr. Michael Mayer began his study of Tai Chi Chuan and Qigong with me in Berkeley, California. With continuous diligence, devotion and skill he grows and ages with me as faithful student and friend. It delights my eyes and warms my heart to witness the masterful way Dr. Mayer integrates the ancient wisdom of East with the psychotherapy of the West.

– Fong Ha, One who practices Tai Chi and Qigong

Bodymind Healing Psychotherapy

Ancient Pathways to Modern Health

Michael Mayer, Ph.D.

Orinda, California

Bodymind Healing Psychotherapy: Ancient Pathways to Modern Health
  by Michael Mayer, Ph.D.

Copyright © Michael Mayer, Ph.D., 2007
Cover Art © Mark Henson, 2007
Cover Design and Text © Michael Mayer Ph.D., 2007
Second Printing, 2007

All rights reserved. No part of this publication may be reproduced in any form by any means, electronic, mechanical, photocopying, recording or otherwise except brief extracts for the purpose of review, without the permission of the publisher and copyright owner.

Published by Bodymind Healing Publications
Orinda, California

*This book is dedicated to healing the healer in each of us...
and to those who by necessity, calling, or love
have devoted their life energy to this path.*

Table of Contents

SELECTED BODYMIND HEALING PSYCHOTHERAPY PRACTICES AND TREATMENT PROTOCOLS XV

LIST OF CASE ILLUSTRATIONS XIX

ACKNOWLEDGMENTS XXI

AUTHOR'S NOTE XXV

PREFACE XXVII
- My Life Path: Two Streams Joining *XXVII*
- My Professional Background: Tai Chi, Qigong, Psychotherapy, and Bodymind Healing *XXVIII*
- Overview of this Book *XXXI*

INTRODUCTION: PSYCHO-ENERGIA: THE LOST SOUL OF PSYCHOLOGY XXXIII
- What is Bodymind Healing Psychotherapy? Definition of Terms *XXXIII*
- Qigong: Ancient Cross-Cultural Path to Modern Health *XXXVII*
- Integrating Qigong and Psychotherapy *XXXVIII*
    - A Turning Point Patient: Carpal Tunnel Syndrome *XXXVIII*
- Summary of the Book *XLI*

SECTION I: INTEGRATIVE MEDICINE, BODYMIND HEALTHCARE, AND ANCIENT SACRED WISDOM TRADITIONS 1

CHAPTER 1: INTEGRATIVE HEALTHCARE AND MIND-BODY MEDICINE 3
- The Healthcare Crisis *3*
    - A Poignant Case Illustration: Lower Back Surgery *4*
- Impediments on the Road to Integrative Healthcare *6*
    - Corporatization of Health *6*
    - The Heads of the Hydra: Medical Dogma, Western Isolationist Worldview, Entrenched History, and the FDA Not Serving the Public Interest *11*
    - Western Medicine: Its Gifts and Limitations *12*
- Efficacy of Complementary and Alternative Medicine *13*
    - Overview of Complementary and Alternative Medicine (CAM) *14*
    - Mind-Body Medicine *15*
- Tai Chi and Qigong: Age-Old Methods of Mind-Body Medicine *17*
- Psychotherapy and Behavioral Healthcare: Two Streams Become One *21*

CHAPTER 2: INTERDISCIPLINARY AND CROSS-CULTURAL RESEARCH — SOURCE OF CLINICAL MODELS FOR MIND-BODY HEALING 23

- The Need for Interdisciplinary, Cross-Cultural Models of Psychological Healing 23
- Integrating Meditation into Western Psychotherapy 24
- Towards a Well-Rounded Psychotherapy: The Psychotherapeutic Mandala 34
    - The "Axis Mundi" of Bodymind Psychotherapies: Eugene Gendlin's Focusing Method 36
- Psychobiology, Psychoneuroimmunology, Stress, and Healing 38
- Qigong as a Form of Hypnosis 40
    - Qigong and Leading-Edge Hypnosis Research Know — It's Not Just about Relaxation! 42
- Psychoanalysis, Energy, and the Body 42
- Shape-Shifting, Clinical Hypnosis, and Ancient Qigong 44

CHAPTER 3: ENERGY PSYCHOLOGIES: TAPPING THE HEALING POWER OF THE BODYMIND 47

- Energy Medicine 47
- Energy Psychology: An "Einsteinian" Approach to Psychotherapy 51
    - The Origins of Energy Psychology 52
- Breadth of the Field of Energy Psychology 52
- The Emotional Freedom Techniques 54
- Energy Psychology Research 55
    - Use in Disaster Relief 57
    - Research on Tapping Acu-Points: Do Specific Points Matter? 59
- The Benefits and Problems with Energy Psychology 60
- Bodymind Healing Psychotherapy's Approach 70

CHAPTER 4: THE GROUND OF ENERGY PSYCHOLOGY: MODERN METHODS & ANCIENT ROOTS 73

- The Age-Old, Broader Traditions of Energy Psychology 74
    - Hypnotic Anchors and Ancient Sacred Wisdom Traditions 76
    - Depth Psychology, Ancient Sacred Wisdom Traditions, and Energy Psychology 78
    - Qigong: A Hypnotherapeutic Anchoring Method 79
- Storytelling as Qigong and Trance-Formation 82
- Widening the Breadth and Depth of Energy Psychology: Qigong, Imaginal Traditions, and Shape-Shifting 84
- The Physician's Staff: Co-Optation and Denigration of Aesclepius 85
    - The Double Snake: The Mental Image/Body Energy Dialectic 88

Table of Contents

- Bodymind Healing Qigong Practices to Activate State-Specific Transcendent Altered States *90*
    - House of Five Doors: Bodymind Doors to Opening to Energy Trance States *90*
    - 1. Activating the River of Life through Microcosmic Orbit Breathing: *91*
    - 2. Experiencing the Light of Qi: Using a Candle *95*
    - 3. Introductory Exercises for Experiencing Qi: The Energy Ball between Your Hands *96*
    - 4. Intention and the Direction of Your Qi. The Interface between Imagination and Energy *97*
    - 5. Rocking Back and Forth to Create a Healing Trance: Tai Chi Ruler *99*
- Beyond Qigong as Qigong Movements: Activating the Core Energy of our Being *101*
- Transcending and Transmuting Imaginal Traditions *102*

SECTION II: BODYMIND HEALING PSYCHOTHERAPY: THEORY AND CLINICAL APPLICATIONS 103

CHAPTER 5: BODYMIND HEALING PSYCHOTHERAPY: THE PSYCHOTHERAPY OF SHAPE-SHIFTING 105

- The Marriage of Psychotherapeutic and Energetic Approaches to Bodymind Healing *105*
- The Most Profound Qigong is Following Your True Life's Path *105*
- The Center-Post of Bodymind Healing Psychotherapy: The Transcending/Transmuting Dialectic *106*
- Bodymind Healing Psychotherapy's Full-Spectrum Approach to the Image/Body Energy Dialectic *107*
    - Shape-Shifting, Metaphors, and Psychological Transformation *110*
    - The River of Life: Healing with the Transcending/Transmuting Dialectic *112*
- The Ten Psychoenergetic Holographic Dimensions of Bodymind Healing Psychotherapy *116*
    - Qigong and Tai Chi: A Soulful Practice for Bodymind Healing *118*
- Summary of Applications of Bodymind Healing Psychotherapy in Psychotherapy and Behavioral Healthcare *120*

CHAPTER 6: ANXIETY AND PANIC DISORDERS 121

- Anxiety Disorders: Socio-Political and Economic Background *121*
- Alternative and Complimentary Approaches to Treating Anxiety *121*
    - What Qigong Offers to Anxiety Treatment *122*

- Bodymind Healing Psychotherapy's Ten Psychoenergetic Holographic Dimensions Applied to Anxiety/Panic Disorder *122*
    - Case Illustration: Panic Disorder *123*
    - Standing like a Tree Qigong — Finding Your Stance *132*

CHAPTER 7: QIGONG AND BEHAVIORAL MEDICINE: AN INTEGRATED APPROACH TO CHRONIC PAIN 133

- Case Illustration: Qigong with a Disabled Car Accident Victim *133*
- Pain and Economics *133*
- Research on Complementary Treatment of Pain *133*
    - Research on Qigong and the Treatment of Pain *134*
- Methods of Qigong and Hypnosis: Partners in Pain Relief *135*
- Dealing with Various Types of Pain: The Medicine Wheel of Possibilities *140*
- "Focusing" on the Meaning of Pain *142*

CHAPTER 8: TRAUMA AND POSTTRAUMATIC STRESS 145

- The New Biology and Somatic Approaches to Healing Trauma *145*
- Using Qigong to Modulate -the Sympathetic Nervous System Stress Response *147*
- Depth Psychotherapy and Trauma *149*
- Bodymind Healing Psychotherapy's Approach to Trauma *149*
    - Case Illustration: Treating the Long-Term, Re triggered Effects of Past Physical Trauma *150*

CHAPTER 9: ADDICTIONS 153

- Bodymind Healing Psychotherapy for Addictions *153*
- The BMHP Process for Smoking Addictions *154*
- Case Illustration: Binge Eating *159*
- Sacrifice: A Key Tool in Addictions and in Therapy in General *160*
- Twelve Step Programs *161*
- Case Illustration: Working with Codependence — A Kabbalistic/Qigong Perspective *161*

CHAPTER 10: INSOMNIA 163

- Research *163*
- Bodymind Healing Psychotherapy Treatment Protocol for Insomnia *164*
- Case Illustration: The Unresolved Issues that Invade Your Sleep *167*
- Alternative Visualization Methods *169*

Table of Contents

CHAPTER 11: HYPERTENSION 171

- Research *171*
    Qigong Research *171*
- Qigong and the River of Life: A Quick Fix for Hypertension? *172*
- Case Illustration: The Hypertensive Executive — What Lies Beneath the Surface? *173*
- Chinese Medical Approach to Hypertension *174*
- Case Illustration: Is Qigong Palatable to Fundamentalist Christians? *176*

CHAPTER 12: DEPRESSION 179

- Research: Medication Versus Behavioral Health *179*
- Exercise *179*
- Qigong: An Exercise that Is More than Exercise *180*
- Bodymind Healing Psychotherapy's Integrated Approach *181*
    Case Illustration: "I Never Had a Happy Moment." *181*

CHAPTER 13: ADDITIONAL EXAMPLES: SYNDROMES AMELIORATED BY QIGONG AND BODYMIND HEALING PSYCHOTHERAPY 183

- Arthritis, Joint Problems, and Musculoskeletal Disorders *183*
- Diabetes *191*
- Headaches *192*
- Raynaud's Syndrome *193*
- Stomach Disorders *193*
- Addendum: Bodymind Healing Resources for Chronic Diseases, Cancer, and Death and Dying *195*

CHAPTER 14: QIGONG PSYCHOSIS 197

- Case Illustration: "I'm Going to Cut My Wife's Head Off with My Samurai Sword" *197*

SECTION III: ANCIENT SACRED WISDOM TRADITIONS, QIGONG, AND PSYCHOTHERAPY: PRINCIPLES, METHODS, THEMES, AND BENEFITS 199

CHAPTER 15: PSYCHOTHERAPY AS CHANGING YOUR LIFE STANCE .201

- Shape-Shifting and Changing Your Life Stance *201*
    Case Illustration: Social Phobia *201*
    Case Illustration: Impulse Control — The Exploding Karate Kid *203*
    Case Illustration: Finding the "Right Man" *205*
- Enhance your Stance: Melanie Klein's "Depressive Position" and Qigong *206*

CHAPTER 16: INCORPORATING PATIENT GESTURES: TAPPING ON THE WISDOM OF THE PRIMORDIAL SELF 207

- The Taoist Initiate Who Sees the Sacred in Everyday Movements *208*
- Tapping the Metaphorical Wisdom of the Bodymind Using Internal Martial Arts *208*
- Phenomenologically Based Internal Martial Arts *209*
  - Case Illustration: Sexual Abuse and Fist under Elbow *209*
  - Case Illustration: The Absent Father and Karate Chop Point Patient *210*
  - Case Illustration: The Placating Professor and the Sword Mudra *212*
- Why Tap on Points on the Body When You Can Tap on the Wisdom of the Primordial Self? *213*

CHAPTER 17: AFFECT MODULATION AND TAI CHI 215

- Parallels Between Affect Modulation and Tai Chi *215*
- Case Illustrations: Affect Modulation Enhanced by Tai Chi Postures *216*

CHAPTER 18: PSYCHOTHERAPY AS AN INTERNAL MARTIAL ART: ATTACKING YOUR PATIENTS TO HEAL THEM 219

- Broadening Psychotherapy with Interdisciplinary Somatic Practices *219*
- Language, Tai Chi, and the Body *220*
- Verbal Tai Chi and the Subtle Art of Bantering: Case Illustration of Obsessive-Compulsive Disorder *220*
- Attacking Your Patients to Heal Them: Case Illustration of the Wife of the Verbally Adept Salesman *224*
- Tai Chi Practices to Enhance Empowerment and Change Your Life Stance *225*

CHAPTER 19: HEALING WITH THE ELEMENTS AND TRANSPERSONAL HYPNOSIS 227

- Transpersonal Psychology and Healing *227*
- Transpersonal Hypnosis and Healing with the Elements *228*
  - Case Illustration: Writer's Block *228*
  - Case Illustration: Flying Phobia *231*
- Anchoring State-Specific States Using the Five Elements of the Internal Martial Arts *233*
- Four Elements of Constructive Communication of Negative Feelings *233*

CHAPTER 20: THE MYTHIC JOURNEY PROCESS: CREATING YOUR OWN STORIES TO HEAL YOUR RELATIONSHIPS 237

- Mythology: The Key to the Door of Your Psyche *237*
  - Identifying and Overcoming Our Inner Demons *238*
  - Petrifying Fear: The Story of Perseus and Medusa *238*

Table of Contents

- Focusing and the Mythic Journey Process *240*
- The Mythic Journey Process *242*
    - Case Illustration: A Critical Perfectionist's Mythic Journey Process *244*
    - Case Illustration: The Passive-Aggressive Ostrich — Healing Trauma and Withdrawal *248*
    - Case Illustration: The Desperately Grasping Parrot — Healing Abandonment and Neediness *250*

CHAPTER 21: WHAT QIGONG AND PSYCHOTHERAPY GIVE EACH OTHER 253

- What Psychological Traditions Give to Qigong? *253*
- What Psychotherapy Gives Qigong? *254*
- What Qigong Gives Psychotherapy and Behavioral Healthcare *255*

CHAPTER 22: ETHICS OF INCORPORATING QIGONG INTO PSYCHOTHERAPY 259

- Informed Consent for Experimental Methods in "Emerging Areas." *259*
- Transference Issues and False Hope *260*
- Scope of Practice Issues *260*
- Standards of Care *261*
- Areas of Competence *261*
- Multiple or Dual Relationships: Mixing Qigong Outside and Inside of Therapy. *262*

SECTION IV: ANCIENT SACRED WISDOM TRADITIONS: TRAINING GROUND FOR THE MODERN PSYCHOTHERAPIST 267

CHAPTER 23: QIGONG/TAI CHI AND ANCIENT SACRED WISDOM TRADITIONS: ADDING TO THE TOOL KIT OF THE MODERN THERAPIST 269

- Psychotherapy Training: Modern Clinician as Carrier of an Ancient Lineage *269*
- Tai Chi/Qigong: Transposing Ancient Methods into Healing Clinical Interventions *271*
- Activating the Therapist's Energy with Animal Qigong *274*
- Does the Therapist-in-Training Need to Practice Tai Chi or Can One Imbibe the Essence of Tai Chi Without Practice? *274*

CHAPTER 24: HEALING THE HEALER: BODYMIND HEALING QIGONG'S TWENTY-MINUTE PRACTICE ROUTINE 277

- The Bodymind Healing Qigong Twenty-Minute Routine *278*

AFTERWORD 293

APPENDIX I: Bodymind Healing Psychotherapy (BMHP) Contributions to the field of Bodymind Healing...................... 297

- Contributions to Psychotherapy and Behavioral Healthcare 297
- Contributions to Energy Psychology 299
- Contributions to the Traditions of Qigong and Tai Chi 300

ILLUSTRATIONS 301

NOTES 303

REFERENCES 325

INDEX 351

SELECTED BODYMIND HEALING PSYCHOTHERAPY PRACTICES AND TREATMENT PROTOCOLS

Chapter 2: Interdisciplinary and Cross-Cultural Research — Source of Clinical Models for Mind-Body Healing

- Gendlin's Focusing method

Chapter 3: Energy Psychologies: Tapping the Healing Power of the Bodymind

- Emotional Freedom Techniques
- The Touch of the Elements
- Circle, Stop, Breathe, and Feel Method

Chapter 4: The Ground of Energy Psychology: Modern Methods & Ancient Roots

- Bodymind Healing Qigong Practices to Activate State-Specific Transcendent Altered States
    1. *Activating the River of Life through Microcosmic Orbit Breathing*
       Macrocosmic Orbit Breathing
       Full Extension Breathing
    2. *Experiencing the Light of Qi: Using a Candle*
    3. *The Energy Ball between Your Hands*
    4. *Intention and the Direction of Your Qi*
    5. *Tai Chi Ruler*

Chapter 5: Bodymind Healing Psychotherapy: The Psychotherapy of Shape-Shifting

- The Full Spectrum of BMHP Symbolic Process Methods
    1. *Fairy tales, myths, and teaching stories from ancient sacred wisdom traditions*
    2. *Transpersonal Hypnosis*
    3. *Bodymind Healing Qigong Methods*
    4. *Activating the River of Your Life*
    5. *The Mythic Journey Process*
    6. *Dreams*
- The *River of Life* Practice
- Ten Psychoenergetic Holographic Dimensions of BMHP
    1. *Taoist Breathing Techniques and Hypnosis*
    2. *Self-soothing*
    3. *Focusing on Felt Meaning*
    4. *Psychodynamics*
    5. *Cognitive Restructuring*

- 6. Energy Psychology Methods
- 7. The Belly Massage of Chi Nei Tsang
- 8. Acupressure and Acu-yoga
- 9. Bodymind Healing Qigong
- 10. Symbolic Process Approaches to Healing
- A Soul-Oriented Qigong and Tai Chi

Chapter 6: Anxiety and Panic Disorders

- Ten Psychoenergetic Holographic Dimensions of BMHP (illustrated in a case example)
  Taoist Breathing Techniques and Hypnosis
    Elevator Breathing
  Chi Nei Tsang (belly massage)
  Focusing
  Psychodynamics
  Self-soothing Using Acupressure Points
  Cognitive Restructuring
  Dreamwork

Chapter 7: Qigong and Behavioral Medicine: An Integrated Approach to Chronic Pain

- Yin-Yang Balancing Method
- The Energy Hula Hoop
- Finding the Healing Ball of Qi with Your Hands
- Yin-Yang Balancing Method and Touch

Chapter 9: Addictions

- Treatment Protocol for Smoking and Other Addictions
- The Sacrificial Object Method

Chapter 10: Insomnia

- Treatment Protocol for Insomnia

Chapter 11: Hypertension

- Bodymind Healing Qigong practices for Hypertension

Chapter 13: Additional Examples: Syndromes Ameliorated by Qigong and Bodymind Healing Psychotherapy

- Bodymind Healing audiotapes illustrating the *River of Life* practice for chronic diseases and cancer

Chapter 15: Psychotherapy as Changing Your Life Stance

- Enhance Your Stance: Melanie Klein's "Depressive Position" and Qigong

Chapter 16: Incorporating Patient Gestures

- Incorporating Patient Gestures (illustrated in a case example)

Chapter 17: Affect Modulation and Tai Chi

- Affect Modulation and Tai Chi (illustrated in a case example)

Chapter 18: Psychotherapy as an Internal Martial Art: Attacking Your Patients to Heal Them

- Verbal Tai Chi (illustrated in a case example)
- Cultivating the Art of Bantering (illustrated in a case example)
- Attacking Your Patients to Heal Them (illustrated in\ a case example)
- Tai Chi Practices to Enhance Empowerment and Change Your Life Stance

Chapter 19: Healing with the Elements and Transpersonal Hypnosis

- Transpersonal Hypnosis and Healing with the Elements
- Anchoring State-Specific States Using Tai Chi
- Four Elements of Constructive Communication of Negative Feelings

Chapter 20: The Mythic Journey Process: Creating Your Own Stories to Heal Your Relationships

- Mythic Journey Process

Chapter 23: Qigong/Tai Chi and Ancient Sacred Wisdom Traditions: Adding to the Tool Kit of the Modern Therapist

- Tai Chi Push Hands

Chapter 24: Healing the Healer: Bodymind Healing Qigong's Twenty-Minute Practice Routine**

1. *Standing Meditation Qigong: Revitalizing Your Energy Bank Account*
2. *Dispersing Stagnant Qi*
3. *Tai Chi Ruler*
4. *Ocean Wave Breathing*
5. *Moving a Snake through the Joints, Dipping Your Hands into the Waters of Life, and Opening Your Heart to the Heavens*
6. *Crane Walking and Flying*
7. *Walking Meditation Qigong*
8. *Wuji Standing Meditation*

* These are some of the most essential Bodymind Healing Psychotherapy Practices.
** See also the Index under "Qigong practices," and see Volume I for the complete ten sets of Bodymind Healing Qigong practices.

LIST OF CASE ILLUSTRATIONS

Introduction: Psycho-energia: The Lost Soul of Psychology
Carpal Tunnel Syndrome

Chapter 1: Integrative Medicine, Bodymind Healthcare, and Ancient Sacred Wisdom Traditions
Lower Back Surgery

Chapter 4: The Ground of Energy Psychology
Healing Depression and Other Psychological Issues with Singing Sacred Songs

Chapter 6: Anxiety and Panic Disorders
Panic Disorder

Chapter 7: Qigong and Behavioral Medicine: An Integrated Approach to Chronic Pain
Qigong with a Disabled Car Accident Victim

Chapter 8: Trauma and Posttraumatic Stress
Treating the Long-Term, Re-triggered Effects of Past Physical Trauma

Chapter 9: Addictions
Binge Eating
The Case of the Batterer and the Baby Grand Piano
Working with Codependence — A Kabbalistic/Qigong Perspective

Chapter 10: Insomnia
The Unresolved Issues that Invade Your Sleep

Chapter 11: Hypertension
A Group Demonstration of Reduction of Hypertension
The Hypertensive Executive – What Lies Beneath the Surface?
Is Qigong Palatable to Fundamentalist Christians?

Chapter 12: Depression
"I Never Had a Happy Moment"
Treating Depression with Your Healing Song

Chapter 13: Additional Examples:
Irritable Bowel Syndrome

Chapter 14: Qigong Psychosis
"I'm Going to Cut My Wife's Head Off with My Samurai Sword"

Chapter 15: Psychotherapy as Changing Your Life Stance
Social Phobia
Impulse Control – The Exploding Karate Kid
Finding the "Right Man"

Chapter 16: Incorporating Patient Gestures: Tapping on the Wisdom of the Primordial Self
Sexual Abuse and Fist under Elbow
The Absent Father and Karate Chop Point Patient
The Placating Professor and the Sword Mudra

Chapter 17: Affect Modulation and Tai Chi
Healing Trauma with Fist Under Elbow
Balancing Boundary Setting with Welcoming
Grasping the Bird's Tail (Single Ward Off)

Chapter 18: Psychotherapy as an Internal Martial Art: Attacking Your Patients to Heal Them
Verbal Tai Chi and the Subtle Art of Bantering – Obsessive Compulsive Disorder
Attacking Your Patients to Heal Them: Wife of the Verbally Adept Salesman

Chapter 19: Healing with the Elements and Transpersonal Hypnosis
Writer's Block
Flying Phobia

Chapter 20: The Mythic Journey Process: Creating Your Own Stories to Heal Your Relationships
A Critical Perfectionist's Mythic Journey Process
The Passive-Aggressive Ostrich: Healing Trauma and Withdrawal
The Desperately Grasping Parrot: Healing Abandonment and Neediness

See also the Index under "Case Illustrations."

Acknowledgments

There is a creative source of energy in the universe that can be tapped upon if we can find the way to dowse for it. There have been many names for this wellspring. The Greeks called it the Fountain of the Muses, and conceptualized it as created by Pegasus, the magical winged horse, after he was liberated from Medusa's head when it was severed by Perseus. As Pegasus leaped up to the sky, he tapped with his feet on a local mountain out of which sprang the Fountain of the Muses. Rupert Sheldrake called this field of inspired creativity the "morphogenetic field"; Carl Jung called it the "collective unconscious." Laszlo (2006) drawing from Cheney's (1996) ideas about the Akashic records called it the "A-field" — the all pervasive information field which contains the imprint of the Self on the eternal, universal, electromagnetic atmosphere of primary substance (as cited in Krippner & Conti, 2006, p. 97). Many authors have given credit to this field for the source of their inspiration; Mendeleev's periodic table of elements, and many musical works, such as that of Beethoven and Mozart, gave credit to this mystical source of knowledge and creativity. Some call it God.

This is not a state relegated only to special people. Most of us have the experience of receiving messages from some unexplained source, some higher power "speaking" to us at the beginning of, or at sometime during our day. Part of our work as human beings is to distinguish whether these messages are a call from this "higher Self," or a projection from a more limited aspect of ourselves. Rationalists would say this voice comes from our mind's synthesis of information and intuitive leaps. Those who have a spiritual stance toward life consider it to be more than that; perhaps, as Native Americans say, it's the voice of *Wakantanka*, the great spirit or the great mystery. There are at least as many stances toward the ineffable as there are feet of human beings.

The fact that such creative surges often come when our conscious mind is least active (in the world of sleep) gave rise in psychology to theories of "the unconscious," and the understanding that rational thought is just one bandwidth of consciousness. Energetic bandwidths like REM sleep and Delta wave sleep give access to other energetic bandwidths of consciousness that are equally important to our functioning and to our identities as human beings.

Regardless of what we call this creative source, for a period of one year, from the spring equinox of 2005 through the spring equinox of 2006, virtually every morning I would wake up flooded with what felt like a compelling force leading me to what I was supposed to write that day. My job was to scribble down the notes first thing in the morning, as I woke from immersion in the hinterworld of sleep, so I wouldn't forget. And then, in-between my patient sessions, and before workshop planning, I felt compelled to continue to write down what had come through me that morning. Though this period of creative flow built upon the edifice of my past writings, experiences, and thinking, which helped to gestate these perspectives, there was a felt sense of being a captive of something greater than what my rational mind could generate. So, first and foremost I must acknowledge that this book stemmed from this creative source, though my twenty-seven years of private practice as a psychotherapist helped to open the door to the creative message of this book and gave it an appropriate container to hold its contents.

In the context of my discussion in the "Preface" of two streams becoming one, I acknowledged how my thirty years of training with Sifu Fong Ha and other Qigong masters helped to form the container of my knowledge. I'd like to thank once again my Sifu Fong Ha and those other masters to whom he brought to train us, including Han Xingyuan, Cai Song Fang, and Sam Tam. As well, my Qigong knowledge and practice were enhanced by my work with Bryan O'Dea at the Acupressure Institute of Berkeley, and training in the animal forms of medical Qigong with Sifu, Dr. Alex Feng. My training was also enhanced by a wide number of medical Qigong masters with whom I was able to learn from at various conferences where I was presenting. The National Qigong Association and the East West Academy of Healing Arts are two of these organizations. An avid addict of Qigong, I have also appreciated the knowledge gleaned in workshops from of the teachings of Kumar Francis, Luke Chan, and Sat Chuen Hon. My friendship, sharing, and collegial relationship with Taoist scholar Ken Cohen was an important influence on my knowledge base in the arena of Qigong healing.

There were many influences of my early psychological training and on what was to become Bodymind Healing Psychotherapy. At the forefront was Dr. Eugene Gendlin, for whom I served as Focusing training coordinator. John Beebe, M.D., a Jungian analyst, Sam Keen, author extraordinaire; Bill McCreary, Ph.D.; and Gordon Tappan, Ph.D. influenced me as they served on my doctoral committee. And my early clinical supervisors, Larry Jaffe, Ph.D. and Ron Levinson, Ph.D., also deserve thanks. Many authors had a strong influence on my development, including James Hillman's archetypal psychology and Carl Jung's teachings about symbolic process. Various theorists of traditional psychotherapies — such as psychodynamic/neoanalytic, cognitive/behavioral, existential/humanistic, and transpersonal — and as you will see, authors of the newly emerging energy psychology also had a major influence on my perspective. As well, authors in the area of behavioral medicine and medical hypnosis were important influences, so I'd like to thank, Ken Pelletier, Ph.D., Ernest Rossi, Ph.D., and Robert Sapolsky, Ph.D. Many of these authors are listed in the reference section in the back of this book. As a child who was taught to kiss a book if it fell on the ground (due to my family's belief in the sacredness of books) I am grateful to the authors whose books deserve to be kissed even when not on the ground.

Regarding the influences upon Bodymind Healing Psychotherapy from the wider age-old, cross-cultural traditions and esoteric sources that have helped to broaden my perspective to psychotherapy, I have appreciated the writings of Mircea Eliade and Joseph Campbell on cross-cultural mythology, Felicitas Goodman's teachings about postural initiation, Edward Edinger's approach to psychotherapy as alchemy, and C.A. Meier's insights about psychotherapy as an initiatory process. And my personal meetings with Dane Rudhyar and Manley Hall will always be with me.

It is most customary to thank individual people in an "Acknowledgment" section, but other spheres of existence have been equally significant in helping authors write through the ages. Therefore I'd like to honor my temple, *Chochmat Halev,* meaning Wisdom of the Heart, for helping to restore my soul after long hours of writing. No less a temple is the special place in nature where I go to restore my soul. In this healing environment, which I call Bear Creek Mountain, I play my flute, practice Qigong, and watch the still egret, with one foot in the water and one foot on land, as he reflects in the water waiting for some morsel to emerge from the depths. I watch

Acknowledgments

in awe the quick turns of the white terns, as their mastery of flying and diving into the depths could inspire the most blocked writer to shift into a new direction. And the deer who jumps over bramble bushes, that can't impede its grace, could help even the most civilized amongst us to remember the power of primordial movements to overcome obstacles. This book surely benefited from an infusion from such spheres.

To acknowledge a major source of my instilled love for learning, I want to thank my parents, Abraham and Freda Mayer, who devoted a good portion of their lives to providing the fertile soil from which I could grow and get the best education possible. My father would oftentimes jump up from the dinner table and go to the encyclopedia when a difficult question was asked; and as my mother served delicious food, my father came back serving morsels of wisdom, transmitting to me a love of research. And, my mother's "emotional intelligence" was also high quality food for thought. Without my parents' loving efforts and sacrifices, the seeds from which this book was planted would have never met the ground.

In the preface of this book I thanked Dr. Len Saputo with whom I co-founded the Health Medicine Institute, for his assistance in grounding my knowledge base in this medical setting. I also thank him for reading over the first chapter of this book and giving me feedback. I also want to express my appreciation to my other fellow multidisciplinary health professionals there, such as Colette Devore, acupuncturist; Steve Milligan, chiropractor; Bill Kneebone, chiropractor; Dr. Calista Hunter, M.D.; June Engle, M.D.; Linda Chrisman, bodyworker and trauma specialist; and Phillip Scott, Native American chief and ritualist. They helped me to see the power and potential of collaborative relationships in integrative medicine.

As well, to those other readers who gave me feedback on my book, I'd like to thank Tarra Christoff, Mark Fromm, Ph.D., Gareth Hill, Ph.D., Jean Hayek, Sandy Rosenberg, Ph.D., Larry Stoler, Ph. D., and David Weinstein.

You've heard about the Triple Goddesses in ancient mythology. I had them working with me on this book. Tracy Chocholousek's dedicated efforts helped with copy and conceptual editing — like the sword given to heroes in Greek myths by Athene, she helped me to cut out non-essential elements and streamline my words and phraseology. Natasha Fischl, with her Master in Computer Science degree from UC Berkeley, showed devoted commitment to the book not only in formatting it with awesome skill in Adobe InDesign, but also in assisting when various technological problems occurred. When I thought I was stuck with a computer monster in a maze in the underworld — she, like Ariadne, came to my rescue and led me out to the light of day. Karin Kinsey of Dolphin Press did the final touches on formatting and, like a Goddess of the Sea, helped me to navigate through choppy ocean waves helping me to find my way home.

AUTHOR'S NOTE

The practices, ideas, and suggestions in this book are not intended as a substitute for medical attention. When considering applying these methods to various health related issues, please consult with your medical doctor and/or other appropriate health professionals. Though benefit can be gained by reading about the integrated solutions to bodymind health issues included in this book, due caution should be exercised in undertaking the inward journeys suggested here. Such inner exploration is best done with a licensed mental health professional. For lay readers, please discuss these methods with your current health professionals to see whether, or how, they can be incorporated in your treatment. For more information on trainings in your area, or finding a therapist trained in, or certified in, these methods please see www.bodymindhealing.com.

Preface

It is probably true that, in general, the most fertile developments in the history of human thought are born at the intersection of two currents of ideas. These currents may originate in the midst of totally different cultural conditions, in diverse epochs and places. But from the time that they effectively meet and maintain a relationship sufficient for a real interaction to take place, one can hope for new and interesting developments to occur.

— Werner Heisenberg

My Life Path: Two Streams Joining

My current life path began when, as a young boy, I sat on a large rock in the woods overlooking the place where two streams joined as one. While other kids were out playing baseball or drinking beer, I was more fascinated by the sound of two streams joining. This was long before the Western culture I knew, heard about meditation.

Native Americans teach that the elements of nature that draw us in our early years symbolically express a calling, leading towards our future destinies, or our "medicine ways." For me this proved to be true. In workshops I teach, after telling this story I ask participants to think about an element of nature which drew them in their childhood, and to reflect upon what it says about their destiny. I now invite you to do the same.

Long before I knew my destiny was to explore the Way of integrating the streams of body and mind, ancient and modern, East and West, my early years were spent huddled over books. I was only vaguely aware that my posture was being affected by my hunching over them. Books were my lovers and I carried the mark of a young man who spent much time embracing them — scholar's shoulders, they were called. As a child, my parents taught me that a book was a sacred thing; if I dropped one, I was supposed to pick it up and kiss it. Brought up by a family of intellectuals whose patriarch was a lawyer, I spent my youth in intellectual arguments trying to show how smart I was. The "Mind" was my God.

As time went on I became aware of the dark side of the worship of this deity. My relationships suffered from endless debating, and constrictions appeared in my body from excess mental pursuits. After being admitted to George Washington University School of Law in the early 1970s, I made a decision to forgo a career based on argument, conflict, and the worship of mind to pursue the study of healthier ways of speech and Being through the study of psychology. When my father expressed his disappointment, I said to him, "Don't worry Dad, I'll still be a lawyer, it's just that I'm going to be a lawyer for the mind, body, and spirit." And so I enrolled in a graduate psychology training program at the New School for Social Research in New York City.

As my studies of psychology and psychotherapy progressed, I found that there was more to healing than modern psychology was giving me. My worship of the old, constricted deity of

Mind had taken its toll. My neck was subluxated to such a degree that for years I found only temporary relief after going to chiropractors, orthopedic specialists, and various other mind-body healers.

My Professional Background: Tai Chi, Qigong, Psychotherapy, and Bodymind Healing

My early training in psychotherapy helped me to understand why there was such an imbalance between my mind and body, which manifested in my neck. However, healing did not come from this knowledge alone; instead, my pain led me to the path of the wounded healer, setting out on the quest to find healing.

The waters of a second stream were needed to heal the imbalances of my life. I was ripe for the growing movement that sought an integrative approach to healing body, mind, and spirit. In the early 1970s I went on a "quest to the West" where graduate programs existed that allowed one to study holistic ways of healing the psyche. At Saybrook Institute, I discovered a program that incorporated holistic psychology, which provided me the opportunity to study a wide variety of ancient healing traditions in the course of obtaining my doctoral degree. In addition to traditional psychological methods, I was able to study symbolic process traditions of the so-called "Western Mystery Traditions" (Matthews, 1986), including dreamwork, mythology, alchemy, and astrology. I wrote two books on these subjects: *The Mystery of Personal Identity* (Mayer, 1984), and *Trials of the Heart* (Mayer, 1995).

I knew that integrating the body was crucial to my quest for my own healing as well as to help in the healing of others; and so I went looking for a tradition of bodily healing to integrate with my mental/emotional healing path. I served as Dr. Eugene Gendlin's Focusing training coordinator of the San Francisco East Bay area for ten years. *Focusing* is a method of body-oriented psychotherapy that pays attention to the felt sense in the body in such a way that felt meaning of body blocks emerge and a felt shift of energy happens thereby. This method helped to transform my way of being, as I hope it will do for you.

As I moved down the stream of my life, I helped to co-found the Transpersonal Psychology Department at John F. Kennedy University — a place where East and West, body and mind were integrated in the training of therapists; I taught there for twelve years. Integrating different traditions became a trademark of my work as a therapist; I called the method I developed, *Integrative Depth Psychotherapy*, which I later changed to *Bodymind Healing Psychotherapy*. Following the publication of my book, *The Mystery of Personal Identity* (Mayer, 1984), at JFKU I taught the first course to be offered in an accredited university on integrating astrology and psychotherapy. In 1979, *The Mystery of Personal Identity* won the World Astrology Prize from the Astrological Association of Great Britain for introducing a new phenomenological theoretical framework using astrology as a tool to explore one's life meaning rather than objectifying the correspondence between cosmos and personality. A key concept of this three-semester, graduate psychology course was how to use astrology in counseling without ever mentioning the word "astrology," i.e. using astrological metaphors (such as fire, earth, air, and water) to reframe psychological issues, to transform pathological ways of viewing one's self and one's relationships, and to find

Preface

new meaning in one's life by using this transpersonal tool. Following the theme of incorporating ancient sacred wisdom traditions to expand the healing tools of modern psychotherapy, I also taught symbolic process courses to psychotherapy interns at JFKU for five years. I wrote *Trials of the Heart: Healing the Wounds of Intimacy* (Mayer, 1995), to show how ancient myths can help couples deepen their perspective regarding the lessons that intimate relationship provides. The *Mythic Journey Process* I developed in this book was a tool for therapists to use to help their patients ground archetypal myths using their bodies' "felt sense" and Gendlin's Focusing method, while telling their life stories. Again, my medicine way of "two streams joining" appeared as I attempted to bring together the stream of Jungian/archetypal psychology with the stream of body-oriented psychotherapy.

A major point in my healing came when I met Master Fong Ha, a lineage holder of one of the great rivers of bodymind healing knowledge based in ancient Chinese traditions and a greatly respected teacher of the art of Tai Chi Chuan. Master Ha represented a lineage that came through Dong Yingjie, a famous Yang stylist, and Yang Shouzhong, a lineage holder of the Yang family style of Tai Chi. In 1974. As I was looking around at many teachers of Tai Chi to help me "get into my body," I chose Fong Ha as my *sifu* (teacher) not because of his credentials, but because of the quality of his movements, embodying solidity and grace, and his personality, which was open and explorative. I felt a cross-discipline identification with him, in that just as I was seeking a psychotherapeutic style that was not rigidly attached to a single method as the answer to the quest for wholeness, Fong Ha was seeking the same in the area of the body. Throughout the three decades I have studied with him, I have had an opportunity to grow with him as he has invited various masters from China to teach us. Three of these teachers who had great influences on my development were standing meditation masters, Han Xingyuan — a master of the *Yi Chuan* (the mind or intentionality behind the various systems of Chuan); Sam Tam — a master of Eagle Claw, Yi Chuan, and Tai Chi; and Cai Songfang — a master of *Wuji Standing Meditation*. *Wuji*, according to the Taoist classic, the *Tao te Ching*, is the void or stillness from which our life energy derives.

From my study in the circle of Fong Ha, at his Integral Chuan Institute, I was able to find an age-old tradition of bodily wisdom that helped to heal my imbalances. I went on from there to the Acupressure Institute of Berkeley to further my study in oriental methods of healing and received a certificate in acupressure in 1990. For many years I kept separate the knowledge derived from my Tai Chi, Qigong, and acupressure training from my work as a therapist.

I was trained to believe that there were problems, detriments, and dangers involved in integrating Eastern modalities with Western psychotherapy, and I internalized and adhered to these beliefs. Some of these relevant concerns will be reviewed in Chapter 2 and Chapter 22. For example, psychology as a profession has a history of looking askance at integrating Eastern modalities and body practices in part due to the belief that they are transcendental in nature. Later we shall see how integrating "transcendent and transmuting" approaches is a key dialectic of an integrative paradigm of healing. Perhaps it was the call of the "two streams joining" of my childhood that gave me the courage to remember my purpose and find my way to a place of more expansive vision.

Combining the Eastern methods of Tai Chi, Qigong, and acupressure self-touch with other body-oriented traditions helped me to find the path that I was seeking to heal the body/mind split that was so much a part of my early life. Through the practices I learned over the years, I was able to find the way to heal the blocked energy in my neck, and, as well, to find a bridge between traditions of the mind and body. Some of these traditions that have influenced me and later became fundamental parts of Bodymind Healing Psychotherapy include various approaches to Western psychotherapy such as: self psychology, psychodynamic and object relations theory, cognitive-behavioral psychotherapy, energy psychotherapies, symbolic process traditions, and Dr. Eugene Gendlin's Focusing method. Also, hypnosis and acupressure became vital parts of the integrative paradigm I was in the process of developing.

I took the knowledge I had been accumulating and taught the first program in the United States to master's level counseling students on the integration of Tai Chi, Qigong, and psychotherapy at John F. Kennedy University. This three-semester class ended with a counseling case seminar where students were able to apply their knowledge to cases in their internship program. Later, I was grateful that the California Institute of Integral Studies invited me to teach the first two classes ever offered on the integration of Qigong and psychotherapy to doctoral students. Then I taught courses in Eastern perspectives on healing at San Francisco State University for three years, bringing this knowledge base to undergraduates — just as I would have liked to have happened for me in my early years.

While I was training therapists, I was also deriving my knowledge from my private practice as a psychologist, learning from my experience with my patients to whom I am most grateful. My specialty became self-healing methods for physical and mental health problems. My dharmic agenda was to reach a wider audience, and to impact the way our culture looks at physical and mental health. My stream joined the larger stream of fellow travelers in mind-body medicine. At this point in our culture's evolution, where corporate greed and multibillion-dollar pharmaceutical companies' agendas rule our approach to health, it is helpful to step out of the tide of commercialism and wonder what a more person-centered, holistic approach would be. What would be an approach that honors the wonders of modern medicine and gives due weight to the ancient reservoir of knowledge held by time-tested methods of age-old healing traditions? This type of approach, which is still evolving, has been called, *integrative medicine.*

My interest in this path led to my co-founding and practicing as a psychologist and Qigong teacher at the Health Medicine Institute (HMI) in Lafayette, California where a multi-disciplinary team of health practitioners practice integrative medicine, and where I worked for three years. Some of the illustrative cases that I put forth in this book come from my experience at HMI, others from my three decades of private practice as a psychotherapist.

It has been my great pleasure to have had opportunities to share the methods I have developed with staff at hospitals, students at universities, and in workshops around the country in venues such as Alta Bates and Mt. Diablo Hospitals, Bryn Mawr College, Institute of Imaginal Studies, Saybrook Institute, the National Institute for the Clinical Application of Behavioral Medicine, and Esalen Institute. I am grateful to now be offering two certification programs — one in Bodymind Healing Qigong and another for Bodymind Health Professionals.

Preface

Overview of this Book

This book is the second of a two-part series, called *The Tao of Bodymind Healing*. Volume I, *Secrets to Living Younger Longer: The Self-Healing Path of Qigong, Standing Meditation and Tai Chi* is about Qigong and psychotherapy, with the emphasis on Qigong. The current book, Volume II, *Bodymind Healing Psychotherapy: Ancient Pathways to Modern Health*, is about psychotherapy and Qigong, with the emphasis on psychotherapy. This book emphasizes the incorporation of Qigong into both the psychotherapy and behavioral health arenas. Although Qigong originated in China, one of my favorite sayings is that Qigong is not just Chinese. All around the indigenous world, energy and intention, movement and metaphor have been used as sources of healing. Though the Chinese have done perhaps the best job in keeping intact the knowledge of specific methods of energy healing, in the first volume of this set, and now here, we shall see how a broad array of traditions contribute to the root system of an integrative healing paradigm. You will see how what is to be integrated in this book is a much deeper and fuller stream than just integrating Qigong and psychotherapy.

In this volume, you'll learn how to use a variety of ancient pathways from both Western and Eastern traditions to help heal the mind and body such as: (1) Chinese medicine approaches including Qigong and self-touch of acupressure points, (2) A full-spectrum approach to symbolic process methods that include psycho-mythological inner work using techniques such as the *Mythic Journey Process*, and the *River of Life Process*, which integrates guided imagery with *Microcosmic Orbit Breathing*, (3) Kabbalistic processes, and (4) Methods drawn from ancient traditions of meditation and postural initiation. Bodymind Healing Psychotherapy artfully weaves these somatic and imaginal methods from ancient traditions together with modern psychotherapy methods.

The two books can each stand alone, yet are best when read as a two-volume set. Thus, those who are more interested in Qigong may want to read the first volume, and they will also get information on the importance of the psychological dimension to make their Qigong practices more whole. Likewise, those who are more interested in psychotherapy may read just Volume II, and will get some information on Qigong. Like a yin–yang symbol, a dot of each tradition is in the half-circle of the other. In actuality, energy and psychotherapy cannot be separated into different volumes, nor into different facets of a whole crystal — each are integral parts of the whole gem of holistic healing.

In the chapters that follow, you will see how I have integrated the images of the stream of life and my Taoist practices into my work with patients. For example, one cancer patient, with whom I used an image of a stream in my hypnotherapeutic approach with him, told me that his chemotherapy and radiation left him so dry that he could feel no moisture. He said he felt so much like a dried out tree next to a dried out river that he could not even imagine a tree with moist leaves. I changed the metaphor, and by following his exhalation down into the roots of the dried out tree he was able to imagine and feel a drawing up of moisture and energy from an underground aquifer. A healing practice emerged for him that I later developed into an audiotape for other cancer patients. Many have felt inspired and alleviated of their suffering when listening to the tape and meditating on the cover image of a tree by the river.

Figure 1: Finding your Hidden Reservoir of Healing Energy

In the pages that follow you'll be initiated into the healing pathway that I have been on for over thirty years, which I have used with myself, in workshops, in training many hundreds of psychotherapy interns, and in my private practice as a therapist. Comprising the Eastern part of the stream, are the Taoist meditation practices of cultivating Qi are the waters of life for this healing paradigm; comprising the Western stream, and flowing in its waters, are Gendlin's Focusing and other Western psychotherapy traditions.

You will see how my medicine animal name, "Michael, Two Streams Joining" has influenced my work in bringing together, body and mind, East and West, Qigong and psychotherapy. In addition, you will see how following the medicine way of my name has led me to bring together other things often separated in the field of psychotherapy and mind-body healing. Throughout this book, Bodymind Healing Psychotherapy, following the tradition of synthesizing opposites, brings together approaches in mind and body, image and instinct, Western and Eastern, energy healing practices with modern bodymind healing methods, and ancient sacred wisdom traditions with modern psychotherapy. I consider it a great blessing to have you join me sitting at this place where two rivers become one; and I hope what you hear helps you, as it has me, to serve in the healing of your Self and others.

Introduction: Psycho-Energia: The Lost Soul of Psychology

When I was in my master's degree program in the early 1970s, as part of my training to become a psychotherapist I learned that psychology began in the laboratory of Wilhelm Wundt in Leipzig, Germany in 1879. I got the answer to that question right on my final exam along with the "fact" that "psychology" meant "the study of the mind;" and I graduated *cum laude*. However, like so many other psychology students, I sensed that my interest in psychology — this deep-seated territory in the depths of humanity — must have much earlier roots. I wondered where and when?

In my doctoral psychology program I learned from reading James Hillman's (1975) *Revisioning Psychology* that the word "psyche" derived from the Greek, meaning "soul," and that the phenomenology of the soul consisted of its being comprised of elements such as fire, earth, air, and water (p. 127). Psychology, according to this viewpoint, is not just about the study of mind; it is about other elements of being too, such as: the fire (the energy of our Selves), earth, (grounding our Selves through body methods), air (yes, of course mental/cognitive methods are important, and so is the breath), and water (feelings are a key, as is developing the ability to modulate appropriately the watery, affective dimension of life). This definition gave me and many other budding psychotherapists room to expand the narrow range of modern psychology and connect the substance of "the Self"[1] with ancient sacred wisdom traditions.

What is Bodymind Healing Psychotherapy? Definition of Terms

I coined the term *"Bodymind Healing Psychotherapy"* (BMHP) to incorporate the breadth and depth of this approach to psychotherapy. It includes Western forms of psychotherapy such as psychodynamic, self-psychology, cognitive-behavioral therapy, and clinical hypnosis; and, as well, BMHP draws upon other various ancient sacred wisdom traditions to integrate their wisdom and healing methods. Symbolic process methods, like Jungian/archetypal inner work, are a key component to this approach. BMHP also includes Eugene Gendlin's Focusing method and my *Bodymind Healing Qigong*[2] program as center-posts of its approach to healing mind, body, and energy — as will be explicated further in the following chapters.

The Term "Bodymind"

The term *"bodymind"* captures the need for modern psychology to resolve the mind-body split of Cartesian dualism. This idea is getting increased notice in the field, not just for academic and philosophic purposes, but because it relates a fundamental truth. Mind, body, and spirit may seem separate; but if we stop and reflect on them, all three levels exist as one inseparable whole in our everyday experience. For example, when we feel angry, our face turns red, thoughts of aggression may fill our minds, and we may become out of harmony with our higher cognitive capacities, unable to differentiate between rage and constructive critique, or between blame and constructive expression of anger.[3] Similarly, we may lose connection with our higher intention and spiritual purpose — to approach the offending person with a higher intention, to clear things, and to have things be different in the future.

The first use of the term "bodymind" in Western thought, that I am aware of, came from Ken Dychtwald whose book, *Bodymind*, was written in 1977. Many people now use the term "mind-body" to describe this integration; but I prefer putting the body first in our overly mental culture, where cognitive therapy is perhaps the best-known form of therapy and the most recognized treatment of choice for many conditions. Joining the two words, "body" and "mind" into one word "bodymind" expresses the core philosophic belief of Eastern thought — that body, mind, and spirit are one inseparable whole. "Bodymind Healing" is a term that emphasizes the need to activate all aspects of ourselves to achieve optimal mental, emotional, and spiritual health.

In the chapters that follow we shall see how integrating the body into psychotherapy has been shown by clinical research to be crucial to the process of healing. We will see how the body has formed a key building block of modern psychology in spite of the fact that many still associate psychology with the study of the mind. We will add to the tradition of somatically oriented psychotherapy by drawing from cross-cultural ancient sacred wisdom traditions, and methods of postural initiation including Qigong.

The Concept of Energy

Likewise, though some respected psychologists have recognized the importance of human energy on the range and depth of psychology, the concept of "energy" has yet to make it into greater public awareness. For example, from the time of Freud, with his ideas of *energy cathexis* (the directing of energy to zones of the body) and *energy fixation,* energy has been known to be a key component of psychological healing. And Wilhelm Reich, with his bio-energetic approach, developed a whole theory of psychology based upon energy, the body, and the breath.

The Term "Self-Healing"

The term "*Self-healing*" has a depth of meaning behind it. As was discussed in Volume I, the term "*Self*" with a capital "S" was initially coined by Carl Gustav Jung to mean a "Self" broader than the ego—a Self that incorporates the archetypes of the collective unconscious. Thus, the path of *individuation*, according to Dr. Jung, is to form an *ego-self axis*, whereby the personal ego is connected with the transpersonal elements of the psyche. Later in Dr. Jung's work, he spoke of the importance of the *psychoid* (body-centered) elements of the psyche in the individuation process. When the term "Self," in Self-healing, is used in this book, it is meant to convey not only the psychoid dimension of the Self, but also the incorporation of the healing elements of the surrounding universe. The healing powers of the Self blossom when the archetypal possibilities of embodied life are brought to fruition. This follows the viewpoint that in order for the Self to be whole, the mind-body-universe split needs to be resolved, which can be accomplished through incorporating bodymind healing practices from the East — such as the ones outlined in this book.

Introduction

The Terms "Transforming Your Life Stance" and "Shape-shifting."

All psychotherapies have their theories regarding what creates change. In general, psychodynamic therapists emphasize the insight gained from going back to our families of origin, cognitive/behaviorists emphasize changes in beliefs and behavior, humanistic/existential clinicians emphasize choice, Jungians emphasize the role of symbolic process, and Dr. Eugene Gendlin emphasizes the felt bodily shift and new meaning that comes at key moments of change in psychotherapy. BMHP draws from all of these traditions, and as seen in Chapter 2, it creates a mandala of psychotherapies, an overarching psychotherapeutic metasystem. In addition to this metasystem perspective, BMHP draws from certain traditions of change stemming from the ground of ancient sacred wisdom traditions. From these traditions there are three interrelated concepts woven together throughout this book. (1) Transforming your life stance (2) Shape-shifting (3) Repairing and cultivating your primordial Self.

Change needs to be embodied change, thus the use of the concept "transforming your life stance." This is one of the quintessential elements of BMHP. Influenced by the traditions of Standing Meditation and postural initiation outlined in Volume I, and the recent advances showing the importance of the body in the role of psychological healing (van der Kolk, 1994, 2002), BMHP places the literal/physical and symbolic elements of transforming one's life stance at the hub of the wheel of its theory of change. Another way to speak of changing our life stance is to use the practices and metaphors of "shape-shifting."

From the two volumes of *The Tao of Bodymind Healing* you'll learn that one of the earliest roots of psychotherapy involved traditions of shape-shifting that used transfiguring metaphors and practices to enhance the process of psychological transformation, loosen up fixated life patterns, and help to change a person's life stance. Virtually all age-old cultures have myths of the shape-shifting of human being into forms that have an ability to heal and transform their souls. The two volumes of *The Tao of Bodymind Healing* series unfolds this perspective and takes us on a journey to the age-old traditions of our trans-temporal compatriots; we will draw from the teachings of cross cultural mythologies and shamanism, the first holistic healing center of the Western World (the temple of Aesclepius), the Kabbalah, as well as the traditions of postural initiation in Native America, Greece, India, and China. In Volume II, I will specifically apply this age-old knowledge of shape-shifting to help those in modern psychotherapy to increase vitality, add depth, promote healing, and discover the multifaceted form of our true selves. We'll harness somatic and imaginal methods from these traditions and show how they can be useful for modern psychological and physical health; and we'll see how modern psychoneuroimmunological research and state-specific state of consciousness research supports their efficacy.

The Term "Primordial Self"

When I speak of the *primordial Self,* I am referring to the deep ground upon which the psyche is built — the elements that comprise the substrate of the soul. The online version of *Merriam-Webster Dictionary* defines the etymology of *pri·mor·di·al* this way: "Middle English, from late Latin *primordialis,* from Latin *primordium* origin, from *primus* first + *ordiri,* to begin. *Prime, Order* means 1a: first created or developed *Primeval,* 1b: existing in or persisting from the beginning (as of a solar system or universe) <a *primordial* gas cloud> 1c: earliest formed in the growth of an individual or organ."

In colloquial usage, we, as modern people, sense that when we talk about our selves we usually are speaking of the culturally embedded modern selves that we are, with our personal histories. We owe it, perhaps, to the Jungians to recognize that there exists a deeper self, a Self of the collective unconscious — and when one gets in touch with that Self, a deep layer of healing may emerge.

Literary critics adopted the term "primordial" from Jung's theory of the collective unconscious composed of archetypal symbols. *Britanica Online* says that a *primordial image* is a character, or pattern of circumstances that recurs throughout literature and thought consistently enough to be considered universal. Such primordial images and archetypal symbols include the snake, whale, eagle, and vulture. An *archetypal theme* is the passage from innocence to experience; *archetypal characters* include the blood brother, rebel, and wise grandparent. Jung defined an archetype as an "energy potential."

But long before Jung used the term "primordial," in the Western mystery tradition, both Christian Gnosticism (Matthews, 1986) and the Jewish Kabbalah (Hoffman, 1981) described the importance of activating the energies of the "primordial human," called *Adam Kadmon*. In Gnosticism, activating Adam Kadmon was an important part of "realizing the macrocosmic signatures within man the microcosm" (Matthews, 1986, p. 146.) The Kabbalah states that, "in the form of Adam Kadmon (the primordial human) the powers of the divine *Sefirot* also flow within each of us" (as cited in Hoffman, 1981, p. 55). The Sefirot are the Jewish archetypes of creation and symbolize the ten archetypal spheres of the tree of life, such as the paired opposites of strength and compassion.

However, we don't need to look at the cultivation of the primordial Self as something esoteric. In psychotherapists' everyday practices the activation of the primordial Self is a common marker of psychological growth. For example, recently I worked with a woman who had a very demeaning husband. She had been trained in her Middle Eastern family to always defer to men. After three sessions of working on this issue, and practicing how to appropriately express her feelings to her husband, she came into our fourth session with happy tears. She reported that she finally spoke up to her husband about how she wanted a change to take place in their relationship regarding his demeaning communication. She found the Self she was before acculturation — a Self who felt free to express her primordial need to be respected as a person, regardless of what her culture taught about the subservient role of women. Surprisingly to her, he received her comments well and agreed to work on this.

In the East, the concept of the primordial Self can be seen in the Buddhist idea of "finding the face of yourself before you were born," i.e. before the conditioning of life covered over your essential nature. In Taoism, cultivating the primordial energies of the universe was viewed as an essential part of developing the whole person. In China, Taoist adepts spoke of a *primordial Qi* (*yuanqi*) that becomes separated into two essential souls and makes up the living person — the *hun,* or spirit soul of celestial origin, and the *po,* or material soul that belongs to earth. At times

Introduction

various animal forms of movements were suggested to develop the initiate's primordial Qi; and it was said that for those following these movements "the hundred diseases will not arise."[4]

The importance of incorporating animal movements in developing the primordial Self was captured well by Laurens Van der Post after time he spent with the Kalahari Bushman. He said,

> *We can not recreate the original wilderness man ... But we can recover him because he exists in us. He is the foundation in spirit or psyche on which we build, and we are not complete until we have recovered him.*

The implications for bringing imaginal and somatically based ancient sacred wisdom traditions into psychotherapy and behavioral healthcare are breathtaking. I learned in my early training from studying the research of Harvard doctor, Herbert Benson (1983), that breathing was important in evoking the relaxation response; later I discovered from many psychoneuro-immunological researchers — including Ernest Rossi (1986), Jeanne Achterberg (1985), and Robert Ader (1991) — that not only does the relaxation response feel good, but also it has been scientifically shown to activate various aspects of the psychoneuroimmunological system, the parasympathetic nervous system, the brain, and electromagnetic elements of the body for healing. Little did I know that my path would lead to a thirty-year training curriculum in Qigong and Tai Chi — two significant, time-tested relaxation traditions from the East, as well as other age-old traditions of cultivating and recovering the primordial Self.[5]

The Term "Vital, Primordial Self"

When I use the term "*vital, primordial Self*," a double *entendre* is intended. First, it is "vital" (of key importance) to be with our primordial Selves at key moments in our lives. Secondly, the term "vital" is used to connote aliveness and a fullness of energy. This is a key concept in psychology, not only for depressed patients, but for anyone who wishes to live a life filled with meaning and purpose. We all hope that psychotherapy may help us access our vital reservoir of energy at those times when we are blocked because of an old psychological complex or a difficult life situation. Whether those blocks are from fear of rejection or inhibitions in being true to ourselves, summoning forth our coping skills requires us to draw from a place deeper than our entrenched, reactive patterns. How to do this is "the grail quest" of everyday life, the quest to bring liquid flow back to a depleted land. And so it is interesting that psychology has yet to draw from these age-old traditions that specialize in the cultivation of vital energy, and that have been a part of our ancestral, cross-cultural lineage as human beings for thousands of years.

Qigong: Ancient Cross-Cultural Path to Modern Health

One of the oldest energy-enhancing healing traditions is *Qigong*. Qigong is a many-thousand-year-old method of cultivating the energy of life by using posture, movement, breath, sound, touch, and awareness.[6]

In Volume I, Qigong was shown to be not just a Chinese tradition of healing. Using and respecting the healing power of the energy of life is a fundamental part of virtually every indigenous culture on earth. In Volume I we saw anthropological evidence for the existence of these traditions of "postural initiation" in China, India, Greece, Israel, and in Native America. I also discussed how in virtually all religions of the world, the concept of "the energy of life" forms a fundamental aspect of our relationship to God, whether it is in the Taoist idea of *Qi* (also spelled *chi*), the Hindu idea of *prana*, or the Kabbalistic idea of *chiyyut*. I discussed the research showing how the Buddha was trained in traditions of energy cultivation; and I showed how pictures of the Dancing Shiva reveal this tradition of moving with divine energy.

Here in Volume II, I propose that it is time to more fully incorporate the healing knowledge of these traditions into modern psychotherapy. In this volume, I show some of the reasons why these traditions have been kept out of Western psychotherapy. As one example, I illustrate how psychotherapy is unconsciously rooted in the alchemical tradition of "transmuting" (working through) psychological issues, in comparison to certain Eastern "transcendent" (rising above) approaches. Later, in Chapter 5, you will see how this false dichotomy can be rectified through the "transcending/ transmuting dialectic," thereby incorporating the benefits of both traditions for healing. In a broader sense, we will see in the following chapters how to incorporate the valuable contributions that each part of the healing mandala of cross-cultural traditions have to healing the whole, vital, primordial Self.

Integrating Qigong and Psychotherapy

The integration of Qigong and psychotherapy did not come easily for me. Like many other Western-trained psychologists, I had been trained in keeping separate the realms of psychotherapy and spiritual traditions. As a matter of fact, it was as if I was a "split personality," a psychologist by day, and an avid Tai Chi and Qigong practitioner in my off hours; I kept the two worlds completely separate. In Chapter 22, I review some of the well-founded reasons for keeping such traditions apart; as well, throughout this book, I discuss reasons for bringing these traditions together.

A Turning Point Patient: Carpal Tunnel Syndrome

All therapists have their turning point patients. For me, one of these patients was a medical student who was working on a research project that required a lot of writing. In our depth psychotherapy sessions, he was often distracted by his diagnosed condition of carpal tunnel syndrome. At that time in my evolution I was very careful about dual relationships, having been trained in the potential dangers of mixing other disciplines with psychotherapy (see Chapter 22). So I thought, why not just refer him out? What happens if using these health methods stops him from getting appropriate medical treatment? What happens if the complementary treatment doesn't work and it produces a transference issue that interferes with the therapeutic relationship?

While "Boris" was working mainly on issues with his father, who was a medical doctor, and the childhood physical abuse that occurred in this relationship, week after week he came into our session with his arm in a sling and a splint due to his diagnosed condition of carpal tunnel syndrome. The physical therapist with whom he was working said to keep his arm still and she worked with him each week to strengthen his wrist through various exercises. One day my compassion was stronger than my considerations about being unduly cautious. I mentioned to Boris that I had something to tell him about my life that normally I would keep to myself, but that could be relevant to him healing his wrist. He expressed appreciation for my caring, and we agreed we would continue our longstanding practice of clearing any negative feelings, if they arose for him through this process. I then told him that I practiced Qigong, and that some research showed (Garlinkle, 1998) it was better to use a relaxing, energizing movement method to promote healing rather than to use splints and not move. I suggested that we might try to use this Qigong method, which combined stillness and movement, to explore together, like scientists researching, to see if these methods helped him. He agreed.

First, I asked Boris to do the breathing method that, from our work together, had become one of his favorite ways of relaxing. As you will see later, this method is called *Microcosmic Orbit Breathing*. Boris and I had never before discussed its roots in Qigong and Taoism. On this day we repeated this breathing method to activate a trance-like state. Then I asked him, as he inhaled, to imagine that he was in water up to his shoulders and that his hands were just floating up, wrists leading the way. From this position, on a long, un-forced exhalation, I directed him to press the heels of the hands down slightly all the way to the level of the belly. He repeated this quite a few times, and by the end of the session his pain had reduced from a self-reported 8 on the subjective units of distress scale (SUDS are measured on a ten point scale, ten being the most stress) to 2 SUDS. Readers of Volume I will notice that this is the first Tai Chi movement called, *Commencement*, or *Raising and Lowering the Qi*. Instead of practicing the movement while standing, with Boris we practiced it from a sitting position.

I was glad I had suggested to Boris to clear with me any negative feelings, because in the next session he came back and said, "OK, you told me to express my feelings to you, well here, you're going to have it." He went on to express his anger that, "Sure, the hypnosis and Qigong thing" I did with him worked in the session; but afterwards, when he was working on his research project, the carpal tunnel syndrome just came back. Then he added, "My father was right about this Eastern stuff not working."

This was a good lesson for me in explaining new methods and their wider theoretical foundations more carefully. I explained to Boris that the underlying philosophy of Eastern methods of healing was not based on a one-time fix model. Even with Western drugs one has to continue a medication regimen; and there are usually side effects with Western medications. We discussed how his body was signaling him that he needed to get up and take more breaks. We discussed how Qigong was "a practice," not a one-time curative event. So, Boris went home that week and did the *Raising and Lowering the Qi* movement (see Volume I). He came into our next session without his brace for the first time in months. In subsequent months, Boris never again needed his brace. He said that the pain would come back when he was working too long, but that he was learning to use his pain as a signal to relax and practice his Tai Chi. He was grateful I had stretched the therapeutic boundaries to introduce him to what he now described as "this cool new behavioral health method."

In addition to the healing that occurred, our process helped deepen our relationship and helped Boris begin to individuate from his father. Boris saw the limitations of his father's myopic view that Western medicine was the answer to all health concerns. It helped to further validate his choices to take some of the new courses offered in his medical school on alternative therapies, and it gave him strength in the future to stand up to his father when their opinions differed.

Throughout the book you will read about more of my turning point patients. For example, in Chapter 6, you will hear about a patient with a panic disorder who gave me the encouragement to bring my work with Qigong further into my work with depth psychotherapy patients. In Chapters 6 to 13 you will see how I began integrating my work with Qigong and other ancient sacred wisdom traditions with a wide array of patients and a wide variety of conditions.

Other psychotherapists and practitioners of mind-body healing have also seen the value of integrating ancient sacred wisdom traditions with these modern disciplines. For example, Jungian analysts use symbolic processes derived from age-old sources, transpersonal psychology (Wilber et al., 1986) incorporates a variety of aspects of ancient sacred wisdom traditions into its healing repertoire, and Jon Kabat-Zinn (1990) has brought Mindfulness Meditation into behavioral health treatment. Throughout this book, I will touch on the wider literature of these authors and others in the field who have traveled these pre-technological pathways. However, my main aim is not do to a historical review of those who have traveled these pathways. The particular traditions and approaches of BMHP, though influenced by these authors and approaches, stands on its own ground, rooted in its own unique place where two streams become one. This approach, for example, is the first, to my knowledge, to integrate Qigong and depth psychotherapy. Also, though it uses symbolic process modalities derived from ancient traditions, BMHP is the first, to my knowledge, to integrate the body into a non-directive symbolic process modality — the way I have done in the *Mythic Journey Process* by blending Gendlin's Focusing technique, Qigong, and psycho-mythology. Likewise, to my knowledge, BMHP is the first to draw on the shamanic traditions of shape-shifting, and blend those concepts and practices (including the animal forms of movement) with modern psychoneuroimmunological research and ideas about change in the modern psychotherapeutic setting. Just as a tree sinks its root system into the ground to establish many routes in its search for water, so is it my hope that modern psychotherapy and behavioral health will benefit from the access-ways developed here, in Bodymind Healing Psychotherapy.

There has been an unfortunate carry-over into psychotherapy of the necessary axiom in our government of the principle separating church and state. In the realm of psychotherapy, this separation does a disservice to the concepts of holistic healing and integrative healthcare. As we shall see in Chapter 2, various "religious" traditions of meditation, spirituality, mysticism, and ancient sacred wisdom traditions that formed the early root system from which religions developed, have, for the most part, been kept out of the realm of psychotherapy. Maybe some elements of their viewpoints were reluctantly incorporated and put to the side as a division of "religion" in the mainstream American Psychological Association; yet they have been seen as adjunctive tools in psychotherapy practice at best. To this date, the Association of Transpersonal Psychology has not been admitted into this mainstream organization, and Jungian psychotherapy still exists outside the norms of traditional academic training programs. Mainstream psychology has often viewed such traditions with suspicion or disdain, as if they were old primitive methods before "real psychology" was developed.

Introduction

In Chapter 4, I touch on some of the historical background of how such ancient traditions were split off from modern healing methods, while at the same time some of their methods and symbols were co-opted by the newly emerging civilization. I show how, to some degree, caution about incorporating these pre-modern technologies has merit, because the two traditions stem from different roots. I coin the term, "transcendent/transmuting dialectic;" and show (in Chapters 4 and 5) how these equally valuable root systems can enhance the strength of the many-branched tree of psychological healing, rather than dichotomize Eastern and Western healing philosophies. My hope is that the integrative approach presented in the following chapters will interest others in further exploration of how these traditions can be used to complement treatment in psychotherapy and behavioral healthcare, and to help to repair and cultivate our vital, primordial Selves.

Summary of the Book

This book is divided into four sections. *Section I* is about integrative medicine, bodymind healthcare, energy psychology, and ancient sacred wisdom traditions. It is the preamble to introducing Bodymind Healing Psychotherapy's integrative methods for psychotherapy and behavioral healthcare in the section that follows. In *Chapter 1* the current crises in Western healthcare will be addressed. We will see how Integrated Healthcare, in general, and some specific mind-body approaches to healing are key elements that can aid in helping our civilization deal with these crises. These methods will be shown to be not fringe science, as some assume; but methods that have some of the most solid research supporting their efficacy (Pelletier, 2000). *Chapter 2*, attempts to "re-member" (put back together the disjointed members of) the shattered gem of bodymind healing by showing how interdisciplinary and cross-cultural research can become a source of clinical models for mind-body healing. Here, new biology, meditation, somatic mind-body methods, psychoneuroimmunology, clinical hypnosis, and ancient cross-cultural healing traditions will join forces to help heal the dysfunctional splits inherent in psychotherapy and behavioral healthcare. In this chapter, I "re-vision" the framework of psychotherapy with a mandala of psychophysiological healing. And, a Native American medicine wheel is used to order the spokes of the proposed integrated circle of bodymind healing traditions. *Chapter 3* explores the paradigm shift that is taking place incorporating energy medicine with biochemical approaches; and focus within this emerging tradition is placed on the emerging field of energy psychology. Here, I discuss research and discuss the value and problems with energy psychology, as it exists in this pre-paradigmatic stage of development; and I advocate for the deepening and broadening of the roots of the field of energy psychology. Then, *Chapter 4* explores these ancient roots and suggests that this emerging mind-body healing tradition can be strengthened by integrating Qigong, depth psychotherapy, and symbolic process modalities. A brief historical perspective is presented on how the ancient roots of energy medicine and energy psychology were "surgically removed" from current Western medical and psychological paradigms. I suggest that by reintegrating these age-old traditions, we may bring new vitality and healing ways to our modern clinical settings.

Section II contains the approach to psychotherapy and bodymind healing which I have been developing over the last three decades, called Bodymind Healing Psychotherapy (BMHP). *Chapter 5* introduces this ten-leveled holographic system which integrates traditional forms of Western psychotherapy, clinical hypnosis, Dr. Eugene Gendlin's Focusing, Eastern energy healing traditions, and symbolic process healing methods. In *Chapters 6-14* case illustrations will be presented of patients from the integrated medical clinic I co-founded, patients from my private practice, and students from my workshops and certification programs.

The case examples in this book are being used for illustrative purposes. Sometimes these cases are composites, names are always altered, and details are changed to dis-identify patients, protect their identities, and to focus on the task at hand — to illustrate how ancient sacred wisdom traditions, in general, and Qigong, in particular, can aid patients' healing in psychotherapy. They are discussed for heuristic reasons to outline an integrative methodology that will differ depending upon a given patient's needs.

The case illustrations in *Chapters 6-13* show how BMHP can aid in the treatment of anxiety, chronic pain, trauma, addictions, insomnia, hypertension, depression, and various other behavioral health issues. My aim is not to list every conceivable psychological issue, but instead to give an overview of how this approach applies to some common conditions treated by everyday clinicians. So, a few conditions are grouped together in *Chapter 13* including: arthritis, joint problems, musculoskeletal disorders, carpal tunnel syndrome, fibromyalgia, diabetes, Chrone's disease, headaches, Raynaud's syndrome, stomach disorders, etc. I do not mean to imply that any of these traditions deserve less space than those conditions that receive a whole chapter. In addition, so that it is clear that I do not hold Qigong or any ancient tradition as a panacea, I close this section with *Chapter 14* on Qigong psychosis in order to show one of the contraindications of excess Qigong practice. Throughout these chapters I will weave together the various facets of BMHP and show how they function together through these case examples.

Section III shifts the focus from case examples to general principles and themes of BMHP and how they can enhance the practice of psychotherapy and behavioral healthcare. Though case examples are also used in this section, the intention here is to expand the perspective of the current practice of psychotherapy to include ancient sacred wisdom traditions, in general, and Qigong, in particular. For example, in *Chapter 15*, you will see how psychotherapy involves "changing your life stance," as I draw upon ancient psychological ideas about shamanic shape-shifting. In *Chapter 16*, I focus on noticing patient gestures at key transformative moments in psychotherapy, and show how knowledge of Qigong and Tai Chi movements help to harness the healing elements that arise from the patient's primordial Self at such moments. *Chapter 17* shows how affect modulation skills (Schore, 2003), one of the center-posts of modern therapy, are enhanced by knowledge of ancient sacred wisdom traditions. *Chapter 18*, presents how psychotherapy can be viewed as verbal internal martial art training — for example, you see how "attacking your patients to heal them," i.e. using verbal role play, but having the role of somatic processes and the internal martial arts tradition in the background of the therapists' awareness can be helpful to the therapeutic process.[7] In *Chapter 19*, you will see how the ancient idea of healing through the elements can contribute to healing various psychological issues, such as writer's block, as we integrate concepts of transpersonal psychology into our healing equation.

Introduction

Throughout, I show how an in-depth knowledge of these age-old traditions, like Qigong and Tai Chi, is not necessary for clinicians to integrate the essence of these ancient sacred wisdom traditions into their practices. Though it is useful to have knowledge of these traditions, clinicians can be aware of body movements at key moments, use metaphors of the elements of nature to enhance healing, and bring in elements of self-touch and self-soothing without extensive training. Of course I believe that sinking one's roots into these healing methods buried deep in the rich soil of pre-technological traditions is beneficial; but it is not necessary. *Section III* ends with the *Mythic Journey Process* that I developed in the 1980s as my contribution to the use of symbolic process modalities in psychotherapy. My aim then was to ground the Jungian active imagination process in the body; and here at this time, I wish to reintroduce this method as a tool to complement the therapist's repertoire, as the use of this somatically based storytelling method as a narrative psychotherapeutic tool is one key way to facilitate a patient's transformation.

Chapter 21 reviews what Qigong gives to psychotherapy, and what psychotherapy gives to Qigong. For example, I discuss how when Qigong is integrated with psychotherapy, along the lines that BMHP suggests, it can help in some of the following ways. It can: Activate state-specific states of consciousness that are both relaxing and energizing; provide useful behavioral health methods beneficial for those suffering from depression, addiction, and sympathetic nervous system overload; introduce a bodily base for developing affect modulation, affect tolerance, and a cohesive center to deal with life issues; and provide beneficial methods for "healing the healer. Finally, in *Chapter 22*, I address some of the ethical and dual relationship issues involved in introducing new paradigms and experimental procedures, such as Qigong, into psychotherapy.

In Section IV, I focus further on how Qigong, Tai Chi, and ancient scared wisdom traditions can be helpful in "healing the healer." *Chapter 23* shows how the initiatory elements of Qigong and Tai Chi can be helpful to center the therapist; and in *Chapter 24,* an abbreviated form of the ten-system Bodymind Healing Qigong practice is presented. This abbreviated set developed from a request by Dr. Wayne Jonas, past director of the National Institute of Health, Office of Alternative Medicine, who asked me to create a less extensive form of my set to be included in a new book he was writing. Though I usually have resistance to abbreviated work, the honor of being chosen by Dr. Jonas to do this gave me the impetus to extract the essence of my ten sets so that busy modern people could get the essence of the energy and benefits of Qigong practice in a shorter time period. For health professionals and others who do not have the time in our busy culture to practice the whole Bodymind Healing Qigong set, I see the merit in creating a twenty-minute set that can be practiced at the beginning, middle, or end of a busy day. In this volume, although I have included illustrations of some of the practices to which I refer, illustrations of the complete Bodymind Healing Qigong set can be seen in Volume I or in its accompanying Bodymind Healing Qigong DVD.

The Afterword of the book brings the reader full circle to reflect upon how the streams of body and mind, East and West, ancient and modern can join to help heal patients in psychotherapy and in our healthcare system. The book is intended for professional audiences and the intelligent general public as an introduction to this integrated healing paradigm which adds its perspective to the wellspring of emerging bodymind healing traditions. As well, in the middle chapters (6-13), the methods for healing common issues such as anxiety, chronic pain, trauma, etc., are written with hopes that they will provide healing pathways for members of the general public who struggle with such issues. For members of the public, please read the guidelines in the author's note about consulting with appropriate health professionals. For ease of reading I have included a list of case illustrations and Bodymind Healing Psychotherapy practices in the front section of this book. Please see Appendix I for a summarized list of the contributions that this book, and BMHP, makes to the fields of psychotherapy, behavioral healthcare, energy psychology, and Qigong.

SECTION I:
INTEGRATIVE MEDICINE,
BODYMIND HEALTHCARE,
AND ANCIENT SACRED
WISDOM TRADITIONS

Like the meridians as they approach the poles,
science, philosophy, and religion are bound to converge
as they draw nearer to the whole.

— Pierre Teilhard de Chardin
The Phenomenon of Man

CHAPTER 1: INTEGRATIVE HEALTHCARE AND MIND-BODY MEDICINE

> *"What is the most important lesson that I derived from these ten encounters over the span of 70 years? Americans think of illness and disability as a condition that can be fixed by an expert, in this case a physician. Accordingly, they want more medicine, more research, and more physicians — all with a lower cost and equitable distribution. This was the case in 1930 and it is still the case at century's end. However the fact that each individual is ultimately responsible for the maintenance of his or her own health is a lesson that most Americans still need to learn."*
>
> — Professor Eli Ginsberg,
> *Columbia University*[1]

The Healthcare Crisis

Currently the United States and much of the rest of the world is experiencing epidemics of chronic and degenerative illnesses such as a cardiovascular diseases, cancer, diabetes, arthritis, and depression. We live in an era in which we have a hard time trusting our Western doctors, and doctors have a hard time trusting themselves. Medical errors are reported, even in the *Journal of the American Medical Association (JAMA),* as being the third leading cause of death in the United States. And according to the 2005 Commonwealth Fund International Health Policy Survey, researchers who interviewed patients suffering from a serious condition that required intense medical treatment, or had been admitted to a hospital for a condition other than a routine pregnancy, found instances of improper treatment 34 percent of the time.[2]

How can this be the case? I was brought up trusting the medical system. With a revered uncle who was a doctor and director of a hospital clinic and a family doctor who would visit us when we were sick, I was trained to have the utmost respect for the medical system. Then when the rebellious '60s took place and the *Fireside Theater's* album came out saying, "Everything you know is wrong," I started reexamining many of my previous assumptions. Like many, I was awakened to disturbing realties as I began to take in this new knowledge.

How could so much that we thought we knew about our trusted medical system be wrong? Everyday we read stories of the problems in our newspapers. Women who took estrogen, and believed their doctors' advice about the best treatment for their menopausal symptoms, now read stories in their local newspapers that estrogen may speed senility and create other health problems.[3] A doctor friend of mine who prescribed it for her patients for many years, with a guilty, pained look on her face, expressed feeling duped by the previous research. When doctors have relied on pharmacological companies, and even their own medical journals for accurate information, their trust has oftentimes been misplaced.[4] According to an article in the *New England Journal of Medicine,* a group of prestigious medical experts declared that the pervasive influence of drug company money is distorting doctor's treatment decisions and scientific findings (Angell, 2000). They called on their colleagues to adopt far reaching new conflict of interest policies. According to David Rothman, professor of social medicine at Columbia University Medical Center, drug companies spend $13,000 per physician annually (as cited in Connolly, 2006).[5]

"A definitive review and close reading of medical peer-review journals, and government health statistics shows that American medicine frequently causes more harm than good," according to a group of well-respected researchers.[6] They cite statistics from reputable sources to back up their claims: A *JAMA* study (Lazarou, 1998) reports that the number of people having in-hospital, adverse drug reactions (ADR) to prescribed medicine is 2.2 million.[7] In 1995, Dr. Richard Besser, of the Center for Disease Control, said the number of unnecessary antibiotics prescribed annually for viral infections was 20 million. Dr. Besser, in 2003, refers to tens of millions of unnecessary antibiotics,[8] he wrote, "Adverse drug reactions are the fourth leading cause of death in America. Reactions to prescription and over-the-counter medications kill far more people annually than all illegal drug use combined."[9] In a Congressional oversight investigation in 2001 it was reported that there were 7.5 million unnecessary surgical procedures resulting in 37,136 deaths at a cost of $122 billion (based on the U.S. dollar value in 1974).[10] *JAMA* (1987) similarly reports high percentages of unnecessary surgeries.[11] In 1995, researchers testifying before the Department of Veterans Affairs estimated that of 250,000 back surgeries in the U.S. at a hospital cost of $11,000 per patient, the total number of unnecessary back surgeries each year in the U.S. could approach 44,000, costing as much as $484 million.[12]

A Poignant Case Illustration: Lower Back Surgery

To put a face on the human toll of this problem, "Jerry," a young, previously very athletic man in his early 40s, suffered from a back injury and "failed back surgery syndrome." When Jerry first came into our Health Medicine Institute (HMI),[13] he could barely walk and was shuffling his feet in pain; he told us his story. Jerry had undergone two operations on his back and for the last eight months there had been no improvement. Jerry was assigned to a group of practitioners at our clinic, a Western doctor who used light therapy (a photon emission stimulator), an acupuncturist, a bodyworker, a chiropractor; and he was assigned to me for psychotherapy, behavioral healthcare, and Qigong. In my first session with Jerry he told me how, when he went to the surgeon and had the regular tests performed, there was a pivotal moment when the surgeon pressed on a point between the bones and where they meet about an inch above the first and second toes. When severe pain shot up his body, according to Jerry, the surgeon replied, "I'm sorry son, but that's a sign that you need surgery." At HMI, our clinic's acupuncturist, told Jerry that the point touched on his foot was an acu-point in Chinese medicine called Liver-3, which is one of the most sensitive points on the body that will hurt on virtually anyone. This was one more item on the list of Jerry's dissatisfaction and rage at the medical system that had failed him.

In my three sessions with Jerry, in addition to supportive psychotherapy I taught him a method of Qigong breathing called *Microcosmic Orbit Breathing*. As Jerry did this type of breathing, along with the guided imagery method of imagining a river flowing through his tension, deep, sobbing tears arose. In the midst of his tears, Jerry said, "I know that if I had done this type of thing there could have been hope for my self-healing and maybe not needing the surgery." Though we will never know if his remark was an exaggerated feeling of the moment or the truth, during one of our sessions together Jerry reported a big reduction in the amount of pain that he felt — from a 9 at the beginning of our session to a 2 at the end. The methods I used for his chronic pain will be explained later in this book (see Chapter 7). In the three sessions I had with Jerry I taught him slow gentle movements such as *Tai Chi Ruler* (for an illustration see Chapter 24), self-touch acupressure points, *Microcosmic Orbit Breathing*, and guided imagery methods to facilitate his re-empowerment and to provide him with self-healing methods to complement the other treatments he was receiving at our clinic. After two sessions our administrative staff told me that workman's compensation said they would not pay for any psychotherapy, behavioral health treatments, nor for any further treatments from me. I had one more follow-up session with Jerry to review the self-healing methods that we had practiced so he could integrate them with his work with others in our clinic. He expressed regret that workman's compensation would not pay for any further treatments.

Workman's compensation had paid for two operations for Jerry — one surgery from the back of the spine, another going in from the front of the spine. Jerry said that workman's compensation paid $80,000 for each operation. In our clinic, with our combined integrative approach, and within six months, Jerry's health was restored and he was fully functional and able to go back to work and participate in athletic activities again. The total bill for our clinic was about $4000, and workman's compensation fought our clinic every step of the way for payment to each practitioner, including payment to our Western medical doctor. Our chief financial officer estimated that she spent thirty hours to finally receive payment for the $4,000 billed. I was never paid a dime for my three sessions with Jerry.

There are many systemic problems overarching the Western medical system. Sometimes it seems like the consumer needs to be like the Greek hero Heracles in his quest to behead the many-headed Hydra.

> *Heracles tried to sever the Hydra's many heads, but found that another one always grew back. Finally his friend and charioteer, Iolaus, held a torch to the severed head and cauterized the wounds.*

There are so many bureaucratic and corporate mouths to feed that the consumer must find a way to avoid the dysfunctional rage and the urge to hack at these heads that seem so resistant to defeat. Each of us needs to embark on our own hero's journey to find the light that comes from the torch of our inner charioteer to heal and cauterize our own wounds, and those of the Western medical system. For many nowadays, finding that light comes from the new promise of integrative healthcare (Blount, 1998), a field that involves combining the best of Western healthcare with the time-tested wisdom of other healing traditions.

Impediments on the Road to Integrative Healthcare

Corporatization of Health

Our health has been reduced to the role of a minor character in a play directed by corporate market forces. Like in Greek mythology, when naïve Persephone is raped and abducted into the underworld by Hades to later return to the earth to become a mature woman, so are our views of health maturing as we realize that we have been abducted by the dark forces of corporate healthcare.

Realizing that the tobacco companies cared more about profits than about our health was surprising to some; but the extent to which these companies went to suppress information and threaten the whistle-blower Jeffrey Wigand, was an eye opener to many. But what was most disheartening to mindful consumers was the extent to which the tobacco industry's crimes against humanity were a symbol of a larger problem — the corporatization of healthcare. We learned that corporations no longer are held by the original intent of the founders of our constitutional government to serve the public interest;[14] and we learned that the statement in the movie, *Wall Street*, that "greed is good" is even being applied to people's health.

There seems to be increasing awareness that, regarding medication and healthcare, our government is not serving as our protector against corporate greed. At a conference sponsored by the National Institute of Health, Dr. Thomas Bodenheimer, an internist at University of California San Francisco said, "Conflict of interest is associated with intentional bias in the conduct and publication of drug trials" (as cited in the *San Francisco Chronicle,* August 16, 2000).

Though we hear of meetings at the Food and Drug Administration (FDA) to increase safety and oversight regarding medications,[15] reports have made suspect the role of our government and FDA in insuring our safety. The FDA does not seem to be able to be trusted to protect the Persephone in each of us from embarking upon our underworld journey.

In meeting with the Senate Finance Committee, Dr. David Graham, who was associate director for science and medicine in the Office of Drug Safety, questioned the FDA review process. He called the FDA's approval of the arthritis drug, Vioxx, "The single greatest drug safety catastrophe in the history of this country or the history of this world" (as cited in www.mercola.com). The short trial that was approved by the FDA proved problematic; it was later discovered that there was increased risk of heart attacks and strokes among Vioxx users, which did not happen until after they took the drug for eighteen months. Graham went on to cite the following statistic: A staggering 88,000 to 139,000 Americans suffered heart attacks and strokes as a result of taking Vioxx, and 30 percent to 40 percent of those died as a result. But this is not a single drug issue; in addition to Vioxx, Graham named five other drugs that are putting the lives of the public at risk. The five drugs in question are: Meridia, Crestor, Accutane, Serevent, and Bextra.

And even more disturbing is that Dr. David Graham was exiled from his work reviewing drugs and put to work in the office of the commissioner for blowing the whistle on this issue.[16] In a recent interview, Dr. Graham said that since the time that he appeared before the Senate Finance Committee to announce to the world that the FDA was incapable of protecting America from unsafe drugs, "very little has changed on the surface and substantively nothing has changed.

As currently configured, the FDA is not able to adequately protect the American public. It's more interested in protecting the interests of industry. It views industry as its client, and the client is someone whose interest you represent. Unfortunately, that is the way the FDA is currently structured."[17] Dr. Graham tells the following story, "a former office director for the Office of Drug Safety criticized me and tried to get me to change a report I'd written on another drug, Arava — he said to me and to a colleague who was a coauthor on this report that 'industry is our client.' I begged to differ with him. I said, 'No, industry is not the client, it's the American people, the people who pay our taxes.'"[18]

For those who want to discount Dr. Graham as just an isolated, disgruntled employee, note also that Andrew Mosholder was prevented from disclosing conclusions about the effects of antidepressants on increased suicide rates among children. The FDA said if he released data he would be subject to disciplinary action. He was urged to delete material from his statement to the Senate Finance Committee.[19]

With so many of the basic elements of our health no longer able to be put in the trusted hands of others, the modern consumer must be aware of those items in the marketplace that are visits to us from Hades, who abducts us into an underworld journey of ill health. When we want the sweet things of life and reach for the sweetener Aspertame, we might want to review the research on its neuro-toxicity (Lean & Hankey, 2004). What is more American than milk and cookies? Yet even here the needs of corporate profits stand between a mother and child when they reach for that glass of milk. From the movie *Corporation* we learned that Fox News suppressed the story about the harmful bovine growth hormone in our milk supply.

Corporatization of healthcare is now the norm of our culture where bottom line profits become more important than serving peoples' health needs. It is now difficult to separate our healthcare from the corporate interests that profit from our illnesses. According to the principle of vertical integration, corporations are increasingly involved in multiple levels of a market in order to insure maximum profitability. One corporation can contribute to a cause of an illness, produce a profitable "fix" to that illness, and corner the market so that other equally or more beneficial alternatives are reduced as options for consumers (Ausubel, 2000, p. 319).

For example Zeneca Corp. makes about one half of their profits of $500 million per year on the drug Tamaxofin. At the same time they produce herbicides such as Acetochlor, which is a known carcinogen. Its Perry Ohio chemical plant is the third largest source of potential cancer-causing pollution in the United States, emitting 52,000 pounds of carcinogens into the air in 1996. Their top executives populate the boards of many major treatment hospitals. Additionally, Zeneca founded and helps fund Breast Cancer Awareness Month while conspicuously failing to mention environmental causes (Ausabel, 2000, p. 319).

In the arena of psychology, the effect of corporations is also insidious. The American Psychiatric Association (APA), for example, gets significantly more money from drug companies' advertising ($13 million) than from membership dues ($10 million).[20] Though some psychiatric drugs have proved beneficial for patients, we must question how much economics has biased the search for healing alternatives to medication. For example, regarding the increased prevalence of attention deficit hyperactivity disorder (ADHD) even though the *Physician's Desk Reference* specifically states Ritalin, "should not be used in children under six years of age," U.S. physicians wrote 200,000 prescriptions in 1993 for children ages five and younger (Black, 1994). When looked at through the perspective of Wall Street and the profits coming to the pharmaceutical industry from the 3-5 percent of American school children who took Ritalin in 1994, the economic incentives are compelling (Robbins, 1996, p. 159). But aren't our children worth the least detrimental and most helpful care? Many of the issues are complex regarding psychiatric medications, and a balanced view is needed; however, one can not help but wonder what approach our country would take if we were truly looking for the best health options for such disorders.

Along these lines, it is interesting to note a study of 13 adolescents with an average age of 14-and-a-half years and a diagnosis of ADHD, who were taught Tai Chi for 30 minutes, twice a week for five weeks. The Conners Teacher Rating Scale was used by the subjects' teachers to evaluate their behavior prior to the Tai Chi classes, during the classes, and two weeks after the classes ended. The twenty-eight-item scale rates overall hyperactivity, as well as subcategories of anxiety, asocial behavior, conduct, dreams, and emotions. Results of the study showed that the adolescents' teachers perceived them as less anxious, emotional, and hyperactive. These improved scores also remained consistent throughout the two-week follow-up period, without Tai Chi" (Hernandez-Reif, 1998). If studies like this were borne out with larger numbers of students, using Tai Chi as one of the first lines of treatment (along with better funded counseling programs, dietary advice, and other non-invasive methods), it could provide an alternative that would avoid drug side effects and the stigma of being on medication. Also, such natural approaches could help build self-esteem and instill a message about dealing constructively with emotions rather than taking a drug to make them go away.

A survey of California's doctors by the California Medical Association (CAM) showed 75 percent of doctors were increasingly dissatisfied with their profession, with 43 percent saying that they were planning to retire earlier than planned, move out-of-state, or change professions, and 9 percent reported planning to reduce time dedicated to direct patient care.[21] Dr. Jack Lewin, chief executive officer of the CAM, said that doctors feel oppressed by an environment dominated by health maintenance organizations.

In the arena of psychotherapy as well, psychologists are increasingly dissatisfied with the reduction of fees and the paperwork required by managed care companies. One of my colleagues quipped, "I'm tempted to give the analogy to my patients — If you were going to go to a mechanic to get your car fixed, would you ask if he accepted your insurance card, which would require about an extra twenty minutes of work documenting the reasons for their repair? By the way, there may be another phone call or two required to make sure your paperwork is in order and that this is a valid claim. And, Mr. Mechanic, would it be O.K. to have your payment delayed for two to three months with possible phone calls and 'phone jail' while you are waiting to hear why the records were lost? One last item, Mr. Mechanic, my insurance company requires you to take a 40 percent cut in pay ... So, when can you begin the work?"

Since most consumers place cost reduction at such a high priority level, they do not often think about what the macro-environment is doing to their allied health practitioners. Corporations as well as consumers may eventually become more aware of the connection between health practitioner's dissatisfaction and deteriorating care; and perhaps an enlightened pubic will eventually change corporations control and influence, despite their vast reservoirs of money often being able to defeat single-payer plans (where consumers pay their health providers directly). Health practitioners, for the most part, much prefer these single-payer plans, or even government run options, to corporate-managed care with its reduced reimbursement rates, unwieldy paperwork, and excessive profits which go into corporate coffers. Twenty-one percent of healthcare costs are now spent on paperwork for insurance administration and an additional 13 percent is used to cover other administrative tasks, such as maintaining medical records.[22] Now we know where some of those dollars, coming out of practitioners' salaries and adding to consumers costs, are going.

Many in the United States have been willing to put up with this state of affairs because we have been living with an idealized image that the U.S. has the best medicine in the world. The truth is that even though we spend more per capita than any other country, our healthcare is not among the world's best (Reinhardt, 1996; Starfield, 2000; Fox, 2006), in spite of the propaganda we are fed. For example, our infant mortality rate is higher than many countries' where far less is spent on healthcare. In Shanghai, China the infant mortality rate is 9.9 out of 1,000, whereas in New York City it is 10.8 per 1,000. Beneath the statistics lie systemic problems that involve our country's $20 billion "birthing industry."

John Robbins's (1996) book, *Reclaiming Our Health,* contains an overview of some of these issues. He argues that the various interests of the birthing industry have led to procedures that often go against what would be most natural, and best, for women and their babies. And, he puts forth the case that this is one of the major causes of our high infant mortality rate. First, he describes the issue of birth position — where mothers in labor in hospitals are told to lie down on their backs even though research has shown that this is one of the worst possible positions for labor to progress (Robbins, 1996, p. 43). Robbins says that this position, used for the convenience of the hospital staff, lessens the flow of blood and oxygen to the uterus and the baby, reducing the effectiveness of the contractions, increasing pain, and contributing significantly to feelings of distress.

Second, is the fact that the United States has one of the highest cesarean rates in the developed world. Although cesarean sections are done for a variety of reasons, one reason in the U.S. seems to be because there have been many lawsuits involving claims that a cesarean was not done, or was done too late. Therefore in order to protect themselves from these lawsuits, doctors and hospitals perform cesarean sections more frequently. Robbins gives another reason for the high cesarean rates — the medical system makes more money from cesareans and these operations can be performed at the convenience of the obstetrician and the hospital. For those who would doubt the economic motives behind the high cesarean rates, it is interesting that when a Kansas health maintenance organization, Total Health Care, changed its policies and began to reimburse doctors equally for cesarean and for normal deliveries, the cesarean rate dropped from 28.7 to 13.5 percent in one year (Silver & Wolfe, 1992). But women are not told as part of their informed consent that this procedure increases the likelihood of mothers facing increased complications, and babies experiencing greater life-threatening problems (Wagner, 1993; Rosen, 1989).

Thirdly, depending on the surgical orientation of the obstetrician, they sometimes tell women not to eat during labor in case surgical anesthesia is needed. Robbins says that the irony is that this makes surgery more likely since the woman becomes famished and tired, and uterine contractions are weakened. The variety of ways that the hospital experience leads women to go against their own natural inclinations can lead to an increased need for medications like pitocin, which produces violent birth contractions, increased pain for the mother, and damage to the fetus (Barcia, 1972). Many of the above issues lead to an increased need for birthing mothers' needs for pain medication, which can lead to neurological impairment in their children (Korte, 1992, p. 124).

Fourthly, are the problematic aspects of fetal monitoring devices. Robbin's says that this procedure, which requires two electric catheters to be inserted through the woman's vagina, leads to rupture of the bag of water which protects the infant and thereby deprives a baby's head of the protective cushion of water needed during contractions; and thereby it may "cause the very distress it is supposed to detect" (Robbins, 1996, p. 49). Many studies published in medical journals cite that such monitors cause greatly increased rates of fetal and maternal distress, and triple the number of cesarean sections with no improvement of infant outcome (Levino et. al., 1986).

Though certainly there are beneficial aspects to the various advances in modern obstetrics, particularly in cases of birth complications, Robbins presents a powerful case about the systemic problems involved including the deliberate attempt by the American Medical Association to suppress the beneficial role of midwives in birthing. Robbins cites many studies that show when midwives are allowed to manage births, neonatal death rates reduce, and superior outcomes often result (Levy 1971; Korte, 1992, p. 57; Hinds, 1985). In this same book, with endorsements from Dr. Deepak Chopra and Dr.. Andrew Weil, are disturbing discussions about the role economics has played in choosing profits over health in a wide variety of other health-related arenas such as estrogen replacement therapy and cancer treatment.

While the economically driven machine of Western medicine sells us the notion that we have the most effective medical system, the corporate interests that control the airwaves are oftentimes demeaning of alternatives (Rampton & Stauber, 2001). Along these lines, the American Medical Association (AMA) has deliberately used hard-ball monopolistic practices to undermine the public's confidence in alternative healing methods even though scientific research has shown many of these methods are beneficial to people's health. The Manga Study in Canada found chiropractic treatment more effective than conventional Western treatment (Manga Report, 1994), as did the *British Medical Journal* find chiropractic treatment more effective than conventional Western treatment for lower back pain (Cichoke, 1995). However, the AMA waged a two-decade battle to eliminate chiropractic competition. This culminated in a U.S. Supreme court verdict in 1990, which let stand a 1987 verdict by a U.S. district court judge determined that the AMA was guilty of "lawlessness of conduct" that "constituted a conspiracy among the AMA and its members ... in violation of Section 1 of the Sherman Act" (Robbins, 1996). Going along with the same dominator-style power tactics, while AMA President Morris Fishbein was on a retainer making more money from the Phillip Morris tobacco company than he was from his AMA salary, he fought to undermine the Hoxsey cancer treatments. Eventually the Fitzgerald Report from the U.S. Senate in 1953 declared that a conspiracy had been undertaken by the AMA, the National Cancer Institute, and the FDA to suppress a fair investigation of Hoxsey's methods (Robbins, 1996; Ausabel, 2000). And in spite of California psychologists winning the Capp vs. Rank case, which allows psychologists to have hospital privileges, the hospital establishment did its best to prevent psychologists from gaining these privileges over several decades.

It is beyond the scope of this book to discuss the similar ways that the AMA has spear-headed campaigns to undermine the public's confidence in homeopathy, herbal medicine, midwifery, and many alternative cancer treatment methods, in spite of supportive research regarding the efficacy of these treatment methods. Reading Robbins's, *Reclaiming our Health,* is a good place to begin your immersion in this eye-opening literature and reevaluate your thoughts in light of the evidence presented in his book.

After extensive research on the economics and politics of our medical and psychiatric systems, one past president of the American Psychological Association said, "The health of our country is suffering because government is not willing to pay the political and economic costs to overcome the vested interests that prefer the status quo" (Fox, 2006).

In a program on 60 Minutes (CBS, 2006) it was reported that hospitals often charge the public two to ten times more than they charge the insurance companies for the same treatment.[23] Senator Charles Grassley, head of the Senate Finance Committee, is one of the people investigating this price gouging. No wonder problems in meeting medical expenses comprise 50 percent of bankruptcies in our country. The *60 Minutes* report on this issue focused on the poignant stories of two families who were unable to meet these inflated prices. Here is an example of how television, as a medium, can produce a state-specific state of consciousness where we may watch such news with intellectual interest, and a brief feeling of outrage, then quickly lose awareness that we are all potentially one medical emergency away from being these families — when our health, finances, and the health and finances of our beloved family members could be at stake.

The Heads of the Hydra:
Medical Dogma, Western Isolationist Worldview, Entrenched History, and the FDA Not Serving the Public Interest

There are many other "heads of the hydra" in the marketplace. In addition to the ways in which corporations stand in the way of a more humane healthcare system, entrenched beliefs have also stood in the way of developing a more integrative healthcare system. The time has come to use what is most efficacious — putting aside ideology in service of people's health. We may not be aware that our attitudes about how to approach illness contain unconscious ideology. For example, images of war pervade many modern approaches to disease, i.e. "the war against cancer and drug abuse" and medications as a "therapeutic arsenal." But, as leading-edge doctors have pointed out, *war against* is not necessarily the best course of action to take with many modern diseases (Weil, 1995).

Many are suggesting that rather than seeing disease as an opportunity to attack the enemy, disease can often be looked at as a guide in the healing process. Disease in this sense is a messenger trying to get our attention or a life process that can activate our healing resources. The mind becomes key in such an approach. For example, though the bacterium Heliobacter pylori is correlated with ulcers, many people infected with this germ do not get ulcers if their relationship to stress is changed (Weil, 1995, p. 91; Pelletier, 2000).

Until approximately three hundred years ago, virtually all medicine treated body and mind as an integral whole. However, just as the United States trampled over the Native Americans, denigrating anything other than modern Western values, so have we steamrolled over other philosophies and worldviews that have their merit and value.

With the advent of the Enlightenment of the eighteenth century, its mechanistic and reductionistic scientific model led to the separation of mind and body (Engel, 1977; Hahn et al, 1990). This eighteenth century paradigm of conventional medicine achieved its heights when it helped to end the infectious disease epidemics of the early twentieth century. Modern scientific biomedicine helped control many of the infectious diseases that were formerly the major causes of morbidity and mortality such as small pox, tuberculosis, and cholera.[24] So, it is natural to be appreciative and even become dependent on something that we think can save us from death. As aware consumers, we need to be careful not to over-generalize; and we need to be circumspect as to where we place our faith.

Western Medicine: Its Gifts and Limitations

The diseases that are killing people in developed nations are no longer these infectious diseases, but rather chronic, degenerative diseases such as heart disease, high blood pressure, cancer and diabetes, for which there is no pharmacologic "magic bullet" (Lehrer and Woolfolk, 1993). These diseases are inextricably related to psychological, lifestyle, environmental, and psychological factors (Pelletier, 2004).

Even in the area of chronic and degenerative diseases, and in many of the other areas where Western medicine has made significant contributions, leading-edge doctors are finding that complementary methods are helping improve their patients' health. The well-known Dean Ornish program has shown that diet, moderate exercise, and yoga can prevent relapse among heart surgery patients (Ornish, 1993). At the University of Massachusetts, Dr.. Jon Kabat-Zinn (1990) conducted a study of patients with a variety of chronic diseases who engaged in an eight-week program of meditation. Participants in the program experienced less pain, anxiety, and depression than patients treated with conventional medications.[25]

Western medicine's advances are not limited to infectious disease. Benefits of Western medicine come in many forms to citizens of the modern world. Eye surgery and new heart valves are great blessings to those whose body parts are failing. Stints and heart replacement surgeries help extend the life of cardiac patients. We've come a long way from pulling our teeth out by tying a string to a door; the benefits of modern dentistry include root canal surgery, composite fillings, and deep cleaning that helps us maintain our teeth and health into our later years. Stem cell research holds great hope for healing some major maladies such a paralysis, heart disease, etc.[26] The accuracy of modern medical interventions is aided by diagnostic methods using equipment such as magnetic resonance imaging (MRI), electroencephalograph (EEG), electrocardiogram (EKG), and electromylogram (EMG). And for type one diabetes, glucose and insulin monitoring devices, insulin, and insulin pumps help patients cope with this condition and extend their lives through the benefits of modern science and inventions.[27] And, on the horizon are the potential benefits of methods such as nanotechnology.

Western medicine is undeniably a valuable contributor to the world's healing traditions. But, with its position of power in Western culture, Western Medicine must take care to follow the Hippocratic oath and "do no harm." Using its political power to stop efficacious alternative healing treatments from being duly incorporated is a violation of their sacred oath, and a betrayal of the father of their tradition. Hippocrates, the father of Western medicine, was an Asclepiad physician — and the temple of Aesclepius was the first integrated healing center in the West, practicing surgery, gymnastics, hands-on healing, catharsis in the Dionysian theater (the origin of psychodrama), and dream incubation. But not only has modern Western medicine attempted to undermine the holistic vision of its father, it has attempted to do so with its great-grandfather. The teacher of Aesclepius was Chiron, from whom derives the word "chiropractic." In this light, our previous discussion about the AMA's attempt to denigrate chiropractic care is interesting — maybe we have a new term, "a double Oedipal complex," which involves unconsciously attempting to slay both your father and your great-grandfather.

"Integrative medicine" was borne from the desire to take the best of all medical traditions. It involves being open to cross-cultural/cross-temporal healing methods while at the same time taking a balanced approach to examining the appropriate role of each discipline in an individual's healing.

Efficacy of Complementary and Alternative Medicine

In addition to corporate profit motives and an entrenched biochemical, reductionistic worldview, another entrenched dogma has stopped integrative healthcare from being accepted. "There is a ubiquitous notion that conventional medicine is grounded in evidence-based research while integrative medicine is not. That assertion is grossly inadequate," wrote Dr. Kenneth Pelletier (2003, p. 38), author and leader in the arena of integrative medicine. As we shall see in the next section on Complementary and Alternative Medicine and mind-body medicine, these are some of the most efficacious and well-researched methods. Dr. Pelletier goes on to say that it is important to challenge both conventional and integrative medicine to meet a higher standard. (Pelletier, 2003).

Out of this quest for health models that work, and irrespective of their political placement in the mainstream health hierarchy, was born "evidence-based" medicine. This approach pays homage to the randomized double-blind, controlled trials (RCT), but does not rely solely upon RCT. This approach integrates clinical expertise, epidemiological studies, and occasionally even anecdotal evidence, with the best clinical research (Pelletier, 2000, p. 53).

Overview of Complementary and Alternative Medicine (CAM)

The natural healing force within each one of us is the greatest force in getting well.

— Hippocrates

Due to the current crisis in healthcare, it is no surprise that there has been the birth of an alternative/complementary healthcare movement. Complementary and Alternative Medicine (CAM) refers to a broad range of healing philosophies, approaches, and therapies that mainstream, Western medicine does not commonly use, accept, study, understand, or make available. A few of the many (over 650) CAM practices include the use of acupuncture, herbs, homeopathy, therapeutic massage, and traditional oriental medicine to promote well-being or treat health conditions. People use CAM treatments and therapies in a variety of ways. Therapies may be used alone, as an alternative to conventional therapies, or in addition to conventional mainstream therapies, in what is referred to as *holistic* — which generally means that they consider the whole person, including physical, mental, emotional, and spiritual aspects (NIH, 2001; Pelletier, 2000, p. 36).

Since a study by Dr. David Eisenberg (1990) in the *Journal of the American Medical Association* showed that more people were going to complementary/alternative practitioners than to Western doctors for their health problems, and spending $ 14.7 billion, our culture took notice. Then increasing attention was paid when Dr.. Eisenberg repeated his classic 1990 survey, and he and his colleagues at Harvard Medical School found that this number of visits increased by 47 percent from 1990 to 1997 for a total of 629 million visits (Eisenberg, 1998). All around us we see examples — in our friends, loved ones, and associates — of the widespread use of "complementary" forms of healthcare so that now the non-traditional has become traditional.

Actually it is a very interesting twist of words, and a fallacious hypnotic induction to say that the "traditional methods" such as acupuncture, Qigong, Ayurvedic treatments, herbs, etc. used all over the world for centuries are "non-traditional," and that the relatively new methods used by the modern corporate medical industry are "traditional." It seems as if we have arrived in Aldous Huxley's (1969) *Brave New World* where "double think" is pervasive: up is down, down is up, and traditional is non-traditional. It would be more accurate to refer to age-old healing practices as "traditional," and modern medicine as "modern."

As of 1998, and due in part from the Eisenberg studies, there were an increasing number of CAM courses offered in medical schools — 75 percent reported offering elective courses in CAM or including these topics in required courses. Of the 123 courses reported, 84 were stand-alone electives, 38 were part of required courses, and 1 was part of an elective. Common topics included chiropractic, acupuncture, homeopathy, herbal therapies, and mind-body techniques (Weizel, 1998).

However, in spite of the great need for more research in the area of CAM, the budget of the National Center for Complementary and Alternative Medicine in 2005 was only $123 million whereas the proposed budget for the National Institute of Health is $27.3 billion.[28]

Mind-Body Medicine

> *Healing is not just a property of the physical body, we are all mind-bodies, so that healing, like health and illness, must also be psychosomatic*
>
> — Andrew Weil, M.D.

Within the arena of complementary medicine is mind-body medicine — the umbrella under which this book stands. Stemming from the work of Herbert Benson, M.D. at Harvard, relaxation methods are one of the key ingredients of mind-body therapy.[29] According to well-known researcher Dr. Jeanne Achterberg, among the interventions constituting mind-body healthcare are clinical biofeedback, autogenic training, Jacobson's progressive relaxation method, the "relaxation response," hypnosis and self-hypnosis, yoga, various forms of meditation, deep relaxation, and Qigong (Achterberg et al., 1992). In the chapters that follow we will focus on how to integrate Qigong, and to more fully fit it into the medicine wheel of other mind-body healing traditions.

A 1996 National Institute of Health panel was instrumental in opening the door to using relaxation methodologies in the traditional United States healthcare system when it concluded that "integrating behavioral and relaxation therapies with conventional medical treatment is imperative for successfully managing these conditions." The panel did not endorse a single technique, but said a variety of them worked as long as they included two features —"a repetitive focus of a word, sound, prayer, phrase, or muscular activity, and neither fighting nor focusing on intruding thoughts" (Hilts, 1995, p. 45). When done this way the panel concluded that these techniques "can lower one's breathing rate, heart rate and blood pressure."[30] We shall later see how Qigong fits these guidelines well.

In the last section we spoke of the ubiquitous notion that mind-body medicine is not based on solid research. Though you will not hear it reported in the mass media, among the CAM interventions, mind-body interventions (MBIs) are supported by the greatest body of scientific evidence for the greatest number of conditions for the largest number of people (Michaud et al., 1998; Pelletier, 2000).

One of the most well-designed overviews of MBIs was conducted by Dr. John Astin of the Complementary Medicine Program at the California Pacific Medical Center in San Francisco. According to Astin and his colleagues,

Drawing principally from systematic reviews and meta-analyses there is considerable evidence of efficacy of several mind-body therapies in the treatment of coronary artery disease (e.g. cardiac rehabilitation), headaches, insomnia, incontinence, chronic low back pain, disease and treatment-related symptoms of cancer and improving post-surgical outcomes. We found moderate evidence of efficacy for mind-body therapies in the areas of hypertension and arthritis. There is now considerable evidence that an array of mind-body therapies can be used as effective adjuncts to conventional medical treatment for a number of common clinical conditions. (Astin et al., 2000)

For example, among the areas of MBIs where there are extensive randomized controlled trails and/or systematic reviews indicating strong to moderate evidence of efficacy are: (1) cardiovascular disease (Dusseldorp et al., 1999; Linden et al., 1996); (2) hypertension (Jacob et al., 1991; Linden & Chambers, 1994; Schneider et al., 1995); (3) insomnia (Morin et al., 1994); (4) general pain syndromes (NIH panel, 1996; Seers & Carroll, 1998); (5) lower back pain (van Tulder et al., 2000); (6) headache (Haddock et al., 1997); (7) fibromyalgia (Hadhazy et al., 2002) (8) arthritis self-care (Lorig et al., 1984; Superio-Cabuslay et al., 1996); (9) surgical outcomes (Dreger, 1998; Johnston & Vogele, 1993) and (10) adjunctive MBIs in cancer treatment (Devine & Westlake, 1995; Meyer & Mark, 1995; Redd et al., 2001).[31]

"The evidence of the clinical efficacy of Mind-Body Medicine in these above listed conditions is at least as good, if not better, than many common conventional interventions being used on a daily basis," according to the well-respected researcher of mind-body medicine, Dr. Kenneth Pelletier. (Pelletier, 2004, p. 28) He is former clinical professor of medicine at Stanford University School of Medicine, a clinical professor of medicine at the University of Maryland and the University of Arizona Schools of Medicine, director of the American Health Association, and author of more than two hundred professional papers. Dr. Pelletier makes the point that mind-body medicine is often overlooked because the intervention or cure does not exist "outside" of the individual, independent of "inside" changes in attitude, lifestyle, and orientation toward self and environment (Pelletier, 1995; Kabat-Zinn, 1996) Also, mind-body medicine recognizes that healing is not always synonymous with complete cessation of all physical symptoms. "It is not simply 'mind over matter;' it is rather that mind matters" (Pelletier, 1995).

With a medical system so tied to economic interests, it is important to realize that many natural things we can do for our health are more beneficial than traditional or complementary medicine. Listen to the way that Dr. Pelletier (2000) puts it in his book, *The Best Alternative Medicine*. Tongue in cheek, he says that it should not be so surprising that mind-body interventions are so efficacious.

> *For a moment reflect on a "breakthrough" intervention now being supported by decades of research from the National Institutes of Health. This breakthrough has been acknowledged by the American Medical Association and the United States Surgeon General. It has the documented effect of reducing virtually all forms of illness. It helps patients prevent or recover from high blood pressure, diabetes, osteoporosis, breast cancer, arthritis and chronic pain. It improves mental function, sleep, weight loss and muscle mass, and extends life expectancy. Miracle drug? New product of advanced genetic engineering? ... None of the above. It is ... exercise. Exercise is more important for health than most of the more exotic forms of CAM, and a great many forms of conventional medicine. (Pelletier, 2000, p. 34)*

Given this understanding of the importance of exercise, it is interesting that Tai Chi and Qigong are not more widely known than they are since they represent some of the most time-tested methods of beneficial exercise. They are low-impact so that instead of producing many of the injuries associated with running — including joint problems and injuries from running on hard pavement — these age-old practices provide benefits without negative side effects.

Tai Chi and Qigong: Age-Old Methods of Mind-Body Medicine

One of the aims of this book is to help Qigong to be more appreciated for its mind-body health benefits. Not that Qigong should need me as an advocate. For centuries before the term "mind-body medicine" was coined, Qigong and Tai Chi were two of the oldest methods of mind-body medicine empirically shown to positively effect the mind and body of the practitioner.

> *Qigong is a many-thousand-year-old method of cultivating the energy of life using movement, breath, static postures, awareness, sound, and touch.[32] Tai Chi is perhaps the best-known method of Qigong.*

It has been estimated that in Beijing alone, 1.3 million people practice just one form of Qigong every day (Tai Chi), and that in China as a whole, eighty million people practice Qigong everyday.[33] So maybe, even though as citizens of the United States we may have been trained to look down at other cultures, we might wonder what these empirically tested methods have to offer our healthcare system.

According to a 2002 National Health Interview Survey, about 950,000 American adults have practiced Qigong, and 5 million Americans have practiced Tai Chi (Barnes et al., 2004). *The Wall Street Journal* called Qigong, "the hottest trend in stress relief" (Weil, 2004). Dr. Andrew Weil (2004) says, "I often recommend Qigong as a relaxation method, and also think it can be an important part of a well-rounded fitness program ... Plus research in Asia suggests that practicing Qigong regularly can lower blood pressure, reduce the frequency and severity of asthma attacks, promote the healing of ulcers, reduce arthritis pain and even enhance immunity (Weil, 2004, p. 1)." *Time Magazine* called Tai Chi "the perfect exercise" (Gorman, 2002).

The many systems of Qigong are ancient methods of cultivating the body's vital energy, called Qi (also spelled chi). They use movement, breath, posture, awareness, sound, and touch and are one part of the multifaceted system of Chinese medicine. To understand Qigong in a more comprehensive way, we must realize that just as the term "psychotherapy" is a catchall term including many branches such as cognitive-behavioral, humanistic, Freudian/neo-analytic, Jungian/archetypal, and transpersonal, so are there many branches of Qigong. And each branch is important to understanding the whole of Qigong.

Qigong, itself, is a multifaceted tradition including methods in: (1) movement and stillness (Cohen, 1997; Ha, 1996; Mayer, 2004); (2) external emission for healing (Cohen, 1997); (3) medical self-healing methods (Chuen, 1999; Francis, 1993; Johnson, 2004); (4) spiritual practices (Cohen, 1997; Luk, 1972; Sha, 2003; Mayer, 2004); (5) internal alchemy (Luk, 1977), (6) internal martial arts and *nei jia* (O'brien, 2004); (7) inner power/*nei kung* (Danaos, 2002); (8) stretching/*daoyin* exercises (Kohn, 1989); (9) medical Qigong (Johnson, 2000; Sancier, 1996); (10) Taoist meditation (Kohn, 1989); (11) animal forms of Qigong (Feng, 2003; Mayer, 2004); (12) self-defense methods (Chia, 1986; Francis, 1998; Mayer, 2004; Ming, 1986; O'Brien, 2004); etc. In common to all branches of Qigong is that, at its roots, Qigong contains a treasure house of ways to cultivate the energy of life for a multiplicity of purposes.

Many scholars believe that Qigong began at the time of the Yellow Emperor, 2690-2590 B.C., when the theoretical foundation for Chinese medicine was laid.[34] The movement of the body's energy for healing purposes probably goes back as far as the earliest humans. Our earliest ancestors must have touched their own and other's bodies when ill or wounded, and learned movements to heal themselves, like rocking back and forth. In terms of definitive evidence, Qigong practices date at least as far back as 168 B.C., when, in the King Ma tomb, forty-four standing and seated Qigong postures were depicted in a chart with associated commentaries and prescriptions for various diseases. In Volume I, I discussed how the term "Qigong" (work, or play, with Qi, the energy of life) as a therapeutic art was first used in 1936 in a work by Dong Hao entitled, *Special Therapy for Tuberculosis: Qigong*. But Qigong derived from Taoist methods of *daoyin* (leading and guiding the life force of the universe, an old tradition with written sources that go back to at the time of Taoist Master Xu Sun who died in 374 A.D.).[35] However, way back further than this, and in Volume I, I show the ancient cross-cultural roots of Qigong in shamanic practices that formed the roots of cultures in Native America, Greece, India, Japan, and China and of various religions including Buddhism, Hinduism, Judaism, and Taoism.

Western culture was first introduced to the pain-reducing effects of Chinese Qigong in 1971 when the *New York Times* columnist James Reston had an emergency appendectomy with acupuncture needles, no anesthetic, and felt no pain. Since that time, a wave of interest has gradually grown in investigating the wider dimensions of Qigong. The PBS special with Bill Moyers interviewing Dr. David Eisenberg introduced the Western TV audience to the use of Qi in medical treatment in Chinese hospitals. A number of well-respected authors have written on the applications of Qigong in medical settings including Michael Lerner (1994) in his *Choices in Healing*,[36] and Dr. David Eisenberg's *Encounters with Qi: Exploring Chinese Medicine* (1995).[37] As of this date, there have been seven international conferences reporting research results. At these conferences[38] numerous studies from China reported Qigong's positive effect on a wide variety of diseases including kidney disease,[39] chronic hepatitis,[40] cancer,[41] and paralysis due to stroke.[42] The problem has been that many of these studies do not meet Western research methodology standards. However, as we will see below, there are many studies from well-respected journals supporting the efficacy of Qigong with a wide variety of health problems; and the International Society for the Study of Subtle Energies and Energy Medicine (ISSSEEM) has complied hundreds of studies and papers on the uses of energy in healing.[43]

Just how Qigong creates a healing response is still a matter of speculation. Researchers are still in the process of trying to determine the extent to which the energy spoken of in many ancient healing traditions exists, or whether the healing response to Qigong is a function of hypnosis, biochemical reaction, endorphin response, etc.[44] This subject is beyond the scope of the purpose in this book to explore the clinical usefulness of Qigong as a complementary tool to help our healthcare crisis.

Mainstream medicine often speaks in a derogatory way about alternative modalities for their lack of solidity of research, including the lack of randomized controlled trials (RCTs). In my peer-reviewed articles on this subject I, myself, have been critical of Qigong research methodology standards in many cases (Mayer, 1999, 2003). To stay balanced — in addition to looking at the political and economic factors about why more research is not done in these areas — it is important for those who criticize to realize that as much as 20-50 percent of conventional care, and virtually all surgery, has not been evaluated by RCTs. Richard Smith, editor of the *British Medical Journal* says, "Only about 15 percent of medical interventions are supported by solid scientific evidence ... this is partly because only 1 in 5 of the articles in medical journals are scientifically sound and partly because many treatments have never been assessed at all" (Smith, 1991, p. 798).

It is true that Qigong is not a panacea, and research in many cases is not up to modern standards. In my peer-reviewed research of Qigong, I have pointed out problems in the research methodology (Mayer, 1999, 2003.) However I conclude these articles by writing,

> *Although many of the studies of Qigong practice and hypertension have methodological flaws ... which may account for some unknown portion of improved health outcome measures ... we should be circumspect before fully discounting positive effects reported in mortality rates, incidence of strokes and retinopathy (Kuang, 1991), and other positive outcome measurements in patients who have suffered from long term hypertension (Kuang, 1991; Jing, 1988; Wu, 1993), or chronic renal failure (Suzuki, 1993). These represent significant numbers of long-term sufferers of severe hypertension. Even if methodological flaws such as expectancy biases and placebo effects contributed to positive results, the results need to be considered seriously in an area that has such significant health ramifications. (Mayer, 2004b, p. 132)*

In addition to addressing research methodology issues, I have tried to bring objective balance to the idealization that some have about Tai Chi and Qigong. I have addressed issues regarding transcendence of psychological issues to my Qigong colleagues (see Chapter 5); and I have spoken about how an excess of Qigong practice can even, on some rare occasions, lead to psychotic symptomatology (see Chapter 14). There is even a diagnostic category called "Qigong psychotic reaction" in the *Diagnostic and Statistical Manual (DSM IV-R)* of the American Psychiatric Association (2000, p. 902).

However, even though there are problems at times with Qigong and Qigong studies, significant research from substantial sources is beginning to accumulate, including respected scientific journals regarding Qigong and Tai Chi's efficacy in helping in the areas of: (1) cancer (Chen, 2002); (2) asthma (Reuther, 1998); (3) chronic pain (Wu, 1999); (4) diabetes (Iwao et al., 1999); (5) fibromyalgia (Astin et al., 2003; Mannerkorpi & Arndorw, 2004); (6) heart rate variability (Lee et al., 2002); (7) long-term disabilities (Trieschmann, 1999); (8) neurological illness (Weintraub, 2001); (9) Parkinson's disease[45] (Schmitz-Hubsch et al., 2005); (10) shingles[46] (Irwin, 2004), (11) preventing falls amongst the elderly (Province et al., 1995); and (12) reducing strokes and increasing blood flow to the brain for subjects with cerebral arteriosclerosis (Sancier & Holman, 2004). As well, many articles on Qigong's general health benefits have appeared in a variety of professional journals concerning: (1) attention deficit hyperactivity disorder and Tai Chi (Hernandez-Reif et al. 2001); (2) Qigong's multiple cardiopulmonary, musculoskeletal, and postural benefits as a therapeutic exercise approach (Wolf et al., 1997); (3) the anti-aging benefits of Qigong (Sancier, 1996); and (4) multifaceted benefits of Qigong in increasing bone density (Chen et al, 2006) and boosting the immune system, (5) psychosocial health of elderly with chronic physical illnesses (Tsang et al., 2003), etc.[47]

In Volume I, Appendix I (Mayer, 2004b), I outlined how the Bodymind Healing Qigong system I have developed over the last thirty years may be applied to various health issues including hypertension, chronic pain, joint problems, etc. Some Qigong practitioners may find beneficial other Qigong practices than the ones I have mentioned there, and all such Qigong practices would benefit from further controlled research to determine which methods work best when, and for which types of people.

In the following chapters, though I will discuss in more depth some of the scientific and clinical research on the efficacy of Tai Chi and Qigong, one of my major aims will be to present how Qigong and broader bodymind healing methods can be integrated into psychotherapy and behavioral health private practice. An interesting set of issues emerges as one considers blending such seemingly different traditions. One of these issues I call the "transcending (rising above a psychological issue)/transmuting (working through an issue) dialectic." We shall see how Qigong and other traditions of relaxation can help a person to *transcend* many issues by activating an altered state of consciousness — which may have healing effects — yet the concern is that such methods may not help a patient to work through, or *transmute* deep-seated issues, which may producing longer-lasting healing results. Later in this book we shall see how, even though such traditions are excellent for relaxation, empowerment, and many other health-related benefits, the traditions come to their fullest fruition when they serve as an integral spoke in the wheel of integrative medicine, and as an integral spoke on the psychotherapeutic wheel. We will see how such traditions benefit from joining hands with other traditions like Western psychotherapy which can be considered a "transmuting tradition" (see Chapter 5); and we will address the ethical and dual relationship issues regarding bringing these traditions into the psychotherapeutic setting (Chapter 22). We will see how combining the benefits of Tai Chi and Qigong with the transmuting elements of Western psychotherapeutic and behavioral health methods can combine into a powerful integrative treatment method for alleviating our current health crisis.

Psychotherapy and Behavioral Healthcare: Two Streams Become One

It is often assumed that psychotherapy and behavioral healthcare are two separate disciplines. This viewpoint is framed by the notion that there are internal neurotic or psychotic psychological problems that are best served in the psychotherapeutic setting; and that there are physical health or medical problems that are best served by a medical doctor or alternative/complementary health practitioner.

But another, more holistic way to look at this is that these two streams are not, in the deepest sense, separate. When people suffer from anxiety they have some physical manifestation of that problem — maybe it manifests in their stomachs as irritable bowel syndrome, or just queasiness. Likewise, when people suffer from hypertension and go to a Western doctor for medication or to a behavioral health specialist — whether it is a biofeedback expert or a psychologist — the question should be asked, "What is going on in their lives that is manifesting that physical disorder?" The truth of mind-body unity is often violated when "God in a pill," is prescribed, thinking we can take a capsule rather than come to terms with the underlying mind-body-spirit root of our life issues.

There is a growing body of evidence that physical disease and psychological issues are inextricably interrelated. A study of 6000 seriously depressed people found them to have almost twice the risk of suffering a heart attack — a greater risk than either smoking or having elevated cholesterol (Cohen et al., 1998). People with higher levels of hostility and cynical mistrust of others and the world are at significantly higher risk of heart disease. In one study, physicians with the highest scores on a measure of hostility at age 25 were seven times more likely to die by age 50 (of all causes, not just heart disease) than those with low scores (Barefoot et al., 1993). Individuals with the greatest amount of job-strain, i.e. occupations where they have high demands but relatively low decision latitude or control of their work, are almost four times more likely to suffer a heart attack. This is equivalent to the increased risk a person has from smoking or elevated cholesterol (Karasek et al., 1981). Lynch (1977, p. 113) documented the multiple problematic psychosocial issues and events that negatively impact coronary patients; and he discussed how hospitalization is often the signal that the precipitating psychosocial events have created an avalanche leading to body breakdown or even death. Ryke Geerd Hamer, M.D. (1997) noted that cancer often comes secondary to a person experiencing a trauma that "catches them totally off guard, a shock against which one is totally powerless and defenseless" (p. 3). Dr. Hamer's research suggests that a trauma can create a lesion in the brain, which sets up a corresponding lesion in the body. These brain lesions can be identified using CAT scans; and Hamer has identified specific sites in the body where corresponding lesions may occur.

The first thing that many think when they have stress in their bodies is that they should go to a physician for medication or to a behavioral health consultant to learn relaxation methods, take a yoga class, or do some biofeedback. The suffering person hopes that they can transcend the effects of stress through the right medication or a well-chosen relaxation method. In the next chapters we will see how the healing methods of depth psychotherapy can add a transmuting tool to help work through of the elements at the root of stress. Epictetus, the famed Greek philosopher, said, "It's not what happens to you but how you react to it that matters." Attitude and psychological response patterns have long been known to play integral roles in life and health.

I once heard a lecture by Harvard-trained Dr. David Eisenberg after he returned from China. He made note of a general trend that was exemplified by a woman admitted into a Chinese clinic with neurasthenia (anxiety) and was treated with acupuncture. Though her anxiety was temporarily relieved, the root of the social problem — her husband was taken away from her to serve the state, and her anxiety about the same thing happening to her sons — was not addressed. Certainly transcendent relief (as people often get from acupuncture treatment) is an important aim of health professionals, but in order for people to transmute the underlying real life issues at the root of their problem, the people themselves — along with their beliefs, attitudes, and the life pathways upon which they travel — need to be at the center of integrative healthcare.

In the following chapters I will attempt to create such an integrative methodology that combines transcending and transmuting elements — an integrative health mandala. This combination that I call the "transcending/transmuting dialectic" forms one of the center-posts of Bodymind Healing Psychotherapy.

CHAPTER 2: INTERDISCIPLINARY AND CROSS-CULTURAL RESEARCH — SOURCE OF CLINICAL MODELS FOR MIND-BODY HEALING

Once upon a time the primordial shaman traveled to the top of a sacred mountain and from his secret hiding place spied on the gods and goddesses who danced around a sacred crystal ball that glowed in the dark. When these divine Beings were in need of healing, they went to this ball, put their hands to it, and healing came. When the Gods slept, the shaman grabbed the ball and ran down the mountain with it. Just as he had the thought, "Now I'm going to be the greatest healer of all times," he slipped and fell. The sacred crystal ball shattered. Some say that our very human race was created from this sacred gem and that each human being carries a piece of the divine gem of healing. Others say that the healing traditions of the world were created from the pieces of this crystal ... and that it is the purpose of this modern era to put back the pieces of this gem into its original wholeness, and stop arguing about whether ours is the best piece.

— As told by Dr. Michael Mayer
From the *Shamanic Sacred Oral Archives*

The Need for Interdisciplinary, Cross-Cultural Models of Psychological Healing

We are in an era where the old, narrow field of psychology is joining forces with a wide variety of other disciplines to expand its terrain, and thereby increase its ability to heal. As a family member may be healed by rejoining with his or her family, so does psychology benefit from its relationship with its wider family of interdisciplinary and cross-cultural healing traditions.

Various leading-edge thinkers are now advocating that the realm of psychological healing must be made wider and deeper, in order to plummet the unfathomable depths of the human condition (Schore, 2003; van der Kolk, 1996). We have known for some time now that our psychological problems surface in distorted beliefs, social problems, undeveloped emotional intelligence, and early childhood fixations; and we now know that our psychological problems are isomorphically[1] reflected on the physical level in biochemical imbalances and brain dysfunctions.[2] But what Western culture is just beginning to learn is how our psychological conditions are also co-created with, and healed by, other facets of the whole grand crystal of life.

The esteemed psychologist Allan Schore (2003) begins his classic text *Affect Regulation and the Repair of the Self* with a first chapter called "Interdisciplinary Research as a Source of Clinical Models." One of his major points is the need to include the areas of neurobiology, psychobiology, and the understanding of brain functioning, in order to fully understand and heal attachment disorders.

Adding his voice to the idea of expanding psychology's parameters is Psychiatrist, Dr. van der Kolk, author of over one hundred abstracts and journal articles and three books in the field, and director of Boston University Medical School's Trauma Department. In his book on traumatic stress, he wrote, "In multicultural societies, the importance of drawing on the healing customs of the past from various cultures can all too readily be forgotten" (van der Kolk, 1996, p. 551). Dr. van der Kolk advocates appropriate use of methods from spiritual and religious traditions to aid in the healing of trauma.

It is within this context of broadening and deepening psychotherapeutic tradition that this book will focus on bringing to light other facets of the grand crystal of healing the psyche in order to form an integrated, multidisciplinary whole. This chapter will address the clinical usefulness of some of these interdisciplinary and cross-cultural, cross-temporal traditions such as: meditation, symbolic process traditions, cross-cultural mythology, body therapies, psychobiology, psychoneuroimmunology, clinical hypnosis, Qigong, and shamanism. Later in the book you shall see how these and other interdisciplinary and cross-cultural, cross-temporal traditions give form to the approach I call Bodymind Healing Psychotherapy.

Integrating Meditation into Western Psychotherapy

What happens when two major intellectual and practical disciplines from separate cultures and contexts — both of which seek to understand, heal, and enhance the human mind — first come into contact after centuries of separate development? This is one of the questions of our time, a question which is increasingly pressing as the meditative and Western psychological disciplines now meet, challenge, and enrich one another in ways that are only beginning to be understood.

— Dr. Roger Walsh
University of California College of Medicine

Benefits and Problems with Integrating Meditation and Psychotherapy

Among the many healing traditions from which psychotherapists now draw is meditation. Before integrating new disciplines into psychotherapy, psychologists have been careful to weigh the potential advantages and disadvantages with a keen eye on research. Let's first look at some of the reservations that psychologists have had about incorporating meditation into psychotherapy, and then explore some of the benefits that have been discovered.

In my early psychotherapy training I was taught that the integration of meditation with Western psychology and psychotherapy should be avoided for a variety of reasons. Meditation was described as a form of dissociation, false transcendence, or defensive regression. Another line of critique stated that meditation and psychotherapy have different purposes that may not blend.

Engler (1986), who is both a teacher of Buddhist meditation and a psychiatrist, differentiates between the seemingly different goals of psychotherapy and Buddhist meditation. Following a psychodynamic line of critique, he explains how, according to object relations theory, the major cause of psychopathology is the lack of a sense of self caused by failures in establishing a cohesive, integrated self, resulting in an inability to feel real. In contrast, Buddhist psychology says that the deepest psychopathological problem is the presence of a self, the "clinging to personal existence." Though Engler points out these seeming differences in purpose of the two traditions, he questions whether or not these two goals are mutually exclusive and suggests that one might be a precursor of the other, when he humorously concluded, "You have to be somebody before you can be nobody." Epstein (1986) disagrees with Engler's contention that meditation is only appropriate for those already possessing a "fully developed personality." He conceded that some people who are attracted to meditation have pre-oedipal issues and narcissistic pathologies, but argues that Buddhist meditation may play an effective role in the resolution of infantile, narcissistic conflicts. Another problem Engler (1986) noted, is the tendency of people following spiritual meditative traditions to develop idealizing transferences to meditation teachers — reflecting a need for acceptance by or merger with a source of idealized strength and calmness.

Carl Jung (1936) also warned about the problems of using Eastern psycho-technologies due to the possibility of psychotic decompensation and self-inflation as a result of identification with archetypal material emerging from the unconscious; he suggested that these pitfalls can be avoided by cultivating the ability to consciously understand unconscious material (pp. 232-234). And those who follow a Jungian orientation today, such as James Hillman, point out the different purposes in the two traditions. According to Hillman (1976), spiritual disciplines are oriented toward "peaks" and the work of the spirit, and psychotherapy is by nature involved in the "valleys" and the work of the soul.

Though the above critiques have validity in given cases, we will see below that much research in the field points to cases where transcendent experiences from meditation have led to beneficial states of awareness. Noble (1987) reviews studies which show that subjects who have had peak experiences are less authoritarian and dogmatic, and more assertive, imaginative, self-sufficient, and relaxed. He reports that, "such experience increased significantly with overall gain in psychological maturity score ... transcendence can present participants with a total existential shift in which their experiences of self and of the world, their orientation in space and time, their emotional attitudes and cognitive styles, and perhaps even their entire personalities undergo a profound change" (Nobel, 1987). Wuthnow (1978) showed that peak experiences were positively associated with introspective self-aware and self-assured personalities and with a greater sense of meaningfulness and purposefulness in life. Wilber (1980, 1986) says that meditation is not a way of digging into lower and repressed structures of the submerged unconscious; he says it can be a way of facilitating emergent growth and development of higher structures of consciousness.

Among the psychological benefits, meditation has been reported to help:[3]

1. Develop a relaxed state of awareness and reduce stress (Almas, 1988; Kabat-Zinn, 2003). This state of relaxation is useful with stress disorders and helps to ameliorate insomnia, eating, anxiety, panic, and phobic disorders (Miller et al., 1995).

2. Provide cognitive benefits by helping patients understand their own mental processes and preoccupations, develop the "observing self," and gain the ability to shape or control mental processes (Deatherage, 1975). A central effect of meditation is calming the mind and reducing anxiety (Taylor, 1988, p. 35).

3. Inhibit unwanted behaviors such as the ones listed throughout this section.

4. Develop a compassionate relationship one's life issues, and enhance a patient's psychological inner work (Rinpoche, 1993). Studies have shown that when compassion is being cultivated through meditation, practitioners have demonstrated uniquely high gamma EEG profiles (Davidson, et al. 2003; Goleman, 2003).

5. Reduce anxiety, hostility, and depression together with enhanced subjective well-being (Shapiro & Astin, 1998).

6. Alleviate human suffering by activating the experience of the "real self," and help to establish an observing self (Deikman, 1982).

7. Induce an altered state of consciousness (Shapiro & Giber, 1978).

8. Increase self-awareness of mental and emotional states, gain mastery over instinctive, compulsive reactions, gain insight into one's true nature and into reality, encourage exploration of religious themes, images, and feelings, and expansion of ego consciousness into a more universal consciousness (Odanjnyk, 1988).

9. Foster maturation — because meditators tend to score higher on measures of moral and cognitive development, self actualization, coping skills and defenses, and states and stages of consciousness (Alexander & Langer, 1990, Alexander et al., 1991).

10. Develop equanimity which overlaps but extends beyond Western concepts of "affect tolerance" and "emotional resilience" to include, not only tolerance, but even serenity in the face of provocative stimuli (Goleman, 2003; Travis et al., 2004). (See below, for preliminary experimental support from measures of emotional stability and startle response.)

11. Serve as a self-regulation strategy that leads to improved self-control and self-esteem (Anderson, 2000), increase higher empathy ratings, increase measures of interpersonal functional and marital satisfaction (Tloczynski & Tantreills, 1998).

12. Provide self-treatment regimens that are highly efficient for the use of the therapist's time, and therefore are cost-effective.

13. Produce a transcendent state, allowing one to go beyond his or her habitual perceptions or conditioning of self and roles, culminating in peak experiences. This state is called by different names in different traditions such as *samadhi*, *satori*, or enlightenment (Delmonte, 1987; Noble, 1987).

14. We will be proposing that, in addition, Qigong meditation also can help to *anchor*, a state of awareness that helps facilitate ego cohesion in maintaining one's center when meeting the emotional tides of life (Bandler & Grinder, 1979).

Concluding his review of the benefits and problems with integrating meditation and psychotherapy, Bogart (1991, p.1) wrote,

Are meditation and psychotherapy compatible? While meditation leads to physiological, behavioral, and cognitive changes that may have potential therapeutic benefits, psychoanalytic and Jungian critics claim that meditation is regressive, fosters dissociation, and neglects the unconscious. In contrast, transpersonal theorists contend that, when used with attention to assessing the individual's developmental stage and choice of an appropriate method, meditation may promote inner calm, loving kindness toward oneself and others, access to previously unconscious material, transformative insight into emotional conflicts, and changes in the experience of personal identity.

Meditation Research

Be open-minded, but not so open-minded that your brains fall out.

— Groucho Marx

Psychotherapists are known to use elements of meditation in their practices to help patients in a variety of ways (Sperry, 2001; Segall, 2003). Following is some more detailed research on the benefits of meditation for use in the psychotherapeutic setting.

In Walsh's (2006) review of the psychological benefits of meditation, he cites studies reporting enhanced capacities in attention, thought, cognition, lucidity, emotional intelligence, and equanimity calculated by measures of emotional stability, startle response, motivation, and moral maturity. After reviewing critical studies and meta-analytic reviews of the literature, Walsh (2006) concludes that, "Despite conceptual and methodological flaws, the current literature suggests that meditation can have significant psychological and somatic effects and therapeutic benefit" (pp. 230-231). (For those who wish to examine more critical reviews of methodological and conceptual limitations in the design of meditation research, see Baer (2003) and Canter & Ernst (2003).)

Regarding the behavioral healthcare benefits of meditation, it has been shown to be effective with hypertension and hypercholesterolemia (Schneider et al., 2005); asthma, stuttering, hormonal disorders, type two diabetes, premenstrual disorders (Murphy & Donovan, 1997); immune function in cancer patients, reducing symptoms of distress in fibromyalgia and cancer patients, and decreasing pain in multiple chronic pain syndromes (Carlson et al., 2003); and treatment of psoriasis, prostate cancer, and artherosclerosis (Kabat-Zinn, 2003; Zamara et al., 1996). A dramatic study, and one that warrants replication, demonstrated improved psychological functioning and reduced mortality among individuals in a nursing home who were taught Transcendental Meditation (Alexander et al., 1989).

In some cases, advanced meditators have demonstrated unique capacities such as voluntary control of the autonomic nervous system, lucid dream sleep, dramatic reduction or possibly eradication of drive conflicts (Jonte-Pace, 1998; Wilber et al., 1986), and detecting fleeting facial micro-expressions of emotion more effectively than any other group—including CIA agents, who were the second to the top scorers. One study on advanced meditators indicated their enhanced ability to respond with subjective compassion and objective relaxation while observing a video of a severely burned patient — after measuring their micro-expressions and startle response through video observation, the chief researcher reported findings that in thirty-five years of research he'd never seen before. (Goleman, 2003).

In the ongoing investigation of the use of meditation to enhance psychological functioning, a neuroscientist at the University of Wisconsin's new $10 million W. M. Keck Laboratory of Functional Brain Imaging and Behavior, Richard Davidson, compared some of the Dalai Lama's most accomplished practitioners to control subjects. From his research published in the Proceedings of the National Academy of Sciences in November 2005, the Dalai Lama's monks showed an increased "neuro-plasticity" in their brains, and increased gamma waves — some of the highest frequency and most important electrical brain impulses. Davidson says that this research is important in showing the positive effect that mediation has on the inner workings and circuitry of the brain.[4]

With all the positive research emerging in the field it is understandable that the Harvard mental health newsletter recently reported that meditation is now being incorporated into psychotherapeutic practice. Dr. Michael Miller (2005), editor of the newsletter, wrote, "The introduction of meditation practice into cognitive-behavioral therapy may represent a further stage in the historical evolution of psychotherapy ... merging cognitive techniques and meditation ... they call the 'third wave' of cognitive-behavioral therapy."[5]

It is important to point out that meditation is not a panacea for the wide range of issues affecting the human condition in dealing with the vicissitudes of life. Jack Kornfield (1993), who is both a psychologist and meditation teacher, adds an important grounded perspective to this discussion. He says,

> *For most people, meditation practice doesn't "do it all"... there are many areas of growth, (grief and other unfinished business, career and work issues, certain fears and phobias, early wounds and more) where good Western therapy is, on the whole, much quicker and more successful than meditation ... Does this mean we should trade meditation for psychotherapy? Not at all.*

Choosing among the tools from psychotherapy and meditative approaches does not need to be an either/or proposition. In everyday practice many therapists "titrate" their patients, i.e. move back and forth, between guiding them through transcendent meditative states and doing the work of transmuting psychological complexes.[6] The well-rounded psychotherapist does not dichotomize between using tools from psychotherapy and meditation traditions; instead, he or she carefully chooses from both traditions, while always keeping in mind the individual needs of each patient. For example, for a bipolar patient in a hypomanic phase, a therapist would not introduce a Kundalini Yoga energizing practice, but a therapist might incorporate, along with traditional psychotherapy and appropriate medication, a Taoist breathing method or postural practice like Standing Meditation Qigong to help the patient sink his or her Qi, find his or her center-line, and discover central equilibrium. As such integration takes place the clinician honors the ethical caveats involving experimental treatments in emerging areas (see Chapter 22).

In this chapter, my aim is not to identify which types of meditation have been shown to be most beneficial for which issues, nor is it my aim to review the hundreds of studies over the last four decades that identify the positive elements of meditation regarding psychological and physiological benefits, but rather my goal is to give a brief overview. Determining which meditative methods are best for which life issues is an important next step for researchers. It is my belief that when there is as much funding to differentiate such benefits among styles of meditation as there is for pharmaceutical research, we will have reached the mythic "golden age."

Differences in Styles of Meditation

Part of the problem with discussions of meditation is that there are so many different types, and what is true about one type, may not be true for another; as well, a style that is good for one person may not be good for another.

Walsh (2006) defines meditation as a family of self-regulation practices that focus on training attention and awareness in order to bring mental processes under greater voluntary control and thereby foster general mental well-being and development, and/or specific capacities such as calm, clarity, and concentration. Although the above definition focuses on mental parameters, Walsh adds that there are also body-oriented practices — such as yoga, Tai Chi, and Qigong — each of which are meditative traditions that add elements such as controlled breathing, body postures, body movement, and energy manipulation. He points out that different styles of meditation vary in terms of type of attention, the relationship to cognitive processes, and regarding the goals.

In a course I taught at San Francisco State College, for the final project, I had students choose and practice a form of meditation that went contrary to their normal style of dealing with life. For example, an intellectual person might practice Bhakti Yoga (yoga of the heart); students who identified as heart-centered practiced Jnana Yoga (the yoga of mental wisdom); students who were unfocused practiced concentrative meditative disciplines; those who were obsessively focused took up spiritual practices involving letting go; avoidant students practiced methods to enhance being present such as Vipassana Meditation; and those who felt they were overly-mental practiced a body-oriented spiritual tradition such as Tai Chi.[7]

Differences in consciousness attributable to different meditative paths have long been recognized. In a classic study it was found that yogis practicing their form of meditation (Anand et al., 1961) were oblivious and unreactive to the world as measured by an EEG, whereas Zen Meditators become keenly attuned to the environment (Kasamatsu et al., 1969.)

With so many different types of meditative approaches from which to choose, psychotherapists who consider incorporating a style of meditation into their practice need to be cognizant of the stylistic differences, and how those differences may affect their patients.

Explanations for Meditation's Healing Effects

Just as there are many different styles of meditation, so too are there many explanatory models for its healing effects. Some traditional explanations are metaphoric such as: purifying the mind, freeing it of illusions and conditioning, and awakening it from its usual trance; other explanations include calming disturbances, rebalancing mental elements, enlightening practitioners, and uncovering true identity (Walsh, 1999). There are also physiological explanatory mechanisms such as: reduced arousal, modified autonomic nervous system activity, stress immunization, and hemispheric synchronization and laterality shifts (Cahn & Polich, 2006).

When we, as Westerners, look at meditative traditions we often try to "decontextualize" them to see how they can be of use to our culture. In anthropological terms this can be the trap of adopting a purely etic (outsider) perspective, rather than both etic and emic (insider or native) perspectives. Having immersed myself in the practices of Qigong and Tai Chi for about the same thirty years that I have been practicing psychotherapy, I hope to be able to justly represent both an etic and emic perspective in the two volumes of this series on the *Tao of Bodymind Healing*.

It is important to note that when one tries to explain meditation based upon Western psychological and philosophical explanations, there can be a danger of inappropriate reductionism (Frankl, 1967; Rosch, 1999; Wilber, 2000). The state of meditation has been described as self-hypnosis, or a relaxation response (Benson, 1984); it has been pathologically compared to dissociation and defensive regression; and it has been neurally reduced to nothing more than brain mechanisms and biochemical reactions.

All of these Western etic perspectives and interpretive reductions can lead to a "colonization of the mind," as well as the loss of the richness and uniqueness of these meditative traditions and the valuable complementary perspectives they offer (Walsh, 2006). Thus Walsh suggests that there are three Piagetian stages of the process of integrating psychotherapy and meditation:

> *The first is one of mutual enrichment via "pluralism" and "accommodation," moving from ... assimilation (forcing novel ideas into preformed conceptual categories) to accommodation (expanding and enriching conceptual categories). The second is an "integrative" stage in which the process of mutual enrichment, both theoretical and therapeutic, becomes increasingly systematic. The third stage is "integral" (Wilber, 2000) as the processes of mutual enrichment and integration lead to, and are conducted within, an increasingly comprehensive, coherent, and holistic conceptual framework, adequate to both meditative and psychological traditions.* (Walsh, 2006, p. 228)

There are currently many emerging integrative movements and psychologies such as cross-cultural psychology, integral psychology (Walsh & Vaughn, 1992; Wilber, 2000; Cortwright, 2007 in press), psychosynthesis (Assagioli, 1965), Ridwan/Diamond Heart (Almas, 1988), transpersonal psychology (Wilber, 1986), and integrative psychotherapy (Arkowitz & Mannon, 2002). Many of these approaches are on the path to creating an integral vision to enhance global cross-fertilization and mutual enrichment of cultures. Walsh (2006) says that, "this could be one of the defining processes and opportunities of our time."

The intention and hope behind the two volumes of this book is to serve to create such an "integral" approach to Eastern and Western healing practices — most specifically an integration of Qigong and psychotherapy. Some could introduce a Qigong movement into psychotherapy and call their approach "integrative." As will be shown, Bodymind Healing Psychotherapy, with the intention of congruence with Walsh's integral stage, is more comprehensive and coherent with a holistic conceptual framework. Volume I focused on the multifaceted dimensions of the meditative traditions of Qigong and Tai Chi; Volume II focuses on how those traditions, as well as other ancient wisdom traditions, can aid the healing process in psychotherapy and benefit behavioral healthcare.

Qigong: Some Specific Benefits of this Meditation Method

Let's look at some of the specific ways in which Qigong benefits psychotherapy. Although some of these benefits have been mentioned earlier in this chapter (when illustrating the research on meditation), here, I have included them for emphasis, and with additional details regarding, specifically, the benefits of Qigong as a particular style of meditation. With the following research and examples, I hope to provide clear and concise answers to the questions: What are the unique attributes of Qigong as a style of meditation? And why is it chosen, in this book, as one of the major methods to be integrated with psychotherapy practice?

1. Qigong fits well into the guidelines stated by a National Institute of Health panel (NIH, 1996), which concluded that integrating behavioral and relaxation therapies with conventional medical treatment is imperative for successfully managing these conditions. The panel did not endorse a single technique, but stated that a variety of techniques worked in lowering one's breathing rate, heart rate, and blood pressure as long as they included two features: (1) a repetitive focus of a word, sound, prayer, phrase, or muscular activity, and (2) neither fighting nor focusing on intruding thoughts. Repetition is a key element in activating healing processes — for example, in energy psychology, repeatedly tapping on points while focusing on new constructive beliefs has been related to greater treatment success rates (Andrade & Feinstein, 2003). In the Eye Movement Desensitization and Reprocessing (EMDR) method, the eyes repeatedly moving from side to side while constructive beliefs are being stated, is believed to be integral to positive treatment outcomes. If repetition is such a key to healing why not further investigate Qigong and Tai Chi traditions — which, for thousands of years, have developed sophisticated ways to use whole-body repetition of movement, repetitive movements for isolated body parts, and repetition of sounds to promote healing.

2. Qigong doesn't only activate a relaxed, altered state, it activates a "state-specific state" (Tart, 1968; Rossi, 1986) that is both relaxing and empowering.[7] This state is called "*sung*," relaxed awakeness. It can be helpful for alleviating symptoms of stress, as well as for empowering those who have deficits in the areas of self-assertiveness, those who are victims of trauma, etc.

3. Qigong not only produces a relaxed state of awareness, but also, in its unique way, provides a pathway to develop qualities seen as useful by therapists who integrate meditation into psychotherapy. Qigong and Tai Chi can reciprocally inhibit unwanted behaviors adding to Wolpe's (1958) behavioral approach; it can aid in developing an observing self, adding to Deikman's (1982) transpersonal perspective; and it can

help to cultivate "a cohesiveness of self" adding to Horner's (1990) psychoanalytic methods. Qigong can help to *anchor* that state of awareness that helps to facilitate ego cohesion in maintaining one's center when meeting the emotional tides of life, adding to Bandler and Grinder's (1979) hypnotherapeutic approach to anchoring. Qigong, like many forms of meditation, can help us to develop a compassionate relationship to our life issues.

4. Qigong traditions, particularly Tai Chi, can help traumatized patients regain a safety zone in their bodies.

5. Qigong adds an energy cultivation practice beneficial to those who are depressed or suffer from sympathetic nervous system overload — such as in cases of fibromyalgia, chronic fatigue, trauma, etc.

6. The well-known relaxation and energizing attributes of Qigong have been applied to many issues that psychologists see in their everyday practices — including insomnia, anxiety, joint problems, energy deficiency, chronic pain, etc.

7. Whereas some meditative traditions are oriented to transcendence, Qigong and Tai Chi are, for the most part, body-oriented traditions,[9] which cultivate "a cohesiveness of self," (Horner, 1990). From an integrative perspective, the way Tai Chi and Qigong are usually practiced, they do not specifically focus on psychological issues (such as early emotional wounding and negative beliefs); however, I shall put forth the case that oftentimes shifts in a person's psychological stance in life can be a result of this practice. As we shall see in the chapters on Bodymind Healing Psychotherapy, an approach that specifically incorporates the psychological dimension and these body-oriented practices can synergistically combine for the benefit of the whole person.

8. Qigong and Tai Chi are multifaceted traditions that are not only meditative but can also be seen as forms of hypnosis, and therefore may result with similar health benefits known to be related to hypnosis (Rossi, 1986, 1988). Both have an empirically time-tested record for enhancing health for a multiplicity of health-related conditions (Sancier, 1996; Pelletier, 2000).

9. The relaxation model of meditation's therapeutic effectiveness is often associated with the psychological theory of *reciprocal inhibition*. Wolpe (1958) hypothesized that a phobic reaction would extinguish if it could symbolically occur in the presence of an incompatible response such as relaxation. This is one of the foundations of modern behavioral self-control strategies, though it is usually done with relaxation responses such as breathing methods or Jacobson's relaxation methods.

However, in keeping with BMHP's integrative perspective, if not integrated into the wider realm of psychotherapeutic knowledge, Qigong and Tai Chi could suffer from many of the problems concerning meditation traditions listed earlier, such as "false transcendence." In this sense it is wise to follow Deikman's (1982) advice that "Meditation is an adjunct to therapy, not a replacement for it" (p. 143).

Chapter 2: Interdisciplinary and Cross-Cultural Research

In the following chapters I will put forth the proposition that Qigong and Tai Chi are more than just meditation traditions — they have the ability to add to other fields of experience that are pivotal to modern health and modern psychotherapeutic healing as stated in the points listed above. For example, Tai Chi and Qigong have significant similarities with, and can make a contribution to the field of medical hypnosis with its time-tested, empirically proven track record of producing health changes. Qigong and Tai Chi are forms of exercise, ideal for the sedentary lifestyle issues that are a significant contributor to the health problems of our modern world. And, as we will see in later chapters, when integrated into the practice of psychotherapy the problems regarding false transcendence can be counter-balanced.

While reading this you may be thinking, Isn't it a little absurd to have a person get up and move around in psychotherapy, when stillness is needed to dive within and get insights about one's life? It is a common misperception to think of Qigong as just involving movement when, in fact, a key part of Qigong practice involves static postures.

In Volume I, I discussed how the Buddha was trained in the warrior class and in internal martial arts before he became the well-known advocate for enlightened mindfulness in everyday life. In his early years he learned both standing and sitting static meditation postures that incorporated methods of psychological transformation and physical empowerment (Tomio, 1994). I discussed there how even before Buddhist times, methods of postural initiation, which combined states of stillness, relaxation, and energy cultivation, were part of cross-cultural methods of spiritual transformation, survival, and health. In Volume I, I discussed how there was a diaspora of integrated holistic traditions of mind-body healing, and how Qigong and Tai Chi today are stripped of some of the wider dimensions of mind-body healing that were part of its Buddhist and shamanic underpinnings (Tomio, 1994; Goodman, 1990). In Volume I, I took steps towards restoring the holistic foundation of Qigong and Tai Chi along these lines.

Many therapists use and teach relaxation methods to provide their patients a tool with which to handle the stresses of life. Such breathing methods can be used to help anchor patients in a state of consciousness that gives them the ability to cope with inner and outer life stressors. In this sense, the altered state that these breathing methods activate are somewhat like a medication that a psychiatrist prescribes. They activate a safety zone that facilitates inward accessing of deeply held material, and create an island in an overwhelming sea that provides ground from which new psychological edifices can be constructed. We will see how the many-year-old tradition of Qigong has sophisticated breathing methods that enhance a state of relaxation and can add to current treatment methods.

In Volume I, I emphasized how Qigong could be made more whole by incorporating the fields of Western bodymind healing methods and psychotherapy. Now in Volume II, one main area of focus is to establish how psychotherapy can benefit from the practices of Qigong. Here we are challenged to stretch our limits and wonder how to incorporate these traditions of postural initiation into psychotherapy.

There are many forms of Qigong, some well-suited to be incorporated within the psychotherapeutic setting (see Chapters 4 and 5), and some that can be used as an adjunctive method of self-healing outside of the psychotherapeutic setting (see Chapter 24). Also, it is important for the psychotherapist to be aware of contraindications to doing various types of Qigong. For example, there is a type of Qigong called "external emission Qigong" where the healer holds his or her hands up in various postures that are reported to emit healing energy to the person in need of healing. In my opinion, this type of Qigong is not suited to the psychotherapeutic setting because, regardless of the objective reality of its efficacy, this method can create a "giving away" of the patient's power to the therapist in a way which is contraindicated in the psychotherapeutic setting.

Towards a Well-Rounded Psychotherapy: The Psychotherapeutic Mandala

In my first book, *The Mystery of Personal Identity,* I put forth the notion of using the astrological mandala as a psychotherapeutic meta-system (Mayer, 1984). To update this idea we could imagine a circle of healing traditions operating together as an integral whole. Each therapist could create his or her own healing mandala (Arguelles, 1972). For example, my mandala would have Gendlin's Focusing method at the center. In the lowest area of the circle, corresponding to underworld journey, would be placed psychodynamic and object relation theories. In the upper part of the circle would be cognitive-behavioral approaches. On the right side of the circle would be intersubjective and relational approaches. Since the astrological mandala includes elements of fire, earth, air, and water, the elements of healing would all participate together as an integral whole. Just like astrologers look for the angles of relations (aspects) between planets (Rudhyar, 1970), so then would we look for the interconnections between therapies instead of looking for which one is the best, thereby avoiding projecting a Western competitive worldview onto psychotherapeutic healing. As has been called for recently, the psychotherapeutic profession, upon taking this integrative view, would draw on the arena of brain research, the new biology, various psychotherapies, and ancient sacred wisdom traditions.

Chapter 2: Interdisciplinary and Cross-Cultural Research 35

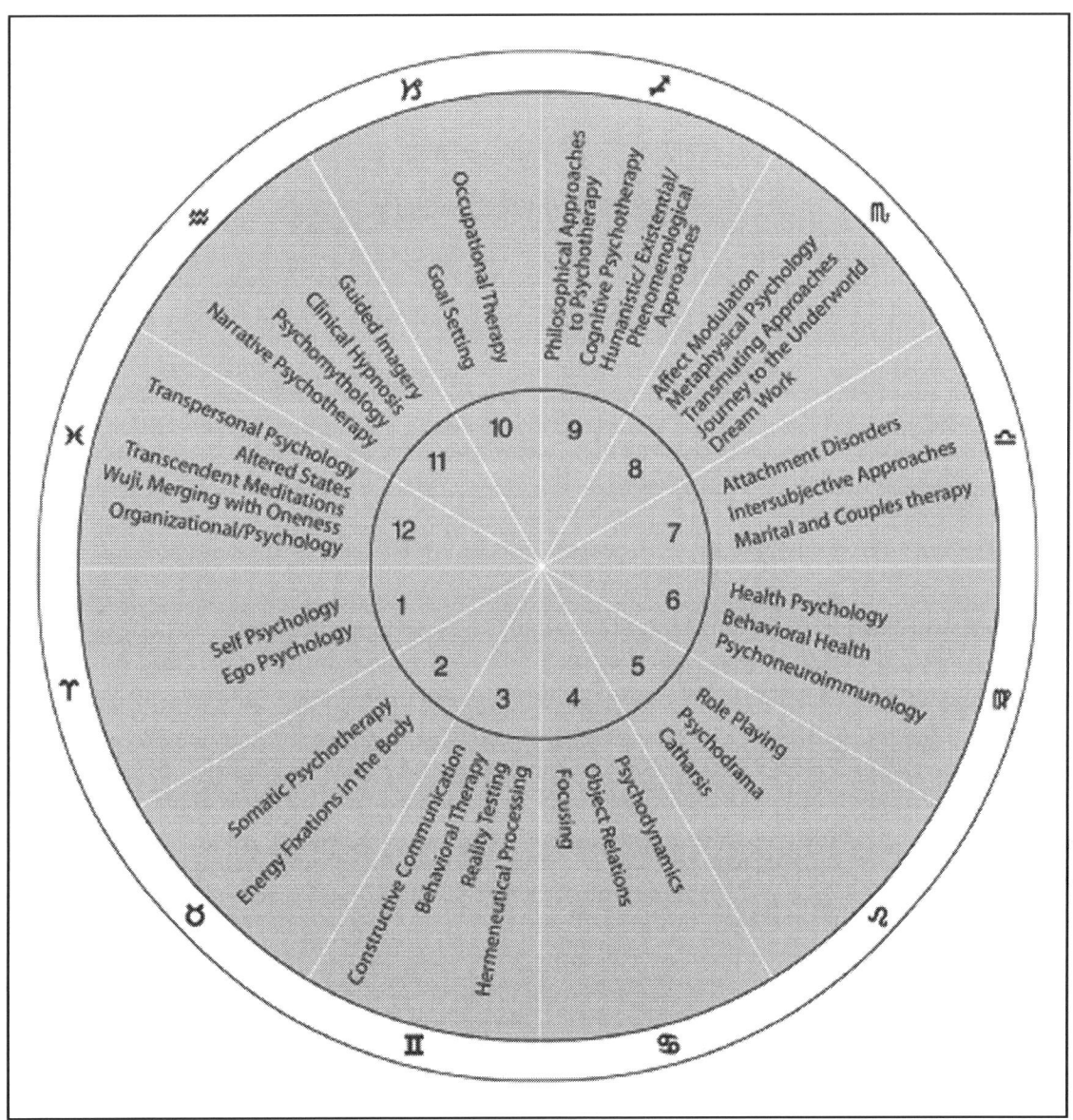

Figure 2: Psychotherapeutic Mandala

The important part of this mandala is not which psychotherapeutic system fits into which of the twelve pieces of the pie.[10] Each system, depending upon its attributes focused upon at a given time, may be inserted into a different part of the wheel. For example, psychoanalysis fits with the astrological fourth house symbolizing the home, since to a great extent it delves into the past home life of the individual. However, when we focus on psychoanalysis' interpretive orientation of giving meaning to experience, we might then place psychoanalysis in the ninth house of philosophy. The important part of creating a psychotherapeutic mandala is creating a well-rounded ordering principal and centering device for the therapist. Just as the martial artist uses the ancient circle walking of the Pa Kua to center him or herself (Smith, 1972), or the Native American uses the medicine wheel to put all things in creation into a interrelated whole (Storm, 1972), so can the modern therapist use the psychotherapeutic mandala.

The "Axis Mundi" of Bodymind Psychotherapies: Eugene Gendlin's Focusing Method

*The heart has its reasons
of which reason knows nothing.*

— Blaise Pascal

Every year one of my colleagues asks me to be a guest speaker for his graduate psychology class in body-based psychotherapy.[11] The essential theme of my presentation there is that Eugene Gendlin is an unrecognized hero of the psychotherapeutic tradition. In the 1970s he was named the most distinguished professional psychologist of the year by the American Psychological Association. He won this award for his research exploring the question, What is the essence of what makes psychotherapy work, regardless of the name of the type of psychotherapy? He got doctoral students to interview a large number of people who had been in a wide variety of different therapies and ask them to reflect upon the moments that most created change in their psychotherapy. Using a phenomenological research methodology, he then had the students write up the themes that emerged. From listening to these tapes he extracted out his *Focusing* method, which replicated the essence of what made psychotherapy work for these people. He found that when people reported moments of unclarity about what they were feeling, they paused and tuned into a body sense where they might find a word, image, or phrase that was close, but not an exact fit with the felt sense of the problem. Then they would "resonate" those words, images, or phrases to get an exact fit with the felt sense of their problem until they experienced an "ah–ha." At this point the patient would experience a "felt shift," and new meaning would arise. From these interviews, Dr. Gendlin created the six steps of the Focusing process which are outlined below, and can be found more completely described in Dr. Gendlin's *Focusing* book (1978).

1. Clearing a space
2. Finding the felt sense of the problem
3. Finding a handle-word, image, or phrase
4. Resonating
5. Asking
6. Receiving

Just as ancient sacred wisdom traditions and symbols can help us to order psychotherapies by using psychotherapeutic mandalas, so the concept of "*axis mundi*,"[12] helps us to see the value of Gendlin's Focusing. Cross-cultural mythologies speak of the importance for the initiate to create an *axis mundi* to become centered in his or her world. For example, in the Roman mysteries of Mithras and in Tai Chi, the initiate imagines his or her spine aligned with the axis of the earth so that his or her spine connects heaven and earth. The reason Gendlin's approach can be seen as an *axis mundi* for the psychotherapist of any tradition, is that Dr. Gendlin has the body sense at

Chapter 2: Interdisciplinary and Cross-Cultural Research

the root of his approach and meaning-making at the top. Regarding psychotherapeutic healing, a major axis of healing comes from the ground of the body and felt experience, and then the felt experience is transformed by the new meanings discovered.

Two of the key things that Gendlin's method adds to psychotherapeutic tradition are (1) an emphasis on the role of the body and felt meaning, and (2) the indication of an energy shift in the process of healing the psyche. Brain research confirms the substantial impact of this inner work through documented changes in EEG patterns of the brain at the moment of a person's "felt shift" (Don, 1977).

While serving as Dr. Gendlin's Focusing training coordinator for ten years, with his approval I added the idea of using Taoist methods of relaxation to his "clearing a space" step, and wrote a little blurb for the *Association of Transpersonal Psychology Newsletter* in the early 1980s, and an article which included these methods in Dr. Gendlin's *Focusing Folio* journal (Mayer, 1982). In later sections of this book we will see how the Taoist method of *Microcosmic Orbit Breathing* complements the use of Gendlin's Focusing as a core method of Bodymind Healing Psychotherapy. When lecturing to graduate students, I am still in touch with the contribution that Dr. Gendlin made to the field by this method of direct reference to the bodymind to create change in psychotherapy. I say that Dr. Gendlin's work stands at the center of the continuum of mind and body psychotherapies, and that it is an invaluable method for allowing meaning to emerge directly from the body's "felt sense."

In actuality, separating body and mind is a false dichotomy based upon "Descartes error" (Damasi, 1994). Descartes posited that our existence stems from our thinking function, i.e. I think therefore I am. As modern neuroscience has confirmed, body is in mind, and mind is in body (Pert, 1997). However, for heuristic purposes we can say that there is a continuum of bodymind therapies. On one end of the continuum we have seemingly body-based healing methods such as Rolfing, massage, acupuncture, etc. In actuality — as anyone who has participated in somatically oriented therapies knows — mental images and issues from the past that are "stuck in the cells" frequently emerge and are often released in this work. This has been called, "the issue is in the tissue." On the other hand, we have apparently mentally-based healing modalities like cognitive therapy, behavioral therapy, talk therapies such as psychoanalysis, etc. As practitioners are beginning to learn, when the body isn't incorporated in these "mental therapies," they do not function as well.

One example of successful blending of the body with mind-based therapies can be seen in Francine Shapiro's (1995) EMDR work. When a patient states a limiting negative belief using cognitive restructuring, she asks the patient for a number on a subjective unit of distress scale (SUDS), "10" being the worst you ever felt, and "0" being totally relaxed. This provides a body-based measure to go along with a cognitive therapy. When the patient finds a new, more truthful or constructive belief, the person tunes into the body sense that is created with that new belief. As reported in her work with trauma, posttraumatic stress disorder, and other psychological issues, the therapist would then work with the patient until he or she comes down close to a 0 SUDS level, based on his or her body sense. Dr. Peter Levine's (1997) "somatic experiencing method" draws from the way animals heal from trauma in order to provide methods such as shaking and reenactment to human sufferers.

Brief Overview of Body Therapies

Behind your thoughts and feelings, my brother,
there stands a mighty ruler, an unknown sage
— whose name is self.
In your body he dwells; he is your body.

— Friedrich Nietzsche
Thus Spoke Zarathustra (1954, p. 34)

There is a longstanding history of body-oriented therapists such as Wilhelm Reich (1970), Alexander Lowen (1971), Stanley Kelleman (1985), and others who have confirmed the importance of the role of the body in healing (Murphy, 1992). Deri (1990), in the *Psychoanalytic Review*, reminds us that the ego functions within the context of a total psychobiological organism, and warned of "the danger of a purely psychological mode that disregards the unavoidable psychosomatic oneness of a functioning human being." In the era of brain and biological research, the importance of the role of the body has been further substantiated in both the area of psychotherapy and in the field of behavioral medicine.

Western civilization's mind/body split is manifested in the somatic symptoms that are seen in most psychotherapists' everyday practices. An over-anxious, obsessive patient suffers from irritable bowel syndrome; a housewife who holds back her anger and is overly placating suffers from fibromyalgia; a manager at a local company, while trying to make it and not feeling up to the task, suffers from hypertension. Without meaning to be categorical or interpretive regarding causal factors of these complex and ideographic conditions, the point is that "physical" and "psychological" are interrelated conditions (Gatchel & Blanchard, 1993). Many therapists are growing to realize that the two must be treated as an inseparable whole, for example by blending relaxation methods (such as Jacobson's) and delving into how psychological patterns are rooted in cognitive and psychodynamic issues.

Psychobiology, Psychoneuroimmunology, Stress, and Healing

The field of psychobiology was one of the first where psychologists incorporated new advances in the physical sciences and brought them to the arena of bodymind healthcare. Beginning with the work of Walter Cannon (1914), who spoke of the stress response in the 1920s, in the 1930s, one of the grandfathers of Western stress physiology, Hans Selye showed that stress caused increased illness through its effect on the immune system.[13] There are many interesting intricacies in the research. For example, the stress response itself does not cause illness, it is the prolonged repeated stress without rest that damages the immune system and is correlated with disease (Sapolsky, 1998).

Dr. Herbert Benson, president of Harvard Medical School's Mind/Body Medical Institute, is most associated with coining the term "relaxation response." He showed the role of the relaxation response in ameliorating hypertension and cardiac problems.[14] Dr. Benson said, "relaxation, meditation, and prayer have begun to find a place in medicine, not only because of support in scientific studies, but because of the possibility that these techniques might reduce medical costs" (Hilts, 1995, p. 45).[15]

From the early days of research on stress and the relaxation response, the whole field of bodymind medicine and psychoneuroimmunology has blossomed, with solid evidence for the relaxation response and the mind to effect healing in a wide variety of conditions. Robert Ader, who coined the term "psychoneuroimmunology," showed that animals' immune systems could be conditioned to extend their life spans (Ader et al., 1991). The fields of bodymind medicine and hypnosis demonstrated the ability of the mind to: modulate the autonomic nervous system and blood flow (Barber, 1978, 1984); ameliorate the alarm response (Cheek, 1969; Rossi, 1973, 1980), heal Raynaud's disease, (Conn & Mott, 1984; Jacobson et al, 1973); and reduce hypertension and cardiac problems (Benson, 1983; Gruen, 1972; Schneck, 1948; Wain, Amen & Oetgen, 1984; Yanovski, 1962). As well, bodymind healing methods have demonstrated the ability to enhance the immune response (Black, 1969; Hall, 1982-83; Lewis, 1927; Mason, 1963). For a more complete list of conditions successfully treated with clinical hypnosis see Rossi (1986, p. 110) and Cheek (1988).

It has been estimated that 50 percent of all primary care consultations and physical disorders are attributable to somatization — the phenomenon wherein a patient presents with a physical symptom that can not entirely be explained by a physical disorder (Brown et al., 1971; Roberts, 1994). This process arises when an individual "hides" from threatening psychological information that expresses (or "transduces") his or her emotional distress into physical symptoms (Wickramasekera, 1998).

Wickramasekera hypothesizes and presents evidence for the fact that somatizers have various risk factors: first, either a high hypnotic ability (as measured by scores of 12-9 on the Harvard Group Scale of Hypnotic Ability), or a low hypnotic ability (as measured by a score of 3-0); and secondly, a high score on the Marlow Crown Scale (17 or higher), which measures the capacity for blocking aversive perceptions, memories, and moods from consciousness — a process that appears to operate by promoting inattention to aversive situations and by amplifying positive situations (Crown & Marlow, 1980). Gutherie (1998) adds to this line of research by arguing that somatization is essentially a normal process that most people experience. He believes that it is better to look at the spectrum of somatoform disorders in normal people who do recognize the significance of psychological factors in the development of their symptoms, rather than study those unaware "true somatizers" who are at the risk of developing persistent symptoms. Awareness of the mind-body connection is an important key to healing a large variety of common complaints including headaches, irritable bowel syndrome, etc.

One way of interpreting the insights of this research is by recognizing that there is a basic human need to go into an altered state — whether we call this state love of God, mystical experience, or hypnotic trance. When we are unable to tap into this state, our propensity to embody the suffering of life increases. From a spiritual point of view, when we incarnate the issue in our body, we have the opportunity to work on it. At one end of the continuum, patients who are overly empathic and tend to merge with others often end up absorbing the issues of life. On the opposite pole, those who are overly critical, such that they cannot go into an altered state, similarly take on the issues of life in their bodies, due to not having the capacity to merge with the divine healing source of their own creation.[16] There is less opportunity for imbalances to arise in the body when we "follow the middle way." (Sounds like an experimental proof of Taoist philosophy.) This adds substance to the psychospiritual dictum that: when we bring our issues into the light and work with them instead of falsely transcending them, we have less of a chance of taking on the issues of life in our bodies.

In later chapters I advocate an approach that combines Qigong with Western psychotherapy in order to resolve those imbalances which create somatization. I suggest balancing the altered state of Qigong by using Gendlin's Focusing method along with the insights that arise from Western psychotherapy in order to become aware of the felt meaning of what arises when doing various Qigong practices.

Tai Chi and Qigong, the embodiments of Taoist philosophy, have the middle way as a conceptual stance, and have practices to cultivate this stance. For example, when a practitioner imagines standing like a tree, he or she balances being in a trance state and remaining open to all things, while at the same time having "bark" and boundaries to protect from the forces of the impinging world. In hypnosis, a person might be induced to imagine standing like a tree, but Qigong goes further. In Qigong, a sophisticated method is practiced whereby the practitioner is trained in postural details of this standing meditation, *Standing like a Tree,* which cultivates boundaries and openness simultaneously, and tests whether or not a practitioner is grounded like a tree when someone pushes on him or her (see Volume I).

Qigong as a Form of Hypnosis

Just what hypnosis is, is a matter for speculation. The term was originally coined by a Scottish physician, James Graid, who thought it was a form of sleep, and used the Greek word *"hypnos"* for sleep. By the time that he and others realized it was not sleep, the term had caught on and was never changed. Franz Mesmer used it and referred to it as "animal magnetism," and Freud used it but gave it up for "the talking cure." Milton Erickson is perhaps the most successful modern user of the storytelling methods of clinical hypnosis. The most common definition of *"hypnosis"* today establishes it as an altered state rather than as a simple response to suggestion (Crasilneck & Hall, 1985). There is increasing research showing the physiological changes that take place in hypnotized subjects, including functional studies of the brain utilizing MRIs, PET scans, and biochemical studies of receptor alteration (particularly in the dopamine system); and there are hypnotizability scales such as the Harvard, Stanford and Hypnotic Induction Profile (Gross, 2002). An overview of theories of hypnosis can be found in the texts of Crasilneck and Hall (1985), and Lynn and Rhue (1991).

The elements constituting Qigong and hypnosis are overlapping circles. Research differentiating various types of Qigong from various types of hypnosis, in terms of the type of trance state induced, could provide clinical models where each could be used for its own particular merits. Many elements used in clinical hypnosis have similarities with, or perhaps in some cases may even derive from, Qigong and Tai Chi. For example, in one of the most common methods of trance induction, "the hand levitation method," the subject is told to first take a deep breath and then "imagine a string around your hand, attached perhaps to some balloons gently pulling your arm up to induce a light, feathery, floaty feeling" (Crasilneck et al., 1985, p. 72). Those familiar with the first movement of Tai Chi will notice the similarity to position one, *Commencement*. And in Tai Chi the instructor will often suggest an image to go along with this practice, such as imagining your arm floating up in water, or imagining you are pulled by a string attached to a star in the heavens. In hypnosis, such inductions create an altered state of consciousness and allow a "letting go" of the normal everyday world. This helps one enter into a state where ordinary habitual patterns can be let go of so that the realm of the imaginal can enter and create new realities. Next, this altered state is used to create a metaphor, which brings forth a new state of awareness. For example: just as your hand can float up with no seeming effort, so can you let go of your anger about your recent job loss, and allow yourself to open to new possibilities as life leads you to naturally rise to the occasion and find your next job.

The understanding of the first movement of Tai Chi can add to the technology of the arm levitation method. First, the instructions about the breath in many hypnotherapy inductions are not as sophisticated as in the many-thousand-year-old Tai Chi tradition. Advising one to "hold the breath," as some health practitioners do, can actually create tension. In Tai Chi, as the hand rises, the practitioner is advised to be aware of a natural, slow inhalation synchronized with the movement — this complements the natural rising of energy — and a slow exhalation complements the letting go. Many who are trained in arm levitation are trained to do it with a locked elbow and a straight wrist. In Tai Chi, the elbow is unlocked, which adds to the ability to let go. The wrist initially rises higher than the hand to facilitate the energy to rise, and as the arm comes down, the wrist lowers slightly further than the hand, along with slightly filling out the lower back (*Ming Men*), to sink the body's energy (*Qi*). Also, synchronizing the breath and movements with exact postural understanding adds an inherent health-producing component, i.e. this movement is used to release tension in the arm for conditions like carpal tunnel syndrome.

One of the aims of this book is to show how Qigong adds to the tradition of medical hypnosis. Like medical hypnosis, Qigong uses the power of imagery and relaxation to induce an altered state of consciousness and to increase one's receptivity to change longstanding patterns. Here I put forth the hypothesis that as a body-oriented method, Qigong has an added benefit — to facilitate the movement of energy directly to the place in the body where the energy is blocked. In alignment with its roots in Chinese medicine, Qigong helps us to understand the underlying roots of fixated patterns — particularly when used in conjunction with Western psychotherapeutic methods. Questions have often been raised about whether Qigong is "just hypnosis," as if that would be a bad thing. Given the wealth of evidence, some of which is touched upon above, hypnosis research is valuable in showing just how powerful the mind/imagination is in promoting healing. Though Qigong rests on the foundation of mind-body medicine and relaxation methods, it does something more — it not only helps the person to relax, but activates a vital energy state that re-empowers.

Qigong and Leading-Edge Hypnosis Research Know — It's Not Just about Relaxation!

Leaders in the field of clinical hypnosis wonder what hypnosis really is? Dr. Rossi recently pointed out that hypnosis is not just a state of relaxation. There has been a longstanding debate in clinical hypnosis called the "activity-passivity paradox" (Gorton, 1957, 1958). Gorton's papers on physiology of hypnosis show that both sympathetic (arousal) and parasympathetic (relaxation) are part of hypnosis. More recent research shows that the nature of arousal or relaxation is dependent on the type of suggestion made during hypnosis. (Sturgis & Coe, 1990, p. 205).

The paradoxical nature of hypnosis's ability to activate rather than relax is demonstrated by a study that reported significantly higher norepinephrine levels in a hypnotized group of patients undergoing angioplasty than in the control group (Weinstein & Au, 1991). One would expect that if hypnosis does cause relaxation, then those patients who were hypnotized would have a lower arterial catecholamine level than their controls. This was not the case. Just the opposite occurred.

The evolving literature in the field of medical hypnosis show that hypnosis utilizes both the active and passive branches of the autonomic nervous system, thus leading to an expanded model of the psychobiological domain of therapeutic hypnosis (Harris et al., 1993; Rossi, 1982, 2000.)

In the light of hypnosis research it is interesting to note that, for centuries, Qigong has trained people in achieving states of reaction which combine relaxation and energization. Just like the Whorfian hypothesis shows that Eskimos have many names for snow due to their increased need for this specific knowledge in their environment; so in the area of the internal martial arts, when your life is at stake, a well-grounded understanding of different energetic states is needed. Thus a major part of training in Qigong is understanding and a achieving a state called *"sung"* in Chinese, or relaxed awakeness. And in *Yi Chuan* (mind or intention) *Qigong,* the practitioner is trained in a variety of combinations of relaxation and energizing methods using breath, posture, and mental intention. For example, the practitioner trains in letting go to a state of total relaxation in the midst of attack, or holding a stance like a cat, totally relaxed yet ready to pounce. In Chapter 8 we will see how the new biology, combined with Tai Chi and Qigong practices, can aid in the healing of posttraumatic stress.

Throughout this book, we will see how Western medical hypnosis and the age-old art and science of Qigong can join hands to serve the healthcare needs of the modern world.

Psychoanalysis, Energy, and the Body

Even in the most seemingly non-energy, non-body-oriented therapy, energy and the body are perceived to be key to healing. Freud borrowed the term *cathexis* (Freud, 1933, 1990) from the Greek to speak about the direction of energy to different zones of the body, which was a fundamental aspect of his bodily oriented psychosexual phases. And Freud's notion of *libido* was a sexually focused way of talking about life energy that could be sublimated into creative and intellectual pursuits. Freud places the body in a primary role when he said, "The ego is first and foremost a bodily ego" (Freud, 1923, p. 16).

In modern psychology there exists a lack of appreciation for Freud's emphasis on energy and the body, perhaps because he didn't specifically use energy-oriented or body-oriented methods in his therapy, despite the fact that they underlay the very foundation of his seemingly intellectual psychoanalysis. And his clinical treatment methods, in line with the prevailing *Weltanschauung* of his era, were cognitive and non-body-oriented. Later we shall see how Bodymind Healing Psychotherapy adds various body-oriented practices to psychoanalytic concepts — for example, I might recommend touching the heart (acu-point CV-17) to add a body-oriented practice to the psychological need for self-soothing. In general, we shall see how the new integrative methods BMHP proposes weave together psychodynamic, energetic, and body-oriented dimensions.

Likewise in neo-analytic thought, psychoanalysts such as Deri (1990) warn of "the danger of a purely psychological model that disregards the unavoidable psychosomatic oneness of a functioning human being." Margaret Mahler (1952) says that, "the core of ego development, the first orientation toward external reality, is the differentiation of the body image which is the psychic representation of the bodily self." A major part of psychotherapeutic process is to examine old representations of the Self that are encoded in the body and to transmute them into new self-representations.

I shall later show how the age-old traditions of shape-shifting and postural initiation can complement this psychoanalytic "transmuting of introjects" (Kohut, 1977). Psychoanalysts in the area of self psychology speak of how early childhood experiences with caregivers provide and "directly affect the energetic vigor and structural cohesion of the self" (Wolf, 1988, as cited in Schore, 2003, p. 117). When there are later problems in regulating and modulating affect, many self psychologists (Mollon, 2001; Schore, 2003) look to early experiences of interaction with the caregiver to help in activating the function of the self that has to do with "vitalization and soothing" and "co-creating states of maximal cohesion" (Schore, 2003, p. 115). I suggest that a natural complement to these psychoanalytic ideas is to draw on methods from the many-thousand-year-old tradition of Qigong that specializes in vitalizing, self-soothing, and creating states of maximal cohesion.

Shape-Shifting, Clinical Hypnosis, and Ancient Qigong

Human Beings, in our deepest essences are 'shape-shifters.' We are elements of creation: fire, earth, metal, water and wood. We are empty space, as modern physics shows us. Qigong practices show us how to change our life stances by becoming like a tree, or moving like a silk worm reeling silk, transforming our identities with the lightness of Being that can be as colorful as that of a butterfly. And if current research is accurate, when we shape-shift into the appropriate element for the occasion, and return to our primordial selves, natural health is restored and we live younger longer.

— Michael Mayer, Ph.D.
Secrets to Living Younger Longer
The Self-Healing Path of Qigong, Standing Meditation and Tai Chi

In Volume I, I discussed how long before modern clinical hypnosis and Western bodymind healing research existed, there were traditions that helped a person heal by assuming postures of stillness and using the imagination. Repeating the story told in Volume I, we once again see how in shamanic literature, "shape-shifting" into different postural forms is linked to becoming all things, animal and human. In the Pacific Northwest it's told this way:

> *A Native American fisherman paddles his kayak into an unknown bay. As he walks, exploring into this untouched new territory, he hears uproarious laughter and cautiously follows the sound until it leads him to the mouth of a cave. After carefully creeping through a great cavern, he sees, gathered around a great roaring fire, animals of all varieties, large and small, playing a game that makes them laugh from the depths of their different souls. The game is "shape-shifting" and they are embodying the postures of different forms, then changing into those forms. The fisherman is in awe as the animals turn into human form, and the human turns into animal forms. (Gore, 1995, p. 14)*

This story symbolizes the cave of our everyday lives where we shape-shift from one state of consciousness to another, fueled by the fire of our intention. The power of shape-shifting from one stance to another to break fixated life stances and activate the healing power of "the universe of possibilities," was known in many ancient cultures. In ancient Greece, Epimenides, an initiate of this tradition, was said to have slept in a cave in Crete for years and used "rituals demanding patience, involving watching animals and following them in their movements" (Kingsley, 1999, p. 215). He was called to Athens to heal people from a plague. In Epidaurus in ancient Greece, where Western medicine originated at the world's oldest holistic healing center, shape-shifting into another identity was one of the essential elements of healing rituals. The Aesclepian priest would advise the sick to go to the Dionysian theater. Instructions were given to play a particular part in a play, or to wear a mask so that a new energy would be activated in the psyche of those in need of healing. These masks, or "*personae*," are the root of our contemporary word "person." So, by assuming the face and adopting the stance of another person or animal, a pathway to healing could emerge.[17]

We do not need to think of shape-shifting as some overly esoteric concept, or something relegated only to ancient initiation rituals. In our everyday lives the bodymind shape-shifts as we embody the continuum of ways of being in any sphere. To illustrate this point in the sphere of self-esteem let's take a look at how, when we shape-shift into various different psychological life stances, the chest expands and contracts in various isomorphically representative ways. Assume the chest position of arrogance, and your chest will push overly outward. Self assuredness also expands the chest out; but not so much. Being balanced with regard to the fact that you are the most special person in the universe, and at the same time just a piece of dust, may bring your chest into a centered position. Self denegration leading to a deflated stance can puncture the sphere of open-hearted Self appreciation; and feeling worthless totally collapses the chest. So, even though throughout this book I will be addressing how shape-shifting can be activated by processes from a wide variety of healing traditions, such as symbolic process methods and various Tai Chi and Qigong postures, shape-shifting and changing your life stance is a natural part of everyday life.

Recent modern research into multiple personality disorder adds to our understanding of how the power of changing our life stance and state of consciousness affects health and healing. It was discovered that a multiple personality diabetic had one or more separate personalities that did not suffer from diabetes.[18] Allergies present in one personality were often not present in other ego states — for example, allergies to orange juice and cats. Research by various doctors shows that in different identity states extraordinary bodily changes take place in visual acuity, brain-wave patterns, and changes in slowing down the aging process. This supports the belief by researchers that both dissociative and altered states facilitate healing.[19]

Not just in multiple personality states, but in other states of consciousness as well, many health conditions are associated with "state-specific states of consciousness" (Tart, 1968; Rossi 1986).[20] When shifting our consciousness, health conditions oftentimes disappear. For example, Milton Erickson once cured a woman from her orange juice allergy by age regressing her to the time of the negative association to orange juice. As the "state dependent memory hypothesis" (Tart, 1968; Rossi, 1986)[20] and psychoneuroimmunological research evolved, it was shown that when we use the powers of the imagination to enter into an altered state, we can create another reality in which disease and general imbalances of body, mind, and spirit can be healed (Ader & Felton, 1991). For example, it is now common knowledge that by activating the relaxation response and imagining we are someone, something, or somewhere else, the immune response is activated and healing oftentimes occurs. For a taste of this experience, try taking a few slow natural breaths, and imagine you are sitting in a beautiful spot in nature with your back against a tree overlooking a river. As you breathe, feel the changes that come to your Self and body.

Throughout the following chapters, my hope is to add to the theoretical underpinnings of state-specific literature, proposing that the energetic component of state-specific states of consciousness is an essential concomitant aspect of healing — and as fundamental as memories and behaviors. Different psychological dysfunctions have corresponding differences in the flow of Qi. By using various types of postures, breathing methods, visualizations, self-touch, and movements from the age-old Qigong tradition, the clinician may help the patient activate a state-specific state of consciousness that enables him or her to tap into the energy of the primordial Self. We will see how this has potential for healing imbalances in commonly treated problem areas such as anxiety, chronic pain, trauma, etc.

Byron Katie, Cognitive Psychotherapy, and Shape-Shifting

In the following chapters I will be putting forth the thesis that many current well-known and leading-edge psychotherapies, consciously or unconsciously, incorporate body-oriented and energy-oriented methods of bodymind healing. Additionally, we will see how these therapy modalities either draw from, or can be enhanced by, an understanding of the perennial roots of pre-modern, psychoenergetic traditions.

For example, the popular method of Byron Katie (2002), who wrote the book, *Loving What Is*, includes a four-step method for psychological clearing, which may be used when finding yourself stuck in dysfunctional belief patterns. Although it has not been sufficiently researched, many people report having benefited from asking these four questions: (1) Is this completely true? (2) Can I really know that it's true? (3) What do I get when I hold that belief? and (4) Who or what would I be without that belief?

From the perspective of shape-shifting, the last of Katie's questions, "Who or what would I be without that belief?" induces a change in life stance. That is, it induces a person to shape-shift into another "subpersonality," a state-specific state of consciousness that does not imbibe the negative beliefs. Also, it can help to deactivate entrenched psychological complexes. For example, for people who hold a victim stance in life due to a perceived past injustice, if they follow the Katie process, they may find that they relish blaming another, and get a feeling of pumped up power that helps to assuage past feelings of disempowerment. They may finally realize that this is not serving them or their health and they may find that without this belief they would be a more loving, healthier, less-poisoned, more empowered, and less stuck person. From this viewpoint, such shape-shifting often takes place in the subpersonality work that is part of many psychotherapies such as psychosynthesis (Assagioli, 1965). Shape-shifting also takes place in modern well-established therapies — for example, in cognitive psychotherapy when a person discovers a new, more functional belief, or in psychoanalysis when a person withdraws a projection — though such psychologists might not conceptualize it in this way.

Even without an awareness of the dimensions of the body and the bodily energy that is shape-shifted in such a change of awareness, it is possible that the person's life stance may change including psychobiological, psychoneuroimmunological, and neurochemical concomitants. In the following chapters I will show the benefits of incorporating the conscious use of energy psychologies and ancient sacred wisdom traditions into modern psychotherapy. We will see how this integration can enhance the depth and cultivation of human beings' ability to shape-shift into states of consciousness that serve the need for emotional liberation from unwanted psychological complexes and dysfunctional ways of being, thereby leading to greater bodymind health.

CHAPTER 3: ENERGY PSYCHOLOGIES: TAPPING THE HEALING POWER OF THE BODYMIND

Energy Medicine

There is a profound evolutionary shift taking place in the world that can be seen in the growing recognition of the fundamental role that energy plays in healing (Benor, 1992). Dr. Robert Becker was one of the grandfathers of this field of "energy medicine" in the West. In the early 1980s he was one of the first scientists to measure the "current of injury" associated with healing wounds and bone fractures. In his early research on the healing and regeneration of salamanders, which some mark as the beginning of the new scientific revolution in energy medicine, he showed that the control system that started, regulated, and stopped healing was electrical (Becker, 1985, pp. 235-236).

Becker's work built upon the work of other scientists such as Harold Burr, a neuroanatomist at the Yale School of Medicine who in the 1930s measured the electrical field around an unfertilized salamander egg and found that it was shaped like a mature salamander, as if the blueprint for the adult was already there in the egg's energy field (Burr, 1972). Most interesting was his discovery that physical illness is preceded by changes in an organism's electromagnetic field (Burr & Northrup, 1935). Another scientist Owen Frazee reported in 1909 that passing electrical currents through water containing young salamanders speeded up the regeneration of amputated limbs (as cited in Becker, 1985, p. 82).

Since that time, there have been numerous solid research studies showing the efficacy of various forms of energy in healing. The International Society for the Study of Subtle Energies and Energy Medicine (ISSSEEM) has complied hundreds of very well-researched studies,[1] as has the excellent scholarly research compendium of Daniel Benor (1992). For an easier read, Dr. Richard Gerber (1996) presents a good overview of the field in his book *Vibrational Medicine*, as does Andy Baggott (1999) in *The Encyclopedia of Energy Healing*.

Some have described this paradigm shift as a revolution, signaling a move from a "Newtonian" to an "Einsteinian" medicine model. As paraphrased from Gerber (1996, p. 43),

> *Newtonian thinkers see the human body as a series of intricate chemical systems powering a structure of nerve, muscle, flesh, and bones. The physical body is viewed as a supreme mechanism, intricate physical clockwork down to the very cellular structure. Einsteinian Medicine sees human beings as networks of complex energy fields that interface with physical/cellular systems. There is a hierarchy of subtle energetic systems that coordinate electrophysiological, hormonal, and cellular structure of the physical body. It is from these subtle levels that health and illness originate. These unique energy systems are powerfully affected by emotions, spiritual balance, nutrition, and environment. They influence cellular patterns of growth.*[2]

This revolution is affecting a wide variety of disciplines including physics,[3] biology (Pert, 1997; Lipton, 2005), and medicine,[4] and can no longer be considered fringe science — in various of its aspects, it is now considered to be mainstream. Western knowledge of energy in the human organism has come a long way from believing that nerves are the only part of the body that contain electricity. We now know that the body emits a broad spectrum of electromagnetic and acoustic radiation that has been measured by magnetic resonance imaging (MRI), electroencephalogram (EEG), electrocardiogram (EKG), electromylogram (EMG), thermography, and ultrasound. These instruments are used to monitor and diagnose diseases.

Behind the everyday use of instruments to measure energies lies an epochal change in the foundation of science. It was Dr. Lipton (2005), cell biologist and author of *The Biology of Belief*, who wrote that the pyramid of science is changing. With this shift at the bottom of the pyramid showing physics changing from a Newtonian mechanistic view to one of quantum mechanics, energy and energy fields have come to the forefront of importance. He says that once the bottom of the pyramid of science in physics shifts, so do all of the levels need to shift — chemistry, biology, and psychology.

Dr. Lipton wrote that, "Though mass consciousness is currently imbued with the notion that genes control the character of our lives, the results of the Human Genome Project completely undermine the long-held concept of genetic determinism. Once thought to be in the domain of the genes, the control of health and behavior are now dynamically linked to the environment, and more importantly, our perception of the environment." Dr. Lipton puts forth the case that we need to focus on "epigenetics," (the controlling realm above the arena of the genes), to discover a broader realm of causative factors than found in genetics. In his "new biology," among the key elements of the epigenetic environment upon which Dr. Lipton (2005) focuses is energy, which plays a key role as information in biological systems (p. 114). Dr. Lipton cites the early work of Dr. McClare (1974), who compared the efficiency of information transfer between energy signals and chemical signals in biological systems and found that energetic signaling mechanisms such as electromagnetic frequencies are a hundred times more efficient in relaying environmental information than are physical signals such as hormones, neurotransmitters, etc. According to Lipton (2006), "The speed of electromagnetic energy is 186,000 miles per second, while the speed of a diffusible chemical is considerably less than 1 centimeter per second."

Although Western medicine uses instruments such as the EEG to read energy fields, it hasn't taken the next step in understanding the role energy plays in other ways, according to Dr. Lipton. He shows how animals, from single cells to humans, transduce environmental stimuli into physiological and behavioral responses. Dr. Lipton says that scientific research has revealed that "every facet of biological regulation is profoundly impacted by the 'invisible forces' of the electromagnetic spectrum ... electromagnetic radiation regulates DNA, RNA and protein synthesis, alters protein shape and function, and control gene regulation, cell division, cell differentiation, morphogenesis (the process by which cells assemble into organs and tissues) hormone secretion, nerve growth and function ..." Dr. Lipton laments that "though these research studies have been published in some of the most respected mainstream biomedical journals, their revolutionary findings have not been incorporated into our medical school curriculum." (Lipton, 2005, as cited by Feinstein & Eden, 2006b). Most importantly for the purposes of this book, he speaks about the implications of this for the field of psychology, and shows how the newly identified cellular mechanisms include master switches through which our thoughts, attitudes, and beliefs create the conditions of our body and of our place in the world.

Energy medicine is increasingly becoming a part of the new theoretical underpinnings of "a medicine for the twenty-first century." Candace Pert, Ph.D., author of *Molecules of Emotion: The Science behind Mind-Body Medicine*, and research professor at Georgetown University School of Medicine, calls this revolution, "New Paradigm Medicine." She says that, "While not well understood, subtle energies can be operationally defined as energies that cannot be measured using existing instrumentation but which, like gravity, are known for their effects. Energy is also hypothesized as being somehow involved in the elusive link between chemistry and consciousness" (Pert as cited in Feinstein, 2004). Other frontier scientists report being able to measure "the biofield," with sensitive magnetometers such as the SQUID (Rubik, 2002). The biofield is comprised of an extremely weak but measurable electromagnetic field with its own waveform, intensity, polarity and modulation patterns that surrounds all living systems. And for those of us that believe that only big things can create big changes, it should be pointed out that Becker found that tiny currents, on the order of a billionth of an ampere, were more effective than larger currents in stimulating tissue regeneration (Becker, et al., 1977).

Modern science has demonstrated that electromagnetic fields of the body are generated during various biological processes including rapid cell division, during natural growth processes such as growth of bone cells following fracture, intense nervous activity associated with mental processes, and various pathological conditions such as abnormal cell growth with diseases like cancer. The distinction between conservative medical practitioners and the new proponents of energy medicine is summed up well by one of the early researchers in the field, Dr. Glen Rein; he wrote:

> *It is now well known that the human body emits a broad spectrum of electromagnetic and acoustic radiation. Traditional medicine looks at these as by-products of biochemical reactions in the body. They are not considered by most biomedical researchers to be involved with the basic functioning (or healing) of the body. The basic tenet of energy medicine is that these fields are not only involved with functioning of physical/chemical body but regulate these processes. (Rein, 1992, p. 7)*

Dr. Rein is not alone in his views. A variety of scientists are now documenting how organizing fields of energy may be responsible for directing genes and biochemical processes like a conductor directing an unimaginably big orchestra (McTaggart, 2003, p. 45); these organizing fields direct biochemical processes as decisively as a magnetic fields aligns metal filings (Liboff, 2004). This paradigm shift has major implications for an expanded approach to medicine.

Energy medicine is used in the treatment of disease. It is now commonplace to hear of athletes using transcutaneous electrical nerve stimulation units (TENS) to deal with the effects of pain. Nurses in many hospitals use energy healing methods (approved by the North American Nursing Diagnosis Association) such as therapeutic touch and its cousin, healing touch, to treat their patients; and there is research accumulating to show the efficacy of touch in reducing anxiety among institutionalized patients (Gagne and Toye, 1994), alleviating depression in breast cancer patients (Nurse Healers-Professional Associates, 2000; Moreland, 1997), enhancing immune system response (Quinn & Stelkaudal, 1993), and speeding wound healing (Wirth, 1991). At leading-edge hospitals, energy medicine is being explored in a variety of ways. For example, at Columbia Presbyterian Hospital in New York, cardiac surgeon Dr. Memmot Oz has had Julie Motz, an energy healer, use energy emission methods with her hands prior to, during, and after surgery for heart replacement surgery. It has been reported that there are less cardiac rejections when such energy medicine procedures take place.[5]

Treatments that influence the brain's electrical activity are being used to overcome a range of psychiatric and other medical disorders. The magnetic stimulation of specific areas of the brain has been shown in double-blinded, placebo-controlled research to help with major depression that did not respond to other therapies (Fitzgerald, 2003), and with bipolar disorder (Rohan, 2004). The surgical implantation of deep brain stimulators that deliver targeted electrical stimulation in the brain have helped thousands of patients with Parkinson's disease to better control their symptoms; and these brain pacemakers are also used with some success to stimulate the vagus nerve in treating severe depression, obsessive-compulsive disorders, and other neurological conditions (Archart-Treichel, 2003).

Differentiating between the energy that is electricity and the energy that is constellated in various human emanation and self-cultivation traditions is part of the work of the field of energy medicine. There is much research in each of these areas that is worthy of efforts to further replicate and substantiate initial results. For example, Dr. Bjorn Nordenstrom (1983) has experimented with electricity's effect on tumors and reports a cure or prevention rate in ten out of twenty patients.[6]

Chinese medicine in the form of acupuncture is now a well-accepted part of Western complementary healthcare, and is a licensed health profession in many states. Scientific evidence is mounting to support the long-held, empirical claims of acupuncturists. Among the mental health conditions that the World Health Organization lists as being responsive to acupuncture are anxiety, depression, stress reactions, and insomnia. An acupuncture needle inserted into a specific point on the toe can be seen in a functional MRI as affecting blood activity in the brain — though no nerve, vascular, or other physical connections are known to exist there (Cho, 1998). Another study using an MRI demonstrated that stimulating specific points on the skin not only changed brain activity, but also deactivated areas of the brain that are involved with the experience of fear and pain (Hui, 2000).[7] Other components of the Chinese medical tradition, such as Tai Chi and Qigong, are also gaining acceptance. The *Journal of the American Medical Association* published a study showing that Tai Chi prevented more falls amongst the elderly than nine other forms of Western exercise (Province, 1995). Qigong is taught at California Pacific Medical Center in San Francisco and other leading-edge medical institutions. There are Qigong studies showing beneficial results on hypertension (Kuang, 1991), and many medical disorders (Sancier, 1996). Determining which type of energy medicine should be used for different conditions, and at what times, is a next step for researchers.

An overview of the emerging field can be found in Feinstein & Eden's (2006b) article *Six Pillars of Energy Medicine* which puts forth the following strengths of energy compared with the traditional medical model. This article backs up these propositions with scientific research:

- *Pillar 1*: Energy medicine can influence certain fundamental biological processes in ways that conventional medicine cannot.
- *Pillar 2*: Energy medicine embraces modern physics in ways that conventional medicine has not, resulting in greater methodological precision and flexibility.
- *Pillar 3*: Energy interventions are faster, more efficient, and far safer than chemical interventions in biological regulation.
- *Pillar 4:* Energy interventions are available that can be readily, economically, and non-invasively applied.
- *Pillar 5:* Patients can utilize energy medicine techniques on a back-home, self-help basis.
- *Pillar 6*: Energy medicine focuses on the total person.

Energy Psychology: An "Einsteinian" Approach to Psychotherapy

This energy medicine revolution is in the early stages of affecting psychology. In the previous chapter I mentioned how energy has always been an important concept in psychology in the work of early seminal leaders in the field (Freud, 1923, 1933; Reich, 1949; Lowen, 1975); and there have been a number of other authors who have spoken about the importance of integrating the energetic dimension (Seem, 1989; Requena, 1989) and Chinese medicine (Hammer, 1990) into psychology.

Just as there has been a shift from a Newtonian to an Einsteinian approach to medicine, in the chapters that follow we shall see how an Einsteinian approach to psychotherapy and behavioral healthcare puts energy at the forefront of what composes, transforms, and heals the psyche. We now know that matter is a form of energy and that harnessing the power of energy has vital, peaceful uses in the external world, as well as in the world of medicine. Likewise, the psyche is composed of energy, and harnessing its power and using it to bring vitality, peace, and healing to our inner worlds is an equally important endeavor.

There is a new growing field called "energy psychology." Already, it has many publications[8] and a national organization, the Association for Comprehensive Energy Psychology (ACEP) with a membership (in 2005) of 781 health professionals from a wide variety of health occupations, including approximately thirty-nine medical doctors. David Gruder, Ph.D., together with his wife Rebecca and with Dorothea Hover-Kramer co-founded ACEP in 1998. The articles of incorporation as a non-profit were approved in December of that year, and the organization opened to membership in the spring of 1999.

The Origins of Energy Psychology

As I discussed earlier, with the founding of psychology being credited to modern researchers like Wilhelm Wundt, a similar issue exists in the arena of energy psychology. Credit for the founding of energy psychology is given to a modern psychologist, Roger Callahan, the originator of "Thought Field Therapy." Callahan built upon the work of Psychiatrist John Diamond (1979) who integrated the acupuncture meridian system and muscle testing from applied kinesiology to assess the flow of life energy through the meridians (Goodheart, 1964). Callahan believes that emotional disturbance is caused by "perturbations in the thought field," and that accurate diagnosis is necessary to "unlock" these perturbations. His approach uses applied kinesiology for assessment, and uses algorithms involving tapping acupuncture meridian alarm points along with his proprietary Voice Technology method to treat psychological conditions. From these beginnings have come what are known as "meridian-based therapies." Meridian-based therapies often claim instant cures of a wide variety of psychological problems including phobias (Callahan, 1985; Nims, 1998); and there is anecdotal and early positive research evidence to lend support to some of these claims (Andrade & Feinstein, 2004). Differentiating how and for whom these methods work is one of the next steps that needs to be taken for this branch of energy medicine to be better accepted by mainstream approaches.

In this pre-paradigmatic stage of energy psychology's evolution (Kuhn, 1996), there are a wide variety of bases for what various psychotherapists see as defining energy psychology. What some view as essential, other energy psychologists may not find beneficial or important. As we will see below regarding "muscle testing" stemming from applied kinesiology, some energy psychologists use it and some don't. Likewise with "tapping algorithms" there is wide divergence regarding its usefulness, clinical efficacy, and importance. In a pre-paradigmatic phase it is natural to want to determine the scientific validity of the methods used, and as a field grows, research separates the "wheat from the chaff," showing which methods work for which disorders and for which people. In the pursuit of validating research, one should keep in mind that psychotherapy is an art as well as a science, and that subjective and objective are both important parts of the whole spectrum of research (Jonas, 2000).

Breadth of the Field of Energy Psychology

There is a wide range of psychological methods subsumed under the umbrella of what is now called "comprehensive energy psychology." To delineate some of its methods we can begin with the Callahan (1985) method of Thought Field Therapy (TFT), and outgrowths of Callahan methods including those loosely defined as "meridian-based methods." One such method is the popular Emotional Freedom Technique (EFT) developed by Gary Craig (1995) — who doesn't think the order of treatment algorithms really matters and who doesn't claim, like Callahan, that his EFT derives from diagnosis. Other comprehensive energy psychology methods such as the Tapas acupressure technique (Fleming, 1996), Seemorg Matrix method (Clinton, 2002), and Hover-Kramer's biofield methods (Hover-Kramer, 1996, 1997) rely on other major energy systems such as chakras and biofields.

In this rest of this chapter I will give an overview of the field, outline the treatment methods of one popular energy psychology technique (Craig's EFT), touch on energy psychology research, and explore some benefits and problems with current energy psychotherapy. Later in the following chapters we will see how Bodymind Healing Psychotherapy expands upon energy psychology. But first, to get a sense of the breadth of the field, I will delineate some of the following categories:

Tapping and Other Treatment Methods

Some energy psychotherapists use an elaborate series of acu-points called algorithms to treat various disorders (Callahan, 1985; Craig, 1995); others say that just one point is needed (Gallo, 2002, p. 36). Some use these algorithms in conjunction with other methods such as eye movements, as we will see below (Craig, 1995). Some energy psychology methods do not use tapping — Nims uses a "cue" to produce energetic shifts rather than tapping (as cited in Gallo, 2002, p. 79), Clinton's Seemorg Method (2002) holds chakras rather than tapping, and Diepold advises touching and breathing rather than tapping as the preferred method (as cited in Gallo, 2002, p. 18).

Muscle Testing as a Form of Assessment

There are energy psychology methods that use muscle testing as a key method of assessment (Gallo, 2000), and other energy psychologies that do not use muscle testing, such as the Tapas acupressure technique (Fleming, 1999), the negative affect erasing method (Gallo, 2000), and the Emotional Freedom Technique (Craig, 1997).

Energy Psychology: Integrated with a Wide Range of Therapies

Though there are those who look at energy psychology methods as stand-alone treatments, the majority of those who describe themselves as energy psychotherapists integrate their methods with a broader base of psychological methods and traditions. For example, energy psychology methods are being integrated with many forms of therapy including: transactional analysis (Lammers, 2002), Adlerian psychology (Wheeler, 2002), Eye Movement Desensitization Reprocessing (Hartung, 2002), and hypnosis (Gross et al., 2002; Pulos, 2002). Energy psychology is also being integrated with some aspects of cognitive (Craig, 1995) and psychodynamic (Nims, 2002, p. 81) therapies.

Energy Psychology in Medical Settings

Energy psychology has been integrated as a behavioral healthcare tool in medical settings for: phobias of medical devices, needle phobias, fears of dying, highly stressed caregivers, chronic pain, pediatrics, cardiac care, surgical phobias, etc (Green, 2002). In a broader definition that includes Qigong, energy psychology is being used for hypertension, chronic pain, insomnia, etc. (Mayer, 1997b, 1999, 2003, 2004).

Scope of the Field

To get a sense of the points of both agreement and controversy in the field, a survey was conducted at the Fifth International Energy Psychology Conference held in May 2003 in Phoenix of 265 participants who identified themselves as energy psychology practitioners with a substantial base of experience. The professional affiliations of those who participated included approximately 10 percent psychologists, 10 percent social workers, 40 percent mental health or marriage, family, and child counselors, 3 percent physicians, 6 percent nurses, 5 percent other licensed health care providers, and 26 percent unlicensed counselors. Approximately 65 percent considered energy psychology their primary, or one of their primary, psychotherapeutic modalities; 35 percent considered it secondary to another modality (Feinstein, 2004b).

In the survey, 35 percent agreed that there are "effective" and "ineffective" points. Thirty-five percent felt that virtually any subset of the acu-points typically used within energy psychology could bring about the therapeutic effect, and 30 percent were in the middle or offered no opinion. Identical percentages were found in relationship to the importance of the order in which the points were stimulated, with 35 percent feeling that it mattered and 35 percent feeling it did not matter.

In the survey, 40 percent felt that energy checking (presumably with muscle testing) is a critical tool in energy psychology, 30 percent felt it is not, and 30 percent were in the middle or offered no opinion. Sixty percent believed that energy checking could accurately assess the state of a meridian, less than 1 percent disagreed, with the remainder saying they were in the middle or did not know. Fifty percent believed that energy checking could also yield reliable answers to questions that go beyond the immediate meridian response, 10 percent disagreed, and 40 percent were in the middle or offered no opinion. Twenty percent felt it was important in a reasonable proportion of cases to assess and treat the specific meridians involved in the problem, 20 percent did not, 40 percent were in the middle, and 20 percent offered no opinion.[9]

In summary, there is a large range of opinion within the field of energy psychology about what constitutes the field and which treatments are best at which times. It is in this sense that the field of energy psychology is in a pre-paradigmatic phase (Kuhn, 1996), as is the research of discovering which methods work best with which people.

The Emotional Freedom Techniques

There is a wide range of energy psychology methods. Among the most popular is Gary Craig's Emotional Freedom Technique (EFT). The basic recipe for EFT as cited in the *EFT Manual* (Craig et al., 1995, 1997, pp. 31-32; Feinstein, 2004, p. 27) is as follows:

1. The Setup. Repeat this affirmation three times: "Even though I have this____, I deeply and completely accept myself." While continuously rubbing the sore spot on the chest (upper left or upper right) or tapping the Karate Chop point (SI-3)

2. The Sequence. Tap about seven times on each of the following energy points while repeating the reminder phrases at each point *

Here I list only the EFT Eight Point Treatment Chart (Feinstein, 2004, p. 27):
EB (Beginning of the Eyebrow) = BL-2 (Bladder Meridian)
SE) Side of the Eye = GB-1(Gall Bladder Meridian)
UE (Under the Eye) = St-1 (Stomach Meridian)
UN (Under the Nose) = GV-26 (Governing Vessel Meridian)
Ch (Between Chin and Lower Lip) = CV-24 (Conception Vessel)
CB (Collarbone) = K-27 (Kidney Meridian)
UA (Under the Arm) = SP-21 (Spleen Meridian)
* In Craig's full method other points are also used. BN, Th, IF, MF, BF, KC (see Craig's *EFT Manual*, 1995, 1997, p. 3; or go to www.emofree.com)

3. The Nine Gamut Procedure. Continuously tap on an acu-point on the back of the wrist called "the gamut point," where the bones of the little finger and ring finger meet (acu-point TW-3) while performing each of the following nine actions:
   (1) Eyes closed (2) Eyes open (3) Eyes down right (4) Eyes down left (5) Roll eyes in a circle (6) Roll eyes in other direction (7) Hum two seconds of a song (8) Count to five (9) Hum two seconds of a song.
4. The Sequence Again. Tap about three times on each of the energy points listed in step 2 above, repeating the "reminder phrase" at each point, i.e., EB, SE, UE, UN, CH, CB, UA, BN, TH, etc.

As do many current mind-body health practitioners, Craig has his patients assess their subjective units of distress (SUDS) level before and after treatment. This serves as an "objective/subjective" method of measuring change.

Energy Psychology Research

Many of the leaders in the field of energy psychology, like David Feinstein (2002), Donna Eden (1998), and Fred Gallo (see Gallo, 2002, for a good overview of leaders in the field) are part of this movement that is stretching psychology's limits and bringing the body and energy back into a field that once placed an overemphasis on mind and participated in the mind/body split. And, there is a growing research base that lends credence to the efficacy of some or many of its methods.

As Feinstein (2004) points out in his article, one of the ways to gain confidence in a early proposed therapy is to look at doctoral dissertation research. Three dissertations that have investigated the efficacy of energy psychology procedures found positive treatment outcomes — two based on systematic observation of individuals who received treatment, and a third based on a controlled experiment. The first, using objective measures such as standard anxiety inventories, demonstrated significant improvement in 48 individuals plagued with public speaking anxiety, after just one hour of treatment with TFT. Following the treatment, the subjects reported decreased shyness and confusion and increased poise and interest in giving a future speech. Treatment gains were still present on four-month follow-up interviews (Schoninger, 2001). A second dissertation followed 20 patients who had been unable to receive necessary medical attention because of intense needle phobias. They, too, showed significant immediate improvement after an hour of TFT treatment and on one-month follow-up interviews (Darby, 2001). A third dissertation investigated the effects of TFT on self-concept with 28 subjects who presented with a phobia. Two self-concept inventories were administered a month prior to the treatment and then two months after the treatment. Again, the TFT treatment reduced the phobias substantially, and in this study, significant improvement was also found in self-acceptance, self-esteem, and self-congruency two months after the treatment. A wait-list control group of 25 subjects did not show improvement (Wade, 1990). (See www.innersource.net for David Feinstein's *Energy Psychology Interactive CD*, which includes a video of acrophobia, the phobia of heights.)

As the emerging field of energy psychology has been incorporating tapping, touch, and other energy healing methods into psychotherapy (Gallo, 2002), it is beginning to investigate the efficacy of energy-based, psychophysiological approaches in a more scientific manner. One controlled study was conducted in Brazil by principal researcher Joaquin Andrade, M.D. (Andrade & Feinstein, 2003). Over a five and a half year period approximately 5,000 patients, diagnosed at intake with an anxiety disorder, were randomly assigned to an experimental group (involving imagery and self-statements paired with manual stimulation of selected acupuncture points) or a control group (involving cognitive-behavior therapy and medication). Ratings were given by independent clinicians who interviewed each patient at the close of therapy — at one month, three months, six months, and twelve months. The raters made a determination of complete or partial remission of symptoms or no clinical response. The raters did not know if the patient was in the experimental or control group. At the close of therapy 63 percent of the control group were judged as having improved, and 90 percent of the experimental group were judged as having improved. Fifty-one percent of the control group was judged as symptom free, and 76 percent of the experimental group was judged as symptom free. At one year follow-up, patients receiving acu-point treatments were less prone to relapse or partial relapse than those receiving CBT and medication as indicated by the independent raters' assessment and corroborated by brain imaging and neurotransmitter profiles from a sampling of the patients.

Brain mapping revealed that subjects whose acupuncture points were stimulated tended to be distinguished by a general pattern of brain wave normalization, which interestingly, not only persisted at the twelve month follow-up, but also became more pronounced. In neurotransmitter profiles with generalized anxiety disorder, acu-point stimulation was followed by norepinephrine levels going down to normal reference values, and low serotonin levels going up. Parallel electrical and biochemical patterns were less-pronounced in the CBT medication group. In a related pilot study by the same team, the length of treatment was substantially shorter with energy therapy and related methods than with the CBT and medication (mean = 3 sessions vs. mean = 15 sessions. (See www.innersource.net)

One problem with using brain wave research is that at this early stage in understanding the individual variations and meanings of activation of different centers in the brain, the cautious observer can't determine with certainty the validity and reliability of the results (Carey, 2005).

Since the Andrade study was initially envisioned as an exploratory in-house assessment, not all the variables that needed to be controlled in robust research were tracked, not all criteria were defined with rigorous precision, the record-keeping was relatively informal, and source data was not always maintained. Nonetheless, the studies all used randomized samples, control groups, and blind assessment. The findings were so striking that the team decided to report them. More detailed reports of some of the studies are being prepared for submission to scientific journals. If subsequent research corroborates these early findings, it will be a notable development since a combination of CBT and medication is currently the established psychological standard of care for anxiety disorders. Since tapping is just one of the methods of Qigong, it will be interesting to see what happens when the wider range of Qigong methods are examined with more sophisticated research protocols.[10]

Brain research shows some promise in assessing efficacy of energy psychology treatment methods. A study by Swingle et al. (2000) examined the changes in brain activity using an EEG. The patients with successful outcomes who were treated for phobias after a car accident showed increases in brain amplitudes related to mental quiescence (increases in slow 3-7 Hz brain waves in the occipital region), whereas those who reported immediate improvement but did not sustain improvement on three month follow-up, showed trends opposite to those clients who sustained improvement. In another study by Swingle et al. (2000), children diagnosed with epilepsy were treated with EFT and after two weeks of daily in-home treatments, they experienced a significant reduction in seizures accompanied with improved EEG measures.

Use in Disaster Relief

Any new discipline trying to gain acceptability must prove itself in many spheres. In this light, it is interesting to hear about the use of energy psychology in treating trauma victims in Kosovo. Over the past six years, Carl Johnson, Ph.D., a clinical psychologist retired from a career as a PTSD (posttraumatic stress disorder) specialist with the Veteran's Administration has frequently traveled to the sites of some of the world's most terrible atrocities and disasters to provide psychological support based in energy psychology methods.

In an article in a journal published by the Institute of Noetic Sciences it was reported that the first 105 people treated in Kosovo by Johnson and his colleagues were followed for eighteen months after their treatments (Feinstein, 2006). He wrote, "The results are astounding. These 105 victims of ethnic violence were suffering from the post-traumatic emotional effects of 249 discrete, horrific self-identified incidents, from torture and rape to witnessing the massacre of loved ones. For 247 of those 249 memories, the treatments (using Thought Field Therapy)... successfully reduced the reported degree of emotional distress not just to a manageable level but to a 'no distress' level ('0' on a 0-to-10 Subjective Units of Distress scale). The memories, of course, remained, and though they were no less horrific, they were no longer emotionally disabling" (p. 18).

For a more complete description of the work of Dr. Johnson see the aforementioned article (Feinstein, 2006) where poignant case illustrations and graphs of the research results can be found. Johnson made nine trips to Kosovo between February 2000 and June 2002. His later visits were as much to train local healthcare providers in TFT as to treat additional patients. He also received follow-up information on approximately three-fourths of the initial 105 people treated, primarily from two physicians who participated as translators in the initial treatments and who continued to care for the individuals who received the treatments. Interestingly, according to this report, once a memory had been cleared of its emotional charge, it remained clear. The initial treatment had proven a potent and durable healing in all cases. The physicians eventually did ask Johnson to see two of the patients a second time, and their problems — similar though less intense than the original memories — were treated. The chief medical officer of Kosovo (the equivalent of the U.S. Surgeon General), Dr. Skkelzen Syla, stated in a letter of appreciation:

> *Many well-funded relief organizations have treated the post traumatic stress here in Kosovo. Some of our people had limited improvement, but Kosovo had no major change or real hope until we referred our most difficult trauma patients to [Dr. Johnson and his team]. The success from Thought Field Therapy was 100 percent for every patient, and they are still smiling until this day [and, indeed, in the follow-ups, each was free of relapse]. (as cited in Feinstein, 2006, p. 19)*

When we hear stories like those about the work of Dr. Johnson, we may wonder how generalizable these results are. In addition to the Kosovo data, various other personnel of disaster relief organizations have reported positive results in Rwanda, New Orleans, and with Tsunami victims. In each case, when a team went into a disaster area, beyond the team's own case reports and outcome evaluations, local observers in positions of authority offered strikingly positive post-deployment assessments, most often with invitations or appeals for return visits. Pierre Llunga, the director of the El Shaddai Orphanage in Rwanda (he also serves as a university professor and holds a Ph.D. in geology), in a letter to the TFT Trauma Relief Team members who worked with the orphanage, noted simply, "Our life has been changed in a better way." In requesting a return visit he asked for "more people if possible."

Likewise, all three of the local organizations in New Orleans that had invited the TFT Trauma Relief Team to work with people following Hurricane Katrina requested additional treatment and training from the team. An unsolicited letter of appreciation was sent from Dwayne Thomas, M.D., chief executive officer of the Medical Center of Louisiana at New Orleans to members of the TFT Trauma Relief Team about a month after their first visit to New Orleans. He wrote, "As you know, our staff has been through (and continues to experience) a significant amount of primary and secondary trauma. We have offered staff many different interventions … the overwhelmingly positive response to the [TFT] therapy was a welcome and delightful surprise for us all."

Charles Figley, Ph.D., founder of the Green Cross and a leading figure in trauma treatment noted that, "energy psychology is rapidly proving itself to be among the most powerful psychological interventions available to disaster relief workers in helping the survivors, and as well as the workers themselves" (as cited in Feinstein, 2006).

Questions have been raised by psychologists in the media about whether going into the field with unproven treatment methods that have not been scientifically examined can produce harm. This is a legitimate concern; and it is not easy to produce rigorous research when a therapy team goes into an area where a disaster has recently struck, particularly when the team is traveling to a culture with which it has little familiarity. The number of variables needed to be controlled for scientific research is extensive, and opportunities to set up stringently controlled research conditions are highly restricted. For more information about the use of energy psychology in disaster relief, see https://energypsych.org/article-feinstein4.php.

Another question about generalizability of energy psychology relates to how broad-based the types of positive treatment effects are. It is known that EMDR (Shapiro, 1995) similarly began with impressive results with posttraumatic stress patients; the positive results of the method later showed that it was effective with other syndromes as well. From this, and other evidence, we know it will take time, and further research, to determine the extent of energy psychology's efficacy and generalizability.

One important criteria, before the mental health field is willing to accept a new experimental method, is to examine new procedures in professional journals. In many reputable journals, articles are beginning to appear. A study published in the *Journal of Clinical Psychology* examined whether the effects of energy psychology procedures were due to placebo; and it explored the question of how much improvement could be gained in a single session with individuals who volunteered to receive help with irrational fears of insects or small animals, including rats, mice, spiders, and roaches. The energy psychology approach was compared with a relaxation technique that uses diaphragmatic breathing. Significantly greater improvement was found, based on standardized phobia scales and other measures, in the group that received the energy psychology treatment. On follow-ups, 6–9 months later, the improvements held (Wells et al., 2003). A study conducted at Queens College in New York to see if these findings could be replicated produced markedly similar results (Baker & Siegel, 2005). Other studies are in progress.[11]

Research on Tapping Acu-Points: Do Specific Points Matter?

With preliminary evidence suggesting that the procedures used in energy psychology are more effective than relaxation training in the treatment of a phobias, a next logical question is whether it matters which points are tapped. Is there something about simply tapping the body that has a curative effect? Or is there really something unique about the points that were identified in ancient China? Here the evidence is mixed. An early investigation of this question suggested that in treating 49 people with height phobias, those who tapped the traditional points showed significantly more improvement than those who tapped "placebo" points (Carbonell, 1997). In a subsequent study, published in the medical journal *Anesthesia & Analgesia*, treatments that involved stimulating acu-points were applied by the paramedic team after a minor injury, compared with treatments that stimulated areas of the skin that are not recognized acupuncture points. Again, the treatments that used the traditional points were more effective, resulting in a significantly greater reduction of anxiety, pain, and elevated heart rate (Kober et al., 2002). A third study used a randomized, controlled, double-blinded design in treating 38 women diagnosed with clinical depression (Allen, Schnyer, & Hitt, 1998). The researchers compared the use of acupuncture points (during twelve treatment sessions over an eight-week period) specifically selected for the treatment of depression, with acupuncture points usually used for other ailments (also twelve sessions over eight weeks), and a waiting-list control group that received no treatment. Following the acupuncture treatments, 50 percent of patients who received the depression protocol showed no sign of the disorder, while only 27 percent of the patients in the other two groups experienced relief of their symptoms. Following the initial clinical trial, the women from the other two groups were administered the depression treatment over an eight-week period. Seventy percent of them experienced a drop in depressive symptoms, with 64 percent showing complete remission according to *DSM IV* criteria. These findings suggest that targeting the proper points was an important ingredient of the treatment.

A fourth study, however, did not detect a difference between tapping traditional points and tapping non-acupuncture points in treating fear — though both tapping procedures proved more effective than no treatment (Waite & Holder, 2003). While serious questions have been raised regarding some of the conclusions reached by the authors of this study (Baker & Carrington, 2005), there is also clinical evidence suggesting that stimulating certain points not identified in traditional acupuncture may have therapeutic effects. While this is an area where further study is clearly needed, research in China suggests that the stimulation of many of the traditional acupuncture points — with their lower electrical resistance and higher concentration of receptors that are sensitive to mechanical stimulation — produces stronger electrochemical signals. Many acupuncture points are also believed to have specific effects, such as to increase serotonin levels and to strengthen or sedate the energy flow to a particular organ.

For more information on research on energy psychology see www.energypsych.org, www.innersource.net, and www.emofree.com.

The Benefits and Problems with Energy Psychology

A. Tapping Points

In Chinese medicine there are many ways to activate acu-points — needling, electrical acupuncture, pressure, tapping, heat, light touch, circling, and by intention. We have mentioned that there is a divergence of opinion among energy psychologists regarding bringing meridian-based tapping into psychotherapy. There is research that points in the direction of these tapping methods being clinically useful in many cases (Andrade & Feinstein, 2003). And, there has been much speculation as to why tapping works when it works. Alongside the Eastern perspective that tapping meridians activates the energetic rivers of the life force in our bodies, one plausible Western explanation is that tapping helps to break up energy fixations; and as Freud put forth, fixations are one of the major impediments to mental health. It makes intuitive sense that tapping may facilitate the breaking up of fixations. In particular, when integrating the somatic dimension into a modern psychology, which has otherwise relied on mental solutions to psychological blockages, we can posit that integrating the tapping of the body may add needed energy to help get people out of habitual ruts. In addition, it should be remembered that tapping is not usually done alone in energy psychology, but is done in conjunction with addressing negative cognitions and beliefs with phrases such as, "Even though I am___, I can still love and accept myself." This statement originally came from Callahan to treat "psychological reversals" which was TFT's explanation of self-sabotage. This phraseology is now expanded by others in the field in such ways as, "Even though this problem is currently ruling my life, I choose to be patient while I discover new and surprising ways to overcome it." Using such transformative cognitions helps to honor what I shall later describe as the "transcendent/transmuting dialectic."

Even though the EMDR method's originator, Dr. Francine Shapiro, does not consider herself an energy psychologist, and she emphasizes information reprocessing as the key to EMDR patient successes, her work can be viewed as a form of energy psychology. Dr. Shapiro (1995) suggests that neuronal bursts caused by eye movements may be equivalent to a low-voltage current and therefore responsible for synaptic changes. She says, "It may be that the repetitive action of any ... alternative stimuli — or even repetitive bursts of attention generates such a current. The shifting of the synaptic potential of the neural networks that include the dysfunctional material may cause the information to undergo progressively more processing with each set, until it arrives at an adaptive resolution" (p. 316). Others hypothesize that EMDR's positive research results are based in part by re-energizing neural pathways in, amongst other areas, the orbital frontal cortex by breaking up old patterns of fixations there. In a similar way, perhaps tapping on meridian points breaks up fixations in these channels and clears pathways allowing life energy to flow naturally.[12]

Among the various rationales for tapping is a behavioral psychology explanation. One of the foundations of modern behavioral self-control strategies is behavioral psychologist Wolpe's (1958) theory of reciprocal inhibition. Wolpe hypothesized that various maladaptive patterns would extinguish if they could symbolically occur in the presence of an incompatible response, such as relaxation. Psychologist Jim Lane believes that EFT's tapping method reduces central nervous system hyperarousal to provide rapid desensitization of triggers, and depotentiates limiting cognitive beliefs along the lines of reciprocal inhibition.[13]

The reciprocal inhibition point of view leads to using tapping while the patient focuses upon, or says, words related to the old negative cognition, dysfunctional state or belief, i.e. "tapping away" the old dysfunctional belief. This is believed to send deactivating signals to areas of the amygdala that regulate emotional arousal (Feinstein, 2006c, p. 2).

However, since the field of energy psychology is still in a pre-paradigmatic phase regarding techniques and theoretical frameworks, there currently exist other theoretical frameworks with differing methods of application that serve the same purpose as tapping. For example, for those who favor the viewpoint that the purpose of various energy psychology methods (including tapping, humming, and eye movements) is to anchor new states of awareness, they would apply these methods while focusing upon, or stating, a new life-enhancing belief. Deactivation versus anchoring do not need to be mutually exclusive theoretical frameworks or treatment methodologies. Further research is needed to determine which theoretical viewpoints, with which accompanying treatment protocols, work best for which issues.

There is neurophysiological theoretical support for physical explanations of the merit of tapping. Dr. Ruden (2005) gives a neurobiological hypothesis that tapping creates affect activation and glutamate release, and that following the tapping with a combination of serotonin and GABA prevents the restoring of the fear response by de-linking the conditioned stimulus to the unconditioned fear stimulus pathway. Dr. Goodheart reports that tapping on the left side of the head along the temporal sphenoidal line around the ear fosters an acceptance of positive statements such as "I am worthwhile," while tapping on the right fosters an acceptance of negative positive statements such as "I am not worthless." He speculated that by tapping on these sites, the filtering system is temporarily disengaged, allowing the assimilation of desired messages (as cited in Gallo, 2002, p. 47).

On the other hand, there are a variety of energy-based psychotherapists who do not consider tapping to be useful, and report non-beneficial or detrimental results. For example, the founder of the Seemorg Matrix method, Clinton (2002), found that in her clinical experience, "tapping on points jangled some of my clients and increased their anxiety and fear, we discovered that holding each chakra in turn by contacting it with the center of the clients palm seems to produce a deeper, more peaceful, more thorough treatment. This has become the preferred, though not the only method" (p. 95). Clinton not only holds chakras that are out of balance, but also has patients simultaneously touch other chakras that can come to the aid of the out of balance chakra. Nims (2002), after practicing Callahan's method for many years, found that tapping was not necessary, and that verbal or nonverbal cues were just as, if not even more, effective. Another leader in the energy psychology movement, Diepold (2002), says that he developed the touch and breath method to move away from tapping because he found that,

> *Colleagues using Thought Field Therapy reported that patients sometimes made statements about tapping that reflected criticism or discomfort ... such as, 'This is silly. This looks stupid. I can't do this in public ...It hurts if I tap too hard. Tapping distracts me.' This type of response compromised compliance with follow-up treatment and homework. Additionally some patients who are victims of abuse either refused to tap, or took tapping as an opportunity to hurt themselves. (p. 20)*

Another issue is that acupuncture, and the wider Chinese medical traditions in which it is embedded, has a wider knowledge of points oriented to a patient's ideographic (unique) condition, as assessed through pulse and tongue diagnosis. Energy psychologists should be open to drawing further on that knowledge base as treatment protocols are established. A question arises — since an acupuncturist would not necessarily use the same points used by an energy psychologist to heal various disorders, has energy psychology discovered a shorthand method that could be a major step forward in helping the evolution of energy based healing traditions? In supporting this position, we would need to include the research on understanding how the mind (placebo effect, better called the "belief effect") has been shown in meta-analytic studies to be responsible for approximately 55 percent of cures (Rossi, 1986 p. 15-19); so we can imagine how adding the psychological dimension to tapping just a few well-chosen points could create powerful healing effects.

Distraction:

Another major concern that clinicians have about tapping is that it may temporarily distract/dissociate patients from their issues, thereby preventing a longer lasting "working through" of psychological issues. One way of measuring whether this is the case is through longitudinal research, i.e. examining how long a patient's reported changes last. From the Andrade & Feinstein study (2003) and from brain change studies (Swingle et al., 2000) the research points to many patients' maintaining long-term changes over time as a result of tapping and many of

EFT's broader methods. As discussed earlier, there are plausible theoretical reasons as well as a neurobiological basis for the positive results (Ruden, 2005). Further examination is needed of such research methodology issues, some of which will be addressed below.

Though there are probably degrees of truth in all viewpoints regarding the advantages and disadvantages of current tapping techniques, as will be explained in subsequent chapters, Bodymind Healing Psychotherapy (BMHP) prefers to have, as a first line of treatment, activating "the energy of the core Self" through a variety of other methods. In addition to the issues listed above, my concern from a psychological viewpoint is that the number of points touched in various algorithms may lead to an obsessive dependence on points rather than on the "real Self" to produce change.

In the sections that follow I will discuss how the transcending/transmuting dialectic is a key variable to consider. Does tapping create a false transcendence, i.e. a rising above and avoiding one's issues rather than a real working through? It should be remembered that tapping in energy psychology is usually done in combination with other psychological methods, not as a stand-alone treatment. I will address this further in the section on research below.

Qigong and Tapping

As an ancient sacred wisdom tradition, Qigong has much to add to modern discussions on touch and tapping, since Qigong is a method of cultivating the energy of life through a variety of means — one of which is touch. Since Qigong used various methods of touch for thousands of years before modern energy psychology took on some of these methods, it is reasonable to think that Qigong might have something to add to our knowledge. In Chapter 6, there will be more discussion on how self-touch of various points on the body is an important part of Bodymind Healing Psychotherapy and Psychospiritual Postural Anthropology in treating anxiety disorders. Volume I of this book showed how touch and tapping is incorporated in various parts of the Bodymind Healing Qigong system — for example, in *Wild Goose Taps its Chest*, *Tapping the Belly Clock*, and in *Beating the Heavenly Drum*.

As Eskimos have many names for snow, so Qigong has a wide range of touching and tapping methods. In Master Lam's (1999) book about *Yi Chuan* healing (my home Qigong tradition), he discusses touch in relationship to the different elements — fire, earth, metal, water, and wood. To exemplify: fire energy, in the *Yi Chuan* system, presses and withdraws suddenly like a plunger unblocking a drain; earth involves slow circling movements; metal touch flows from surrounding tissues to the place where it is needed (metal is an inward movement like a caravan closing in on itself for protection against hostile outer forces); water energy places the hand over an injured spot and makes sustained vibrations downward, as if sending signals inward to the skin, muscle, and bone; and wood energy moves outward from the center.

So, once a more fully developed paradigm of psychological energy healing is created, we can begin to wonder what conditions will be best-served by energy psychology's stimulating touch method of tapping. It makes intuitive sense that it may be best in situations where increased energy is needed, for example in a case of depression. In certain cases of hypertension, tapping touch may be too activating rather than self-soothing.

The wider Chinese medical tradition incorporates Qigong in its treatment protocols along with acupuncture, herbs, and touch methods (such as *Tui Na*, acupressure, etc.); the Chinese tradition often prescribes Qigong movements so that a patient will have self-healing methods to use between sessions, and for health maintenance in general. In its broadest definition, "Qigong" means cultivating the energy of life and includes self-touch of points in a variety of ways. I remember from an acupressure certification program that I took, my instructors would talk about applying more pressure for deficiency conditions and using softer touch for conditions of excess.[14] As clinicians integrate the verbal/cognitive dimensions of energy psychology into their practices, further research will be needed regarding which type of touch is best-suited for different conditions, rather than having a "one size fits all" touch protocol.[15]

While in this pre-paradigmatic phase, it would be beneficial to draw from the many-thousand-year-old empirical tradition of Qigong, and its accumulated wisdom, to find the most healing movements and places to self-touch for our patients, in order to enhance energy psychology's healing repertoire.

B. Muscle Testing

Though not all energy psychologists use muscle testing, myself included, there is a body of research that points to the validity (Perot et al., 1991) and reliability (Frese et al., 1987) of this technique. Others report various problems with muscle testing. There is, for instance, a difference in the amount of pressure that is required to test whether an indicator muscle locks following a statement the subject believes to be true, as contrasted with a statement the subject believes to be false. And just because a subject believes something to be true does not mean that this belief is necessarily true. Also, since subtle energies are involved, and if the mind influences subtle energies, then the practitioner's and the subject's beliefs, expectations, and hopes must be prevented from skewing the outcome if the test is to be accurate. Firm conclusions cannot be drawn from the research and many of the most-respected energy-oriented practitioners emphasize that energy testing is as much an art as it is a science (Durlacher, 2002).[16]

Some of those who use muscle testing have raised questions that simple changes in language can effect the test (Monte, 1999). Even experienced clinicians report inconsistent results, raise questions about the intentionality of the muscle tester, have concerns about incongruence between the subject's rational and emotional response to some stimulus, and raise issues about how conscious or unconscious "experimental bias" can creep into results and create confounding variables (Durlacher, 2002; Wiseman et al., 1997). Some energy psychotherapists who use muscle testing use it not as an objective method of assessment, but more like an attunement experience to train the intuition of the therapist and patient.

Bodymind Healing Psychotherapy does not use muscle testing due to a variety of reasons. The muscle testing method originally came from the chiropractic profession, and, as psychotherapists, a different set of factors needs to be considered in this realm of experimental treatments and potential dual relationships, i.e. mixing different elements can at times produce benefits or create problems (see Chapter 22).

In addition to my not having sufficient training in this method, not being inclined in this clinical direction, and having the aforementioned reservations, another concern I have is that muscle testing can potentially set up transference problems in depth psychotherapy. For example, it may create expressed or unexpressed trust issues, i.e. "Is my therapist pressing harder because he/she wants a certain outcome?" Even if this is not true, the suspicion may influence trust in subsequent therapy. For example, for low hypnotizables (Wickramasekera, 1998) this may be more of a factor than for high hypnotizables. For high hypnotizables it places reliance on an outside agent (the tester) or a body part (a muscle), and takes the patient away from reliance on his or her own emotional core. More research is needed to validate these hypotheses, and to determine for which people muscle testing works, and for whom it may create problems in a psychotherapeutic relationship. Some of the transference issues involved with doing ethical energy work in a therapeutic context are addressed in the book *Creating Right Relationships* (Hover-Kramer & Murphy, 2006). BMHP favors using a SUDS scale (subjective units of distress scale) for an objective/subjective measurement of treatment results because it directs the patient to his or her emotional core and it helps to develop the hermeneutic (Warnke, 1987) of exploring inner knowing.

Bodymind Healing Psychotherapy's Perspective on Muscle Testing

BMHP prefers, as a first choice in assessment methods, the use of the body's felt sense. By allowing words and images to arise from this felt sense and resonating them back to the body to find a fit, the resultant hermeneutical process helps a person to discover an inner knowing and uncover his or her own unique felt meaning of a life issue (Gendlin, 1962, 1978). This seems to be more psychologically congruent with a self-empowering psychotherapeutic process. So many people in our culture have alexithymia (difficulty putting feelings into words), or more psychodynamically put, have a problem "differentiating their affects." Thus, when a change does or does not take place after a given psychological intervention, rather than testing a muscle for confirmation, I favor an approach that allows patients to tune in and "inwardly search" (Bugenthal, 1978) for their own new state of being, drawing from the center of themselves. This promotes development of affective states.

A Tai Chi Perspective on Muscle Testing

Finally, since BMHP draws much of its knowledge from the Qigong/Tai Chi traditions, and because these traditions teach that the primordial Self is most developed when awareness is brought to one's center-line, the training is to de-emphasize putting awareness and emphasis on the muscles. Muscle testing in this regard moves contrary to the Taoist principle of cultivating the center in the belly (*Tan Tien*) and the center-line (*axis mundi*).[17] So we see how the principle of depth psychotherapy concerning developing and putting awareness on one's emotional core is more closely aligned with the Taoist Tai Chi practice of putting awareness on the center of oneself physically and spiritually.

On the other hand, all healers have their own specific tools that work for them — so for those who are inclined to use muscle testing, I hope the above discussion will add to the hermeneutics of the dialogue as the field circumambulates the issues concerning which techniques are most helpful in facilitating the transformative process for different types of people.

C. Quick Fix Mentality

Many energy psychology methods claim instantaneous results (Callahan, 1985; Nims, 1998), or results that are "usually permanent" (Craig, 1997, p. 33). And there are many initial studies lending support to energy psychologies effectiveness with certain issues such as anxiety (Andrade & Feinstein, 2003), phobias (Callahan, 1985), trauma (Feinstein, 2006), etc. Energy psychology seems less effective with conditions that have a strong biochemical etiology such as major endogenous depression, psychosis, bipolar disorders, personality disorders, and dementia (Andrade and Feinstein, 2004).

Generally speaking, BMHP prefers as a working model, the "practice model" versus the "quick fix model." It is the experience of most patients and most psychotherapists that although the process of "transmutation" from psychotherapeutic inner work sometimes moves forward in leaps and bounds and often provides transformative "felt shifts," it is more helpful to think of change as an ongoing process. For example, with a case of public speaking phobia, there are many methods that can bring a person back to the state-specific state of consciousness that was experienced in a transformative moment in therapy. Some of these methods include: inner work uncovering psychodynamic roots, working with various cognitive psychotherapy methods, and finding anchors (whether from energy psychology or other hypnotic anchors). However, this most often requires the use of a "re-membering" process when past triggers get reactivated. In this respect it is important to distinguish between psychological first aid and long term healing (Feinstein, 2006c). Furthermore, pushing the idea of instant cures can lead to shame in those who don't have such positive instantaneous results; it can also lead to false reports to please the therapist, thus resulting in the so-called "halo effect."

Though it is very fitting with our modern "God in a pill" culture, where managed care measures "cost savings" by claims of "instant cures," it is the position of BMHP that the preoccupation with quick cures are often antithetical to true lasting change and healing that comes over time from the "working through" process. From a Taoist perspective, not trying to change, can activate change.

There is a need to be circumspect as we look at "instant cures" in order to determine how much the healing is due to real, lasting change versus a halo effect that occurs through hypnotic induction. For example, in one demonstration of "instant cure" I witnessed at a conference, a well-known leader in the field said to a woman reporting change in a major issue, "not only has that changed; but while we changed that, I also affected 1,370 other related issues." Since most people in the audience were caught in that hypnotic, authority-laden, group consciousness that often surrounds leaders, no one challenged this authority figure. Unable to believe my ears that the leader was serious, I asked one of his most ardent followers, "Was this leader kidding?" He replied, "Yes, I know, I've tried to get him to tone down that type of thing."

It should be noted that spontaneous remissions and miraculous "cures" are possible and have been reported at many healing places with many legitimate healing modalities, whether it be Lourdes in France, John of God in Brazil, Olga Worral, etc. (Benor, 1992; Weil, 2004). So, it should not be a surprise that these occurrences could take place through an energy psychology approach.

A variety of issues still need further examination. What creates physical versus psychological "cures"? What types of psychological issues are most affected by energy psychology, and of those, which are most likely to have a quick healing take place? For example, what is the difference in quick healing results between working with energy psychology methods with core life issues and with a simple phobia? Also, the repeatability of cures is certainly a desired goal at the forefront of a Western scientific paradigm; but in the Einsteinian era of quantum principles, sometimes the healing of one person by a given healer may not be repeatable for another person. This is not a reason to discard the method. The reasons for healing a given individual are multifaceted, including the power of the so-called "placebo effect."

A "practice model" is inherent in Qigong practice and in the BMHP approach to psychotherapeutic change. In subsequent chapters we will see examples from the last few years of my clinical practice in BMHP that confirm for me that quick, lasting results from some energy psychology and BMHP methods are possible; but as well, I have often found that long-term depth psychotherapy is required to produce lasting change, particularly with core life issues. Toward this end, I use the ten levels of BMHP (see Chapter 5), which includes traditional psychotherapeutic methods, energy psychology techniques, Qigong, and symbolic process methodologies.

D. The Depth of the Energy Psychotherapy Traditions

Certainly those in the energy psychology field are aware that there exists an older tradition of energy psychology. Many energy psychologists make reference to traditions such as Chinese medicine, Hindu Chakra systems, etc. As a matter of fact, another name often used for energy psychologies are "meridian-based psychologies," thus showing their oriental origins. Energy psychology's common use of acu-points along the meridian systems further indicates its connection with ancient sacred wisdom traditions like acupuncture. One intention of this book is to expand the foundation of energy psychology — to root it more firmly in the ancient sacred wisdom traditions that I believe best represent its foundations. Also, though energy psychologists have contributed much to the holistic healing traditions of the world by adding energy healing methods (such as touch of acu-points) to cognitive and other forms of modern psychotherapy, in the following chapters I will show how symbolic process traditions and other tools of depth psychotherapy can add vital ingredients to the healing methods of modern energy psychology, and can, in turn, add to an integral bodymind healing psychotherapy.

E. Political Problems with Modern Energy Psychology's Founder

A problem with basing energy psychology's efficacy on the ground of Roger Callahan's work is that he has had some political problems with the American Psychological Association (APA), which has had unfortunate effects on the growth of this approach.

One issue is that Callahan claims his Voice Technology method (VT) cures virtually all psychological problems with 98 percent effectiveness (according to a personal communication by

Dr. Larry Stoler, current president of the Association of Comprehensive Energy Psychology). In addition, the training in his VT method is extraordinarily expensive — he charges $100,000. At the current time the APA is not giving continuing education units for training in energy psychology in part due to its association with Dr. Callahan's work; however, continuing education courses have been approved on a case by case basis by the mandatory continuing education accrediting agency for licensed psychologists (MCEP) in California. MCEP has taken this position in part due to the efforts of the well-respected Dr. David Gruder, one of the past presidents of the Association for Comprehensive Energy Psychology (ACEP). As the field of energy psychology continues to be broadened and put on a more comprehensive base, and its efficacy is more firmly established, hopefully the APA will reconsider the value of giving CEU's to psychologists who want to learn more about well-founded energy psychology approaches. I feel honored that the continuing education courses that I offer, which incorporate elements of energy psychology, have been among those approved by MCEP.

F. Research Methodology Issues

Some issues in need of further examination are:

1. Population Selection Biases/ Dropouts from Treatment.

Who are the people that do and don't respond to these methods? And why? Selection biases are one commonly addressed research methodology issue. For example, are the people from groups where the group energy creates "the weekend effect?" (an effect where workshop participants get a transformative experience that doesn't last). Are the people for whom the treatment "instantly works" highly susceptible? Or do they tend to cluster in particular personality categories as measured by standard psychological tests? Are the reported successes in groups and in individual sessions from those who are highly hypnotizable? (This could be measured by using one of the standard measuring scales of hypnotic suggestibility[18] with those who report positive results compared with those who drop out of treatment or who do not report success.) All of the above issues relate to the generalizability of energy psychology methods.

2. Longitudinal Research.

What are the long-term lasting results of these methods? Rossi (2002) wrote that,

> *Whenever a new and numinous method or psychosocial belief system is introduced it will usually be able to boast a number of fast converts who will report marvelous results. It is likely that this immediate positive experience come from highly suggestive 5-10% of the general populations who have a special talent for mind–body accessibility and healing. Only later, when the larger proportion of the population that does not have such talent complains of lack of success does the novelty numinosum neurogenesis effect loose its psycho-genomic potency. (p. 194).*

In the Andrade & Feinstein (2002) study this doesn't seem to be the case because of the reported longitudinal results (follow-up over time). One study of EFT examined workshop participants, pre and post workshop, and showed a significant decrease (P > 0.0005) in all measures of psychological distress at a six month follow-up (Rowe, 2005). There are various research methodology issues with studies of this nature — for example, the workshop particpants may have been operating under a halo effect, which can create a bias due to a desire to validate one's workshop experience; and also, groups of this nature may have a selection bias that is not representative of the wider population or clinical population encountered in mental health practices. In a study by Wells (2003) on the effectiveness of EFT versus abdominal breathing in the treatment of animal phobias, the results indicated that a thirty minute EFT treatment produced significantly greater improvement, and this improvement was maintained for six to nine months. Though these studies are promising regarding the lasting effects of certain energy psychology methods, further research and replications of these studies are necessary to make any definitive conclusions.

Studies from other journals also point in the direction that energy psychology results appear to last over time in some other specific cases — for example, in cases of acrophobia (Carbonell, 1997), blood injection injury phobia (Darby, 2001), and trauma (Diepold & Goldstein, 2000). Swingle et al. (2000) reported results of two treatments of EFT for PTSD symptoms and found significant positive changes in brain waves and stress symptoms at a three month follow-up. For more on issues involving research, see Gallo's (2004) review of some of this literature (Gallo forthrightly acknowledges that these studies are not from peer-reviewed literature and are lacking in sufficient research design).

In fairness, it should be mentioned that a double standard is being applied when a short-lasting treatment is expected to produce long-lasting results in order for that method to be worthwhile. As Gallo (2004) points out,

> *It is interesting that the same level of criticism is not invariably raised when a psycho-pharmacological study demonstrates that a benzodiazepine or a beta-blocker is able to relieve anxiety or deter a phobic response. Follow-up studies would seldom support the effectiveness of the psychotropic in relieving the phobia or anxiety disorder over time, after the agent has been discontinued. Nonetheless, the ability of a treatment to afford even temporary relief is considered acceptable by the medical community and as far as the general public is concerned.*

As mentioned above, we need to be mindful of the potential detrimental effects that the expectation of one-time cures can have on patients. A primary concern in the field of psychology is whether such claims may lead to shaming people for whom the methods do not work, or lead to a halo effect through over-reporting positive results. One variable to consider in measuring the success of a treatment is to measure drop-outs from treatment. In some energy psychology studies this is not a reported variable. I suggest that such data be systematically reported in the ongoing evolution of research in the field in order to determine what kinds of people drop out from treatment and for what types of people the treatments work.

3. Face Validity

One type of validity is called "face validity," which means, on the face of the proposed study, does it seem that this method measures what it claims to measure and produce the changes it claims to produce? The experience of most clinicians supports the belief that a working through process is usually necessary to create change. Although sudden shifts do occur, and transformative experiences do happen in therapy, the repetition compulsion often emerges as old habits reemerge. Thus a method that claims or implies instant results that last without practice over time meets with skepticism concerning its face validity. This doesn't mean the method is not valid, it just means that the method fights an uphill battle against human experience. Certainly there are times that instant, long-lasting transformation occurs; but the job of research is to determine for what types of people, with what conditions does this change maintain over time with or without continuous application of the treatment methods.

Bodymind Healing Psychotherapy's Approach

It is one aim of this book to widen the foundation of the existing field of energy psychology by incorporating a deeper substructure to support the edifice of this emerging field. I propose that integrating Qigong (known to be one of the five branches, or, some say, the very roots of Chinese medicine), depth psychotherapy, and symbolic process approaches into energy psychology will contribute to not only the greater field of psychotherapy, but also to our current bodymind health crisis.

In the following chapters you will see how different elements of the bodymind healing traditions can add to the energy psychology tradition in some of these specific ways:

Going Beyond Mechanistic Approaches: Phenomenologically Based Anchoring Methods. In Chapter 16 we will see how Bodymind Healing Psychotherapy (BMHP) favors, as a first line of treatment, the use of a patients' own gestures at the moment that a felt shift takes place in order to anchor state-specific subpersonalities involved in that change. Though tapping is used, BMHP also uses points that are metaphorically congruent with meanings known to, and agreed upon, by the patient. For example, if I suggest that a patient taps on his or her chest (acu-point CV-17) to anchor a state of being with the heart, its meaning is clear to the patient.

Emphasizing the Meaning of Points. In energy psychology when the patient is instructed to tap on various points, the meaning of those points is not usually discussed in detail. Bodymind Healing Psychotherapy proposes that "meaning" is a key healing agent, and is a significant component of activating "the mind-body trance state." For example, we will see in Chapter 16 how discussing the meaning of the "Karate Chop" point, and its association in acupuncture theory with activating the yang meridians associated with the back of the spine, helps a patient to develop a metaphorical "spine." One can think of explicating the meaning of acu-points to patients as a method of further enhancing the placebo effect, thereby potentially increasing the positive elements of hypnotizable effects, or simply empowering them with a sense of being included as a partner in understanding the deeper meanings of their treatment. By including the patient it helps create a connected understanding, rather than a disconnected state where only the therapist holds the esoteric knowledge of the deeper meaning of the points. To withhold such information from patients could potentially cause counter-therapeutic, unintended consequences.

Adding Breath to Touch. Diepold (2000) proposes a "touch and breathe" method as an alternative to tapping. This coincides well with the acupressure and Qigong methods of treating conditions of excess. As an addition to this approach, I propose a "circle, stop, breathe, and feel method" to be incorporated with energy psychology, particularly in cases involving conditions of excess such as high stress and hypertension (particularly with hypertension based in the Chinese category of "excess liver Qi rising"). I originally learned the circle, stop, and feel method from *Yi Chuan Qigong* Master Han Xinyuan in 1976 as part of our Standing Meditation Qigong training. I introduced it into my own Standing Meditation practice and to my students in the 1980s to help prevent stagnation of Qi. I learned that this method was also part of the touch methods of "polarity therapy" developed by Dr. Randolf Stone, when I was introduced to this method of self-touch by Kozoko Onodera, director of the Polarity Therapy Center of Berkeley in the late 1970s. When I was trained at the Acupressure Institute of Berkeley in 1990, I found that this was a basic method of acupressure training. During these years, from the early 1970s to the mid-1990s, I began to gradually introduce these methods as an adjunct to my psychotherapy and behavioral health practice.

Hidden in the circle, stop, and feel method is an activation of the *wuji* state, which is a central notion to the altered state induced by static forms of Qigong practice. I defined "*wuji*" in Volume I as: the void, the mother of Qi, and discussed this more fully there. Here, the process of stopping after the circling can induce the practitioner into the *wuji* state. The circling movement helps to activate the Qi. In moving from circling to stillness and back to stillness, the practitioner repeats the cosmogenic creation myth of Tai Chi — moving from "no-thing" and stillness to movement, and back to stillness. The beauty of this simple movement is that elaborate conceptualizations are not needed and the movement has the potential to accomplish this *wuji* state when done properly. If difficulties arise in inducing this altered state, other aspects of the BMHP methods can be introduced to transmute issues that are in the way.

Adding Depth Psychotherapy to Energy Psychology. The tradition of depth psychotherapy has not been sufficiently incorporated into energy psychologies. In the following chapters we will see how symbolic process traditions, a key element of depth psychotherapy, can be integrated into energy psychology.

Moving Beyond Imagery: The Felt Kinesthetic Sense of the Rivers of Qi. In Chapter 4 we will see how BMHP's methods contain ways to combine imaginal traditions with the long-known rivers of Qi in the body through the use of breath and movement.

My Goal

As a presenter at energy psychology conferences, I envision my purpose is to further define the roots of energy psychology as not having derived from any modern researcher, but from the ground of ancient sacred wisdom traditions and depth psychotherapy. The particular roots of the bodymind healing tradition that is the subject of this work are grounded in cross-cultural traditions of postural initiation and various ancient symbolic process traditions including mythology, alchemy, and astrology. The following chapters will show how a deeper connection between the field of energy psychology and these traditions, particularly Qigong, can help reconnect modern psychology with primordial wisdom and practices that honor our psychological ancestors. Most importantly, my aim is to help modern people suffering from the vicissitudes of modern life, the human condition, and from deep-seated psychological wounds and issues.

CHAPTER 4: THE GROUND OF ENERGY PSYCHOLOGY: MODERN METHODS & ANCIENT ROOTS

Once upon a time a stream passed through many different kinds of terrain. It had its falls over great cliffs and its twists and turns, but it enjoyed the adventure of traveling alone. It had acquired considerable skills in overcoming barriers, but one day it reached the sands of the desert and found that as fast as it ran into the sand, its waters disappeared. It was in an "existential crisis," suffering from feelings of emptiness, stagnation, dryness, and being cut off from the circle of life.

The stream was convinced that its destiny was to cross the desert, and yet there seemed to be no way. Then a hidden voice from the sands whispered, "The wind crosses the desert, and so can the stream. By hurtling in your own accustomed way you cannot get across. You will either disappear, or at best, you'll become a stagnant marsh." You must allow the wind to carry you over to your destination by allowing yourself to be absorbed in the wind."

This idea was not acceptable to the stream. After all, it had never been absorbed before. It didn't want to lose its individuality. And, once having lost it, how was the stream to know that it could ever be regained? The sands replied, "The wind performs this function. It takes up water, carries it over the desert sands, and then lets it fall again. Falling as rain, the water again becomes a river."

"How can I know that this is true?" "It is so, and if you do not believe it, you cannot become more than a quagmire, and even that could take many, many years; and it certainly is not the same as a stream." "But can I not remain the same stream that I am today?" "You cannot in either case remain so," the whisper said. "You are called what you are even today because you do not know which part of you is the essential one."

When the stream heard this, certain echoes began to arise in its thoughts. Dimly it remembered a state in which it — or some part of it, had been held in the arms of a wind. With this thought the stream let go for a moment, and lo and behold, it started to rise up. It was scary — as if the essence that it had identified with for a long time was evaporating away. But this awe-filled evaporation process did indeed bring an experience of a deep, long-forgotten part of its identity.

As the stream continued to rise up with a feeling of elation, memories of its long journey alone began to coalesce. The stream remembered how it had fallen from its home in the clouds after early wounding in its life, and had withdrawn to an isolated life, bound by the banks of the river of duality. With this depressing realization it noticed its form change into a dark cloud. Remembering all the time spent lost from its connection with all things, the stream felt very sad.

With this awareness, tears started to roll down its face. It noticed that the tears fell in the form of rain, down to the sands below, beginning the process of watering new seeds, which would eventually grow into flowers.

The stream realized that the cycle of its journey had not been meaningless. It appreciated the cycle of creation and learned something from every part of it. At this moment the stream was filled with electricity as it appreciated the cycle of aloneness and togetherness, merging and separating. Lightening and thunder filled the heavens as the stream felt the wholeness of its essential nature.

— Idres Shah's
The Stream and the Sands
Revised by author from Tales of the Dervishes:

The Age-Old, Broader Traditions of Energy Psychology

There are a broad, unfathomably deep number of traditions of energy healing and energy psychology that go back to ancient times. Actually, Western medicine is one of the world's only healing traditions that does not utilize these concepts. Due to our mechanistic bias, we seek answers to questions about our health and disease in physical structures, biochemical processes, and atomized parts. In ancient traditions the human organism is seen as comprising more than a physical body. In the age-old yogic tradition, for example, the energy of consciousness manifests in successively denser forms, determined by its energetic frequency, culminating in physical tissue (Rama et al., 1976). Even sophisticated theorists in the West such as Victor Frankel (1967) with his "dimensional ontology" have warned about the "reductionism" inherent in taking a whole phenomena and reducing it to one or more of its parts (like the proverbial blind man and the elephant story where one part is focused on losing the whole). Thus, we need to re-member the wider energetic dimensions of being human as we reflect on healing the mind, body, and spirit.

This should not be news to anyone, since we all know that the energy of the human body is, and has been through the ages, the foundation of human health. When our energy is high, our immune system is strong; and when our energy is low, we become vulnerable to disease. It has also been known through the ages that healing depends on energy, that energy is the foundation of life, and that without energy we die. In our everyday lives we seek to increase our energy by the way we eat, the way we exercise, and the lifestyles we choose. In fact, much of our everyday lives involves a process of making choices about activating or relaxing our energy.

Low energy is the not-so-hidden epidemic of our times. It seems that Starbucks and other coffee houses are appearing in our neighborhoods faster than restaurants. As a culture, we are starved for energy and gravitate towards almost anything that promises to give it to us. According to a Gallup Poll, 40 percent of all Americans report a significant daytime tiredness. Low energy laments are the most frequent complaint pharmacists and physicians hear from their patients. Many surveys indicate that fatigue and lack of energy is the most common complaint and symptom reported to physicians. For example, 37 percent of 500 patients in a Boston health center survey

Chapter 4: The Ground of Energy Psychology

reported feeling tired. Outside the doctor's office, shopping carts in corner store pharmacies are filling up with popular energy boosters. Whole Foods reports that natural energy supplement sales are up by 15 percent over last year. Our energy level is an indicator of our overall health. Those who are energetic are generally healthy, whereas those who are tired all the time are usually ill or about to be ill. A Yale University assessment of over 300 nurses found that energy levels had the highest correlation with general health status. Energy was also found to be the best predictor of both physical and psychological health over time (Graud & Childers, 2005).

What if we could tap into a source of energy that is within us and all around us? Over the eons, ancient sacred wisdom traditions have found many ways to activate the energy of life. It is crucial for our health and our lives that we, too, draw from these age-old roots. Just like it takes gas to move a car, so it takes energy to move the human psyche to a new place. Amongst the age-old traditions that enable the psyche to move to new places are bodymind-oriented traditions such as: methods of postural initiation (Goodman 1990; Mayer, 2004) like yoga (Rama, 1976; Shearer, 1982); meditation (LeShan, 1974); sacred forms of dance (Tomio, 1994); methods of self-touch (Gach, 2004); and touch by others (Brennan, 1990).[1]

In the following chapters, we will see how modern bodymind healing methods, Western psychology, and ancient sacred wisdom traditions can join to help heal "the energy crises" of modern times. These traditions do more than just help restore energy to the depleted; they are at the core of "healing" in the deepest sense of the word. The earliest energy psychology was created to bring the energies of the life of the individual human soul back into balance. These age-old esoteric psychological traditions believe that many human disorders start in the energies at the archetypal level (from, for example, human tendencies to hold anger, be frustrated by unfulfilled desires, be anxious about not living up to our own or other's expectations). They believe that disorders manifest in the human mind and are incarnated in our bodies in areas of increasing levels of energetic density, i.e. these imbalances then manifest in the musculature and finally the spine. From this perspective, life is looked at as a school for learning how to deal with these issues, and then returning to the source of creation.

Finding the way to return to the source of creation, and to thereby renew ourselves, has been a central subject in cross-cultural mythology (Eliade, 1965). Each different tradition has its own way of conceptualizing this process of returning to the source of the healing energy of the cosmos. For example, in the Taoist tradition it is believed that prior to creation, the void (or the mother of Qi) existed (*wuji*), from that was born the two (Tai Chi), then the five elements, and from there was born the myriad of things. In Taoist practice therefore, when a person gets lost in the myriad of things, he or she repeats the creation myth in reverse and returns through various practices (such as Tai Chi) to the mother of Qi, and is then bathed in the womb of life energy found in static forms of meditation (see Volume I). In particular, the first and last Tai Chi non-movement is a static form of meditation, which is meant to lead to the initiate's dissolving into a *wuji* state. In the Greek tradition this was called a *"catabasis"* (a reverse birth) and was enacted by the initiate being drawn, feet first, into a cave, where a transfiguring underworld journey then took place. For the initiate, this *catabasis* process reportedly included learning to see human souls as stars, waiting for a transformative dream before exit was allowed, and recovering laughter (Meier, 1967, pp. 100-112). In cross-cultural shamanic traditions, the "loss of soul" was treated by a shamanic journey (Eliade, 1964; Ingerman, 1991). An important element of many such traditions is how to keep connected to "sacred space" after returning to the "real world." A Native American shaman might keep his eagle feather or a sacred pipe or a shield of his medicine animal as a power object to remind him of his journey to the "other world."

Hypnotic Anchors and Ancient Sacred Wisdom Traditions

> *And so God says to us, "Make for me a holy place so that I can dwell inside you. Yes, it is possible to stay connected with me at all times in all places, even as you engage in the life of the world."*
>
> — Rabbi Shefa Gold
> Commentary from the *Old Testament*[2]

In modern hypnotherapeutic parlance, *"anchors"* (Bandler & Grinder, 1979) are used as cues to bring back healing states of consciousness. We can think of an anchor as a weighted object dropped by a boat over a hidden treasure; when an anchor is put down and a storm blows the boat off course, the anchor can bring the boat back to the desired spot to recover the treasure. In hypnotherapy, an anchor brings a person back to a treasured, "state-specific state of consciousness" (Tart, 1968; Rossi, 1986); this experience can be kinesthetic, visual, auditory, or olfactory (Bandler & Grindler, 1981)

Ancient energy psychology has a treasure house of such anchoring methods that go back to ancient times, long before hypnotherapy coined the idea. Long before energy psychology introduced the idea of using humming a song as part of the Nine Gamut process (Craig, 1995) to balance the brain, songs were used in ancient sacred wisdom traditions to heal. Found within the deeper mysteries of the Jewish tradition, there are songs to help heal virtually every psychological malady.[3] For example, one orthodox Jewish man with whom I was working was suffering from severe negative thinking and resultant depression. Among other aspects of our depth psychotherapy, he found that singing the song, "This Too Is for the Good" *(Gam Zeh Tovah)* was helpful in countering negative cognitions when they arose. When he did this practice he experienced a felt shift from a negative constricted feeling into a bodily felt sense of open-heartedness.

As I spoke about in the last chapter, Bodymind Healing Psychotherapy holds a "practice model" as its basic stance, rather than a one-time fix model. Within this model, both transcendent and transmuting songs have their place. For example, the Jewish song that honors the oneness of all life *(shama),* is used to enter into a transcendent altered state whereby one arises from the differences and oppositional elements of life to "re-member," and get back in touch with the oneness of all creation. On the other hand, as black "soul music" taught us, and other traditions know as well, it is oftentimes most helpful to choose a song which goes into the pain and transmutes it. For example, one female patient, who had just lost a long-term relationship and didn't know how she could ever put her life back together again, found herself singing Tom Petty's, "I'm free falling," in the shower. In conjunction with our longer-term therapy work together, she used this song to identify with everything in the universe that falls, is freed up to create new realities,

Chapter 4: The Ground of Energy Psychology

and survives. This became her anchor when she was in the midst of her deepest pain. It helped remind her, along with the "cognitive restructuring" we did (see Chapter 5), that like the seeds of an oak tree falling to the ground, life goes on.

Kinesthetic anchors and the human body have also been used by a variety of cross-cultural traditions for anchoring altered states. Long before energy psychology used tapping of points to facilitate transformation, Christians, using the sign of the cross, tapped their bodies to anchor their connection with Jesus. Interestingly, the specific points tapped in the sign of the cross by Christians (the third-eye point (GV-24.5), the heart (CV-17), and the lung points (Lu-1)) are sacred energy points according to pagan and oriental traditions. Though Christianity derived the points of its cross from older pagan traditions, it holds these traditions in low regard, and does not complete the lower part of the bodily cross by tapping the belly. Perhaps this is to bring forth the transcendent state of consciousness they wish to emphasize, while eliminating the lower connection with the earth point in the belly. This can be juxtaposed to those traditions, such as the Taoist tradition, which emphasize tapping on the power-center of the belly *(Tan Tien)*; a tradition like this is therefore, in this respect, more aligned with what are commonly described as "God immanent" traditions.[4] God immanent traditions emphasize how the sacred is manifested in all creation — the earth and the body.

In the Jewish tradition, *Tefillin* — small leather boxes containing the sacred pathway of the Jewish holy book the *Torah* — are wrapped over key points on the body as prayers are said or sung. The points on the body where the boxes are placed, where knots are tied, and even where the leather thongs are wrapped are key points for healing and opening spiritual states of consciousness (Schram, 2002). For example, the place where the Tefillin box sits on the forehead (Governing Vessel, DU-24) is referred to in acupuncture literature as the *Spirit Court,* which is said to calm the mind, balance the spirit, and is used to treat mental diseases. The place on the occiput where the Tefillin knot is tied is called *Wind Mansion* (DU-16) in Chinese medical literature and is widely used as a treatment for both concentration and memory and to treat dizziness, stroke, aphasia, and headache. The places where the leather thongs of the Tefillin are wrapped create pressure at key acupressure points such as the point on the wrist called *Ghost Heart* (Lu-9) — in acupuncture literature, this point is recommended to treat agitation and is reported to be calming to the mind. Dr. Schram, a researcher who is familiar with both acupuncture and Tefillin wrapping says, "regardless of the belief system behind the procedure, it seems clear that putting on Tefillin is a unique way of stimulating a very precise set of acupuncture points that appears designed to clear the mind and harmonize the spirit" (Schram, 2002, p. 8).

In ancient sacred wisdom traditions, not only is the kinesthetic sense of the body used to activate and anchor altered states, but so are auditory and visual representational systems used for such purposes. In these traditions, one of the key ways whereby the energies of the lost soul were brought back into balance was through listening to a story, visualizing its landscape, and identifying with its characters.

The most primordial imaginal method of introducing new states of consciousness and balancing our human psyches is found in the process of dreaming. Almost every night, built into the human organism, our inner dream weaver tells us a story that has the potential to bring us back into balance, if only we can assimilate the message being sent. Thus, in the *Talmud* (the

Jewish interpretive text of the *Old Testament*) it says that, "a dream left not interpreted is like a letter left unopened." A key element of depth psychotherapy is to help a person interpret these messages from the unconscious (Freud, 1899; Jung, 1974; Hillman, 1975; Gendlin, 1986) and use the images in the dreams to anchor new ways of being.

As we will see, symbolic process methods and imaginal traditions are like waking dreams (Watkins, 1984) that can help a person change his or her life stance. From a hypnotherapeutic viewpoint these are primarily visual anchoring methods that bring a person to state-specific states of consciousness associated with new states of awareness.

Depth Psychology, Ancient Sacred Wisdom Traditions, and Energy Psychology

The term "*depth psychology*" was initially coined by the Zurich psychiatrist Eugen Bleuler (*Tiefenpsychologie*) "in order to indicate that Freudian psychology was concerned with the deeper regions or hinterland of the psyche also called the unconscious. Freud himself was content just to name his method of investigation ... psychoanalysis" (Jung, 1953, p. 259). Bleuler wanted to shift attention from taking things apart to seeing them in depth, and to establish a different ground that was less scientific and more metaphysically philosophical; he proposed "depth psychology" as the "appropriate" name for psychoanalysis (Hillman, 1979, p. 24).

Bleuler's different ground was not a new ground. I discussed earlier how modern psychology is replete with incidents of taking concepts from older traditions and insufficiently honoring their historical roots, i.e. that psychology was claimed to be founded by Wilhelm Wundt in his laboratory in Leipzig Germany, and that energy psychology was claimed to be founded by Roger Callahan. Similarly, depth psychology had roots in an older tradition first tapped upon by Heraclitus, who brought together psyche, log*os,* and *bathos* (depth). With Heraclitus, the image of depth was designed to throw light on the outstanding trait of the soul and its realm (Snell, 1960). Heraclitus's famous quote, "You could not find the ends of the soul, though you traveled every way, so deep is its logos," led those who followed this path of *psyche* to the realm of symbols and mythology. Freud, as one who followed this path, took many of his early core concepts from mythology — for example, his well-known *Oedipus complex*, and the death principle, *Thanatos*. Jungian analysts are the theorists best-known for tapping on this older tradition of "soul making" (Hillman, 1975, p. 67) by taking psychology down into the underworld realm of Hades more than into the transcendent upper realms symbolized by Zeus (Hillman, 1979, p. 27). Many Jungian analysts, along with other therapists from different backgrounds, use symbols, imaginal methods, and stories as their key tools to gain access to these depths.

The depth psychotherapist often uses storytelling from the treasure house of symbolic process traditions to open a patient to new awareness. For example, using the last mystery play of the ancient world, *Amor and Psyche* (Neumann, 1956), the therapist might mention how a woman needs to learn to say "no" as did the character, "Psyche," when the lost souls in the river Styx begged her to give up the coin she needed for the ferryman, Charon. Thus Psyche could complete her journey to and back from the underworld. Or, for a man with similar problems with boundaries, the therapist might mention the story of *The Odyssey* (Houston, 1992). Remember how Odysseus wisely put wax into his ears and tied himself to the mast of his ship, whereas the sirens' songs drew his men to jump off the ship to their death onto jagged rocks? Symbolic stories enable sensitive listeners to transform old, deeply rooted patterns and, in terms of my thesis, shift their energetic state.

A wealth of symbolic process and imaginal practices can be found in so-called mystery religions, initiatory traditions (Campbell, 1978; Hall, 1988; Kingsley, 1999; Steiner, 1973; Matthews, 1986), and as part of cross-cultural mythologies (Neumann, 1954; Eliade, 1964). Symbolic process healing methods were a fundamental part of the earliest pre-religion called "*shamanism*" (Eliade, 1964; Campbell, 1988) and were part of the repertoire of the world's religious leaders (Schure, 1977). Metaphors deriving from chemical/metallurgic processes (Edinger, 1985; Eliade, 1956) or from celestial bodies (Rudhyar, 1970; Mayer, 1984) were used to help individuals see how their own transformative processes could be aided by connecting with the symbolic energies of the wider whole of which we are a part. These symbolic process traditions formed the early foundation of modern depth psychotherapy (Jung I-XX; Hillman, 1975; Meier, 1967); additionally, these traditions showed that the link between symbol and transformative energy was part of this foundation. For those who doubt the connection between symbol and energy, it is important to remember that Jung defined an archetypal symbol as an "energy potential."

Though these and other similar traditions lie at the roots of modern energy psychology, we will now focus on the aspects of these traditions that have direct clinical relevance to Bodymind Healing Psychotherapy. First, let's look at the clinical tools that can be used in that place where the two streams of bodily energy and imaginal processes explicitly join.

Qigong: A Hypnotherapeutic Anchoring Method

Long protected by the Great Wall of China, Qigong is one of the oldest among these intact traditions that delineates a wide spectrum of methods for energy healing. My viewpoint is that one main purpose of these traditions is to aid in the process of anchoring with state-specific, sacred altered states of consciousness. The postures and movements of Qigong and Tai Chi that are proposed in this book offer both kinesthetic and visual ways of anchoring these primordial states of consciousness to individuals in need of a new "life stance."

I propose coining a new term, "*transpersonal state-specific states of consciousness*," to refer to the orientation of many ancient sacred wisdom traditions to provide transpersonal anchors to help connect people to specific healing states. I use the term "transpersonal," as did Dane Rudhyar, one of the first people to use this term in 1930, to refer to the movement of divine energies "beyond" the ego, but also to refer to a descent of spiritual energy "through" the person (Rudhyar, 1975, p. 38). For example, Hebrew letters in the Kabbalah are taught to denote transpersonal state-specific states of consciousness (Suares, 1973, 1976) as represented by particular sounds, (i.e. "B" denotes a grounded state corresponding to the number 2, whereas "M" brings forth a more soothing melodic state); particular yoga postures bring forth openings to specific healing states; and similarly, each Tai Chi/Qigong posture represents a transpersonal state-specific state of consciousness that can bring people into an altered stated beyond their everyday life stance.

As well, the Tai Chi/Qigong postures can bring on specific needed healing states. For example, the *Bear Walking* posture evokes a state of grounded power (see illustration in Volume I)

Volume I showed how Standing Meditation (*Zhan Zhuang*) helps people to practice "rootedness" through the posture, *Standing like a Tree*. Here in Volume II, specific Standing Meditation Qigong practices can be adapted to "treat" different bodymind psychological states. Typically in Standing Mediation Qigong practitioners are advised to stand with their weight over the *Bubbling Well* points (K-1), located slightly forward of the center of the ball of the foot. But there are also "prescriptive" methods to help initiates "shape-shift" into stances that can be helpful to balance specific, off-centered aspects of their way of being. For example, for the practitioner who is overly aggressive, the *sifu* may suggest that he or she adapts to bring the center-line a bit further back; if someone is held back in his or her way of being, it may be suggested to shift his or her awareness more forward.

Tai Chi/Qigong: A Rosetta Stone for State-Specific, Healing Altered States

Just as the Rosetta Stone, discovered in 1799, gave us access to the ancient realm of Egyptian language and ways of seeing the world, so is Tai Chi/Qigong a "Rosetta Stone" that provides us access into the healing, altered states of consciousness of ancient Taoist/Buddhist/shamanic traditions of postural initiation.

I propose that we think of each Tai Chi/Qigong posture as part of a healing alphabet. Alphabets contain the keys to open state-specific domains of experience. The English alphabet opens a different domain of experiencing the world as compared to the Egyptian hieroglyphics or the Hebrew alphabet (Suares, 1973). "Right brain alphabets" open still another kind of state-specific realm; music in the form of rock and roll opens a different domain as compared to Indian ragas. Likewise each posture in the "alphabet of Tai Chi/Qigong" can form and induce different transpersonal state-specific states of consciousness. Just as the right brain language of music can help us attune to and play with these specific healing, soothing universal vibrational frequencies and rhythms, so can Tai Chi/Qigong.

In Volume I, I explored how every Tai Chi posture has four different levels of healing purpose. Each posture is for healing, spiritual unfoldment, self-defense, and "shape-shifting" the practitioner's life stance. There I also looked at how two-person, self-development exercises can help bring healing, balance, and states of equilibrium to practitioners. Exercises such as *Cultivating the Golden Ball* (rolling back, adhering with, and yielding to one's partner) can teach us how to flow where there was rigidity, respond with non-reactive no-force to impinging and assaultive force from another, and counter the instinctual sympathetic nervous system fight, flight, and freeze tendencies. One of the greatest secrets of this alphabet is that it is not the letters themselves that contain the greatest treasures of the language, but the space between the letters. In music the notes are fundamental, but the silence after the notes is one of the gifts of this language. Likewise, in Tai Chi/ Qigong the space between the movements is key — the quality of stillness between the movements and the state of relaxation that one carries into the movement is a fundamental aspect of this right brain language. Also, the images that are behind the movements (letters) are a fundamental aspect of this language. Here in Volume II we will see further how this alphabet can be applied to the psychotherapeutic and behavioral health setting.

Chapter 4: The Ground of Energy Psychology 81

Imagery: The Missing Ingredient in Qigong's Definition

"*Qigong*" is usually defined as work (*gong*) with the energy of life (*Qi*), and is associated in popular culture with practices that synchronize movement and breath. Earlier I defined Qigong in a fuller way: "Qigong is a many-thousand-year-old method of cultivating the energy of life through breath, movement, posture, touch, sound, intention, and awareness." However, this definition leaves out a key element, as Qigong also includes the cultivation of the energy of life through imaginal methods. This addition is not a new idea, but it is nevertheless frequently left out of academic definitions, and is little-known in popular conceptions of Qigong. Yet it is a part of most teachers' presentations of Qigong practices.

In virtually all facets of Qigong, the use of imagery is a key element. For example, in animal forms of Qigong practitioners are taught not only to imitate the physical movements of a given animal, but to focus their intention on imbibing the spirit of that animal and imagine that they are the animal, while moving and while still. In Standing Meditation Qigong practitioners imagine standing like a tree, visualize having roots to develop rootedness, and imagine swaying and circling in the wind to develop flexibility and prevent the stagnation of Qi. The depth of an initiate's practice of developing rootedness is then tested by the master teacher who pushes on the acolyte in order to test what he or she has cultivated rootedensss (*sili*), i.e. to see if the imaginal has become real. Likewise in Taoist Qigong Meditation, (often called Taoist Internal Alchemy), static Qigong postures are combined with various visualizations to cultivate energy and to heal the body and mind (Kohn, 1989, 2001; Luk, 1972, 1977). For example, practitioners imagine mixing fire and water to balance the internal elements of their physical and mental states.

In Qigong, one key addition to modern guided imagery traditions is that visualizations are mixed with somatic practices. For example, practitioners may do more than just think about adding water to the imbalance of excess fire in their body, they may swallow saliva (Luk, 1977) and on the exhalation imagine and feel the saliva descending to the belly (*Tan Tien*) — this reduces excess fire and increases parasympathetic nervous system relaxation. In general, Qigong is a buried treasure house containing ways to bring balance and healing to the human body through visualizations on the elements of life and by providing practitioners with pathways to spiritual unfoldment.

In a moment, I will discuss how combining imagery and body practices can be helpful to the Western bodymind healing tradition. But first I want to stretch the definition of Qigong and make the case that imaginal traditions, such as storytelling, myths, and imagery, are themselves forms of Qigong; and even when the body isn't explicitly mentioned, these traditions help us to cultivate the energy of life.

In Volume I, I introduced Bodymind Healing Qigong as a ten-system integration of my thirty years of training with some of the most respected masters of these traditions. I showed how this tradition had static (Standing Meditation) and moving components, and how imagery enhanced Qigong practices. I discussed how this particular synthesis, which evolved from my healing work, is a physical exercise system, a Self-healing pathway, a spiritual practice, a method of transforming one's life stance, and a way to find one's ground in the midst of the emotional crosscurrents of everyday life. Then I began to show how Western bodymind healing methods could broaden Qigong. Here in Volume II, I want to do the converse, and show how Qigong can benefit and enhance the tool kit of the Western bodymind healing tradition with its imaginal and hypnotherapeutic methods.

Storytelling as Qigong and Trance-Formation

Regarding the use of story to expand our spiritual horizons, I began this chapter with an old Sufi teaching story called *The Stream and the Sands*. This story is a good example of how storytelling can be a form of Qigong (cultivation of the energy of life). At a moment of existential despair, when we are feeling isolated or disconnected from our purpose in life, when we hear a story like this, a "trance" may be induced that helps us remember how we have become constricted by our identification with the narrowing banks of the stream of life or have become separated from others and from the spirit of the universe from whence we came. Maybe the story helps us get in touch with how its part of the experiment of human evolution to feel such separation so that we can manifest the individual destiny of our separate selves. Or maybe it helps us remember that we pay a price when we forget the bigger picture of how we are, in truth, children born from, and for, the wider universe. When we lose sight of these messages, we run into the desert of life. A story like this can open our consciousness to remember our wider selves, and, for the sensitive listener, it may bring about a change in the body's energy.

A story like this can open us to an experience of oneness with all of life, which is a fundamental purpose of many cross-cultural spiritual traditions. There are many paths that can lead us to this state of oneness. For example:

- We've seen above how sacred songs are used to enter this state, such as the singing of Jewish *Shama,* which honors and helps us to merge with the oneness of life. In the Kabbalah, this state is called *Ain Soph* — the origin of the energies of the archetypes (*Sephirot*) of creation.

- In esoteric psychology, astrological symbols are used to help us realize how our personal identities are formed from the energies of the universe (Rudhyar, 1970). This may help us reconnect with the wider whole of which we are a part (Mayer, 1984).

- Taoist Qigong physical practices along with accompanying visualizations are meant to activate *wuji*, a return to the void, the mother of Qi.

- A Native American listens to the creation stories of the tribe and their descent from the animals and forces of nature and experiences the interconnectedness with "all of my relations" in life — the trees, four-legged ones, the insects, the earth, and *wakantanka* — the great mystery behind the energy of the universe.

- Buddhist meditation practices facilitate a letting go of the attachment to the individual, isolated ego; and such sayings as "the sky and the palm of his hand are the same in the mind of the Buddha," refer and lead the practitioner to the path to find this state of consciousness.

In terms of esoteric or transpersonal psychology, these are all cross-cultural "dissolving practices," which help the listener to let go of the experience of the separate Self and merge with the source of life. The story of *The Stream and the Sands* is the Sufi imaginal induction into this energetic state of dissolving into the source of the stream of life, entering into the stream of life, and returning again to its source. This back and forth play of life helps to induce the astute listener into a state-specific state of consciousness that opens up a wider universe of meaning and has energetic correlates.

Stories, Myths, and Fairy Tales Used to Help Heal Archetypal Issues of the Human Condition

Imaginal traditions contain multifaceted tools for cultivating the energy of life, psychologically and spiritually. In the storytelling and symbolic process traditions listed above, the listener is induced into a transpersonal energy state that can be helpful in expanding his or her spiritual horizons. Other types of storytelling and symbolic process traditions can heal more specific issues, like certain blocked archetypal issues of the human condition, such as being different or being narcissistically demanding of attention. In all these cases it is the bodily energy/image dialectic that is key to healing.

Mythological stories in general (Larsen, 1990; Heuscher 1974), and the stories of Greek mythology in particular, have been used as methods of transforming our relationship to the archetypal issues of life. (Neumann, 1956; Kerenyi, 1951; Barring, 1991; Mayer, 1994). Earlier I discussed how the Greek stories of *Amor and Psyche* and the story of *The Odyssey* function this way. In more modern times, psychologists like Bruno Bettleheim (1977), with his *Uses of Enchantment*, and hypnotherapists like Milton Erickson (Zeig, 1985) have also used stories to heal archetypal issues of the human condition. Though they did not mention energy per se, as listeners we know that it is fundamental to the experience of hearing a transformative story to feel a shift in energy, along with a shift in consciousness. A basic fact of the deeper dimensions of human experience is that images, myths, and stories activate energy in us, as does physical exercise.

Remember back when you were a child and one of your parents told you a story. As my father read me *The Ugly Duckling*, I remember feeling a sense of energy rushing through the core of me — I, too, was different like the ugly duckling, and my differences now had meaning. A sense of strength came into my body where before there was a debilitating sense of doubt about my differences.

When parents tell their whining children about *The Boy who Cried Wolf*, a receptive child may put some reins on his or her incessant crying-out for attention. Stories and symbols have the power to transform energetic states and create new worlds of possibilities. In the *Bible*, in the Gospel of John, the connection between the power of the word and story is known to be associated with creating new beginnings — "In the beginning was the Word, and the Word was with God, and the Word was God." Likewise, hypnotherapists who are adept in the use of stories know that physiological correlates accompany the opening of consciousness that occurs when a story is heard (Achterberg, 1985); also, they know that this bodymind shift that takes place has the capacity to create new realities (Zeig, 1985; Wallas, 1985).

If while listening to a story we could use sensitive instruments to examine our neurochemistry, we surely would be able to measure a healing biochemical change. And if we had instruments that were subtle enough to measure our Qi, we likewise might be able to detect a qualitative or quantitative change in our energy state after a meaningful story is told. This goes along with Oschman's (2000) contention that the whole body is electromagnetically linked through the fascia and connective tissues, such that it forms an undivided energetic matrix.

Widening the Breadth and Depth of Energy Psychology: Qigong, Imaginal Traditions, and Shape-Shifting

> ...the path to heaven doesn't lie down in flat miles.
> It's in the imagination with which you perceive this world,
> and the gestures with which you honor it.
>
> —Mary Oliver
> *Winter Hours*

Milton Erickson (1948/1980), the master hypnotherapist and storyteller, has shown that stories, words, and images create an altered state of consciousness within which the patient can reorganize his or her inner psychological life. He says, "It is this experience of re-associating and reorganizing our own experiential life that eventuates in a cure of bodymind symptoms, not the manifestation of responsive behavior which can, at best, satisfy only the observer" (p. 38).[5]

Those who think the field of energy psychology consists simply of tapping meridians, muscle testing, etc are taking too narrow a view of this age-old, multilayered, fertile field. It has long been known, at least since the time of the temple of Aesclepius (from the end of the sixth century B.C. to the end of the fifth century A.D.), that energy is key to healing. Energy is not just the energy of our body, but also the energy of the universe. This energy is activated through a wide variety of ways. Some of these energetic pathways lying in the lower layers of our psychological/archeological dig are: physical exercise, tapping, touching, moving like the animals, standing like a tree, self-soothing, loving, dissolving practices, and the power of the energy of symbols and stories to heal.

A carefully chosen image or story has the capacity to "shape-shift" us into new life pathways and change our life stance. When hearing the story of *The Boy who Cried Wolf*, the incessantly demanding child may experience "a shape-shifting" into a more self-contained state. Listening to the story of *The Ugly Duckling*, the inadequate, collapsed-chested person who is ashamed of his or her differences may experience his or her bodymind change into a stance of confidence.

When hearing the story of *The Stream and the Sands*, the alienated person who lacks purpose, may begin to be transformed into an energetic state filled with a sense of connection to the wider whole of which he or she is a part. Just like physical stances in the tradition of postural initiation (see Volume I) can shape-shift us into new life stances, so can images, symbols, and stories.

I will be putting forth the thesis that these age-old shape-shifting traditions have two poles, or two rivers, that become one to the aware observer. One polar end of the continuum uses imagination to heal the "soul." Here, by speaking the metaphors of life, the adept of this language uses the elements of life to heal.[6] We have just seen how the seemingly non-energetic concept of "symbols" is a significant method of activating energy (as when a story such as *The Stream and the Sands* is told). At the other end of the continuum are bodily energy traditions rooted in age-old shamanistic practices — for example, the internal martial arts tradition, Qigong, Tai Chi, and Taoist alchemical meditations. As outlined in Volume I, these psychophysiological, imaginal healing traditions are cross-cultural and cross-temporal and existed in various forms in such places as Native America, India, Asia, and Greece.

One of the first scholars to speak of "the imaginal," and coined the phrase "imaginal realm" was the French philosopher Henry Corbin (2001). In his study of Sufi and Persian texts he discovered that in these literatures there was believed to be a realm that existed above our ordinary three-dimensional consciousness. One of the students of his work summarizes his view of the imaginal this way,

> *While some aspects of the imagination are clearly contrived, these texts suggest that there is also a place in our imaginations where things are "real," in the sense that they are not being "imagined" by someone, but are images that have some kind of integrity or existence on their own. Thus the imagination appears to have two aspects: one intentionally fabricated; the other presents itself to us intact. Corbin used the term "mundus imaginalis" (imaginary realm) to differentiate between the "imaginary" (i.e. something equated with the unreal or with fantasy) and the "imaginal" (i.e. a world that is ontologically as real as the things we see or touch or know intellectually) .... In Corbin's view — and that of archetypal psychology — the images that come from the mundus imaginalis are a reality in some dimension other than the sensible and intellectual dimensions that we are most familiar with and have been taught to value and respect.* (Frenier, 2006)

The Physician's Staff: Co-Optation and Denigration of Aesclepius

Why have traditions of energy psychology and energy healing not been more incorporated into Western healing and psychotherapy? Though storytelling is commonly used in modern psychotherapy, when stories are told, the energetic component of their ability to heal is not often explicitly recognized. And with body energy practices, they are usually placed out of the realm of psychotherapy or are often viewed with denigration.[7] There are some justifiable, modern reasons for viewing energetic traditions with caution — with some cases of psychotic breaks being caused by the "Primal Scream" type of therapies in the 1970s. But there are more deeply rooted historical reasons for the resistance to incorporating energetic methods into modern psychotherapy and behavioral healthcare.

The central symbol of Western medicine is the staff of the Greek God of Healing, Aesclepius, with a snake winding around it. This image speaks to us in timeless metaphorical language about how, at the core of healing, the movement of energy winds up and around the spine.

Why is the very thing that the staff of Aesclepius symbolizes so ignored and devalued by the medical profession that adopted it? In the fifth century A.D., the early Christian emperors, such as Theodosius II, destroyed the Aesclepian temples. When visiting these temples scattered all around the ancient lands of Greece, whether it be Epidaurus, Acrocorinth, or Athens, we see statues with cut-off arms, legs, and heads — the violent remnants of the battle against paganism. The rubble that now lies in the place of edifices to the "God of Healing" serves as a potent symbol for the destruction and denigration of ancient holistic methods of healing.

When we look at the symbol of Western medicine of a snake winding up and around a staff, whether it is on an ambulance or in a doctor's office, we may not realize that this symbol was co-opted from the temples of ancient Greece. The emerging Western civilization took the symbol because the Asclepiads were revered in the Mediterranean world for their healing abilities — to take the power of that symbol added to the respect of the "new medicine." It would be lopsided to discount some of the scientific advances that have grown since the time of this old, empirically tested approach to healing — such as polio vaccines and many surgical advances including organ-replacement surgery, sterilization of medical equipment, etc. However, we might also wonder what was lost from the old traditions that were co-opted. In our modern culture that looks down on the ways of our ancestors, sometimes a visit back to our grandparents yields an archeological treasure house of valuable knowledge that helps us in the present. Can this ancestral knowledge help us on our quest to find answers to the modern healthcare crisis?

The temple of Aesclepius was the first holistic healing center of the Western world. Here, surgery was performed and a gymnasium was provided for exercising. The central symbol of Aesclepius symbolizes the old tradition of energy healing. Hands-on healing was an integral part of the treatment as shown by the fact that Aesclepius's teacher was Chiron, from whom derives the modern word "chiropractic." We do not know exactly what Aesclepius's training regimen was; however, we may surmise from Chiron living in a cave and his name being associated with a race of centaurs (half man/half horse) that perhaps he transmitted teachings of shamanic animal movements to Aesclepius. As part of the tradition of holistic healing in the temple, an Aesclepian priest would often prescribe as a treatment the patient going to the Dionysian theatre. There he or she would put on a mask (*personae*, the origin of our word person); this was one of the early derivations of modern psychology's psychodrama. We might also wonder whether animal movements were prescribed as part of the cure; for example, a shy or depressed person may have been told to put on the garb of a lion and act out that part in a play. Some say it was from this Dionysian theatre at the temple of Aesclepius that the word "catharsis" derived. Honoring the importance of the world of images, dream incubation was a fundamental part of healing here. When a patient had a healing dream, the Aesclepian priest would take this as a sign that a healing had taken place and that it was time for the patient to leave the temple. So, Sigmund Freud (1899, 1965) wasn't the first to use, *The Interpretation of Dreams*, as a key to psychological healing.

The early Christians waged a battle against worship of the old deities like Aesclepius in their attempt to promote the belief in one God and Jesus as his only son who had miraculous ability to heal. The Aesclepian temples were a threat to the belief that Jesus, as son of "the one and only God," was the only one who could bring back people from the dead. But myths of Aesclepius say that he also succeeded in raising the dead, such as Glacous, the son of Theseus; and, as well, there were miraculous cures attributed to him including restoring eyesight to people who were blind from birth, and instantaneous cures of the lame and paralyzed.[8]

Denigration of the snake seems to be built into the myths of our modern Western culture. In the *Old Testament* it was the snake that tempted Eve into "original sin." One hypothesis for why the snake was devalued is that it was associated with the sexuality and promiscuity of the old Goddess religion. According to Merlin Stone (1976), the snake was vilified to stop the sexual practices of the followers of the Goddess religion who mated with men out of wedlock as they participated in snake dancing rituals. The Israelites, and the tribe of Levites in particular, wanted to be able to determine the identities of their children, which could not be done if the Goddess' orgiastic practices were followed. Thus came the establishment of a monogamous religion, centuries of sexual repression, and an ethos that constricted, denied, or transcended the body. Some of the remaining effects of these historical roots are easy to identify, such as women in the Victorian era dressed in corsets. Other factors are more subtle and form an unconscious part of our everyday Western culture that is cut off from the body.

*The right way to wholeness is made up
… of fateful detours and wrong turnings.
It is a "longissima via," a path
that unites the opposites
in the manner of the guiding caduceus,
a path whose labyrinthine twists and
turns are not lacking in terrors.*

— C.G. Jung
Psychology and Alchemy

Figure 3: The Double Snake

Modern civilization is living in the karmic rubble of Aesclepius's disjointed body. Our mythos of worshipping one God up in the heavens has disconnected us from the pre-modern belief in the West, and, from the Eastern-influenced belief that our feelings and our own body's energy is sacred and needs to be valued in everyday life as "a pearl of great price."[9]

In pre-Christian traditions, images of the snake were associated with healing. Whereas Aesclepius's snake is depicted as a single snake winding around a staff, an even older image of the *caduceus* of Thoth (in Egypt), or Hermes in Greece, shows a double snake winding around a staff. Many meanings are associated with the double snake. Some say that Hermes' healing came from being able to ascend to the heavens, as well as, being able to guide others on the path to the underworld (Pedraza, 1977). Since symbols are, by their nature, expansive in nature, no one fixed meaning can be attributed to them; only in the individual process of hermeneutical (Warnke, 1987) interpretation can we find their meanings.

The Double Snake: The Mental Image/Body Energy Dialectic

I like to think of the symbol of two snakes winding around a staff, the *caduceus of Hermes*, as representing two healing powers: the activation of bodily energy and the use of imagery. These have long been known to be important healing powers which wind up the staff, or spine, of ancient healing methods. We can give ourselves poetic license and imagine that the Aesclepian single snake symbol of holistic healing unifies these two snakes of bodily energy and image.

The idea of the interrelatedness of bodily energy and symbolic image is a center-post of the psychology of Dr. Carl Jung who said, as mentioned earlier, that archetypal symbols are "energy potentials." A key element of Jungian psychotherapy is to get in touch with the power of a symbol, and thereby transform energy, which leads to a change in an old pattern of behavior. We have seen from our earlier discussion of *The Stream and the Sands*, *The Boy Who Cried Wolf*, and *The Ugly Duckling* that image and stories are connected with activating energy and inducing shape-shifting. Towards the end of Dr. Jung's life, he changed his idea that archetypes were *psychic*, meaning "of the mind," to archetypes being *psychoid*, i.e. of the mind and body. It is this conceptual shift that provides the foundation from which we are to build.

In Volume VIII of his collected works, Dr. Jung (1960) addresses a key concept of his depth psychology that archetypal image and instinct represent two ends of a continuum (pp. 211-215). Using the analogy of a spectrum, he spoke of instincts being related to the infrared end of the spectrum of healing, and imagery being related to the ultra-violet end of the healing continuum. In BMHP the instinctual end of the continuum is represented by the primordial traditions of the body, including Qigong, breathwork, etc. The imaginal dimension of healing comes from symbolic process modalities. Regardless of whether we want to conceptualize it as a spectrum or a double snake, let's take the next step in our exploration of how bodily energy and symbolic process are transformative tools for the primordial staff of healing.

It is somewhat surprising that psychotherapy has not done more to incorporate bodily energy practices into its healing toolkit, particularly during the era of expanding its horizons into the arena of behavioral healthcare. In Chapter 2, I briefly reviewed body energy practices in psycho-

Chapter 4: The Ground of Energy Psychology 89

therapy, but here we will show how bodily energy healing tools can be integrated with the realm of symbolic process, and vice versa.

Why bring the body into the equation when our intention, our symbols, and the images themselves have such transformative power? The answer to this question is that there is a difference between visualizing a river and swimming in one; there is a difference between imagining we are exercising and actually moving our bodies. In internal martial arts training, a common combined physical and imaginal practice is to imagine that you are being attacked in order to increase energy and proper alignment of physical postures. Most of us don't need a scientific analysis to differentiate the neuro-chemical distinctions between just imagining and combining the imagination with a physical practice, we can sense the difference.

The question of which should be at the forefront, the mind (intention, symbols, and images) or the body, has been a matter of controversy in the mind-body healing professional community. At one conference I attended, Dr. Larry Dossey was the keynote speaker, and at a big banquet with about a hundred tables of leading-edge healing practitioners, he gave a presentation on the theme, following up on several of his articles (Dossey, 1992, 1994), that its time to go beyond energy psychology and see that "intention" is the key to psychological healing. I raised my hand and somewhat shyly came to the microphone. Thinking about my twenty-five years of training in the *Yi Chuan,* where I learned the value of integrating intention and energy, I questioned, "Is not to split energy and intention a false dichotomy?" And then I continued, "If the two were not intimately connected why, in the research of Dr. Bernard Grad in his experiment at McGill University (Gerber, 1996, p. 78) with various subjects holding and intending to send healing energy to barley seeds in water, did depressed people (with low energy) suppress plant growth and non-depressed people have significantly better results in facilitating plant growth?"

In a banquet room of about 500 people there was dead silence. Dr. Dossey paused while pondering for what felt like a full sixty seconds. He then did something that made me respect him even more than I had before, he said, "I don't know the answer to your question; but I'm gong to think about it." At the next conference where Dr. Dossey and I were both presenting, I ran into him in the men's room and jokingly reminded him who I was, "Remember me? I'm the heckler they send to harass you and ask impertinent questions at all the conferences." He laughed and invited me to sit with him at his dinner table. We had a chance to further discuss that important ontological question about the roots of modern bodymind healing, during which time I told him how my practice in *Yi Chuan Qigong* over the last twenty-five years had led me to the experience of these two streams joining. He kindly gave me a backcover quote for my last book saying that it was, "A splendid break-through which will certainly contribute a new slant to meditative practice."

Following the river which flowed from that experience, this book's orientation is about how energy and intention can be better partners in healing. Each of us may find an inclination in our work to focus on one or the other; but, like the yin-yang symbol of the Tao, a colored dot of energy is in the half-circle of intention, and the opposite colored dot of intention is in the half-circle of energy.

Next we will delineate a graduated approach to the continuum of symbolic process work that emphasizes various combinations of the mind and body, intention and energy. The spectrum of symbolic process inner work when combined with the body, involves a continuum that moves from stories/images with no explicit body dimension integrated into their use, to bodily traditions with no use of images. It should be noted that even with no explicit body dimension, the power of story affects the felt experience of the body; and when a person does a somatic practice the mind is affected.

Bodymind Healing Qigong Practices to Activate State-Specific Transcendent Altered States

I have just shown that the body (and the body's energy) is "in the mind of" imaginal traditions. Likewise, the mind is a vital component in traditions of the body. Not only do words and images have the capacity to put us into trance, but also so do postures and movements of the body. Explicitly combining visualization traditions with the age-old knowledge base of Qigong can add to the bodymind's ability to promote healing.

Following the theme of the wisdom of the story, *The Stream and the Sands*, the practices that follow are age-old methods of initiating us into the experience of being like the stream — letting go, evaporating, and dissolving into the winds of spirit. These practices are oriented to help us return to the energy from whence we came, thereby reclaiming our birthright to remember the experience of what it is like to be "light-er."

Each of the following practices emphasizes a different part of the experience of activating these energies. There are many ways to experience Qi — through activating the power of the mind, through feeling it in our hands, through movement, and through the breath and the relaxation response. In truth these aspects all operate together; but because of our different proclivities and "representational systems,"[10] different people may have an easier time focusing on one over the other. Each of the following rivers provides a different way to merge into the ocean of Qi (*wuji*), which the Taoists believe is the source of life's energy.

From the hypnotherapist's perspective these practices create "trance states," or "altered states of consciousness," that can open us to the experience of transcendent energies and thereby facilitate the creative reorganization of the psyche. From the Taoist practitioner's perspective, they provide keys that open the doors to Qi — the domain of state-specific transcendent altered states of consciousness. (In the following chapter, the transmuting dimensions of psychoenergetic work will be introduced.)

House of Five Doors:
Bodymind Doors to Opening to Energy Trance States

To illustrate the importance of combining the mental/imaginal dimension with the body, and the body with the mental/imaginal dimension, the rest of this chapter outlines, in detail, various doorways to healing trance states. The following methods serve as a proto-introduction to Bodymind Healing Qigong, and illustrate how Qigong (cultivating the energy of life) can be done with or without moving the body. Starting with a breathing practice, there are then four other "doors" which blend image and body, with increasing emphasis on the body. These five methods are called:

- Activating the River of Life through Microcosmic Orbit Breathing
- Experiencing the Light of Qi
- The Energy Ball between Your Hands
- Intention and the Direction of Qi
- Tai Chi Ruler

1. Activating the River of Life through Microcosmic Orbit Breathing:

Microcosmic Orbit Breathing is the method referred to in *The Secret of the Golden Flower* (Wilhelm, 1931, 1963). It was long used in secret Taoist initiatory training to achieve such a deep sense of relaxation that it was reported "to help one return to being like a fetus again." It was claimed that this breathing technique, when done properly, could help people regain their youthfulness and vibrancy — that in practicing it people could experience golden energy radiating from their bodies, and become like a golden ball or a golden flower (Wilhelm, 1963; Mayer, 2004).

As you practice this method, be open to notice how it changes the way you experience yourself along with any changes in energy that you feel. The steps of *Microcosmic Orbit Breathing* (Wilhelm, 1931; Cleary, 1991) are as follows:[11]

- *Begin by focusing on the breath moving up the spine, arising from a point at the bottom of the spine at the perineum, (the Huiyin point between the anus and the genitals). Feel this as a natural rising (as a helium balloon, when inflated, naturally rises up to the sky) rather than as a forced inhalation. Then imagine the breath coming over the top of the head (to the Baihui point), where the lines of the ears meet at the top of the head, the "soft spot" on a baby's head.*

  While you are doing this practice, the tongue touches the palate right behind the teeth, connecting two of the major meridian lines in the body. The one up the back, the Governing Vessel, is called the Du or also Tu Mei; the one going down the front of the spine, the Conception Vessel, is called the Ren or Jen Mei.

- *On the exhalation, focus on the breath coming down the front of the body until it reaches the belly (Tan Tien) and feel the pause after the out-breath.*

  The length of the breath that is associated with the development of Qi is called "long-breath." To find it we imagine that our exhalation is like a tire that has a slow leak in it and someone is sitting on the tire. This can be differentiated from short breath that is like a blow-out in a tire. Long-breath builds Qi and gives us a grounded feeling.

- *The movement of the breath downward continues to the perineum. Here you pause on out-breath until it naturally arises for a new cycle up the center of the back (Du).*

♦ *If at first you have a hard time feeling the energy, don't try to force it. You might try to imagine it as water by visualizing a waterfall pouring down from over the top of your head, then flowing down your body like a river as you exhale. If you feel blockages hampering the water from moving down the body, don't try to force it through. Instead, continue to breathe and imagine the constriction to be an ice-block that will melt in time by the gentle warming of the waters by the sun. As the breath comes down to the belly imagine that you are coming to a still pool or a calm sea where you can come to rest. Feel your river expand as it meets and dissolves into the sea.*

In many forms of meditation, breath is a primary object of focus, and images like the sea can aid the experience of meditation. The sea is an apt metaphor for representing the mind; on the surface it tends to be choppy, with waves of thought or emotions taking us in one direction then the next, subject to the whims and rough weather of the outer environment. In meditation in general, and in *Microcosmic Orbit Meditation*, as you breathe for a while, you may find your jumpiness settling down. Beneath the waves of the sea of life you find a calmness in the sea deep below. There are still currents deep below the surface of the ocean, but they have a different quality than the ones on the surface.

There are similarities and differences here, as compared to other forms of meditation, which would be too extensive to outline here. Discovering or returning to a calm place beneath the crosscurrents of life is one theme shared by many forms of meditation. All forms of meditation induce "state-specific states of consciousness" (Rossi, 1988) that have their own unique attributes. What is unique in this Taoist alchemical breathing method is the particular ways in which it combines the focus on the breath, particular body parts, energy, and imagery. Each adds a vital component to the whole, with a multiplicity of purposes:

Specific Healing Attributes of Microcosmic Orbit Breathing

♦ *Exhalation and Sinking Qi*: Reversing the Sympathetic Nervous System's Fight, Flight, and Freeze Responses. According to ancient Qigong empirical research, focusing on the out-breath and the pause after the out-breath, helps to "sink the Qi." According to modern bodymind healthcare practitioners it is used to reverse sympathetic nervous system overload and induce a parasympathetic nervous system relaxation response. When we are afraid, the instinctive fear response induces us to hold our breath, our energy rises, and energy goes out to our extremities as our bodies get ready for "fight or flight." Microcosmic Orbit Breathing can help to reverse the fear response by using a breath that emphasizes letting go, and focusing on energy traveling down the inner center-line to the belly.

♦ *Focus on the Belly*. By bringing awareness down to the belly, we return to the center of ourselves, the place where our umbilical cord connected us to our mothers. We thereby metaphorically and organically connect ourselves with the protective center of ourselves. The exact place of focus is called the *Tan Tien*. Considered by the Taoists to be the center of the body, it is located approximately three fingers-width beneath the navel, and inwards toward the center of the body. This zone of the body is sometimes referred to as the "*Sea of Elixir*" (*Qi Hai*). In *Webster's* dictionary, "*elixir*" is defined as "a substance held capable of changing base metals into gold." Regardless of the objective truth of these esoteric claims, many who practice focusing on their bellies while meditating report different types of ideas rising to the surface of awareness about their lives — ideas that seem to come from a deeper place. From a psychological perspective, using a metaphor of changing lead into gold enhances the psychic intention and the state-specific state of consciousness to open such transformational potential.

- *The Center-Line of the Body — The Conception and Governing Vessels*. The notion that particular parts of the body or particular meridian lines have their own inherent power is a supposition of empirically tested Chinese medicine. Some recent research has shown that particular meridian lines activate parts of the brain not activated by sham needles. Such a study using a MRI showed that needles inserted into particular points on the bladder meridian, not on the bladder, activated parts of the brain associated with the bladder (Cho, 1998).

The meridian lines focused upon in *Microcosmic Orbit Breathing* travel up and down the spine, and are known to be among the most important meridian lines. So, we might expect that placing our attention on these meridians may have more impact than other areas of the body on which we could focus.

- *Imaginal Methods Hidden in Microcosmic Orbit Breathing — The Sea of Elixir, the Golden Flower, the Golden Ball*. Imaginal methods are also used in this classical practice. The practitioner visualizes the breath going up and down the spine, and uses descriptive metaphors like the *Sea of Elixir*, the Golden Flower, or the Golden Ball. As mentioned earlier, these images may increase one's propensity to enter into an altered a state of consciousness. I have added to the classical method of *Microcosmic Orbit Breathing* the practice of imagining the exhalation turning into a river and allowing the image of the river to merge with the sea in the belly (see Chapter 5, the *River of Life* practice).

- *Circular Breathing*. The circular breathing pattern of the "microcosmic orbit" makes intuitive sense regarding its healing import. Some breathing methods focus on rapid in-and-out breaths while forcing the breath up the spine, visualizing the breath as a square pattern, or holding the breath after the inhalation. Here in the *Microcosmic Orbit* method we have a circular breathing pattern that flows up, down, and around the spine. From the perspective of Taoist Qigong this emphasis on circular, rather than linear or square, facilitates a return to the more primordial and circular realm of womb-like existence. It makes sense that this type of breathing would be a good balancing method for a culture like ours, which has the tendency to be linear, square, fast-paced and oriented to bringing energy straight up to the head.

While presenting a workshop on the East Coast, I heard a radio program where a breath expert suggested, "square breathing." Compare for yourself how you feel with the rounded methods, and metaphors of *Microcosmic Orbit Breathing*, and which works best for you.

Microcosmic Orbit Breathing is a center-post of Bodymind Healing Psychotherapy, and in many of the chapters that follow, I adapt it to deal with various psychophysiological issues including hypertension, insomnia, chronic pain, and anxiety. In the next four practices we will see how this type of breathing adds to the trance state of combined imaginal and body-oriented methods.

Some support regarding the healing power of *Microcosmic Orbit Breathing* comes from a preliminary study by Dr. Leonard Lascow who is doing groundbreaking research in exploring the effects of different states of consciousness and intentionality on tumor cells. In one of his comparative studies of biological responses to different intentions he discovered that focusing intention on the phrase, "return to the natural order and harmony," produced a 39 percent inhibition in tumor cells. The intention of "unconditional love" neither stimulated nor inhibited cell growth, and *Microcosmic Orbit Breathing* produced a 41 percent inhibition (Lascow, 1998, p. 306).

Though Dr. Lascow's experiment showed that *Microcosmic Orbit Breath* affected these cells more than other methods did, there are many aspects of the research methodology that were inadequate for substantial claims to be made. For example, we do not know whether for in a larger sample of subjects, some people would find different types of breathing to be more or less effective. It would be interesting to expand upon the type of research. Regardless of the comparative scientific merits of each type of breathing for different people in different circumstances, from a purely phenomenological viewpoint, the specifics attributes of this type of breathing, the particular metaphors used with this method, and the focus on the center-line of the body could intuitively be expected to produce a powerful type of meditative response.

Macrocosmic Orbit Breathing

Macrocosmic Orbit Breathing expands on the breathing method above (Huang, 1974). On the exhalation, instead of going down to the belly (*Tan Tien*) or the perineum, the practitioner allows the breath to descend all the way to the ground, by experiencing the breath going down through the bottoms of the feet (Kidney-1). From a synthesis of various sources, I developed a practice that further extends the imaginal dimension of this breathing exercise (Luk, 1972; Huang, 1974; Schafer, 1977; Ulansey, 1989). Have you ever, on a starry night, been fixated on the Big (or Little) Dipper, sensing there must be some mystery and magic to its existence that you wish you could draw from? If so, try this method:

> *On your next inhalation imagine the breath going all the way up the spine, out the top of the head (Baihui), to a star above your head; on the exhalation send the breath down to the central core of the earth. Then imagine that you are becoming an "axis mundi" (Eliade, 1959) as you imagine your spine aligning with the earth's axis and becoming the central axis that unites heaven and earth. As you align with the pole star above your head, picture the rest of the Big Dipper; and on your exhalation, imagine its bowl spilling out loving energy from the universe and your heart.*

In this practice your bodymind becomes aligned with the macrocosm, the spiritual energies of the wider universe. Here in *Macrocosmic Orbit Breathing*, once again, the focus is on the breath; but the imaginal dimension adds to its transpersonal healing power. I like to call this breathing method "*Full Extension Breathing*," due to the breadth of what it encompasses.

2. *Experiencing the Light of Qi: Using a Candle*

This practice emphasizes the imaginal door to a trance state by using a Qigong exercise with no Qigong movement. Here we see how the integration of other dimensions — Taoist breathing methods, classical hypnotic types of verbal instructions, a spiritual viewpoint of letting go and being non-attached — all come together to enhance the felt sense of energy as we identify with, and visualize being, a candle. It is classically reported that the experience of activation of Qi is like activating the light of the human energy field.

> *Sit in a dark room with a candle as your only source of light. Notice your breath coming in and going out through your nostrils. Find a "long-breath," as in the previously mentioned practice. Imagine breathing light into your heart on the inhalation, and out from your heart on your exhalation. Imagine that you are this candle, and the glow around it is the glow that is around you. Practice this combination of visualization and breathing for about five minutes, or longer if you are so inclined.*
>
> *Practice with an attitude of doing "no-thing," i.e. not trying to do anything, not trying to have any experience in particular, but just waiting to experience what arises from being with your breath. If nothing happens you might imagine that the candle has a living consciousness that knows it will take a long time for you to find the way. You simply have not yet become one with it; and loving and letting go are sometimes difficult for us all to do. The candle has compassion, for it knows from direct experience what it means to have its light extinguished. Maybe it is that awareness of losing and rediscovering light that enables the candle's compassion to fill the dark space of your room with its gentle glow. Though sometimes you have constricted and forgotten to breathe, and the loss of oxygen has made you lose your light, re-lighting it has always been just a breath away. On one of your exhalations — whether it will be now or tomorrow or even sometime when the candle is not lit — you may let go and remember and experience this again, knowing the eternal candle is always lit and emitting loving kindness, even when you forget that it is there.*

"*Identification*" is one of the primal psychological mechanisms. In the animal kingdom it's called "*imprinting*," and can be seen when a young bird instinctually follows and imitates its mother; it does the same with a human, if that person appears at a key developmental period. In the human kingdom, a young child identifies with his or her parent's behaviors, and gradually introjects those ways so that they become integral parts of the Self. We take on the attributes of that with which we identify.

Identification is one of the primary means of creating an altered state of consciousness that promotes healing. It has long been known in cross-cultural shamanic literature that healing is induced by having a person identify with an element of nature with which he or she is out of balance. In Native American shamanic methods of "soul retrieval," the spirit of the eagle is called forth, and through identification with the farthest seeing bird, the spiritually lost individual may be lifted above current life problems and find his or her vision restored in the process. Healing by identification is rooted in the idea set forth in the *Upanishads*, "By seeing oneself in all beings and all beings in the self, enlightenment is found." According to ancient philosophy, all elements of the universe are contained in the Self, such as fire, water, earth, and air.

Modern hypnotherapists use identification with the elements of nature to create a healing trance state. From the above exercise you may have experienced the mind's ability to activate the felt experience of the glow of light, the energy called Qi. Is this an illusion? There are many examples of using imagery to heal (Rossi, 1986; Achterberg, 1992). In the Simington Cancer Clinics, the person suffering from cancer identifies with the pictures of the healthy white blood cells (macrophages) that surround and attack the cancer (the T and B cells). This significantly activates the healing response of the bodymind (Lerner, 1994, pp. 163-166). It would be interesting to do a scientifically controlled experiment studying what happens to cancer cells, or to the immune system in general, when one meditates on various different objects of nature, including candlelight.

3. Introductory Exercises for Experiencing Qi: The Energy Ball between Your Hands

While the above exercise emphasized the visual channel to activate Qi, this next static Qigong exercise emphasizes the kinesthetic channel to activate Qi.

> *Find a comfortable sitting posture. In Taoist Qigong it is often suggested to place both feet flat on the floor and sit on the edge of the chair so that your back is straighter. Sitting in this way is an energetic improvement on the half or full lotus positions where some Qi is blocked in the legs. For three to five minutes, notice your breathing becoming longer and deeper; notice the pause after the out-breath and how your in-breath arises from that pause. Once you feel a state of calmness, with your palms facing each other, place them about six to eight inches apart, in front of your heart, forming an imaginary ball. Remember when you were a child and open to playing games? Pretend that you can feel a magnetic field in your hands. As you try to pull your hands apart, the magnetic field slightly inhibits their expansion. Next, try to press your hands together. Again, imagine that your hands are two, opposite-poled electromagnets that have a hard time coming together.*
>
> *You may begin to feel the ball of energy that inhibits the hands from coming together, and the electromagnetic force that prevents them from pulling apart. This can happen the first time you try this exercise, or it may take a few days, weeks, or months of practice.*

In the tradition of hypnotherapy the idea of "natural magnetic forces" of our bodies is used for bodymind healing (Rossi, 1988, pp. 38-42). Whether we want to think of this sense of energy as real or imagined, the state of consciousness we enter can be used to draw forth our healing resources. In the Taoist tradition, Qi is held to be as real as physical matter.

If, in doing the above exercise, you experienced a feeling of energy or relaxation, imagine this feeling spreading through your body as you let go on your exhalation—through your arms, trunk, pelvis, and finally legs and feet. Eventually you may find that energy will move to a particular part of your body just by thinking about that part of your body and allowing your exhalation to move through it. For example, do the above exercise with your hands on your thighs face up or face down. Just focus your intention on one hand and notice what sensations develop in that hand. Maybe you'll feel it tingling, growing warmer, more relaxed, or more energized. Eventually you'll develop confidence in your mind's ability to focus healing energy.

The hands are a very powerful tool used through the ages to promote healing (Brennan, 1990). In a study reported in *Taiji Magazine*, Luke Chan (1995) reports on a Qigong clinic in Zhining, Qinhuangdao Province, China where Dr. Pang Ming, a Western and traditional medical doctor, combines technology from the West with Eastern healing methods.[12] At his clinic, Qigong masters place their hands over, or on, patients who have cancer, while the cancers are viewed on an ultrasound screen (pp. 34-35). Usually, in his method of *Chilel* (called *Zhineng Qigong* in China) a *wuji* state is activated by linking with the love and compassion of the "10 million" fellow practitioners worldwide. This may add to the power of the trance state and, perhaps, to non-local field effects. Chan, one of the best-known teachers of this method, reports witnessing bladder cancer disappear in a matter of minutes while a Qigong teacher worked on a patient; he has a videotape of the process.[13] It will be interesting to see whether such reports will prove valid when put through the scrutiny of modern scientific observers. For now, we can use the reports to add to the activation of a positive mental set. If, when we try and don't succeed to activate Qi for our own healing purposes, we need to be careful not to judge ourselves and create constriction in the rivers of our Qi. Instead, we should view our psychospiritual practice as one that involves patience, non-attachment, and an opportunity to explore the healing potential of Qi.

4. Intention and the Direction of Your Qi. The Interface between Imagination and Energy

It has long been known that imagination creates changes in consciousness and the body. Less known is the fact that by combining breath with imagery, the experience of energy and its healing effects can be amplified and directed within the body.

> *As a personal experiment, try using Microcosmic Orbit Breath and imagine a stream coming down the front of your body as you exhale. Then imagine that the river of breath goes down to your left thumb. Do you notice any different sensations there, tingling, warmth, etc? Then imagine that the river is flowing to your right thumb. Do you notice the sensations shifting to the other thumb?*

For those who have doubts about the ability to focus energy and think it is just a "head trip," it is interesting to note that Dr. Basmajian, a physician and scientist, published an article in *Science Magazine* providing evidence that human beings could learn to voluntarily control a single cell (as cited in Achterberg, 1985, p. 199). When very small electrodes that could measure electrical activity of a cell were inserted into a motor nerve cell, and auditory feedback was given to the person when that cell would fire, the person could quickly learn to fire it at will.[14] Though Basmajian's study shows us that there is evidence that human beings can learn to voluntarily control the electrical activity of a single cell, such power should be used cautiously. Be careful not to focus too much on an area that is in need of healing, because there is already often an excess of energy in that place. It is better, as discussed more fully in Chapter 7 (discussion of *The Yin Yang Balancing Method*), to focus on the river of Qi that moves through that blocked area than on the spot itself. Trust that the overall energy in your bodymind can, in time, restore balance; and instead of focusing on the inflamed area, I recommend focusing on the belly (*Tan Tien*) or the heart or on the opposite side of the body to promote balance. Most importantly, remember to try not to use force. And remember that it is not you who is doing the healing; it is the loving energy of the universe that heals you.

When I was told by Sifu Ha to practice Standing Meditation for 100 hours over a few months, I (as did many other students of this art) began to experiment with my imagination, intention, and the resultant shifts of energy that coincided with these shifts in awareness. This tradition is called the *Yi Chuan*, which uses the mind or intention to better cultivate our relationship with the elements of the universe. But we need not immerse ourselves in a Chinese tradition to experiment with such states of awareness. Dr. Leonard Lascow (1998), in his book, *Healing with Love*, has similarly experimented with how different states of awareness effect healing. For example, he has done some initial experiments comparing different state-specific states such as letting go of desires, focused intention, and *Microcosmic Orbit Breathing*. His preliminary research, that was cited earlier, showed the ability of *Microcosmic Orbit Breathing* was able to affect cancer cells (Lascow, 1998, p. 306). And for those who doubt the ability of love to heal you might want to check out the study reporting that rabbits that were touched and shown affection developed less arteriosclerosis than those fed the same poor diet and were not touched and loved (Nerem, 1980).

The important point is not to discover which laboratory experiments work the best, in general; but instead, to discover for yourself, when you need a shift in consciousness, which practices work best for you. One of the major themes of this book is that when we change our intention we "shape-shift" into a different state of consciousness, which thereby brings on correlating psychophysiological changes.

Throughout this book we will see how the combined use of intention, breath, and awareness has created healing results for many of my patients. In Chapter 7, using the case of a woman who had a crushed leg in a car accident, we'll see an example of how the combination of *Macrocosmic Orbit Breathing*, visualizations, and Qigong were able to eliminate her need for pain medication and reduce and eliminate her pain. In Chapter 16 we will see how a woman in psychotherapy was helped to stand up to a dominating, overbearing father by using a Tai Chi stance where she

Chapter 4: The Ground of Energy Psychology 99

simultaneously set a boundary and also expressed a welcoming intention. Shifts of intention help us to shape-shift and draw from the universal archetypal energies to heal our life issues.

5. Rocking Back and Forth to Create a Healing Trance: *Tai Chi Ruler*

Finally, we will see how bodily oriented Qigong movement exercises have their own state-specific attributes. In the exercise below, be aware of how just physically doing this practice activates a trance state, but also be aware of how adding the particular imaginal exercise enhances the experience of Qi. Along the lines of Chapter 2 and the discussion of brain research, it could be hypothesized that activating the meaning centers of the brain (the amygdala, cingulate cortex, etc.) adds to the experience of energy and the ability to enhance bodymind healing.

To explore your healing resources, in a standing or sitting position, place your hands around your ball of Qi and begin to rock back and forth (illustrated in the *Tai Chi Ruler* practice, Chapter 24). The rocking motion activates the healing response, as a mother instinctively knows when she rocks her infant when he or she is upset. Rocking back and forth soothes and heals. Blind people also intuitively do this movement to activate their Qi. Rocking back and forth activates energy by alternately filling and emptying the opposite poles of yin and yang. Magnetic fields, piezoelectric effects, are generated this way; and if we are sufficiently relaxed we will find the magnetic field where yin and yang play, and we will go into trance. To do the moving Qigong movement called *Tai Chi Ruler*:

> *Put your right foot slightly in front of your left foot. The left foot should be at a 45-degree angle. Both knees are always bent. As you rock forward onto the right foot, hold the ball of Qi and integrate movement with the exhalation. Make sure your center-line doesn't go over your right foot. As you rock forward, the ball is relatively close to the body and moves down to the area of the belly. As you rock forward, exhale and pause. Imagine returning stress or toxic energy to the earth, which welcomes it as fertilizer. As you rock back into your left foot, the ball rises up with your in-breath. The ball rising on the inhalation is further out from the body than it was on the downward arc of the exhalation. Along with the in-breath, imagine drawing in healing energy from the earth, until your hands, still in the shape of the ball, arrive at the level of the shoulders. The front of your right foot has risen on the in breath, with the heel still on the ground. If your back foot is at a 45-degree angle you will naturally feel a stretch in your lower back. This area is called the Ming Men, one important gateway of vital energy. Continue with your exhalation, moving your hands back downward. Next, for balance, switch the position of the two feet so that the left foot is forward and the right one back.*

This exercise is excellent for combining imagination and movement to activate a trance state. Use it to practice healing a particular part of the body. (As with all exercises, do not to use them as a substitute for medical attention if needed.) These movements form part of a traditional Taoist exercise system called *Tai Chi Chih*, or *Tai Chi Ruler*.

The idea of "the ruler" implies that this method is a way to take measure of the day or of our internal universe — to feel the measure of the quality of the ball of energy we carry with ourselves today. We can imagine that we hold the earth itself in our hands. What kind of earth do we want — a peaceful one or an uptight, rushing, anxious one? Through the exercise of *Tai Chi Ruler*, we practice finding the felt sense we desire, and having "the whole world in our hands."

With a little practice we may begin to experience the ball rising by itself along with our breath. Hypnotherapists conceptualize such a state as one of arm levitation or ideodynamic hand signaling; and they use such a trance state to promote body/mind healing (Rossi, 1988, pp. 39-46). Whether we want to conceptualize this as a trance state or as an experience of Qi, the spiritual technology of ancient Qigong practice may lead us to feel as if we are in a tub of water that goes up to our shoulders. As happens when we are in water, the hands float up to the surface with no muscular action needed. Taoist texts tell us that this is one of the signs of Qi — a sense of movement that happens by itself, with no effort, like floating up in water. A Taoist hypnotherapeutic healing induction can be created as we rock back and forth in the *Tai Chi Chih* tradition:

> *If you just experienced the transformation of the air into water, can you allow the gravitational force of the water to carry your stress or dis-ease downstream to the earth below as your hands move downward, or will it float away up to the sky as you let go and your hands rise upward?*

There is a depth of healing potential in this movement. In more advanced training with this method, we discover how when the toe is raised the lower back is slightly pushed back, "filling the hollow." Thus, this practice is a good preventative medicine for lower back problems. This movement is also a secret method for reversing the normal fight-flight response of the body. Normally, when we are attacked the sympathetic nervous system brings the energy up to the head and extremities as the fear response of the body kicks in. Here we follow the fear response upward with the hands as we inhale, but at its peak, we bring the energy down to the lower back (*Ming Men*). Then we draw the energy downward with our exhalation as we let go. As we discussed in the *Microcosmic Orbit Breathing* method, we sink our energy to the belly (*Tan Tien*), but here the Qi is grounded even more by integrating hand movements and body posture. No wonder this method is being used in trauma trainings by the world-renowned Psychiatrist Bessel van der Kolk in his training of trauma therapists.

> *Why shouldn't psychologists and workers in behavioral healthcare be armed with the full spectrum of bodymind and symbolic process modalities for the benefit of healing our patients?*

Beyond Qigong as Qigong Movements: Activating the Core Energy of our Being

All of the Qigong practices in this chapter, whether they involve using imaginal processes or the body, activate healing energy at the core of our being. When someone thinks about medical Qigong they may think about many movements with captivating names like *Dragon Rises to the Heavens*, *Healing the Internal Organs*, or *Raising and Lowering Qi with Heavenly Palms*. But the activation of Qi may be a more simple thing. I remember in one of my medical Qigong trainings, I, and many of my fellow students, were looking forward to learning loads of new moves from a world-renowned medical Qigong master, Sat Chuen Hon. He began the workshop stating that Western medicine focuses on curing disease and that Chinese medicine is not disease-focused; instead, Chinese medicine focuses on restoring equilibrium to the whole system. He took out a ping-pong ball, dented the ball, and then asked the assembled group of health professionals including Western doctors, nurses, etc. what to do to cure the dent. One person said, "Let's get a needle with a hook on it and stick it into the dent and pull it back out." Many people gave their suggestions while Master Hon made a seemingly unrelated request — "Can someone please get me a cup of tea?" Meanwhile, another medical professional suggested that we take the needle and go into the other side of the ping-pong ball to push out the dent that way.

A few moments later, the meaning of Master Hon's request became apparent — he put the ping-pong ball into the tea, and the ball expanded back to its original state. He continued his lesson by saying, "By surgically operating on the ping-pong ball you may have temporally cured it, but you also may have irreparably damaged it. By increasing heat, and using natural elements as a first resort, we can facilitate the healing of the ping-pong ball and ourselves." Then he went on with his lecture about how, through cultivating the essence of a human being's vital energy and expanding it from the center, many diseases on the periphery of the body can be healed. He talked about the natural balance of fire/heat and water/cool in the body and how one key principle of healing is how to recreate balance when these forces are in disharmony.

As discussed in Volume I, virtually all Qigong masters would agree that the best way to activate "the ping-pong ball" of our life energy is to practice Standing Meditation. As my Sifu, Fong Ha puts it, "It is Standing Meditation Qigong that best fills our Qi bank accounts."

But, there are many ways to go to the center of our Selves and find our inner heat, and there are many ways to find our ability to cool ourselves down when we are overly active. Qi may certainly come from physical exercises like Qigong, but the energy of life also comes from the center of our Selves when we are in the state of imagining. Activating our Qi by guided imagery methods can help us transmute blocked mind-body issues as we identify our dysfunctional beliefs and work through the issues that create the "dent in the ball of our lives."

Transcending and Transmuting Imaginal Traditions

The methods delineated thus far in this chapter have been transcendent methods, that is, they activate healing energy that helps us to rise above life's problems. Some experience this as taking a bath in the source of life's energy, adding weight to the Taoist claim in *The Secret of the Golden Flower* (Wilhelm, 1963) that *Microcosmic Orbit Breathing* practices lead to an experience of the *Sea of Elixir*. These methods provide an introduction to the continuum of practices that aid in the cultivation of the transcendent energy of life for bodymind healing. They provide the building blocks for other methods, which will be introduced in the following chapters, which are transmuting in nature and enable the specific working through of psychological complexes.

SECTION II:

BODYMIND HEALING

PSYCHOTHERAPY:

THEORY AND CLINICAL

APPLICATIONS

*My philosophy is that psychological issues and bodily disease
are "divina afflictios" (divine afflictions)
giving us opportunities for psychospiritual growth, soul-making
and finding the source of healing.*

– Michael Mayer

CHAPTER 5: BODYMIND HEALING PSYCHOTHERAPY: THE PSYCHOTHERAPY OF SHAPE-SHIFTING

*The history of science is rich in the example of the fruitfulness
of bringing two sets of techniques,
two sets of ideas,
developed in separate contexts for the pursuit of new truth,
into touch with one another.*

— Robert Oppenheimer
Science and the Common Understanding

The Marriage of Psychotherapeutic and Energetic Approaches to Bodymind Healing

What is *"Bodymind Healing Psychotherapy?"* In order to help a patient face the challenges of everyday life, a therapist must be able to weave together psychological theories and healing methods that fit the unique person and moment. Practicing the art of psychotherapy also requires transcending methodologies in order to meet a person in that place of raw humanness where contact is made with the deep source of one's being. In this spirit, Bodymind Healing Psychotherapy draws from traditional forms of psychotherapy, energy psychology, bodymind and symbolic process approaches to healing, hypnosis, psychoneuroimmunological research, and ancient sacred wisdom traditions.

The last chapter explored how the streams of Qigong and imaginal processes can merge into a bodymind healing Qigong to enhance each tradition's healing effects.[1] In this chapter we will see how Bodymind Healing Qigong (BMHQ) stands as a center-post within the terrain of an integrative Bodymind Healing Psychotherapy (BMHP). We will broaden the imaginal/somatic dialectic to include transmuting as well as transcending methods, and then show how a wider range of depth psychotherapeutic methods enhances this energy psychotherapy that uses Qigong.

The Most Profound Qigong is Following Your True Life's Path

*People say that what we're all seeking is a meaning for life.
I don't think that's what we're really seeking.
I think that what we're seeking is an experience of being alive,
so that our life experiences on the purely physical plane
will have resonances within our own innermost being and reality,
so that we actually feel the rapture of being alive.*

— Joseph Campbell

A fundamental thesis of this book is that the most profound Qigong, the deepest way to activate the energy of life, is to follow your true life's path, unencumbered by distorted psychological issues. These issues, a natural part of the school of human life, make us notice them when they encumber the flowing river of life in our bodies, minds, and relationships with others. It is these issues that send us on healing journeys for psychospiritual growth, soul-making, and finding the source of healing. Qigong, in its narrowly defined sense of using movements synchronized with breath, is just one way of restoring balance and energy to our out-of-balance lives.

As discussed earlier, some of the origins of psychotherapeutic healing can be found in traditions of energy psychology. In the introduction to this book we saw that the earliest use of the Greek term "*psyche*," meant "soul." Hillman (1975, 1976) differentiates this term from the word, "*pneuma*" or spirit, which has a more transcendent meaning. One classical idea about the psyche was that it was considered to be composed of the energies of the elements of the universe such as fire, earth, air, and water (Rudhyar, 1970; Hillman, 1975, p. 127).

The earliest energy psychology in the West was created to bring the energies of the unique human soul back into balance; this was done through storytelling and the use of other symbolic process (also called imaginal) methods to help change one's way of being and way of seeing the world (Neumann, 1954, 1956; Campbell, 1978; Eliade, 1958, 1964; Edinger, 1985; Rudhyar, 1970; Jung, I-XX; Houston, 1992; Hillman, 1975; Kingsley, 1999; Schure, 1977; Steiner, 1973; Mayer, 1984, 1993). I call this imaginal, somatically based, energetic path, a "'trance-forming' of one's life stance." (Mayer, 2004).

The Center-Post of Bodymind Healing Psychotherapy: The Transcending/Transmuting Dialectic

> *"Call the world if you please the veil of soul-making.*
> *Then you will know the purpose of the world.*
> *Can't you see how necessary it is*
> *to have a world of pains and troubles*
> *to school the intelligence and make it soul."*
>
> — John Keats

In the last chapter I delineated Bodymind Healing Qigong symbolic process methods that were transcendent-oriented, and I explained how these methods can activate a healing energy that helps us to rise above life's problems and take a bath in, what may be experienced as, "the source of life's energy." I hope you had an experience like this with *Microcosmic Orbit Breath*, imagining you were a candle, holding an energy ball, directing energy with intention, or with rocking and visualizing healing energy in the *Tai Chi Ruler* exercise.

Here, and in the chapters that follow, I will begin to introduce "transmuting traditions," and show how they can be blended with "transcending traditions" for an integrative mind-body healing psychotherapy. Transcending and transmuting dimensions refer respectively to whether healing methods are used to rise above, or work through a life issue.

Chapter 2 gave an overview of the critique of psychotherapy traditions that incorporate meditation and do not use various depth psychotherapy tools, including those of symbolic process. The critique stated that by using spiritually transcendent methods, the transmutation of psychological complexes will not occur, but will be bypassed and then reappear the next time an associated trigger touches off the complex. It is the viewpoint of BMHP that dichotomizing between transcendent and transmuting needs of the patient in psychotherapy is a function of the Western dualistic mind. Such dichotomization does not do justice to the holistic spirit of healing in the deepest sense of the "perennial philosophy" (Huxley, 1970); nor, as we will see, does it meet the healing needs of an integrative depth psychotherapy.

In his book on psychotherapy and alchemy, Dr. Edinger (1985), the well-respected Jungian analyst, discussed how there is both a time for rising above in the alchemical container of psychotherapy, and a time for descent into the dark places that need to be traveled. The time for rising up to the top of the alchemical container is called *sublimatio*. In the last chapter we saw some methods for rising up in the container of life to feel our unity with the water of life (exemplified by the story of *The Stream and the Sands*). Metaphors, in general, move us to connect with the wider whole of which we are a part; and, as well, they can have both transcendent and transmuting dimensions. There is also a need in depth psychotherapy to transmute the base substances of the psyche. This requires a descent into the *negredo*, the "dark stuff," where the base matter, the "lead," of the psyche is submitted to various alchemical operations and "turned to gold."

Greek mythology can be seen as a coded language, using images of the gods/goddesses and their stories as pathways for describing how to heal the psyche (Hillman, 1975; Kerenyi, 1979; Barring & Cashford, 1991; Mayer, 1994). In this sense, we can look at: the gods/goddesses of the earth as symbolizing practical ways of dealing with life, divinities of the sky as symbolizing transcendent pathways, and the underworld divinities as transmuting transformative paths. And so it is in psychotherapy — there are times for practical interventions, times for transcending, and times for transmuting.

Bodymind Healing Psychotherapy's Full-Spectrum Approach to the Image/Body Energy Dialectic

When I was training master's level students in a psychotherapy program in the 1980s, I taught a course called *Symbolic Process Approaches to Psychotherapy* for five years. In that class, and in the last chapter, I discussed how I borrowed from Carl Jung's idea of a spectrum of instinctual and symbolic processes. From this I showed how symbolic processes modalities could be integrated with body-oriented practices such as a Taoist breathing method and Qigong movements. In that course, which later became one of the foundations of BMHP, I delineated four dimensions of the spectrum of symbolic process work:

1. *Directive or non-directive dimensions:* Refers to whether the therapist or the patient comes up with the images.

2. *General or ideographic dimensions:* Refers to whether the method is unique to the individual.

3. *Transcending or transmuting dimensions:* Refers to whether the symbols are used to rise above or work through a life issue.

4. *Body-oriented or image-focused:* Refers to the somatic or imaginal orientation of a healing method.

We can think of the components of these four dimensions of the spectrum of symbolic process methods, not as fixed opposites, but rather more like a Taoist *yin-yang* symbol — with a black dot of *yin* in the white *yang* half circle, and the white *yang* dot in the black *yin* half circle. A portion of each quality resides in its opposite end of the spectrum. This metaphor can help us realize that these are fluid rather than fixed separate categories. For example, using this kind of Chinese non-dualistic thinking, we can see that (1) a directive, therapist-guided symbolic process method often constellates a patient's own spontaneously arising, non-directive imagery, (2) a general archetypal theme can transform an individual's life issue, and an individual's personal imagery may become an archetypal teaching story for others, (3) a transcending tradition (such as a breathing method) may evoke the transmuting of psychological issues; and the transmuting of a longstanding pattern may help one to breathe a relaxed sigh of relief, which can lead to a transcendent state, and (4) body-oriented traditions evoke images, and imaginal traditions evoke affective states in the body.

As we keep in mind the Taoist *yin* and *yang* symbol, various types of symbolic process traditions will now be delineated, serving as a heuristic device to be used in a non-categorical way.

The Full Spectrum of the Bodymind Healing Psychotherapy Symbolic Process Methods:

Bodymind Healing Psychotherapy (BMHP) contains a full-spectrum approach to the continuum of mind-body uses of different symbolic process modalities combined with certain body-based energy practices. The full-spectrum symbolic process approach looks like this:

1. *Fairy tales, myths, and teaching stories from the world's ancient sacred wisdom traditions.* (Directive, transcendent, general/archetypal and imaginally oriented.)

    In the last chapter I showed how age-old fairy tales like The Ugly Duckling or The Body Who Cried Wolf have the power to change consciousness and create an energetic shift. We saw how the teaching stories from the world's sacred wisdom traditions, such as the story of The Stream of the Sands, are another example of a directive symbolic therapeutic method of psychospiritual healing. The use of myths in psychotherapy to heal was explored in-depth in my book, Trials of the Heart: Healing the Wounds of Intimacy (Mayer, 1984) and is beyond the scope of this book.

2. *Transpersonal Hypnosis.* (Directive, ideographic, transmuting, imaginal.)

    I used this term, "transpersonal hypnosis," in my symbolic process classes in the early 1980s to describe a therapist-directed, storytelling method I developed that was meant to add to the field of hypnosis an emphasis on connecting patients with the wider whole of which they are a part. This method draws on the elements of nature to facilitate healing and has both imaginal and somatic components. Some of the somatic healing components involve focusing on the breath and constellating bodymind blockages related to life issues by using the River of Life practice. Transpersonal hypnosis[2] uses Gendlin's body-oriented Focusing method (Gendlin, 1978) to transmute these bodymind blocks by creating a felt shift as healing meanings emerge from the body's felt sense.

BMHP's method of transpersonal hypnosis is illustrated in Chapter 9 regarding its use in psychotherapy for addictions, and in Chapter 19 for working with writer's block and encumbrances to the creative process. In Chapter 19 we will see specifically how transpersonal hypnosis uses symbols of the elements of nature to connect us to the healing power of the wider whole of which we are a part. After all, the very definition of "symbol" derived from the word "sym-bolon," which referred to a stick that was divided in half to symbolize and serve as a token receipt of the sale (Edinger, 1972). Just as these sticks were reminders of a greater unity, symbols today help reconnect us with the wider whole of which we are a part.

3. *Bodymind Healing Qigong Methods.* (Directive, general, transcending, body-oriented with imagery.)

   In the last chapter I introduced various Bodymind Healing Qigong methods, and showed how they could help to enhance transcendent imaginal traditions. In the following chapters we will see how many of the practices of BMHQ can enhance behavioral health treatment and depth psychotherapy. Breathing methods, postures, acupressure self-touch, and Tai Chi and Qigong movements, when appropriate, can be incorporated to aid the treatment of anxiety (Chapter 6), chronic pain (Chapter 7), trauma (Chapter 8), hypertension (Chapter 11), etc.

4. *Activating the River of Your Life.* (Directive + non-directive, general + ideographic, transcending + transmuting, imaginal oriented with use of the body.)

   This method will be introduced later in this chapter, and is one of the core methods of Bodymind Healing Psychotherapy. Using a combined directive and non-directive method, the therapist directs the patient to the river of his or her breath and suggests the visualization of a river in the body. But then, unique images arise non-directively from the patient's unconscious as he or she focuses on body blocks that are in the way of the river's flow. This method combines Taoist Microcosmic Orbit Breath, visualization, and Gendlin's Focusing. It combines transcending and transmuting, directive and non-directive, body and mind.

5. *The Mythic Journey Process.* (Directive + non-directive, ideographic + general, transmuting, imaginal + incorporating the body.)

   This method is a combined directive and non-directive method whereby people can create their own stories using imagery and body-oriented tools in order to create a transformation in their life myth and life stance. The Mythic Journey Process helps people create a waking dream as they tap into the creative source of the inner "waking dream-weaver" from where healing images arise. I developed this process in the early 1980s to be a body-oriented, active imagination process. (See Chapter 20.)

6. *Dreams.* (Non-directive, ideographic, transmuting, imaginal.)

   Finally, dreams are one of the most important parts of symbolic process work. They give us a glimpse into a non-directive approach created by "the master of symbolic process" — our unconscious mind. As used here, "non-directive" is not really accurate because, in fact, we get a glimpse of direction from a transpersonal source. Once we begin to enter into a hermeneutic (Warnke, 1987) with "the genie" in dreams; we may find ourselves in a state of inspired awe, as we question what is meant by the images.[3] Dream interpretation is a significant element of depth psychotherapy and of Bodymind Healing Psychotherapy. As in the Aesclepian temples, dreams give a sense of when therapy is coming to a close, as you will see in the next chapter with the case of "The Waitress with the Dream of the Flower Tattoo." Most importantly, dream images contain transformative energy potential and, in accordance with the thesis of this book, they allow us to "shape-shift" into other ways of being when we "gestalt" the dream, i.e. become its characters. There will be some examples of how dreams play a part in BMHP in the next chapter on anxiety/panic.

Shape-Shifting, Metaphors, and Psychological Transformation

One of the deepest symbolic process methods stemming from cross-cultural mythologies and ancient initiatory paths is shape-shifting. This archetypal concept lies at the roots of the earliest "psychotherapy" and uses tranfiguring metaphors to describe the process of psychological transformation. Oftentimes the process of transfiguration was expressed in terms of a change from a human form to an animal form. In fairy tales, like *Beauty and the Beast* or the *Frog Prince*, the characters were transformed from a human being into another form as a punishment for some transgression; then a loved one came to the rescue to shape-shift the human being back to his human form. In Chinese folklore the Monkey King learns to shape-shift into seventy-two different forms, learns to fly, does battle with demons, and even challenges the Gods as he learns lessons about his arrogance (Shepard, 2005). Greek mythology is filled with rich metaphors of such shape-shifting — as when Circe turned intruders on her island into swine, Athena transformed Arachne into a spider for challenging her as a weaver, and Artemis transformed Acteon into a stag for spying on her in her bath. In European legends human beings shape-shift into werewolves and vampires. "Almost every culture around the world has some type of shape-shifting myth" (www.en.wikipedia.org/wiki/shapeshifting). As I have pointed out throughout this book and I have discussed extensively elsewhere (Mayer, 1993), those who see myths with a psychological eye understand that these stories hold keys to using the imagination to aid the process of psychological transformation. In particular, in Chapter 2 we saw how modern research on state-specific states of consciousness shows that when a person imagines entering into such states, healing can emerge; and I have discussed how somatic practices (that were practiced in the Dionysian theater at the temple of Aesclepius, amongst Native Americans, and in Qigong practice) can aid in healing the psyche.

Found in the *Upanishads*, one of the clearest statements ever made about the "psychology of shape-shifting" alludes to this deeper purpose of the use of metaphor. It reads, "By seeing all beings in yourself, and yourself in all beings, enlightenment is found." Not only do the Hindu gods and goddesses shape-shift into animals and other aspects of nature as part of their evolution, so do we in our self-healing process, as we become the elements of our wider nature.

Nature not only represents different aspects of the Self, but we *are* nature. When we are out-of-balance with those elements of our primordial Selves, images and metaphors from nature restore our connection to the "Way of things."

Metaphors are a particular use of symbol that creates a likeness between our lives and the wider whole of which we are a part. Metaphors from nature have long been used to help facilitate the healing of the psyche, and have been used in psychotherapy (Asch, 1955; Mayer, 1977; Wallas, 1985) and in clinical hypnosis (Achterberg, 1985). This process is inherent in the deepest layers of our psyches as they manifest in our dreams. Take the example of a modern psychotherapy patient who, during a time of a stressful job relocation, dreams of his healthy bonsai tree that survived its transplanting into a bigger pot. Realizing the likeness between his life and the bonsai tree, he gets a sense of power to cope with the transplantation going on in his life.

Metaphors give wisdom and healing; but in creating a likeness between our narrow Selves and the wider whole of which we are a part, much more happens. A fundamental part of the suffering of civilized men and women comes from being out of touch with nature, our nature — and, as when we are actually out in nature, an experiential journey takes place as we "re-member" our connection with the elements of our wider nature.

Psychotherapy without nature is a psychotherapy that attempts to resolve the suffering of civilized women and men within the civilized office. Metaphors help to bridge the gap between civilized people and the world of nature, thereby calling on the wider sphere of nature's healing powers to help us. Later, in Chapter 19, in the case example of a patient with writer's block, and in Chapter 9 on healing addictions, we will see the clinical application of how the elements of nature, imagined and experienced in vivo, can be used to facilitate a transformative healing of blocked life energy.

"Shape-shifting" is one way to harness the power of metaphor in order to make psychotherapy a deeper, more transformative process. In the West, as in the East, it has been known that shape-shifting is a fundamental part of the path to self-knowledge. In Greek mythology,

> *Proteus, the old man of the sea, changed his form from a lion to a snake, and from a leopard to a tree. When Menelaus needed information from him to find his way home, Menelaus disguised himself as a seal and waited with the rest of Proteus's flock until Proteus returned to his true form, and then he got the information he needed.*

Similarly, each of us moves through various forms in our everyday lives; sometimes we feel powerful like a lion, or as if we are slithering around like a snake, or grounded like a tree. After going through our ups and downs and surfing in the waves of our emotional nature, eventually we may find our true form[4] and our way home. BMHP proposes that body movements and postures, as well as metaphors representing nature, can help the lost soul find its way home.

This power that symbolic processes have as tools for depth psychotherapy comes from the fact that symbols, metaphors, and images precede language and therefore exist at a more primordial level of the psyche. For example, in the Jewish Kabbalistic tradition, Hebrew letters symbolize primordial sounds, each of which has its own inherent meaning (Suares, 1973, 1976). And an image of an object invokes a deeper primordial healing realm than does the reified term that represents that object. For example, when someone tells you that you are as strong as a tree, you may say, "thanks," and the message may not go very deep. But if you take a moment to "shape-shift" into the tree, to feel and imagine your roots descending into the earth, you may experience how you are rooted in your family relationships and in connection to your own religious/spiritual path. You may come to see that it is from these roots that you draw your strength, thereby deepening the personal meaning and healing power of the tree.

It is in this light that images like the tree or the river are used in BMHP. When we create a likeness between ourselves and an object in nature, we may shape-shift into that object, imbibing its needed quality for our healing. Next we will see how the river in the *River of Life* practice functions as a shape-shifting metaphor for healing the psyche.

The River of Life: Healing with the Transcending/Transmuting Dialectic

The *River of Life* (ROL) is a key method used in BMHP to activate both transcending and transmuting dimensions; and it will be an essential treatment method used in most of the following clinical chapters. Its imagery and breathing methods are oriented to activate the transcendent energy of life and induce a felt experience of the glow of our natural being. But the *River of Life* exercise also contains a transmuting dimension as it directs the river of one's life energy to come up against bodymind blockages, then helps a person to focus on those blocks, and finally uses appropriate aspects of the ten-leveled methods of BMHP (explicated next in this chapter) to transmute those blocks. The "river" in this process is not an intellectual symbol, but rather it evokes the essence of "riverness" as an archetypal force, with all of its inherent power to cleanse, take us on a journey, etc. So, in the ROL practice we "shape-shift" into assuming the attributes of various aspects of a river.

As a metaphor, the river provides many psychotherapeutically useful elements, such as:

- ♦ A metaphor for the soul's journey through life.
- ♦ A felt experience of Qi down the front, central meridian (Conception Vessel, *Ren Channel*, also called the *Jen Mei* or *Jen Mo*).
- ♦ A way to activate blocks in the body and psyche, and bring them to the surface where the underlying issues can be brought to light and undergo a process of transmutation.
- ♦ A tool to dissolve blocks in the bodymind, and restore flow to frozen, stagnant, fixated bodymind issues and bring forth new healing psychological meanings.

Throughout this book, and in the case illustrations, we will see each of these different attributes of the river emphasized at different times depending upon the clinical need. For example, in Chapter 20, in the *Mythic Journey Process,* the ROL's ability to constellate the soulful experience of a person's life journey is emphasized. In Chapter 8, in the case of a man suffering from the long-lasting effects of unremembered sexual trauma, the ROL helps to bring those hidden memories to the surface and, in conjunction with other aspects of BMHP, helps facilitate a process of transmutation. The metaphor of, and the experience of, the inner river gives us a powerful tool that integrates psychological and energetic healing powers.

In the last chapter, I outlined *Microcosmic Orbit Breath* and the practice of focusing on the energy up the back (Governing Vessel, *Du Channel,* also called the *Tu Mei* or *Tu Mo*) and down the front of the body (Conception Vessel, *Ren*). In BMHP, the use of the metaphor of the river adds to the healing effects of *Microcosmic Orbit Breathing.*

A river is a powerful hypnotherapeutic image that can constellate the river of one's life experience. By combining the image of the river with a breathing method that activates the primordial central energy channel (Conception and Governing Vessels) of the bodymind, the practitioner is further induced into the experience of the river's "psyche/somatic realness." The tradition of BMHP proposes that adding this central channel breathing method (*Microcosmic/Macrocosmic Orbit Breathing*) to the process of imagining a river helps us to further "re-member" the river within us.[5]

Interestingly, I recently learned from my colleague Hana Matt, who teaches World Religions at various universities, that in the mystical Jewish tradition the linking of the long exhalation with saying various divine names was used to produce psychological change. Avraham Abulafia, a famous Kabbalist who lived in Spain (1240-1290), used a method that is somewhat similar to the *River of Life* practice that I developed. The experiences that Rabbi Abulafia had were so powerful that he thought he could convert the Pope to Judaism, and he set off to Rome to prove his point. About one of the processes that Abulafia taught:

> *The human being is tied in knots of world, time and persona... and if one unties the knots in oneself, one may cleave to God.... This process is accomplished with the help of repeating the Divine Name on the long deep out-breath. One must link and exchange a name of the unwanted behavior with a Divine Name. The extended slow deep breathing renews one and loosens the tied pattern. And then the use of the Divine Name re-ties the loosened state. By this loosening and re-tying you will strip off your binding constraints ...and dress yourself in a new form.*
>
> — Avraham Abulafia
> *Otsar Eden Gamuz*
> (As cited in Idel, 1988, p. 135)

In another of Abulafia's writings, called *Hayyei Ha-Olam Ha-Ba,* he said that this repetition of the Divine Name with breathing in a slow deep rhythm is a way to attain spiritual energy and help to "Enter the Spiritual Stream." In addition to using the image of the stream, which is central to BMHP's approach, Abulafia's imagery is also striking when he says that as you draw down the Divine Supernal Force with your breath that "Your two nostrils are the chariots which force the female aspect of God (*Shekhinah*) to dwell in you ... and eighteen long breaths give you vitality of the soul (*Hai*)." Another Rabbi, Rami Shapiro, in his book, *Minyan*, says that this repetition of the Divine Name used by the Kabbalists helps one to get rid of unwanted thoughts and behaviors, as your breath slows and deepens. This practice in Kabbalah is called *Gurushin*, meaning "dispelling," and in the Bible this method of quieting the mind and stepping back from unwanted patterns is called *Hagah* (Shapiro, 1997).

In light of one of the essential themes of this book regarding the importance of tapping into the ancient roots of psychotherapy, it is interesting that "repetition" of eye movements in EMDR while substituting more truthful or constructive cognitions with unwanted thoughts, and repeating tapping movements or sounds in energy psychology, have similarities to these age-old Kabbalistic practices. Likewise in Bodymind Healing Psychotherapy's practices, to dispel unwanted psychological patterns we link the image of the *River of Life* with the long out-breath, while substituting truthful or constructive cognitions, repeating Qigong movements, or adding the use of other Western and Eastern transformative methods.

Whether you use the methods of EMDR, energy psychology, or Bodymind Healing Psychotherapy, if you find these practices of exchanging names and repeating movements, sounds, songs, words, or touch to activate altered states to be so empowering and transforming that you want to let the world know about it, take care not to get inflated from your experience. When Rabbi Abulafia went to Pope Nicholas III, the pope ordered him to be burned at the stake; fortunately for Rabbi Abulafia because the pope succumbed to a stroke, he was instead just jailed for a short time (www.en.wikipedia.org/wiki/Abraham_Abulafia).

In the *River of Life* practice below, and the way the practice is developed in the following chapters, there are some similarities to the above Kabbalistic practices; yet we will see how in Bodymind Healing Psychotherapy's ten levels there are many other principles for, and ways of, "untying the knots," or melting the ice blocks, in order to, "... strip off your binding constraints ... and dress yourself in a new form."

And, if you think that blending breath with healing words or images is just an esoteric method for pre-modern times listen to what Dr. Herbert Benson, M.D. Professor of Medicine, Harvard Medical School, Chief of Behavioral Medicine at New England Deaconess Hospital says,

> *Over the course of time your brain develops certain physical conduits that determine how you habitually think, act, and feel. These conduits are your "wiring." Your wiring can become so fixed as to make changing your behavior nearly impossible. When you try to change a deep-seated habit, your best intentions are not enough. Change is not merely a matter of will. Habitual thoughts, feelings and behaviors become hard-wired into your brain, and you cannot change them until you change the wiring. You have to make a physiological change in the brain's old wiring before you can successfully imprint new wiring. Many studies have shown that periods of deep breathing and repeating the Divine Name on the exhale, bring this about. It makes the brain and nervous system more pliable. This is called "neural plasticity." This deep breathing and repeating the Divine Name releases the hold that the old wiring has on your brain and nervous system and allows you to imprint new neural pathways. This enables you*

to alter the way you think and act, and you create new and additional connections that can, with repetition, come to dominate the old connections, helping to solidify the new thoughts and behaviors. This practice causes the two hemispheres of your brain to begin to exchange information more freely causing them to function in sync with each other. Then your mind tends to operate more creatively, you process information more effectively and you are capable of understanding things in different ways. The is called "cognitive receptivity." Because you are more receptive to new information and new ways of thinking about old situations, you are open to alternative ways of handling situations. This allows you to make lasting changes in your mind and behavior. It allows for a more successful re-imprinting of the mind. It rewires the brain with the new behaviors that you want.

— Dr. Herbert Benson
The Maximum Mind (as paraphrased by Hana Matt from Benson, 1975, 1975b, 1984)

The *River of Life* practice, outlined below, contains a blend of guided imagery, hypnotherapy, a Qigong breathing method, and Gendlin's (1978) Focusing. As mentioned earlier, this method combines a directive, transcendent imagery practice with a non-directive, transmuting "focusing" process on the crux of our blocked life issue. The transmuting dimension is further enhanced by combining the *River of Life* exercise with elements of modern psychotherapy, as is explained in the section following this exercise.

The River of Life Practice

Step 1: Breath: Microcosmic Orbit and the River of Your Life:

> *As your breath comes in, imagine it rising up your back. It rises all the way to the sky. Then as you exhale, feel the breath going down the front of your body. Notice how your exhalation gets longer and longer and deeper and deeper the longer you are aware of your breath. Don't try to force your breath deeper. Then imagine that this out-breath is a river that is traveling down the front of your body. The longer and deeper your breath is, the longer and deeper is your inner river. Focus on the pause at the end of your exhalation, as it brings you to an inner peaceful pool slightly below your belly. After that pause by your inner peaceful pool, the river continues to flow down to the ocean beneath your feet. Then the breath rises again for another cycle up your back.*

Step 2: Using the Breath to Constellate Bodymind Blockages:

> *Your life has been a journey down a river that came from the mountains; and it will eventually reach the sea. Right now on your life's journey there may be some issue that is constricting or blocking the flow of the river of your life. On the next downward cycle of your breathing, notice where the river doesn't flow smoothly in your body and allow an image to arise that represents a block in that place on the river of your life energy. Maybe the encumbrance feels like a boulder or an ice block.*

Step 3: Transmuting Body Blocks:

> *As you sense any block in the river of energy, "focus" (Gendlin, 1978) on that body sense and allow a word, image, or phrase to emerge from it as you ask the question, "What is this all about?" Don't try to think of an answer; allow a response to rise to the surface as if something stuck was being shaken loose from the bottom of a riverbed. Then "resonate" that word, image, or phrase back to the body sense to see if it gets the crux of what that block is about. Once you hit the bulls-eye of meaning, you will often notice a "felt shift" occur ... perhaps a sighing breath may release a sign as you find what that block is all about.*

The above method, the *River of Life*, is a key practice of BMHP. These three steps are just the beginning of the process. In many of the subsequent chapters we will see how to build upon this practice in different ways to fit different circumstances. Once the patient's issue is constellated, then the next transmuting elements of BMHP may be applied. Some of these transmuting methods are: cognitive-behavioral therapy, various psychodynamic approaches, energy psychology methods, self-soothing, and various transmuting symbolic process approaches to psychotherapy. (The application of many of these methods are illustrated in Chapter 6.) In its broadest scope, BMHP weaves together transcending and transmuting dimensions to create an integral healing approach for psychotherapy and behavioral healthcare.

The Ten Psychoenergetic Holographic Dimensions of Bodymind Healing Psychotherapy

In addition to Bodymind Healing Psychotherapy's imaginal and somatic approaches, it also contains an integrative psychotherapeutic approach to heal the psyche, by bringing back into balance, imbalanced elements of the psyche.

In the following chapters, we will see how BMHP includes Western forms of psychotherapy including psychodynamic psychotherapies, self psychology, cognitive-behavioral psychotherapy, and energy psychology. BMHP also includes ancient sacred wisdom traditions including Qigong, in the broadest sense of the word. From the perspective of the wider purpose of this book, we can see the limitation in thinking of Qigong as just a physical exercise to create energy in the body. There are other ways to "cultivate our life energy," i.e. by working on all psychospiritual facets of ourselves. A person's life stance at a given moment, and the energy that expresses that life stance, does not change through the medium of the body alone. Instead, as proposed in BMHP, healing is best-done by integrating the following methodologies and traditions which address the aforementioned facets of ourselves — body, mind, and spirit. These various, integrative dimensions are outlined below.

The Ten Psychoenergetic Holographic Dimensions of Bodymind Healing Psychotherapy

1. Taoist Breathing Techniques and Hypnosis (Most often using the *River of Life* practice)
2. Self-soothing
3. Focusing on Felt Meaning
4. Psychodynamics
5. Cognitive Restructuring (plus using a body-oriented SUDS scale)
6. Energy Psychology Methods, including Eye Movement Desensitization Reprocessing (EMDR)
7. The Belly Massage of Chi Nei Tsang (Chia, 1990)
8. Acupressure: Phenomenological Approach, and Acu-yoga (Gach, 1981)
9. Practices from Bodymind Healing Qigong[6]
10. Symbolic Process Approaches to Healing

Bodymind Healing Psychotherapy is "psychoenergetic" in that it combines elements of modern psychotherapy and hypnosis with ancient Taoist energy healing methods. The dimensions of this method are "holographic" in that each part actually contains the whole. In order for any one dimension to function properly, the others must be present. In practice, the clinician or individual using this approach moves from one part of the hologram to the other, as needed. While one dimension is being focused upon, the other parts of the whole need to be present. For example, even though Taoist breathing techniques and hypnosis enable us to relax, the underlying psychodynamic patterns that create our tension may not be transformed. Thus, we need to have the psychodynamic dimension present.

Another example — if we merely understand how our fear of having our vulnerability exposed is a psychodynamic issue stemming from our family of origin, but we don't feel a felt shift in our body through a body-oriented technique like Gendlin's Focusing, the insight may not develop deep roots, and may be short lived.[7] Also, crucial to psychological healing is the need to cognitively restructure our old thought forms, such as "I can't trust being vulnerable with anyone," into new thought forms, such as "I choose to be in a world where I can be vulnerable with at least some people." BMHP adds to cognitive therapy a bodily dimension (as do other therapists like, Shapiro, 1995) by using a subjective units of distress scale (SUDS) to make sure the cognition is congruent with the "real self." As well, having patients check-in with their bodies serves to ground new beliefs. The energetic dimension catalyzes the whole mix.

It should also be noted that many aspects of current energy psychologies are included within the above structure. Meridian tapping is part of Qigong, and part of Bodymind Healing Qigong. However, tapping fits into a larger framework of self-touch methods, because in Qigong tapping is looked at as a yang method that increases energy, and in psychotherapy there are times when relaxing yin methods are more appropriate. Therefore self-touch methods from acupressure, such as the "circle, stop, feel method" are used to open the energy of meridians along with psychotherapeutic methods. Although at certain times, specific acu-points are chosen by the therapist, BMHP favors a phenomenological orientation where the patient touches him or herself, trusting how the natural, primordial expression of movement and self-touch arises from the unconscious (see Chapter 16). Many energy psychologies use cognitive therapies as their underlying tools; and, as mentioned in the example above, just as Shapiro's EMDR (1995) uses a body-based SUDS scale to determine the felt effect of a change in belief, so too does BMHP. The Emotional Freedom Technique (EFT) has some excellent bodily and verbal healing methods that are used and adapted to BMHP. For example, as a person says, "Even though I _____, I can still love and accept myself," BMHP adds touching the heart (Conception Vessel-17) for self-soothing purposes, and touching the belly (*Tan Tien*) to help further ground in the body the new cognition. The verbal "self-soothing" dimension of such new healing beliefs are central to EFT and psychodynamic theories (Kohut, 1977), and BMHP's self-touch methods can easily be integrated with their treatment protocols. Likewise, the hypnotherapeutic idea of "anchoring" is used in BMHP to ground the state of consciousness and new belief that has been activated, so that patients can carry this new body awareness into their everyday lives.

Qigong and Tai Chi: A Soulful Practice for Bodymind Healing

> *You could not find the ends of the soul though you traveled every way,*
> *so deep is its Logos.*
>
> — Heraclitus

Finally, although Qigong is usually associated with a transcendent spiritual path; I suggest adding a "soul-oriented" practice of Qigong and Tai Chi to expand the somatic dimensions of psychotherapeutic healing. Esoteric psychology says that our souls consist of our unique constellation of the elements such as fire, earth, air, and water (Rudhyar, 1979; Hillman, 1975, p. 127). Qigong can aid in the cultivation of, and healing of, the elements of our soulful selves. As discussed in Volume I, Qigong and Tai Chi can help to ground us (earth), activate our energy (fire), help us to flow with life (water), and help us activate our transcendent states (air). But now here, in Volume II, we can more clearly see some of the elements that would specifically comprise a "soul-oriented" (Hillman, 1975; Moore, 1992) Qigong and Tai Chi. From a behavioral healthcare perspective, while one is practicing Tai Chi and Qigong, instead of solely focusing on transcendent, spiritual aspects induced by these practices, one can focus on the memories, emotions, and images that arise, making it into a "soulful practice." For example, when we are practicing Standing Meditation, oftentimes, particularly after we have been practicing for a good amount of time, shaking will spontaneously arise in an area of the body that has been blocked. Instead of just appreciating the process of release, we can ask ourselves, "Which of my life issues am I now releasing?" Then, as the body is shaking, we can appreciate the issue that is being released; and we can practice cognitive restructuring, as we say our truthful or constructive new belief.

For example, a perfectionistic person might say while his or her leg is shaking, "I'm letting go of my life-long stance of being self-judgmental and fearing rejection." When the shaking stops, the person might say, "I can feel the solidity of my new stance."

Another facet of a soul-oriented Tai Chi relates to a proposition put forth in the last chapter on the ancient roots of modern energy psychology. There I spoke of how a major theme of cross-cultural ancient sacred wisdom traditions is how to shape-shift from one state of consciousness to another with conscious choice. Modern hypnotherapeutic traditions speak of this as an "anchor," that facilitates the movement from one state-specific state of consciousness to another.

In Volume I and now in Volume II, I have been showing how Tai Chi is much more than a physical practice, it is an initiatory tradition that has a wide variety of transformative effects. For example, I suggest that Tai Chi is a good practice for learning how to smoothly shape-shift from one state-specific state to another. A basic theme of Tai Chi training is to shift from a state of oneness with the universe (*wuji*) to moving into the world of opposites (Tai Chi). In this training the initiate practices alone, and with others (*Tai Chi Joining Hands* practice), to try to maintain a state of relaxation (*wuji*) as the oppositional forces of life push on him or her. When under stress, different specific body postures and principles become anchors to bring the initiate, back to the state of equilibrium and back into harmony with the universe. Every individual stance, and the transitions between those stances, can be such anchors. Depending upon the particular form of Tai Chi, there are between 24 to 108 stances, more or less. For example, the initiate slowly transitions from *White Crane Spreads Wings*, symbolizing a transcendent bird-like state, to *Brush Knee Forward*, one of the most assertive yang movements in the Tai Chi set.[8]

Though usually the initiate isn't explicitly told that Tai Chi is a specific training for joining his or her transcendent and assertive selves, this shape-shifting is implicitly embedded in the transition from one posture to the next. With the conscious awareness that the movements involve shape-shifting from one stance to another, a research hypothesis to be explored would be that this awareness may lead to an increased ability to access such chosen psychological states, i.e. that the practice would further generalize to everyday life.[9] As we will see in subsequent chapters, various Tai Chi postures can function to anchor, signal, and evoke desired state-specific states of consciousness (see Chapter 16). Similar to classical conditioning where Pavlov's famous bell was paired with food, and eventually the bell alone produced a salivary response, here various elements of Tai Chi positions may become associated with activating desired state-specific states.

In Tai Chi practice there are many types of "anchors" that become a signal (bell) to change from one state to another. In addition to each specific posture being an anchor for state-specific states, the act of shifting weight can anchor a felt experience of filling or emptying the Self. And rocking back and forth slowly from one posture to another simultaneously signals the bodymind to enter into a relaxed smooth flow and at the same time activates energy. (As noted in Chapter 4 the unique attribute of the "Tai Chi alphabet" is that the space between the letters is as important as the letters themselves.) Most importantly, the breath alone may become a signal to change from one state to another. In Tai Chi training it is said that eventually just the breath, the intention, or the associated sinking of Qi is enough to recreate the desired state.[10]

From the outline of the ten levels of Bodymind Healing Psychotherapy above, we can see that Bodymind Healing Qigong movements are one dimension of this approach, and are part of a wider system. In my attempt to make the essence of this tradition accessible to modern psychotherapy, I extracted certain elements of the tradition — such as the use of particular styles of breathing, the awareness of sinking of the Qi on the exhalation, the visualization of animal postures, and the awareness of one's life stance — to make this tradition more accessible to Western psychotherapy.

From this wider psychotherapeutic perspective we can see that the practice of Qigong methods can be used to constellate, work with, and focus upon the body blockages that reflect the encumbrances to the soul's journey. We just saw this outlined in the *River of Life* practice. In the chapters that follow, we will see many examples of this method and other Qigong methods combined with psychotherapeutic processes used to transmute psychological issues and create "soul." Most specifically, in the chapter on the *Mythic Journey Process*, we will see not only how the breathing methods of these oriental traditions facilitate the journey into our mythological inner worlds; but we will see how other somatic attributes of the internal martial arts traditions help to anchor the felt shifts created in telling our stories. These methods bring out a soulful dimension to the psychotherapeutic process.

Adding to psychotherapy, the internal martial arts traditions enhance patients' abilities to go through their "underworld journeys."[11] In the following chapters we'll hear the stories of those who have met and engaged in the process of transforming their demons. For example, we'll hear about a case of a woman who had a passive-aggressive style of withdrawal under stress, and for whom the combination of internal martial arts training, animal forms of Qigong, and the *Mythic Journey Process* helped her to shape-shift into a healthier way of being (Chapter 20). And we'll hear about a man with no internal martial arts training who was cut off from his instinctual self and had lost the ability to banter, and how verbal martial arts and affect modulation skills helped him to better defend himself verbally (Chapter 18). The combination of internal martial arts and psychotherapy are an ideal mix to repair and cultivate the vital, primordial Self.

Summary of Applications of Bodymind Healing Psychotherapy in Psychotherapy and Behavioral Healthcare

The following chapters illustrate the various facets of Bodymind Healing Psychotherapy in action. In these chapters, BMHP will be applied to issues including chronic pain, writer's block, addictions, insomnia, trauma, hypertension, workaholism, carpal tunnel syndrome, etc. We will see how Qigong (in the broadest sense of the word) can be integrated with psychotherapy and behavioral healthcare. Obviously, the clinical examples given in these chapters are not proof of the efficacy of BMHP, they are meant, instead, to serve illustrative purposes. Further research is needed to determine with which individuals, and at which times, these methods are most efficacious. Furthermore, BMHP is not meant to be a stand-alone methodology, but rather its intention is to take its stance and join hands with other healing methods in the vibrant mandala of integrative healthcare. To begin to illustrate the breadth and depth of BMHP, the next chapter shows how BMHP is applied to anxiety disorders, specifically with the case of a young woman with a panic disorder.

CHAPTER 6: ANXIETY AND PANIC DISORDERS

Anxiety Disorders: Socio-Political and Economic Background

Anxiety and panic are some of the most common issues treated by therapists in our culture. The National Institute of Mental Health estimates that anxiety disorders afflict 8 percent of the population. Three million Americans are said to suffer from panic disorder or recurrent attacks of anxiety, while eleven million suffer from such variations as phobias, obsessions and compulsions, and chronic levels of apprehension and dread (Breggin, 1991, p. 220).

Many millions of people in our culture use medication for anxiety, creating a multibillion-dollar pharmaceutical industry.[1] A wide variety of questions have been raised as to whether it might be better to make fewer trips to the pharmacy (Altrocchi, 1994).[2] The side effects of anti-anxiety drugs are many, including severe withdrawal symptoms and "rebound anxiety." The use of the medication can even eventually cause an increase of the very symptoms that the drug is supposed to ameliorate. Some medications may even cause brain damage (Breggin, 1991, pp. 244-253.) Also, once a person begins to take these drugs it is difficult, if not impossible, for a therapist or a client to determine whether therapeutic improvements are result of the medication or the other components of the therapy.

Whether or not these drugs are worth the side effects is a complex question that needs to be decided by each individual. There are certainly times when medication seems necessary, for example, when there is an imminent danger to self or others. And many people find anti-anxiety medications help them function when they feel at a loss to do so. But, natural caution dictates that psychotherapeutic methods should be tried first, before using medication. If these methods fail, then we may choose to move up the hierarchy of responses.

Alternative and Complimentary Approaches to Treating Anxiety

In 1991, the Office of Alternative Medicine was mandated by Congress to encourage and support the investigation of alternative medical practices. The ultimate goal was to integrate validated alternative medical practices into health and medical care. The conclusion of the National Institute of Health panel (1996) was that, "Integrating behavioral and relaxation therapies with conventional medical treatment is imperative ..." The panel did not endorse a single technique, but said a variety of them worked to lower one's breathing rate, heart rate, and blood pressure."[3]

Various forms of meditation techniques have been shown through reputable studies to effect anxiety and panic attacks. In one study, Dr. Kristeller, from the University of Massachusetts Medical School's Department of Behavioral Medicine, in conjunction with Dr. Kabat-Zinn researched the effects of Mindfulness Meditation training at their stress clinic and "found that both anxiety and depression dropped markedly in virtually every person in the study" (Kabat-Zinn, 1990, p. 336).

What Qigong Offers to Anxiety Treatment

Having practiced and taught Qigong for over twenty years, I began to wonder whether elements of Qigong could help psychotherapy patients suffering from anxiety disorders. As a traditionally trained psychologist, I was suspicious of claims that any single type of physical intervention could be a panacea for anxiety.

Our anxieties have deep roots in our character structures, our introjected family of origin messages, our beliefs, and in the very condition of being human. The roots of our problems cannot be superficially remedied by a drug, or by the activation of chemicals in the brain that are stimulated by Western forms of exercise, or even by meditative techniques such as Qigong.

In this sense, anxiety is not, in its deepest essence, a demon to be slain or defeated. Since the time of the cavemen and cavewomen, anxiety has operated as a signal to warn of danger. Homo sapiens would not have survived without acting on their anxieties about that noise the saber-toothed tiger made in the woods at night. Likewise today, anxiety signals the fight or flight response in the modern individual who faces the dangers of modern society; as well, it signals us about emotional threats, and it lets us know when we've strayed from our life's purpose. To attempt to slay anxiety is to attempt to destroy the barometer of our souls.

However, despite our philosophical understanding that anxiety has purpose, anyone who suffers from an anxiety disorder knows how vital it is to find a moment of relief from its debilitating effects. Relaxation tools can provide these moments of relief, thereby serving as anchors in the sometimes chaotic or overwhelming sea of life. Once relaxed, we can get in touch with our observing selves in order to reflect upon our issues. Qigong, with its breathing methods and internal martial arts techniques, has evolved over many thousands of years to help us cultivate the awareness and ability to meet fearful situations by cultivating "a neurophysiology of harmony" (Diepersloot, 1995, p. xvi).

Combining psychotherapy, hypnotherapy, and Qigong provides both therapist and client with the ability to integrate two disparate modes of healing — transcending and transmuting. Qigong and hypnosis give us the ability to relax, center, and transcend our ego's limitations by tapping into a wider source of energy — the energy of life, called *Universal Qi*. We thereby can get distance from the "demons of life," and meet them from a place of connecting with the powerful energy of our transpersonal Selves.[4] On the other hand, Western psychotherapy provides the skills to go into, understand, work through, and transmute our underlying psychological patterns — including debilitating forms of anxiety.

Bodymind Healing Psychotherapy's Ten Psychoenergetic Holographic Dimensions Applied to Anxiety/Panic Disorder

In the last chapter I discussed how Bodymind Healing Psychotherapy is a psychoenergetic, holographic approach that integrates Western psychotherapy and Qigong. Here again, for the ease of the reader, I repeat BMHP's ten psychoenergetic, holographic dimensions in order to reiterate my approach and clearly demonstrate how these ten dimensions apply to the treatment of anxiety and panic disorders. Though these ten dimensions often progress in order, they can also emerge organically, in their own time and way, in the therapeutic process. In some cases, one or more levels may be omitted. The ten dimensions may eventually be seen as a hologram, each part containing the others.

1. Taoist Breathing Techniques and Hypnosis (Most often using the *River of Life* practice)
2. Self-soothing
3. Focusing on Felt Meaning
4. Psychodynamics
5. Cognitive Restructuring (plus using a body-oriented SUDS scale)
6. Energy Psychology Methods, including Eye Movement Desensitization Reprocessing (EMDR)
7. The Belly Massage of Chi Nei Tsang (Chia, 1990)
8. Acupressure: Phenomenological Approach, and Acu-yoga (Gach, 1981)
9. Practices from Bodymind Healing Qigong[5]
10. Symbolic Process Approaches to Healing

Following is a case example to illustrate many of these BMHP methods, as they combine Taoist healing techniques with traditional forms of Western psychotherapy,[6] in the case of a woman with severe anxiety manifesting as a panic disorder.

Case Illustration: Panic Disorder

The story of a young woman we'll call "Shelly" is one of those turning point cases that helped to create Bodymind Healing Psychotherapy. Working with her on her panic disorder helped me to see the limitations of my approach to psychotherapy, because certain elements of my approach that had worked with so many other patients, did not work with Shelly. Therapists grow, and the field of psychotherapy grows, as we meet the limitations of our methods. I owe Shelly a debt of gratitude for showing me how each of the ten components of BMHP were necessary for her healing. But in addition, through our work together she helped to forge a pathway that has led me to help many subsequent patients over the years.

Shelly was a 23-year-old woman who had just landed her first job as a graphic artist for a big company. When she first came into my office she was very stiff and her face was frozen, showing almost no emotion. She told me:

> *Whenever too many jobs back up, I have to leave my cubicle. I tell my fellow employees that I have to go to the bathroom—but in reality I'm sweating, heart palpitations and dizziness come over me like an unwanted plague. Sitting on the toilet seat in the bathroom with the door closed, I hope no one will discover what's going on with me. Finally the panic lessens.*

Shelly was literally petrified that her boyfriend and friends would find out about her attacks and reject her. Before our therapy Shelly suffered from adverse side effects from medications used to alleviate her anxiety, so she wanted to find an approach that did not require medication. She told me that she had been to a psychiatrist who, according to Shelly, "tried to push on me the idea that my issues related to the fact that I had been adopted when very young." She left treatment with the psychiatrist because she felt that her anxiety couldn't have anything to do with her early life since she had such a loving relationship with her adopted parents.

After establishing rapport with Shelly, and sending her to a doctor who ruled out medical complications, I wanted to first help Shelly control her symptoms.

Taoist Breathing Techniques and Hypnosis

One popular behavioral method for treating anxiety, phobia, and panic attack is *systematic desensitization*. In this method, a patient's fear is desensitized by combining a state of relaxation with imagining moving closer to the feared object — in this case, the fear of being overwhelmed by the multi-tasking required at work. Shelly's anxiety was so strong that she had a difficult time finding a sense of relaxation with traditional therapeutic methods, such as Jacobsen's technique of tensing and relaxing each part of the body.

Elevator Breathing

After establishing Shelly's openness to experimenting with alternative treatments, I taught her how to activate a deep state of relaxation by using a technique called *Elevator Breathing*, a variation on the *Microcosmic Orbit Breathing* method illustrated in previous chapters.[7] The Taoists believe that healing states can be activated through such techniques of using the breath to "sink the Qi" to the *Tan Tien* area.

> *Notice your out-breath, the pause after the out-breath down in your belly, and the in-breath that comes from there. As you inhale, imagine your energy rising up from the basement below your navel, and up to the crown of your head connecting to the heavens above. As your breath goes out, imagine an elevator descending down to a point just below the belly (Tan Tien). With each succeeding exhalation you'll sink down a little deeper into yourself. Notice how many floors you go down on each breath. How low and how high does your elevator travel? Allow your breath to take your elevator to the level to which it wants to go, without trying or forcing.*

> *The length of the breath that is associated with the development of Qi is called "long-breath." To find it, we imagine that our exhalation is like a tire that has a slow leak in it, and someone is sitting on the tire. This can be differentiated from short breath that is like a blow-out in a tire. Long-breath builds Qi and provides a grounded feeling.*

> *Don't try to force the breath in and out; just notice your natural breathing. As your rate of breathing slows down naturally, the length of time of each part of the process will take longer to complete. For example, if at the beginning you count to four for*

> *each in-breath, pause, and out-breath, after doing a few cycles, the count for each phase of the cycle may increase to seven.*
>
> *Using a water metaphor may further induce the feeling of the descending of the breath and thereby the sinking of the Qi. Imagine that your fingertips and bottoms of your feet are like hoses with the central faucet being just below the belly button. As you breathe out, the water flows down to the sea, carrying out stress and toxins, and relaxing you. On the inhalation, new fresh "water" (or energy) comes in from the universe around you, and the ground under you. Just like water eventually wears away rough spots on a river bank, so will the energy you're contacting wash over your tension and naturally wear it away as it travels down to the sea.*

The Taoists believe, (and virtually anyone can experience, as Shelly did), that breathing out, with focus on this central meridian line, does indeed give the feeling of "sinking the energy (Qi)" as this many-thousand-year-old tradition reports.[8] For virtually every patient with whom I have tried this method, it was of major significance in reducing their panic attacks. But for Shelly, it only provided minor relief. I discovered later that this was, in part, because of how critical she was of herself, and that she feared I would judge or abandon her if she did it wrong.

Chi Nei Tsang — Belly Massage

In addition to the *Elevator Breathing* technique, another Taoist technique can be helpful for treating anxiety, as this one proved to be for Shelly. Following is an adaptation of this technique called *Chi Nei Tsang*:[9]

1. *As you are lying down, place your hands on your belly. Just feel your inhalations and exhalations; notice the way you normally breathe, and whether your hands rise or fall as you breathe in. The Taoists say that in natural breathing, called diaphragmatic breathing, as the breath comes in, the stomach should inflate and the hands should rise. As you breathe out, your stomach should deflate and your hands should follow the falling of the stomach.*

2. *Follow the breath out and, using your hands, press firmly, yet sensitively into whatever tension you feel there. Gradually increase the pressure on the succeeding out-breaths. On the inhalation, let the hands slightly rise and follow the stomach back up. When you feel a spot that is painful, imagine that you have the healing hands of a spiritual Being (your Self) who is sending loving energy to your belly. You'll know when you've spent long enough on a spot by the release you feel.*

3. *Imagine a clockwise spiraling circle around your navel. Imagine that the top of this circle extends out as far as your rib cage, and the bottom extends to your pelvic floor. Picture this circle to be like a clock. On each point on the clock, 12, 3, 6, 9, or all the points in-between, make little circling movements, pressing in with your hands until you reach the point of greatest depth in your body at the end of your exhalation. Then stop and feel.*

Shelly found this processes to be helpful. For the first time, she was able to feel a sense of having some control over the anxiety in her body without psychiatric medication. Though she was very happy to have found some momentary symptom relief from her feelings of anxiety, the symptoms returned between sessions. And though she gradually learned to use these methods herself outside of our sessions, the work was far from complete. In the realm of psychological/spiritual interface, it is often the case that if the psychological complex behind a life issue is not "worked through," the spiritual altered state accessed may not be long lasting. In such instances, the transcendent state merely serves as a temporary anchoring — similar to the effects of a drug. This is the land where spiritual traditions can benefit from psychological knowledge regarding how to transmute the underlying issues.

Psychological knowledge helps us come to terms with our panic in a variety of ways by helping us to: understand how it developed, develop new coping skills, activate new cognitive methods including modulating catastrophic thinking, transmute dysfunction messages, and foster a compassionate relationship towards our issue. In this way, anxiety becomes the dragon's claw that grips us, taking us, sometimes against our will, on a journey of emotional evolution.

Reframing the Meaning of a Symptom

Though BMHP most often uses cognitive restructuring as its preferred cognitive method, here with Shelly I first started with another cognitive therapy method — reframing. Psychotherapy research teaches that a panic attack is often based on fear of fear, and that reframing "fear" as a normal part of the human condition can help to reduce the escalation of anxiety into panic. Reframing a symptom with a metaphor from nature or the outside world, helps to de-pathologize a quality of being and to begin a healing process with it. For example, I pointed to the electric outlet in my office to reframe Shelly's fear. I told her that, "A wall socket can handle just a certain amount of voltage. Just as the fuse box and circuit breaker in the house shuts off the power to give the current running through the line a rest, so do our bodies signal us when we go into overload. Sweating, dizziness, and tightness are "friends" reminding us that we need to find a way to relax." Shelly felt a sense of relief after hearing this metaphor, as if she could accept that maybe her symptom of overwhelm had a purpose of reminding her to relax. We will see how another purpose of this symptom was to initiate her into a transformative inward journey to heal longstanding life issues.

"Focusing" on the Felt Meaning of Anxiety

Shelly felt incompetent and troubled that she didn't know what her feelings of panic were about. Once again, this is where psychological knowledge and Western psychotherapeutic methods help us to discover the specific unique meanings of our individual feelings. One such method is Gendlin's *Focusing* (Gendlin, 1978).[10] The process, as I have adapted it to combine with BMHP, consists of the following six steps:

1. *The first step involves learning to "clear a space" from painful feelings, and the "subpersonality" (Assagioli, 1965) that is associated with those feelings. As mentioned in Chapter 2, I added to the Focusing technique the idea of imagining a river traveling down the "macrocosmic orbit"*[11]

Chapter 6: Anxiety and Panic Disorders 127

>   on the exhalation in order to further facilitate clearing a space from these distressing feelings.[12] Through this integration of Qigong and Focusing, a temporary, healing dissociation from our issue can be created. In this combined method, on the exhalation we imagine negative feelings releasing down the river of breath and coalescing into an image of that subpersonality at a distance from us. This honors Focusing's emphasis on finding the right amount of "breathing room" from our issues, not too close, and not too far. It is from this "right distance" that we can get a "felt sense" of what this issue is "all about."
>
> 2. Secondly, we find a "felt sense" of the issue. A "felt sense" can be distinguished from a feeling by the fact that it is unclear, is experienced as more holistic, and it combines meaning with a body sense. The unclear sense in the body is a place where the meaning feels like it's "on the tip of our tongue," The difference between a feeling and a felt sense is like the difference between being immersed or drowning in the water of a feeling, versus sitting next to the river of our experience and noticing words or images arise that capture the essence of what that feeling state is all about. This involves not thinking about the issue, but directly referring to the body in this state-specific meditative state and allowing meanings to arise. (This is a key component of the transmuting dimension of the River of Life practice.)
>
> 3. Third, we find a "handle word or image" that opens the door to the description of that sense.
>
> 4. Fourth, we "resonate" the emerging thoughts or images back with the body sense to see if we're hitting the center of the target.
>
> 5. Fifth, we "ask questions" of the felt sense, such as "What's the worst thing about this issue?" "What's so ____ about this whole issue?" or " What's the crux of this issue?" We wait until one of the images, words, or sounds gives us the sense that we've discovered the felt meaning of the issue and a "felt shift" occurs.
>
> 6. Sixth, we "receive" the information we get from our bodymind with appreciation, and explore where the information leads us in terms of life changes.

As Shelly embarked on the journey of "focusing" on the tension that blocked her inner river, she discovered a "held back" feeling in her jaw and heart. When she resonated the words "holding back" with the felt sense of all this she realized, "No, it's more like I feel 'ashamed' that, I don't have it together." Though this was an important step at getting closer to the crux of what Shelly's panic was all about, identifying this feeling of shame still didn't produce a "felt shift." Still another level of descent into "the underworld" was needed for Shelly to transmute this issue at a deeper level.

Psychodynamics

The question, "What feels so scary about not having it together?" enabled Shelly to find the bulls-eye of felt meaning, and led her to the psychodynamic roots of her current issue. As she continued to "focus" on the unclear felt sense of "what this whole thing was all about," an image came to her mind. The image of an infant being given away brought tears to Shelly's eyes, and at first she said, "No, it couldn't be about this."

But as the tears turned into sobs, she realized that the deepest, earliest root of this issue was her feeling of being rejected by her birth parents. Though her past psychiatrist had been correct in his assessment, I believe that because he told her his interpretation, rather than allowing it to come from her own bodymind, the interpretation did not take hold, and instead produced a defensive reaction. Shelly knew she hit the target of felt meaning, because she felt it arise from the depth of her own guts. For the first time, she was able to cry about this abandonment. She realized that the fear of being rejected by her friends nowadays felt similar to her fears that her adopted parents would reject her if she didn't meet their standards. We then worked on developing the re-parenting tools needed to soothe herself.

Though Shelly had this deeply cathartic experience, and for awhile the panic attacks subsided at work, soon her panic returned, and scared her. This led to a next layer of her process, and a next level of the development of Bodymind Healing Psychotherapy.

Self-Soothing Using Acupressure Points: The Tao of Re-Parenting

The Tao of re-parenting uses the felt sense in the body and imagery to facilitate the re-parenting of vulnerable emotions. First we try to find an image and felt sense of our actual parents soothing us, but if blocks exist, archetypal imagery can be used to find an energetic connection with a universal mother or father figure.

In the beginning, Shelly held a pillow and tried to imagine her mother soothing her by being compassionate and non-judgmental about her problems getting enough things done at work. Since her natural parents had rejected her, and though there was much love with her adopted parents, Shelly realized she didn't fully trust the unconditional love of her adopted parents. Because she had a hard time finding a self-soothing figure in her personal life, she searched for an archetypal image that could accept her the way she was. Mother Teresa came to her mind, followed by a reduction in her anxiety level from a 7 to a 4 on a SUDS scale of ten.[13]

Chinese medicine, with its knowledge of the acupuncture and acupressure points, complements this imagery work well. Along with using archetypal or personal healing imagery, the therapist can suggest that the patient self-touches an acupressure point on his or her heart with the right hand, and a point just below the navel with the left hand. These points can provide an anchor, so that anytime an unwanted feeling arises in the patient's life, these points can be touched, outside of the session. Similar to when the master hypnotherapist Milton Erickson (Rosen, 1982) said, "My voice will go with you," here the tool of self-touch goes with the patient and serves as an anchor in difficult circumstances, even outside of the therapeutic encounter. One anchoring point that often proves useful is Conception Vessel-17, located at the center of the heart *chakra* according to Taoist theory; and according to Chinese medicine, this point functions to "unbind the chest" (Deadman, 1998, p. 518). This point, also called the *Sea of Tranquility* (Gach, 1990), is on the center-line of the breastbone, four finger-widths up from the base of the breastbone, in an indentation there. To contact our heart's energy we touch this point with the middle finger of the right hand or the whole hand, make small circles, stop, breathe, and feel the energy.[14]

Shelly practiced this method, and with the middle finger of the left hand she also touched her *Tan Tien* acu-point, beneath the navel. The Taoists believe this point is the power center of the body. Shelly was the first patient with whom I tried this physical method of self-soothing, suggesting it to her as an experiment. She later described this self-soothing as one of the most beneficial tools of her therapy.

Self-soothing is deemed by psychoanalytic psychotherapists to be important to repairing the Self (Kohut, 1971, p. 64; Pearlman & McCann, 1992), particularly when soothing was not provided by a person's early primary caretakers (Schore, 2003, p. 171). Bodymind Healing Psychotherapy proposes that physical self-touch of the body, in general, and on particular acu-pressure points on the heart (CV-17, also called Du-17) and the belly (Ren-6, *Tan Tien*), adds a key dimension to self-soothing. I have had many patients tell me that this is one of the things they most remembered about our therapy.

After my work with Shelly, I was feeling that sense of accomplishment and personal satisfaction that comes from having discovered a new addition to the realm of psychotherapeutic healing. I presented this at a few major conferences to the acclaim and appreciation of my colleagues, as I wanted to spread the word and see if it worked as well for their patients as it had for mine.[15] Then one day while I was doing some anthropological research I saw the picture below:

Figure 4: Chiltan Spirit Posture

I was amazed when I saw this picture of the *Chiltan Spirit Posture*, which shows standing figures that have one hand on the heart and the other on their belly (Goodman, 1990). It was exactly what I was doing with my patients. I discovered that this posture was found in Alaska, Arizona, and Tennessee, on the Northwest coast of America, among the Olmecs in Central America, in Bolivia, as well as in Asia in the valleys of Uzbekistan (Gore, 1995, pp. 60-61). At first I felt deflated that the contribution that I thought I had made to the field of psychology was known back so many years ago. But, then I felt a sense of deeper satisfaction that I was aligned with my psychological colleagues from ancient times who took the time to carve out in wood this healing totem, rich with potential healing meanings. Re-discovering this self-soothing gesture was another step on my path of traveling into the earlier roots of psychotherapeutic healing "before modern psychology 'began' in the laboratory of Wilhelm Wundt."

Though we cannot be sure of what meanings these totem carvers intended, it can prove phenomenologically enlightening to follow the tradition of psychological archeology that was developed by Dr. Felicitas Goodman (1990) and her colleagues, and explore holding postures and repeating hand gestures used by indigenous traditions. From doing so, I felt a renewed sense of connection with the importance of a primordially based psychotherapy.

Drawing from psychotherapy's age-old indigenous origins provides a deeper root system that helps all the branches of modern psychotherapy. Touching the heart and belly have cross-cultural healing significance from the chakras of Hinduism to the energy centers of Taoism, and as we see, are also represented in Native America. Chinese medicine gives us more than just these two points to help alleviate anxiety. For example, Kidney-1 (located on the ball of the foot, in the middle, slightly in front of center, toward the toes) is particularly helpful for public speaking phobias. This point is also helpful to ground energy, bringing it down from the head, at times when the ego experiences fragmentation under stress. The Kidney meridian in Chinese medicine is used to deal with the polarity of fear and vitality/strength.

Cognitive Restructuring

Cognitive restructuring could be defined as a type of spiritual transformation of the mind — a spiritual exercise.

— L. Rebecca Propst (1981)

In the process of touching acupressure energy points or doing various movement-based interventions, it is helpful to do "cognitive restructuring" (Beck, 1979). And it was also an important key, as we shall see in a moment, for Shelly's healing. Recently, cognitive therapy techniques have been combined with somatic interventions. For example, in Dr. Shapiro's Eye Movement Desensitization Reprocessing (1995), the patient is instructed in using particular movements of the eyes along with restructuring their beliefs, i.e. instead of an abused person being fixated on a negative cognition such as, "The world is an unsafe place," they might instead verbalize a truthful or constructive new cognition like, "It's over; I'm safe now." In Thought Field Therapy (Callahan, 2001) and in the Emotional Freedom Technique (Craig, 1995) a patient taps on various locations on the body while saying such constructive new beliefs such as "Even though I am not a great public speaker, I can love and accept myself the way I am."

Such restructuring of statements creates a positive transcendence by allowing the mind to access our compassionate observing self, who is then able to put the symptom with which we are identified into proper perspective. When the statement is truthful or constructive it also allows a transmuting of a dysfunctional false belief. Before and after treatment, a measurement is often taken on a SUDS scale. For example, a patient can say, "I can feel O.K. about myself even though I still feel a little____," and then check their SUDS level to determine how much they were actually soothed by the cognition.

Bodymind Healing Psychotherapy adds to cognitive approaches the power of self-touch of key acupressure points, in order to allow us to dip into and activate the well-known primordial healing streams of the ancient sacred wisdom traditions of our ancestors. For example, as we saw above, touching the *Sea of Tranquility* (CV-17) in the center of the chest may lead to a felt sense of a relationship with our transcendental compassionate Self. When we also touch the belly (*Tan Tien*) we may access the psychoenergetic dimensions of love and power, which may aid us in transforming our relationship with our symptom by providing somatic anchors for the new belief. Finding the specific thought forms that express a person's old and new beliefs is an important key.

In Shelly's case, she began with the catastrophic negative belief, "If anyone knows how messed up I am, I'll be rejected." In the field of psychology, it is well-known that catastrophic thinking is one component of panic attacks. BMHP proposes that adding a somatic component to cognitive therapy helps to develop a more grounded, compassionate way of thinking. Through this work, Shelly developed a new, grounded, more constructive cognition, "I deserve to be loved for the way I am, vulnerable and all. I'm willing to take the risk to put out who I really am, and have people in my life who won't abandon me for who I am." Shelly anchored this new cognition by touching the two acupressure points on her heart and belly, using this BMHP self-soothing method. Her face and breath relaxed. Her SUDS level reduced to zero when she focused on her fear in session; and she said that using the self-touch methods outside of session helped her to maintain the connection to our work, and reduced her SUDS level there as well.

Shelly eventually became more comfortable discussing her anxieties and panic attacks with her boyfriend. Another step forward on her path came after telling her boyfriend her deep dark secret about her panic attacks, after which he shared a secret with her regarding abuse in his childhood. This led to increased intimacy between them. Another sign of Shelly's growth was that she was able to better handle the job stressors of being a graphic artist.

A dream she had at this time provided Shelly with more validation of her inner work. Early on in our therapy sessions, Shelly dreamed that she had a beautifully colored flower tattoo that turned into a grey, lifeless flower. During our termination process, she had another dream that the flower's color returned and was even more vivid than it had ever been before. She interpreted this to mean that trying to hide her fears and invalidating her vulnerabilities took the color out of her Self — now her colorful Self was returning.

Similar to the tradition in the Aesclepian temple that a healing dream signaled it was time to leave the temple; Shelly and I saw this dream as a signal to begin the termination phase of our treatment. We were able to discuss how all the elements with which we had been working, were coming together for her — the breathing, the belly massage, the self-touch, the new beliefs and their connection with her wound from the past. This was a first step for me in confirming the holographic dimensions of the model that was to become Bodymind Healing Psychotherapy. Breathing and self-touch without the cognitive and psychodynamic levels are less complete, as are the cognitive and psychodynamic levels less complete without breath and self-touch. It seems to be best when each level is contained within the other, for example when breath and self-soothing is in the cognition, and the cognitions are in the breath and self-soothing. As discussed in the chapter on energy psychology (Chapter 3), the research on self-touch and cognitive therapy showed that cognitive therapy alone was not as successful, or as long lasting, as when the two methods were used together (Andrade & Feinstein, 2003).

In our termination session, after about six months of therapy, Shelly said, "It's not that feelings of anxiety don't arise anymore; but they haven't turned into panic for a long time because I'm able to soothe myself when they arise. I look at life's difficulties as an opportunity to practice 'sinking my Qi.'"

Standing like a Tree Qigong — Finding Your Stance

I have also found a variety of other Qigong methods to be beneficial to patients suffering from anxiety disorders. For example, Standing Meditation Qigong (Standing like a Tree, or *Zhan Zhuang Qigong*)[16] is a method of psychophysiological healing whereby a practitioner learns to find a relaxed stance in life.[17]

Later, in Chapter 15, you'll hear the story of one of my patients with severe anxiety that stemmed in part from his brother's physical abuse, coupled with the message, "I'm better than you at everything." I believe combining psychotherapy with Standing Meditation practice led to a pivotal moment in his therapy, when he found his stance later in his life and said, "You're not better than me at everything, you're not better at being a kind brother." His new cognition coupled with his new stance became "I deserve to be treated with kindness."

Internalized messages from our childhood often contribute to the scattering of our Qi, or in psychoanalytic parlance, "fragmentation." For this reason, we all can benefit from a practice that uses breath and "stance" to constellate our observing selves. From this place of compassion and equanimity, as we watch abusive thoughts arise, we can find a way to return to our ground in kindness and appropriate self-assertiveness. By integrating Western psychotherapy with the body-mind-spirit healing methods of Qigong, the modern person may benefit from the joining hands of Eastern and Western traditions.

CHAPTER 7: QIGONG AND BEHAVIORAL MEDICINE: AN INTEGRATED APPROACH TO CHRONIC PAIN

Perhaps everything terrible is,
in its deepest being,
something helpless that needs our love.

— Rainer Maria Rilke

Case Illustration: Qigong with a Disabled Car Accident Victim

As a nurse at a local hospital, "Terry" had the best hospital care money could buy when she suffered a terrible car accident that crippled her and necessitated the use of a crutch. Her lawyer referred her to me as part of a lawsuit against the person who crashed into her car, pinning her in so badly that the "Jaws of Life" had to be used to free her crushed foot from the accordionized automobile. For six months she suffered with a bad limp, and anytime she tried to reduce her pain medication, Terry found herself in excruciating pain. The doctor that prescribed the pain medication told her she would probably need it for the rest of her life. By the time she came to me she was developing an addiction to the medication. I advised her to reduce the pain medication under the advice and care of her doctor, so that she would be able to determine to what extent the methods we used in psychotherapy were helping her.

Pain and Economics

Surveys indicate that 11 to 12 percent of the adult population in the United States report difficulties related to chronic pain (Steinbach, 1986). According to *The Pain and Absenteeism Report (1996)*, employee benefit managers believe that 20 percent of their employees suffer from various types of pain conditions; and employees think that more than two-thirds of all full-time employees, the equivalent of more than 80 million people, suffer from pain-related conditions.[1] It's hard to fathom that estimates for the direct and indirect costs of pain-related syndromes in the United States each year range between $90 to 100 billion, and that 20 million tons of aspirin are consumed annually (Taylor, 1991).[2]

Research on Complementary Treatment of Pain

A wide variety of well-documented research studies, and the National Institute of Health's (1996) report in the *Journal of the American Medical Association* shows that strong evidence exists for the ability of various techniques of behavioral medicine to alleviate chronic pain, including techniques in relaxation, hypnosis, and meditation.[3] And moderate evidence exists for results in reduction of pain using cognitive behavioral therapy and biofeedback (NIH, 1996, p. 313). The data of meta-analysis consistently showed positive effects of these behavioral and relaxation programs; though evidence was insufficient to show that one technique was more effective than another in reducing chronic pain. "For any given individual patient ... one approach may indeed be more appropriate than another" (NIH, 1996, p. 315). According to the report, the successful techniques all shared some basic components: repetitive focus on a word, sound, phrase, body sensation, or muscular activity; the adoption of a passive attitude toward intruding thoughts; and a return to the object of repetitive focus (NIH, 1996, p. 314). Though Qigong was not mentioned specifically in this report, the above criteria are the very essence of Qigong practice.

In spite of the beneficial results of relaxation methods in general, and Qigong and Tai Chi in particular, for pain relief, we hear less about these natural, no-side effect alternatives for those suffering from the severe debilitating effects of pain than we do about medication. Fueled by drug company advertising and our cultures' propensity for instant gratification, mass marketing has programmed us to go on a quest for "God in a pill" the moment we feel pain.

Certainly, many people suffering from extreme pain have good reason to be thankful to modern pharmacological and medical advances.[4] The decision between when to use these or other pain reducing drugs and when to try to find a more natural choice is a complex one that needs to be decided by each individual.[5] There are certainly times when the advances of modern medicine can be useful, but it seems that caution dictates that natural methods should be tried first before treatment with medication. If these methods fail, then a person may choose to move up the hierarchy of responses.[6]

Modern neuroscience has demonstrated that many chemicals of the outer world are produced in our brains, like the "natural morphine" found in endorphins. An interesting fact is that 30 to 60 percent of patients will experience pain relief by being given a placebo, i.e. an inert pill.[7] This shows that the mind has the ability to activate inner pain medication if we can learn how to turn the key. The question becomes, How, and to what extent, can we increase our abilities to unlock our natural powers?

In a culture like ours, so oriented to the outer world, we oftentimes forget our inner healing resources, just as we forget the old traditions that existed long before the advent of Western medicine that once held knowledge of how to use these abilities to effect healing.

Research on Qigong and the Treatment of Pain

Qigong is one age-old tradition of relaxation and healing that can help sufferers of chronic pain. There are peer-reviewed (Morris, 2000; Wu et al., 1999) and non peer-reviewed (Jin, 1944; Anderson, 2000) articles showing the benefits of Qigong and Tai Chi for the treatment of pain.[8]

It is interesting that in one of the these peer-reviewed studies (Wu et al., 1999) the researchers chose the most severe patients with complex regional pain syndromes. Even here, this group of researchers, which included two medical doctors, concluded that Qigong practice resulted in reducing pain and long-term anxiety. However, the study emphasized that the Qigong result for pain reduction was transient, and didn't last after the patients stopped practicing. This illustrates one of the problems with scientific research — the wrong question can be asked. The important question is whether Qigong can continue to reduce pain with continued practice.

Qigong and Tai Chi come from a "practice model" of healing — meaning one needs to continue the practice to achieve results. Just as we don't expect pain reducing pharmaceuticals to be taken one time and produce results for difficult pain syndromes, likewise it is unreasonable to expect that the benefits of short-term, time-limited Qigong practice will last without continued commitment. Still, this was a very well-designed study that is important in showing Qigong's beneficial effects even with patients with severe pain.

Methods of Qigong and Hypnosis: Partners in Pain Relief

To return to the case of Terry, with whom this chapter began, our work together helps illustrate how Bodymind Healing Psychotherapy applies the methods of Qigong in a psychotherapeutic or behavioral health setting. I will follow my goal of not being overly esoteric so that a therapist can use language and methods that would not be perceived as "selling Qigong," or advocating an oriental method that might seem strange to some Western patients. This is important in a psychotherapeutic setting where transference issues about a health professional's own personal beliefs need to be given due care, and since part of a psychologist's ethical duty is to present new methodologies as experimental (see Chapter 22). Therefore we shall see how Qigong can be presented under the umbrella of the well-researched field of clinical hypnosis in that Qigong adds another method of "trance induction." A next step for researchers will be to study how Qigong compares to other hypnosis methods regarding how it facilitates a relaxation and healing response

Microcosmic Orbit Breathing

When Terry came into my office, I asked her to give me a current rating of her pain on a SUDS scale — 10 being the greatest it had ever been, and 0 being pain free. She said it was an 8 now because she had reduced her medication, as I asked her to do with consultation with her physician. She wanted to "see what this hypnosis stuff could do" for her.

After taking a case history, I introduced Terry to an approach that integrates Qigong and hypnosis without mentioning a word about Qigong. When presenting the methods to patients, this background can be revealed or not, depending upon the given patient's background and the clinical relationship.

The first step in helping to relieve Terry's pain was to teach her how to activate her Qi by noticing her inhalation coming up the "microcosmic orbit." Classical Taoist literature claims that *Microcosmic Orbit Breathing*, when done properly, can help induce a healing state. As discussed more fully in Chapter 4, this breathing method consists of inhaling and allowing the breath to rise up the back, and on the exhalation, imagining the breath going down to the belly (*Tan Tien*), thus creating a circular circuit of breath.

Macrocosmic Orbit Breathing

After Terry moved into a state of relaxation with *Microcosmic Breathing*, I introduced *Macrocosmic Orbit Breathing* (Huang, 1974), which (as also discussed in Chapter 4) is an extension of the above method whereby the person enlarges the circle of breath, imagining it coming up from the ground over the head on the inhalation, and then down the front of the body on the exhalation.

As discussed in Chapter 5 with the *River of Life* breathing exercise, the use of imagery adds to the healing effects of Qigong.[9] I had Terry imagine a waterfall coming down over the top of her head on her exhalation that became a river flowing down through the front of her body and out her damaged foot.

Terry told me that another health practitioner told her to imagine putting healing energy into the pain in her right leg, but that just seemed to make it more swollen. This illustrates the Taoist notion that when there is an excess of yang, we want to decrease the energy there, not increase it, as may happen when we concentrate too much on a point that is already suffering from excess. I told her to experiment with focusing, not on the spot that was hurting, but on the river above and below that spot. Since she described the pain as having a hot, stuck quality to it, the following image was constellated to use along with her *Macrocosmic Orbit Breathing*:

> *Where you feel the energy blocked, you might imagine it as stuck leaves in a river, or anything else that you picture the block to be, and, without forcing it, notice how many breaths it takes for the cool waters to flow through the dammed up place.*

Visualization is a hypnotherapeutic tool often used with chronic pain patients (Hilgard, 1983). The Taoist parallel and addition to this idea is to use the thousand-year-old understanding of the meridian lines and vital points of the body to activate the vital energy of the body (Qi) to aid this process. Terry visualized the *Bubbling Well* point (Kidney-1) at the bottom of her foot with water being drawn into the body from there, then spiraling up the leg and up the back of the body over the top of the head, to the *Baihui* point.[10] Then Terry visualized it coming down the front of her body and exiting at the foot through the *Bubbling Well* point. The Taoists, and practitioners of Chinese medicine, believe this point is one key place where energy can be drawn into the body, as well as being a point where the waters of life can wash out toxins from the body.

In the first session, Terry's pain decreased to a 2 SUDS level. She was amazed because this was the most pain-free she had been without medication since her accident six months before. In subsequent sessions, Terry learned these and other methods to use with her pain. In our second meeting she was able for the first time to experience a 0 SUDS level. With the consent of her doctor, she started to use medication on a less frequent basis. In the third and subsequent meetings, we focused our efforts on achieving this state outside of session.

Yin-Yang Balancing Method

One other method I taught Terry to ease her pain was the *Yin-Yang Balancing Method*. I derived this method from a hypnotherapeutic technique called "pain transferal" (Hilgard & Hilgard, 1983, p. 65; Crasilneck & Hall, 1985, p. 105), which involves a person imagining the transferal of his or her pain from one to another part of the body.

By adding to this the idea of *yin* and *yang* in Taoist theory, we have the benefit of adding a many-thousand-year-old understanding of the pathways of energy in the body, thereby allowing

Chapter 7: Qigong, Behavioral Medicine and Pain   137

the person to transfer the pain, or energy, by coming into alignment with a ready-made stream. Whether we want to believe that this stream is "real," when we visualize it, and imagine that it is real, our mind activates our healing powers.[11]

In the *Yin-Yang Balancing Method*, a person imagines more energy flowing through the *yin* (cold, weakened) part of the body and less energy going through the *yang* (hot, strong, acutely injured) part of the body. Terry learned to imagine and experience her breath turning into warm water flowing through her uninjured left leg, and cooling gentle waters flowing through her injured leg.

Terry learned to play with the sensations, and to control and trick her body. Never mentioning a Chinese word or the term "Qigong," I introduced her to an idea from the tradition of *Yi Chuan* (the mind or intention behind the various systems of Chuan) that energy (Qi) follows intention (Yi). While she was in a relaxed trance state, I gave her the hypnotic suggestion that her left leg was the one that was in the accident instead of the actually injured, right leg. She did indeed experience that this left ankle felt very painful. Then I brought her out of trance and she was able to see how powerful her mind was in creating pain. When I presented this case at one conference, I was criticized for using hypnotherapeutic methods to create pain. However, this temporary "creation of pain" serves the higher purpose of helping a patient to discover the role of their mind in creating, controlling, and healing pain. After seeing how her mind alone could create pain in her left leg, I taught her how to release this pain by imagining a river of breath coming all the way down to the bottom of the foot (Kidney-1). As a further way of working with left-right imbalances and one-sided pains common in many cases of chronic and acute pain, I introduced her to the following method, which I call the *"Energy Hula-Hoop."*

The Energy Hula-Hoop

1. *Imagine a vertical hula-hoop with water flowing through it, circling through the points on both ankles and going up to the hips.*

2. *Between the two feet there is a break in the hula-hoop, where, when desired the water can be released to the earth.*

3. *Breathe in and up through the left leg around the hips and on the out-breath down and out the right leg and foot.*

Each time the sensations of pain arose in her right or left ankle, I asked Terry to imagine what it felt like. At first the hula-hoop was blocked like stuck leaves where her injury was, but gradually, as she imagined the water flowing through the leaves, she felt the blockage clear. While she was playing with her mind-body connection, she forgot which leg was the one in the accident.

Finding the Healing Ball of Qi with Your Hands

The use of various postures is another Taoist contribution to alleviating pain. One posture involves experiencing the magnetic force between the *Laogong* points in outstretched palms to enhance the healing ability and cultivate the Qi (vital energy) in our hands.[12] A world apart and a thousand years later, directing a patient to imagine that there is a force that attracts outstretched hands together is well known in hypnotherapy. In the Stanford Hypnotic Clinical Scale, one of the methods used to assess a patient's ability to enter into trance is by having them practice this method.[13]

Another hypnotherapist who uses the outstretched hands to create trance is Dr. Ernest Rossi. He uses it for the purpose of ideomotor (ideodynamic) signaling to measure the patient's responsiveness to the inner work occurring. According to Rossi (1988), "If your creative (healing) unconscious is ready to begin therapeutic work, you will experience those hands moving together all by themselves to signal yes; but, if there is another issue that you need to explore first, you will feel those hands being pushed apart" (p. 39).

In Qigong practice, a similar posture is held, though the methodology is more intricate (having developed over thousands of years) and the intention is broader. The two traditions could benefit much from learning from each other. The hypnotherapist focuses on using the outstretched hands to create a "trance" and to facilitate the reorganization of the psyche. For the practitioner of Qigong, the energy in the outstretched hands is developed for the purpose of self-defense, personal empowerment, and healing acute and chronic disease. As well, a long Taoist lineage promotes the practice of meditation in these postures in order to find keys to open the energy gates to the spiritual healing energy of the body and the cosmos.[14] Cultivating the energy in-between the hands is viewed as a way to affect the universe of energy that the practitioner holds, qualitatively and quantitatively.

For example, the *Yi Chuan Qigong* tradition is oriented to cultivating a "ball of Qi," which can then be used for whatever purpose the practitioner chooses.[15] "Yi" translates as intention, and "*Chuan*" literally translates as fist. But the esoteric meaning of holding the five fingers into a fist is to grasp, or bring into a whole, the healing energies of the five elements: fire, earth, metal, water, and wood. Depending upon the practitioner's intention, the *Yi Chuan* postures can be used for self-defense, healing, personal empowerment, or transforming Qi into *shen* (spirit). The outstretched hands in the position used in the Stanford scale and by Rossi is virtually identical to position number six of the eight postures used in the *Yi Chuan*.

In this tradition, a period of sitting or standing in stillness is advised as a first step before raising the two hands into a fixed posture.[16] These meditation positions are very specific and are oriented to developing the body's energy in a multiplicity of ways.

There are many postural elements to be aware of while practicing Sitting or Standing Meditation. For example, while sitting, place yourself on the edge of the chair, the spine is straight, chin slightly tucked, hands are face-down on the knees, and your feet are straight forward and under the knees. For Standing Meditation, the hands are by the side, the feet straight forward, knees slightly bent, chin slightly tucked, and the pelvis is slightly tucked so that the *Ming Men* (located behind the *Tan Tien*, in the center of the lower back) is filled out.[17]

The spine is naturally stretched by these methods so that the Qi sinks and the spirit is raised. Once in position, the practitioner may be instructed to practice *Microcosmic Orbit Breathing* for a few minutes, to focus on the natural breath, or to focus the intention on the *Tan Tien*.[18] Then the teacher may tell the practitioner to allow the hands to rise, as if in water, until they are in front of the heart. In this movement, the palms are facing each other as if they are holding a helium balloon, the elbows are slightly away from the body and are not locked. The practitioner continues the breathing techniques mentioned above with the hands in this position, and then is instructed to see if he or she can experience a "stickiness" as the hands are gently pulled apart, away from the ball of energy. Likewise, the person is instructed to try to compact the ball of energy and see if he or she can experience its substance (see Chapter 25, *Ocean Wave Breathing*).

In more advanced practice, a student of the tradition learns to direct the Qi of the meridians with his or her intention. One method is to focus the intention on one hand and note any sensations or energy that follow the movement of awareness (as we did in the similar practice in Chapter 4). Small, circular hand movements are sometimes used to enhance this direction of healing energy into the *Laogong* points in the center of the palms or fingertips.[19] For example, in the *Tai Chi Ruler Qigong* tradition (*Tai Chi Chih*), wooden balls are held between the palms and circular movements are practiced to open the *Laogong* points.[20] The practitioner is also instructed in how to cultivate Qi by moving the hands in small circles without the ball there.

It would be heuristic to further explore how the combination of hypnotherapeutic visualization techniques with Qigong postures enhances "trance" and healing. In my private practice, for example, I may ask a client to imagine the following:

> *The ball that you feel in your hands can be filled with whatever you desire, and its energy can be directed to wherever you choose. First, you might imagine that the love in your heart enters into the balloon. Then, just as when earlier you felt energy enter into one hand through the direction of intention there, so can you feel its energy spread throughout the body wherever you want to direct it. By letting go on your exhalation and imagining the compassion of your heart melting any ice blocks in the rivers of your Qi, you can gradually let go of tension in your body and direct that liberated healing energy to wherever it is needed.*

Acupressure Points and Pain

In various Qigong traditions (such as acupressure), touch is used to focus the Qi. By teaching psychotherapy clients to touch their own acupressure points, rather than a practitioner touching them, various ethical and clinical problems can be avoided (Kilberg, 1988, pp. 487-491; Goodman, 1988, pp. 492-500).

Getting back to the case of Terry, after she learned to hold her hands apart to activate the experience of the ball of Qi in her hands, we moved on to practice how she might now direct that energy for her own self-healing. I showed Terry how to use the *Yin-Yang Balancing Method* combined with touch. When the inside of her ankle hurt, she learned to touch and direct healing energy to points on the outside of the ankle more strongly, as she either very lightly made contact with the inside point that hurt, or didn't touch the inside point at all as she directed her healing intention to the point from a few inches away.

When Terry touched a point in the little hollow anterior to the outside ankle bone (Gall Bladder-40) known to be beneficial to ankle pain, she reported a release of the pain down to a 0 SUDS level within ten exhalations, accompanied by a perception of green light filling the room. (Terry had never had an experience of seeing light like this before.) If the outside of the ankle hurt, we would have similarly had her experiment with touching a point next to the inside of the ankle bone (such as Kidney-4). Also, Terry learned to press acupressure points more strongly on the ankle opposite to the one that was hurt, and to touch points on her hurt ankle more softly, or not at all. This helped her to learn to balance the energy in both legs. In the very first session that she tried this, she had the experience of creating that balance.

Terry began to see her homework as a spiritual practice to learn to work with her pain and let it teach her. She imagined opening her heart to send love to the hula-hoop of her pain. She also reported an experience of the water in the hula-hoop dissolving into water vapor and leaving her body — as the boundaries between herself and the world dissolved into a pleasant feeling of lightness and heaviness combined. If an old Taoist was listening to modern Terry, he or she might describe the boundless feeling she experienced as *wuji*, described in ancient texts as the void, emptiness or healing reservoir from which Qi derives.[21]

After five sessions Terry felt like she no longer needed to see me because she was able to achieve a 0 SUDS pain level anytime she did the above practices. In addition, she noted improvement in her ability to walk during this time (though from a scientific standpoint we cannot know whether this improvement in ability to walk was a function of time and would have occurred without treatment).[22]

An important final note of caution: Not all people will find relief from these methods as quickly as Terry did. From the perspective of Qigong, the path to spiritual growth involves more than just getting rid of pain, it involves letting go of "trying" to get rid of pain. "Trying" constricts the river of Qi, "letting go" to our process allows the river to expand and find its natural course. There may be moments when we hit into rocks in the downward currents of the river of our pain; these moments can serve as reminders to breathe in and out of our pain to find our center as we ride the rapids of physical and emotional agony. At other moments our breath leads us to merge with *wuji*; and we are held in the warm embrace of the ocean of energy that is the mother of all life.

With any technique we need to be careful that we don't produce a personal attribution of shame when a "cure" doesn't come as quickly as we might like. Hence the distinction between "cure" —the absence of symptoms, and "healing"— an attitude that whatever life presents us with is an opportunity for psychospiritual growth in the midst of suffering. Many patients who have described more severe and long-lasting pain than Terry, report being thankful that they have Qigong as a partner that gives them breathing room and helps them to find a compassionate relationship to being with pain.

Dealing with Various Types of Pain: The Medicine Wheel of Possibilities

Each different type of pain leads us on a journey to different methods from the wide variety of healing traditions. Native Americans would say that each place on the "medicine wheel" has its value (Storm, 1972). For example, sometimes the pain, due to a subluxated vertebrae, may be best helped by a chiropractic adjustment. At times when through our own Qigong practice we are unable to remove a given energy block, an acupuncture treatment may help. When a person is too debilitated to practice Standing or Sitting Meditation, maybe doing yoga postures while lying down will be the best way in which to breathe and work with the pain. Sometimes prayer may help (Dossey, 1993).

It is in these various ways that pain leads us on a journey to rediscover the natural healing elements of the world around us. The most basic elements of the yin and yang of life, such as hot and cold, may become the medicine we need. We might experiment with using ice packs during the early phases of an acute injury, and warm compresses during the later stages; or in the case of chronic blockages, we might find that going back and forth between warm and cold packs may do the trick. An herbalist may have information to remind us that the world of nature is our ally (Heinerman, 1988). Homeopathic remedies (Edinger, 1985) are based on the notion that "like cures like." They use the minutest amounts of a substance to create a healing response in our immune system — for example using a highly diluted amount of nettles to heal pain. Homeopathic treatment opens our minds to wonder about the healing potentials of the things around us that we take for granted.

Western doctors and medications may help us to appreciate being part of an evolving civilization, for the pain-killing medications used by modern pharmacology often derive from the biological intelligence that has been developing for eons in the natural world. For example, a new pain relieving drug, SNX-111, is a synthetic copy of a natural neurotoxin isolated from the venom of sea-going snails.[23]

Qigong energetic practices can be viewed as a center-point in the "medicine wheel approach" to pain; they can be combined with any other approach, including pharmacological. For example, in a research study in China, 127 patients with advanced cancer were divided into two groups — a Qigong practicing group and a control group that did not practice Qigong. Both groups took medication. The Qigong group improved significantly compared to the control group in the following measures: strength, appetite, diarrhea free, weight gain, and in their immune systems' phagocyte rate. In addition, the Qigong practices helped to ameliorate the effects of the medications (Sancier, 1996).[24]

Each different type of pain initiates us into the lessons of its own particular pathway. At times, finding ways to distance ourselves from the pain is helpful. We use our breath to find a calm place inside where we know we have pain, but are not identified with that pain. We may thereby learn to cultivate concentration and equanimity in the midst of our suffering. At other times, we may choose to go into the pain. Buddhist Mindfulness Meditation practice can be very helpful at such times — to be with the sensation of pain instead of distancing from it.[25] As we explore its various qualities, such as temperature and tightness; metaphors may arise of pinpricks, knife stabbing, or demons grabbing our stomachs while we "shape-shift" into yogis, or internal martial artists, or any subpersonality that can explore and handle the elements of pain. Something about us may indeed transform in the "being with it" — a self-sufficient, isolated person may reach out for others, or a critical, judgmental person may finally find compassion for his or her pain instead of fighting against it.

"Focusing" on the Meaning of Pain

> *Our complexes are not only wounds that hurt and mouths that tell our myths, but also eyes that see what the normal and healthy parts cannot envision ... Afflictions point to gods, gods reach us through afflictions.*
>
> — James Hillman

Every pain contains a message that has its own unique meaning and its own voice. If we listen to its message, we are led to appropriate action. Sometimes our stomach pain says that a certain food is disagreeable to us, other times, that pain may mean that a psychological issue needs to be faced. Learning to read the deeper messages behind our feelings is the missing ingredient in "symptom relief" schools of thought on pain.

Western psychotherapy has many tools to discover the meaning of pain. For example: psychoanalysis uses free association, phenomenological methods allow a person to explore his or her own unique experience, hypnotherapeutic traditions have contributed imagery and relaxation methods, and cognitive-behavioral psychology has contributed techniques involving shifts in attitude, distraction, and imagery. Gendlin's Focusing (1978), as outlined in detail in Chapter 6, involves a six-step process for finding the felt meaning of any psychological issue, including pain.[26]

For example, using the Focusing method, one man in his early 40s focused on the thoughts that arose while breathing into, and out from, his chronic lower back pain. He remembered repeated beatings with a wire coat hanger by his mother when he was a child. He was able to begin a process of working through his feelings about this, and releasing the held emotions that had been stored there for years. In the case of a placating, continuously smiling teacher who focused on her recurring headaches, she realized that they often occurred when her husband didn't help with the housework and meal preparation. By being conscious of the meaning of her pain she was able to work through a longstanding message from her matrilineal lineage that "women are supposed to grin and bear it." When she expressed her feelings, including anger, she noticed that her headaches disappeared.

Generally speaking, in cases of internally generated pain such as headaches, muscular aches, and energy blockages, stress begins at the level of mind, signaling us that inner emotional reprogramming needs to take place. These symptoms, or off-centered patterns, first manifest on the level of Qi, then are translated into the musculature, and finally may manifest as spinal subluxation. By using psychotherapy in conjunction with Qigong practices, we can work on realigning ourselves and finding our center in the midst of the crosscurrents of our emotional terrain. The *Yi Chuan Standing Meditation Qigong* practices discussed earlier can be particularly helpful in this regard, for experiencing and realigning structural deficits that derive from our genetic and characterological makeup.

Conclusion

This chapter began by referencing the 1996 *Journal of the American Medical Association* report from the National Institute of Health panel's review of numerous, well-designed studies of pain relief. The panel concluded that chronic pain could be significantly reduced with a wide variety of behavioral and relaxation methods.

In the foregoing case illustration of Terry, we explored how Qigong can be an addition to the relaxation and hypnotherapeutic methods that have been used to alleviate the suffering of people with chronic pain. As a practitioner, I have appreciated seeing the positive effects of these age-old Chinese methods in my private psychotherapy and behavioral healthcare practice on Western patients with a wide variety of acute and chronic, pain-related syndromes including cancer, multiple sclerosis, and back and neck problems.[27] As well, I feel grateful for having the opportunity to stand at a place and time where the streams of Western behavioral medicine and ancient Qigong practices can merge together to benefit people in healing body and mind.

In the next chapter I will go more deeply into the realm of psychosomatically based pain and how Bodymind Healing Psychotherapy methods helped a man who had physical back pain that was rooted in a previous trauma.

CHAPTER 8: TRAUMA AND POSTTRAUMATIC STRESS

*Trauma often disconnects a person from her or his center or self–
the essence of positive emotional wisdom and guidance
that is best equipped to guide us.*

— Asha Clinton (2002)

The New Biology and Somatic Approaches to Healing Trauma

Since both Qigong and Tai Chi have self-defense and empowerment methods at their core, it is natural to look at what they, and other body-oriented, mind-body methods might contribute to those suffering from posttraumatic stress. First let's take a look at the growing field of stress research, where recent research helps us understand more about the role of brain and biochemical reactions in the creation of, and healing of, stress.

In his book, *Why Zebras don't get Ulcers*, Robert Sapolsky (1988) shows that when our bodies face stressors perceived as life endangering, in order to maximize our power our arteries constrict like a hose maximizing its powerful force. However, this adaptive stress response, when prolonged, creates excess glucocorticoids, which lead to certain physiological dysfunctions. When primordial survival mechanisms are activated in modern high stress situations for which they were not designed, they are no longer adaptive. Thus, a big key to transforming locked-in, stress responses is to use various bodymind healing methods that unlock such non-adaptive patterns.

The field of "new biology" has also contributed to this understanding. Dr. Bruce Lipton (2005), one of the foremost thinkers in the field of the new biology, says that there is a primordial, psychobiological ground to the stress response. As we approach danger we activate the hypothalamus, pituitary, adrenal, (HPA) axis; this stops our ability to fight disease as we focus on survival. When our "survival-self" hears the sound of a lion, our bodies halt the fight against infection in favor of mobilizing energy for flight and fight. The HPA axis interferes with our ability to think clearly. The forebrain center of logic is significantly slower than the reflex activity controlled by the hindbrain. Stress hormones constrict the blood vessel in the forebrain, thus reducing its ability to function (Lipton, 2005, p. 150). This sheds some light on why, when we are fixated in a state of over-stimulated sympathetic nervous system over-arousal, we develop various chronic diseases and lose our ability to think clearly. Many of my patients, and I'm sure other therapists' patients, feel a sense of profound appreciation when hearing about this research. One patient cupped his hand to his head in a gesture of relief and said, "Now I understand why I've always felt like I was stupid when I was in a major conflict."

In the arena of posttraumatic stress, there have been many contributions to understanding why the role of the body is significant to healing. Dr. van der Kolk, the prolific author of one hundred articles in the field, says that, "The basic assumption that finding words to express the facts and feelings associated with traumatic experiences can reliably lead to a resolution turns out to be wrong" (van der Kolk, 2002, p. 62). His research in brain functioning shows that when trauma occurs, the trauma is held in the right brain where it is inaccessible to verbal therapies.

He posits, and much research is now confirming, that for many conditions, psychotherapies that incorporate the body are more successful than traditional therapies (Shapiro, 1991; Andrade & Feinstein, 2003; Wells et al., 2003).

Dr. van der Kolk and others have therefore reoriented their research direction due to understanding the importance of the body in healing. For example, infants have demonstrated the ability to heal from trauma and stress from being touched, making sounds, and through movements such as rocking. (van der Kolk, 1995). Another author in the field, Dr. Levine (1997), author of *Waking the Tiger: Healing Trauma,* draws from animal sources showing the way that animals, such as impalas, heal from trauma. He explains how, when being chased as prey, once the impala's fight, flight, or freeze response is activated, it will often play dead. When the impala stops moving, its predator, the cheetah, takes its awareness off the impala, and the impala escapes. The impala then heals through shaking, and by replaying the trauma by reenacting with fellow impalas the drama of the cheetah attack. This has formed part of Dr. Levine's method of *Somatic Re-experiencing,* i.e. using the body to heal from trauma.

In realizing the importance of the body in healing, Dr. van der Kolk became interested in new methods of therapy such as Eye Movement Desensitization Reprocessing (EMDR). In EMDR (Shapiro, 1995) traditional cognitive restructuring[1] is combined with a body-oriented approach of moving the eyes back and forth across the center-line. This method has shown promising results with posttraumatic stress, though it is still unclear as to exactly why. Some posit that it breaks up fixations in the brain where "dead spots" stop normal cognitive functioning from operating (Ruden, 2005). The key to a person's healing from trauma is to be able to be in the present, rather than react with the inflexible responses based upon the past trauma. Drawing from theories in physics many therapists are now pursuing a "bottom up" (meaning from the body to the mind) approach.[2]

Researchers like Dr. van der Kolk put forth experimental evidence from brain scans about the effectiveness of various types of body-based psychotherapy approaches in healing trauma (van der Kolk, 1996, 2002; Rauch et al., 1996). One of the keys to healing posttraumatic stress is the stimulation of the meaning reorganization centers of the brain such as the amygdala (LeDoux, 1986, 1992), where new metaphors and new contexts emerge. After body-based therapies such as EMDR, brain scans do show a reactivation of these and other important areas of brain functioning (van der Kolk 1996, 2002; Shapiro, 1996).

The importance of the role of the body in healing was seen in the chapter on energy psychology. In Chapter 3 we saw how preliminary research in the field of energy psychology, substantiated by brain wave imaging and independent raters assessments, shows that meridian-based tapping plus cognitive therapy is more effective than cognitive therapies alone in dealing with anxiety (Andrade & Feinstein, 2003). Some postulate that one of the key elements of body-oriented energy psychology, such as tapping on acu-points on the body, may have a neurobiological basis behind its ability to work (Ruden, 2005).

In this era of bringing body-oriented approaches into psychotherapy, Qigong and Tai Chi have much to offer to help reverse sympathetic nervous system overload that comes from the fight, flight, or freeze response. As internal cultivation (*neigong*) traditions (Cohen, 1997; Kohn, 1989) they have developed over many centuries to help reverse the flight, fight, and freeze response for purposes of health and self-defense.

So, it is no wonder that a psychiatrist such as Dr. van der Kolk is experimenting with using Qigong in his trainings of trauma therapists. From the catalogue at his workshop on *Frontiers of Trauma Treatment* given at Esalen Institute (February, 2005) he says that, "Recovery needs to incorporate physical experiences that contradict feelings associated with helplessness and disconnection. The goal of treatment is to help bring the traumatic experience to an end, in every aspect of the human organism. This includes experiencing physical mastery to initiate new ways of perceiving reality and promoting new behavior patterns." In his workshops, towards this end, Dr. van der Kolk incorporates yoga, EMDR, Mindfulness Meditation, theater, breathing, touch, and Qigong.

I feel very honored that he is using my *Bodymind Healing Qigong DVD* in his trainings of trauma therapists. In addition, to its long history of helping practitioners move from sympathetic nervous system overactivation to parasympathetic nervous system relaxation, Qigong and Tai Chi have other benefits. For example, Volume I discussed how Qigong and Tai Chi's various movements activate *sung*, defined as "relaxed awakeness;" so these traditions both relax and re-empower — a valuable contribution to those suffering from trauma. A wide variety of Tai Chi and Qigong movements can also be useful for establishing new state-specific states of consciousness that "contradict feelings associated with helplessness and disconnection," as is shown in the case illustrations throughout this book.

One of the unfortunate outcomes of early childhood trauma is the development of "reactive instead of stable attachment styles." (Schore, 2003). This is one of the most common problems standing in the way of making relationships work for those who have suffered from childhood trauma. In cases of early childhood trauma, or where general experiences of the stability of the self was not nurtured, or where there was neglect or ongoing maltreatment (Briere, 1997), Tai Chi and Qigong have the potential to be ideal complementary practices to psychotherapy. Those with reactive attachment disorders oftentimes respond to life stressors with retriggered fear and the activation of emotionally labile qualities rather than with modulated coping strategies. Tai Chi and Qigong can help to develop a cohesive center when the everyday issues of life assault or impinge upon ones sensibilities; and they can provide a bodily base for developing affect modulation and affect tolerance.

Using Qigong to Modulate -the Sympathetic Nervous System Stress Response

Tai Chi Ruler (for an illustration see Chapter 24) is one such exercise that helps to reverse the fear response in the body by the action of simultaneously lifting the hands while sinking the body's energy to the center of the body in the belly and lower back (the *Tan Tien* and *Ming Men*). As an example, I recall a perfectionistic manager of a local company who was preparing to be a witness in a court case involving the murder of a family member. As part of his psychotherapy we practiced *Tai Chi Ruler*; he found the body movements and the sinking of the Qi to be helpful to ground himself in a state that countered his introjected paternal critic and the resultant obsessive need to get everything right. Then, at trial, with reported success he touched his belly (*Tan Tien*) as a cue to remind him of the sinking of the Qi that he had experienced with the *Tai Chi Ruler* practice in his psychotherapy sessions to anchor this centered subpersonality. This is similar to the common behavioral treatment method "systematic desensitization" where the relaxation response is used to reciprocally inhibit an unwanted behavior (Wolpe, 1958). Instead, here we are using Tai Chi and Qigong movements to de-condition and reciprocally inhibit an unwanted response.

Many times the circumspect clinician will find it impractical or incongruent with modern psychotherapy to ask a patient to stand up and practice *Tai Chi Ruler* in a session. So, psychotherapists can extract out the essence of the internal martial arts tradition to help patients in a variety of ways. For example, patients can be introduced to the *Elevator Breathing* method (see Chapter 6) as a way to sink their Qi without doing a Qigong movement. In the following chapters we shall see various examples of how patients can significantly increase their relaxation response, producing useful effects for psychotherapy and behavioral healthcare.

Dr. van der Kolk (1996) says that the first task of treatment is for patients to regain a sense of safety in their bodies; "Assault victims often benefit from 'model-mugging' programs, and physical challenges such as Outward Bound programs. Many women whose bodies have been violated report having been able to regain a sense of physical safety with the help of therapeutic massages" (p. 18).

One of the deepest injuries of severe trauma is that it "disconnects a person from her or his center or self — the essence of positive emotional wisdom and guidance that is best equipped to guide us." (Clinton, 2002, p. 101). Multimodal treatment approaches are a key element of many psychotherapeutic approaches that attempt to help restore patients' connection with the core of themselves. Finding a new ground of safety in one's body is a key to healing. As this ground in safety is found, emotional work can begin and over-reactivity can begin to be modulated. For example, Krysal (1978), Pennebaker (1993), and Nemiah (1991) have all discussed the critical importance of learning to identify and utilize emotions as signals rather than as precipitants for fight and flight reactions.

BMHP proposes that many elements of the internal martial arts tradition, such as learning to sink Qi in response to an imagined or actual aggressor, can be beneficial in finding a new ground in safety in the patient's body. Once this ground is re-established, then the patient can begin the inner work required to heal from his or her trauma.

Helpful Methods from Qigong and Tai Chi

In general, the practice of Tai Chi and Qigong have long been used to reprogram the body and the nervous system to re-establish a neurophysiology of harmony. Not only in the East, but in the West as well, enactments of physical movements have been a part of the healing process. For example, we spoke earlier about one of the rituals of the first holistic healing temple in the Western world, the temple of Aesclepius. As part of the healing process, people would be sent to the Dionysian theater to act out a part in a play, which would be helpful to their healing.

With respect to healing trauma, when appropriate, I have suggested to my trauma patients that they practice various Animal Qigong movements or other aspects of the Bodymind Healing Qigong tradition. Tiger movements from *Yi Chuan Qigong* (see Volume I) are one type of practice that has particularly helped quite a few of my patients in reestablishing power in the re-empowering phase of treatment. A rape victim still carrying the trauma ten years later reported having benefited from the courage to practice *Tai Chi Push Hands*; she reported that these practices taught her how to feel in her body the ability to use her gentleness and a yielding movement to turn back an aggressive force of an attacker. Certainly due caution needs to be exercised in not being overconfident of our abilities to fend off an aggressor; here I am addressing the re-empowerment that is part of the recovery phase in trauma care.[3]

Depth Psychotherapy and Trauma

Healing of trauma involves much more than just finding safety and groundedness in the body. What depth psychology teaches is that oftentimes the psychological results of trauma "develop not in response to the trauma per se, but in reaction to the fantasies through which it gets an attributed meaning." (Kalsched, 1996, p. 95). Thus a fundamental aspect of psychotherapeutic healing is to help patients come to terms with the meaning of the trauma. It is common for those who have been a subject of abuse to develop patterns such as withdrawing from conflict, being a victim, or being an unconscious perpetrator — because, "when innocence has been deprived of its entitlement it becomes a diabolical spirit." (Grotstein, 1984).

In Dr. Kalsched's (1996) profound book called *The Inner World of Trauma*, he says that one aspect of the depth psychological answer to healing such patterns is through *lumen* (light) and *numen* (meaning). This type of "light" that heals trauma in the Western mystery tradition has been called *lumen naturae* (the light of nature), or *soma pneumatikon* (spirit body), which is related to the body's animating spirit. Dr. Jung, drawing from an old alchemical text, put it this way, "There is in the human body a certain aethereal substance ... of heavenly nature, known to a very few, which needeth no medicament, being itself the incorrupt medicament." (Jung, 1955, para., 114n).

The parallels between the Western notions of this healing *lumen* and the Qigong practices that have remained intact in the East are striking. I propose that these *lumen*-generating practices can be incorporated to help heal trauma. Likewise, regarding the healing tool of *numen*, after going though the descent into the felt darkness of the traumatized complex, a key moment in healing often comes when the patient finds a new meaning, such as "this abuse led me to be a healer, helped me to be more sensitive to the suffering of others." We will show how finding a new meaningful life stance is a key element in the *Mythic Journey Process* and in various other aspects of the Bodymind Healing Qigong tradition.

Bodymind Healing Psychotherapy's Approach to Trauma

In many of the following chapters case illustrations of patients are presented who could as easily have fit in this chapter on abuse, instead I will use their cases to illustrate other important themes of Bodymind Healing Psychotherapy. For example, in Chapter 16 on incorporating patients' gestures, we will hear about a case of a female victim of sexual abuse who naturally came up with a posture like the Tai Chi movement, *Fist under Elbow*, which helped to give her a sense of safety and groundedness in her body. This helped her to have the confidence to deflect the assaultive energy she felt coming from aggressive men. She reported that the sense of groundedness that developed from her Standing Meditation and Tai Chi helped give her a safety zone, where she was better able to differentiate men's intentions and better able to modulate her responses to men. In Chapter 15, about changing your life stance, we'll hear the story of a young man who was the victim of his brother's physical abuse, and how Standing Meditation Qigong helped him find his stance of power with his brother.

In the chapter on the *Mythic Journey Process* (Chapter 20) we'll see an example of a woman who was a rape victim, and had passive-aggressive tendencies that were endangering her marriage. A combination of psychotherapy, learning the animal movements of Qigong, and a *Mythic Journey Process* helped her to realize she was being "an ostrich rather than an openhearted crane." She reported that all of the above traditions, including doing the *Crane* movement from the animal forms of Qigong, helped her to transform her withdrawing pattern and develop a more open, modulated and expressive communication style with her husband.

It is important to remember the advice in Chapter 4 from "The Master with the Ping Pong Ball," that isolated movements may go along with the technique-oriented Western mind; yet the real key to healing involves filling the dented ping-pong ball of our lives with the "warm tea" of our life energy. This is analogous to the wisdom of the Western mystery tradition that we just discussed regarding finding the *lumen naturae*. The wide range of psychotherapeutic and Qigong methods are part of the process of finding our inner heat, and recovering our inner illumination. Specific movements like *Tai Chi Ruler*, Standing Meditation Qigong, and *Tiger* or *Crane* movements can be an integral part of reconnecting to a life stance that shape-shifts a trauma victim back into being grounded in his or her primordial Self. Also, the *Mythic Journey Process* can be part of the process of transmutation of our self-identifications.

Case Illustration: Treating the Long-Term, Retriggered Effects of Past Physical Trauma

The following case shows how, even without doing Qigong or Tai Chi, and even without doing a *Mythic Journey Process* with patients, a psychotherapist can facilitate the healing of trauma with Bodymind Healing Psychotherapy methods. By extracting certain aspects of the essence of these traditions, we can use the *River of Life* practices and help patients shape-shift into new stances grounded in new meanings.

As an example of how BMHP functions in the case of a past trauma affecting a patient's physical health, "Gerry," a single father in his early 40s, was referred by an orthopedic doctor to our integrative medical clinic. While Gerry was taking out the garbage one day, his back went into spasm. For three months he was not able to walk up the stairs to the second floor of his house; he switched bedrooms with one of his children downstairs so he could avoid the arduous trip up the stairs. One surgeon already recommended surgery, and our orthopedic back specialist wanted to see what a non-invasive approach could accomplish before he concurred with the first doctor's opinion.

In our second session, after some rapport had been built, Gerry was lying down on the couch in my office in pain. Because he couldn't sit up comfortably in my office, I suggested he take an acu-yoga posture — sometimes called the child's pose while touching Bladder meridian acu-points in the inside corner of the eyes (Gach, 1981, p. 150). While he was in that posture I introduced him to the combination of breathing and guided visualization used in the *River of Life* practice (see Chapter 5) where Gerry sensed a river of energy traveling down his body along with his breath. He described a sensation in his back like a block of ice stopping the flow of the river. I asked Gerry to not try to change this, but just to imagine the sun shining on the block, gradually melting it. I then asked him while "focusing" on the body block to also report any images or words that arose from the block while it was melting. After a few minutes, his subdued crying turned into deep sobbing. Gerry exclaimed, "It couldn't be this, it couldn't be this …"

Gerry then proceeded to tell me how when he was 16 years old he was hitchhiking and he got into a car with two men. They sexually assaulted him, stabbed him in the back, and left him in a ditch. He made his way back to his parent's house, but never told them about this until after our session. When he was a teenager his parents had forbidden him to hitchhike. Gerry didn't want to admit to his parents that they were right about hitchhiking, and so he suffered his shame in silence.

Over the next sessions we worked with healing the trauma of this repressed incident. Gerry released his shame and feelings of victimization by experiencing his anger toward his perpetrators, and forgave himself for not sharing this story with his parents for all of these years. Most importantly, he was able to see that his current pattern of not sharing with others and standing up for his truth was related to this past trauma. He realized that this had been a major factor contributing to his divorce. Gerry saw that "developing spine" in his interpersonal relationships was an important part of his life's meaning and not "holding back" his truth. Gerry found his *numen*.

Not being a therapist who generally believes in miracle cures, and instead knowing that transformation often takes long hard work, I was surprised to hear Gerry's report on his progress. Within a few weeks of this session he was back to his old jogging schedule of running up mountains, and was able to move back to his upstairs bedroom. Not only was there a healing on a physical level, but Gerry also took the metaphor of "the pain held in his back" as a numinous symbol of his life's journey — to work on not holding back his truth, and developing his spine in relationship with others.

Whenever I tell this story of Gerry's transformation I am careful to point out that I cannot be certain that his dramatic change was due to our therapy. Gerry had also been seeing the chiropractor and an acupuncturist at our clinic. However, I must say that I believe that the type of integrative treatment for patients with certain somatic complaints will be the standard approach to medicine sometime soon in our twenty-first century — using the least intrusive and most cost-effective methods first before moving to costly, more invasive methods.

CHAPTER 9: ADDICTIONS.

Bodymind Healing Psychotherapy for Addictions

Carl Jung once said that only "a radical rearrangement of consciousness" could have any lasting effect on individuals suffering from chronic addictions (Sparks, 1993). Using the etymological definition of the word "radical" as meaning "returning to the roots," from the perspective of Bodymind Healing Psychotherapy, one aspect of addiction involves returning to the roots of the "ego-Self axis." This requires not only dealing with the ego's dysfunctional coping strategies that first led to the addiction and replacing them with more healthy coping strategies, but also it requires helping patients' higher Selves find a pathway to link to the wider whole of which we are a part.

The following method can serve as an adjunct to either a broader psychotherapy or a Twelve Step approach to healing addictions. It is useful for those who suffer from addictions, as well as for the helping professionals who serve them. It is a way to help overcome addictive patterns and return to the roots of the primordial Self who basks in the natural ways to feel "high." A basic instinct, fundamental to being human, is the ability to enter into altered states naturally, for example through breathing, rocking, moving, imagining, etc. It has been hypothesized that one of the roots of addictive processes is our culture's lack of adequate initiation rites where the individual learns to find natural ways to link with the higher power that is the source of our life's energy — by whatever name we call it, and through whatever means we access it.

The resources we need to cope with a difficult world are within us, if we could just take the time to tap these inner wells. Our body's biochemistry activates endorphins when we are in need of pain relief; our breath can put us into a pleasurable altered state as we activate our parasympathetic nervous system and the well-documented relaxation response occurs; and our imagination creates images that have neurobiological correlates so that we can not only imagine a river, but also experience its healing effects.

Next I will outline the BMHP method for addictions, using cigarette smoking as an example. This method can be done in one or more sessions by health professionals, or as a self-practice method by those who suffer from addictions. The process can be done in its entirety, as it exists below in its five parts, or it can be trimmed to suit individual needs. While describing the method, I incorporate the case of "Mary," a married woman who worked in the mail sorting room at a local corporation and who was smoking about a pack a day. She came to me after hearing from our clinic that I did hypnosis for smoking addictions. She said that a close friend of hers had just died from emphysema; this finally motivated her to try to stop.

The BMHP Process for Smoking Addictions

Preliminary Questionnaire for Smoking and Other Addictions

1. *Take a History:* When did smoking begin? What were the psychological reasons for beginning? What feelings were associated with these times — i.e. feeling insecure and trying to fit in with peers, not feeling cool like someone who you admired who was following this addictive pattern, shame over not living up to some standard. Do you realize that your smoking, or following some addictive pattern, was because you didn't know another way of coping with this feeling? Was it your way of medicating this feeling? What was that feeling?

2. *Past History of Attempts to Stop:* What methods were tried? What happened?

3. *Reasons to Stop:* What are the reasons you want to stop smoking now? What kind of negative effects has this addiction had in your life?

4. *Triggers:* What are the current places that trigger you — that are your most chosen locations where you self-medicate rather than using alternative methods of coping? What are the feelings associated with those trigger times? Where do you feel these triggering stresses in your body? Does some image express what that feels like? For example, maybe it's at work when you are overwhelmed with all that you have to do.

This was the case for Mary as she worked in the mail sorting room. In her "overwhelm" she felt like electrical wires shooting out electricity in all directions with no ground.

5. *Identifying a Favorite Object:* What is your favorite flower, animal, and place in nature? What is your favorite houseplant? (This will be used later as a sacrificial object.)

Part 1: River of Life Preparatory Induction

1. *Breathing:* Check abdominal breathing by putting one hand on your belly. As you inhale does your stomach go out? — this is correct abdominal breathing. Then use *Microcosmic Orbit Breath*. Naturally inhale and feel the breath rising up the back; on your exhalation feel the breath coming down the front of your body. Notice how long the out-breath lasts, and be aware of the pause after the exhalation. As you are noticing the out-breath going down your body your eyes will naturally feel like dropping or closing.

2. *Imagine a River:* Picture the most beautiful river you've ever seen, or the most beautiful one you can imagine. What kind of trees and flowers are growing next to it? How fast is it flowing? Perhaps you can hear it rushing or dribbling over rocks, or smell some element of nature around the river. As you breathe out, imagine that river flowing down the front of your body. The longer your exhalation the deeper the stream. Don't try to let go of tension but just imagine the river flowing over that tension, as if water was flowing over leaves or encumbrances and gradually freeing up the

blockages so that they get washed down stream. At the end of your out-breath the river comes to a still pool where you are seated with a nice tree against your back. What's your favorite tree? Feel its strength supporting you. This is the river of your life. Get a sense of how it has rained down from the heavens, came down through the mountains, and formed your life-stream. Maybe some images will come up about those places where the river became constricted or blocked as you felt _____. (Fill in your own feeling here that you medicated through your substance of choice.)

3. *Identifying Your Triggers:* Picture the time in your life right now that you find yourself getting most triggered. What time of day is it? Where are you? Can you picture something, some color or object that is in those surroundings? Can you feel how your body gets some certain feeling, perhaps a blockage, when that situation exists? Imagine that blockage as an ice-block (or choose your own image) in the river.

4. *Coalescing Your Blockage into a Belief:* "Focus" on that felt sense of your body block and what it's all about. Can you get a sense of a belief, phrase, or image that gets the worst of it? For example, Mary's sense of overwhelm was associated with the belief, "I'm a failure for not being able to get done as much as other employees." Give yourself a number of how strong you feel this on a SUDS scale — 10 being the most you have ever felt stress and 0 being totally relaxed. Mary was a 9 on this scale. Imagine writing this belief on the ice-block, and feel how the issue blocks the river of your breath.

5. *Restructuring Your Belief:* What is a more constructive or truthful belief (not necessarily a more positive belief)? Mary first came up with a belief of, "I'm acceptable the way I am with all my limitations." This brought her SUDS level down to a 6. I asked Mary how much she believed this statement on a 10-point scale (10 being the most) and she said, "not that much." What would be a more truthful or constructive belief? She said, "Even though I am slower than others, I deserve to be loved the way I am." This brought her down from her original 6 to a 3.

6. *Self-Soothing*: Put one hand on your heart and one hand on your belly. As you say your constructive belief, imagine that you have in your hands the love that you've given to another at a time when they were in difficulty. Or imagine the person that has most loved you and imagine his or her hands on your heart. How many breaths does it take to let that love in?

7. *Identifying Underlying Psychodynamics:* For some people, or in depth psychotherapy, more rounds may be necessary to get to the crux of what is creating the block. Both Mary's mother and father had high expectations for her and were always comparing her to other children and to her brother. She remembers being hit on a few occasions where she brought home a "bad" grade (C) in school. She was criticized rather than coached. So, not living up to other's expectations activated a sympathetic nervous system fight, flight, and freeze response.

8. *Melting Your Blockage with Compassion:* Go back to your breathing and see the old ice block with the negative belief written on it. Imagine, as you are touching your heart, that the compassionate light of the sun is shining on the ice-block. The sun shines on everything on the earth regardless of how light or dark, good or bad it is. Gradually the sun melts the ice. Don't try to do anything, just let the sun's love melt your ice gradually. Sometimes this takes a short time, sometimes a day, sometimes it takes longer. Allow the love of the sun to turn the ice into water. As you let go with your exhalation, can you feel the water flow all the way down to the still pool within you?

Part 2: The River of Life Practice Targeted to Smoking and Other Addictions

1. Imagine that you are sitting with your back against a tree by the side of this river. In front of you is a fork in the river. Recognize that you are at a turning point in your life, "a fork in the river." Imagine walking alongside one of the two rivers. In and along this river are cigarette butts, and the river is an ugly yellow color. You continue to walk down the river where there are dead flowers and dying trees along its banks. Be aware of your own sensitivity to these life forms as if you could hear them crying out in pain from dying from the tobacco-laced river. Eventually you've walked past many crying life forms: fish lying belly-up, deer lying dead from drinking from the river, etc. Finally you reach the stagnant, putrid pond at the river's end, where cigarettes butts have accumulated over many years. Can you smell it? Allow an image to arise of the many people who thought they could beat the odds and are lying here with emphysema or other diseases — maybe an image will come of one of those people laying in the hospital, attached by a tube in his or her throat to a machine that is breathing for him or her. Here on the river, your favorite animal is laying, making sounds of pain as it takes its last few breaths after being poisoned by the river. You apologize to the animal for your lack of strength to not pollute the river; you make excuses to the animal (all the excuses you usually make about why you can't stop smoking). Your favorite animal looks at you pleadingly, but when it tries to utter something it just emits a hacking cough. You stop and pause and let in the message of this suffering animal, and you think about how this is like the pleading of others in your life who care about you and look pleadingly at you. (Notice how your breath is right now and how your body feels. Do you recognize that this polluted river is one of your choices?)

2. Next, imagine that you are again by the tree at the fork in the river. Feel its strength against your back. Notice your exhalation going to its strong roots. Be aware of the beautiful clear river that flows right in front of you, down the other river fork, and begin walking down that fork of the river. Notice the beautiful flowers, trees, and foliage along the banks. You can even see fish swimming through the clean, clear waters. Be aware of other images that might arise to represent the path that would

emerge in your life if you followed this river. What is the posture that you hold as you are walking with a sense of accomplishment, pride, and strength of character on this path? Notice the admiration from those who you care about, admiring that you have had the strength to choose this path. At times there may be difficulties with this path — your cravings for your old habit of walking down the other stream may produce irritability and headache; but the beauty, power, and flowing vitality of the river you are now walking along gives you the conviction that you are following the path meant for you. Follow the river down to the ocean. As you feel the sand under your feet, you look out to the sea of healthy new life possibilities that await you. What feelings are associated with your sense of accomplishment? And what postural stance do you now embody? Touch or tap on the part of your body that you associate with this new stance to further awaken its energy.

Part 3: Anchoring the Process

Imagine those habitual places where you smoke in your everyday life. Just as you are here in my office now, imagining you are there, so when you are there you can imagine that you are back here in this office, or back in your sanctuary by your inner river. Your breath, and the body part that you've just touched, will be your anchors. This will become your practice one day, one hour, one minute at a time — to choose to travel down the path of the river of increased health.

If you want to smoke, just put your fingers (the opposite hand from the one you use to smoke) up to your lips without a cigarette in them. Say to yourself, "Smoking is a natural desire; but I've distorted the desire to smoke fresh air and replaced it with a toxic mimic (smoking). I will now smoke fresh air." Then, take a few puffs of fresh air through your fingers, and feel the fresh air taking you back to the healthy river of your inner sanctuary.

You have the choice of which river you want to travel down — the one of disease, and shortened life, or the one of _____ (add in the reasons you listed in the Preliminary Questionnaire for why you wanted to stop smoking). The healthy river is one where you will achieve your goal of _____ (add in the reasons you listed for why you wanted to stop smoking).

In the next days or weeks, you'll be making choices between which river you want to travel down. Feel where in your body is located your commitment to walk down the river of your health, and to follow your desire to fulfill the goals you listed above. Touch or tap on that part of your body to anchor that commitment.

Part 4: Post-Session Options

Outside of your Bodymind Healing Psychotherapy session, you have two choices.

1. Throw away all of your cigarettes today, and stop smoking today. Then, when you feel the desire to smoke, try one (or all) of the above practices that worked best for you. If you still can't resist smoking, do the *sacrificial object* method below.

2. With the advice of your medical doctor, smoke more cigarettes than you ever have at one time, until you get sick. By overloading with an excessive, distasteful amount of

cigarettes, this can create an extremely negative association to cigarettes. However, if you still have a desire to smoke at some point, try the *sacrificial object* method below.

Part 5: The Sacrificial Object Method

Save all of your cigarette butts and put them into a big glass of water. Pour the water into your favorite flowerpot or houseplant. Make sure that this plant is in a place that you walk by regularly, or is in a place where you regularly smoke. Create a ritual where you ask for forgiveness from the plant for needing to sacrifice it to benefit you finding your path. Promise the plant that its sacrifice will not be in vain. Tell the plant that you will use its sacrifice to not only follow a healthy life path, but to give to loved ones or the planet in some way that will make this plant's sacrifice more worthwhile. Tell the plant that anytime you see another plant of the same species, you will pay it special attention, water it, and/or send it loving wishes.

Overview of the Process:

This method of smoking cessation provides a means to stop not only smoking, but other addictions as well. The basic components of the protocol are:

1. Establish an altered state of consciousness by *Microcosmic Orbit Breath* and guided visualization of the *River of Life* practice.

2. Imagine sitting at a fork in the river with your back against a tree. Then take a walk alongside one fork of the river imagining the negative outcomes of this addictive path. Walk down the other riverbank imagining the positive outcomes from breaking the addiction.

3. Create a ritual where you have a choice to stop your addictive pattern or transfer harm to some element of nature that is significant to you. This sacrifice should not be taken lightly and is to induce a commitment to use this sacrifice for the world's, and your life's, higher good.

Final Note:

Sometimes our psychological patterns are so entrenched that even the above ritual will not be enough to defeat our inner demons. In this case, the other elements of Bodymind Healing Psychotherapy can be of assistance.

- *Psychodynamic dimension*: Explore the underlying patterns that lead to self-destructive behaviors — What created these patterns in our family of origins? What costs do we pay? What secondary gains come from not changing? And what benefits would accrue from a new path?

- *Cognitive Restructuring and Focusing Dimensions*: What belief(s) stand in the way of changing? And what would be a more truthful or constructive new belief? —"Focusing" on what's behind these patterns and beliefs that are stuck in the body can lead to finding the crux of what keeps these patterns entrenched, and can create felt shifts, new meanings, and new pathways.

- *Symbolic Process Dimension*: Try doing a *Mythic Journey Process* (see Chapter 20) to activate the archetypal layer of the psyche and thereby find a new healing path.

Various other elements from the healing mandala of life are useful: change in diet, increase liquid intake, drink herbal or green teas, aloe vera juice, etc. As Twelve Step programs have taught us that social support is an important part of recovery, make an assessment of who you can call when you are tempted to go back to your substance of choice. Check with your doctor and/or other health professionals for the most current treatment methods. Chinese medicine and herbs and acupuncture have some significant research pointing to their benefits as an adjunct. Find a Qigong movement that helps to remove the stuck energy that comes from detoxifying. In particular, *Tiger Qigong* (see Volume 1 on the *Yi Chuan Tiger*) can help to release irritability and strengthen the lung meridian.

In the case of Mary, when we did a follow-up session three months later, she had totally stopped smoking because she didn't want to "hurt something living (her favorite plant)." She realized that her lungs and her life were also something living. In the process of stopping smoking, Mary realized that she had started smoking again when her mentally ill father had committed suicide, and she had felt responsible. Mary made a choice to embark on a course of depth psychotherapy to heal her patterns of taking on other's issues and feeling bad if she didn't meet other's expectations. She realized that these patterns were affecting her relationship with her husband and made a conscious decision that, "Now that smoking is out of the way, it's time to look at other problem areas of my life." Mary's subsequent therapy regarding these deeper issues is beyond the scope of the current chapter.

Case Illustration: Binge Eating

The process outlined above can be adapted to use for any addiction. For example, "Amy" was binge eating at night. As she "focused" on the feeling she experienced right before eating, she first said it was a sense of being bored. But then a deep feeling of sadness emerged as she realized she had been avoiding dealing with the loss of her oldest brother, who she described as being like a father and her companion. She felt alone and abandoned. Even though Amy was married, when her husband went off to work on his computer at night, she felt abandoned. This paralleled her past, similar feeling of emotional abandonment by her parents.

Amy had been in talk therapy for many years and complained about it not working; and now, in addition, she was taking 60 mg. of Prozac. Amy reported that her psychiatrist said, "You should be over your grief by now," but this just added to Amy's guilt. The self-soothing practice of one hand on the heart and one hand on the belly was helpful in getting Amy out of her intellectual mode of dealing with her loss. Also using the EFT method, "Even though I have pain, I can accept my feelings," was helpful. Her favorite place was the ocean, so it fit in well with the BMHP *River of Life* breathing method. Amy jokingly said that her inner sanctuary of the river merging with the ocean provided her with an "interesting inner movie to watch," and that it helped as a substitute to self-medicating with food.

Sacrifice: A Key Tool in Addictions and in Therapy in General

Sacrifice of something in the real world is an important part of ancient rituals. Our ancient psychological colleagues knew that when they sacrificed a goat or an animal this could lead to a transformative effect on the human psyche. Though we can take pride in that, as modern people, we have evolved to a point where we do not need to sacrifice a young maiden to create transformation in ourselves or in our tribe, nonetheless there is still something useful that can be extracted from such rituals. Sacrifice, when done with mindful awareness, can add psychic energy to produce healing effects. In a primordially based psychotherapy, it is one more tool given by the powers of the universe and nature for our healing.

The Case of the Batterer and the Baby Grand Piano

In the case of Mary we saw how the anticipated sacrifice of a plant helped Mary to save her lungs. It should be noted that the object to be sacrificed needs to be one that is meaningful to the particular patient. In my experience, the anticipated sacrifice of a living thing from nature, or a meaningful object, can be a motivator for many people to stop an addiction.

Off the topic of addictions, I remember a situation where the sacrifice of a meaningful object was a transformative agent in a case of couple's therapy where intermittent battering was taking place. A man we'll call "George" had impulse control problems and had battered his girlfriend on a few occasions. She said she'd give their relationship one last try. After they came to see me, after a few sessions of teaching them non-violent communication, George's partner "Alice," in the midst of tears, said she still didn't trust George. She said she couldn't think of anything that would make her believe he wouldn't batter her again, regardless of the progress that he seemed to make in therapy. I asked George what his most valuable possession was. He replied that his grandfather's grand piano was what his life was about; after a long day at the office, playing a tune on this family heirloom was what he lived for. (He qualified the statement with a wink at Alice, clarifying that she was his grand, grand piano and she was also what he lived for.) I then challenged George about how much Alice really meant to him, and if he'd be willing to put a contract in her safety deposit box that if he ever hit her again, he'd sacrifice his grand piano. He paused for a brief moment and then said, "Yup, I'd be willing to sign." In the sessions that followed, this agreement helped Alice regain her trust, along with the work that they continued to do on their relationship. It worked. After termination, I heard from Alice and George about a year later thanking me for the work we did and letting me know that there were no further incidents of violence, and that they had just been married.

Twelve Step Programs

Twelve Step programs are a useful complementary tool that work well in conjunction with psychotherapy for addictions. In particular for alcoholism, sex and love addictions, and various major drug addictions many people get beneficial results from the philosophy, camaraderie, support, and the spiritual path based on connecting with "a higher power" involved with these programs.

I have had the experience of doing psychotherapy with quite a few people who are simultaneously in such programs. Other patients who do not appreciate aspects of Twelve Step programs for a variety of reasons, will chose to do psychotherapy instead. Depending upon the person, and the severity of the addiction, this may or may not be successful. There have been patients who wanted to avoid such programs; and at times I have suggested that I will work with patients without their entering into a Twelve Step program on the condition that they are honest with me and will agree to go to a Twelve Step program if they slip. Appropriate assessment of the severity of an addiction regarding a person's ability to gain control over his or her addictive patterns without the support of a Twelve Step program is a key element of treatment.

Case Illustration: Working with Codependence — A Kabbalistic/Qigong Perspective

When a loved one is suffering with addiction it tests our own limits and boundaries. Such was the case for a man we'll call "Mark" who had been in depth psychotherapy with me for about six months, working on, among other things, his "reactive attachment style." This had gotten him into problems in many of his relationships, including with his son, over the years. Mark had a 25-year-old son who had recovered from alcoholism due to being part of a Twelve Step program; and he had not had a drink for four years. Yet his son began smoking again.

Mark's mother had died of lung cancer, and during his son's teenage years, before he moved out of the house, Mark had many arguments, to no avail, with him about stopping smoking and drinking.

As part of his therapy during those years, Mark had worked on his codependence, i.e. looking at the sense of self-righteousness that he got from being the all-knowing father. But he noticed that he still had a hard time catching himself from falling into this old, codependent pattern. It was particularly difficult when his son came into town on a vacation after not seeing Mark for about a year, and Mark saw his son smoking. Mark reported that by remembering his breathing, this helped him to sink his Qi and not be reactive. In addition, Mark told me about how he applied a principle he had heard from me many months earlier — when he wanted to tell his new girlfriend how weak she was regarding her over-eating problem. At that point we discussed the principle of *"tsimtsum,"* from the *Kabbalah*, meaning a withdrawal or retreat (Scholem, 1969, pp. 258-264). In the creation myth of the *Kabbalah*, it was said that God created the world by stepping back, and from the space created, the world came into being.

Mark, an orthodox Jew, found meaning in acting out the creation myth of the *Kabbalah* with his girlfriend and with others, by withdrawing into *tsimtsum*. And when Mark's son came into town we were in the process of exploring his affect modulation skills regarding how to balance right assertiveness versus withdrawing and making space. Mark proudly reported to me that although when he saw his son smoking he felt like strangling him with words, he first exhaled and then remembered the stepping back of the *Kabbalah*. During the week that his son stayed in town, he didn't confront him as he had done in the past. At the end of the trip his son told him how much he appreciated his father's not getting on his case about his smoking. Mark replied, "Why should I get on your case? You are an adult now and I know you have the strength to stop when you decide to, as you did with alcohol and with cigarettes in the past."

Mark's son expressed deep appreciation for his father's non-confrontational attitude, and in a few months he quit smoking on his own. When Mark described appreciation for his new changed attitude, he commented on how the *Tai Chi Push Hands* practice that he was learning (from another instructor) was teaching him how to not use force when interacting with others. He said, "This non-force stuff is really beginning to take root in my body."

CHAPTER 10: INSOMNIA

Research

A record 43 million sleeping pill prescriptions were filled the United States in 2005, fueled by almost $300 million in drug companies' advertising, and resulting in more than $2 billion in sales. And, just take in these statistics for a moment: More than 70 million people in the U.S. may be affected by sleep troubles, according the National Institute of Health. The National Commission on Sleep Disorders Research estimates that 40 million Americans suffer from chronic sleep problems, and as many as 30 million more have occasional difficulty sleeping. The use of sleeping pills by adults, ages 20 to 44, doubled between 2000 and 2004, and according to IMS Health, a market researcher, the 43 million prescriptions issued by doctors last year represent a 13 percent increase from 2004. Sleep deprivation and related disorders cost the nation $16 billion in annual healthcare expenses, and about $50 billion in lost productivity, according to the U.S. surgeon general (Laszarus, 2005).

According to Dennis McGinty, a professor of psychology at UCLA who specializes in sleep disorders, insomnia can result from a wide variety of factors, some physiological, some psychological, and some behavioral. But, McGinty says, "one cause that hasn't yet been closely studied by experts is the impact on sleep of American's increasingly stressful lives ... and that's something you can change through your attitude ... by getting more exercise, or by just looking up at the sky from time to time" (as cited in Laszarus, 2005). Rachel Manber, director of the insomnia program at the Stanford Sleep Disorder Clinic says, "the biggest concern is that people are getting swayed by the drug companies' marketing campaign and are accepting that little if any risk is attached to frequent use of so-called hypnotics to catch some shut-eye. This means that people are taking a shortcut to circumvent insomnia, rather than addressing whatever the root causes may be. Sleep problems relay to us a message that something is wrong. Taking medication is the same as killing the messenger" (as cited in Laszarus, 2005).

Solid research shows mind-body interventions to be effective in helping with insomnia. For example, a randomized trial found that cognitive-behavioral therapy (alone and in combination with pharmacologic therapy) was effective in reducing time awake after sleep onset in elderly subjects. Only those subjects treated with the behavioral approach maintained treatment gains at follow-up. While pharmacological treatments produce somewhat faster sleep improvements in the short-term; behavioral approaches show comparable effects in the intermediate-term (4-8 weeks); and in the long-term (6-24 months) behavioral approaches show more favorable outcomes than drug therapies (Morin et al., 1999.)

Regarding Qigong in particular, Dr. Pelletier (2000) reports that, "Qigong exercises helped patients with insomnia, according to a 1996 review of the literature by Dr. Kenneth Sancier, president of the Qigong Institute in Menlo Park, California" (p. 360). In the rest of this chapter I will discuss how Bodymind Healing Psychotherapy integrates some aspects of Qigong along with other BMHP methods for the benefit of patients with insomnia.

Pharmacological treatments have several disadvantages as compared with bodymind healing methods. They oftentimes produce "rebound insomnia" when the patient stops taking the medication; they have side effects; and they dis-empower the person regarding his or her own inner resources. According to a recent report by CNN, taking the most common sleeping medication, Ambien, may be related to sleep walking and "sleep driving" in some patients.[1] For this reason it seems that, at least as a first line of defense, the intelligent consumer would try to use the best mind-body approaches before using medications. Pharmacological treatments fit well with the prevailing Western worldview where "outside-fixes" circumvent the need to do inner work to find healing. Certainly there is a place for using "outer-world" oriented solutions for insomnia. Awareness of the effects of caffeinated drinks and appropriate exercise are keys; and use of medications and herbal remedies such as Valerian (Pelletier, 2000, p. 171) can be important adjuncts to treatment. Be aware of your body's unique reactions to Valerian to see if it has any unwanted side effects. Check with your medical doctor regarding remedies such as Melatonin, which helps some people, but for others it stimulates them, causing nightmares or hangovers, and it may harm the reproductive system (Pelletier, 2000, p. 111)

However, since symptoms are oftentimes symbolic messages from the deep recesses of the unconscious mind, it is important to listen to these messages as learning opportunities. As we move into a horizontal position and go to sleep, we leave the world of everyday life and we get a chance to lie horizontally at one with the truth of our spirit. If issues are in the way of our spirit being at rest, we have a chance to be a peace with these issues before gaining entry into the deeper recesses of the sacred world of sleep.

To address these wider, deeper dimensions of insomnia, Bodymind Healing Psychotherapy uses the following eight-leveled holographic approach:

Bodymind Healing Psychotherapy Treatment Protocol for Insomnia

1. Non-Attachment to Falling Asleep

One major reason why people suffer from various natural autonomic nervous system disorders is that they are trying to force something that is natural. For example, many who are suffering from sexual impotency issues try to force sexuality when the body is trying to express a message. As sexual potency naturally declines in our later years, rather than accommodating to these natural changes, fueled by a culture that worships youth and a drug industry that profits from selling us unnatural fantasies, we buy into an unrealistic vision. I am not speaking against taking an occasional Viagra pill, but more about excessive use of medication in a compensatory manner that damages our health in the short- or long-term (Pomeranz & Bhavsar, 2005). Likewise with anxiety, fighting against it can contribute to panic attacks. So the first step in treatment of autonomic nervous system disorders is to try not to fight something that in many cases is natural, and to say the following when having difficulty sleeping:

Chapter 10: Insomnia

This is an opportunity to catch up on my relaxation/self-healing meditation practice. If I was in a monastery now I'd have to get up to the sound of a bell, and though I would have an opportunity to appreciate this hour of the morning and the silence around me, I'd have to sit up and be in a cold uncomfortable room. Instead now, I can at this hour of the morning, in my comfortable bed, be aware, enjoy my surroundings, and notice my breath. Going into a deep state of trance or relaxation will be as healing for me as going to sleep.

2. Microcosmic/Macrocosmic Orbit Breath and the River of Life Practice

See Chapter 4 where both the *Microcosmic and Macrocosmic Orbit Breathing* methods are illustrated, i.e. notice your inhalation as the energy rises along with it up the back, and on the exhalation notice your energy sink down to your belly, and continue the oval breathing circle from the perineum to the top of your head. Then extend your breathing all the way down to your feet using the *River of Life* practice as discussed in previous chapters (see Chapter 5).

3. Self-Soothing: One Hand on Heart, One on Belly

For more details see Chapter 6.

4. Acu-Point Self-Touch

- Chi Nei Tsang (Chia, 1990) — Making your way around your belly clock, press in gently on the exhalation. (For more on this method see Chapter 6.)

- Acupressure points — It is best to go to an acupuncturist to find which meridian imbalances relate to your ideographic condition, and then to use those acupressure self-touch points on your own. I usually favor the circle, stop, breathe, and feel method described earlier in this book (Chapter 3). Here are some general points often used for insomnia (Deadman, 1998; Gach, 1990):

    - For relaxing the central nervous system — try touching the third-eye point (GV-24.5).
    - For calming the spirit, agitation of the heart, palpitations, overexcitement — try touching the point at the inner wrist-crease in line with the little finger (H-7).
    - For fright, agitation, sadness and worry with diminished Qi, and fear of people — try touching the point where the bent pinky finger hits the crease on the inside of your palm, in line with the little finger (H-8).
    - For relieving nervousness, blocked Qi in the chest/heart, and anxiety — try touching the acu-point on the center of the breastbone three thumbs-widths up from the base of the sternum bone (CV-17).

- For mania, fear, palpitations, nausea, disorders of the chest, and distention in the stomach — try touching a point two thumb-widths above the center of the inner wrist crease (P-6).

- For fear and back pain that make it difficult to sleep — try touching, with your hand or foot, an acu-point in the first indentation directly below the outer anklebone (Bl-62).

- For hypertension, nightmares and deficiency conditions in the elderly — touch the acu-point directly below the inside of the anklebone in a slight indentation (K-6).

- When touching all the above points, use the *River of Life* practice, your own imagery, and your heart's love, to relax and melt into the calm lake of life's energy. In BMHP as we touch these points, when needed, we also integrate the methods below to maximize the healing potential of integrating East and West, transcending and transmuting traditions.

5. Focusing (Gendlin, 1978) on the Felt Meaning of What's Keeping You Awake

See Chapter 6 for the six-step Focusing process combined with BMHP's *River of Life* imagery process.

6. Cognitive Restructuring

What are the thoughts and beliefs that are keeping you awake? Take your negative thought/belief that is keeping you awake. Give it a SUDS level. What is a more truthful/constructive thought? Now what is the SUDS level?

- Practice thought stoppage and thought substitution.

- Serenity prayer: *"God grant me the serenity to accept the things I cannot change, the courage to change the things I can change, and the wisdom to know the difference."* How will worrying about the issues you are preoccupied with right now help, versus, can you let yourself deal with it tomorrow? Imagine your upsetting feeling (worry, anxiety, fear), and on your exhalation imagine letting go of the feeling, watching it float like a dead log downstream.

7. Psychodynamic/Object Relations Issues

The case of "Carl" beginning on the next page will illustrate the importance of this dimension.

8. Bodymind Healing Qigong Exercises

Some of the BMHQ practices that have been reported as useful for those with insomnia are: *Yi Chuan Holding the Golden Ball of the Heart, Tai Chi Ruler, Cloud Hands, Buddha Opens the Heart to the Heavens* — using the sound: *"Ha,"* and *Raising Qi to Heavens & Returning it to Earth* (see Volume I.) Trust your own body regarding which movements or static postures are best for you. For some people, activating *sung* (relaxed awakeness) with a Tai Chi movement helps. While doing Qigong movements, try focusing on one of the acu-points mentioned above. For others, static Qigong postures serve pre-sleep purposes better. For some people, doing Qigong before going to sleep gives a nice balance of relaxation and fuel for the night's journey into sleep; for others it is too stimulating. Listen to your bodymind.

Case Illustration: The Unresolved Issues that Invade Your Sleep

"Carl" was a 45-year-old married man who came to me suffering from insomnia. His past psychiatrist had prescribed sleep medication, but it didn't seem to work. Carl still woke from nightmares with a sense of being invaded. When he came to see me, we began BMHP's integrated treatment approach. Going along with Carl's desire to get off his sleep medication, we worked in conjunction with his psychiatrist to taper off his sleep medication as we began to unravel the deeper meanings of his symptoms.

We discovered that this sense of being invaded in his nightmares was correlated to the fact that his father physically abused Carl in his childhood. His father would barge into his room when he was resting, or even when he was asleep, hitting him for "being bad." In addition to the physical abuse, Carl had internalized messages about not being good enough, resulting from his father's blaming messages when Carl didn't meet his idealistic expectations. When Carl was not functioning well in his work, he felt his boss was judgmental of him, and then he hid his feelings of ineptitude behind a cloak of placating behavior — similar to the way he responded to his father's abuse and demands. Though his boss was different from his father, his emotional body and the hyper-vigilance of his childhood were triggered as he projected on his boss the physical abuse by his father. From not feeling safe to express himself with his father, Carl developed a stance in life which was overly accommodating to others. Adding to his fear of expressing his feelings was the fact that his father had a heart condition. Though Carl had held anger towards his father, he was afraid that if he really expressed himself he would give his father a heart attack. This learned holding-back survival strategy was the same style he used with his boss. But as he continued to hold in his feelings, somatic symptoms began to flare up including neck and back pains. From not expressing and honoring his limits at work he developed repetitive stress syndrome in his right arm; and from the tension that he carried from the accumulation of unexpressed feelings during the day, at night his sleep was invaded by the demonic vestiges of these unworked-through issues.

After doing some good inner work on the above issue with Bodymind Healing Psychotherapy, the pain from Carl's repetitive stress gradually disappeared. He attributed this healing to setting boundaries at work regarding the time he needed to finish projects, and to the various prescribed Bodymind Healing Qigong movements that he practiced.[2]

In our therapy, Carl role-played expressing anger constructively to his father. Then, he finally called his father, after not speaking to him for many years. This led to his father apologizing for hitting Carl in his childhood, and a new relationship developed between them. After this phone call, Carl's insomnia disappeared for a while.

Often in depth psychotherapy, layers of the underlying pattern lie beneath the surface as a psycho-archeological dig takes place. The next layer was the layer of his current feelings about his mother. After his parents divorced, due to his father's physical abuse of both him and his mother, Carl lived with his mother. In one session, while "focusing" on the feeling he had in his body when he woke up, he realized that another layer of his insomnia was about his guilt about not taking care of his mother who lived in a third-world country. As the oldest brother, Carl had been shouldering most of the responsibility for sending money to her. Through the course of therapy he realized that he had been holding back his anger toward his other siblings about their not shouldering their fair share of the responsibility. As he had just learned to do with his father, Carl constructively expressed his feeling to his two siblings. This helped him to let go of some of the burden he was carrying. He also spoke up to his mother to renegotiate the amount of money that he was sending to her. This led to his mother assuming responsibility to reactivate her sewing business to help support herself and decrease some of her dependence on Carl and his siblings.

Carl worked on his beliefs with cognitive and energy psychology methods. Instead of believing, "I'm no good, and I need to do all I can to get other's love, even if it means not having rest myself" (SUDS level 9). Carl's new truthful and constructive belief was, "Even though I have my limits in terms of what I choose to give, I deserve to have people in my life that take responsibility for their own lives, and I will help them to the extent that it doesn't endanger my own health and economic well-being" (SUDS level 1).

Many of the other elements of Bodymind Healing Psychotherapy also helped Carl to maintain an anchor in the state-specific state of letting go of his tension and accepting his chosen limits. Using *Microcosmic Orbit Breath* and visualizing the river washing away the old patterns were keys to his healing, as was practicing *Tai Chi Ruler* at times during the day to let go of tension. When the pattern reoccurred in his bed at night, Carl repeated his new constructive belief along with his *River of Life* practice. While doing these practices, he also found it helpful to press the acupressure point on the inside of the wrist crease in alignment with the little finger (H-7, called *Spirit Gate*), a point often used for insomnia (Deadman, 1998). During one session while holding this point, tears came to Carl's eyes; he said, "It's sad that my mom doesn't have more money." However, Carl realized that his codependent way of trying to fix everything for everyone was putting a financial burden on his relationship with his wife. He said, "It's better to mourn my mom's limits than it was to be in that state of continuous guilt that was stopping my spirit from resting."

By the end of our therapy, Carl's repetitive stress injury had disappeared, and he was speaking up more in his significant relationships. His every-night insomnia had significantly decreased, but it did reoccur when triggers activated him. He told me that when it did reoccur, on somewhat rare occasions, he was able to use our bodymind healing methods to go to back to sleep much more quickly than he had before treatment. Carl had totally stopped all medication.

From Carl's case we can see that those who jump on the bandwagon of medication to alleviate symptoms, (and risk "rebound insomnia" when they get off the medication), are missing the growth potential involved in unearthing the deeper meanings behind their patterns. Also, such inner work enables people to discover self-healing methods as they learn to deal with the underlying issues. It is also important to realize how medication affects our access to dreams. Like physical symptoms, our dreams are messages waiting to be deciphered. By prematurely shutting off the "messenger" with medications, we risk not hearing the message. By using a combination of psychotherapeutic and other bodymind healing methods, the encumbrances in the river of our life energy can be removed and our spirit can find its way to its natural state of rest.

Alternative Visualization Methods

Though the breathing methods of the *River of Life* practice have been effective with most people with whom I have worked over the years, there are a few people who are "meditative-breath resistant." For example, sometimes a person has had a traumatic experience learning to meditate or breathe that is still linked to meditation or breathing. With other people the difficulty may be linked to a perfectionistic critic who compares him or herself to others who "can meditate." Sometimes it helps to apply energy psychology methods (Craig, 1995) like, "Even though I can't relax, meditate, and breath as well as others, I can still love and accept myself." In BMHP this is done while one hand is on the heart, practicing self-soothing. Though the above BMHP methods (cognitive restructuring of the negative beliefs, self-soothing, etc.) can be useful to heal these traumas, occasionally other methods are useful. There are occasions when going to a sleep clinic where differentially diagnosing for sleep apnea and other disorders can be useful. Likewise, changing the form of imagery from a river to a specific place that has been relaxing to the patient can be helpful. Then the patient is instructed to use the above BMHP protocol (not trying to go to sleep, etc.) and to imagine being in that place with or without the use of focus on the breath.

Pleasant dreams....

CHAPTER 11: HYPERTENSION

Research

Hypertension affects 20 percent or more of the adult population in Western societies and is a significant risk factor for stroke, myocardial infraction, and congestive heart failure. These together account for more than 50 percent of deaths in the United States (Wollam et al., 1988). It is estimated that about 50 million Americans have elevated blood pressure, which is defined as systolic blood pressure (BP) of 140 mm Hg or greater, or diastolic BP of 90 mm Hg or greater. (Joint National Committee on Detection, Evaluation and Treatment of High Blood Pressure (JNC-V), 1993).

The problem with conventional treatments that use medication is that patients suffer from high costs and side effects. For example, research points to hypotensive drugs negatively affecting carbohydrate and lipid metabolism (Polare et al., 1989; Medical Research Council Working Party, 1985) mood state, cognitive functioning, and sexual performance (Kostis, 1990). Therefore, a growing body of research in the West has focused upon lifestyle modification as an alternative to anti-hypertensive drugs. According to the Joint National Committee report (JNC-V, 1993), lifestyle modification can provide "multiple benefits at little cost and minimal risk" and may be used as a first step therapy for individuals within a high range of normal or who have Stage 1 hypertension. Lifestyle modifications can also be used for reducing the number and doses of anti-hypertensive medications required (Little, 1991).

Qigong Research

In my earlier two peer-reviewed research articles (Mayer, 1999, 2003), I reviewed 33 studies representing approximately 5545 subjects who used Qigong to treat hypertension. Almost all of the studies suggest that Qigong lowers BP to various degrees over various time periods.

The most in-depth of these studies is the Kuang study (Kuang et al., 1991, updated by Wang et al., 1994), which took place over twenty years. The basic design involved 204 patients with hypertension who were randomly assigned to Qigong practice and control groups. The ages of the subjects were not mentioned. Both groups were given anti-hypertensive drugs. The Qigong group of 104 patients reportedly practiced thirty minutes, twice per day, over twenty years. During the first two months, the BP of all patients dropped in response to the hypotensive drug. Subsequently, and consistently over the period of twenty years, the BP of the group practicing Qigong stabilized while that of the control group increased ($P < 0.01$). Due to the stabilized BP, 48 percent in the Qigong practice group reduced the hypotensive dosage, and for 30 percent in this group, the BP medication was eliminated. In contrast, 31 percent in the control group increased the hypotensive dosage (Kuang et al., 1991). Kuang reports, in his twenty-year study, less cardiovascular lesions ($P < 0.05$), decreased blood viscosity, improved platelet aggregation, decreased triglycerides, and increased high-density lipoprotein cholesterol (HDL-C, good cholesterol) in the groups practicing Qigong. Beneficial changes were reported in total peripheral vascular resistance, plasma cholesterol, and in two messenger cyclic nucleotides (cAMP and cGMP) in the Qigong compared to the control group (Kuang et al., 1991).

Most importantly, in the latest update of the research of Kuang by Wang (et al., 1995), significant differences were reported in subjects who reportedly practiced Qigong for thirty years, thirty minutes twice a day. The accumulated mortality rate was 25.41 percent in the Qigong group and 40.8 percent in the control group. The incidence of strokes was also significantly different in the Qigong practice groups as compared to the control group, 20.5 percent and 40.7 percent respectively. The death rate due to strokes was 15.6 percent and 32.5 percent respectively (P < 0.01) (Wang, 1993, as cited in Sancier, 1996).

I concluded my peer-reviewed research by saying that the weight of evidence of these studies, representing approximately 5545 subjects, suggests that practicing Qigong has a positive effect on hypertension in the following areas: blood pressure, blood circulation, other cardiovascular measures, and other health-related measures including strokes, deaths due to strokes, and overall mortality.

However, I also concluded my review by saying that due to inadequate addressing of methodology issues it was difficult to determine just how effective Qigong is, and what other factors may contribute to the positive effects reported in the studies reviewed. In addition, I suggested the elements of research methodology that needed to be included in future studies. I also said in my final abstract that whether Qigong alone can affect hypertension is not necessarily the most important question. I called for further research to better assess and understand the effect of adding Qigong into an integrated, multifaceted program that selectively incorporates diet, moderate aerobic exercise, relaxation training, and social and psychological dimensions. In this book and in the discussion that follows I address more deeply some of the psychological, clinical dimensions relevant to an integrative approach to treat this major disease.

Qigong and the River of Life: A Quick Fix for Hypertension?

When I was working at the Health Medicine Institute, the medical director, Dr. Len Saputo, with whom I co-founded the clinic, asked me to do a session in a public forum with one of his patients suffering from hypertension. The Health Medicine Forum (HMF) is a leading-edge group of multidisciplinary health professionals trying to combine the best of modern traditional and age-old methods of healing. HMF is part of the movement to bring forth integrative medicine as the norm in the twenty-first century.

In front of an audience of approximately 200 interested people, each doctor or health professional on our panel described how he or she would work with this patient. I always learn so much from hearing the dialogs between ayurvedic doctors, acupuncturists, medical doctors, psychologists, and body workers.

At this HMF event, Dr. Saputo asked me, and one of his patients, who was a man in his late 60s, to take a risk and do something experiential in front of the assembled group. One of the chief medical researchers from a local hospital was there with a blood pressure monitor. He measured the systolic blood pressure rate of the patient at 168. I then did the *River of Life* hypnosis method (see Chapter 5) with this patient in front of the group. Within about five minutes the patient's systolic blood pressure had gone down to 128. Many people in the audience were impressed, as was I; since by nature I'm a shy person, and I wondered what my blood pressure would be in front of such a large group if I was on the spot and having my level of tension measured.

There are many reasons why BP reduction on single occasions is not something about which we should be overly impressed. Let's look at some of these research methodology issues that are important to consider. First, we know that the relaxation response is capable of creating significant positive changes in blood pressure (Jacob et al., 1991; Linden & Chambers, 1994; Schneider et al., 1995). More important than any brief reduction in BP, by whatever means, we would want to know how long such reduction lasts, and whether the hypertensive person can call on this method at times when his or her BP rises. This would be one of the behavioral healthcare tests to determine whether a deeper, longer lasting healing has taken place.

Case Illustration: The Hypertensive Executive — What Lies Beneath the Surface?

In accordance with the viewpoint of BMHP, the deeper psychodynamics, cognitions, and beliefs of a person needs to be worked through before deep, long-lasting healing takes place. I recall a patient who we'll call "Richard," a very wealthy married man and an executive in a local company. Richard's marriage was about to fall apart due to what his wife said was "his inconsiderateness," exemplified by his going out and buying expensive motorcycles without asking her first. An equally important factor in his upcoming divorce was that Richard only slept about four hours a night, and was described by his wife as a "workaholic" who didn't pay enough attention to his young children.

Richard was suffering from severe hypertension, and came to me after hearing about my articles and research on hypertension. Being very busy, he was interested in the quick fixes that he hoped would be part of this "Qigong/ hypnosis thing." He was more than a little upset when, after our first session, I suggested that a combination of marital as well as individual therapy might be important to consider. He reluctantly agreed and later, after a few sessions of both individual and couples therapy, in one of our sessions I asked him to do our *River of Life* breathing method and "focus" on what came up as he followed his exhalation down the river of breath through his body. As Richard "focused" on his body sense he became aware of a high energy, yet disconnected quality to his energy state. As he stayed with the felt sense of this a bit longer, he described the feeling as being like a disconnected live wire, after which a sense of anger arose in him. When I asked him to stay with the sense of anger and ask the feeling, "What is this all about?" another image arose.

Richard remembered a childhood scene from his dinner table when he came home with a "D" on his report card. He vividly recalled his father saying to him in a demeaning tone, "You'll never amount to anything, you dummy." All of his brothers joined in the shaming process. Laughing, mocking, and pointing at Richard, they said, "Don't worry, you can always work on one of Uncle Jimmy's garbage trucks and pick up the garbage from our mansions." At that moment Richard made a promise to himself, "I'll never rest until I make twice as much money as all of you combined."

Indeed, Richard kept that promise and more than fulfilled this goal — but he had forgotten the promise he had a made to himself. He didn't realize how this unconscious motivation was driving him in his current life, and just how literally he was following through on this childhood promise when he said, "I'll never rest."

This insight was the beginning of Richard's changing his behavior. He became aware of the advantages and disadvantages of this compulsion, which had both made him successful, and endangered his health and family. His wife marked this session as the beginning of Richard's change in behavior, which saved their marriage and led to the opportunity to reduce and eventually eliminate his hypertension medication.

There are many interesting clinical points that can be learned from Richard's story. His case illustrates how the "quick fixes" of relaxation modalities may not get to the deeper underlying psychodynamic issues that need to be addressed. Richard shows us the power of using an integrative psychotherapy; and, since one in twenty Americans suffer from hypertension, and 50 percent of Americans may die from its effects (Wollam, 1988), Richard's case has bearing on the importance of a bodymind approach to solving a portion of this health crisis.

Chinese Medical Approach to Hypertension

Regarding a Chinese medical perspective on Qigong and hypertension, we need to be aware that Qigong practices are not so easily oriented towards Western notions of prescribing a single pill or movement. Western, nomothetic (general) categories may provide ease of scientific measurement, but they do not fit into holistic Chinese medical philosophy with its more ideographic (unique) ways of looking at various disorders. For example, the diagnostic category of Western hypertension as perceived in Chinese medicine may be due to a wide variety of energetic imbalances such as "an imbalance of the Yin and Yang functional aspects of Deficient Kidney Yin and Excess Liver Yang, and/ or an overabundance of phlegm and dampness within the body" (Johnson, 2000). In Chinese medicine, two different persons with the same Western diagnosis of "hypertension" may be treated differently depending upon specific diagnostic considerations that come from such general categories and tongue and pulse analysis. Ideographic factors related to the unique patient and the background of the particular Qigong healer/Chinese doctor are also part of the decision about what treatment, or combination of treatments, is chosen. Unique combinations of herbs, acupuncture, and a wide variety of Qigong movements are prescribed based upon what is suited to the individual whole person.

Despite the caveat above, and the insights discussed in Chapter 4 in the ping-pong ball story with Chinese Qigong Master Hon, I wish to suggest some general Qigong movements that may prove beneficial to those suffering from hypertension.

Breathing

One key element that may be a factor in hypertension is when a person's stomach goes in as he or she inhales. In Qigong language, this is called "reverse breathing." In a comprehensive clinical text on Qigong, Johnson (2000) states, "scientific studies confirm that 90 percent of hypertensive patients practice *Reverse Breathing* chronically." Though no reference citation is given for the research behind this claim, many others, including myself, have found that changing habitual reversed breathing is one factor to be considered in restoring parasympathetic relaxation to a person suffering from hypertension.

Standing Meditation Qigong

The Chinese Qigong master with the ping-pong ball (Chapter 4) and my teacher's advise that the key to any form of Qigong is to first balance our energy state with a Standing Meditation practice. In Volume I, I discussed extensively how Standing Meditation Qigong is a method to develop *sung*, or relaxed awakeness. In the last chapter of this book, the illustration and instructions for this essential practice are repeated. My clinical experience shows that it is particularly beneficial for hypertensive patients. This may be due, in part, simply to its effect, like any form of meditation, on getting a person to slow down enough to do the practice. But the specifics of Standing Meditation, and imagining that we are "standing like a tree" rooted in the earth, helps to ground the energy of those hypertensive patients who have a high degree of pressure from the various vicissitudes of life that lead to pent up energy or resentment (excess liver yang). There is some research support for the beneficial elements of Standing Meditation to created balance in life and in the brain.[1]

Qigong Movements: Lowering the Qi with Heavenly Palms

As one common example of a Qigong movement used in the treatment of hypertension, Johnson (2004) suggests that patients be instructed to move their hands with palms downward along the front and side of the body in order to purge and guide the imbalanced Qi so that it descends down the liver and gall bladder channels, or down the torso to the hips. This is a similar movement to the practice suggested in Volume I called, *Lowering the Qi with Heavenly Palms* (See Volume I). Specific acupressure points are also prescribed by Johnson (2004), such as acupuncture point GB-30. And Deadman (1998) uses a variety of points such as Lu-7, LI-4, Lv-3, and K-1 (p. 652). As discussed in Chapter 10 with insomnia, BMHP uses the *River of Life* practice along with those other methods listed while the patient touches these points.

Just as Chinese doctors use acupuncture needles to treat different points for different people based upon their diagnosis of the tongue and pulses, so do I choose different points — either by borrowing the points used in the patient's last acupuncture treatment, points suggested in consultation with an acupuncturist, or based my own assessment of the patient and his or her unique issues. When I suggest points, I hope that I make up for not being a Chinese doctor, and not having sophisticated pulse and tongue diagnosis methods in my tool kit, by helping patients evoke their life energy through various BMHQ methods, with the spirit of Master Hon's "ping-pong ball" discussion in mind. Some of these BMHQ movements include breathing methods that focus on the exhalation and sinking the Qi to the belly (*Tan Tien*), and visualizations such as imagining warm water flowing in down the front central meridian (*Ren*) as in the *River of Life* practice. Sometimes I, and others (Johnson, 1990), use specific sounds to help patients relax and release pent up energy. In BMHQ, I use various non-forced sounds accompanying the exhalation, such as: "ssss" to release excess liver Qi; "ha" to let go in the heart; "whooh" or "chir-ee" to help the vitalizing functions of the kidneys; and "huh" for spleen stagnation. But I prefer a phenomenological approach (see Chapter 5) to all of the above, trusting each patient's own unconscious process to come up with sounds, images, visualizations, and movements that feel right to him or her. Though there is a treasure house of knowledge in the specific series of points chosen by experienced Chinese doctors, the perspective outlined here is a way to pay our respects as Western clinicians to the essence of their tradition. Though limited in our understanding of their breadth of knowledge, Western bodymind health professionals can perhaps add an equally significant knowledge base to the multilayered bodymind methods needed for healing hypertension.

Case Illustration: Is Qigong Palatable to Fundamentalist Christians?

In conclusion, I'd like to mention, as a cautionary tale, a case that reminds us all about the problems that can occur when integrating practices from traditions that may not be familiar to many people in our culture. I tell this story in my trainings so that my students will not make the same error that I once did.

A doctor in our clinic referred a patient to me who was suffering from hypertension. After our first session, his SUDS level went down from an 8 to a 3, and "Paul" asked if there was anything he could do in-between sessions for homework. I suggested that he continue to practice the exercises we had done in the first session: *Microcosmic Orbit Breathing*, the *River of Life* visualization, and the *Lowering the Qi with Heavenly Palms* Qigong movement. I also mentioned that I had a booklet that illustrated these and other Qigong movements that might be helpful. He took this booklet home with him.

In the next session he came in and told me that he was a Fundamentalist Christian and he wanted me to explain to him, "Why are these practices not the work of the Devil?" He went on to explain that he looked at my booklet and in it he saw the exercise called *Buddha Opens the Heart to the Heavens*. He told me that his beliefs were that, "Jesus is the only son of God. It is only through Jesus that a person can find his way to heaven, and that any others were destined to go to hell."

After taking a breath, I complemented Paul on his coming back to this session, and I told him that it showed he was a true Christian by his wanting to discover the truth of things. I went on to explain to Paul that many people misunderstand the idea of the Buddha — that Buddha is not a God, as many believe Jesus is. The Buddha, I explained, is a state of mind that involves compassionate and enlightened awareness, and that any deity may be used in discovering this state of mind. I told him about Tibetan Buddhism where when you do certain practices (*Phowa, Tonglin*) of opening your heart to the compassion and light of the heavens, any deity, for example Jesus, can be imagined to be raining their light of love on you (Rinpoche, 1993, p. 218).

I asked whether he would like to try this and after hearing an affirmative response, I instructed Paul to open his hands to the side and after they were raised over his head, to imagine Jesus in the sky; with a slow exhalation, I instructed him to lower his hands in synchronization with his out-breath and to imagine bringing the love of Jesus down through his body. He reported that his SUDS level went down significantly more when he imagined Jesus's love coming down from the heavens.

Paul thanked me for our work together and said it really helped his hypertension. He then asked me for a referral to a therapist who specialized in a Christian approach to psychotherapy, which I gave him.

This case illustrates, among other things, how important it is to be aware of an individual's cultural and religious beliefs when doing Qigong or any form of therapy.

CHAPTER 12: DEPRESSION

Research: Medication Versus Behavioral Health

Almost 19 million Americans are thought to suffer from depressive disorders; however, only 23 percent of individuals with clinical depression seek treatment, and only 10 percent of these people receive adequate care (Dunn, 2005). The purpose here in addressing this pervasive malady is not to give an exhaustive review of treatment, but to give a sense of how Qigong and BMHP can add to current treatment options.

The literature on the treatment of depression is substantial (Yapko, 1997; Morrison, 1999), showing that cognitive-behavioral approaches can be effective (Beck, 1979). And there is much research also showing that medications can be of help (Morrison, 1999). Sometimes medication can be a useful, and even necessary, tool in treating cases of severe depression, bipolar disorder, and general inability to function. Since there is much conflicting information about the efficacy and side effects of medication for depression, the aware consumer should, in conjunction with consultation with a trusted health professional, do adequate research on the contrasting views regarding medication's benefits versus its side effects (Kramer, 1997; Breggin, 2001).

For example, there are many reports on the detrimental side effects of antidepressant medication. As discussed in Chapter 1, unfortunately our Food and Drug Administration cannot be trusted at this time due to political lobbying by drug companies. One good overview of this literature can be found at www.drmercola.com.[1] Regarding warnings from an international source, the *British Medical Journal* reported increased suicide rates in adults and children taking serotonin re-uptake inhibitors, the most popular form of antidepressants (Moncrieff & Kirsch, 2005). A study reported in *Blood* magazine, reported cases of lowered immune function when taking common antidepressants that target 5 HT uptake and release (O'Connell et al., 2006). And a study from the Northwestern University Medical School says that SSRI antidepressants can cause internal bleeding (http://msnbc.msn.com/id/7876902).[2]

Exercise

With so many potentially negative consequences involved in taking these medications, when they are not absolutely necessary, it seems prudent to start with less potentially deleterious methods. Dr. Pelletier (2000) says, tongue-in-cheek, that, "researchers may have discovered a new 'drug' for depression that promises no medication side effects that almost anyone can take advantage of, and utilize: '*Exercise*'" (p. 34). In fact, it is well-known that exercise is an important treatment component of depression. In a study that involved eight adults, ages 20 to 45 years, who were diagnosed with mild to moderate depression, when researchers looked at exercise alone to treat the condition they found (Dunn et al., 2005):

- ◆ Depressive symptoms were cut almost in half in those individuals who participated in 30-minute aerobic exercise sessions, three to five times a week after twelve weeks.

- Those who exercised with low-intensity for three and five days a week showed a 30 percent reduction in symptoms.
- Participants who did stretching flexibility exercises for 15 to 20 minutes, three days a week averaged a 29 percent decline.

In everyday standard of care, therapists often prescribe exercise to activate energy in depressed patients. So, why not consider using Qigong, one of the oldest exercise systems in the world, for depressed patients? Recent research reported in the *International Journal of Geriatric Psychiatry* adds credence to the intuition that Qigong would be beneficial for depressed patients. In a randomized control trial eighty-two participants with a diagnosis of depression and chronic physical illness were recruited and randomly assigned to a Qigong group or a newspaper reading group. After 16 weeks the members of the Qigong group were significantly improved in mood, self-efficacy, personal well-being, and physical and social domains of self concept compared to the controls (Tsang et al., 2002).

Qigong: An Exercise that Is More than Exercise

BMHP proposes that, in addition to the cardiovascular and energizing attributes of traditional recommended exercise, and in going along with the known benefit of stretching exercises, Qigong and Tai Chi should be considered as recommended treatments of choice — due to their ability to complement other methods of exercise and psychological treatment in the unique ways mentioned throughout this book.

One beneficial, yet unrecognized, attribute of these forms of exercise is that they are easy to use as hypnotic anchors at moments when one is not physically exercising. For example, methods such as the combined breathing methods and meridian visualizations in the *River of Life* practice, and the practices of experiencing the "energy ball" between your hands, can be activated at moments when negative cognitions overwhelm the ego. Likewise, the empowerment postures in the animal forms of Qigong, such as the *Tiger* or the *Bear*, provide state-specific anchors, which can reactivate these state-specific states of consciousness (Rossi, 1986).

The deeper dimensions of Qigong practice involve the very thing that is needed in the sedentary setting of the modern office and modern life — the ability to activate an empowered, energized state when one isn't in the act of exercising. For example, in the *Bear* practice (see Volume I) you first start imagining you are a bear, then practice *Bear Breathing*, and then do various movements to activate the liver meridian, which in Chinese medicine is associated with anger and depression. After the practice, see if you can bring back the energy of the "bear-specific" state of consciousness just by doing *Bear Breathing*. These multiple access channels provide ways to identify with and shape-shift into activating the soft, grounded power of the bear.

Bodymind Healing Psychotherapy's Integrated Approach

Following an integrative treatment approach, Bodymind Healing Psychotherapy incorporates many of the common standards of care, such as cognitive-behavioral therapy. I prefer, as a first line of treatment when appropriate and in conjunction with psychiatric consultation, to use non-medication alternatives to balancing the patient's psychophysiology. Like other health professionals, BMHP practitioners suggest aerobic exercise, but in addition we suggest (with clinical discretion and with appropriate clients) the use of Qigong movements and static non-movements (see Chapters 11 and 22). Regardless of which type of Qigong is integrated into a therapist's practice, Qigong has the potential to be an important adjunct to psychotherapeutic treatment by its ability to activate the energy of a patient's vital, primordial Self.

Case Illustration: "I Never Had a Happy Moment."

"Gloria," was a young woman who, early in our therapy, reported not being able to remember ever having had a happy moment. She was in a relationship with a man who continually made denigrating comments to her thereby adding to her longstanding feelings of worthlessness. Our therapy involved some deep psychodynamic work uncovering how, according to Gloria, "both my mother and father hated me." Her internalization of these self-deprecating messages were what led to her sense of worthlessness. From many undeserved beatings, and from being fearful of communicating her feelings to her abusive father, "learned helplessness" developed and Gloria found herself oftentimes in a victim stance in life. At her job as an executive assistant, she reported being "walked over" by her officemates, and she complained to me about being "totally incapable of asserting myself to my boyfriend and other people, due to freezing up whenever I am criticized."

    The methods of BMHP were helpful in her long-term therapy. As Gloria went back to her early childhood memories, she recalled that she came to her parents as a third child just when her parents were having financial difficulties and didn't want another child. From this realization, Gloria saw how when her parents had deprived her of many of the things that her siblings had received, it was not personal, but circumstantial. She saw the parallels between her relationship with her father, and how she projected and reenacted this old abuse in her current work situation, and in her relationship with her boyfriend. As she "cognitively restructured" her belief about being worthless, she saw that, "I have worth and deserve to be treated with respect." Though this cognition, in conjunction with energy psychology tapping methods, was helpful to some degree, the anchoring was not long lasting or accessible at key moments due to Gloria's severe wounding at an early developmental age.

    Our therapy would be too extensive to outline here, but one more aspect worth noting came from my suggestion that Gloria ask her mother for a good picture of her from her childhood. To Gloria's surprise, she found one where she was smiling. This became a useful anchor for those times when Gloria felt worthless and incapable of smiling about anything. She also found it helpful when I suggested that she try pretending that she was getting $100,000 to act the part of a genuinely happy person in a play. When she acted "as if" she was happy, she was able to "shape-shift" into the long-buried, happy part of herself. After these interventions and for the first time, I saw Gloria smile, and we built on this in subsequent sessions. She learned to focus less on the abuses in her life, and more on how she responded to these things. She began to find things in life for which she was grateful; and she realized that she could find pleasure in taking a self-assertive stance, even if the person didn't respond exactly the way she wanted.

Another anchor we used was the *Bear Breathing* exercise that she had noticed in my book (Volume I). She said, "Since my Teddy Bear was my only friend in my childhood, I thought I'd check out that Bear exercise." In addition to her childhood picture, *Bear Breathing* became another anchor to help empower her at moments when she regressed to her "worthless" self. *Bear Breathing* consists of raising the hands (claws) palm up to the heart on the inhalation, and turning of the palms (claws) downward on the exhalation down to the belly. I believe that the role of the Bear Qigong in conjunction with the broader dimensions of BMHP helped reverse Gloria's learned helplessness and helped her develop a "cohesiveness of self" (Horner, 1990, p. 30). Towards the end of our therapy, Gloria reported that she was now better able to take her stance of power with her co-workers, and eventually, after trying to work things out with her boyfriend and asserting herself to him with appropriate affect modulation skills to no avail, she left him. In our termination session after about year of therapy, she joked about the Bear being her "medicine animal" (Storm, 1972); she said that those things that used to bother her bounced off more easily now that she had this new stance in life. Last I heard, Gloria was in a new relationship with a man who treated her better.

The particular anchors chosen must be suited to the particular person. In Chapter 4, I discussed auditory anchors in the form of songs that have either transcendent or transmuting attributes. These songs can play an important part in the context of a wider psychotherapy process. There I discussed an orthodox Jewish man who was suffering from severe negative thinking and resultant depression. Among other aspects of our depth psychotherapy over a one-year period, he found that singing the song, "This too is for the Good" (*Gam Zeh Tovah*), was helpful in countering negative cognitions when they arose. When he did this practice, it created a felt shift from a negative, constricted feeling into a bodily felt sense of open-heartedness.

In addition, regarding the use of songs in Chapter 4, I discussed the principle of not just singing a happy song, but singing one that is in tune with the pain felt, i.e. like songs from the "Blues" genre of music. Along these lines, I recall the female patient suffering from situational depression from having just lost a long-term relationship, and she didn't know how she could ever put her life back together again. She found herself singing, "I'm free falling," in the shower; and in conjunction with our longer-term therapy she used this song to identify with everything in the universe that falls, survives, and is freed up to create new realities. This became her anchor when she was in the midst of her deepest pain, which helped to remind her, along with her ongoing psychotherapy, that like the seeds of an oak tree falling to the ground, life goes on.

Cultivating the energy of life comes not just through Chinese Qigong practices, but through finding the songs of our heart. (And it doesn't hurt to add a little Qigong rocking or bodily expression of the song while you're singing.)

CHAPTER 13: ADDITIONAL EXAMPLES: SYNDROMES AMELIORATED BY QIGONG AND BODYMIND HEALING PSYCHOTHERAPY

In the appendixes of Volume I, and throughout this book I have addressed a variety of syndromes for which Qigong can play an ameliorative role. In this chapter I will touch upon some of the prevalent syndromes that are affecting a large number of people, and how a combination of Qigong and Bodymind Healing Psychotherapy may be of benefit. Although I will not go as deeply into how BMHP applies to these conditions as I have in previous chapters due to space limitations, it is my hope that you will be able to draw from these earlier chapters and apply the previously outlined BMHP principles and methods to the health issues included in this chapter. It is not my purpose in these clinical chapters to be exhaustive in addressing all possible clinical syndromes, but to lay a groundwork upon which others may build regarding how BMHP and BMHQ may contribute to an integrative approach to our current health crisis.

Arthritis, Joint Problems, and Musculoskeletal Disorders

Arthritis and Tai Chi

There are a number of peer-reviewed research articles from reputable journals showing the efficacy of movement therapy (Van Deusen & Harlowe, 1987) and Tai Chi for a variety of arthritic conditions including rheumatoid arthritis (Kirsteins et al., 1991), and osteoarthritis (Hartman et al., 2000).

Rheumatoid arthritis (RA) is a chronic progressive disease that consists of joint and generalized pain, swelling, stiffness, fatigue, sleep disturbance, weakness, decreased range of motion, and limb deformities. It affects approximately 1 percent of the general population, with women almost three times more likely than men to be affected. This disease's onset occurs most commonly between ages of 20 and 50, with prevalence increasing with age (Young, 1993).

There is increasing evidence that RA is an autoimmune disease (Young, 1993; Sapolsky, 1998, p. 138); and there are many psychological interpretations for why the body activates such a course of action. As related to the discussion in Chapter 2 about somatization disorders, it may be that the body is expressing its limits by attacking that which is hurting it — itself. Some have posited that when the body mistakes itself as an invader and attacks itself, it may be related to psychophysiological issues. For example, a person may be severely overdoing things and not listening to his or her body's limits, or the body may be expressing itself metaphorically. For a more extended discussion see Gatchel & Blanchard (1993), Sapolsky (1998), and Wickramasekera (1998). From BMHP's perspective it is important for each individual to "focus" on the felt meaning behind his or her unique symptoms (Gendlin, 1978). It has been shown that autoimmune disorders are highly correlated to stress, yet it is not the stress itself, but a faulty response to stress that may provide an important clue to healing.

There is increasing research that points to how the consideration of psychological etiology and treatment may be beneficial as one component of an integrated treatment approach. For example, RA has been associated with learned helplessness (Garber & Seligman, 1980; Stein et al., 1988), and a study showed that arthritis helplessness significantly predicted impairment twelve months later, independent of disease activity (Lorish et al., 1992). Among other relevant psychological variables are self-efficacy (Lorig et al., 1989) and disease-related cognitive distortions (Smith et al 1988). An article in the *Annals of Behavioral Medicine* concluded that patients who rely on passive, avoidant, or emotion-focused strategies such as self-blame, or catastrophization for coping with RA typically report lower self-esteem, poorer adjustment, and greater negative affect. The converse is true for those patients who engage in active, problem-solving coping styles (Zautra & Marine, 1992).

Traditional Western research has shown that appropriate exercise can be beneficial with RA patients to increase aerobic capacity, endurance, strength, and flexibility, and to significantly decrease depression, anxiety, and pain (Minor, 1991). An article in the *American Journal of Physical Medicine and Rehabilitation* says that Tai Chi is safe for RA patients and has the potential advantage of stimulating bone growth and strengthening connective tissue (Kirsterns et al., 1991). But studies like this merely begin to demonstrate what Tai Chi is capable of doing. A next step in research would be to do comparison studies between Western forms of exercise and Tai Chi to see which does best for which groups of people and which variables are further enhanced.

In my limited experience with RA patients at the Health Medicine Institute, I found that they usually preferred relaxed Tai Chi movements as compared to more vigorous or forceful Western exercise, due to the unique ability of this art to simultaneously relax and strengthen, and not over-stimulate an already taxed immune and nervous system. Patients who found vigorous forms of Western exercise too much to handle found Tai Chi to be easier to practice. One RA patient found that when she was in her most exacerbated state, physical exercise was out of the question, and even Tai Chi was too much. She found the static forms of Qigong that included slight rocking (like the *Circle that Arises from Stillness* exercise) and just a minimal amount of *Tai Chi Ruler* to both be soothing practices, and both helped her to feel more in control of her pain.

Osteoarthritis (OA) is a degenerative joint disease characterized by degeneration of joint cartilage and adjacent bone that can cause joint pain and stiffness. It is the most common joint disorder equally affecting men and women. There are differences between the treatment of RA and OA that are beyond the scope of this current discussion. For example, injections of various antioxidants, such as superoxide dismutase, to protect cells against damage from free radicals have been used successfully to treat osteoarthritis, but results with RA have been disappointing (Pelletier, 2000, p. 105).

The *World Press* has reported on the benefits of Tai Chi in reducing pain for osteoarthritis sufferers. According to *Reuter's Health* (2005) Dr. Rhayun Song of Soonchunhyang University in Korea, presented his research findings recently in San Francisco at the annual meeting of the American College of Rheumatology. He found that twelve weeks in a Tai Chi program eased women's pain and made their daily activities more manageable. This report states that previous research has suggested that the art, which focuses on improving strength, balance and flexibility through gentle movements, can help treat arthritis and lower blood pressure. Dr. Song reported on his randomized designed trials: Forty-three women were randomly assigned to one of two groups. Twenty-two subjects performed Tai Chi exercise for twelve weeks, while the rest received standard treatment only. After twelve weeks, there were significant differences between the groups. Song reported, "Women in the Tai Chi group reported less pain, less difficulties with daily activities, improved balance, and greater abdominal muscle strength."[1]

Meditation and mind-body interventions have proved beneficial for sufferers of various forms of arthritis (http://nccam.nih.gov/health/meditation). In a study by Dr. Kate Lorig (1984, 1993), of the Stanford University School of Medicine, arthritis patients who participated in a behavioral pain management program experienced an increase in self-efficacy, an average 20 percent decline in pain, and a 40 percent reduction in visits to their doctors. It is promising to hear that this Stanford National Council for Complementary and Alternative Medicine funded program will extend their research to arthritis patients learning Mindfulness Meditation (Pelletier, 2000). Since there are many similarities and differences between Qigong/Tai Chi and these meditative and mind-body approaches, it would be interesting to explore with whom which treatments work best.

From my experience, I've seen that Qigong can be beneficial for many types of arthritic conditions and joint problems. The general axiom is that those who suffer from such conditions need to listen to their own bodies when doing any exercise. In Bodymind Healing Qigong, I advise participants in classes or individual sessions to first build up a sufficient amount of Qi by spending time in static Qigong postures. After building up Qi, then they may flow back and forth from stillness to movement, and back to stillness. *Wuji Standing Meditation* (see Volume I) is ideal for this, if standing is not too difficult for one's condition. If standing is difficult, then the practitioner practices Qigong while sitting or lying down. As discussed in Volume I, an additional aspect of the Taoist notion of going from stillness to movement, and back to stillness, is to first make circles and then go back to stillness. There I spoke about how the grandmaster of my Qigong tradition, Wang Xiangzhai, said, "Big circles are very good, small circles are even better, no circles are best." The idea here is that whether one is sitting, lying down, or standing such practices promote healing.

In BMHQ, after Qi is built up into one's "bank account" and the *Circle that Arises from Stillness* is practiced (see Chapter 24), we add another practice that involves spirals. The three-sequence practice illustrated in Volume I — *Moving a Snake through the Joints*, *Dipping Your Hands into the Waters of Life*, and *Opening Your Heart to the Heavens* (see Chapter 24) — is another practice that may be beneficial, so long as the practitioner listens to his or her own body. To make this practice most beneficial, move back and forth from spiraling to no spiraling movements, finding the stillness in spiraling and the spiraling in stillness.

What integrative medicine adds to the treatment of arthritis sufferers is a multidisciplinary approach beneficial to the condition. At our clinic, in working with such patients, we incorporated acupuncture, bodywork, psychological, and medical advice about dietary changes needed. Natural herbs can also be an important adjunct to treatment.[2]

What Bodymind Healing Psychotherapy, or any psychotherapy, adds here is a supportive place for those who suffer from arthritis to come to terms with the social, interpersonal, and intrapsychic dimensions of the effects of these disorders on one's lifestyle. Some of the relevant components of effective psychotherapy are: using cognitive restructuring to change cognitive distortions, working through patterns of learned helplessness, being aware of issues of secondary gain, increasing a sense of self-control and self-efficacy, using the symptoms as teachers to learn from the body, seeing illness as an initiation onto the path of the wounded healer, and countering self-blame with self-love. In conjunction with these components of psychotherapy, using a blend of cognitive therapy and energy psychology interventions can be helpful. For example, repeating the phrase, "Even though I ____, I can still love and accept myself," can be a key component of the healing relationship to one's self that has corollaries in the biochemistry, energy, and neurophysiology of the patient. The breathing, visualization, and self-soothing methods of BMHP as well can be useful adjuncts to the integrative treatment approach. Further research is needed to substantiate these methods and explore the parameters of which, when, with whom, and how, these methods work best.

Carpal Tunnel Syndrome

In the Introduction I discussed the case of one of my turning point patients who suffered with carpal tunnel syndrome (a syndrome associated with repetitive motion of the hands/wrists that causes chronic pain). Following are some of the key issues that were discussed in regards to how the *Commencement* movement in Tai Chi helped to alleviate his carpal tunnel syndrome.

1. Qigong is not a one-time fix, but instead a method of practice that usually needs to be continued to maintain healing results.

2. When integrating Qigong movements into the context of psychotherapy, the therapist needs to be aware of the transference issues so that the patient will feel free to address any limitations of success.

3. The way in which Qigong is integrated into the psychotherapy is important in order for the therapist to avoid making false promises, as well as in protecting the patient against disappointment. It should be introduced as a scientific experiment rather than promising a "cure."

The Tai Chi movement that was helpful for this patient, called *Commencement* or *Raising and Lowering the Qi* (see Volume I), involves exhaling and pressing the hands down slightly at the level of the belly, bending the wrists just to the point where there is no force, as if the practitioner is pressing a ball slightly down into water. On the inhalation the hands float up as if in water. This practice gets Qi to move through the joints without strain or force.

It is an established fact that mind-body interventions can often be helpful in alleviating the symptoms of carpal tunnel syndrome (Garlinkel et al., 1998). And, it is becoming an established fact that various aspects of Chinese medicine can be helpful in the treatment of carpal tunnel syndrome. In a 1990 study, by Chen (1998), all but one of thirty-six acupuncture patients attained excellent pain relief from carpal tunnel syndrome after treatment. In a follow-up study, twenty-four patients showed 2.5 to 8.5 years of pain relief.[3] In China, Qigong is often used to complement acupuncture treatment.

One basic thing to keep in mind if you are suffering from carpal tunnel syndrome is that usually your body is giving you a message to alter the behavior which is causing the problem.

Chapter 13: Additional Examples. 187

Altering the ergonomics of your work situation, changing the way you put your hands on the computer keyboard, changing your seating, taking more breaks, massaging your wrist with various ointments such as Traumeel (www.healusa.com) are important parts of everyday standard of care.

According to Gach (1990), using the Qigong self-touch methods of acupressure should be a basic part of self-care for those who suffer from carpal tunnel syndrome. Try using the acupoint on the middle of the inner wrist (P-7), and also breathing and massaging with the "circle, stop, breathe, and feel method" on points up this meridian line (Pericardium) up the inner arm. Similarly a point on the middle of the outer wrist (TW-4), and likewise massaging points on this meridian line (Triple Warmer-5) up the outside of the arm can be beneficial.

From the perspective of Qigong, people oftentimes inappropriately focus on the area of the symptom, rather than expanding the focus to include the whole body. Most often there is a constriction in the shoulder muscles around the spine, or even in the hips, that is correlated with the constriction of the nerves and the tightening of the tendons in the wrist. The points listed above are some of the most common points used in carpal tunnel syndrome. However, from the perspective of Qigong and the *River of Life* practice, it is important to focus both upstream and downstream from the apparent point of energy blockage. For carpal tunnel syndrome, imagine opening the river of life with self-massage on points "upstream" in the shoulder muscles, then let your intuition guide you "downstream" and explore points there. For example, massage the meridian line down the outside of the hand, ending at the base of the pinky finger where the crease appears when you make a fist (Small Intestine-3).

When your body is crying out for help, it is also a great time to reach out for help from a loved one or body worker for a nice massage. Remember the principle from the chapter on chronic pain that sometimes it is best not to force touch in areas where there is inflammation. Instead, try touching adjoining areas in order to move the Qi to balance excess and deficient energy, and try exploring using the appropriate element of touch (fire, earth, metal, water, and wood) referred to in earlier chapters (Lam, 1999).

Joint Problems

Regarding Qigong movements for joint problems in general, the first principle is that before moving, learn to experience filling the ball of Qi through *Microcosmic Orbit Breathing* and visualizations. In addition to the principles outlined above for carpal tunnel syndrome, the *Yin-Yang Balancing Method*, as discussed in the chapter on chronic pain, can also be helpful. After checking with your doctor and/or physical therapist, you might try some of the following Qigong movements (illustrated in Volume I). For example, *Horse Whipping Tail* increases circulation to the shoulders and arms. To open the energy of the heart and to get the spiraling energy of the whole body into the meridian lines of the wrist and shoulders, try this sequence: *Moving a Snake through the Joints, Dipping Your Hands into the Waters of Life,* and *Opening Your Heart to the Heavens* (see illustration in Chapter 24). In our clinic, using these movements helped quite a few people in conjunction with other health professionals who used diet, acupuncture, chiropractic, and light therapy (photon emission) as their treatment methods. Depending upon their finances, some patients would see one or more of these health professionals.

Freezing of Joints Due to Stroke — My Father's Physical Therapy

Regarding joint problems, I'd like to share a story about my father, who, after experiencing a stroke, was lying in bed, unable to straighten his leg for quite a few months. One time that I visited him, a physical therapist was trying to help my father straighten his leg by pulling it in the direction that would straighten it. She said to my father, "Come on Mr. Mayer, you know it needs to be exercised to build its strength. Let's do it ten times. Then she began to pull on it … one … two …" My father was not able to do this and I could see the physical therapist and my father getting frustrated. So I asked her if she'd mind my trying something. She said, "Go ahead." I then said jokingly to my father, "Dad, you know that breathing and Qigong stuff I've always been trying to get you to do? Well now I have a captive audience; how about doing an experiment with me?" My father agreed. I asked him to inhale as I moved his leg in the direction to which it could move, and then asked him to exhale as I moved it right up to, but no further than, the place it was stuck. The physical therapist impatiently interrupted and in a demeaning tone, thinking I must be pretty stupid, said, "Of course he can move it in that direction, sir; we're trying to get it to move in the other direction." I told her I understood what she was saying, but asked her to be patient and just watch for a moment. Then I continued to have my father inhale as I bent his leg in the direction which was easy for him; with each exhalation I moved his leg a little further as it was beginning to regain its flexibility. Eventually, after a few minutes, the leg was almost completely straight.

It was an important moment in my life to give this gift back to my father, and to see the physical therapist's amazement as she asked where I had learned this technique, since she had never been shown it in physical therapy training. I explained to her it wasn't so much a technique but a Taoist principle called *wu wei*, or effortless effort.

I explained to her that the Eastern viewpoint on healing is to not fight the current, but to go along with the natural forces of life. Using the body's natural movements the way it wants to go, synchronizing breath and movement, and not forcing, are all important principles of Taoist healing.

Fibromyalgia (FM)

There are a variety of conditions appearing in doctor's offices and hospitals in which the cause of the condition remains unknown. Among these syndromes, such as chronic fatigue and fibromyalgia, we will focus on fibromyalgia. Fibromyalgia is a pain disorder where pain occurs at multiple locations accompanied by widespread stiffness, fatigue, weakness, and irritability. About four million Americans (about 2 percent of the population) suffer from FM, and 90 percent of those are women (Selfridge, 1991). Unfortunately, many in the medical industry often don't take the complaints of this disorder seriously. Instead medical professionals often minimize sufferers' pain with denigrating statements like, "It's all in your head." In the *Journal of Orthopedic Nursing* it was said that, "The cause of this complex syndrome is unknown, and there is no known cure" (Taggart, 2003).

Chapter 13: Additional Examples.

Some researchers in the field look at FM and other related disorders as sympathetic nervous system overload diseases. From the perspective outlined in Chapter 2, one way of looking at this disorder is that it may actually be the body's way of communicating to us that we haven't listened to its expressed limits.

These types of somatization disorders may be the body's way of enforcing relaxation and limit setting, and asking for new lifestyle modifications to be made. However, the term "somatization disorder," does not do fibromyalgia justice, because there are a complex array of biochemical, energetic, and stress-related factors that are correlated with this disorder. To reduce FM to "nothing but psychosomatic" is not helpful.

Numerous research studies indicate that a combination of physical exercise and mind-body therapy is effective in symptom management (Taggart, 2003). In this same orthopedic nursing journal article, the effect of Tai Chi on FM was investigated in a pilot study with a one group, pre-test/post-test design. Thirty-nine participants with fibromyalgia formed a single group for six weeks of one hour, twice weekly Tai Chi classes. FM symptoms and health-related quality of life were measured before and after exercise. Twenty-one participants completed at least ten of the twelve exercise sessions. Although the dropout rate was higher than expected, measurements on both the Fibromyalgia Impact Questionnaire (Buckhardt, Clark, & Bennett, 1991) and the Short Form–36 (Ware & Sherbourne, 1992) revealed statistically significant improvement in symptom management and health-related quality of life.

Even though the research methodology of the above study lacks a control group and follow-up research on the dropouts, its findings on Tai Chi and FM offers some hope in an arena where little hope is given.

In addition to this article in the *Journal of Orthopedic Nursing* there are quite a few articles in professional journals that point to the beneficial effects of relaxation and exercise methods like Tai Chi and Qigong on fibromyalgia (Mannerkorpi et al., 2004, 2005; Creamer, 2000) — there have even been randomized controlled trials supporting the efficacy of Qigong and Mindfulness Meditation in the treatment of fibromyalgia (Astin, 2004).

These studies are particularly significant due to the fact that pharmacological treatments produce unwanted side effects. When I did a training with Dr. Selfridge, at the 2005 energy psychology conference in Baltimore, where I was also presenting, it was reconfirming for me to find that such a leader, and medical doctor, in the field was promoting the beneficial effects of a mind-body-energy approach to healing fibromyalgia. Dr. Selfridge is author of the book *Freedom from Fibromyalgia: The Five-week Program Proven to Conquer Pain*, (Selfridge & Peterson, 2001). In her presentation she spoke about how the common pharmacological treatment of anti-inflammatory medication doesn't usually work. Dr. Selfridge is a medical doctor who is not only chief of the Complementary Medicine and Wellness Center in Madison, Wisconsin, but she is also someone who healed herself from this disorder. Dr. Selfridge spoke about how she believed that fibromyalgia is a "disharmony of the spirit," and she used Chinese medical terms to speak about the disorder. In Dr. Selfridge's (2001) book, she speaks of the need to identify triggers to one's symptoms such as anger and shame, do emotional house cleaning, and use cognitive approaches and journaling to work with dysfunctional beliefs. She advises meditation and breathing exercises as key components of her treatment approach. In addition to those who have found a healing pathway through Dr. Selfridge's approach, another place where behavioral treatment methods have proved effective in treatment of FM is in Nashua, New Hampshire at the Mathew Thornton Health Plan's Behavioral Medicine Pain Program (Pelletier, 2000, p. 85)

Discovering a similar pathway as these leaders in the field, I also developed a body-mind-energy approach to helping those who suffer from this disorder. In my experience with FM patients, I have found that their symptoms often developed during a time of great stress — outer or inner. For some patients, they did not listen to their body's need to relax, for others, they didn't pay enough attention to recharging their batteries, expressing their needs, or setting appropriate limits. It was as if the body was screaming out in multiple locations, "I'm in pain, I'm not going to let you overwork/overstress me anymore." For other patients I've found that some common denominators were inner stressors such as holding in various feelings like anger, or having internalized perfectionistic messages from their families of origin. Identifying beliefs that are relevant to the creation of their symptoms such as, "I can't rest until I get everything done," is an important part of treatment. Often, as discussed in Chapter 2, the roots of somatization disorders seem to come from the body expressing what the voice can't (Gatchel & Blanchard, 1993). So, expressing the unique words and meanings underlying the "somatization" is crucial for each person.

Normally we think of symptoms as something we want to get rid of at any cost. However, symptoms sometimes serve a purpose about which our conscious mind may be unaware. Sometimes an unconscious secondary gain comes from the symptoms, i.e. loved ones finally give desired attention when they see the sufferer's pain. In such cases, expressing one's needs directly and letting in others' caring, can be an important part of the path towards symptom reversal. Another "benefit" that the symptom of pain provides is to stop a person from engaging in the detrimental, self-destructive behavioral patterns that may have created the FM in the first place.

At our clinic, and in my private practice, the BMHP methods discussed in earlier chapters have been a helpful component in an integrated treatment approach to this disorder. For example, I use Focusing to find the felt meaning of the pain, identify the dysfunctional beliefs which led to taking on more stress than the body could handle, and clear the obstacles to expression. Solid clinical evidence in the field has shown hypnosis is beneficial in fibromyalgia.[4] My patients often report that using the particular breathing and hypnosis visualization methods contained in the BMHP process, such as the *River of Life*, have been beneficial. Particularly helpful have been the components of BMHP which involve self-soothing by putting one hand on the heart combined with the energy psychology method (Craig, 1995) of saying, "Even though___, I can still love and accept myself." Other key factors in healing include: finding ways to change dysfunctional lifestyle choices, noticing dietary exacerbations, limiting caffeine intake, and setting appropriate limits with work and family members. Since oftentimes even light touch or moderate exercise can be painful, an adjunctive program of Tai Chi and Qigong can be ideal methods for keeping circulation active and energy alive while not overstressing the body.

Many think of fibromyalgia as a "modern" disease, but Chinese Medical Doctor Xiao-Ming Tian says that the symptom complex now called fibromyalgia has long been known about in Chinese medicine (Selfridge, 2001, p. 19). Since exercise is a key element of activating immune system response, Qigong is a natural practice to try in conjunction with advice from medical professionals. Practicing static Qigong first, until the ball of Qi is filled, and then moving from

Chapter 13: Additional Examples. 191

stillness to movement and back to stillness is a general principal to be honored. Some of the Bodymind Healing Qigong methods that FM patients have reported to be helpful are: cultivating Qi through *Microcosmic Orbit Breathing* (see Chapter 4), Standing Meditation, finding the *Circle that Arises from Stillness*, Walking Meditation, and *Dispersing Stagnant Qi* (see Chapter 24).

Here, as much, if not more so than in other disorders, the axiom is to listen to your body to find the method that is best suited to your individual needs. For example, one fibromyalgia patient couldn't lift her hands above her shoulders to do *Dispersing Stagnant Qi* exercises. By using *Microcosmic Orbit Breath* to fill her ball of Qi, pressing down instead of forcing up, and using self-hypnosis to imagine herself in water — she eventually was able to feel her hands spontaneously floating up until they came up past her shoulders, as tears of joy came to her eyes.

Diabetes

Diabetes is one of those many conditions where patients have much to be thankful for Western medicine's technological advances in the ability to monitor and bring into balance insulin levels. Psychotherapy in general, and Bodymind Healing Psychotherapy in particular, can help Type I and Type II diabetes sufferers to find a self-accepting attitude to the difficulties and limitations that this disease has on their lifestyle.

At our clinic, Qigong and BMHP together represented one spoke of an innovative wheel of treatment. Our multidisciplinary treatment approach was having diabetic patients gain the benefits of leading-edge treatment methods for balancing their insulin levels. For example, acupuncture was used to balance the patient's energy, and, in addition to the standard Western treatment protocols, the doctor at our clinic introduced an experimental, leading-edge technology called *photon emission therapy* for diabetic neuropathy. I heard about many cases and spoke with quite a few sufferers for whom their symptoms of lack of feeling and pains in the legs were healed after Dr. Saputo treated their legs with this "light machine." Further research is needed to determine just how long these effects last, for what types of patients it best works, how much placebo effect is involved, etc.

Qigong can also be a useful complement to Western medicine's contributions. A study in the *Journal of Alternative and Complementary Medicine* reported on an examination of "The Effects of Qigong Walking on Diabetic Patients" (Iwao, 1999).

Here is the abstract from this study:

Objectives: The present study was designed to evaluate the advantages of *Qigong Walking* — a mild and slow exercise that uses all the muscles of the body, in comparison with conventional walking in patients with diabetes.

Interventions: Ten inpatients with diabetes mellitus and associated complications were studied on three different days. One day the patients did *Qigong Walking*, one day conventional walking, and one day they did no exercise. On the walking days, patients walked for 30-40 minutes, 30 minutes after they ate lunch. Plasma glucose levels and pulse rates were measured 30 minutes after lunch, and again, 20 minutes after exercising; that is, 90 minutes after lunch. These data were compared to those obtained on a day with no exercise after lunch.

Results: Plasma glucose levels decreased during both exercises (from 228 mg/dL before to 205 mg/dL after conventional walking) and (from 223 mg/dL before to 216 mg/dL after *Qigong Walking*). In both walking situations, the patients' glucose levels decreased more after exercise than when they did no exercise (229 mg/dL; P<0.025). The pulse rates increased after conventional walking (from 77 to 95 beats per minute; P<0.025), and were higher than those in the group with no exercise (70 beats per minute; P<0.01), and those after *Qigong Walking* (79 beats per minute; P<0.05).

Conclusions: *Qigong Walking* reduced plasma glucose after lunch without inducing a large increase in the pulse rate in patients with diabetes.

After hearing about this study, and in response to a few of my diabetes patients asking about my suggestions for exercise, I suggested that, in addition to following their doctor's advice, they might consider practicing the *Yi Chuan Qigong Walking* from my DVD. After a female doctor at our clinic gave her enthusiastic approval, both patients reported that they enjoyed doing the exercises, and found them helpful in experiencing a sense of relaxation and empowerment at the same time (the Chinese term for this is *sung*).

The bulk of my work with diabetic patients has involved standard psychological treatment for issues involving self-esteem, decreased sexuality, anger at having lifestyle limitations, etc. I have used the Bodymind Healing Psychotherapy methods listed in the previous chapters, particularly focusing on methods of cognitive restructuring. I have also found energy psychology methods beneficial in helping patients establish anchors to self-accepting states. For example, I used this method with one male patient whose negative cognition was: "God must not exist, or I must have done something evil in a past life to deserve to carry this burden and encumbrance on my lifestyle. I'm a weakling who'll never get married." The new constructive cognition for this patient was, "We all have our crosses to bear and this is mine. The empathy for human suffering and other lessons I've learned have made me a better person, and the person with whom I am meant to be will accept all of me." (Concomitant with this statement he reported a shift of SUDS level from an 8 to a 2.) Interestingly, when this diabetic patient said these words, he held an imaginary ball in front of this heart in almost exactly the way it is practiced in *Yi Chuan* Standing and Walking Meditation (see Volume I). We were able to use this posture as an anchor (see Chapter 16) for those times when he fell into his old, self-despairing voice; and we used the holding of the ball and walking with it as a metaphor for walking through life holding a ball of self-acceptance. When doing this posture along with the cognitive restructuring, his SUDS level went down to 0.

Headaches

There is now established literature regarding how inappropriate coping mechanisms are correlated with many headaches, and how mind-body healing methods can be useful in the treatment of headaches (Pelletier, 2000).

After a good differential diagnosis has been done by a health professional, and dietary considerations such as excess caffeine or severe medical disorders such as tumors have been ruled out, mind-body healing methods come to the forefront.

Research in the field of clinical hypnosis shows that when a person imagines a stream coming down his or her arms and imagines it warming the hands, this can be an effective treatment for migraines (Andreychuk & Skriver, 1975). The basic principle regarding headaches and all "somatization disorders" is to wonder about the metaphorical meanings of the symptom so that the symptom becomes a symbol ... for what? One question to ask is: What is making my head ache in my life? Any good therapist can help you do this. Once a reply is found through "focusing" on the felt meaning of the symptom, an opportunity arises to "shape shift" into another way of being that could cope with this situation and the old habitual pattern.

If making the hands warm can be of help, why not use the many-thousand-year-old knowledge base of a tradition that has studied ways to make the hands warm. Qigong static postures, breathing methods, knowledge of meridian lines, and movement methods are ways to tap on a somatic knowledge base spanning the centuries.

Raynaud's Syndrome

According to the *Merck Manual of Medical Information* (1997), "Raynaud's syndrome or phenomenon are conditions in which small arteries usually in the fingers and toes go into spasm, causing the skin to become pale or a patchy red to blue ... Most often it is triggered by exposure to cold, the fingers and toes turn white, usually in a spotty fashion" (p. 136).

Medical hypnosis has also been proved beneficial to healing Raynaud's syndrome through suggestion procedures whereby subjects imagine that their hands are becoming warm (Braun, 1979; Jacobson et al., 1973). Again, why not use the many-thousand-year-old methods of hand warming that stem from Qigong to supplement the behavioral health treatment of Raynaud's syndrome?

I personally suffered from this syndrome, and told the story in Volume I about how Standing Mediation and Qigong breathing methods helped to cure me of this disorder. Since that time, I have helped a few patients lessen and cure their symptoms through the use of the *River of Life* breathing methods. In these cases, I changed the visualization to imagine warm water coming down the river to the hands. In addition to this method, "focusing" (Gendlin, 1978) on the particular issues that are stuck in the river (ice blocks) and allowing the compassionate light of the sun to melt them has been helpful to some patients; and others have benefited from the practice of Qigong and Tai Chi.

Stomach Disorders

For all disorders of this area of the body, it is particularly important to have a differential diagnosis by your physician. The intelligent consumer can also look at the *Merck Manual of Medical Information*.

Crohn's Disease

Crohn's disease is a chronic inflammation of the intestinal wall. Like other diseases of the stomach area, Bodymind Healing Psychotherapy is well-suited as a complementary treatment for treating this disorder since this disease is often rooted in stress and psychosomatic issues. A female doctor who suffered from this disease reported no further symptoms after our bodymind healing psychotherapy alone, with no Qigong or Tai Chi practiced. This example is not provided as evidence of efficacy, since many times Crone's disease is known to remit after short-term episodes. In fact, her symptoms did reoccur later in our long-term therapy when a significant stressor arose in her life. Again, by using BMHP method she was able to alleviate their symptoms with no need for her usual medication. Further research is needed regarding how the specific methods of Bodymind Healing Psychotherapy can become part of an integrated treatment protocol.

Irritable Bowel Syndrome

It is a well-researched fact that mind-body-spirit issues are inextricably connected with irritable bowel syndrome and other functional gastrointestinal disorders (Salt, 2002). These disorders of the gut affect 35 million Americans and comprise 10 percent of visits to medical doctors. It is important to have a differential diagnosis by your physician to approach your treatment in the best way since many gastrointestinal disorders can be mistaken for IBS.

Bodymind Healing Psychotherapy is one of many psychotherapeutic approaches that can be helpful for this disorder. As discussed in Chapter 2, somatization disorders like IBS are often related to a difficulty in differentiating and expressing feelings. The body seems to express "its irritation" by saying, "I'm irritated by ___." Understanding the psychodynamic roots of why a person holds onto feelings rather than expressing them is one step on the path to healing; another step is to examine the beliefs that are in the way of self-expression. Using cognitive restructuring along with somatic anchors, as discussed in other chapters, is one important part of treatment. Qigong and Tai Chi are also natural ways to substitute a relaxation response for a stress reaction. In particular, the patients with whom I've worked enjoy using the *Tai Chi Ruler* exercise while they imagine putting down a ball of tension on their exhalation, and re-empowering their hearts on the inhalation, as the Tai Chi circle moves back into the body (see illustration in Chapter 24.). As well, doing self-applied *Chi Nei Tsang* (Chia, 1990) can be helpful for some people, i.e. using gentle "circle, stop, breathe, and feel" movements, pushing into your belly as you exhale. Before pushing into your belly this way, check with your medical doctor to make sure you have a correct diagnosis.

One female patient, "Edith," the daughter of a medical doctor, was extremely skeptical of any mind-body-spirit connection to her IBS; but through "scientific" exploration and her journaling she realized that every time she had a flare-up there was something serious going on with her son or husband. As soon as her husband and she made-up, all of the symptoms would leave. Through these realizations, she was able to attribute the roots of her inhibition to multiple rapes in her early adulthood; from this trauma she internalized the belief that, "It's best to not be visible." Substituting a more balanced cognition was an important part of her process of change. "I know when to express myself and when not to, due to my wounds; and I'm going to allow myself the pleasure of expressing myself from my center in appropriate situations." When Edith said these words, she assumed a posture where she held her hands in front of her belly. This posture became her anchor (see Chapter 16) to be able to activate this state-specific state of consciousness. In the course of talking about this gesture, I suggested that she might like to practice the *Tai Chi Ruler* exercise. Edith liked doing this as a way, not only to hold her power in her belly center, but also to let go of the ball of inhibition on her exhalation that had been so much of her previous pattern.

Addendum: Bodymind Healing Resources for Chronic Diseases, Cancer, and Death and Dying

Finally for those who wish to see aspects of the Bodymind Healing Psychotherapy approach to other health-related issues in audio and video formats please see the following:

Chronic Diseases

Adding to the research discussed throughout this book and in Chapter 1, I created an audio tape for my patients that takes the listener through a healing meditation. It is called, *Find your Hidden Reservoir of Healing Energy: A Guided Meditation for Chronic Diseases*. This tape also takes the listener through the *River of Life* practice, which is an essential component of BMHP. It is used by some therapists and hospitals to supplement the healing methods of other health professionals, and is a good take-home audiotape to enhance relaxation and healing.

Cancer

In Chapter 1, I reviewed some of the literature in the field about the successful use of adjunctive mind-body approaches to cancer treatment (Devine & Westlake, 1995; Meyer & Mark, 1995; Hamer, 1997; Redd et al., 2001). In addition, I discussed some of the research on the use of Qigong as a complementary treatment helpful in: raising the curative rate, extending the tumor-free survival time of patients (McGee, & Chow, 1994, p. 173), lessening nausea, increasing strength, improving appetite, and bettering the quality of their survival (Sancier, 1996b; Chen, 2002).

There is an audio tape I created from my work with a cancer patient, discussed in the preface of this book, which takes the listener on a *Find your Hidden Reservoir of Healing Energy: A Guided Meditation for Cancer*. It is a duplicate of the above tape on chronic disease; but marketed for use by cancer patients.

Some references for the use of Qigong with cancer can also be found in the appendixes of Volume I.

Death and Dying

A DVD of a presentation I gave on the BMHP approach to death and dying was filmed by one of my students, a medical doctor, and is in the production process.

These last three publications are available on my website www.bodymindhealing.com

CHAPTER 14: QIGONG PSYCHOSIS

Qigong is not a panacea, nor are spiritual practices in general. This is an era where the importance of blending the psychological and the spiritual is apparent. In this spirit, Bodymind Healing Psychotherapy honors the deep, emotional, transformative journey to the underworld, as well as the raising of our spirits through the treasure-house of the cross-cultural spiritual traditions of humankind. The following case illustrates the importance of integration in the realm of psychospiritual inner work.

Case Illustration:
"I'm Going to Cut My Wife's Head Off with My Samurai Sword"

"Mitch" was referred to me by another Tai Chi teacher who said Mitch was one of his most dedicated students. Mitch reportedly practiced up to ten hours day and believed he was an advanced Taoist master. He was convinced that his one remaining obstacle was his wife, and he explained in our first session how his sword techniques were so developed that he thought he could behead her with no anger, just a centered, Samurai slice. I learned that this was not an exaggerated expression of feeling, but something Mitch was really considering doing. When I asked him what led to his wanting to do this he told me his story.

Mitch was secretly financing a woman friend who was in dire straights. This other woman was one of his closet friends from childhood (he assured me that there was nothing sexual between them). He said that his wife would never approve of him giving money to another woman, and that it was essential to his integrity that he be a giving "Master" and not be controlled by a woman's narrow material concerns that went against the flow of the Tao.

Here we see a clear example of how a "spiritual" training without psychological inner work can create dangerous imbalances and delusional thinking. Though I was concerned that this patient could be a "danger to self or others," and I was getting ready to activate Tarasoff procedures,[1] in our very first session, Mitch experienced a shift of perception as I spoke to him as a fellow Tai Chi practitioner. I questioned why, as such an advanced follower of the Way of the Tao, did he not at least trust "the Way of the universe" enough to check out with his wife how she would feel? And even if she reacted negatively, I questioned, "Don't you have the power to sink your Qi into your roots and hold your ground and work out a way both of your needs can be met? Doesn't an internal martial artist use the least force necessary?" At the end of the first session he agreed to try this, to not overreact, and to not "act out" his feelings before our next session.

To his surprise, his wife was not as upset with him as he thought she would be. She understood how he wanted to give to a longstanding friend. However, she did not want to finance this and suggested that they create two separate bank accounts so he could take his gift money out of that account.

This circumvented the immediate threat of danger. In the next sessions, Mitch and I explored the roots of his reactive pattern. His wife's not being there for his needs felt just like his mother who was "always hassling me about the amount of money she was giving me." Mitch's father had died suddenly when he was a child, and his mother was now financing his non-working lifestyle. To make a long story short, in the next sessions, Mitch worked through his rage about his father's "abandonment" of him, and he realized that he had made a decision to do whatever he wanted with his life, since he felt God and others had abandoned him. Mitch's inner work on his issues of entitlement and narcissistic rage over having to be there for other's needs helped him to commit to a new stance in life. He eventually saw how it was to his benefit to hold a job in addition to his training in Tai Chi in order to develop his root in his Self, and in everyday life and work. As he moved on from the feelings regarding his father's death, he found a job to his liking. He saw his relationship with his wife, and others, as an opportunity to practice being as centered in his emotional body, as he felt he was in his physical body. Mitch realized that, due to his wounding and lack of emotional education in his family, he had never learned to "modulate his affects." Additionally, he now saw the benefit of doing "emotional" *Tai Chi Push Hands* with his wife, and his life.

SECTION III:

ANCIENT SACRED WISDOM TRADITIONS, QIGONG, AND PSYCHOTHERAPY: PRINCIPLES, METHODS, THEMES, AND BENEFITS

...classical man saw psychological sickness as the effect of a divine action
which could be cured only by a God or another divine action.
When sickness is vested with such dignity,
it has the inestimable advantage
that it can be vested with a healing power.
The divina afflictio then contains its own diagnosis, therapy and prognosis,
provided of course that the right attitude toward it is adapted.

— C.A. Meier
Ancient Incubation and Modern Psychotherapy

Overview of Section III

Here in Section III some key principles, methods, and themes of BMHP are illustrated with discussion and case examples:

- Chapter 15: Changing Your Life Stance
- Chapter 16: Incorporating Patient Gestures
- Chapter 17: Affect Modulation and Tai Chi
- Chapter 18: Psychotherapy as Internal Martial Art: Attacking your Patients to Heal Them
- Chapter 19: Healing with the Elements
- Chapter 20: The Mythic Journey Process

Each of the chapters in this section is interwoven into a quilt. Each patch (chapter) of the quilt helps to form the whole, and many of patches are repeated in other areas of the quilt. For example, in the psychotherapeutic process of changing one's life stance, the therapist may incorporate a patient's gestures to anchor desired state-specific states, and help the patient to gain affect modulation skills. As patients developmentally mature in their self-expression, develop affect modulation skills, exercise appropriate self-assertion, and learn to banter, they may embody some of the deepest principles of internal martial arts and not use any more force than is needed. So, in each chapter many of the principles from other chapters are co-existent, but one or more of the principles are high-lighted to illustrate the issue in focus.

CHAPTER 15: PSYCHOTHERAPY AS CHANGING YOUR LIFE STANCE

What is the work of works for man
if not to establish in and by each one of us
an absolutely original center
in which the universe reflects itself in a unique and inimitable way
and those centers are our very selves and personalities.

— Tielhard de Chardin

Shape-Shifting and Changing Your Life Stance

Earlier in this book (Chapter 4), I spoke of the Aesclepius temple rituals that involved sending those who needed healing to the Dionysian Theater. This cathartic experience, which could lead to the embodiment of a new life stance, was an important part of people's healing journey in this first holistic healing temple of the Western world. Here people would wear masks of different characters in order to help change their identification with attributes of the character that was associated with their state of "dis-ease." In the earlier sections of this book we saw how the idea of "shape-shifting" into different ways of being has been a fundamental aspect of shamanic traditions the world over — a part of initiatory traditions that were helpful to hunting, empowerment, and healing. In those sections I also discussed topics such as: modern quantum biology, multiple personality research, mind-body medicine, hypnotherapy, and a "state-specific" understanding regarding how consciousness affects physical structure.

In this chapter, case illustrations will show specifically how, from the perspective of BMHP, the psychotherapy process can be viewed as changing the patient's life stance. The state-specific states of consciousness that can be activated by integrating Western psychotherapy and Qigong-related practices can aid the transformative process of shape-shifting to healthier ways of being.

Case Illustration: Social Phobia

Among those cases where a combination of Standing Meditation, Qigong practice, and psychotherapy combine to help a person change his or her life stance, perhaps none are as poignant as the stories of those who gain the strength to stand up to someone who has been abusive to them in their childhood. As reported in Volume I, as a young boy "Stan" was the smallest of all of his classmates and was a gentle and sensitive child. When other kids engaged in cruel jokes and hitting contests, Stan shied away. Because he was so small, kids enjoyed bullying him when he wouldn't fight back. Stan's stance was, in part, constitutional — his mother remembered that he was a gentle child even in his first few years of life.

Contributing to the fixation of this stance into a characterological pattern was Stan's physically abusive brother, who told him, "I'm better than you at everything." By the time he was in his late teens, Stan felt so paralyzed that he developed a social phobia and feared contact with authority figures. He dropped out of college once and complained of multiple somatic issues including developing arthritis in his fingers. In his current occupational setting he couldn't assert himself to his boss to ask for the raise he felt he deserved.

Stan was first a student in my Bodymind Qigong classes, which emphasize Standing Meditation and also include some self-defense training. Then he decided to leave our student/teacher relationship to do Bodymind Healing Psychotherapy with me.[1]

A major turning point in Stan's life was when he found a stance to stand up to his brother through his internal martial arts practices. Though his martial arts practices were important in giving him sensitivity and power, the verbal dimension of his power was equally crucial and needed to be developed through psychotherapy. One of the more significant moments in our therapy occurred after Stan went to his family's home for Thanksgiving and his brother greeted him, "So, after all these years I bet you're still not better than me at anything. Let's go out play some basketball one-on-one."

His brother's demeaning messages had always made Stan cower with anxiety in his stomach. But during this Thanksgiving dinner, after much inner work in therapy and a year of Standing Meditation practice, Stan found his verbal stance to address his brother's abusive message. Stan said, "You know something, you're not better than me at everything." His brother paused for a moment, and said, "What do you mean; give me an example. I'm still better at basketball and at every sport, and I make more money than you." Stan found the stance he had always wanted in his childhood at this moment and continued, "You're not better than me at everything — you're not better at being a kind brother." According to Stan, when he said this to his brother, it stopped him in his tracks and left him speechless for a moment. After apologizing for the way he had treated Stan in his childhood, a new relationship developed between them.

With a combination of his study of the internal martial arts, which emphasize the power of softness, and his therapy, over time Stan transmuted his identification with being an ungrounded, wimpy male. He was able to work through his lack of self-confidence and asked for a raise at work, which he got. He learned to affect his arthritis in his hands with the power of his mind and through the use of acupressure points and the visualization methods that are a wider part of the practice done in Bodymind Healing Qigong.

This was no "total cure," but "a healing." Issues still arose, but through our work together Stan had cultivated a new stance toward his issues, and he had found a way of working with and through them. He now had a clear vision of the path ahead of him, whereas before, his primordial ground was paved over. Stan now recognized that just like his internal arts work takes practice, so does finding his psychological stance. He learned to be aware of how the abusiveness of his brother fragmented his energy. And he learned to practice "cognitive restructuring" when negative thoughts arise for him. Instead of his old thought, "I'm no good and can't stand up for myself," his new, restructured thought and stance became, "I don't deserve to be treated badly despite any of my short-comings; and I will stand up for myself." Then, he breathes and practices returning to his grounded stance of power and self-assertiveness. It also helps that he is now able to use his *Tai Chi Push Hands* practice to play with his brother and demonstrate the power of his softness.

Case Illustration: Impulse Control — The Exploding Karate Kid

This case was reported in Volume I and will be repeated, with some relevant additions, to illustrate changing one's life stance with issues involving impulse control. "Arnie" was a 30-year-old night-shift worker at an industrial firm. Arnie was not one of my Tai Chi students, but in the course of our therapy I referred him to another teacher in order to keep our therapeutic container unencumbered by two different types of relationships.

Arnie came to me on referral from his company's employee assistance program for "exploding on two separate occasions" — one time he put his fist through a window, another time he threw a vial of industrial fluid across the room.

In Chapter 2, I discussed how various forms of meditation may complement psychotherapy by providing ways for patients to: develop an observing self, enhance equanimity, self-regulate and therefore improve self-control, and cultivate affect tolerance and emotional resilience in the face of provocative stimuli.

As part of our psychotherapy with an integral intention (Walsh, 2006), I introduced various meditation methods to Arnie. After introducing him to the *River of Life* meditation method (see Chapter 5) in our sessions, I suggested he try practicing it at home and at work. I hoped, along the lines of the beneficial attributes of meditation listed above and those known to be associated with Qigong meditation, that it would help Arnie to develop some of those qualities, such as: constellate his observing self, change his emotional reactivity, help him to learn to sink his Qi to his belly to find a center there, discover his central equilibrium, reduce fragmentation, develop affect modulation skills, reduce sympathetic nervous system over-arousal, and change his life stance. As part of this meditation practice, Arnie visualized the situations that triggered his loss of impulse control, then noticed the waves of emotion, thoughts, and beliefs that arose; then he returned back to his breath in the *River of Life* exercise. When Arnie was reactive, he said he wasn't aware of his body. Because of this, he reported that it was particularly beneficial to learn to follow the river of his breath down into his body and become more mindful of kinesthetic sensations and bodily holdings. This practice was a first step to help Arnie learn to avoid capsizing, and maintain his central equilibrium in the crosscurrents as he set sail on his journey of transmuting old introjected bodymind patterns of response. To further help develop his observing self I added a dis-identification method from psychosynthesis (Assagioli, 1991) to this practice, i.e. "I have a body; but I am not my body. I have sensations; but I am not those sensations. I have thoughts; but I am not my thoughts. I have impulses; but I am not those impulses. What am I then? I am a pure center of awareness that notices all these things; but I am more than them."

A key moment in therapy occurred when Arnie was practicing the transmuting dimensions of the *River of Life* practice and "focusing" (Gendlin, 1978) on his body sense. He tried to identify the tightness that was there and noticed how puffed out he was in his chest. A memory surfaced of being in gym class as a child and noticing that his chest was caved in and his posture was slouched, whereas other boys' chests were more filled out and their postures more erect. The belief that ruled Arnie's life for the next ten years was forming: "A man is one who doesn't slouch, a real man's chest is pushed out proudly."

This was Arnie's way of expressing a common male theme that: A man is one who doesn't show his vulnerabilities and doesn't cave in to the pressures of life. Many people gave Arnie validation for being able to tolerate more than other guys could. For instance, he worked longer hours than any of the other workers. When anyone needed someone to take over one of the late-night shifts, Arnie was the one that would readily volunteer. He was very well-liked for his willingness to help out anyone who had a problem.

Since Arnie would never "stoop so low" to admit his vulnerabilities or ask for help on his late-night shift, when things bothered him he would oftentimes build up resentment and explode. Also, Arnie started to realize that he had little true intimacy in his life where his true feelings could be expressed and his real feelings be known.

Arnie had been a longtime practitioner of Karate; and at first he balked when I suggested that he might consider trying Tai Chi, the best-known method of Qigong that helps to develop the qualities listed earlier and specifically emphasizes balancing strength and softness. I didn't push this idea on him, but when he saw a man practicing it in a park one day he was struck by its grace and asked me for a referral. I gave him the name of a local teacher I respected. After six months of practice, Arnie began to discover a new type of strength. On one occasion he told me of the insight he had just gotten from his practice of *Push Hands* with another student — he found that "the softer you are, the stronger you are."

The insights he gained went along well with the psychotherapeutic work we were doing. Arnie realized how he was never given any room in his family of origin to speak of his vulnerabilities. His father was a Marine captain who had a very stoical view of what it meant to be a man and "trained" Arnie in this attitude.

Arnie began to develop a new stance in his life: "A man is one who balances strength and softness. A man is one who can be with his whole Self — vulnerabilities and all." Identifying and working with both his old and new life stance was a significant part of a larger psychotherapeutic process. Arnie learned to become more aware of the feelings in his body, and he became better able to differentiate and regulate his affects. He was able to identify when he was caught in his "son of the Marine captain stance," and he was able to be aware, as stressors arose, of his abilities to activate his softer, balanced "Tai Chi stance." Arnie's was able to activate his observing self when stress arose, which led to improved impulse control, enhanced coping skills, and affect tolerance, and which proved particularly useful in the long hours of his late-night shift. The psychotherapeutic process, in conjunction with the various meditation methods discussed above, led to better containment of his feelings and the ability to express them more often in an appropriate way. At a later point in our therapy, Arnie was proud of himself on one occasion for expressing to a co-worker that he was exhausted and irritable on his late-night shift. He asked the co-worker to help him out by letting him catch a twenty-minute catnap, and wake him. To the best of my knowledge, Arnie never exploded at work again.

Chapter 15: Psychotherapy as Changing Your Life-Stance

Case Illustration: Finding the "Right Man"

As reported in Volume I, here, again, is "Rachel" — a bright, vivacious student in her early 30s, who learned Standing Meditation as part of a psychotherapy training process I gave at a local university. The following is a synopsis of a term paper she wrote and discussions I had with her.

Rachel had a history of many short-term relationships. During the time of her training, after a boring evening with her current partner, the thought arose, "He's not stimulating enough for me." Crosscurrents of feelings then took her away from her own center of gravity: "Life is depressing. There must be something wrong with me to be in a relationship that's not more alive. Maybe I shouldn't stay in this relationship any longer."

Rachel reported, after two months of practice, that Standing Meditation was helpful to ground her on her own "Island of Being" in the midst of waves of conflicting thoughts and emotions — waves that in the past made her criticize her partner with derogatory remarks. On this island she had room to cultivate her awareness with some of the methods of Bodymind Healing Psychotherapy that I had given the class to practice.

When Rachel felt that her current partner wasn't stimulating enough, she "focused" on the bodily feeling that emerged as she reflected on the above issue and asked the question, "What's this feeling all about?" As she did the *River of Life* exercise, she felt the loneliness that arose from not being met in the way she wanted to be. She felt a closed door in her heart. She felt deadness there and desperately desired to be saved from the feeling. She became aware of the thoughts, and precisely how they disrupted the flow of her Qi. She reported having difficulty going back to her breathing.

Specifically, when Rachel noticed the thought arise, "He's not enough fun," she become aware that her Qi went up into her head and an angry flushed feeling came into her face along with a contorted turn of the side of her mouth.

In Standing Meditation with psychological intent, we connect the feelings that arise while Standing with our family of origin issues. Self psychology and object relations theorists believe that many of our core patterns develop from introjected representations of early objects such as our parents. Our parents' beliefs, or lives, live in us as object-representations that need to be transmuted in order for us to be our real Selves.

Rachel associated the roots of her feelings with her unhappily married mother who thought her husband was boring, and so gave her the message, "Be careful not to get involved with a boring man." Rachel became aware of the replaying tape of her early family experience, then she went back to breath, back to center, back to her own ground. This insight, and the resulting shift that happened in her body, led her to begin therapy with a therapist that I recommended. She began the process of differentiating her own life from that of her parents; and she began to take responsibility for making things fun in her relationship, instead of "expecting the man to do it."

In the third quarter of her training program, Rachel reported that while practicing the *Opening the Golden Sphere of the Heart* exercise, she found a sense of her own ground and a sense of her Self as a golden ball of energy that was sending out love to her mother. She realized that her mother's message was just a well-meaning attempt to save her daughter from a similar fate. Rachel's resentment of her mother started to melt away as her therapy continued, and she started to take responsibility for initiating humor-full interactions with her boyfriend. The last time I heard from Rachel she reported that once she began to let go of her internalized mother's fear, she was able to see that her boyfriend actually had a dry sense of humor with which she could play.

Enhance your Stance: Melanie Klein's "Depressive Position" and Qigong

According to Melanie Klein's concept of "depressive position," as a person develops and matures, a realization comes that the hated mother is also the mother that one loves. The depressive position takes place when we take in the mother as a whole object. We inhibit our need to attack and contain the feeling in ourselves, thereby tolerating the pain of our loved object's limitations. Klein's theory is insightful regarding ambivalence — one can love and hate the mother or any person and still have a relationship (Grosskurth, 1986).

To add to Klein's ideas of the depressive position as being a way of holding the opposites of good/bad and right/wrong in order to resolve splitting, Bodymind Healing Psychotherapy suggests adding a Qigong posture to practice this stance. While doing the *Yi Chuan Qigong* practice of *Holding the Golden Ball of the Heart* (see Chapter 24 and Volume I), imagine holding a yin-yang ball that holds all opposites — good and bad, right and wrong, and the ideal versus the denigrated self. There is a dot of the complementary partner in each. While holding the ball, allow a half smile to emerge and express itself on your face. Derived from meditation traditions, this half smile says, "I'm not overjoyed because I'm in touch with the dark side and limits of life. Yet it's good to be alive, and to be able to hold all this." Thus, we have what I call (with a half smile), "the Taoist depressive stance."

Just as acupuncturists sometimes suggest Qigong postures to their patients, so do I sometimes, when appropriate, suggest that a patient practice holding this *Yi Chuan Golden Ball, Depressive Stance* posture as homework, with the intent of resolving splitting.

I have spoken about "stances" as one of the keys to ancient traditions of postural initiation. Here we have a practice for "re-membering," and reintegrating the soul-work that is part of a modern primordial psychotherapy. This includes finding a stance that helps to cultivate the "transcendent function" (Stein, 1982, p. 19) that unites opposites.

CHAPTER 16: INCORPORATING PATIENT GESTURES: TAPPING ON THE WISDOM OF THE PRIMORDIAL SELF

Once upon a time a young man decided to go on a quest to the Taoist sacred mountain of Hua Shan to see if his life's meaning could be restored. Although he vowed to fast from all food and wait until a vision came, after three days, nothing happened. Weak from starvation, he fainted in the middle of his prayer circle and gave up his effort.

As he let go of trying, it was then that the founder of Tai Chi Chuan, Chang San Feng, appeared and offered to teach him how to move like the animals to restore his vital energy, and how to find his Primordial Self by filling his body with the powers of the heavens and the earth.

And so this initiate learned how to move like a Snake Creeping Low. In addition to learning the physical movement, the snake taught him to descend into his darkness and find the way through his pain. Another week was devoted to watching and imitating the movements of a White Crane Spreading its Wings. Mimicking the crane, the initiate put one foot in the water, and spread his not-so-imaginary wings. Into his awareness came a vision of how to step into his pain, and yet find a Transcendent Self that could observe his emotional process with non-attachment.

After 40 nights on the mountaintop, learning from the animals, studying the ways of nature, and being visited by the spirit of various Taoist Masters, he knew it was now time to leave. As he traveled down the mountain, he was very excited about all he had to teach.

The first person he passed was an old lady who was washing off a glass window with a circular motion. The initiate felt a wave of disenchantment come over him as he realized that she was doing the Tai Chi movement, Making a Circle between the Heavens and the Earth (also called Taoist Immortal Paints a Heavenly Rainbow), just like he had learned it from Yang Luchan, the founder of the Yang lineage of Tai Chi.

"Maybe everyone knows what I know already and will not want to learn anything from me," he thought.

After walking a little further, he saw a man drop something on the ground and bent down to pick it up. "How does this man know the secret movement called Grasping the Pearl at the Bottom of the Sea, which I learned from Yang Cheng Fu? It's supposed to be a secret way to open the lower Tan Tien and ground the body's energy. What I know is nothing special; everyone knows it," he said to himself dejectedly.

Walking a little further he saw a couple in an argument. The woman's arms were outstretched in the shape of a ball in front of her heart as she exclaimed to her husband, "Why can't you just listen to me?" The young initiate now reached his limit, for she was doing the special Holding the Golden Ball of the Heart Meditation posture that he learned from the founder of the Yi Chuan system, Wang Xiangzhai.

Just as he was ready to give up and fall back into the sea of depression he knew so well, he came to a realization that, yes, everyone he saw was doing sacred movements, but most were unconscious of their sacred character. Then he realized that his path was to teach people to appreciate the meaning and beauty of what they were already doing in their everyday lives … that our human movements, and our very Being, are divine gifts — if we could just see them as such.

— Michael Mayer
Adapted and Retold from Shamanic Oral Teachings

The Taoist Initiate
Who Sees the Sacred in Everyday Movements

When I tell this teaching story in workshops, I ask people to notice how their body is positioned, and to appreciate its sacred meaning. For readers now, I advise the same. Maybe your feet are crossed at the ankles, preventing your life energy from dissipating out your feet. Maybe you are touching your head at the temples, unconsciously instilling some idea further into your mind through touch. What is the sacred purpose of your current posture?

Tapping the Metaphorical Wisdom of the Bodymind
Using Internal Martial Arts

Similarly, I began to notice my psychotherapy patients, particularly at key moments of change, move in ways that represent deep, often-unconscious transformative aspects of their psyches. There is a metaphorical wisdom of body language that is expressed at these moments. From my training in the internal martial arts, I noticed that the movements a martial artist uses to confront physical danger are often the same, or similar, to the movements my psychotherapy patients expressed when dealing with emotional dangers. The ancient art of Qigong, of which Tai Chi is the best-known system, contains some of the best and most primordial of these empowering movements. The psychologist who is attuned to those bodily expressions can help to bring to awareness the bodily expression of the primordial Self as it moves toward empowerment and change. The clinician who is aware of these movements and their multifaceted meanings can help to grease the wheels that facilitate movement in the direction to where the patient's psyche is already moving in its natural healing journey. To illustrate this incorporation of patients' gestures, I will use key moments in three different patients' bodymind healing process.

We saw earlier how modern energy psychology uses the tapping of points to move energy and anchor state-specific states of consciousness associated with new constructive beliefs that emerge in psychotherapy. Bodymind Healing Psychotherapy also, at times, uses tapping techniques from meridian-based psychologies. However, I have a preference towards using a patient's own gestures that emerge at the moment a new healing, state-specific state of consciousness is expressing itself through the metaphorical wisdom of body language.

In medical hypnosis, "ideomotor signaling" (Rossi, 1988; Hilgard, 1965) is used to have the patient communicate various things to the therapist, for example to communicate when a trance state has been achieved. Many times, following the therapist's suggestion, the patient moves various body parts when he or she achieves a certain state-specific state of consciousness — for example raising a finger, or nodding the head, when in a relaxed state. The patient notices that, all by themselves, these body movements seem to take place following the therapist's suggestion. For example, a therapist might suggest, "Your hands will come together when your creative unconscious is ready to begin therapeutic work." Or, "When your unconscious has resolved that problem in a satisfactory manner, your arm will come to rest on your lap." These ideomotor signals are interpreted as 'objective proof' that patients can call upon the help of their creative sources whenever they need to" (Rossi, 1988, pp. 38-39).

Adding to this tradition of ideomotor signaling, BMHP proposes that natural movements of the body be noticed at the moment a "felt shift" occurs, and that we view this process in line with the knowledge base of Chinese medicine, Qigong, and internal martial arts traditions. Then, this "whole body, naturally arising, ideomotor signaling," (without prior suggestion on the part of the therapist), can be interpreted as revealing the primordial pathways of the movement of the life force (Qi) as it opens new ways of being and new life stances. Whether or not the therapist knows Chinese medicine or Qigong, the therapist can help the patient to be aware of these body movements so that the patient can further anchor these state-specific states of consciousness for self-healing.

Phenomenologically Based Internal Martial Arts

Case Illustration: Sexual Abuse and Fist under Elbow

A young woman in her forties, who we will call "Elaine," was a psychotherapist and wanted to do a single session with me after one of my workshops. Elaine told me about being molested and raped by multiple family members in her childhood. She said she had done much work with many psychotherapeutic methods including the tapping techniques of energy psychology, but she still reported being overly hyper-vigilant and a long way from developing adequate verbal affect modulation skills.

I like to explain affect modulation to my patients through the metaphor of having the ability to regulate the quantity of affective charge on the dial of one's feelings. At the lowest setting on the dial (0 on a 10 scale) a person would be non-expressive, and with the dial all the way turned up (a 10 on a 10 scale) a person would be totally uninhibited in his or her expression. Modulating affect has to do with turning up the dial to the amount of force appropriate to the situation.

There are striking parallels between the internal martial arts tradition where the practitioner is trained in using only the least amount of force necessary when confronted with an attack, and psychotherapy's concept of affect modulation.

In her practice of affect modulation skills, Elaine used the example of a man who was "coming on to her" in a workshop she had taken in the past. The old patterns that got activated were: feeling like a victim, withdrawing in order to survive in the world, and holding on to over-reactive anger about being intruded upon. She told me that in her current therapy she was working on boundary setting and felt disappointed in herself that she wasn't able to follow through on the work she was doing with her current therapist. She said if she was "more together" she would have said to the man, "Stop coming on to me, this is a workshop." I asked her how she felt about that response. She said that type of boundary setting felt a bit extreme to her. I asked how she would ideally like to handle this man. Elaine paused for a moment and said she'd rather just flick him off as if he was a fly bothering her. At that moment she unconsciously embodied this stance with a gesture demonstrating how she'd like to flick him off. She put her left hand in a fist under her elbow, and her perpendicularly raised right hand flicked to the outside. I pointed out this arm gesture to her and asked her what she felt it expressed. She said that the stance felt so powerful to her that she didn't need to overprotect herself, and yet it made her feel she wasn't so vulnerable that she was at the mercy of someone who was coming on to her in what she felt was an inappropriate manner.

It was amazing to me that Elaine spontaneously moved like this, though she had never taken a Tai Chi class or seen the movement called *Fist under Elbow* (Ha, 1995). We role-played a few examples of unwanted men coming on to her sexually and began the working through process of finding the words to match her new empowered stance. She came up with these words for the man at the workshop, "I appreciate your interest in getting to know me, but I'm trying to concentrate on the workshop, and I have a boyfriend." Elaine felt that this was a more appropriate response from the center of her "dial of feelings." She said that she would take this work we did back to her regular ongoing psychotherapist, as a new place to begin.

This case could just as easily have been included in Chapter 17 on "Affect Modulation" as in this chapter.

Case Illustration: The Absent Father and Karate Chop Point Patient

"Emma" was a liberal arts university student who hadn't spoke to her father for five years. After her parents divorced when Emma was 12 years old, she felt abandoned and rejected by her father and his new wife. Even before this traumatic event, there were a series of times when her biological father didn't stand up for her; for example when she was 11 years old one of his drinking buddies, while drunk, made a remark about her budding sexuality and touched her on her buttocks. Another incident was when her father didn't stand up to his new wife when she broke her word about letting Emma stay at their house. She felt betrayed by her father and felt helpless in a world where "No-one will stand up for me." Also, stemming from her having a very large and angry biological father, and a new physically abusive step-father, Emma developed a pattern of helpless withdrawal when stressors arose in her life.

Chapter 16: Incorporating Patient Gestures

One of her reasons for beginning therapy was to see if she could change her pattern of "taking her marbles and going home," i.e. withdrawing when feeling betrayed by a group of friends — as in her childhood, she felt helpless to do anything about other's uncaring actions.

A large part of Emma's therapy focused on developing affect modulation skills where she learned to get better control of expressing the center point on her dial of feelings — not withdrawing and not attacking (as was discussed earlier and will be discussed further in Chapter 17 on "Affect Modulation"). But here, for our purposes let's hone in on one key therapeutic moment to make a point.

In many energy psychology approaches various combinations of acu-points are tapped as part of meridian-based therapies. One common point chosen as part of a larger sequence of points is found on the outside side of the hand, in the middle, called in energy psychology the "Karate Chop Point." It is acupuncture point Small Intestine-3.

Let's see an example of BMHP's more phenomenologically based energy psychotherapy, which favors using the patient's own movements and his or her unconscious expressed intent. In one session, when Emma was getting ready to see her father after five years of not speaking to each other, she was role-playing speaking up to him. Her negative belief was, "It's no use speaking up, because no one cares about my feelings" (SUDS-8). Her constructive belief was, "I need you to stand up for me and the truth." When Emma said these words, without knowing anything about the meaning of this point, she put her hand down forcibly on the couch, hitting the Karate Chop Point (SI-3). As we worked on her tone of voice, that she felt was somewhat blaming and not clear, she searched for the appropriate way to express herself to her father using my three-step method for constructive clearing of negative feelings (for the complete, four-step process, see Chapter 19).[1] In the course of this role-play she realized that her voice tone would be more constructive if she was simultaneously centered with her strength and her heart. She spontaneously touched her heart when she was talking about this, and put her hand down on the couch simultaneously hitting her Karate Chop Point. Then Emma said the same words, "Dad, I need you to stand up for me and the truth." She described these words and her gestures, which brought her SUDS level down to a 0.

Rather than choosing a series of therapist-imposed meridian points, here we see how the patient's own movements are so naturally healing. The meanings in the points and gestures that naturally arise in patients at key transformative moments are organically emergent expressions of primordial healing energies activated as part of the healing process. These meanings are amplified by the therapist's understanding and exploration of their healing intent. For the patient, the potential for incorporation of new ways of being and the ability to shape-shift into new characterological pathways can thereby be increased.

In this case, the Karate Chop Point (SI-3) is known by acupuncturists and Qigong teachers to be a point that activates the Central Channel that travels up the back (the *Ren Channel*) and controls the yang meridians. Telling this to Emma helped to underline the power she had just felt, and helped her to appreciate the natural intuition of her body's wisdom. The simultaneous action of touching her heart and hitting her Karate Point with her other hand served as an anchor, which she told me she used when she finally cleared some feelings with her father on the phone one day. Her inner work and the way she brought her heart and power together in her communication with her father led to a new father-daughter relationship.

When Emma finally met with her father she became aware of why she had such a problem dealing with him in her childhood and adolescence. He was domineering and left little space for her feelings. Emma described this meeting as being like hot air blowing at her. An image from our anchoring work came to her mind of a mudra that came spontaneously in one of our sessions. She found empowerment in the stance of putting her right-hand palm out in front of her heart and her left-hand palm up right below her chest (duplicating the transitional movement in Tai Chi between *Push* and *Pa Kua Fish,* as illustrated in Volume I). She reported that this posture felt as if her right hand protected her from the onslaught she felt and, at the same time, her left hand expressed receptivity to create a new relationship. In addition, Emma said it was helpful to imagine herself to be "*Standing like a Tree*" firmly rooted in the earth to withstand the assault of her father's forceful style of expression. This posture, which we had practiced in a session one day along with *Macrocosmic Orbit Breathing*, also helped her to find a new adult stance with her father. The affect modulation role-plays she had practiced, along with boundary setting, helped Emma create a new relationship with her father where she felt more comfortable establishing limits and expressing her need for space.

As virtually all therapists know, the reality of psychotherapy process is that one-time fixes do not usually change most longstanding characterological patterns. Continued practice of affect modulation is a significant part of psychotherapy, as it was for Emma.

Case Illustration: The Placating Professor and the Sword Mudra

"Trent," a university professor, suffered from being overly placating, and was self-deprecating in spite of many years in psychoanalysis. Once he let his sick niece, who was his favorite relative, nose-kiss him when she was sick, despite his "knowing better." He got a cold that lasted through much of the winter. This illness motivated Trent to look more deeply into changing this dysfunctional pattern — the cold from his niece became a blessing in disguise.

Trent was very insightful about his problems originating with an abusive alcoholic father who often beat him. When he finally stood up to his father in his teenage years, his father had a stroke, which almost killed him. At that point, Trent unconsciously decided to shut off his power. "My fear of the 'oedipal victory' is behind all this, I know." He also got in touch with how his desire to be adored was behind his placating pattern stemming from what he called, his "abusive, neglecting family."

One current issue he was dealing with was taking on extra administrative work for another professor. While he was talking about this, his fingers naturally went into a clawing position (which had also happened at other points in our therapy), but this time he was touching his thumb to his ring finger. I explained to him that in Chinese medicine this ring finger was associated with the triple warmer meridian having to do with the power of three vital centers in the body — the belly, heart, and third-eye. This meaning was empowering to Trent as he then role-played asserting himself to the officemate who had been taking advantage of his kindness. I also explained to him how this same hand gesture was called "the sword mudra" — two fingers up and holding the ring (and pinky) fingers with the thumb. He felt excited and empowered to begin exploring various ways to assert himself using variations of this mudra as a "hypnotic anchor" to bring him back to this state-specific state of consciousness when his old dysfunctional pattern emerged.

In one session, sweet, placating Trent role-played standing up to his father and said, "Stop telling me I'm a fuck-up, you raging drunk." While holding his fingers in the sword mudra he was more assertive than I had ever heard Trent be in two years of our therapy. When I asked him what he would do next time a cute, sick child wanted to kiss him, he said this mudra would be inappropriate there, it felt more appropriate to do a flick off of the ring finger as if to say, "I'm flicking off my old pattern."

Trent's old belief was, "I need to do whatever I can to get adoration because I'm unworthy of love." Along the lines of asserting his newfound power to me, Trent refused to give his SUDS level, but said he felt a deep, pervasive feeling of sadness. Next a new belief emerged, "I am worthy of love, and I don't need to whore myself." As Trent "focused" on this new feeling that the "felt shift" produced, he experienced a sense of power, like anger, but more like holding a sword of power.

In subsequent sessions it was interesting to see how much Trent, who had been through years of psychoanalysis, and who was also a very intellectual university professor, had deep *chthonic* (meaning deriving from the depths) bodily elements arise in his process. The activation of bodily processes is not limited to emotional types and seems, in my experience, to happen across the spectrum of personality types. In one session, as we were working with his shut-off power deriving originally from his fear of hurting his father, he became aware of his chronically cold hands and cold feet and how they symbolized his cutting off his power to hit his father. At this moment, he again instinctively touched his ring finger with his thumb and described an intense heat arising in his belly. Then his hands shaped into claws as he became aware of his anger, and a buoyant feeling arose along with an image of an eagle. At this moment, his inhibitions regarding his promotional work for a new business he was starting came to mind, and along with this rising heat, a new belief emerged, "I deserve to express confidence and have heat in my life." Then he said, "Even though there are dangers in putting myself out there, it's worth it to soar and enjoy life."

So, here we see how the primordial elements of the psyche — elements of the body and elements of the imaginal realm — arise in everyday process in psychotherapy. These body movements and symbolic images became pathways to help anchor Trent to his primordial Self in situations where he needed to reclaim the power he shut off to protect his father.

Why Tap on Points on the Body When You Can Tap on the Wisdom of the Primordial Self?

In all of the cases above we see how body movements and hand gestures that naturally arise in the course of a patient's therapy can be used to ground, anchor, and amplify the new emerging patterns that arise in transformational psychotherapeutic processes. In this case of "The Placating Professor and the Sword Mudra" it is interesting that Trent instinctively touched the meridian line that energy psychology views as particularly vital. Donna Eden (1998) describes this meridian as key in developing aggressive, defensive strategies for maintaining the body's integrity (p.

244); and energy psychologists use the triple warmer point, TW-3 or the "gamut point" as one of the main points in their healing algorithms.

Rather than choosing unknown acu-points to give the patient or having algorithms as a first-line intervention, I propose that the somatic unconscious wisdom of the patient can lead the astute clinician to harness its primordial wisdom. Standardized points can feel artificial to some patients and may take others away from their experience. BMHP is not adverse to tapping points or introducing them to patients to anchor new beliefs and awareness — because tapping on the empirical, proven power of acu-points has its merits. However, BMHP advocates as a first-line intervention, tapping on the natural arising bodily wisdom of the primordial Self.

Following along the lines of humanistic and phenomenological philosophy, honoring a patients own experience is empowering. Transpersonally oriented therapists believe that honoring the wisdom naturally arising from the body can fill the patient with a sense of awe regarding the mysterious source of healing within; they believe that this source of healing derives from that unfathomable power of the universe that some call "the nameless one." BMHP draws from these traditions, adding that such instinctively arising movements are manifestations of the love of the primordial Self and its life energy (QI), which seeks to restore equilibrium to a damaged world.

In the words of Ralph Waldo Emerson, "What lies beyond us, and what lies before us, are small matters compared to what lies within us."

CHAPTER 17: AFFECT MODULATION AND TAI CHI

> *Health, well-being, and long life can only be achieved by*
> *remaining centered with one's spirit,*
> *guarding against squandering one's Qi,*
> *using breath and movement*
> *to maintain the free flow of Qi and blood,*
> *aligning with the natural forces of the seasons,*
> *and cultivating the tranquil heart and mind.*
>
> — Han Dynasty 200 B.C.E. - 222 C.E.
> *The Yellow Emperor's Classic Book of Medicine*

Parallels Between Affect Modulation and Tai Chi

The concepts of affect modulation and affect regulation have become central to psychotherapy (Shore, 2003). Modern psychological research has shown that those individuals whose sense of self involves a well-functioning pre-frontal cortex can modulate their affective or emotional responses more easily than populations who have suffered a variety of traumas early in their lives (van der Kolk, 1994). Secure attachment to a primary caregiver early in life fosters a sense of self with affective competence (Brier, 1992.) The healthy self has the ability to self-soothe, self-stimulate, tolerate being alone, and tolerate criticism (Pearlman & McCann, 1992). Psychological research in "the era of the brain" has shown how disruptions in early attachment sets the stage for many problems later on, including difficulties managing affect (van der Kolk, 1987).

Long before psychological research saw the importance of affect modulation and finding a balanced expression of the self in everyday life, Tai Chi practitioners were also finding ways in their movements to not be overly yin or yang. For example, in the posture *Single Ward Off* the practitioner is instructed to not be too far forward of too far backward. The instructions for this position are very exact — do not let the knee or your forward arm extend over your toes or you can cause knee injury and you will be aggressively leaning off-center; similarly, the initiate is instructed to not allow the forward arm or knee to move too far back so that you are constricted into an overly withdrawn position. The right palm is facing the chest as if holding a ball, and the left hand is at the level of the belly, palm facing downward (see Volume I). This posture is also called *Grasping the Bird's Tail* and was reported to be used by the famed Chang San Feng. The mythological tale says that though Chang was one of the greatest martial artists, he had such gentleness and receptivity that a bird could not take off from his hand. This was due to his having let go of so much, that when a bird tried to push off of his hand it couldn't, because there was nothing of substance on which to push off.

Case Illustrations: Affect Modulation Enhanced by Tai Chi Postures

Case Illustration: Healing Trauma with Fist under Elbow

How can modern affect modulation theory and the practice of Tai Chi, join hands for each other's benefit? In the past two chapters we have seen examples of the way that Tai Chi and Qigong can aid in the process of affect regulation, though that was not our focus. For example, in the case of Elaine in the last chapter, we saw the importance of affect modulation and finding the center of her dial with an interested man in a workshop. Instead of saying "stop coming on to me, this is a workshop," Elaine found the place in the center of her "affect modulation dial" and said, "I appreciate your interest in getting to know me, but I'm trying to concentrate on the workshop, and I have a boyfriend." In this case illustration we saw how a spontaneously arising internal martial arts posture of *Fist under Elbow*, helped her to find the centered power to regulate her affect so that she could set a boundary in a kind, yet firm way.

Case Illustration: Balancing Boundary Setting and Welcoming

Likewise with the case example of Emma, discussed in the last chapter, we saw how an overbearing father contributed to Emma's belief that "it's no use to speak up because no one cares about my feelings." After years of not talking to her father she realized that a more modulated approach would serve her and her family better. In the course of trying to find such a balanced stance, we saw how a naturally arising Tai Chi posture/mudra emerged where her outstretched, right-hand palm expressed the power of boundary setting, and the left-hand palm up, expressed a welcoming gesture. Even though Emma had never practiced Tai Chi or Qigong, this spontaneously arising movement helped to anchor her at a key moment in her life. When she met with her father, she later reported that keeping this stance in mind helped her to not verbally attack him for leaving the family; yet at the same time she was confrontative regarding asking why he left, and why he didn't stand up for her with his new wife. By being balanced in her approach with her father, Emma was able to fill in many of the missing pieces of her childhood. Though her father appeared as very strong on the outside, Emma grew to see her father's limitations in standing up to women. This helped Emma interpret his not standing up for her less personally, i.e. that his inability to stand up for her was not about her worth. Taking back her power and withdrawing her projections helped her to reestablish a relationship with her father.

Case Illustration: Grasping the Bird's Tail (Single Ward Off)

Another example is the case of "Eve." After her parents divorced in her teenage years, Eve resented having to take care of a chaotic mother and a younger brother. Eve spoke about how she came from a very refined family where expressing limits about taking care of others in the family was frowned upon.

When Eve came to therapy one of her issues that led to significant relationship problems was that she resented taking care of others' needs. Yet, she had never made the connection between her current pattern and her parent's divorce and the early caretaking role that was forced upon her in adolescence. In addition, Eve was a regular at the local body worker's table, as she somatized her held back feelings so that her body ended up expressing the issues with which her voice had difficulty. Neck pain was a common symptom for Eve.

Eve practiced Tai Chi with another Tai Chi teacher and sometimes we would use the metaphors from her Tai Chi practice to communicate about affect modulation issues. Eve had a group of friends with whom she enjoyed socializing. Though Eve had warm feelings towards one of her friends, she described this friend as very emotional and needy. On one occasion Eve wanted to go away on a retreat with another member of their close-knit group with whom she shared a particular spiritual path. Her emotional friend started crying when Eve told her about this on the phone. Eve felt guilty about setting boundaries and her old neck blockage became activated. In our BMHP, as Eve "journeyed to the underworld" she realized that the feelings she had now, paralleled her feelings about having to take care of her mother and brother after the divorce. She was made to feel wrong when she didn't help in her family and now a similar guilt was arising. In the course of our work together, I expressed the basic axiom of BMHP and other forms of therapy, "Life is a school and everyday life stressors give us the lessons to learn." Adding to this idea is the metaphor that life is a spiral, and if there was a block at one turn of your spiral, the same block will emerge at a later turn on your spiral (in your life) when you have acquired more developmental abilities to find better coping skills to resolve the issue.

In our first role-play with her newfound strength, regarding her friend's disappointment Eve said, "It's not my job to fix it." Her old belief was, "Others aren't strong enough to be there for me" (7 SUDS level). Her new belief, "Others are responsible for taking care of themselves." Tapping on her belly to ground that statement, she shifted to a 3 SUDS level with a renewed sense of power; but her neck still felt twisted. I asked her to imagine expressing this to her friend, and Eve said, "I feel twisted in my neck when you cry and beg me to have you come along. It's not my job to shield you."

Eve realized that though this helped to release tension in her neck, she didn't feel that this would be appropriate to say to her friend. This is where the meeting of affect modulation skills and Tai Chi helped Eve. She realized that at the top of her affective dial was rage at her friend for crying. At the bottom of her dial was her desire to leave the relationship so she wouldn't have to take care of her any more.

At this point Eve used the metaphor of her Tai Chi posture *Single Ward Off* (discussed at the beginning of this chapter) and said that this posture, and particularly her out-stretched upward right palm facing her heart, and the back of her hand warding off an aggressive force, helped her to ward off her feelings of projected guilt. In the Tai Chi literature this upward hand is described as turning over slightly as if something is spilling out from the heart — this helped Eve search for a compassionate response to her friend. The downward facing left hand by her belly helped her feel grounded. This posture served as a state-specific anchor for Eve when she spoke to her friend the next day. Eve found the middle of her dial, "I'm sorry you're hurt, and feel touched you want to be with us. But I'd like uninterrupted time with you, and it wouldn't be that way with our other friend on this particular retreat. Let's do it another time later this summer." Saying this to her friend led to a deep conversation about the things they shared and the things they didn't; and it helped Eve to hold her ground in her separation/individuation process with her friend.

Standing Up to the Veterinarian after Her Dog Died

Another example was after Eve's dog was "put to sleep" and the veterinarian was giving Eve a lot of specific information about the type of drugs used and how the Vet had done the best she could. Eve's old placating pattern began to come up in this situation with the Vet. This feeling was accompanied by a smiling response that we had identified as related to her false self who had to pretend that she was happy taking care of her mother and brother. Eve reported that in this situation with the Vet that the memory of her Tai Chi *Single Ward Off* stance helped her transform her placating ways. We discussed how her outward right hand expresses holding on to the ball of her heart's truthful power, and how this stance also anchors her in not overextending herself while at the same time being compassionate toward another. Eve proudly told me that something clicked for her at that point. She knew she had to find a different stance to honor her memory of her dog and what he taught her about being with her natural instincts. Eve's observing self was then activated as she noticed that one part of her wanted to smile to make the vet comfortable so she wouldn't feel guilty, and another part of her wanted to scream at the vet and say, "Shut up, I need to mourn." She remembered her affect modulation dial and her Tai Chi *Ward Off* posture, and so she said, "Thanks for your help and knowledge but right now I need some space to myself."

So, affect modulation skills and various Tai Chi postures are a natural complement to developing the ability to regulate our affective states and be appropriate to the situation. In the next chapter we will see another variation on the theme of how the marriage of internal martial arts and psychotherapy can help patients in their process of modulating affect and developing self-assertion skills.

CHAPTER 18: PSYCHOTHERAPY AS AN INTERNAL MARTIAL ART: ATTACKING YOUR PATIENTS TO HEAL THEM

*Tai Chi, the Supreme Ultimate, the immense absolute
is the expression of the Great Harmony
— the balance and mutual support of Yin and Yang.
Whether boxing with your shadow
or engaging in the complexity of life and things,
The Supreme Ultimate within and around you
secures the potential for harmony and ease
in every moment of the eternal present.*

— Wu Wei, Legendary Qi Master

Broadening Psychotherapy with Interdisciplinary Somatic Practices

In Chapter 2, I described a new era blossoming in psychotherapy where interdisciplinary and cross-cultural research are being used as a source of clinical models for mind-body healing (Shore, 2003; van der Kolk, 1996). There we saw the benefits and contraindications for integrating certain spiritual traditions and psychotherapy. I said that I would address the potential problems with introducing "spiritual methods" into psychotherapy, and in subsequent chapters I have done so. For example, I showed how Bodymind Healing Psychotherapy integrates both transcending and transmuting dimensions to avoid the concern about false transcendence that therapists have regarding spiritual forms of psychotherapy.

In Chapter 8 on "Trauma," we heard psychiatrist Dr. van der Kolk, the medical director of the trauma center at Boston University School of Medicine, speak about how the first task of treatment for trauma patients is to regain a sense of safety in their bodies. Dr. van der Kolk went on to say that assault victims often benefit from "model-mugging" programs, Outward Bound programs, and therapeutic massages. He advocates appropriate use of methods from spiritual and religious traditions to aid in the healing of trauma (van der Kolk, 1996).

Along these lines I propose that Qigong can be useful not only as an extrinsic, adjunctive activity to be recommended to help trauma patients get a sense of safety in their bodies, but also for its wider range of clinical usefulness. Throughout this book I have been showing how Qigong, Tai Chi, and ancient sacred wisdom traditions can be woven directly into the fabric of psychotherapy and behavioral health practices. In this chapter, I go into more depth on how Qigong and Tai Chi can be woven directly into the psychotherapeutic process.

Verbal therapy on the surface may seem to be an intellectual oral pursuit. In the following pages I wish to show that behind words are stances, body expressions, and internal martial moves. And I hope to demonstrate how awareness of psychotherapy as an internal martial art enhances psychotherapy.

Language, Tai Chi, and the Body

A number of psychologically oriented authors have questioned how much psychological language itself is responsible for a lack of soulfulness in our modern lives. Robert Bly has suggested that psychological thought has contributed to the effeminization of men. James Hillman and others have questioned whether the obsession with growth and focus on victimization by our parents has turned us into a cult of child worshipers. In my first book, *The Mystery of Personal Identity*, I stated that the language through which we describe ourselves colors the way that each of us sees ourselves. It becomes the lens through which we view our identity and the structure through which we experience our life's meaning. In this book and my second book, *Trials of the Heart*, I, along with many other authors, I talk about the language of myth and story as an *anecdote* (sic) for the language of "dry psycho-logeeze" (Mayer, 1984, 1993).

How much does our psychological language and style of talk stop a naturalness of self-expression in our emotional lives? Are the waters of life being put into culverts that make expression civilized, yet take out some of the essential minerals in the process? Does politically correct psychological language take the Qi out of verbal intercourse?

When we use the language of Tai Chi to conceptualize our way of speaking we have a language that gives us room to be with our primordial Selves. We wonder what it means to respond from our *Tan Tien* (the center below our navel), or our heart center in our verbal interactions. Words come from our bodies, and each of us can feel it when we are responding from our disconnected heads — our words lack power.

Part of the initiation into the Taoist art of Tai Chi Chuan is to practice bringing the embodied metaphors of these arts into our everyday interactions. Using only the amount of force necessary to deal with an oncoming force, so as not to inflict unnecessary damage, is one basic rule of the play of *Tai Chi Push Hands*. Psychotherapists will notice the similarity between the concept of using only the least necessary force and the concept of "affect modulation," having control of the dial of one's emotions so one doesn't turn up their emotion too high in rage, nor too low in inappropriate withdrawal. Tai Chi gives an embodied practice for activating the affect modulation dial of the bodymind; psychotherapy provides practice in "emotional" *Push Hands*, i.e. appropriate verbalizing of emotional expression.

Often in my psychotherapy practice I do not even use the language of Tai Chi — instead the metaphors become translated into the language that is most appropriate for a given client. For example, I may use the language of tennis or another sport. But the important question is, How do we be with our primordial Selves in the difficult encounters of everyday life?

Verbal Tai Chi and the Subtle Art of Bantering: Case Illustration of Obsessive-Compulsive Disorder

"Bob" was a young man who suffered from an obsessive-compulsive disorder. He was addicted to being a perfectly refined good boy, and was like the proverbial centipede, who in thinking about his next step was often frozen into inaction. He was continuously the butt of co-workers' jokes in his job as a phone intake worker at a local company because, as he believed, "I am such an easy target." When a co-worker who continually took great joy in mocking Bob said that a sandwich he was eating "looked like it came out of someone's ass," Bob didn't know how to respond. He reverted to his old standby that he had done all of his life — playing the part of a fool, pretending to enjoy being the butt of everyone's joke. He held his nose, and acted out eating his sandwich of feces. Everyone laughed, but inside, Bob felt humiliated and wished he could find a way to stand up to this verbal bully's continuously demeaning remarks.

Bob was the butt of everyone's jokes since high school. His inability to banter with his high school buddies led to feelings of shame and a self-identification of being a man unable to fend for himself. We may all underestimate just how much the ability to banter is crucial in psychological development, particularly for a man and perhaps also for women, to keep our power with others.

The word "bantering" etymologically derives from the old English "to cook properly, not overcook and not undercook." This meaning shows us psychologists the early roots of "affect modulation" in verbal intercourse. The *Oxford English Dictionary* (1979) says that the first known use of "bantering" may have come "from bullies in White Friars," in old England and that etymologically it relates to the word "roasting." Indeed, finding a defense against aggressive language does involve the ability to take some raw insult and roast it over a fire. This requires cooking the comment in such a way that we don't quite "burn the other," but transform its rawness into something palatable and more easily digestible. The process of roasting in early times required turning a piece of meat around on a spicate, which requires a careful turning so that the meat comes out "just so." When we attack someone back, we are just as raw as the attacker. We have not yet added the civilized element of bringing it into contact with our inner flame where our inner alchemical vessel contains it and subjects it to heat for the purpose of transforming the substance of the remark into something of great value. Bantering is a civilized art of using the heat of aggression in a playful manner. "Indulging in good humored jest," the *OED*'s definition of bantering is exactly this. It has the potential of bringing people closer together if we can alchemically process the heat.

There was a psychodynamic aspect to Bob's pattern of holding back his aggressivity. Early in his therapy, Bob realized that his early inability to respond to insults was rooted in his relationship with his father. When he would respond assertively to his Dad's put-downs of him, his Dad would just walk away. Bob felt castrated, abandoned, and learned to hold back his aggressive impulses. From his many years of therapy in his adolescence, Bob learned to respond to insults by expressing his feelings and saying how that hurt him or made him angry. His father still withdrew and said, "Well if it hurts you or makes you angry I just won't say anything. Have it your own way." This sulk-withdraw pattern further added to Bob's fear of self-expression and lack of natural aggressivity.

But, how does a person take such a psychodynamic insight and turn it into fire. Certainly Bob's uncovered anger at his Dad was part of the "recovery process;" but Bob was suffering from "a bantering disability" that made him feel crippled with his father and with his co-workers. He desired to verbally joust with his Dad, and others who put him down, to find those "just so" remarks that would make his point.

In our therapy, to help Bob explore how his natural style of expression actually felt, we set up a ten-point affect modulation scale, (10 feeling like a hit in the center of the target and 0 being a miss). He imagined expressing to his co-worker, "I don't like it when you say those kind of things to me. It makes me angry, and I wish you'd stop it." This "expression of true feelings" that therapists often suggest may be highly appropriate with someone with whom you are in an intimate relationship, but not with everyone. Different strokes are needed with different folks. Or to carry the "roasting" analogy through, each occasion requires turning the expression around the spicate on the fire to find the right amount of heat. Communication of real feelings is only one of the many forms that the "fire" of our expression can take.

Bob imagined that his co-worker would respond to his real feelings of hurt and anger by saying "I was just kidding when I made the remark about the food, why do you take things so seriously?" These are the kinds of things this co-worker had said to him in the past when Bob tried to stand up to him, and it had left Bob even further humiliated. Due to numerous years of psychotherapy, Bob had learned how to express himself in psychologically real ways, but he had not learned how to use his fire in such a way that he had bantering skills. In his interactions with others he often felt "roasted," rather than the other way around. Therefore, in this case, Bob rated his "psychologically real" response as a "1" on our ten-point affect modulation scale. It felt good to be real, but left him feeling ineffective and humiliated.

Bob realized that this situation called for firmer boundaries around "the ball of his Self," rather than being so open and vulnerable about his feelings. Bantering was what was needed. Bob used the metaphor of the ball of his Self though he practiced no internal martial arts, nor did he know I was a practitioner. Since Bob was an avid tennis player, we used the analogy that he didn't want to hit the ball softly into the net, letting his co-worker win the point, he wanted to hit the ball in the center of his racket back to his co-worker.

Bob's first attempt at bantering was an assertive, "fuck you," but he felt it didn't hit the center of the racket. Bob felt that using that language would be like throwing your racket at the other player because you didn't like the other person's shot. Bob tried on another response that felt a little closer to center, "Do you always put down what other's are eating like that? I wonder how often you go out with people to eat, and how many have puked on you." Bob felt that this rated a "6" in that it got out some of his aggression but still might be too aggressive for the particular work situation he was in. The response that felt closest to the center of his tennis racket was to say in a light-hearted, humorous, but semi-real way, "Thanks for your comments, now that I've lost my appetite will you pay me for the sandwich I'm not going to eat, or should I take you to small claims court." Bob gave this a "9" on the scale because he liked the fact that this let the co-worker know that it upset him, it wasn't inappropriately aggressive, and was assertive enough to "roast the co-worker." It let his co-worker know that the raw, uncivilized remark should cost him something.

Another example of something that happened to Bob took place when a woman called up the company where he answered the phones. She asked him what was going on with a story about his company that had been on the nightly news two months earlier. When Bob responded that he didn't know, she replied, "How could you not know about that? Do you come from Mars or something?"

Chapter 18: Psychotherapy as an Internal Martial Art

"No, do you?" This was Bob's first reactive attempt to practice bantering in our session the next day. This rated low on his ten-point scale at a "2." Though it did put the statement back on the other person, it was overly defensive and he felt it was immaturely "tit for tat." When he responded with, "Last time I checked I wasn't" or "Yes I am, but please don't let anyone know," he felt a little better and rated those responses a "6" due to adding in some humor to break his tension. A psychologically real response of, "It hurts me and makes me angry when you put me down that way. I can't know every story that every member of the public wants to know," rated slightly worse. Bob rated that response a "4," commenting that though it might feel good with an intimate other, it was inappropriate and too self-disclosing in this situation.

Bob's favorite response was, "Sorry I don't know everything that you want me to, but I am very much an earthling, and like many of us from this planet I have many things going on in my complex life. I can't keep up with every story. Since I'm a fellow earthling and care about your and other's needs, I'd be glad to find the latest on that story for you." Bob also wanted to add a clause to the last statement, "Even though by your attack on my limitations it seems like you may be from the red planet of war." But though this last clause felt good to say in therapy, Bob felt the first part of his response had the appropriate amount of caring for others required by his phone intake job. However, it felt good to him that he was developing his bantering ability more so he could come up with remarks that allowed him the pleasure of letting out some of his anger through sarcasm, turning the caller's attack back to her.

What Bob was practicing is very much like *Tai Chi Push Hands* — using the other's force to circle the energy back to the other practitioner. Tai Chi teaches using the least amount of force necessary to achieve one's desired result. In this case Bob found the amount of force that would fit with his job, and used a tennis metaphor to describe his sense of achievement. The way Bob put it was, "I don't need to throw my tennis racket at her;" instead, by saying "we are both earthlings" he felt he made his tennis point.

Each of us has our own ten-point scale where a particular remark feels "just so" given our needs and the appropriateness of a given situation. When reading the above practice, in affect modulation each of us may not find Bob's scale fitting with our sensibilities; each of us has our own dial of affective and effective bantering. We know when a remark is "just so" — like a tasty morsel, an oral zone treat that tastes good as we put our tongues around our palate. It is this that heals our "bantering disability."

Where do we go to learn the art of bantering? Maybe we are lucky, and our rivers of Qi are flowing naturally enough so that our instincts allow bantering to simply come forth. If not, we may pick it up in our early schooling in interactions and modeling from our peers or parents. Bantering involves the subtleties of communication, and since, like communication in general, it is so vital to a healthy life, we would hope it would be part of "education" (which means "to draw out" what is deep inside). Unfortunately, in a culture that emphasizes "the three R's," and with cutbacks in school counseling programs, there is often not enough education about the psychological needs of sensitive or emotionally blocked youngsters. They may get A's in English, but get wounded in their interactions with peers. Education of the heart, and of activating the primordial Self, would be a blessing to our children and our society.

I am reminded of a story in the Fairfax, California Spirit Rock Meditation Newsletter about how a 6-year-old girl named Mattie was teased by her schoolmates by being called "four eyes" because she wore glasses. After speaking to her mother, a meditator, about this, she went back armed with the words she needed and finally said to her abusers the next time they insulted her, "Having 'four eyes' isn't such a bad thing. You might do better if you had four eyes: two eyes to see the world, a third eye in the middle of your forehead for wisdom, and another eye in your heart. If you had four eyes instead of two, you probably wouldn't be putting me down for my limitations."[1]

From "the mouths of babes" and from the eyes of the six-year-old inside of each of us, like Mattie, we all are on the path of learning and practicing the heartfelt art of bantering.

Attacking Your Patients to Heal Them: Case Illustration of the Wife of the Verbally Adept Salesman

As part of teaching patients how to recapture the long lost art of bantering, a therapist can role-play the important characters from the patients' lives to help them recover aspects of their primordial Selves that may have been damaged or not developed in childhood. One woman who was in the midst of a divorce complained that she could not stand up to her husband during the divorce proceedings. She complained about his arrogant, non-yielding style of communication. The psychodynamic root of "Rebecca's" falling into a victim stance was that she was repeatedly hit in childhood. One vivid memory came from when she was eight years old and was hit and pulled out of bed for not cleaning her room. From this and other traumatic experiences she developed a belief that, "Nice girls don't get hit."

In present time, in the course of a divorce with her husband, he wanted to see the kids Wednesday nights. The problem was that this was the only fun night she had available to spend with her kids. As she "focused" (Gendlin, 1978) on her bodily felt sense, she realized that her fear of self-expression was rooted in her fear of being hit or judged. "If I don't give someone what they want, I feel that I'm bad and selfish."

In the course of our therapy Rebecca often went into a victim stance complaining about her husband being too good of an arguer because he was a salesman and being able to "convince anyone of anything;" and, she said, he usually demeaned her in the process. I role-played with her and asked her to stay in touch with her body as I said some things to her. I then role-played her salesman husband asking her to buy my office chair "What's wrong with you that you won't buy my office chair for $500? It's a great deal. You must be a terrible business woman and have no sense."

Some of the purposes for this role-play were to teach Rebecca to:

1. *Learn to shift from a victim stance to one of expressed power:* This is often called "response-ability," i.e. the ability to effectively respond to another rather than put the emphasis on the other's expression.

2. *Differentiate between when someone is merely angry or raising his or her voice versus when someone is blaming her and making her wrong:* In this regard, I differentiated between

raising my voice in anger because I was upset that she would not buy the chair versus being abusively demeaning to her and making her wrong for not buying it.

3. *Learn to express herself, modulating affect appropriate to the intent of the other person.*

In our role-play Rebecca was able to stand up to me and say, "If I don't give you the money you are asking me for, there's nothing wrong with me and I don't deserve to be treated badly or be blamed. I resent you making me wrong to manipulate me into giving something I don't want to give." Our role-playing helped Rebecca stand up to her husband and negotiate various key points in her child custody and divorce agreement.

Both of these examples, the case of Bob and the case of Rebecca, show how the clinician who wants to use the essence of Tai Chi as a verbal martial art in psychotherapy can do so with no Tai Chi training.

Attacking your Patient's Choice of Clothing

As in the last example with Rebecca, attacking a patient's clothing in a role play can provide a way for the patient to learn how to shift from a victim stance to an empowered stance, differentiate various voice tones and intentions of the attacker's dysfunctional communication, and learn to modulate affect with an appropriate response. So, instead of attacking Rebecca for not buying my chair, I could have criticized her choice of clothing in a role play. After assessing the patient's ability to handle such role plays, the clinician's aim is to find some less charged life sphere that can give the patient a chance to get some distance from the everyday life issue that triggers a defensive or overly reactive response. Similar to a boxer being coached on how to use a punching bag or to respond to a punch while wearing protective gear, "practicing one's moves" in psychotherapy gives a person the chance to develop skills to use later when entering into the "ring of life." Such methods give patients an opportunity to learn to breathe when attacked or criticized, reverse their instinctual fight, flight, or freeze response, and develop new response patterns thereby. Qigong and BMHP can add key elements to such role plays. For example, Qigong can add relaxed breathing methods that help patients sink their Qi to the belly center (*Tan Tien*) rather than hold their breath in fear; and these combined methods can add the use of self-touch to anchor the place in the person's body that is activated in the new life stance.

Tai Chi Practices to Enhance Empowerment and Change Your Life Stance

There are other dimensions of how to use the interface of Tai Chi and psychotherapy together to enhance a patient's well-being. For example:

1. When appropriate, a therapist can suggest that an abused patient take Tai Chi classes. I have had the experience in my Tai Chi classes of teaching other therapists' patients who have been sexually and physically abused,[2] and seeing them benefit from *Tai Chi Push Hands* to regain a sense of safety in their bodies.[3] There are a variety of consid-

erations as to which type of "martial art" is chosen. Some prefer model mugging or a hard style martial art like Karate. Tai Chi is not as cathartic or as physically oriented to self-defense as are certain other martial arts, and it is better suited for those who wish to find a gentle approach to discovering their internal power. As has been said in other parts of this book, it is important not to be overconfident in your abilities when viewing Tai Chi or any other martial art as a method of self-defense.

2. Examples are given throughout this book of the use of the integration of psychotherapy with Tai Chi, Qigong, and Standing Meditation to help a person shape-shift into new life stances. These stances enable the person to access state-specific states of consciousness that help the person cope with external and internal stressors, and develop the ability to better self-assert, modulate affect, and banter. For example, in Chapter 15 we saw how "Stan" was able to banter with his brother's longstanding derogatory, castrating comments such as, "I'm better than you at everything," when Stan replied, "You're not better at being a kind brother." We will see in Chapter 20 on the *Mythic Journey Process* how "Roberta's" passive-aggressive "ostrich behavior" was transformed though a combination of psychotherapy with another therapist, a *Mythic Journey Process*, and the practice of certain animal form movements to help her recover her primordial Self-assertion abilities.

CHAPTER 19: HEALING WITH THE ELEMENTS AND TRANSPERSONAL HYPNOSIS

Oh, what a catastrophe for man when he cut himself off from the rhythm of the year,
from his unison with the sun and the earth.
Oh, what a catastrophe ... This is what is the matter with us.
We are bleeding at the roots,
because we are cut off from the earth and sun and stars ...
We plucked it from its stem on the Tree of Life,
and expected it to keep on blooming in our civilized vase on the table.

— D. H. Lawrence

Transpersonal Psychology and Healing

When I was training graduate students in transpersonal psychology programs over a twelve year period of time, I defined *"transpersonal psychotherapy"* this way: "Transpersonal psychotherapy is an integrative approach that combines traditional psychotherapy with ancient sacred wisdom traditions; it emphasizes how healing comes from the wider whole of which we are a part."

Transpersonal psychology has been called the fourth force of psychology along with the humanistic/existential, cognitive/behavioral, and Freudian/neo-analytic psychologies. However, those in the field of transpersonal psychology do not look at their tradition as separate from mainstream psychologies. Bodymind Healing Psychotherapy, in part, builds upon a foundation in transpersonal psychology.[1]

The shift from traditions that honored the elements of the wider whole of life to modern culture's anthropocentric focus has been part of the ongoing march of civilization. Historically, the disconnection of humanity from nature has roots in the shift from the worship of Goddesses in the second and third millennium B.C. to the worship of a deity of the heavens (Stone, 1976). And so the archetypal image of the sacred in Western civilization has become a disembodied one — a male God living in the upper stratosphere on a throne. Adding to humanities' disconnection from reverence of the earth, the philosophy of atomism growing from seventeenth century Europe put forth the case that a human being is an isolated fragment in an alienated universe. Central to this viewpoint was "Descartes error:" "I think therefore I am," as contrasted with: "I feel therefore I am" or "I am a child of God (a spiritual power in the universe) therefore I am." Virgil, the famous classical author of the *Aeneid*, said, "We make our destinies by our choice of Gods" and therefore we create our own chosen "reality bubble" by worshiping the mind, feelings, or our view of the Creator of Life.

The rise in Western technologies and philosophies are all part of the benefits and detriments of modern civilization. On the positive side, we have created comfort and safety from some of the elements of nature with our air-conditioners and heaters. The chemical elements of the earth have been harnessed to fight malaria, polio, and other health conditions. Yet these advances have repercussions in the way we have disrespected endangered species and looked at them as "things" for us to use — as Americans did while killing the buffalo during the conquest of the United States. Our reliance on medications, and drug company greed, has produced side effects like the heart attacks from medications like Vioxx, and has led our healing efforts away from trusting the elements of natural life in our bodies and in the surrounding universe (such as natural herbs).

Recently there has been a balancing of this disconnection from our roots in nature and the universe. The new physics is at the forefront of showing how human beings are in fact condensed light and how our physical bodies' separation from the surrounding universe is an illusion. Many authors and others have shown the modern world the reality of this knowledge in the area of quantum physics (Capra, 1975; Peat, 1997). And members of the new biology movement, such as Bruce Lipton (2005), have shown how our human connection with the wider universe is even true on a cellular level.

The need to reconnect with the wider whole of which we are a part is a key element for healing our psyches as well. According to ancient Chinese medical philosophy, the universe, the human body, and mind were composed of five elements — fire, earth, metal, water, and wood. In pre-modern medicine, when a person was ill and out of balance, an analysis was made regarding which element was in excess or deficiency. Then, herbs were given and points on the body were either needled with acupuncture or touched with acupressure to return the energies of mind, body, and spirit to harmony with the natural balance of life. In Western esoteric traditions the initiate was tried by the four elements (not five): fire, earth, air, and water. The Greeks of classical antiquity believed that the soul itself was composed of a vaporous substance formed out of the four elements, and that healing the soul took place when these elements were in balance.

Transpersonal Hypnosis and Healing with the Elements

Case Illustration: Writer's Block

Honoring this idea of healing with the elements, I developed the concept of *transpersonal hypnosis* in the 1980s. A patient, we'll call her "Marcy," found the metaphor of the elements of nature to be particularly transformative to her writer's block. A student in her early 20s, Marcy was enrolled in a program for young screenplay writers. After she took a workshop of mine, I had a chance to work with Marcy for only two sessions since she lived out-of-state.

When Marcy came in for our first session she told me she hadn't been able to write on a play she was working on for three months, and was considering leaving her program. Her closest friends were also writers and seemed to be turning out articles and producing plays without the problems Marcy was experiencing. She felt like a failure.

She told me first, in detail, how hard she had tried to find a way through her writing blocks. She felt defeated and was coming to the conclusion that she just didn't have it, that she needed to recognize that she was an awful writer.

Marcy was expecting me to tell her she was a good writer, as all of her acquaintances had; so she was taken aback when I told her that she was overlooking just one thing — that of course she was a terrible writer — that everyone is. I told her that her problem was fighting this basic truth. She was at first startled, because everyone else was trying to comfort her by attempting to convince her that she was a good writer. This paradoxical intention method (Frankl, 1967) used in psychotherapeutic healing and clinical hypnosis is also fundamental to Taoist healing — by not trying to make things happen, things happen. By being "nothing special," a very special human quality emerges.

Marcy came to me as a psychotherapy patient in part because she knew that I had written a prize-winning book; she thought that even though she wouldn't have enough time to do depth psychotherapy with me, she had heard that sometimes results could be achieved in a shorter time. She thought that since I had written a book maybe I could give her some advice. Creating a bond with her as a fellow writer who is also often blocked, I told her the story of how I learned about writing blocks from writing my doctoral dissertation, which later turned into my book *The Mystery of Personal Identity*. I told Marcy how I was blocked on how to start my writing for a period of six months. I saw a sign of relief wash across her face as if to say, "If a prize-winning writer can be blocked for six months, maybe it's not so bad that I'm blocked for three months."

Drawing on the old tradition of using stories to heal, I continued and told Marcy my story of writing my dissertation:

> *One day, completely depressed, I gave up and walked outside for a breath of fresh air realizing that I just didn't have what it took to write. As I breathed in the fresh air, all of a sudden an idea came to me, and from there my dissertation grew. I realized that the idea came "from the air" and I started to joke around with myself that this is how the quote, "the idea came out of thin air" arose. Maybe, I thought, other writers had discovered this same truth that I had ... that they couldn't write either, and that ideas come from the air. I wondered whether in ancient times astrologers knew this, and that's why they said that knowledge is associated with the air element. I got so invigorated by this hypothesis that the energy carried over into my writing and ideas started flowing forth for a chapter or so. I would just go out for a breath of fresh air when I got stuck and an idea would come to me.*
>
> *I was getting pretty self-assured, thinking that I could just call on the air element to write, when one day, working on the second chapter, it came again. I was completely blocked. I went outside and nothing happened as I tried to invoke the air element. Day after day I would go for walk and nothing came. I let go to the knowledge that I was just no good at writing, and decided to take a shower to get away from it all. While I was in the shower, I started to relax and realized how critical I was of myself. I became more aware of how I wouldn't let anything out before my critic would beat me up and say that I was no good. I realized that I had done this all of my life, and mourned how difficult my schooling had been for me. I realized that I needed to keep my critic out of the first draft of my writing and only let it come in on later drafts. As my tears merged with the water and I let go, an idea emerged for a blocked section in my writing. I realized the great healing power of water, and I appreciated that by my letting go to be with the power of the water element that it could write through me.*

Then I thought, all I need to do is take showers when I get stuck, get in touch with the water element, and I'll be healed. But eventually, I got to the place that even a shower didn't help. I went to the refrigerator took out a piece of bread to escape the fact that I couldn't write at all. As the bread grounded me I got in touch with how a grounded experiential flavor was missing in the theoretical section that I was working on in my book. I realized that the earth element was speaking to me and helping me to be more grounded in my approach.

It was only after all this, and still many times hitting into writing blocks even though I breathed fresh air, took showers, and ate bread, that I fully recognized my foolishness as a writer. I now knew that I couldn't write at all, and that it was the elements of creation that wrote through me, in their own time and in their own way. I realized that my attachment to being able to write was similar to my attachment to having a given element heal me. Like my attempt to control the writing process itself, I had become attached to trying to control the elements of creation to write through me. I then deeply realized that it was only in letting go of trying to control the elements of writing, and being open to what comes, that the appropriate element of the universe could come to my aid and help in my healing.

In our two allotted sessions we were able to schedule in California, Marcy and I also touched upon the roots of her blocks in her inner critic and we worked as much as possible in our sessions along the lines of Bodymind Healing Psychotherapy to work through these energy blocks regarding writing. We identified one of her family of origin issues of being an overachiever to please her parents. By practicing cognitive restructuring, she learned to change her negative belief from, "I need to be a great writer to be worthwhile," to the belief, "My destiny as a writer is waiting to be drawn out of me by the elements of the universe around me." Marcy's SUDS level significantly decreased with this new belief, showing that her bodymind was beginning to metabolize the new way of seeing her path as a writer. She also appreciated the self-soothing she experienced when she touched her heart, since she was self-described as "such a mental person."

Marcy also requested some Bodymind Qigong Movements to help her with the tension that accumulated when she was writing, and I was able to briefly show her some such as: *Opening the Shoulder Well* — the wood element of BMHQ (see Volume I), *Tai Chi Ruler* — for general relaxation and balancing of energy, and *Moving a Snake through the Joints* — to release common body areas that accumulate tension while writing.

After our sessions and telling this transpersonal teaching story to Marcy, I didn't hear from her for about a month, then I got a phone call from her saying that she broke though her writing block one night while looking into her fireplace. Marcy told me that the metaphor of "fire" created a felt shift for her. She said that while looking there she realized how she had always tried to be a bright light in her parent's eyes, and how comparisons with other relatives had stifled her own natural fire within from burning. Looking into her fireplace she got in touch with the natural fire she had left behind as a child. I only heard from Marcy one last time when she graduated from her writer's program and thanked me for the influence that our session and the elements of life had on her writing.

How is transpersonal hypnosis different from traditional hypnosis? For one, they have different philosophical foundations. In traditional hypnosis a story is used to reframe a current life experience and create a new way of seeing the world. In "transpersonal hypnosis" there is an explicit opening to a reality that is connected with the primordial powers of the universe, and respect for its inherent powers.

However, it is not so much the method that is important here as the experience of being "called" by something — some power greater than our egoic selves. When we experience our life as "a calling," and the problems that arise in everyday life as an initiation by the elements, purpose enters into our lives, and a calling is indeed undertaken.

We now know that reactivation of the center of our brains, where the meaning centers such as the amygdala lie, is an important part of healing trauma and restoring energy to the Self. Anyone who is a writer knows that mini-traumas are a part of the writer's everyday life. As Thomas Mann said, " A writer is one for whom writing is more difficult than it is for other people."

Many of the dimensions of Bodymind Healing Psychotherapy can be helpful to clearing writing blocks. In addition to the elements of nature, and the psychodynamic and cognitive distortions needing to be cleared, so can the movements from Bodymind Healing Qigong listed above be of help to clear the body of encumbrances that block the muses of writing from coming forth. These all are necessary tools for the writer's toolbox — just as much as are pens and paper.

Case Illustration: Flying Phobia

The following case shows how synchronistic happenings in the therapist's office can be integrated into a session for healing — another example of how sensitivity to the healing elements of the universe, as they synchronistically intercede into a session, can become hypnotic anchors to aid the process of transformation.

A corporate manager, "Barry," who never before had a fear of flying, developed a phobia after the infamous wave of terrorist airplane incidents of September 11, coupled with an incident when a plane he was on hit an air bump, "dropping what must have been 1000 feet." As he imagined going on his next speaking engagement, his SUDS level was an "8". Barry's process further illustrates the multilayered approach of BMHP (outlined in Chapter 5) as he explored his "journey to the underworld." Some of these layers coincide with the steps of BMHP, and some (as we see above) are broader in scope.

- *Breath and Imagery*: We first did the BMHP process of using *Microcosmic Orbit Breath* and the *River of Life* visualization. As Barry focused on a body sense that felt like an ice block in his upper stomach, he said, "We're going to die." Next, doing cognitive restructuring he said, "There's a small chance of dying." But this created an unexpected rise rather than a fall in his SUDS level reported to be "6.5".

- *Focusing:* On the next level down in the underworld, as he "focused" on the his body sense as he imagined flying, he became aware of a lack of control and not trusting many aspects of life, including trusting the airplane. From this, his SUDS level raised even higher to a "7.75".

- *Psychodynamic:* He said this feeling of fear felt similar to when he was a child and was afraid of going out to a playground due to killings in his neighborhood.

- *Self-soothing:* The self-soothing that had been helpful to Barry in the past didn't seem to work for him as he attempted to not try to change this inner child's feeling, but to accept him where he is.

- *Energy Psychology:* Barry tried out the statement, "Even though I have this phobia I can love and accept myself," but this intervention from the Emotional Freedom Technique didn't produce a SUDS reduction because more work still needed to be done on the psychodynamic layer. His father's message was "buck up and get over it." Measuring himself by his father's expectations hindered Barry's ability to relax and find a compassionate relationship to his issues.[7] Paralleling his process of measuring himself up against his father's standards, Barry also measured himself against other managers in his company "who didn't have such fears."

- *Teleology:* Once the psychodynamic layer was brought into awareness, the teleological level could be explored. Etiology involves a focus on past causes, whereas teleology involves the forward-oriented purpose of a symptom. Barry became aware that his sensitivities to the fearful realities of life, such as planes crashing, was his talent and curse. As he accepted his path as a wounded healer, a felt shift happened and a real self-acceptance and self-soothing could begin. Then the use of self-soothing touch brought him to a 1 SUDS level.

- *Practice:* Barry became aware that his upcoming plane ride was an opportunity to practice re-parenting and self-soothing as he accepted his very nature of being a sensitive individual.

- *Synchronicity of the Healing Elements:* Just as we were doing this inner work, we heard the synchronistic sound of a dove cooing right outside my office. Barry interpreted it to be saying, "I fly every day and though there are hawks and potential dangers, I find peace." A 0 SUDS level occurred at this point.

This well-respected manager now flies to speaking engagements around the country, and although anxieties arise, he uses his self-soothing touch, the various layers of BMHP, and his power symbol (medicine animal) of the dove to aid him in his process of "re-membering" his primordial Self.

Barry's process illustrates how the various dimensions of a person's "journey to the underworld" are implicitly part of the realm of everyday clinical practice and psychological healing; however, many clinicians may not explicitly describe their work this way. This multilayered way of conceptualizing the patient's journey adds a psychospiritual depth to the process. Barry's case shows how certain energy psychology methods, though helpful, don't always result in one-intervention cures. Healing the primordial Self often involves not only incorporating the relaxation response, self-soothing, self-touch, the cognitive layer, the psychodynamic layer, and time; but sometimes it also it involves a little help from the synchronicity of some higher power that lies behind the workings of this wonder-filled universe.

Anchoring State-Specific States Using the Five Elements of the Internal Martial Arts

It should be noted that there are three styles of internal martial arts. Tai Chi, Pa Kua, and Hsing-I. In Volume I, I outlined the *Healing the Internal Organ* sets which correspond to the five elements (fire, earth, metal, water, and wood). Movements from these sets can be used as hypnotic anchors in BMHP along the lines suggested throughout this book. Body movements for activating the five elements are also contained in Hsing-I (Smith, 2003) and are part of Bodymind Healing Qigong Level III training. When appropriate, I suggest that patients practice a movement from these sets to help anchor an element that is helpful for their healing, and to help them cultivate a missing aspect of their primordial Self. For example, in one session with Barry I chose the metal element to help him to cut through his introjected father's message to "buck up." Interestingly, the movement in Hsing-I involves bringing the right hand down like a knife in a slicing motion, leading with the side of the hand. This point is the same point used in energy psychology (SI-3) called the Karate Chop Point. Barry felt empowered when doing this movement along with saying, "I can cut through my father's bullshit and finally be compassionate with myself." When his father's voice came to mind on plane trips, Barry used his right hand in this mudra to anchor this new state-specific state of consciousness.

Four Elements of Constructive Communication of Negative Feelings

The ancient idea of using the elements of life to heal can be applied in our modern age to psychotherapy with individuals, as well as couples. In my last book on couples therapy and intimate relationship (Mayer, 1994) I outlined the four-step method that I have used with couples for the last twenty-five years. It takes the elements of pre-modern Western psychology — fire, earth, air, and water — and shows how these can be brought together as healing elements of constructive communication. Following is this four-step method:

1. *First express your intent in communicating your feeling. For example, "There's something I want to clear up with you because I care about you, and this issue is affecting my feelings about our relationship." (Fire — raises the intentionality to a higher level, like fire ascending.)*

2. *Distinguish between the whole person and the behavior you don't like. "I love you and care about you deeply, but the mess you leave in front of the closet is really getting to me." (Air — distinguishes between the whole and the parts.)*

3. *Express your feelings as "I feel" statements.* "Dealing with this mess is really making me angry. I notice myself walking around feeling resentful for hours after coming into the room and I don't like being this way." In the water stage it's important to distinguish between your feelings ("I feel ..." statements) and blame or name-calling ("You are ..." statements). (Water — expresses the hot and cold of your inner river of experience.)

   A way to get in touch with and deepen "the river of your communication" comes from first "focusing" on your body sense (i.e. clenched jaw). Then resonating a word with this sense until it feels like a match ("I feel ... angry"). Then, to get the felt sense, asking yourself, "What gets me so much about this issue?" (or "What makes me so angry?"). And waiting for an answer, "What gets me so much, about the mess is that it makes me feel out of control. It makes me feel scattered, like the way I am when I'm messy. And just like I'm impatient with my own scatteredness, I get that way with yours. I guess I have to admit that I have a hard time with not having my own way, and it scares me to reflect upon whether I'll ever be able to make it long term in a relationship because of my issues with this kind of thing."

4. *Ask for what you want. Frame the issue as a problem that the two of you have.* "I wonder how we can work this whole thing out. I'd like to be able to find a solution to this together because I'm at the point of tearing my hair out." This is the bargaining phase. Remember you're not necessarily entitled to get what you want, but you do deserve to be able to ask for, and dialogue about, it. "How about agreeing to at least put your clothes over there, out of the way instead of in the middle of the room." (Earth — finding practical solutions to the problem.)

In the above elements of constructive communication, therapists will recognize certain things that are standard in the field. For example, the using of "I feel" versus "you are" is a basic of every psychotherapist's training, though few would recognize that we are calling on the qualities of the water element of expression when doing so. Bodymind Healing Psychotherapy puts such elements of effective communication back into connection with the elements of the wider whole of which we are a part in order to further enhance interpersonal communication. For example, if we start off by saying to our partner, "I'm angry with you for leaving your clothes out in front of the closet," the offending party may get defensive. There is less of a chance of evoking or provoking defensiveness if the communicator says, "I'd like to clear something with you because you are my partner, and I'd like to tell you something so I can let go of holding on to it, and so we can find a way to work with this dynamic in the future" (Fire). This prepares the person to receive the feeling. Likewise with all of the other elements, by operating together each element is enhanced by the wider whole. In my book *Trials of the Heart: Healing the Wounds of Intimacy* (Mayer, 1994) I give many examples of how this process helped to improve couples' relationships and marriages.

The following is an updated version and graph of this process that shows how both communicating parties can use it together. One important thing to note is how the "responder" first needs to empathically listen to the "initiator's" communication process until the initiator feels heard. After the initiator is heard, then problem solving and bargaining can occur (Earth.)

Chapter 19: Healing with the Elements and Transpersonal Hypnosis

THE FOUR ELEMENTS OF CONSTRUCTIVELY EXPRESSING NEGATIVE FEELINGS

STEP	PERSON A *The Initiator*	PERSON B *The Responder*
1	Express your intent in communicating your feeling. (Fire)	*
2	Distinguish between the whole person and the behavior you don't like. (Air)	*
3	Express your feelings as "I feel" statements, not "you are" statements. (Water)	*
4	Ask for what you want. (Earth)	*
5	*	Empathize with PERSON A's feelings until you are sure PERSON A has been heard accurately. Make sure you see PERSON A's acknowledgement that he or she feels empathized with.
6	Respond to PERSON B, letting him or her know if you felt that he or she "got" what you said and felt in Step 3. If PERSON B is missing something, let him or her know what's missing. (PERSONS A and B go back and forth between Steps 5 and 6 until PERSON A feels heard.)	*
7	*	Respond to what PERSON A asked for in Step 4, and tell him or her what you are willing to do with regards to that issue.
8	Problem solve together, propose and discuss possible solutions, come to a conclusion.	Problem solve together, propose and discuss possible solutions, come to a conclusion.
9	Close the circle. Tell the other how you feel about the process	Close the circle. Tell the other how you feel about the process.

Figure 5: Four Elements of Constructively Expressing Negative Feelings

* *During this time in the process, this person is silent, empathetically listening.*

CHAPTER 20: THE MYTHIC JOURNEY PROCESS: CREATING YOUR OWN STORIES TO HEAL YOUR RELATIONSHIPS

We have not even to risk the adventure alone, for the heroes of all time have gone before us; the labyrinth is thoroughly known: we have only to follow the thread of the hero path. And where we had thought to find an abomination, we shall find a god: where we had thought to slay another, we shall slay ourselves; where we had thought to travel outward, we shall come to the center of our own existence; and where we had thought to be alone, we shall be with all the world.[1]

— Joseph Campbell

In Chapter 1, I discussed how one of the field of psychotherapy's critiques about meditation and the emerging energy-based psychologies was that they lacked a depth psychological perspective and methodology. Throughout this book I have shown that there is more to energy-based psychologies than the technologies of tapping and muscle testing. The whole realm of Qigong (including breath, movements, postures, and awareness) as well as symbolic process modes of inner work can be included under the emerging "re-membering" of the ancient roots of modern psychology. Ancient sacred wisdom traditions are key elements to unlocking the treasure house that is the human psyche.

In the 1970s and 1980s, my work in integrating psychotherapy and the Western mystery traditions culminated in the development of the *Mythic Journey Process*. This process was first outlined in the last chapter of my book, *Trials of the Heart* (Mayer, 1994), and is now updated here. Among the various psycho-mythological and symbolic process methods used nowadays to facilitate healing, this method is unique in how it is not as tightly structured as guided imagery, and therefore allows one's own tale to freely emerge. However, the method also has a structure to it that provides river-banks through which one's unconscious stream of imagery can flow and be guided.

Mythology: The Key to the Door of Your Psyche

Ancient myths are becoming new resources for the human venture. Joseph Campbell's written works and interviews gave the study of world mythologies increasing respect. James Hillman, Sam Keen, Robert Bly (1990), and a vast number of Jungian-oriented authors have shown the importance of ancient myths and storytelling to bring soul to modern culture.[2] It seems that we are in an age of mythological renaissance. It is a time when the mythic "Sword of Excalibur" can rise again — a time for reviving the gods and goddesses of imagination to give meaning to modern life.

Throughout the ages, mythic stories have been passed down describing the deep inner transformations of the psyche. We've seen how these legends can show us oceans of possibilities within us and help us begin the odyssey that will transform our souls. Today, with the many different religious and mythic traditions, we are in a unique position — we are able to set sail and find our own myths on an even larger ocean. We can create our own mythic journeys from all past mythic literature and our imaginations.

Our very lives are mythic journeys, and when we depart, it is not our bones that will be left, it is our stories. They are our link to immortality. Yet the importance of stories and myths have not been integrated as a formal part of our education.[3] We are told stories by our parents and teachers, but we are not trained in their deeper mysteries: their ability to soothe the soul, transform, awaken, and heal us.

To understand the essence of the healing power of myth, we must first explore its primary ingredient — symbol. A symbol is to a story what a note is to a song. Edward Edinger has pointed out that the early use of the Greek word "*symbolon*" referred to a stick that was used in a trading agreement.[4] To mark the transfer of ownership of an object from one person to another, a stick was divided in half to symbolize the sale. Just as these sticks were reminders of a greater unity, symbols today help reconnect us with something larger than ourselves.

Everything is part of a greater whole. Just as a lung is part of a human body and its identity must be understood within that whole context, so we as human beings, in order to fully comprehend our identities must connect ourselves to a wider whole. The secret of myth's healing power comes from how it helps us to create a likeness between us and an aspect of the surrounding universe. This likeness is a particular use of symbol — a metaphor.

In the *Mythic Journey Process*, we create a likeness between our current life situation and a person or situation of ancient times, and we make room for the power of imagination to enter through this likeness.

Identifying and Overcoming Our Inner Demons

Whether you are the most positive, rational thinker in the world or a traditional religious person who is against iconic pagan imagery, we all have our problems, obstacles, and demons lurking under the veneer of our lives. It is these archetypal aspects of the human condition that the *Mythic Journey Process* brings forth. By facing the particular "demons" behind our psychological problems we can deal with suffering at its root (Hillman, 1975). Picturing the form of the demon, and how we will address it, changes confrontation into adventure. The demon may turn out to be the monster of our fear. The giant may be our inertia or suppressed power. By directly facing and dealing with the demon, we can rediscover our lost selves and gain access to the treasure of our inherent nature.

Throughout time, myths recorded the numerous ways that heroes have confronted various demons. Whether it was by attacking, wrestling, or feeding them, each encounter offers us an approach to a present-day demon.

Petrifying Fear: The Story of Perseus and Medusa

Hearing a story, which contains a problem like ours helps us face our demons and feel less alone in our suffering. For example, maybe our partner continually gets angry when we come home late from work. Perhaps we fear that the relationship is endangered because we need our freedom, or perhaps we feel smothered but are petrified to discuss it because our partner reacts so strongly.

A mythic analogy to this situation can be found in the tale of Perseus and Medusa, where we are Perseus, and Medusa represents our angry partner. In this myth, Medusa's face was so horrifying that it had the power to petrify into stone the people who dared look at it. Using the example above and reading this story, we may see that maybe we are not dealing with our own personal neurosis, but with a wider, universal issue — the petrifying fear of a powerful figure. Instead of feeling alone and isolated, we can feel linked with those ancient heroes who struggled with monstrous embodiments of the same forces with which we are now coping. What once felt like neurotic suffering becomes an adventure as we explore how our problems were dealt with in the mythic past.

In order to save Perseus from being turned into stone, Athena, goddess of wisdom, gave him a shield to reflect Medusa's image. By looking into the shield instead of looking directly at her face, Perseus was able to approach Medusa and behead her. We might look to the myth of Perseus and Medusa and wonder, "What in my life could function like Perseus's shield?"

We can reflect on our situation aided by the distance our own inner shield gives us. Let's imagine that we realized that in the past we felt petrified of hurting our mother or being rejected by her when she disapproved of and limited our behavior. We gave in to her demands as a child in order to survive. And perhaps we developed a pattern of constantly giving in to others' demands for fear of hurting them or being rejected by them. Metaphorically speaking, we may have turned to stone inside, acceding to the demand, but with a stiff upper lip, resenting the restriction. A pattern may have developed to withdraw in other ways in our relationships.

Reflecting on our partner's image in the mirrored shield, we might be able to understand his or her issues better. Perhaps our partner was feeling a loss of control in the relationship or wasn't feeling needed or cared about. Reflecting upon what caused the anger rather than reacting to it, we can "behead the monster," i.e. diffuse our reactivity.

Reflecting in such a way in the midst of seemingly monstrous emotions requires the proper implements. Perseus was given an adamantine sickle and winged sandals by Hermes, and a helmet of invisibility by Pluto. We must learn what these implements mean and learn how to use them so that we are prepared when we meet the Medusas in our life. In the above example, perhaps the sword's parrying ability would be useful in its ability to point to the real issue, slice through the mire, and to find the truth of the underlying feelings.

Perseus's sickle was adamantine (made of the hardest stone). Today we know that the hardest stone is diamond, but any stone that is very hard has sustained years of pressure by the earth's forces. If it is a diamond, it has become clarified. Perhaps the myth is telling us that we must be patient in regards to the hard-to-bear forces in our situation. There is a purpose behind the pressure — to create something that is clear and of great value. The image of this sword tells us that we must combine the qualities of hardness (not being weak about the "hard truth") with the softness of a sickle's curve. On the one hand, we cannot passively cave into our partner's demands, we must be strong in our assertion that there is more here than meets the eye. But the soft lunar curve must also be present in the discussion, reflecting on both partners' underlying issues. A straight-edged sword approach will not do. If we point our sword in a judgmental way, the mythic solution will not be found.

The imagery tells us that at a certain point in exploring our different viewpoints, Hermes's winged sandals might be useful to guide us into the underworld to see our own issues — our feelings of being smothered and our partner's difficulty with feelings of neediness.

Discussing these feelings can give us winged sandals that transport us to the upper regions, as Hermes's sandals transported Greek heroes to that place of compassionate perspective. This takes place only if we are able to keep our ego under the "cap of invisibility." If we are enraged by our partner's neediness, or we withdraw in anger, the hero's goal will not be accomplished.

In one version of the myth, after Medusa was beheaded, Pegasus the winged horse emerged and as he ascended, he kicked a mountain top from which sprang one of the fountains of the Muses. Indeed, when two people work through issues such as these, a wellspring of creative energy is released. We may learn to humorously dramatize our issues or be awed by the insight they bring. Love may be reborn.

Remember that Perseus's quest was for Andromeda, his beloved, who was chained to a rocky cliff. Medusa's head and the weapons that he accumulated in his quest were used to free her from the dragon. Often it seems that our beloved is chained to a rocky cliff and that the relationship is tottering on the edge. Ultimately it requires a quest like Perseus's to rescue the feminine in us, and in our partner. The feminine symbolically represents that lunar quality of inner reflection that must be rescued from the hard rock of rigidity.

Myths record the tests and trials of the human spirit. They are keys to the psyche's secrets, which are brought to life by our imagination. Just as it takes a combination of factors to create a rainbow (light, water, and a person at the proper angle), so do myths provide illumination when we see a story from a particular angle. There is no one correct angle from which to interpret a story, each angle produces its unique vision that is meaningful to us at a given time.

In the *Mythic Journey Process*, when we feel lost, we can create our own stories and use the symbols that arise from our inner vision to help us find the way into the cave of our unconscious. Here we can meet the demon, wrestle with it, and find the jewel of our own Self.

Focusing and the Mythic Journey Process

The *Mythic Journey Process* is a way of harnessing the ancient power of myth to work through modern-day problems. It combines elements of the Focusing technique with archetypal psychology.

Eugene Gendlin is a modern-day hero in the field of psychology who researched the factors that produced change in the psychotherapeutic setting. In his study at the University of Chicago,[5] Dr. Gendlin analyzed tapes of different therapies to discover what factors were present in successful therapy. The Focusing process (Gendlin, 1978) was developed from this research. Gendlin proposed a way to develop our body's felt sense as a guide to new meanings and fresh perspectives on life's problems. He found that a felt energetic shift ("felt shift") occurred when a person found new meaning for a life problem. The *Mythic Journey Process* adds to Focusing the richness of symbolic language.

The *Mythic Journey* exercise consists of starting with our bodily felt sense of a chronic physical or psychological problem, and then telling a story about this problem, transposing it into ancient times as we did with Medusa. While the story is being told, we continually refer to the bodily felt sense, noticing how it changes along with the development of the story. We can reach a point where the story begins to tell itself and experience a felt shift and new meaning regarding our problem.

The *Mythic Journey Process* is a modern-day embodiment of the ancient mythic journey to the underworld. Just as the mythic Greek hero Theseus used Ariadne's thread to find his way into and out of the underworld labyrinth to free the captive children from the monstrous Minotaur, so do we use our bodily felt experience as a thread into and out of our psychological underworld to liberate the energies of our inner experience. The steps of the Focusing process become guideposts along our path.

In Focusing's first step, called "clearing a space," we find a friendly relationship to a life issue by saying, "Everyone has their stuff to deal with and here's mine. If I had a friend, I wouldn't be hard on him for having this to deal with." Since we are often harder on ourselves than we would be on a friend with the same problem, we need to find a relationship to ourselves that is like the relationship that we would have to a friend with a similar problem.

Dr. Gendlin also found that an important factor in successful therapy was a person's ability to use his or her body's felt sense to create movement in therapy. In his book, Gendlin (1978), gives an example of a traditional couple (pp. 45-50). A wife at home cleaned the table. A man returned home after getting a job promotion and, in his excitement, knocked the milk onto the table that his wife had just cleaned. The woman became aware of her bodily feeling of anger and began the Focusing process. She "resonated" the word "anger" against the felt bodily sense of the issue surrounding her husband's promotion. She then stopped for a moment and said, "No, that's not quite right. I'm not sure what I felt, but it's not quite anger." For some people this can be a difficult moment, "I don't know what I am feeling." In Gendlin's Focusing process, we learn to trust an unclear "felt sense" and wait for something to emerge. While staying in touch with the unclear feeling of "a hole in my stomach," the woman above realized, "It's not so much anger; what's getting me the most is the void I feel about being left behind in my life." At this point she sighed and there was a "felt energetic shift" in the way her body carried the problem. (We can see here in Dr. Gendlin's work the phenomenological core of a primordial energy psychology.)

In the Focusing technique, our bodily felt sense can be used as a guiding light. We can imagine that the woman might be guided to express her feelings to her husband and be comforted, or she might look for a way to develop her life further.

The healing role of the body has long been recognized in mythology. Modern-day students of mythology, however, often fail to give the body due respect. Body feeling and archetypal image are mutually interdependent systems; they are isomorphic translations of each other into that other medium. Without the interweaving of body and myth, healing is not complete.

The insights gained from Gendlin's Focusing technique, coupled with mythology, can be an important next step in mythic voyages. Many of the subtle elements of the Focusing technique are integrated in the counseling setting, but to delve into these elements in depth goes beyond the scope of this section.[6]

Prelude to the Mythic Journey Process

The inner journey in the *Mythic Journey Process* parallels journeys to the underworld that have been spoken of by the earliest healers of the psyche.[7] Shamans and temple priests of the mystery schools have spoken of it as a journey into the body of the earth or into the dark caverns of the unconscious. Myths suggest ways to prevent us from getting lost.

As modern people we can use Focusing on our experience and felt sense in combination with the *Mythic Journey* to follow Theseus's path. We can join these methods to serve as our thread through the psychological underworld to find and liberate the energies of the natural child within.

The *Mythic Journey Process* starts with a grounding exercise that helps clear a space where we find our center, our inner pillar. Using a Taoist breathing technique, we can experience the *Tan Tien* center below the navel. When the breathing meditation is done properly[8] this center can become a pillar to return to when fear is encountered in one's inner labyrinth.

The Mythic Journey Process

The *Mythic Journey Process* begins with a breathing meditation combined with Focusing's "clearing a space" step, and an imagery exercise.

> *Notice your exhalation ... the pause ... and how the inhalation comes naturally from this pause. After a few cycles, notice how your body feels different and notice the way you have settled down to be in contact with the ground under you. Are you held off the ground in any way? Feel how being with your breathing cycle can help you let go to the ground under you, so that you are simply here.*
>
> *If there is any residual tension in your body, just notice it in a way that establishes a compassionate, friendly relationship to it. If a friend of yours had a similar tension, you'd find room to accept him, in spite of the issue. Find this relationship to any tension in your body, letting the natural breathing facilitate the friendly relationship. During the following process, when something arises that you want distance from, just breathe this way and return to the relaxed place, your inner pillar.*
>
> *One way to combine the breathing meditation with searching for an issue is to imagine that as you breathe out, it's like letting go of some of the tension in your body and lowering a bucket into the well of your Self, deep beneath the surface tension that you may be carrying at this moment. The bucket is tied to a secure pillar at the top. As you breathe out and lower it, you come to a place where your breath pauses before you take in the next breath. As you pause, it's as though the bucket is waiting for something deep within to fill it, some issue that stands in the way of you feeling all right. As your breath comes in, the bucket rises. It may take quite a few exhalations (lowering of the bucket) until something from deep within you comes into your bucket.*

Chapter 20: The Mythic Journey Process

The first step of the *Mythic Journey* consists of finding an issue and an associated bodily felt sense of this issue, just as in the Focusing technique. For some people the body sense comes first, for others the issue emerges first. If the body sense comes first, do you know what this body sense connects with in your life? If the issue arises first, do you feel where this issue lies in your body? You might start by proclaiming, "Everything in my life is completely alright," and noticing what issue(s) arise(s) to contradict this. With each issue that emerges, you establish a compassionate, friendly relationship to it. Create enough distance so that you can say, "I recognize you're there, but I'm not going to work on you right now. Maybe I'll come back later." Imagining yourself somewhere else in the room, feeling the way you do when you are with this issue, is one way to clear a space.

Give yourself time to notice, as issues pop up, how they affect the subtle barometer of your body. It is from your body's reaction that you'll know which issue to choose to work with. As you approach this "friend" you can get a felt sense of the issue.[9] For further aid in getting the felt sense, sometimes it helps to say, "I could feel completely fine about this whole thing." The voice inside which says, "No I couldn't feel fine about this," is the felt sense.[10] What's this sense all about? Wait for something to come up from the felt sense. See if you can distinguish between trying to think about it, and just having something emerge from the sense itself. It may be a word or an image or a sound — trust whatever comes for you. To get a "handle word or image" for this felt sense of the issue, just wait as if you are a fisherman by an ice hole. You can't rush a fish onto the hook. Just wait for what pops up from your body's sense of the issue as a whole.

What word or image seems to resonate with the sense of what this issue is all about? You'll know that you have something that resonates by the response that your body gives — the way its movement is facilitated when something gets to the crux of the matter.

What's the "worst thing about this issue" for you? At this point it helps to actually write down the issue on a piece of paper along with the bodily feeling you've noticed. Note bodily feelings in parentheses. For example:

Issue:

Body sense: (Write this in parentheses)

Handle word/image:

The worst of it: Ask various questions to the felt sense, such as: What's the worst of it? What's the crux of this issue?

Then the mythic dimension begins.

The Mythic Dimension

The first part of the mythic dimension of the *Mythic Journey Process* is to take your issue and the associated bodily felt sense, and create a story about a character in ancient times who had the same problem. Begin by writing, "Once upon a time ..."

There will be three parts to the mythic dimension. First, describe the problem you are facing in mythic terms — where does this mythic character live in terms of terrain and surroundings, etc. How did this problem come about? Was it created in a relationship with a young prince or princess's mother and father, the king and queen? Use your own characters and imagery. (The second two parts of the mythic dimension will be illustrated in the following case example.)

A key element is transposing the felt sense of your own obstacle into mythic terms. What created this problem in the character's life? Was a curse or spell put on you? For what reason? By whom? Give an actual face or name to the "demon," and write it in capitalized letters to personify it, i.e. Fear, Blame, Self-doubt, etc. Naming or "facing" the specific demon is very important (Hillman, 1975).

Case Illustration: A Critical Perfectionist's Mythic Journey Process

For example, one perfectionistic patient's issue was an intense criticizing that led to attacking his partners. The following *Mythic Journey Process* was written at a key point in "George's" long-term therapy.

> *Issue*: My difficulties with relationships
>
> *Body sense*: (Clenched jaw)
>
> *Handle word/image*: Anger. He imaged his "demon" to be a serrated sword. Then this patient, who we'll call "John," proceeded with part one of the mythic dimension and developed the felt sense of this demon into the following story.
>
> *The worst of it*: No one is good enough; I'll never find anyone with whom to have a long term relationship.

Once upon a time:

> *The Serrated Sword of Criticism was given to my father's father many generations ago when he was down and out. He sat on a mountaintop praying for power and the ability to support his family when a mountain demon came to him and gave him a serrated sword with a mountain emblazoned upon it. He said that the cuts made with it and the blood on it would proportionally increase the sword's power and would help him ascend the mountains of earthly life to be great, admired, powerful, and respected. He was told to make a family crest of it, and begin practicing with his own family.*
>
> *Indeed, great power and admiration came to this family of swordsmen and women through the generations. Though wounds occurred and blood was let increasingly, the Sword's power was the key focus of the family. Applause was given at the family dinner table for the great swordplay of the day, whether it was against the bulls killed for dinner or the other swordsmen defeated. Even family wounds inflicted, were respected if done in a skillful way.*

Chapter 20: The Mythic Journey Process

The second part of the mythic dimension of the *Mythic Journey Process* describes how impossible it seems to defeat the demon, and the problems it has caused. What methods have you tried that haven't worked to defeat it? Transpose these methods into mythic terms. For example, John added to his story:

> *Although our royal family attained a castle on a mountaintop and much power in the world through our fine discriminating cuts, the prince's life was not a happy one. As great a swordsman as he was, as admired as he was, he was alone most of the time.*
>
> *The problem was the sword, the very one that had given him such pleasure in his youth, the one for which he and his family had been admired for generations. When it was handed down to him, it went out of control. Each time it would become unsheathed, it would cut anything he looked at in a discriminating way. It cut all of his lovers to bits. The prince tried to break the sword, but many generations of power made it unbreakable. He tried to get rid of it at an Eastern religious temple; he denounced it, and tried to bury it. But he felt impotent without it, and had trouble climbing the castle steps if the sword was not in his belt. (slumped chest, feeling of being defeated)*

Accentuating how impossible it seemed to defeat the demon brings out the "soulful dimension" (Hillman, 1976) and can help prevent Pollyannaish solutions. Again check back with your body's felt sense and note it in parentheses here.

Concluding part two, make a statement that addresses, What is the specific nature of the impasse? What is the specific obstacle or demon the character is dealing with? How, specifically, do you feel knowing that nothing can be done to deal with it? This is "exploring the resistance" mythically. For example, from John's story:

> *The prince felt that he could not give up the way of the sword for he was too good at it, and it was too much a part of his nature. Yet, at the same time, he could not live with it. There seemed to be no end to the loneliness and the guilt that the prince felt over cutting up his lovers. The Critical Sword seemed all-powerful. (Depressed, hollow feeling in my chest.)*
>
> *The prince used his discriminating insight to see where the power of the sword came from. He relaxed and sensed the presence of the old mountain demon above him. Above him and to the right he noticed a demon called "Smug-faced Pride."*
>
> *It added an electric glow to the sword each time the prince said, "Look at what an adept swordsman I am." Upwards and to the left the prince was able to sense the presence of another demon, "Needy-faced Expectation." It added a desperate, angry, war-like hacking motion to the sword each time the prince said to others, "If you aren't the way I want you to be, I'll cut you up to fit into the 'right' mold."*

The third part of the mythic dimension begins with writing the words, "Then one day …" Then one day, what happened? Let some solution to the impasse come to you. Give it time. If no solution arises in you to break the impasse, then think about who could deal with this demon? Imagine some heroic figure, animal, or mythic creature and see what happens when it meets your demon. Use your creative story-writing capacity to let the story tell itself. Continuing his story:

> *Then one day, while the prince was depressed and looking into a mountain lake, he began to reflect upon whether he wanted to be a swordsman if it meant having no love. (Something lets go in my chest area; a sense of openness comes there as I sigh.) At that moment a Maiden of the Lake[11] appeared with the golden sword Excalibur that had been thrown back into these waters many years ago.*
>
> *Tears came to his eyes as he explained that he could not go on being a swordsman if there was no love in his life, and yet he could not give up his family's path either. He asked for her help.*
>
> *With compassion, the Maiden of the Lake taught him the one movement that the mountain demon had neglected to teach his forefather many years ago. She instructed him to feel with his heart before he was about to use the golden glowing sword, and caress it as if it was a beloved from whom he was asking guidance. Then he was to look at the polished mirror that the sword's metal became, reflect as he was doing in the lake when he met her, and ask for guidance on how to use the sword in the service of love and truth.*
>
> *As the prince followed her instructions, he noticed that as he held this sword in front of him, a ray of light came from his heart and bounced off the sword. His eyes could direct it, but only when they were reflecting inward with clear intent. "This light," the Maiden of the Lake said, "had the ancient power to transform anything that he wanted to heal."*
>
> *The Maiden said that this was the true power of the sword that had been lost through the ages. She explained that before the sword was used for fighting, it was used for directing energy to points on the body that were in need of healing. She told him stories of how her teachers of the Golden Age used this sword in daytime to bring the healing power of the sun, and at night to bring the powers of the stars to earth. All this was done with the same meditation that she had just given him — using the powers of reflection and the power of the heart's glow.*
>
> *With the Maiden of the Lake before him, the prince felt his heart's desire to be a healer and he reflected upon the mountain demon above him. A light went to the demon and transformed him into a beneficent mountain spirit whose purpose was to help others to climb to their own heights. (A feeling of fullness in my chest.)*

As he reflected on the electric light around "Smug-faced Pride," this conceited demon changed to a healing ally. The smug expression changed to a smile like the Buddha's as he realized that "skill" is not one's own, but is borrowed from the powers of the universe, the stars, the sun, and the earth.

As the prince reflected upon "Needy-faced Expectation," he realized that much of the world's and his own suffering came from this demon's misplaced needs for power over others, for false security, ego recognition, and worldly success. With the sword's light on this demon, a new power came to the sword — a compassionate understanding of human foibles. A new form of sword dancing came from this transformed demon which gave the prince's movements a heartfelt, gentle, slicing motion, as when a person cuts a flower for a loved one, and in the cutting wants the flower to suffer as little as possible. As when the sword-masters of ancient times had cut a field of wheat with deep appreciation for the forces of nature that went into producing the growth of the plant, so would the prince try to appreciate that which went into the growth of all that he was to use his sword upon. The prince vowed to make it his new practice to have tenderness when he used his sword to point out the places that became un-centered in his own and other's everyday life.

When the prince returned home, he created a new family crest with the Golden Glowing Sword of the Heart over the Critical Serrated Sword. The Maiden of the Lake's sword had the power to stir the prince's compassion. In the future, when the Critical Sword came out, the Maiden's sword was there to help remind the prince that its sharp power was to be put to a healing rather than a destructive use. This was not easy work, but at least now the prince knew what the work of his kingdom was. When the old sword arose, his work was to reflect on it with the heart meditation that he had learned, and thereby bring love and compassionate understanding to the kingdom. (Open-hearted glowing feeling in my chest, and hope through my whole being — a feeling like I've found what my life work is.)

Your story does not have to have a happily-ever-after ending. Simply note your actual sense of the issue and transpose it into mythic terms. Sometimes "time" is an important force to integrate into the story. Remember it took Moses forty years in the desert to complete his destiny. What is the destiny, the purpose for which your character is going through his or her trials and tribulations? Sometimes this dimension of meaning and purpose can contribute to a felt shift.

After you reach a place in the story where it feels complete for the moment, notice your body's felt sense and note it in parentheses at the end of the story.

Bring the adventure of this character back into your own life now. Reflecting on his or her quest, what can you learn form the character's adventure? How does your own path feel different now?

Reflection on the Mythic Journey Process

Many people experience new meaning emerging from their story and note that, at a certain point in writing, they find the story writing itself. Some report that it is as if something was overtaking their writing and giving them a solution. It is unimportant whether one calls this, in ancient Greek terms, a muse, our higher Selves, right brain function, the healing mind/energy of the universe, or intuition. The felt energetic shift that happens and the new meaning and perspective born on a blocked life issue help us to heal regardless of what one calls the source of healing.

When people are stuck in a critical part of themselves, as was "The Prince of the Serrated Sword," there are a variety of ways to create a shift in life stance. Tai Chi *Sword Dancing* practice, or Western psychotherapy and its symbolic process methods, when combined with Gendlin's Focusing, all can go right to the crux of the psychological problem, and can create a felt shift in a person's life stance. All are paths that lead to learning to wield a sword with compassion.

In this example of a *Mythic Journey Process*, the prince had to find a new life practice to change his "critical serrated sword way of being" to be a compassionate coach of his own and others' limitations. As we saw earlier Dr. Jung knew that body and archetypal image are two ends of a spectrum and healing can enter from the infrared or ultra-violet end of that spectrum. Or as the ancient Taoist alchemist would put it, intention (Yi) follows energy (Qi), and vice versa. So, "working on our life energy" involves working on all psychospiritual and bodily facets of ourselves. A person's life stance at a given moment, and the energy that goes along with it, does not change through the medium of the body alone.

Case Illustration: The Passive-Aggressive Ostrich — Healing Trauma and Withdrawal

In the middle of my five-day Bodymind Healing Qigong workshops, participants do a *Mythic Journey Process*, and then have the option to incorporate a Tai Chi or Qigong movement that helps to anchor the felt shift that oftentimes takes place at the end of their mythic journeys. So, I invite readers of this book to do the same. Perhaps some Qigong animal form, sword dance, or some other posture or movement of your own choosing will help you to embody the shape-shifting that may take place in your *Mythic Journey Process*. If you are so inclined, I invite you to do the movements in this book, use your own movements, or go to the more complete set of movements from Volume I, which has an accompanying Bodymind Healing Qigong DVD. Though Tai Chi, Qigong, or other movements are not necessary for the *Mythic Journey Process*, they do help to bring out a somatic dimension, which has the capacity to increase the method's transformative possibilities. In this sense, Volume I and Volume II of this work form a circle — like two uroboric dragons biting each other's tails and feeding each other, so does the Qigong emphasis in Volume I feed the psychotherapeutically oriented bodymind healing practices emphasized in Volume II, and vice versa.

The combination of these different facets of BMHP can be seen in the example of "Roberta," a young female student who had a pattern of passive-aggressive behaviors at significant times in her life. Roberta was engaged in psychotherapy with another therapist to work on her passive-aggressive tendencies because they were getting in the way of her intimate relationships, particularly with her husband. She also did the *Mythic Journey Process*, Tai Chi, and the animal forms of Qigong with me, as part of her Bodymind Healing Qigong certification program. Here we can see how the *Mythic Journey Process* can combine to help heal trauma, and enhance a healing experience of shape-shifting from one life stance to another.

> *Issue:* My husband's aggressivity and my withdrawal
>
> *Body sense:* (Anxiety in my stomach)
>
> *Handle word/image:* Ostrich hiding my head in the sand
>
> *The worst of it:* I feel like a weakling not being able to stand up for myself

Roberta's *Mythic Journey Process* activated memories of her running away from severe stressors in her teenage and young adult years, including a rape. This "running away" produced a belief that, "As soon as you sense danger, it's better to immediately leave." In her *Mythic Journey* she pictured and felt the demonic forces as Attacking Giants crushing her chest, closing off her ears, making her body tense like taught metal, which resulted in her running away from these feelings like a "Fearful Ostrich." Through her *Mythic Journey Process* she realized that this was an overreaction to many things that were not as dangerous as the rape of her youth. Her excessively reactive pattern resulted in her not listening to her husband when he was giving constructive critiques; instead, Roberta often withdrew with passive-aggressive behaviors such as threats to end their marriage. In her *Mythic Journey Process* her favorite movement from Hua Tao's set was *Crane Opens the Door to the Heavens* (see Volume I). This movement is used as a non-forceful way to split the force of an aggressor. As Roberta got in touch with an image of herself doing this posture, she felt a noticeable felt shift in that her stomach loosened its tight grip and she realized that her husband was often trying to be helpful. We discussed how one of the crane's powers was to peck and differentiate the good food from the bad and spit out what was distasteful. In alchemy this is called the *seperatio* phase (Edinger, 1985).

Roberta realized as her mythic quest that she must assert to her husband what she didn't like about the way he expressed himself rather than withdrawing. She later told me that in her psychodynamic therapy she was learning affect modulation skills to not be overly reactive and express herself appropriately to each occasion. Roberta reported that doing the *Crane* movements were helpful in showing her how to keep her heart open, yet appropriately defended, when needed. Last I heard, her marriage was better and the occurrences of "ostrich behavior" were much less long-lasting. Roberta said that now she almost always caught herself when the body feeling associated with the Attacking Giants came up. She used her anchor of touching the backs of her hands together in the *Crane Splitting* mudra (see Volume I) to find her Crane power, and differentiate what was harmful with what she could deal with as she cleared the way for her heart's grounded expression.

Case Illustration: The Desperately Grasping Parrot — Healing Abandonment and Neediness

The power of "naming," even without any internal martial arts practice, can be an important part of shape-shifting into another life stance. The significance and healing attributes of a mythic name can be seen with "Mary," a woman in her mid-20s who was in therapy for the guilt and desperation she felt from hanging out at various places looking for the man of her dreams. She described her disappointments going home each night without a man. She realized that the rejection she felt was similar to what she felt from her single mother who would often abandon her to go out on dates when Mary was young.

> *Issue*: Finding the right man
>
> *Body sense*: (Hole/emptiness in my heart)
>
> *Handle word/image:* Needy, grasping for someone who isn't there
>
> *The worst of it:* I'll never find a life partner

In doing her *Mythic Journey Process*, Mary took her "needy" felt sense and imagined being a huntress in ancient times. Her demon was a "Desperately Grasping Parrot" who would try to hold onto desired objects with its weak claws. The grasping claws though, would frighten its prey away. It would chatter, parroting back cliches that it had learned in order to impress, but all the chatter only frightened away all the beautiful, wild creatures of the forest.

> *The young princess was originally given the parrot as a present by her mother, the queen, as she abandoned her to go off for greater adventures than could be had with a young child. (Hole in my heart, emptiness.)*

Mary's single mother actually did go out on dates quite often in Mary's formative years, and Mary traced her first memories of this sense of neediness to these times in her early life. She learned to talk incessantly whenever her mother was there, to fill up the silence. She would try to say all the right things, parroting what her mother might like to hear so that her mother might stay with her more.

In her *Mythic Journey Process*, the curse was that the parrot would emerge out of her needy stomach each time Mary went hunting for someone to love. The parrot drove everyone away. The healing intervention came for her "one day" in her *Mythic Journey Process* in the form of the Greek goddess of the hunt, Artemis, who was her favorite Goddess in mythology.

> *One day, when the princess was depressed in the forest because she had not caught anything, Artemis appeared and offered to teach her the secrets of hunting ... how in primordial times the Master Huntress knew that love was something that came from our connection to the whole world. (A sense of rising excitement and a sense of purpose.)*

Chapter 20: The Mythic Journey Process

As if straight out of classical mythic literature, Mary was describing *anima mundi*, soulful love of the world. She was expressing, in her own terms, the classical idea that at a certain point in our evolution, we as human beings transposed this *anima mundi* into *anima personalis*, a love for one human being, hopeful that this one person could contain her love for the world and universe. A large task indeed!

> *Artemis taught the maiden how to hunt by enjoying all that was around her. If no deer came to her, she could still feel love for all surrounding life — the way light bounced over the meadow, the colors at sunset, and her relaxed position against the tree while she waited. Artemis told her that it was only in modern times, when the cult of true hunting decayed, that hunters would be devastated if they returned home without a deer. In primordial times, through the quality of waiting, the Priestesses of the Temple of Hunting always returned home with something of value. Upon hearing this, the princess (stomach opened and relaxed) and her pet parrot were both stilled as never before. (A melting sensation in my stomach.)*

A few months later, Mary related how she sat watching the interesting variation of light shine on the table plants at her favorite local bar. She described a new sense of "life as practice." Though feelings of loneliness still arose, she said that her "hunting" now had a felt sense of adventure to it. A new context emerged, one of practicing the ancient art of "true hunting." She became more aware of her desperate, needy chatter and began to practice being a "Stilled Parrot Who Enjoys the World While Waiting" — her new symbolic name.

Many people who do the *Mythic Journey Process* find a new name for themselves. As in ancient initiatory rituals, it offers a new identity, and a new life stance for the person. It defines a new path and a new practice in one's life.[12] The new name is much like the new name that Native Americans receive in their initiatory rituals in that it holds a power which links the person to a transpersonal purpose, a path to a sacred life, and a destiny worth pursuing.

The *Mythic Journey Process* is a way of responding to those who might ask, "Where are our heroes today? Where are those mythic adventurers who were able to deal with the archetypal demons of their age and open a path for fellow sufferers?

Perhaps, if we follow Ariadne's thread into our own underworlds, our stories, like hers, will be placed in the night sky; they will be like the crown of Ariadne (the Corona Borealis constellation) that Dionysus put there to immortalize her as a guiding light for lost souls to find their way. By opening our mythic imaginations, each of our life stories can become a guiding light for humanity. For who are we but stars in the making, hoping to shed light on the darkness of space and thereby give new life to ourselves, our planet, and to fellow travelers everywhere.

CHAPTER 21: WHAT QIGONG AND PSYCHOTHERAPY GIVE EACH OTHER

Among the things we have explored throughout this book, we have sat at the place where the streams of Qigong and psychotherapeutic traditions become one. In Volume I, it was shown how psychotherapy and traditions of mind-body healing have much to contribute to the tradition of Qigong. Here in Volume II, the emphasis is on what Qigong gives to psychotherapy.

What Psychological Traditions Give to Qigong?

Long before modern psychotherapy existed, "psychological awareness"[1] and mindfulness practice were a part of the static and moving traditions of postural initiation such as Tai Chi/ Qigong. However, those who practice these traditions (such as Qigong) today oftentimes do so without a conscious appreciation of how the tradition can help change their life stance.

Volume I showed how, according to the research of Tomio (1994) and Goodman (1990), there is a long-lost tradition of postural initiation oriented to facilitate a transformational process, a "shape-shifting" of the a person's life stance. In the Buddhist tradition, according to Tomio (1994), this involves a process whereby the practitioner's *klesas* (unconscious patterns such as envy, greed, etc.) are worked on in the process of holding various postures and engaging in various *natas* (physical exercises which utilized sequences of attack and defense). This involves working on the totality of one's life stance (*sthana*), "the totality of a student's perceived and acknowledged mental stance or concurrent position in regard to their self-understanding … [it] was also a term applied to describe an individual's physical condition and health balance" (Tomio, 1994, p. 221). Tomio puts forth the case that the wider tradition called the *Chuan Fa* went through a *diaspora*, but in its earlier form it included healing, self-defense, spiritual unfoldment, and changing the whole of the practitioner's life stance. He defines "*Chuan Fa*" as the associated arts surrounding the *Chuan*. "*Chuan*" usually translates to mean "fist." In my early publications (Mayer, 1996) I suggest the idea that the esoteric meaning of "fist" is the ability to metaphorically hold the five elements — fire, earth, metal, water, and wood — in one's hand. Now, here in Volume II, we see further how the *Chuan Fa*, as it joins with Western bodymind healing methods, can aid in helping us, as modern people, recover the soulful (Hillman, 1975) aspects of our primordial Selves.

In Volume I, and here in Volume II, I suggest that the Western bodymind healing tradition can aid in the repairing of the broken pieces of the *Chuan Fa* by adding to the internal martial arts Qigong traditions, such as Tai Chi and the *Yi Chuan*, in the following ways:

What Psychotherapy Gives Qigong?

Modern psychotherapy has much to offer Qigong practitioners:

1. *Provides a psychological framework and clinical methods for transmuting bodymind fixations.* I have discussed how Qigong and Tai Chi aid Western bodymind health in their ability to create sophisticated state-specific transcendent altered states of consciousness. Conversely, Western psychotherapy aids the traditions of postural initiation by providing a clinical base of knowledge that can give those suffering from various bodymind issues the ability to transmute, not just transcend, the issues that create many bodymind blockages. For example, in the case of Shelly's anxiety (Chapter 6) we saw how relaxation alone, including the induction of trance states, was not sufficient to produce healing. Cognitive restructuring, psychodynamic work, self-soothing and the transformative symbols from her dream life provided some of the necessary ingredients to transmute the psychological patterns rooted in early abandonment and fear of rejection.

    Many concepts and clinical methods of modern psychotherapy are vital in healing the bodymind and activating the core energy of the soul. For example:

    - Positive mirroring of the real self (Kohut, 1977, 1981)
    - Transmuting introjects (Stolorow, 1987)
    - Cognitive restructuring (Beck, 1979)
    - Transforming self-identifications[2] (Jacobson, 1964)
    - Activating the separation-individuation process (Mahler, 1975)

    Listing all of the specific contributions that modern psychotherapy has made to the ability to transmute body/mind fixations and heal the Self would be an overwhelming, extensive, and close to impossible task. Earlier (Chapter 4) I discussed how in Greek mythology the realm of gods/goddesses of the heaven (transcendent states), earth, (practical grounded approaches), and underworld (transmuting) journeys all had their part in a comprehensive mythology. Likewise, modern psychotherapy addresses these zones in its various schools of therapy, which were addressed in Chapter 2.

2. *Deepens consciousness of psychological meanings.* For example, Gendlin's Focusing method can aid a practitioner in becoming conscious of the psychological meanings of body blocks that emerge while holding static postures. As Gendlin has shown, when such new meaning arises, a "felt shift," occurs. From the perspective of BMHP, this is a Western embodiment of one aspect of the age-old tradition of shape-shifting.

3. *Facilitates healing disintegration/reintegration of split-off aspects of Self.* We have seen how these age-old traditions of postural initiation can help heal split-off, dissociated complexes (see the case of Stan in Chapter 5). Many have spoken of the issues of self-fragmentation (Stolorow, 1987) and dissociation (Krippner et al., 1997) commonly arising in the practice of psychotherapy. The psychological inner work necessary to enable one to regain "cohesion of the self" (Horner, 1990) is aided by the Western psychotherapeutic tradition, and I propose that it can be further enhanced by traditions of postural initiation such as Qigong and Tai Chi.

4. *Increases awareness of psychodynamic methods of self-soothing to reverse self-critical internalized messages* (Kohut, 1971, p. 64; Pearlman & McCann, 1992).

5. *Imparts awareness of how illness often manifests from mind to energy, then to feelings, and then to bodily structures.*

6. *Gives affect containment methods to deal with abreaction* (Gallo, 2002, p. 184) *and impulse control problems.* See Chapter 15 for a discussion of a case where BMHP helped a patient with impulse control problems.

7. *Aids in healing trauma — reorganizing meaning.* See Chapter 8 for a discussion of how psychotherapy and Qigong traditions can join hands to help traumatized individuals.

What Qigong Gives Psychotherapy and Behavioral Healthcare

1. *Contains useful relaxation methods.* Dr. Herbert Benson (1983) first coined the term "relaxation response," and showed its ability to ameliorate hypertension and cardiac problems. Qigong fits well into the guidelines stated by a National Institute of Health panel (1996) which concluded that integrating behavioral and relaxation therapies with conventional medical treatment is imperative for successfully managing many chronic conditions including chronic pain and insomnia. The panel did not endorse a single technique, but stated that a variety of techniques worked in lowering one's breathing rate, heart rate, and blood pressure as long as they included two features: a repetitive focus of a word, sound, prayer, phrase, or muscular activity, and neither fighting nor focusing on intruding thoughts.

   Repetition is a key element in activating healing processes. For example, in energy psychology repeatedly tapping on points while focusing on new constructive beliefs is believed to be related to greater treatment success rates (Andrade & Feinstein, 2003); and in the Eye Movement Desensitization and Reprocessing (EMDR) method the repeated movement of the eyes from side to side while constructive beliefs are being stated is also believed to be integral to positive treatment outcomes. EMDR's originator Dr. Francine Shapiro (1995) suggests that neuronal bursts caused by the eye movements may be equivalent to a low-voltage current and therefore responsible for synaptic changes. She says, "It may be that the repetitive action of any ... alternative stimuli — or even repetitive bursts of attention generates such a current. The shifting of the synaptic potential of the neural networks that include the dysfunctional material may cause the information to undergo progressively more processing with each set, until it arrives at an adaptive resolution" (p. 316).

For thousands of years, Qigong and Tai Chi traditions have developed sophisticated ways to use whole-body repetition of movement, repetitive movements for isolated body parts, and repetition of sounds to promote healing.

In addition to Qigong and Tai Chi, Taoist relaxation methods can also be beneficial to enhance the relaxation response. In BMHP, I have emphasized those methods that are easy to introduce into the modern healthcare setting, such as *Microcosmic* and *Macrocosmic Orbit Breathing*.

2. *Activates state-specific states of consciousness that are both relaxing and energizing.* Qigong doesn't only activate an altered state that is relaxing, it activates a state-specific state (Rossi, 1986) that is both relaxing and empowering. It resolves the activity-passivity paradox spoken of in the clinical hypnosis literature (Gorton, 1957, 1958). As Sturgis and Coe (1990) showed, whether hypnosis causes arousal or relaxation depends upon the suggestion made (p. 205). Hypnosis not just about relaxation. Chinese Qigong has known this to be true for thousands of years in its concept called "sung," relaxed awakeness. *Sung* can be helpful for alleviating symptoms of stress, as well as empowering those who have deficits in the areas of self-assertiveness, those who are stuck in victim roles as result of trauma, etc.

3. *Contains specific healing and balancing energetic techniques.* For example: (a) static and moving Qigong from Bodymind Healing Qigong (see Appendix I and Volume I) (b) sounds (c) acupressure points (d) Chi Nei Tsang (e) releasing body blocks/ dispersing stagnant Qi (f) embodying new life stances. (See Volume I or Chapter 24)

4. *Provides a pathway to develop many of the qualities proved useful by therapists who integrate meditation into psychotherapy* (Bogart, 1991). In conjunction with the psychotherapeutic process, Qigong and Tai Chi can help a person to:

    - Reciprocally inhibit unwanted behaviors (Wolpe, 1958)
    - Establish an observing self (Deikman, 1982)
    - Dissolve into the oneness of life
    - Facilitate ego cohesion in maintaining one's center when meeting the emotional tides of life
    - Develop a compassionate relationship to life issues

Chapter 21: What Qigong Gives to Psychotherapy

5. *Enhances development of cohesiveness of self.* Whereas some meditative traditions are oriented to transcendence, for the most part Qigong and Tai Chi are body-oriented traditions that can lead to cultivation of "a cohesiveness of self," (Horner, 1990).[3] Qigong and Tai Chi can facilitate healing the disintegration/reintegration of split-off aspects of Self.

   For example, as discussed in Volume I, in *Yi Chuan Qigong* and Tai Chi practice, initiates are "tested" *(sili)* to see if they can maintain a cohesiveness of self and the sense of the ball of their body when pushed. This is called "maintaining integral force." Various aspects of the ball are tested as to whether one can "bounce," i.e. when pushed does the acolyte fight as he or she is lifted into the air, or is the sphere of the bodily self intact as he or she lands in a new location. This practice is shown in Volume I *(fajing)*. There, I mention that physically doing this practice is not as important as finding the ability to maintain a cohesiveness of self when attacked by the forces of life.

   In Chapters 15-18 we saw how the interface of Qigong and psychotherapy can help one to practice maintaining self-cohesion and change one's life stance under stress The way that Tai Chi and Qigong are usually practiced does not specifically focus on psychological issues (such as early emotional wounding and negative beliefs) and maintaining cohesiveness of the self; however, I have put forth the case that oftentimes, shifts in a person's psychological stance in life can be a result of this practice. As we saw in the chapters on Bodymind Healing Psychotherapy, an approach which synergistically combines both the psychological dimension and these bodily oriented practices can help one to develop many of the qualities associated with ego strength — such as self-cohesion and a stable attachment style.

6. *Helps those with reactive attachment styles to develop a cohesive center when the everyday issues of life assault or impinge upon ones sensibilities, and together with psychotherapy it may provide a bodily base for developing affect modulation skills, and affect tolerance.* (See Chapters 16 and 17)

7. *Adds an energy cultivation practice beneficial to those who are depressed.* (See Chapter 12)

8. *Induces an altered state, helpful in issues with addiction.* (See Chapter 13)

9. *Contributes to the field of clinical hypnosis.* Qigong and Tai Chi are multifaceted traditions that are not only meditative, but they can be seen as forms of hypnosis accompanied by the health benefits known to be related to hypnosis (Rossi, 1986, 1988). They have an empirically time-tested record for enhancing health for a multiplicity of health-related conditions (Sancier, 1996; Pelletier, 2000). Qigong helps to *anchor* (Bandler & Grinder, 1979) state-specific states of awareness (Rossi, 1986) that help the patient to maintain a connection to the somatic ground of new healing pathways.

10. *Aids transformation of self-identifications* (Jacobson, 1964) through the process of invoking state-specific states of consciousness that lead to shape-shifting.

11. *Employs methods helpful to those who suffer from sympathetic nervous system overload, in cases of fibromyalgia and chronic fatigue.* (See Chapter 13)

12. *Helps traumatized patients to regain a safety zone in their bodies.* Qigong traditions, particularly Tai Chi, are especially useful for those who suffer from conditions of sympathetic overload to create somatic safety zones. (See Chapter 8)

13. *Contains useful behavioral health applications.* When appropriate,[4] it is natural for such a time-tested method of behavioral healthcare to be applied to many issues that psychologists see in their everyday practices, including insomnia, anxiety, joint problems, energy deficiency, chronic pain, etc. (See Chapters 6, 7, 19, 13)

14. *Helps to heal the healer.* An integrative tradition includes self-healing, spiritual unfoldment, self-defense, and "trance-forming" one's life stance by "shape-shifting."

15. *Provides a philosophic framework for how healing often comes from mind, to Qi (energy), and then to the body.*

CHAPTER 22: ETHICS OF INCORPORATING QIGONG INTO PSYCHOTHERAPY

Introduction and Summary

Due caution and mindful awareness should be exercised when integrating new experimental methods and modalities with psychotherapy. To summarize, some of the areas that need to be considered by psychotherapists who want to incorporate such treatments are:

1. Informed Consent for Experimental Methods in "Emerging Areas"
2. Transference Issues and False Hope
3. Scope of Practice
4. Standard of Care
5. Areas of Competence
6. Multiple or Dual Relationships: Mixing Qigong Outside and Inside of Therapy

1. Informed Consent for Experimental Methods in "Emerging Areas."

According the American Psychological Association's (APA) code of ethics,[1] for treatment involving "emerging areas" in which "generally recognized techniques and procedures" have not been established, it is important to have informed consent from patients. Some of the elements of informed consent are:

- Voluntary nature of participation — patients must freely and without undo influence express consent.
- Inform patients of the potential risks involved.
- Inform patients about available alternative treatments.
- Inform patients of the developmental nature of the treatment
- Give patients an opportunity to ask questions and receive answers regarding the activities.
- Protect patients from harm.
- Inform patients that they are free to stop treatment anytime they want.
- Have a written informed consent form for patients to sign.

According to Celia Fisher, Ph.D., director of the Fordham University Center for Ethics Education and chair of APA's Ethics Code Task Force, "While psychologists are now required to tell patients if a treatment is experimental, the Ethics Code does not prohibit the use of new treatments, as long as they are based on scientific or professional knowledge."[2]

As we have seen, there is substantial scientific research and professional knowledge that lies behind the individual components of the approach taken in Bodymind Healing Psychotherapy. The base of research on Qigong in behavioral healthcare (see Chapter 1 and 2), the use of medical/clinical hypnosis (Chapter 2), the use of imagery (Chapter 2, 4, and 5), energy psychology (within the parameters spoken of in Chapters 3 and 4), and the transmuting elements of traditional psychotherapy (Chapter 5) have each individually shown positive potentials for patient's healing. Certainly further research is needed to determine which, or what combination of, methods are best in which situations for what types of individuals. As well, further research is needed to see how this approach compares to other, more generally accepted methods in dealing with various conditions.

2. Transference Issues and False Hope

As stated above, the therapist who uses methods stemming from extra-psychological sources should let the patient be part of the process of deciding to use such methods, with full disclosure of the experimental nature of the treatment. It is best to introduce "emerging area" treatment methods as an experiment. Asking for an honest report as to whether this treatment works for the person will increase the likeliness of accurate patient feedback, and will hopefully decrease the potential for activation of the patient's placating false self who may not want to "disappoint" the therapist with unsuccessful reports. Introducing an experimental treatment to patients who have not received relief elsewhere has the potential to create more wounding in those who are already vulnerable to disappointment. Unfulfilled promises can lead to feelings of betrayal and deflated expectations.[3] False promises can impact the therapeutic alliance and may prevent the patient from receiving appropriate treatment from other health professionals. As we saw in the case of the carpal tunnel patient in this book's introductory chapter, it is important to disclose to the patient that Qigong is a "practice" not a one-time fix.

3. Scope of Practice Issues

When a person comes to a psychotherapist who also specializes in complementary behavioral health treatments, the clinician should be working within the scope of practice of the field of psychotherapy. Informed consent mixes with scope of practice in that a patient should be informed about how other traditional treatments may be necessary or beneficial. For example, when working with any behavioral healthcare method in general, and here specifically, when introducing acupressure self-touch or Qigong into treatment, caution should be exercised regarding circumventing needed medical treatment. If a patient suffers from pain and an acupressure self-touch point, relaxation method, or a Qigong movement is suggested,

Chapter 22: Ethics of Incorporating Qigong   261

it may give temporary relief which could stop the person from getting necessary medical treatment — for example, for a malignant tumor. Therefore, the health professional using the aforementioned methods should be mindful of referring patients to medical doctors and other health professionals, when appropriate. Likewise, if Qigong is used to facilitate various facets of psychotherapy, the patient should be informed that traditional treatment might include Jacobson's relaxation method, i.e. tightening and loosening muscles. Or, if using energy psychology, or Qigong in conjunction with energy psychology methods, the patient should be informed that many therapists do not use touching or tapping. Giving a patient choice within the therapist's expanded scope of practice helps the patient to be aware of other treatment choices. Finally, billing of third-party payers for experimental treatments should be done within appropriate ethical and legal parameters and may require consultation with your attorney or professional organization.

4. Standards of Care

All therapists, including those of us who use experimental methods in emerging areas of the profession, are expected to act under the guidelines of standards of care in our profession. For example, "doing no harm" and making reasonable judgments and assessments about when and with whom we are using such methods are essential aspects of professional practice. We operate with the best interests of our patients in mind; and when we make judgments about incorporating such methods, we do so with informed consent as outlined above, and we use these methods with a clear rationale (documented in our case notes) that is within our areas of competence.

5. Areas of Competence

As health professionals, we limit our practice to fall within the scope of our education, training, and expertise. Informed consent, scope of practice, standards of care, and areas of competence are overlapping categories — each a facet of appropriate professional ethics. So, how does the clinician reading this book about Bodymind Healing Psychotherapy proceed to incorporate these methods and make sure he or she is practicing within an area of his or her competence?[4] Surely, adequate training is necessary to incorporate any new method of therapy. However, in this book I have striven to present some methods that the licensed health professional can incorporate without much additional training. For example, many clinicians will be able to incorporate into their current treatment methods certain aspects of the methods introduced in this book such as: breathing techniques (*Microcosmic* and *Macrocosmic Orbit Breathing*), awareness of somatic states that arise at the moment of a felt shift, self-soothing touch of acu-point CV-17, and the phenomenologically based somatic methods suggested for anchoring state-specific states of consciousness to help patients maintain treatment gains. Some of the other methods discussed may require more training — for example, Gendlin's Focusing method, some Qigong movements and acu-point self-touch methods, and some aspects of the *River of Life* practice. It should be noted that the somatic additions to the use of imagery methods (like the *River of Life* practice), and the use of Gendlin's (1978) somatic Focusing method, may produce surprisingly deep abreactions in a shorter amount of time than when verbal psychotherapy methods are used. Most clinicians are probably adept at dealing with such states and previous training in dealing with such abreactive states may suffice, or further training may be necessary. For example, the therapist must be able to facilitate the patient's titration into and out of such states with a grounded safety net that prevents re-traumatization. Many of the BMHP and Qigong methods such as "sinking the Qi," some of Craig's (1995) EFT methods, self-soothing by touching CV-17, etc. can be useful components of such a safety net. For members of the intelligent lay public who read this book and experiment with its methods, it is wise to have a psychotherapist, or a psychotherapist trained specifically in Bodymind Healing Psychotherapy, to help facilitate your dealing with emerging issues.

6. Multiple or Dual Relationships: Mixing Qigong Outside and Inside of Therapy.

In 2002, the APA explicitly defined multiple relationships in its code of ethics, while pointing out that not all multiple relationships are unethical.[5] It wrote:

> *"A multiple relationship occurs when a psychologist is in a professional role with a person and (1) at the same time is in another role with the person, (2) at the same time is in a relationship with a person closely associated with or related to the person with whom the psychologist has the professional relationship, or (3) promises to enter into another relationship in the future with the person or a person closely associated with or related to the person."*

According to Fisher, "We've become more informative by defining multiple relationships and underscoring the fact that multiple relationships that are not harmful or going to impair your judgment or limit your effectiveness are not unethical." Specifically, the standard says that multiple relationships that "would not reasonably be expected to cause impairment or risk exploitation or harm" are not unethical. However, the code advises psychologists to refrain from multiple relationships if the relationship could reasonably be expected to impair the psychologists' professional performance or could exploit or harm the patient.

In mixing Qigong and psychotherapy there is some potential for problematic aspects of dual or multiple relationships to occur. In the rest of this chapter I will address various types and aspects of multiple relationships both outside and inside of psychotherapy sessions.

Mixing Roles: Qigong Teacher and Psychotherapist

First, when a patient sees the same professional in two different settings — for psychotherapy and Tai Chi practice — various problems can arise. Some potential issues are: the person may feel inadequate or not proficient in doing a movement which carries over into the psychotherapeutic relationship, or perhaps something occurs in the class which represents and evokes a childhood wound — for example, a situation of perceived favoritism of another student. If something like this occurs and the patient does not talk about it, a negative influence can spill over into the psychotherapy. This can create an unwanted "negative transference." Thus, some would argue for a "sterile/safe container" in order to protect the patient. In particular, damage can occur to people with limited ego strength, or those who suffer from borderline issues and unresolved "splitting," i.e. over-idealizing in one moment and over-denigrating in the next without being able to hold memory of the constant center.

For these reasons many would argue it is better to keep such relationships separate. The question can be raised, "Why not just refer a patient out to a Tai Chi or Qigong teacher to get the benefits of these traditions?" Most of the time, I believe this is indeed the best course of action, and usually I do refer patients out to another Tai Chi/Qigong teacher. However, there is also a way in which such a viewpoint "suffers" from the Western dualistic bias that favors dichotomy, separation, and specialization; and it therefore may limit the benefits of an integrated, bodymind approach to healing the whole person in the psychotherapeutic and behavioral health spheres. A combination of psychotherapy and practice of that therapist's style of Qigong has the benefit of sharing metaphors that can more easily be incorporated into the psychotherapeutic work.

On this other side of the issue, it is said that if the difficult feelings that arise from the multiple or dual relationship can be acknowledged and explored; those feelings can become a subject to deepen therapy, and can help the person to grow further by constellating these additional issues. This is called the "grist for the mill" viewpoint. Before such mixing of role relationships occurs, careful assessment of a patient is important. The therapist needs to be mindful of his or her own, as well as the patient's, motivation for such mixing in order to ensure it is in the patient's best interest.

Which relationship came first is an important criterion to consider when deciding to mix these relationships, because different issues arise depending upon which relationship is first. For example, if the person was first a Tai Chi/Qigong student, he or she must have informed consent to be aware that the psychotherapeutic relationship is different and that it usually requires safer boundaries than a student/teacher relationship. Also, once the therapeutic relationship begins the student may lose that person as his or her Qigong teacher, depending upon the agreements made. Likewise, informed consent regarding a psychotherapeutic relationship where a patient wants to take a workshop or class requires careful examination by the therapist and the patient regarding possible issues that could arise, which could damage the safety of the therapeutic container. Agreements to talk about feelings that arise is crucial, as is assessing the patient's ego strength, the patient's ability to process issues, and being mindful about motivations of both parties in expanding the parameters of the therapeutic relationship.

One could compare these mixing of roles to the "coaching" relationship. For those who are both psychotherapists and coaches it is advised to keep such relationships separate. A coach is focused mostly on facilitating goal setting and meeting behavioral objectives regarding ones life. Addressing healing of pathological conditions should be clearly separated and coaches are advised to refer out such clients to other psychotherapists when such issues arise. If a coaching client wants to expand a coaching relationship to a psychotherapeutic relationship, the client is advised that it would be best to see another therapist, and if the client insists that he or she wants to expand the relationship to a psychotherapeutic one, they are advised that once they move into a therapeutic relationship, it is best not to move back to a coaching relationship. The coach/therapist should make proper notes of the rationale for such choices and agreements made.

Though there are some analogous elements to the coaching relationship, the relationship between psychotherapy patient and Tai Chi/Qigong teacher seems to be more similar to a psychotherapeutic training institute where the student may mix taking classes from a teacher and being in therapy with that person to get the broadest and deepest immersion into that teacher/therapist's tradition. From the perspective of this analogy, still the clinician should discuss the advantages and disadvantages of such mixing of traditions, and the potential dangers and issues involved. It should be recognized that, as compared to private practice, in a psychotherapeutic institute a broader context and clearer container may ameliorate possible negative effects of blending a therapy and student/teacher relationship. Regardless of the particular place where such mixing takes place, prior to making such a decision a careful assessment of the patient's motivations and object relations should be carefully considered. The therapist should include in his or her case notes the rationale for such choices and agreements made.

For these reasons I usually do not mix the two traditions — though for some students/patients in certification programs I have sometimes mixed these two models using the above considerations. Some of the cautions and considerations discussed above come from my experience with such cases. Evaluative elements of a relationship are another important component to consider in mixing roles, whether it is in a university setting, certification program, etc. Clear agreements should be made in writing. Superego issues may endanger the therapeutic container, and issues in a "sterile/safe container" approach versus a "grist for the mill" approach should be discussed and reflected upon to determine the most appropriate course of action.

Blending Qigong with Psychotherapy

Some might consider mixing Tai Chi/Qigong and Western psychotherapy within the confines of the psychotherapeutic setting a "multiple relationship." Along these lines, it could be said that even though each of the traditions that are part of BMHP have individually shown merit in ameliorating various conditions, the question remains, Is there potential harm, or less clinical effectiveness, when these traditions are mixed? Dr. Mark Fromm, an ethics consultant for the California Board of Psychology, calls this "the Alchemical Error" — the mixing of two or more elements, which may be beneficial individually but don't work together. In a conversation I had with Dr. Fromm, he said, "Fire has great benefits, gasoline can give your car energy, but put them together and you can get an explosion."[6]

This type of intra-session multiple relationship issue particularly relates to the mixing of an oriental tradition such as Qigong with Western psychotherapy, or in integrating Qigong as a form of meditation into psychotherapy. In Chapter 2, I reviewed some of the literature on the integration of meditation and psychotherapy and discussed many of the benefits and problems with that integration. Since Qigong is, in part, a type of meditation, many of the issues addressed in Chapter 2 apply here, i.e. that there are quite a few benefits and some problem areas. I have also shown how some of the concerns about the transcendent dimension of Qigong as a medita-

Chapter 22: Ethics of Incorporating Qigong

tion tradition are resolved by the way BMHP integrates Qigong and the transmuting aspects of Western psychotherapy (see Chapter 5).

Again, the question can be raised, Why not just refer a patient out to a Tai Chi or Qigong teacher to get the benefits of these traditions? Throughout this book I have shown that sometimes this is indeed the best course of action. However, as stated above, at times such a viewpoint may suffer from a Western dualistic bias — which splits the whole and thereby limits the benefits of an integrated, bodymind approach to healing the whole person in the psychotherapeutic and behavioral health spheres. In this sense, Tai Chi/Qigong is similar to a relaxation method introduced within therapy; and as shown in Chapter 2, there is much solid research to support such a mixture.

As stated above, and is equally applicable now, within the psychotherapeutic setting, as far as mixing Qigong and psychotherapy within a session is concerned, it is possible for material from one tradition to spill over from its container and "contaminate" the other. I also mentioned above how if this "spill over" can be acknowledged and explored in the therapeutic context, the therapy may be deepened. (We saw an example of this in the case of the carpal tunnel syndrome patient mentioned in the introduction to this book.) This is called the "grist for the mill" approach to therapy (Alpert, 1971). The issues here are similar to if the therapist introduced any extra-therapeutic method — whether it is Jacobson's relaxation exercise, biofeedback, or Mindfulness Meditation. The aware clinician uses his or her clinical skills to bring any discontent to light, so that such feelings will not harm the integrity of the therapeutic container.

The clinical issues involved here are complex. When I train doctoral psychology students in the integration of Qigong and psychotherapy, this subject comprises a three-hour lecture. Suffice it to say that due caution should be exercised because of the legal and clinical complexities. Some of the issues involved relate to the ones addressed above. A brief but comprehensive review of these clinical issues includes: a careful assessment of the patient's ego strength, written, informed consent and choice, letting a patient know the experimental nature of the discipline that is being introduced, an explanation of the theoretical framework behind the treatment, a clear agreement that the patient can say "no" at any point in doing the practice, an agreement that an honest debriefing will take place after the treatment is tried to assess its efficacy, weighing the advantages of introducing the patient to another practitioner who does the "alternative" practice to avoid dangers, weighing potential legal consequences and risk assessment, and addressing problems in mixing different theoretical orientations involving "transcendence" in Eastern practices versus "working through," which is more emphasized in Western psychotherapy.

In Chapter 11, I gave a case example of when unknowingly introducing a Buddhist Qigong practice to a fundamentalist Christian created a problem by disturbing the therapeutic alliance. I discussed in that chapter some potential ways to deal with this type of problem.

Regarding the advantages of mixing the two traditions, when the above considerations are taken into account, rather than producing an alchemical error by blending the traditions of Qigong and psychotherapy, an alchemical joining may take place, which, like an amalgam of coal and iron creating steel, oftentimes produces something stronger. From psychotherapy's early roots in alchemy (Edinger, 1985), it was said that in the process of psychological transformation, there is a time for keeping things separate (*seperatio*) and a time for bringing them together (*coniuntio*).

In this chapter and throughout the book, I address both the benefits and the contraindications of such blending, and I discuss how to avoid the potential risks.

Regarding the benefits, in Chapter 1, I review the substantial research in respected scientific journals regarding Qigong's efficacy with a wide variety of health-related conditions. And in Chapter 21, I summarize the previous chapters of this book, which show how blending Qigong and psychotherapy: (1) adds a relaxation method that can be a useful adjunct to psychotherapy in a variety of areas including cases of anxiety (Chapter 1 and 6); (2) contributes to clinical hypnosis interventions in psychotherapy by activating and anchoring state-specific states of consciousness that help the patient to activate healing pathways (Chapter 2); (3) brings balance to conditions of sympathetic nervous system overload, and therefore is beneficial in cases of trauma (Chapter 8); (4) helps to activate state-specific states of consciousness that are both relaxing and energizing, and are beneficial in cases of depression (Chapter 12); (5) enhances transformations of self-identifications and changing one's life stance (Chapter 15); (6) enhances developing affect modulation skills (Chapter 17); (7) helps to cultivate self-assertion skills (Chapter 18); (8) adds a body-centered method into therapy that helps to anchor the person and make the person more whole (as discussed in Chapters 16-19); and (9) provides a many-thousand-year-old empirically validated healing technology that can be useful in behavioral healthcare in cases involving chronic pain, insomnia, hypertension, and joint problems (Chapter 7, 10, 11, 13).

Another point regarding boundaries and dual relationships is that if a therapist has a knowledge base that could be useful to a patient and withholds that knowledge, another type of ethical breach occurs — allowing undue suffering when the clinician has tools to alleviate that suffering. We saw examples of how — with careful weighing of the ethical and clinical issues involved — I decided with a few turning point patients, and then with other patients, to incorporate the wider scope of my training and expertise in interdisciplinary, cross-cultural healing methods in order to better treat my patient's issues.

Along these lines, it should be remembered that just as loose handling of boundaries and multiple relationships can be problematic, so too can rigid avoidance of all boundary crossings and dual relationships have a negative affect on treatment. Throughout this book I have cited a substantial body of scientific and clinical research in the field to lend support to the efficacy of somatically grounded, energetically founded, psychological treatment. Therefore, as treatment protocols of BMHP are introduced, the astute clinician should use flexible and personally tailored boundaries to address individual clients' needs and sensibilities. When doing so, a therapist is best advised to articulate and document in his or her treatment plan notes the rationale for such boundary crossing, and consult with experts when appropriate (Zur, 2005).

Since different states, different mental health professions, and different backgrounds necessitate different approaches, it is wise to contact your professional organization, or your attorney, to make sure that the way you choose to incorporate new methods, such as Bodymind Healing Psychotherapy, meets with legal and ethical guidelines.

SECTION IV:

ANCIENT SACRED WISDOM TRADITIONS:

TRAINING GROUND FOR THE MODERN

PSYCHOTHERAPIST

*I swear the earth shall surely be complete
to him or her who shall be complete.
The Earth remains jagged and broken to him or her
who remains jagged and broken.*

— Walt Whitman

CHAPTER 23: QIGONG/TAI CHI AND ANCIENT SACRED WISDOM TRADITIONS: ADDING TO THE TOOL KIT OF THE MODERN THERAPIST

Psychotherapy Training: Modern Clinician as Carrier of an Ancient Lineage

When I co-founded and taught at the Transpersonal Psychology Program at John F. Kennedy University, for twelve years we spent many a faculty retreat discussing what might be the ideal training of a psychotherapist. "*Transpersonal psychology*" was then defined as an integration of all forms of traditional therapy with an added spiritual component. Each of our distinguished faculty members had his or her own particular stance on what would best be included in this ideal training — like allowing students to choose independent studies of the particular spiritual tradition they believed would best help their development as therapists. This integrative view was touched upon and illustrated in Chapter 2, where I put forth one vision of a psychotherapeutic mandala. In this chapter I will describe the viewpoint of Bodymind Healing Psychotherapy on psychotherapy training.

Whenever I watch movies like the *Karate Kid, The Last Samurai*, or the old Kung Fu series, I am always most interested in the particular training methods used. From my training with various masters in the arts of Tai Chi, Qigong, and psychotherapy, I have learned that the specific training regimen shapes the future form of the initiate's way of being. A different character is shaped by hard style martial arts, as compared to Tai Chi training. It is assumed that the best training for a psychotherapist is the officially sanctioned curriculum that includes a broad range of accepted psychological teachings. Some of these include knowledge of cognitive-behavioral methods, psychodynamic interventions, research methodology, ethics training, knowledge of trauma, abuse, etc. Traditional training and supervision provides students with a foundation in the psychotherapeutic practices that have been discovered by the leaders in the field, most of which are supported by clinical research. This helps the initiate to be fluent in the current language in the field and to develop confidence in fitting into these norms; and it trains therapists in recognized healing methods.

But what if an additional type of training that is equally relevant to the study of the "psychology of the soul" was recognized? What would comprise this training? First, it should be said that the skill sets of traditional and non-traditional training are meaningless without our initiation, by the vicissitudes of life, into the path of the "wounded healer" (Harner, 1990). Life's suffering gives birth to deep eyes and a tenderized heart. This "journey to the underworld" brings out our inherent compassion and caring about the suffering of others, and a desire to learn to be of service to the paths of others. This was as true for the ancient shaman of a tribe, as it is for a bodhisattva training in a Buddhist monastery, or a psychology student in a modern university.

In terms of skill sets, in Chapter 2, I advocated for the expansion of psychological training to include interdisciplinary and cross-cultural mind-body traditions including the new biology, medical hypnosis, psychoneuroimmunology, shamanism, etc. There are schools that, in addition to the traditional courses, give their students the opportunity to train in methods on the outskirts of modern psychological life, like the subject areas mentioned in Chapter 2. These schools have offered courses in mythology, somatic approaches to healing, and various ancient sacred wisdom traditions such as Buddhism, Taoism, energy healing, mythology, Chinese medicine, dream work, shamanism, and cross-cultural approaches to healing — just to touch on a few.[1] I don't have the answer as to what should be in the curriculum of training for psychotherapists, but for eighteen years I trained therapists in such programs. From here, in part, grew my particular approach to the sacred and humbling task of choosing what to add to traditional accredited curricula to form the stance of the modern psychotherapist who wishes to draw from a wider root system in order to better serve his or her patients.

Different therapeutic schools advise different approaches to the process of change. It is important to realize that we each have biases toward the particular "temple" in which we have been trained; and we need to be open to learning from other "temples." As discussed in Chapter 2, there is a psychotherapeutic mandala that contains all psychological methods, each of which has its appropriate place and time to be used with particular individuals.

Symbolic Process Training

It has been said that psychotherapy as a profession is an *opus contra naturum*, a great work that goes contrary to the life force. To illustrate what this fundamental principle means — if someone is sad, and you tell them "just be happy," the person will often not feel met where he or she is. Guilt and shame may ensue and leave the person wondering "What's wrong with me that I can't just be happy." Instead, psychotherapy training usually teaches us to meet patients where they are — to empathize with the sadness, explore what it's about, and find what the beliefs are that are contributing to the sadness — before trying to change patients or their feelings.

I once read in a book on the Greek mystery traditions that said there were four known openings to the underworld (Paske, 1982, p. 117). I took this idea to be a symbolic representation of the entryways to going downward into the recesses of the unconscious to tap upon the chthonic layers of the psyche. Since symbols are expansive in nature, what we call these pathways at a given moment can change in the next moment. For example, these four entryways could be: family of origin work, breathwork that takes us down to a deep place of relaxation, tapping on our "midnight sun" — finding the light in the depth of our pain, or somatic methods of contacting our real feelings and being comfortable with our emotional depths.

Symbolic process traditions were at the roots of the founding of the United States,[2] and as well were part of the early founding of psychotherapy. A symbolic process curriculum for budding psychotherapists might be exemplified by including study of some of the following: mythology (Eliade, 1956, 1958, 1959, 1964; Graves, 1955; Houston, 1992), archetypal psychology (Hillman, 1972, 1975, 1976, 1979; Meier, 1967), fairy tales (Colum, 1944; Bettleheim, 1977), alchemy (Edinger, 1985; Eliade, 1956), astrology (Rudhyar, 1970; Mayer, 1984), imagery and healing (Achterberg, 1985, 1992), and metaphors for hypnosis and healing (Wallace, 1985; Zeig, 1985).[3]

Life Is Free Psychotherapy: Using Stories to Find Your Way on Your Mythic Journey

One basic axiom of BMHP is that "life is free therapy," and a chance to develop your inner characters and stories, as you learn how to shape-shift into the appropriate way of being for a given situation. This path is as beneficial for the psychotherapist as it is for the patient. Study of the above symbolic process traditions can open the therapist's imagination to deal with the vicissitudes of the human condition. When patients feel isolated in their suffering, symbolic processes can help to link them to the other heroes/heroines who have traveled before them.

For example, as we saw in Chapter 20, when a man freezes up around a woman, the story of Perseus confronting Medusa helps provide ideas for how to deal with situations where fear turns us to stone. Implements — such as the mirrored shield that Perseus used to not look directly at Medusa — remind us that when caught in our complexes, it is sometimes best to reflect upon what our fear is about, and work it through, rather than looking the other directly in the face (Mayer, 1994, p. 189). Likewise, when a person feels pain about the way he or she is different from others, the therapist's knowledge of the story *The Ugly Duckling* may provide a transformative perspective.

Understanding the archetypal range of psychotherapeutic helping pathways expands the therapist's repertoire, and enables moving around the medicine wheel of possibilities, finding the appropriate method of responding at a given moment. For example, Rogerian therapy emphasizes the Greek nymph Echo; and helping to guide the patient's journey into the underworld emphasizes a "hermetic approach" to psychotherapy (Pedraza, 1977). Each therapist would do well to wonder which temple is behind his or her usual approach, so that myopia doesn't develop. Expanded repertoires emerge by being able to "shape-shift" into other ways of being that stem from other places on the psychotherapeutic mandala (as discussed in Chapter 2).

Symbolic process traditions provide the therapist with ways to expand his or her soulful (Hillman, 1975, 1976) language. All of the above methods, symbols, and metaphors coming from ancient sacred wisdom traditions give the therapist-in-training an additional root system from which to draw. Since it would be too great a task to list all the methods from which a therapist might draw, I will now focus upon the ancient sacred wisdom tradition that has been one of my major roots. I like to think of Tai Chi/Qigong as one of the deep "roots" of an age-old tree, which draws from a rich underground reservoir lying beneath the "field" of modern psychotherapy. Let's see how Tai Chi and Qigong can be beneficial to the modern therapist.

Tai Chi/Qigong:
Transposing Ancient Methods into Healing Clinical Interventions

Tai Chi Push Hands:
Initiation into Healing Psychotherapeutic Interventions

In *Tai Chi Pushing Hands* (also called *Joining Hands*) practice, the practitioner learns to "stick" to his or her partner. When the partner stops the practitioner stops. It is commonplace in psychotherapy training institutions to hear of the principle of "attuning" to your patient's voice tone, manners, and gestures. In Tai Chi training, an additional mechanism exists whereby clinicians can learn to attune to and stick with their patient's process. The Tai Chi adept doesn't let his or her partner get away — as the partner withdraws, the practitioner gently follows the force to the other's center. This embodied process of being trained to "search for the center" goes along well with Dr. Eugene Gendlin's principle of "finding the crux of the issue." This Tai Chi practice is also called "finding the center-line," which means to be aware of the line that connects your *Push Hands* partner to the earth and the sky — a perfect metaphor for the psychotherapist's desire to help patients get in touch with how a given life issue is connected to their everyday life and to the spiritual orientation of their life. Also in Tai Chi, you learn how to use the least possible force to up-root your partner to move him or her to a new location.

If a practitioner is verbally attacked, he or she learns how to deflect the force and "roll back" so that the force isn't absorbed and doesn't get stuck in his or her body. Instead, the practitioner learns how to turn an attacking force back on the aggressor. Tai Chi training is oriented to becoming an "adept of the elements," i.e. learning how to have the appropriate degree of fire, earth, metal, water, and wood when "joining hands" with another. This becomes a training in shape-shifting into the appropriate element that is useful for that moment — for example, the practitioner learns to be like a ball and bounce another person off, or become so rooted like a tree (earth) that it is difficult for someone to push him or her over. In Volume I, *Tai Chi Joining Hands* — as such an initiatory training — was discussed more extensively.

The above practices can become embodied metaphors for the practice of psychotherapy. When I taught my three-semester course to master's level psychotherapy students at John F. Kennedy University, for the first two semesters students practiced Tai Chi, then in the third semester, they applied it to their work with patients in a case seminar. For example, when they were being verbally attacked in sessions, they learned if they could "roll back" and not take on the negative projection of their clients. They explored whether or not they could respond in a grounded, centered way, using the least amount of force to "lead the patient back to his or her center."

I remember one intern who was working with a very narcissistic manager at a local company who said to him, "I know I only gave you one hour of notice rather than meeting your rigid, twenty-four hour policy, but I think you're a really selfish person for charging me when I needed to meet with a prospective, important, business client. I thought you were supposed to be a therapist and a caring person." In our case seminar the intern proudly reported that he was able to remember his Tai Chi training, his breath, and was able to sink his Qi. As he was feeling his longstanding pattern of induced guilt (stemming from his berating mother) the image came to mind of bringing his hands into "roll back" posture as if he had a ball in front of his tense belly. He took the ball of energy and imagined rolling it back, behind, and away from him. Then he imagined joining hands, sticking with the patient as he empathized with the patient's money issues. But he was also able to lead the patient to explore the entitlement issues involved with assuming that others (such as the therapist) didn't have their own lives and boundaries. In addition, on the next metaphorical circle around, the therapist was able to work with the patient's attacking, blaming, guilt-tripping communication style to manipulate others to get what he wanted. This was the crux of why this manager was in therapy. The intern's ability to not get defensive and to activate his own parasympathetic nervous system response as he practiced verbal *Tai Chi Push Hands*, helped the manager to work on his off-centered, reactive style.

Exploring Resistance

One of my favorite sayings, that I was known to say in these graduate training courses was, "You only need to know one thing to be an excellent therapist — Explore the resistance." This statement goes along with the idea that psychotherapy is an *opus contra naturum*; and our job is not to over-push the patient towards healthier lifestyles, but to explore what's in the way. Tai Chi practice teaches us how to stick to another without force. Thus, when another intern had a talented woman patient who was staying home, overeating and avoiding work, he got into a battle with her when he pushed her to keep to her behavioral agreements in therapy to stop eating so much. After supervision and remembering his *Tai Chi Push Hands*, he went back to the next session and explored the patient's resistance to going out of the house. He explored with her about what the underlying beliefs were that got in her way. They discovered that the woman's aristocratic mother looked down her nose at almost everyone, and that she could never meet her mother's expectations. The patient now projected this internalized mother out onto the world, and therefore did what she could to withdraw from the expectations of the world. The intern spoke about how it was helpful to activate in his body the idea of "following" and exploring, rather than pushing — one of the main goals of *Tai Chi Joining Hands* practice.

Tai Chi Roll Back: Embodied Metaphor for Flexibility of Approach

In Tai Chi self-defense, as you practice *Push Hands* you learn that if your push misses the mark, follow with the elbow, and then with shoulder — this is the self-defense application of the Tai Chi movement called *Roll Back*. In psychotherapy training today, many therapists are trained to lead with the "hand" by first working with the patient's behaviors and cognitions of the present moment — if that doesn't work the therapist might put a little "elbow" into it and do a regressive intervention back to the psychodynamics of the family of origin, if that doesn't work the therapist might shift the weight of the intervention into the "shoulder," and choose to go to the archetypal layer.

One example of this internal martial arts metaphor can be seen in an earlier discussed BMHP intervention of self-soothing with the hand on the heart. If that doesn't work because of a lack of intrapsychic self-soothing healing ability, the therapist might follow with his or her metaphorical "elbow" and ask: Who in your life could you imagine soothing you — a parent, friend, or partner? Some severely wounded patients have not had the experience of being soothed in their lives, so a next step is needed — go to the archetypal shoulder — and ask, Who can you imagine in all of mythic history would be able to heal you? Thus the patient can imagine the sun shining on the ice block, or can imagine his or her representation of God. I've only had a few patients in all my years of practice for whom one of these three approaches didn't work due to their having never experienced a feeling of self-love and self-soothing from which to draw. What helped them were two things: (1) finding a picture of themselves as a child when they were happy and (2) asking them, What if someone gave you $100,000 to become an actor in a play who could experience being able to love and self-soothe? This provided the needed anchor upon which they could call.

Activating the Therapist's Energy with Animal Qigong

The practice of the ancient animal forms of Qigong (see Volume I) helps to expand the therapist's repertoire to activate the instinctual energies appropriate to a therapeutic moment. At times being like a tiger is key, at other times activating a transcendent method of rising above like a crane is appropriate, other times delving downward like a snake into a hole, being solid and stable like a bear, playful like a monkey, flexible like a deer. The practices of Hua Tau and other animal forms provide the therapist with useful metaphorical tools and different styles of interventions, and as well, these practices help keep the therapist's Qi flowing — to prevent the stagnation of Qi that is one of the occupational hazards of sitting for long periods and listening to patients issues. For therapists, Tai Chi and Qigong are helpful antidotes to have in your medicine bag.

Does the Therapist-in-Training Need to Practice Tai Chi or Can One Imbibe the Essence of Tai Chi Without Practice?

In all of the above examples, one might ask, Why do I need to know *Tai Chi Push Hands*? I can explore resistance, have flexibility of response, and stick to a patient's process on my own. This is partially true, yet it helps to have such a practice behind you to ingrain these abilities that are present in your body for use at key moments when you are triggered. Just as the continued verbal practice of role-playing in psychotherapy training helps to desensitize reactivity, so can this internal martial art play a useful role in activating the relaxation response and help the therapist to center. Patterns of behavior are formed by the methods of practice we employ.

On the other hand, for those who choose not to spend time practicing this art, maybe you don't need to — if you follow the wisdom of the following story of *The Rabbi in the Woods*. Perhaps, as I have done in this book, you can extract the essence of Tai Chi/Qigong and help to heal people just by hearing about and tapping upon the essential elements of the tradition.

> *Once there was a great Rabbi. When his congregation was ill and suffering, he would take the secret Book of Prayers and go out to a special place in the woods. There, he would sing a special prayer of healing while rocking back and forth in special ways. The people were healed. In the next generation, his lineage holder did not have the book because it was destroyed, but he still knew the prayer, the movements and the sacred spot in the woods. He was able to heal the people thereby. In the following generation, the place in the woods was destroyed through fire, but the next Rabbi could still heal the people with the prayers and movements. Today, the prayers and the movements are lost, but the story of the old ways, and the "re-membrance" it evokes, may still be enough to heal the people.*

Other Beneficial Tai Chi Principles

Some other concepts and principles from Tai Chi that may prove useful for the therapist, whether you practice them or just hear about them, are: the principle of *wu wei*, or effortless effort, which means to not fight resistance, but explore it; and the concept of holding the love of the universe in your hands to promote your and other's Self-healing. It is the perspective of Bodymind Healing Qigong that as powerful as the mind is — being responsible for approximately 55 percent of healing (Rossi, 1986), still, the reality of the body and its ability to heal exists as, at least, an equal partner. Though there is some truth in the *Rabbi in the Woods* story — that thinking about a sacred event can activate aspects of its "state-dependent" character (Rossi, 1988) — thinking about physical exercise is not the same as doing it.

In the following chapter we will see more on how the practice of the methods of Tai Chi and Qigong, and attention to the way they come together in Bodymind Healing Qigong, are useful for "healing the healer."

CHAPTER 24: HEALING THE HEALER: BODYMIND HEALING QIGONG'S TWENTY-MINUTE PRACTICE ROUTINE

The Qigong traditions are thousands of years old:
The fact that Qigong and Tai Chi (the best known system of Qigong)
have stood the test of time attests to their effectiveness.
These fitness practices have been carefully refined over several thousand years.
The various forms of practice can be categorized by their degree of activity,
ranging from completely motionless to very energetic.
They include techniques that are performed in total stillness as meditation
or meditative breathing exercises.
Qigong and Tai Chi also involve gradual movement,
like a dance in slow motion.
Martial arts such as Kung Fu are vigorous forms of Qigong.

— Roger Jahnke [1]
Getting Your Immune System in Shape (2002)

Oh Healer, Replenish thy Self

What do you do to replenish yourself after your healing work with others? Whether you are lovingly present for your friends and family, or if you are a health professional who spends long hours each day helping others, everyone's batteries run down and need recharging.

Qigong stems from a cross-cultural lineage of healers who developed methods over thousands of years to help people cultivate the energy of life. One Qigong form, for example, was developed by Boddhidharma after he saw how the bodies of monks were atrophying from sitting for so long (like our sedentary office workers). The story goes that Boddhidharma went into a deep mediation and stared at a wall to help solve the monks' problem. The legend says that after thirty years of meditating in front of this wall, he came up with one of the systems of Qigong called the "Qigong for Changing the Muscles, Sinews, and Bone Marrow" (*Yin Jing Jing*). So, it is no wonder that Qigong is associated with dissolving one's inner walls.

Many Qigong systems can help restore our vital energy. The one I developed, from training for the last thirty years with some of the most respected Qigong masters, synthesizes ten different systems of Qigong.[2] Because this system takes about one and a half hours to practice, I have been encouraged by others — such as Dr. Wayne Jonas, former director of the National Institute of Health, Office of Alternative Medicine — to develop a shorter twenty-minute routine that is better suited to the busy modern lifestyle. I am grateful that he chose to include my twenty-minute routine in his upcoming book as an aid to others who desire a shorter method that still captures the essence of the many healing elements of Qigong. I now use elements of this shorter routine during breaks with my psychotherapy patients and, as I am pleased to report, so do many other health professionals.

I developed this practice routine to activate some of the key types of energy that healers, and the healer in all of us, need to restore vitality. It includes first doing a prelude exercise of your own choosing, followed by the next eight practices: (1) *Standing Meditation* practices — to return to the source of healing energy; (2) *Dispersing Stagnant Qi* — to clear blocked Qi and cleanse stress; (3) *Tai Chi Ruler* (also called *Tai Chi Chih*) — this rocking method restores equilibrium, soothes, relaxes, and revitalizes just like the poles of a battery or the rocking of a child by a mother; (4) *Ocean Wave Breathing* — recharges the heart; (5) *Moving a Snake through the Joints* — this stretching practice limbers the joints; (6) *Crane Walking and Flying* — lightens the felt sense of the heart, develops balance, and strengthens the legs; (7) *Yi Chuan Walking Meditation* — adds something vital to traditions of Walking Meditation, and is a practice for staying connected to sacred awareness as you walk through life; (8) *Wuji Standing Meditation* — returning to stillness at the end of your twenty-minute routine helps to activate "the myth of the eternal return," (Eliade & Trask, 1954). These eight practices are state-specific practices to restore vitality to various elements of the primordial Self.

The Bodymind Healing Qigong Twenty-Minute Routine

This brief routine takes you from stillness to movement and back to stillness, and helps you find the stillness in movement and the movement in stillness. (As always, consult with your doctor or appropriate health professional before engaging in such physical activities.)

As a prelude to the twenty-minute set, activate your energy in your own chosen way, with your favorite exercise. One of my favorite ways to begin is to first, *Bring the Yang Energy Down from the Heavens*.

> *With your hands at your sides, open the palms to the outside, let the hands rise up the sides of your body above the crown of your head, then bring the heavenly Qi down the front of the body. Three cycles of this movement provides a nice centering practice, and helps begin to create sacred space. To see a pictorial representation of one of the parts of this practice see the Dispersing Stagnant Qi picture later in this section. Secondly, Bring the Yin Energy Up from the Earth. Start with your hands by your sides, then gather up the earth's energy with your hands bringing your wrists together until they cross in front of the heart, palms facing toward your body as if you are holding a ball there. Then open your hands palm outward, spreading your hands apart, out and upward, as they open the energy you've just brought up from the earth to the heavens. Finish this movement by bringing your arms back down to rest at your sides. Three cycles of this movement provides a powerful, expansive opening of the yin energies, and your heart, to the sky — a nice prelude to generating some energy to be applied to the creation of an axis mundi, as you assume the Standing Meditation posture in the short set of BMHQ that follows.*

1. Standing Meditation Qigong: Revitalizing Your Energy Bank Account

A. Standing like a Tree

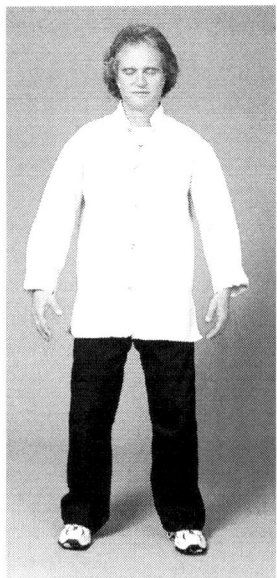

Figure 6: Wuji Standing Meditation

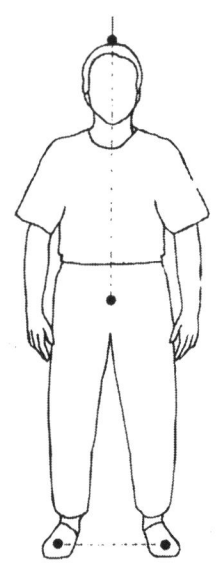

Figure 7: Puppet Dangling from Heaven

Keep both feet parallel, pointing straight forward, between a hip and a shoulder's width apart. The knees are unlocked, approaching being over the toes. The pelvis is slightly turned forward as if you are getting ready to sit down on a stool. The lower back is slightly pushed out so that the lumbar curve begins to disappear allowing the lower back to approach being straight. The chest and shoulders are relaxed, causing a slight rounding of the upper back. Imagine there is a cord descending from a star attached to the top of your head so that you are like a puppet dangling from the heavens. Your chin is slightly tucked. Your arms hang loosely at your sides. The tongue is touching the top of the palate just behind the teeth. The eyes can be open in a soft gaze, half open, or closed. Notice the natural flow of your breath. Pay attention to how long and deep your breath is without trying to force it to be calm. Be aware of any sensations or thoughts that emerge during this practice, while continually returning to your breath.

As you stand, feel the way your spine makes a connection between the heavens above and the earth below. After a number of breaths, imagine yourself as a tree with deep roots. Let your exhalation slowly descend down into your roots. What are you rooted into in your life — family, friends, loved ones, spiritual traditions? Let an image arise of what this root system is like. On your inhalation, imagine drawing in from those roots to strengthen your trunk. Then on your next inhalation allow the Qi to rise up to your branches, reach out for the light, and transform that light into energy as you imagine giving your fruit to others.

The Circle that Arises from Stillness:

After standing for a while — since trees aren't rigid nor are we — allow circles to emerge from your stillness by moving your weight 51 percent over your right heel, then over your right toes, then over your left toes, and then over your left heel. Imagine a snake or a vine spiraling up the tree, bringing the energy of the earth up and around the tree of your spine to the heavens. Stay in stillness for most of the time — practice the Circle that Arises from Stillness occasionally, and then return to stillness.

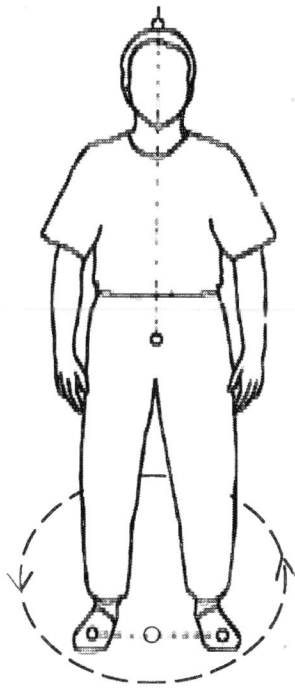

Figure 8: Circle that Arises from Stillness

Bodymind Healing Purpose: Research has shown that this "non-movement" posture increases the coherence in the brain between the two frontal regions, between two occipital regions, and between the left and right temporal areas.[3] This practice is also called Wuji Standing Meditation. *Wuji* means the void, or the mother of Qi, so this posture is considered one of the best ways to fill your "Qi bank account." Stillness is a powerful way to activate the Qi, and is also a way of bringing up the psychological and physical issues that block the Qi. By being with our Selves we initiate a pattern of alchemical transformation which over time dissolves chronic body blockages. During the process tingling, vibrating, shaking, and sensations of asymmetry may occur as blocks in the rivers of Qi shake loose. Don't be alarmed, just breathe through these sensations, practice the *Circle that Arises from Stillness*, or take a break and come back to the practice when you are ready. All these Qi activation signs are ways that the Qi is healing old areas of blockage. Eventually this method may lead you to experience the *Sea of Elixir* — an experience of dissolving into that sea of cosmic bliss (altered state of consciousness) spoken of in the Taoist text, *The Secret of the Golden Flower*.

B. Holding Golden Balls in the Waters of Life

Figure 9: Holding Golden Balls in the Waters of Life

While using the same stance as in the above Standing Meditation, allow your wrists to rise and then, palm down, descend down to the belly area (*Tan Tien*). Then imagine that you are standing in a slowly moving river, your palms are slightly compressing two balls down into the water with just enough pressure so that they are steadied from floating downstream. The energy in your feet sinks down into the streambed, and your knees bend just so much that you take root, which prevents the river from moving you downstream. Stand in this posture for as long as is comfortable (initially 2-4 minutes). If it starts to feel difficult, listen to your body, allow another few exhalations, and return back to Wuji Standing Meditation Posture 1 to refill your Qi bank account.

Bodymind Healing Purpose: This stance comes from *Yi* (intention) *Chuan* (fist, or ability to hold the power of the five elements in your fist) Qigong. One way to use your intention while you are *Holding Golden Balls* is to imagine that you are sending healing energy from your palms (*Lao Gung* points) to some part of the earth that is in need of healing. Imagine that you are sending energy there on your exhalation, and replenishing yourself on the inhalation. This is a favored practice of body workers, acupuncturists (who use the posture to focus their intention on sending energy through the needles), and for healers in general. This posture is also a favored stance for developing *sung* — the Chinese term for relaxed alertness. In the West we have separate terms for "relaxation" and "alertness," but just like the Eskimos have differentiated many names for snow, the Chinese have many names for energy. This state of *sung* can be seen in cats when they appear simultaneously very relaxed, yet ready to pounce.

C. Finding Your Own Stance

Figure 10: Opening the Golden Ball of your Heart

Figure 11: Feeding the World with your Heart (Wild Goose says Hello)

Find your own Standing Meditation posture that expresses the stance you need at this moment. Above are two stances from Volume I: stance one is called *Opening the Golden Ball of Your Heart*, stance two is called *Wild Goose Says Hello and Goodbye*. Both are good for replenishing your heart's energy. For more about the specific healing attributes of these stances, please see Volume I.

2. *Dispersing Stagnant Qi*

After Standing Meditation it is important to disperse stagnant Qi. Begin with your hands by your sides as in Standing Meditation — while breathing in, raise your hands to the sides, palms up, until they are outstretched over your head. As your palms face the top of your head, stop and breathe nice long exhalations. Imagine that your right and left hands are like electromagnets with a yang (right hand) and yin (left hand) polarity. You might imagine that any stagnant energy remaining on your skin after standing is like iron filings. Very slowly and while you are breathing, allow your hands to gradually descend about six inches from your body while the iron filings jump onto the electromagnet from the magnetic attraction.

Figure 12: Dispersing Stagnant Qi

Chapter 24: Healing the Healer: Bodymind Healing Qigong

When you reach the bottom, with your hands by your sides, turn off the electromagnet by letting go with a few long out-breaths.

Imagine that the iron filings are turning into molten lava and seeping back to the iron at the core of the earth. Dispersing Stagnant Qi is done three times: first to clean the skin; second, the internal organs; and third to wash the bone marrow. Other Dispersing Stagnant Qi exercises include massaging and tapping the body, and tapping your toes against the ground — as hoofed animals do when they have stood too long in one place.

For those of you who want to add other *Dispersing Stagnant Qi* exercises to your repertoire, see Volume I, page 101. There you will find the *Three Methods for Electromagnetic Cleansing of the Skin*, which include: self-massage, tapping methods, and *Horse Tapping Feet*.

Bodymind Healing Purpose: According to modern physics, human beings are condensed light. When the light of the universe condenses in our bodies and takes on our emotional and physical blockages, it acts like logjams blocking the free flow of a river. Standing Meditation can constellate and make us aware of these places of stagnant Qi. *Dissolving and Dispersing Stagnant Qi* exercises can loosen the logjams and allow the river of life to flow again to evaporate into water vapor and to transform into space. By moving back and forth from Standing Meditation to *Dispersing Stagnant Qi* exercises, we return to our source as the Beings of light we are. In this exercise, the movement of the hands down the body while focusing on the exhalation is used for those suffering from hypertension to help cleanse the body of stress and help sink the Qi. The sinking of the Qi is accomplished by focusing on the downward movements of the hands while exhaling with long-breath. Johnson (2004) suggests for hypertension that the practitioner imagines sending Qi down the Gall Bladder meridian. For more about Qigong and hypertension, see Chapter 11.

3. Tai Chi Ruler

Figure 13: Tai Chi Ruler-Bringing in Healing Energy

Figure 14: Tai Chi Ruler-Letting go of Toxic/Stagnant Energy

Place the right foot slightly in front of the left. The left foot is at a 45-degree angle and your left big toe is aligned with the middle of the right foot. Keep a fist's distance between the extended backward line of the right foot and the left heel, so there is sufficient width between your feet.

Slowly rock backward onto your left foot, and inhale while your left knee bends and your right toes rise off the ground. Next, breathe out as you rock forward while your back, left heel rises naturally off the ground. Repeat until you feel the sensation of filling and emptying your forward and rear foot, in turn. Your weight, when forward, should be over your right foot, knee bent. When your weight is on your left, back foot, your bent knee approaches being over the front of your foot. Be careful not to extend your forward knee beyond your front toes.

Next, integrate hand movements. Place your hands about 6-8 inches apart, palms facing each other as if you have a ball between your hands. Your hands should be far enough apart so that the upper arms allow space for imaginary little balls to fit in the armpits. As you rock forward, allow the hands to come down to three fingers distance below the navel. As you rock backward, the hands come up and circle inward, towards the heart. As your hands rise up and inward you might want to imagine bringing the loving energy of the universe into your heart, as you say, "I'm bringing in the fresh." As you exhale and breathe out, your hands come down, as if laying a ball filled with your troubles or dis-eases as you say, "I'm letting go of the stale." After about 12 repetitions on one side, switch which leg is forward and repeat the movement to ensure balance between the right and left sides of the body.

Bodymind Healing Purpose: As you practice on the right side you can practice healing a life issue that's been difficult for you — recharging your Self on the in-breath and letting go of tension on the out-breath. As you practice on the left side, create a healing ritual where you put a problematic body part or chronic disease into the center of your circle, the circle of the universe, which as it passes through you brings you back into balance with the healing elements of the universe. This movement is also used for reversing the fear response of the body and balancing sympathetic nervous system over-arousal by focusing on sinking the energy of the body to the lower back (*Ming Men*) as the hands raise up to the top of your circle of movement. For those suffering from trauma (or for all of us involved with the mini-traumas of everyday life) this movement can be helpful to help us let go of stress and re-empower ourselves when used in conjunction with other appropriate psychological healing methods.

4. Ocean Wave Breathing

Figure 15: Ocean Wave Breathing

After you have practiced Standing Meditation for some time, you will begin to feel a natural rocking movement that synchronizes with your breathing. You may notice that your weight shifts back to the heels as you inhale, and your weight naturally shifts onto the balls of the feet as you exhale. From our earliest experiences of being rocked in the cradle, rocking is a primordial way to energize, heal, and soothe the bodymind.

Place your outstretched hands, palms facing each other, in front of your belly. Experiment with synchronizing your hand movements outward and inward from your belly with your breath. It is as if you are blowing up a balloon and then allowing it to naturally inflate and deflate. As the body rocks backward, the breath goes in, and your hands go outward, expanding your ball. As the body rocks forward, the hands come in and the breath goes out, collapsing your ball. As you continue to inhale and exhale, make the arm motions larger and larger.

Bodymind Healing Purpose: This practice can be done with hands in front of the belly or the heart. The belly area *(Tan Tien)* is the physical center of the body where heaven and earth meet. While practicing this movement be aware of how you have been off center this week and allow this movement to recharge and expand your center where heaven and earth join their creative forces. If you do the practice with hands holding the ball in front of your heart, imagine recharging "the battery of your heart" as you are doing your expanding and gathering motions.

5. Moving a Snake through the Joints, Dipping Your Hands into the Waters of Life, and Opening Your Heart to the Heavens

Figure 16: Moving Snakes through the Hip Joint

Figure 17: Moving Snakes through the Shoulder Joint

Keep your legs spread wider than in other Bodymind Healing Qigong movements. As you shift to the right side your right palm faces out next to the right thigh and the back of the left hand slides up your left thigh. Then shift your weight back to the left side as your left palm faces up by your left leg; the back of your right palm slides up the right side of your leg. Practice this movement with focus on the hips first, and then at the shoulder level. Then go back to the hips, but this time focus on moving a spiral through any body part that is problematic. As you spiral a snake through your joints, imagine your spiraling movement going all the way up to the galactic spirals and all the way down to the spiraling forces in the molten core of the earth. Imagine your problematic body part is just a little point in the spiraling forces of life. This exercise is paired with the exercise Dipping your Hands into the Waters of Life where you bend forward, as your shoulders rotate forward and your palms face upward. Then bend backward, Opening your Heart to the Heavens, as you face up toward the sky at about a 45 degree angle as your palms face up. (Illustration not shown). At the end of this exercise, as your hands move up and down your legs, make smaller and smaller spirals until there is no movement at all. Can you experience the spiral in your stillness?

Chapter 24: Healing the Healer: Bodymind Healing Qigong

Figure 18: Dipping Your Hands into the Water of Life

In the Taoist tradition it is said that when you can find the stillness in the movement and movement in the stillness that health and the experience of light in the body can be found. As you are residing in stillness you might imagine the spiraling double helix at the center of your cells vibrating though you are still; and imagine that your cells are electro-magnetic receivers and senders ("nano-antennas") connected with the wider healing forces of the universe — modern science confirms both of these are facts (Lipton, 2005).

Bodymind Healing Purpose: This three-movement sequence (*Moving a Snake through the Joints, Dipping Your Hands into the Waters of Life, and Opening Your Heart to the Heavens*) is an excellent preventative and a complementary treatment for joint, hip, and shoulder problems. It is also useful for chronic diseases that relate to a sedentary lifestyle. The practice, in particular when you go back and forth from movement to stillness is excellent for activating and filling the reservoir of your energy field.

6. Crane Walking and Flying

This is one of a series of Animal Qigong movements based on the Chinese five elements — wood, fire, earth, metal, and water — each of which corresponds to particular organs of the body. For this "fire" posture:

Figure 19: Crane Crosses Wings

Figure 20: Crane Walking

Step out at a 45-degree angle and cross your arms in front of your heart. As your hands rise up and one leg rises up, keep your toe still touching the ground as you become a Crane Walking. When your hands descend they can come to your sides or all the way down (or cross over) in front of your belly where they gather Qi. Synchronize the movement with your breath and repeat on right and left sides approximately four times. (The Taoist method of training is to progress slowly to avoid injury or strain, therefore we do Crane Walking before practicing the next movements.)

After sufficient strength is built up from Crane Walking, you can become like a Crane Flying. Again, step out at a 45 degree angle (as done in Crane Walking), but this time on the inhalation, lift your knee along with raising your arms, so that the knee begins to approach being parallel to your hip. Then, as you exhale allow the hands to descend as if they are sinking down in water.

Practice on both right and left sides and allow the fingertips to flutter slightly as they rise up to activate Qi. Eventually, to strengthen the legs more, hold your posture in the arms raised position for one to five exhalations.

Figure 21: Crane Flying

Chapter 24: Healing the Healer: Bodymind Healing Qigong   289

During these various exercises, experiment with using the sound, "ha" (vocally or sub-vocally) on the exhalation to relax the heart (for hypertension), and to increase the energy of the heart (for hypotension) use the sound "heng" on the inhalation. While being in touch with the life issues in your heart, feel and imagine the healing powers of the Crane bringing your heart back into balance.

Bodymind Healing Purpose: The Animal Frolics were created in the second century A.D. by Chinese physician Hua Tuo who synthesized the shamanic knowledge of the healing power of the elements with Chinese medicine. In the *Crane* postures we are given a way to feel the Qi rise from the earth to lighten the heart, and we are given a way to increase our balance. An article in the *Journal of the American Medical Association* (1995) showed that Tai Chi was a more effective system for preventing falls amongst the elderly than many Western exercise systems. For those with balance problems or with limitations in leg strength: move slowly in your lifelong cultivation practice of *Crane Walking* in order to develop the proper leg strength before moving on to *Crane Flying*. Listen to your body about how long to hold the *Crane Flying* posture with your hands raised. Follow the Taoist axiom, "less is more," to avoid injury and to cultivate your Qi. Also, as we see from the descriptions above, the *Crane* is used to help heal the energy of the heart.

7. *Walking Meditation Qigong*

Figure 22: Walking Meditation Qigong-Holding the Golden Ball

Figure 23: Walking Meditation Qigong-Opening the Heart

Start with your posture as in the Wuji Standing Meditation posture at the beginning of this chapter. While standing, slowly shift your weight from one leg to the other. First your weight is equally balanced; then very gradually shift your weight back and forth from right and left until you can support 100 percent of your weight on each leg as the other leg slowly come in to join it. While supporting all weight on one leg, move the other leg forward in a crescent moon step. Gradually put down your weight, putting first 5 percent, then 10 percent, until the weight is 100 percent over that foot. Then do the same with your next step. Breathe in as your foot comes in toward your ankle, and synchronize your exhalation with stepping down. The spirit of your walking is like a stalking cat. Walk as if there is sand paper under your shoes and you are sanding a deck. For those who have difficulty walking, or those who are recovering from sports injuries or chronic movement disorders, try doing this Walking Meditation with a chair next to you for added support. Practice walking forward and backward. Eventually the practitioner walks while imagining holding a ball in various ways — for example, under your hands as in Holding Golden Balls in the Waters of Life posture (seen above). While stepping down, exhale and press the palms down towards the earth and say, "I let go of the stale," or "I give to the earth." Inhale as you bring your foot toward your ankle and let the wrists rise as you say, "I take in the fresh" or "I bring in the healing energies of the earth."

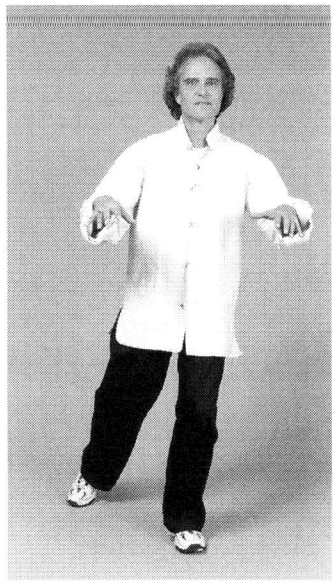

Figure 24: Walking Mediation Qigong-Drawing in Energy from the Earth

Figure 25: Walking Meditation Qigong: Giving Energy to the Earth

Bodymind Healing Purpose: Walking Meditation is excellent for those who have difficulty walking, as well as for those who are recovering from sports injuries, joint diseases, or chronic movement disorders such as Parkinson's or Multiple Scleroses. Walking Mediation is an integral component of the Yi Chuan Standing Meditation Qigong tradition. Walking Meditation is a self-healing and spiritual practice for carrying the Qi that you have developed in Standing to test (*shili*) whether your Qi "breaks" — a metaphor for keeping the centeredness that you have cultivated in the stillness of Standing Meditation.

8. End Your Routine with the Wuji Standing Meditation Posture

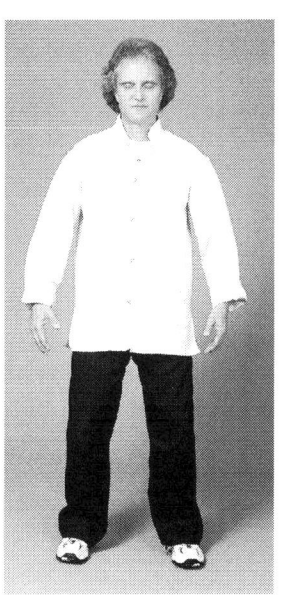

Figure 26: Wuji Standing Meditation Qigong

It is most helpful to end your routine returning to the Wuji Standing Meditation posture. In cross-cultural mythic terms, Wuji Standing activates "the myth of the eternal return" (Eliade, 1954), i.e. renewing your Self by re-establishing a connection to the source of healing energy in the cosmos. In Taoist terms, after moving we return to stillness to honor the Taoist precept that healing energy comes from moving from stillness to movement, and then back to stillness. The key here is to find the stillness in movement, and the movement in stillness.

I am often asked how long one should do each of these practices. The answer is that I don't know how long you should do each of them — but you do. Please listen to your bodymind.

AFTERWORD

Reflections:
At the Source of the Stream of Modern Psychotherapy

In the introduction of this book, I told the story of how I learned in my master's degree program that psychology began in Wilhelm Wundt's laboratory in Leipzig, Germany in 1879. This left me wondering about psychology's origins before that time in one man's laboratory.

I asked and explored the question: What is the source of the stream of thought that has become "psychology?" As I went on a journey upstream I found a worldwide river system of ancient sacred wisdom traditions. I found that astrological metaphors were used to help people connect their personal identities with the universe of which we are all a part. I stripped the astrological language of its deterministic leanings in my book, *The Mystery of Personal Identity*. I showed how, by using a phenomenological theoretical framework, astrological language could become palatable even to skeptics. In the process of integrating this language with transpersonal psychology, I showed how this ancient tradition could be re-visioned in such a way that it could answer critics' concern that astrology could be used as an excuse for one's neurosis, and lead to faulty deterministic thinking that would rob a person of his or her own will. I demonstrated how astrological language could be incorporated into depth psychotherapy to help people find new meaning by seeing how personal identity is connected with the wider whole of which we are a part (Mayer, 1984).

As I continued my journey upstream I found that ancient Greek mythology and the art of storytelling represented some of the oldest forms of psychological healing and could transform the way people look at their problems. The book I wrote at that time, *Trials of the Heart: Healing the Wounds of Intimacy*, culminated in the *Mythic Journey Process*, which showed how to use ancient myths to heal modern day problems. Throughout my journey, I was humbled and overwhelmed by the number of rivers of knowledge that could bring refreshing perspectives from the lands of our psychotherapeutic ancestors. I wondered why people downstream didn't seem to know about these healing rivers, and why these methods weren't more incorporated into the education of modern therapists.

For example, alchemy contains rich metaphors for the various phases of the metallic and psychological processes for turning lead into gold, and for the soul's journey of self-healing (Edinger, 1985). In the Kabbalah of the Jewish tradition, one of the earliest forms of energy psychology talked about how the energy of the universe that is expressed in the archetypes of the "tree of life" comes from *ain soph* (the void, the source of creation, similar to the Chinese concept of *wuji*); and the Jewish prayerful *davening* tradition (rocking back and forth while praying) has songs to help virtually every affliction such as loss of power, and lack of being able to cope with life. Other Jewish sacred songs help the daveners to dissolve into the love of the universe and connect with the source of life's energy. Singing chants and songs from ancient sacred wisdom traditions can add to other psychological inner work similar to the way that energy psychology traditions use humming to help heal the modern day psyche. I've spoken about how the roots of Buddhism contained a tradition of postural initiation that combined "dissolving" practices and working with the *klesas* (emotional issues) on the path to psychospiritual health. In my last book I showed how the traditions of postural initiation and energy healing are part of a worldwide cross-cultural river system of healing the psyche in Greece, Native America, India, and in China in its tradition of Qigong. Among the deep, lost rivers of ancient psychological knowledge that I discovered on my journey were the ancient mythologies of shape-shifting, which contain metaphors for using the imagination to aid the process of psychological transformation. Combining somatic practices, such as Qigong, with these cross-cultural, shape-shifting healing methods helped my patients, students, and me to draw from the elements needed to heal our relationship with our primordial Selves.

And we should remember that beyond all traditions, at the source of all rivers and at the deepest origins of the stream of psychology is a fundamental truth that healing comes from the elements themselves, each of which are expressions of the awe-inspiring, loving energies of the universe — that some call God.

The Deva that Sits at the Place Where Two Streams Become One

In the past, Western culture has looked at the practices and philosophies of indigenous cultures as "less than" Western medicine and psychology. We have treated these age-old practices with an attitude similar to the way the missionaries treated the practices of Native Americans. In midst of the current healthcare crisis, we may do well to investigate and incorporate the teachings of ancient lineages into our current medical and psychological methodologies — by doing so, we honor our ancestors and colleagues who learned to heal from traveling pre-technological pathways. By not including ancient sacred wisdom traditions into our approach to healing the psyche, we commit a crime analogous to our cultures' running over the Native Americans. We get to occupy the land, but we lose the sacred knowledge of how to be with its treasures.

One of the treasures coming from the land of ancient psychology — the psychology of the "soul"[1] — is the notion that there is a *deva* in every location in the natural world. Another name for devas are *elementals,* because they carry the healing powers of the elements of nature (Jung, 1974). It is said that every deva has a form, usually feminine, that communicates to those who listen. There are devas of the waters — *nereads*, devas of the air — *sylphs*, and devas of the earth — *dryads*. These devas are specific to locale and, not being "major deities," they are more humble, more down to earth, and have more intimate personal messages to give us. The male counterpart to devas are *daimons*, such as *Eros*, god of erotic love. Devas and *daimons* occupy a mythic place on the ladder of creation in that they are not gods, yet they are not human beings either — they are beings that travel between the two realms of heaven and earth. Being in touch with their attributes can help us humans to journey in that space.

On one level, this book is a communication from "the deva where two streams become one." Before you dismiss this notion as archaic, or smile thinking this idea is quaint, instead allow yourself to wonder about the places in nature that have drawn you to them, and meditate upon what message is waiting to be drawn from that place in nature. We don't call our deepest ways of being "human nature" for nothing. We are inextricably connected with nature; and our own healing and our messages for humankind come from this connection with the wider whole of which we are a part.

APPENDIX I:

Bodymind Healing Psychotherapy (BMHP) Contributions to the field of Bodymind Healing

Contributions to Psychotherapy and Behavioral Healthcare

1. Offers a ten step holographic, psychoenergetic method (BMHP) which combines traditional psychotherapies (e.g. cognitive/behavioral, psychodynamic/neo-analytic, humanistic/existential, Jungian/archetypal, hypnotherapeutic) with various ancient sacred wisdom traditions (e.g. symbolic process traditions, traditions of postural initiation, cross-cultural self-healing traditions) to contribute towards developing an "integral" psychotherapy (Wilbur, 2000, Walsh 2006). {Chapters 2, 4, and 5}

2. Drawing from ancient esoteric roots, BMHP brings to Western psychotherapy healing methods and perspectives from the Western (e.g. Eliade, 1954, 1958, 1959, 1964, 1965; Neumann, 1954; Needham, 1956; Meier, 1967; Rudhyar, 1970; Campbell, 1978; Jung, Collected Works; Edinger, 1985; Matthews, 1986; Hall, 1988; Goodman, 1990; Kingsley, 1999) and Eastern (e.g. Wilhelm, 1931; Luk, 1972, 1977; Schafer, 1977; Tomio, 1994; Mayer, 2004) mystery and initiatory traditions. {Chapters 2, 4, 5}

3. Adds methods from Qigong and other Bodymind Healing Psychotherapy techniques to the growing field of integrative medicine that is attempting to help resolve the current healthcare crisis. {Chapters 1, 2, 5-14}

4. Shows how Qigong in general, and when combined with BMHP in particular, can aid in healing psychological issues in a wide number of areas. The tradition contains useful relaxation methods, activates state-specific states of consciousness that are both relaxing and energizing, provides specific healing and balancing energetic techniques, helps to reciprocally inhibit unwanted behaviors, provides methods to help dissolve mental and somatic fixations, facilitates ego cohesion by helping our central equilibrium when meeting the emotional tides of life, helps develop a compassionate relationship to life's issues, enhances development of cohesiveness of self, enhances stability for those with reactive attachment styles, helps with developing affect modulation skills and affect tolerance, adds energy cultivation practices beneficial to those who are depressed, induces an altered state which is helpful in issues with addiction, aids in transformation of self identifications, adds beneficial methods for those who suffer from syndromes involving sympathetic nervous system overload, and provides tools to allow trauma victims to regain a safety zone in their bodies. {Chapter 21}

5. Reveals specific approaches and methods from the tradition of Qigong to aid treatment of behavioral healthcare patients suffering with specific conditions such as:

anxiety, chronic pain, hypertension, insomnia, carpal tunnel syndrome, addictions, joint problems, depression, energy deficiency, etc. {Chapters 5-14}

6. Enhances "subpersonality work" and hypnotherapeutic methods of trance induction by activating state-specific states of consciousness with an expanded view of cross-cultural traditions of shape-shifting. The symbolic process and somatic dimensions of shape-shifting traditions are combined and utilized to help the patient in psychotherapy cultivate new life stances. {Chapters 2, 4, 5, and 15}

7. Contributes to the hypnotherapeutic tradition by coining the term, "transpersonal state-specific state of consciousness" to refer to the orientation of ancient sacred wisdom traditions to provide transpersonal anchors to help connect the person to specific healing altered states. I use the term "transpersonal," as did Dane Rudhyar, one of the first people to use this term in 1930, to refer to the movement of divine energies "beyond" the ego, but also to refer to a descent of spiritual energy "through" the person (Rudhyar, 1975, p. 38). Each Qigong/Tai Chi posture is like a letter in a Rosetta Stone of an ancient language of the bodymind — a link to a long-lost, right brain alphabet. Each letter (posture) represents a transpersonal state-specific state of consciousness that can bring a person into an altered state beyond his or her everyday life stance; as well it can bring specific needed healing states through the person. {Chapter 4, 5}

8. Adds to the hypnotherapeutic technique of ideomotor signaling the method of "whole body, naturally arising, ideomotor signaling" to help patients harness the primordial pathways of the movement of the life force as it emerges at moments of "felt shift" in psychotherapy. Patients in psychotherapy, particularly at key moments of change, express movements that represent deep, often-unconscious transformative aspects of their psyches. The movements a martial artist uses to confront physical danger are often the same, or similar to, movements which spontaneously arise in a person as he or she deals with emotional dangers. This book, and the practices that lie at its foundation, can help healers learn to become more aware of the body's expression of the primordial Self as it moves toward empowerment and transformation. The ancient art of Qigong, of which Tai Chi is the best know system, contains some of the best and most primordial of these empowering movements. The clinician who is aware of these movements and their multifaceted meanings can help to grease the wheels and facilitate movement in the direction to where the patient's psyche is moving, on the path of its natural healing journey. {Chapter 16}

9. Delineates a full range of symbolic process methods for psychotherapy by adding the power of somatic processes in general, and Qigong techniques in particular, to ground and further bring out the power of imaginal methodologies. {Chapter 4 and 5}

10. Combines Gendlin's Focusing (1978) with Taoist breathing methods and the use of a mythic storytelling method (the *Mythic Journey Process*) to create important bodymind healing tools for psychotherapists. {Chapter 20}

11. Introduces the term "transcending/transmuting dialectic" to differentiate aspects of psychospiritual traditions that can help people rise above versus work through their life issues. BMHP focuses on how specifically Qigong, when integrated with Western psychotherapy, can have both attributes. {Chapter 5}

12. Introduces the *River of Life* practice which combines a Taoist breathing method and visualization techniques to help patients activate a transcendent state-specific altered state and transmute their psychological issues. {Chapter 5}

13. Adds to the Jungian notion of the psychoid nature of archetypes by further integrating the body with Jungian symbolic process methods, as in the *Mythic Journey Process*. {Chapter 4 and 20}

14. Introduces a method of "transpersonal hypnosis" — a directive, storytelling method that adds to the field of hypnosis an emphasis on connecting patients with the elements of the wider whole of which they are a part. {Chapter 19}

15. Provides practices and perspectives from ancient sacred wisdom traditions, including Qigong, to enrich the field of psychotherapists' vision and aid in expanding therapists' repertoire of clinical interventions. {Chapter 23}

16. Provides Qigong practices to aid in the process of "healing the healer" to help mental health professionals "recharge their batteries." {Chapter 24}

17. Extracts the essence of Qigong/Tai Chi so that a therapist can use key elements of these traditions without practicing Qigong movements or ever mentioning a word about Qigong. {Chapter 5 and 18}

Contributions to Energy Psychology

1. Proposes using phenomenologically based anchoring methods. BMHP adds a phenomenological orientation to energy psychology methods, i.e. choosing the patients own movements at the moment of a "felt shift" to anchor new state-specific states of consciousness as a first-choice method. The most common meridian tapping methods are seen as just one of many energy psychology techniques that are part of researchers' differentiated attempts to determine which methods are best for which people at which times in this pre-paradigmatic stage of energy psychology's development. {Chapter 3, 4}

2. Advocates for explaining the meaning of acu-points used in treatment. In current energy psychology treatment, often the patient is instructed to tap on various points, but the meaning of those points is not usually discussed in detail. Bodymind Healing Psychotherapy proposes that "meaning" is a key healing agent, and is a significant component of activating "the mind-body trance state." I believe that including the patient's understanding helps create a mindful, connected awareness, which has many positive consequences. {Chapter 3 and 16}

3. Adds depth psychology methods to energy psychology with a focus on symbolic process methods, including the *Mythic Journey Process*. {Chapter 4 and 20}

4. Broadens the field of energy psychology by including Qigong. {Chapter 3 and 4}

5. Expands the foundation of energy psychology by introducing relevant historical foundation material and age-old methods. {Chapter 4}

6. Adds to the self-touch methods of energy psychology the circle, stop, breathe, and feel method. {Chapter 3}

Contributions to the Traditions of Qigong and Tai Chi

1. Broadens the definition of Qigong by including the use of imagery methods, i.e. Qigong is a many-thousand-year-old method of cultivating the energy of life through the use of posture, movement, breath, touch, sound, awareness, and imagery methods. Also, it broadens the definition of Qigong to include non-movement, energetic, psychological states that cultivate the universal life force, i.e. the most profound Qigong is following your true life's path. {Chapter 4 and 5}

2. In Volume I it was shown that each Tai Chi posture has four different purposes: healing, spiritual unfoldment, self-defense, and to change the practitioners life stance. In Volume II, we see that each Tai Chi/Qigong posture is part of a healing alphabet that can form and induce different state-specific states of consciousness that can be useful to Qigong practitioners and to the psychotherapeutic or behavioral health setting. {Chapter 5 and 16}

3. Reveals how Qigong/Tai Chi are "soulful traditions." Qigong and Tai Chi have been seen as spiritual traditions. This book is the first to show how Qigong is also a "soulful tradition" following in the path of depth psychologists such as Hillman and Moore. For example, while one is practicing Tai Chi and Qigong, instead of placing most emphasis on the transcendent, spiritual aspects induced by these practices, one can also focus on the memories, emotions, and images that arise in the practice — making it into a "soulful practice." {Chapter 5}

4. Shows how the meaning-making orientation of psychotherapy can add to Qigong by bringing psychological awareness to the postures and movements. This psychological awareness can help Tai Chi and Qigong practitioners to better use their practice to change their life stance. {Chapter 5 and 15}

ILLUSTRATIONS

Figure 1: Finding your Hidden Reservoir of Healing Energy from Dr. Mayer's Audio Tape. Cover Design: Eleni Rivers — XXXII

Figure 2: Psychotherapeutic Mandala — 35

Figure 3: The Double Snake from www.dictionary.com/images — 87

Figure 4: Chiltan Spirit Posture from Gore, B., (1995) *Ecstatic Body Postures*, Santa Fe, N.M.: Bear & Company, (with permission). — 129

Figure 5: Four Elements of Constructively Expressing Negative Feelings updated from Dr. Mayer's book *Trials of the Heart,* Berkeley, CA, Celestial Arts, 1994 — 235

Figure 6: Wuji Standing Meditation — 279

Figure 7: Puppet Dangling from Heaven — 279

Figure 8: Circle that Arises from Stillness — 280

Figure 9: Holding Golden Balls in the Waters of Life — 281

Figure 10: Opening the Golden Ball of your Heart — 282

Figure 11: Feeding the World with your Heart (Wild Goose says Hello) — 282

Figure 12: Dispersing Stagnant Qi — 282

Figure 13: Tai Chi Ruler-Bringing in Healing Energy — 284

Figure 14: Tai Chi Ruler-Letting go of Toxic/Stagnant Energy — 284

Figure 15: Ocean Wave Breathing — 285

Figure 16: Moving Snakes through the Hip Joint — 286

Figure 17: Moving Snakes through the Shoulder Joint — 286

Figure 18: Dipping Your Hands into the Water of Life — 287

Figure 19: Crane Crosses Wings — 288

Figure 20: Crane Walking — 288

Figure 21: Crane Flying — 288

Figure 22: Walking Meditation Qigong-Holding the Golden Ball — 289

Figure 23: Walking Meditation Qigong-Opening the Heart — 289

Figure 24: Walking Mediation Qigong-Drawing in Energy from the Earth — 290

Figure 25: Walking Meditation Qigong: Giving Energy to the Earth — 290

Figure 26: Wuji Standing Meditation Qigong — 291

NOTES

Introduction

[1] The term Self is deliberately spelled with a capital "S" in many places in this book, following Dr. Carl Jung's pointing out, as a key element of his analytic psychology, that a depth psychological perspective on healing necessitates a Self wider than the ego. Dr. Jung felt that this Self, which he spelled with a capital "S," was defined by an axis between the collective unconscious, the home to the energy potentials (archetypes of the collective unconscious), and the ego. Throughout this book I will build on this foundation to show that the *psychoid* (body-oriented, rather than just mentally psychic) nature of the archetypes includes body, mental and energy components, and when these elements combine, verbal therapy is best able to reach the goal of healing the primordial Self.

[2] *Bodymind Healing Qigong* is a synthesis of ten systems of Qigong derived from my thirty years of training. See Mayer, M. H. (2004b). *Secrets to living younger longer* (Vol. 1), op. cit.

[3] See Mayer, M. H. (1994). *Trials of the heart*, op. cit., for the four-step method I developed for constructive clearing of negative feelings. This method is also offered free on my website: www.bodymindhealing.com/services

[4] This information came from a workshop I did with Taoist Scholar Livia Kohn (1989, 2001) that derived from early medical manuscripts dating from the early Han dynasty, i.e. the late second century B.C.E. The fruits of her research will be appearing in her next book *Chinese Healing Exercises* (forthcoming). I was fortunate to get a preview of this book in her workshop at the National Qigong Association. The statement about the animal movements comes from page 2 of an unpublished manuscript Dr. Kohn gave to students about the animal forms, and the bird form.

[5] Some of these age-old traditions to be touched upon in this book are ancient sacred wisdom traditions such as symbolic process traditions of alchemy, astrology, and mythology. Also incorporated in Bodymind Healing Psychotherapy's (BMHP) definition of *primordial Self* are the teachings contained in my first two books, *The mystery of personal identity* (1984) and *Trials of the heart* (1993) regarding the use of symbolic process traditions to activate the elements of the primordial Self for ourselves and our relationships. It should be noted that this concept of the primordial Self incorporates the concept of "progressions" in our natal birth-chart, and so it is not a regressive moving back to an idealized past self, but instead it represents a progressing, learning, evolving life force. Similar therefore to Carl Jung's ideas about the axis that connects the ego and collective unconscious to form the Self, my concept of the primordial Self contains an axis (*axis mundi*) that connects the "face before you were born," the instinctual and archetypal aspects of the Self, and the absorbed learning of that Self as it progresses through time. Also underlying BMHP's definition are the teachings from my last book, *Secrets to Living Younger Longer* (Mayer, 2004), which shows the importance of Bodymind Healing Qigong practices to help cultivate the primordial Self — particularly animal movements stemming from static and dynamic postural initiation traditions. Now in this book, *Bodymind Healing Psychotherapy*, my viewpoint is presented on the psychological/emotional/affective dimensions of what it means to connect with our primordial Selves.

It should be noted that there are many pathways to the primordial Self, in addition to the ones mentioned above. Teilhard de Chardin, perhaps captures best my meaning of the primordial Self when he wrote,

> *What is the work of works for man if not to establish in and by each one of our selves an absolutely original centre in which the universe reflects itself in a unique and inimitable way, and those centres are our very selves and personalities.*

[6] For those not familiar with Qigong, please see the index of this book for references to definitions and research on this many-thousand-year-old branch of Chinese medicine.

[7] In Volume I (Mayer, 2004b, op. cit.) I outlined some of the principles of the internal martial arts tradition. For example, Standing Meditation is a way to enhance your life stance and find "your spine" in everyday life. With sufficient long-term training, "no-force" methods have been used as a way to defend against physical attack, but I emphasize how the embodied metaphors of the stances and movements of the internal martial arts tradition are an opportunity to practice becoming "an adept of the elements," i.e. developing the appropriate inner psychological balance of fire, earth, metal, water, and wood in everyday encounters. For more on the internal martial arts tradition, see Cohen (1997) and Francis (1998).

SECTION I

Chapter 1

[1] In the November 3, 1999 *Journal of the American Medical Association (JAMA), 28*(17), 1665-1667.

[2] July 26, 2000 *JAMA* Report, *284*(4), 483-485. Other sources cite evidence for medical errors and iatrogenic (physician-caused) reasons being the number one cause of death, (see http://www.mercola.com/2003/nov/26/death_by medicine.htm). The Commonwealth Fund International Health Policy Survey (2005) was reported on www.mercola.com/2005/nov/17.

[3] According to a report by the *Journal of the American Medical Association* and Dr. Stephen Rapp, project investigator for Wake Forest University. As reported by the *Los Angeles Times*. In the *San Francisco Chronicle,* (2004, June 23). Estrogen may speed senility, study warns.

[4] In a World Health Organization press release, Bulletin #9, December 17, 2001, Jonathan Quick, director of Essential Drugs and Medicines Policy for the World Health Organization (WHO) wrote, "If clinical trials become a commercial venture in which self-interest overrules public interest and desire overrules science, then the social contract which allows research on human subjects in return for medical advances is broken." Former editor of the *New England Journal of Medicine* (NEJM), Dr. Marcia Angell, struggled to bring the attention of the world to the problem of commercializing scientific research. In one of her articles, Angell, M. (2000, May 18). Is academic medicine for sale? *New England Journal of Medicine, 342*(20), 1516-1518, Dr. Angell called for stronger restrictions on pharmaceutical stock ownership and other financial incentives for researchers. She said that growing conflicts of interest are tainting science. For a current article on this issue discussing how, though some limited progress has been made, there are still serious problems regarding federal scientists receiving illegal income from drug firms see, Beamish, R. (2006, Sept. 13). Federal scientists pay small price for illegal income, *San Francisco Chronicle* (quoting NIH spokesman John Burklow), p. A7.

[5] Connolly, C. Doctors urge ban on gifts from drug firms. *Washington Post*. In the *San Francisco Chronicle,* (2006, January 25). p. A6.

[6] Null, G., Dean, C., Feldman, M., Rasio, D., & Smith, D. (2003, November 26). Death by medicine. Retrieved from http://www.mercola.com/2003/nov/26/death_by_medicine.htm

[7] Lazarou, J., Pomeranz, B., & Corey, P. (1998). Incidence of adverse drug reactions in hospitalized patients. *Journal of the American Medical Association, 279*, 1200-1205.

[8] Rabin, R. (2003, September 18). Caution about overuse of antibiotics. *Newsday*. Also see http://www.cdc.gov/drugresistance/community

[9] This statistic was reportedly from a *JAMA* article, see http://www.mercola.com/2005/aug/30/secrets_of_the_fda_revealed_by_top_insider_doctor_part_3.htm

[10] Calculations detailed in Unnecessary Surgery section, from two sources: http://hcup.ahrq.gov/HCUPnet.asp and United States Congressional House Subcommittee Oversight Investigation. (1976). Cost and Quality of Health Care: Unnecessary Surgery. Washington, DC: Government Printing Office. Also see Leape, L. (1992). Unnecessary surgery. *Annul Rev. Public Health, 13,* 363-338. And see an article on Dr. Mercola's website, Null, G., Dean, D., Feldman, M., Rasio, D., & Smith D. (2003,

November 26). Death by medicine. As retrieved from http://www.mercola.com/2003/nov/26/death_by_medicine.htm

[11] According to http://www.mercola.com/2003/nov/26/death_by_medicine.htm, a 1987 *JAMA* study found the following significant levels of inappropriate surgery: 17 percent of cases for coronary angiography, 32 percent for carotid endarterectomy, and 17 percent for upper gastrointestinal tract endoscopy. Using the Healthcare Cost and Utilization Project (HCUP) statistics provided by the government for 2001, the number of people getting upper gastrointestinal endoscopy, which usually entails biopsy, was 697,675; the number getting endarterectomy was 142,401; and the number having coronary angiography was 719,949.13 Therefore, according to the *JAMA* study, 17 percent, or 118,604 people, had an unnecessary endoscopy procedure. Endarterectomy occurred in 142,401 patients; potentially 32 percent, or 45,568, did not need this procedure. And 17 percent of 719,949, or 122,391 people, who received coronary angiography were subjected to this highly invasive procedure unnecessarily.

[12] Testimony to the Department of Veterans Affairs' Chiropractic Advisory Committee; George B. McClelland, D.C., Foundation for Chiropractic Education and Research: March 25, 2003. http://www.fcer.org/html/Research/VAtestimony.htm. Also see www.mercola.com?2003/nov/26death by medicine_ref.htm

[13] The Health Medicine Institute (HMI) in Lafayette, California is a multidisciplinary team of health practitioners who practice integrative medicine, which I co-founded with Dr. Len Saputo, and where I practiced for three years. www.healthmedicineinstitute.com.

[14] For more information on the history of corporations see Nace, T. (2003). *Gangs of America: The rise of corporate power and the disabling of democracy,* (San Francisco, CA: Berrett-Koehler). He discusses the case of "Santa Clara County v. Southern Pacific Railroad (1886)" (p. 231). This case's decision is cited as having established that corporations are "persons" for purposes of applying the equal protection clause of the 14th Amendment, which had been enacted to protect the newly freed slaves in the states of the former Confederacy. For the full story on this complex case, see Chapters 9 and 10 of the aforementioned book. According to Nace, The Supreme Court did not actually decide the case that way, but the crooked clerk who wrote the abstract on the case had ties to the railroad industry. Subsequent Supreme Court decisions were based on that abstract, thus confirming its legality, and thereby gave corporations more and more "rights," which are at the root of many societal problems. Also see www.poclad.org, i.e. The Program on Corporations, Law, and Democracy. This website provides links from which you can learn how initially corporations were there to serve the public interest, and then got their charter from the king and government and served at the behest of the people. This website contains a discussion of how the situation has degenerated into corporate power becoming the powerful entity that it is, which serves its own, rather than the public's, economic interests.

[15] Kaufman, M. (2005, February 16). Oversight panel to monitor safety of drugs. *San Francisco Chronicle.*

[16] See www.drmercola.com Vioxx/DepressionWhistleBlowerMyHero/12-18-04.html. Also see Kaufman, Ibid.

[17] Food and Drug Administration (FDA) employee and Vioxx whistleblower Dr. David Graham, Dr Graham points out several conflicts of interest between consumers and drug companies: (1) "When a serious safety issue arises at post marketing, the immediate reaction is almost always one of denial, rejection, and heat. They approved the drugs, so there can't possibly be anything wrong with them. This is an inherent conflict of interest," (2) The "gorilla in the living room" is new drugs and approval. Congress has not only created that structure, they have also worsened that structure through the Prescription Drug User Fee Act of 1992 (PDUFA), by which drug companies pay money to the FDA so it will review and approve their drug. For industries, every day that a drug is held up from being marketed represents a loss of $1-2 million of profit. The incentive is to review and approve drugs as quickly as possible and not stand in the way of profit making. The FDA usually cooperates with that mandate. See http://www.mercola.com/2005/aug/13/fda_david_graham.htm.

[18] From the interview with Dr. Graham and Manette Loudon, which was reported to a Senate hearing in response to a question by Sen. Charles Grassley (R-Iowa). For the whole interview see http://www.mercola.com/2005/aug/30/secrets_of_the_fda_revealed_by_top_insider_doctor_part_3.htm

[19] The FDA tried to tailor a report on antidepressants, as reported by the *Washington Post*. In the *San Francisco Chronicle*, (2004, September 24). p. A4.

[20] See July 26, 2000 *Journal American Medical Association*, 284(4), 483-485.

[21] Colliver, V. (2001, July 14). *San Francisco Chronicle*, p. A5. Reporting on survey from the California Medical Association.

[22] Colliver, V. (2005, November 11). *San Francisco Chronicle*, p. C1. Reporting on a research study published in the Winter issue of the *Journal of Health Affairs (2005)*, authored by Dr. James Kahn of the Institute of Health Policy Studies at UCSF.

[23] This program, aired on *60 Minutes* CBS TV on March 5, 2006 was in part drawn from Michael Rosenbaum's research "Is the price right?"

[24] However, even these diseases had already declined to a very low incidence, prior to successful medical interventions. Declines were predominantly due to public health measures such as improved sanitation, safer water, improved housing, and more widely distributed food for better nutrition (McGinnis & Foege, 1993).

[25] Pelletier, K. R., (2000). *The best alternative medicine*, (New York: Fireside), p. 65. See also Kabat-Zinn, J. (1990). *Full catastrophe living*, (Delta), p. 336.

[26] See NBC's *60 Minutes* program, about Dr. Robin's research, aired on February 26, 2006, produced by Tanya Simon. Californians passed Proposition 71, showing the will of the people of California to contravene against the Bush administration's attempt to limit new stem cell line research.

[27] Francis, Z. (2005, August 1). Diabetes care has come far, and the future is very bright. *Oakland Tribune*, p. 7.

[28] Information retrieved from the website http://www.whitehouse.gov/infocus/medicare/health-care/health-budget.html

[29] I say more about the relaxation response in the following chapter, where I show how it is a key ingredient to psychotherapeutic healing. Then I examine the cross-cultural understanding of the relaxation response and Dr. Rossi's current research in medical hypnosis. You will also see how relaxation is one part of a wider phenomena which includes both the relaxating and energizing effects of trance states.

[30] Reprinted in *Qi: Journal of Traditional Eastern Health*, (1995). 5(4), 45. In reference to an article in the *New York Times* by Phillip Hilts. Also see National Institute of Health Technology Assessment Panel, (1996, July 24). Integration of behavioral and relaxation approaches into the treatment of chronic pain and insomnia. *NIHTAP*, 276(4), 313-318.

[31] For a more complete listing of studies see Pelletier, K. R. (2004, January-March). Mind-body medicine in ambulatory care. *Journal of Ambulatory Care*, p. 14.

[32] Actually Qigong can be considered broader than even the above definition. Since Qigong includes all forms of activating the vital energy of life it also incorporates the whole of Chinese medicine including acupuncture, herbs, moxibustion, etc. However, it is most often associated with the definition outlined in the text.

[33] The Beijing estimate is from Eisenberg, D. (1995). *Encounters with Qi*. (W. W. Norton), p. 207. The estimate of 80 million Qigong practitioners in China comes from September 1996, *Life Magazine* article, The Healing Revolution.

[34] Some historical researchers date Qigong to at least as far back as 168 BC, where, in the King Ma tomb, forty-four standing and seated Qigong postures were depicted in a chart with associated commentaries and prescriptions for various diseases. Cohen, K. (1990, Fall). Qigong: Cultivating the vital breath. *ISSSEEM*, 1(2), 9. Some speak of its origins in the *Yi Ching*, the book of changes. One source describing the history of Qigong is Ming, Y. J. (1985). *Chi kung: Health and martial arts*. (YMAA Pub.), Chapter 1.

[35] For more information on the origins of Qigong see Cohen, K. (1997). *The Way of Qigong*, (Ballentine Books), p. 13. Reference Despeux, C. (1988). *The marrow of the red phoenix: Health and long life in*

16th century China, (Paris: Guy Tredaniel), p. 10. Also see Kohn, L. (2001). *Daoism and Chinese culture*, (Cambridge, MA: Three Pines Press), p. 195.

[36] Lerner, M. (1994). *Choices in healing*. (Cambridge, MA: MIT Press), p. 389

[37] Eisenberg, D. (1995). *Encounters with Qi,* (W. W. Norton).

[38] A Qigong database of 1000 abstracts of the papers presented from these proceedings, including articles from 160 scientific journals, has been prepared by the Qigong Institute of San Francisco, 450 Sutter St. #2104 S.F., CA 94108. At the "First World Conference for Academic Exchange of Medical Qigong" which was held in Beijing in October 1988 many scientific papers were presented giving data to support claims of the effectiveness of Qigong in healing. Of 137 papers presented, only three were from the United States, one from Canada, almost all of the others were from China. The research described in the abstracts does not always meet strict scientific standards; but taken as a whole, the favorable results suggest that there should be more rigorously done follow-up studies to determine how Qigong can improve Western healthcare.

[39] Lu, Guangjun, (1993). Second World Conference for Academic Exchange of Medical Qigong. Record 8010, Database from Qigong Institute of San Francisco.

[40] Shen, Fudao, Hubei College, Wuhan China, 1993. Second World Conference. See record 8090 Qigong Institute Database.

[41] Wang, S., Henan Tumor Hospital, Zhengzhou, China Annual Conference. Since 1985, cancer patients have been prescribed long-term Qigong exercises side-by-side with being given routine treatments such as chemotherapy, radiotherapy, and surgery. Results seem to show that this combination of Qigong-chemotherapy in the management of cancer has the advantage of raising the curative rate, extending the tumor-free survival time of the patients, lessening nausea, increasing strength, improving appetite, and bettering the quality of patients' survival. See McGee, C., & Chow, E. (1994). *Miracle healing from China,* (Coer d'Alene, ID: Medi-Press), p. 173.

[42] See McGee, C., & Chow, E. (1994). Ibid, pp. 203-210.

[43] For copies of their materials and conference proceedings contact ISSSEEM, 356 Goldco Circle, Golden, CO, 80403.

[44] Many psychophysiological measures are affected by practicing Qigong. There are psychophysiological correlates to the relaxation response including change in brain wave patterns, neurochemical release, etc. One research study from Japan indicates Qigong's ability to effect the immune system and endorphin levels. In this study, a sitting control group experienced a 35 percent decrease in endorphins after one hour sitting, whereas the Qigong group showed an increase in endorphins after practicing Qigong. Higucchi, Y. (1996, September). Endocrine and immune response during Qigong meditation. *Journal of International Society of Life Information Science (ISLIS), 14*(2). Many questions remain as to whether studies on *Qi* have proved the existence of Qi, or whether some epiphenomenon is being measured. One researcher, Voll, measured the electrical conductance of the skin above individual acupuncture points of Qigong practitioners, and significant differences were found. It should be kept in mind that this doesn't necessarily measure Qi, it measures "its" effects. See Sancier, K. (1995). The effect of Qigong on therapeutic balancing measured by electro-acupuncture according to Voll. *Acupuncture and Electro-Therapy Res. Int. Journal, 19*, 119-127. See reports of Feng Li Da's ability to increase or decrease bacteria cell growth with Qigong, in Mcgee, C., & Chow, E. (1994). *Qigong: Miracle Healing In China,*(Coer d'Alene, ID: Medi-Press). Likewise, this study points to the effects of a Qigong master's hands over a medium and doesn't necessarily show whether Qi exists. In the past, Western scientists have viewed with skepticism the actuality of energy existing in the meridians of the human body, but recent research is exploring the ancient notion that meridian lines of energy in the body in fact exist. On the side of Qi being objectively real see Kaptchuk, T. (1983).*The Web that has no weaver,* (NY: Congdon & Weed). Thermally sensitive film shows Qigong masters' emission of energy down lines similar to classical acupuncture meridians in Lerner, M. (1994). *Choices in healing,* (Cambridge, MA: MIT Press), p. 389. Credit should be given to the early research of Becker, R. (1985) who has shown the healing effects of electrical energy in a Western context (pp. 234-237). Also see Serizawa, K., et al. (1964). *Individual pattern changes in the distribution of skin temperature and electrical*

resistance, (University of Tokyo School of Medicine); and *The distribution of skin temperature and point meridian phenomena*, (1976), as cited in Teeguarden, I. (1987, p.23). *The joy of feeling*, (Japan Pub.). In general, see the vast literature on acupuncture. A hypothesis for this stage of our knowledge is that Qigong practice simultaneously induces effects in many areas of human anatomy: energetic dimensions, brain wave functioning, biochemical measures such as endorphin levels, etc.

[45] Schmitz-Hubsh, et al. (2005, October 14). Qigong exercise helps to reduce the motor and non-motor symptoms of Parkinson's disease: A randomized controlled pilot study, *Movement Disorders*. The abstract reads as follows: "Irrespective of limited evidence, not only traditional physiotherapy, but also a wide array of complementary methods are applied by patients with Parkinson's disease (PD). We evaluated the immediate and sustained effects of Qigong on motor and non-motor symptoms of PD, using an add-on design. Fifty-six patients with different levels of disease severity (mean age/standard deviation, 63.8/7.5 years; disease duration 5.8/4.2 years; 43 men {76%} were recruited from the outpatient movement disorder clinic of the Department of Neurology, University of Bonn, Germany. We compared the progression of motor symptoms assessed by Unified Parkinson's Disease Rating Scale motor part (UPDRS-III) in the Qigong treatment group (n = 32) and a control group receiving no additional intervention (n = 24). Qigong exercises were applied as 90-minute weekly group instructions for 2 months, followed by a 2 months pause and a second 2 month treatment period. Assessments were carried out at baseline, 3, 6, and 12 months. More patients improved in the Qigong group than in the control group at 3 and 6 months ($P = 0.0080$ at 3 months, and $P = 0.0503$ at 6 months; Fisher's exact test). At 12 months, there was a sustained difference between groups only when changes in UPDRS-III were related to baseline. Depression scores decreased in both groups, whereas the incidence of several non-motor symptoms decreased in the treatment group only."

[46] Of the UCLA Neuro-psychiatric Institute in Los Angeles, Psychiatrist Michael Irwin, M.D.'s 2004 study reports that three Tai Chi classes a week for 15 weeks boosts shingles immunity by about 50 percent. He wrote, "There's nothing currently available to boost shingles immunity to match what we did … We found significant improvements in the older adults who practiced Tai Chi and their ability to carry out day-to-day tasks." This research was reported by www.ivanhoe.com who offers medical alerts by email.

[47] An overview of Tai Chi and Qigong research can be found at www.Qigonginstitute.org, where also can be found the Computerized Qigong Database, referenced in the 2001 *Jour. of Alt. and Comp. Med.*, 7(1), 93-95. Here you can search a wide variety of medical applications of Qigong. Also see www.worldtaichday.org, for a good layperson's overview.

Chapter 2

[1] *Isomorphism* is one position on the so-called "mind body problem." Dualistic approaches say that mind and body are two separate entities; monistic approaches say mind and body are one. "Isophormism" derives from the terms iso=same, morphic=structure; it means that mind and body are the made of the same stuff and are translations of each other into different mediums. Isomorphism has important implications for psychotherapy and bodymind healing (McDougal, 1911, op. cit.).

[2] Sapolsky, R. M. (1998). *Why zebras don't get ulcers*. (New York: W. H. Freeman and Company). Rossi, E. (1986). *The psychobiology of mind-body healing: New concepts of therapeutic hypnosis*, (New York: Norton).

[3] For a review of the issues involving combining meditation and psychotherapy see Walsh, R., & Shapiro, F. (2006, April). The meeting of Western meditative traditions and Western psychotherapy. *American Psychologist*, op. cit. Also see Bogart, G. (1991). Meditation and psychotherapy: A review of the literature, *The American Journal of Psychotherapy*, op. cit.; this article is available online at www.buddha.net/medpsych.htm. For a general review of the literature on the science of meditation see www.noetic.org/ions/medbiblio/ch1.htm. Later in the book we shall explore various problems with incorporating methodologies from other cross-cultural traditions.

[4] Kaufman, M. (2005, January 3). Meditation gives brain a charge. *Washington Post*, p. A05. Newsweek interactive. See www.washingtonpost.com. Or for more information on the extensive literature on the efficacy of meditation in treating various health-related conditions such as heart disease, rheumatoid arthritis, chronic diseases, etc. see http://nccam.nih.gov/health/meditation.

[5] Meditation helpful in psychotherapy, *Harvard Mental Health Letter*. Reported in *ASI Washington*, June 24, 2005.

[6] In the trainings done by Peter Levine (1997), author of *Waking the tiger: Healing trauma*, one of the methods he teaches for dealing with trauma patients is "titrating," i.e. going back and forth from going into the trauma and coming out of the trauma, so that the ego isn't overwhelmed. Thus one can learn to handle the reactivated traumatized state.

[7] One of the books for this course was by Le Shan, L, (1975). *How to meditate*, (Bantam). In Chapter 5, pp. 32-46, he reviews various styles of meditation.

[8] See note 20 at the end of this section for a distinction between the terms "state-dependent" (Rossi, 1986, 1988) and "state-specific" (Tart, 1968) states of consciousness.

[9] There are Qigong traditions, such as Taoist Alchemy, which are oriented to transcendence. However in the main traditions, Qigong and Tai Chi foster greater bodily awareness and being in the present. It is true that psychotherapy is oriented more to being present in one's "emotional body," and for that reason the blending of traditions is beneficial to incorporate presence of both greater body awareness (which can develop from Qigong) and emotional self-awareness (which comes from Western psychotherapy).

[10] The houses of the astrological chart correspond with the signs of the zodiac, but according to astrological theory, the houses symbolize how various energies manifest in everyday life (Rudhyar, 1970). Thus the first house, Aries, symbolizes the personality and how the ego manifests and rises to life. The second house, corresponding to Taurus, symbolizes what one possesses, one's body, etc. The third house, Gemini, symbolizes one's immediate environment and communication. The fourth house, Cancer, symbolizes deep feeling, inward journeys and the home. The fifth house, Leo, symbolizes children and self-expression/catharsis. The sixth house, Virgo symbolizes perfecting details, and getting one's health together. The seventh house, Libra, symbolizes relationships to others. The eighth house, Scorpio, symbolizes deep emotional inner diving, and is the house of metaphysics. The ninth house, Sagitarrius, is the house of philosophy, and higher knowledge. The tenth house, Capricorn, is the house of occupational work. The eleventh house, Aquarius, is the house of fixed knowledge of the archetypal possibilities of life, friendships, and meaningful goals, groups, etc. The twelfth house, Pisces, is the house of feelings for humanity, institutions, letting go, etc. For more information on the astrological signs and houses see Rudhyar, 1970; Rael, 1980; Mayer, 1984.

[11] St. Mary's College, Moraga, California.

[12] Eliade, M. (1959). *The sacred and the profane*, (New York: Harcourt, Brace, & World), p. 36-47. The "axis mundi" is the central axis referred to in cross-cultural mythology which brings the initiate to experience "the center of the world."

[13] Mason, J. (1975). A historical view of the stress field. *Journal of Human Stress 1*, 6; Mason, J. Ibid, part II, *1*, 22. Selye, H. (1975). Confusion and controversy in the stress field. *Journal of Human Stress, 1*, 37.

[14] Benson, H. (1983). The relaxation response and norephinepherine: A new study illuminates mechanisms. *Integrative Psychiatry 1*, 15-18. Benson, H. (1983, July). *The relaxation response: Its subjective and objective historical precedents and physiology. Trends in Neuroscience*, 281–284.

[15] Hilts, P. (1995, Winter). Spiritual side finds favor in medical field. *Qi: Journal of Traditional Eastern Health & Fitness, 5*(4), 45. Reprinted from the New York Times.

[16] It has been hypothesized that going into an altered state is one of the fundamental needs of being human. Some say that the vast drug problems in our culture are a distortion of our basic need to "get high." Such inductions into altered states have been a fundamental part of initiatory rituals in past indigenous cultures.

[17] At the Aesclepian temples it was reported and engraved in stone that miracle cures took place, such as curing people who were blind from birth, and curing the lame so they could walk again; and there were even stories about Aesclepius raising the dead — like Glaucos, the son of Minos, and Hippolytos, the son of Thesues. The mind, "noo-therapeia," was key in the healing process. Papadakis, T. (1988). *Epidauros*. Zurich and Athens: Verlag Schnell.

[18] Chopra, D. (1990). *Quantum Healing*, p. 122, reports a study by psychologist Daniel Goleman.

[19] Braun, B. (1983). Psychophysiologic phenomena in multiple personality and hypnosis. *American Journal of Clinical Hypnosis*, 26, 124-35. Murphy, M. (1992). *The future of the body: Explorations into the further evolution of human nature*. (Jeremy Tarcher), pp. 242-245. For more information on the ability of the realization response, psychoneuroimmunology, and Qigong to effect healing, see Appendix 2 of Volume I (Mayer, 2004b). The most recent term in the DSM-IV for multiple personality disorder is "dissociative identity disorder."

[20] In the literature in the field, the terms "state-dependent" and "state-specific" states of consciousness are often used interchangeably. Charles Tart (1968) was one of the first consciousness researchers to use the term "state-specific;" Rossi (1986, 1988) and other hypnotherapeutic researchers seem to favor the term "state-dependent." Throughout this book I will mostly use the term "state-specific" due a preference for emphasizing the way that hypnotic anchoring, imagery, and somatic practices create states which are specific to the unique methodology used to create that state of consciousness. It is not necessarily always "dependent" upon that method of evocation. For example, one may be introduced to a feeling of letting-go by imagining a river washing away tension; that letting-go feeling may also be induced by breathing or other specific methods.

Chapter 3

[1] For copies of their materials and conference proceedings, contact ISSSEEM, 356 Goldco Circle, Golden, CO, 80403, or www.issseem.org.

[2] Paraphrased from Gerber, R. (1996). *Vibrational medicine*. (Bear & Co.), p. 43.

[3] The most well-known physicist who put energy at the forefront of investigation about the nature of the universe was Albert Einstein, who led us to the worldview that matter and energy are inter-convertible aspects of the same basic reality. Also see Popp, F. A., Li, K., Hung, K., & Gu, Q. (Eds.). (1992). *Recent advances in biophoton research*. (Singapore: World Scientific). General reviews of numerous studies can be found in Gerber, R. (1996). *Vibrational medicine*, (Bear & Co.).

[4] Benor, D. (1993). *Healing research*, op. cit.; Rubik, B., Walleczek, J., Liboff, A., Hazelwood, C., & Becker, R. In Swyers, J., et al. (Eds.). (in press). *Expanding medical horizons: Report to NIH on the status of alternative medicine*, (Washington, DC: US Gov't Printing Office). For general review and leading-edge research in this field, see *Subtle Energies Journal*, ISSSEEM, Goldco, Colorado, phone 303-278-2228. Also see Becker, R. (1990). *Cross-currents: The promise of electro-medicine*, (Tarcher/Putnam); Sancier, K. (1996). Medical applications of Qigong. *Journal of Alternative Therapies for Health and Medicine*, 2(1). Cohen, K. (1997). *The way of Qigong*, (Ballantine Books).

[5] For a description of Dr. Mehmet Oz and Julie Motz's work, see Benor, D. (1992). *Spiritual healing: Scientific validations of a healing revolution*, pp. 95-96. I was very fortunate to have had the opportunity to do a workshop with Julie Motz, sponsored by our clinic, the Health Medicine Institute.

[6] Nordenstrom, B. E. (1983). *Biologically closed circuits: Experimental and theoretical evidence for an additional circulatory system*, (Stockholm, Sweeden: Nordic Medical Publications). See Heilberg, E. (1993, Winter). *ISSSEEM*, 4(4), 5. One must be cautious about interpreting this research because electricity has been shown to increase as well as decrease tumors.

[7] An interesting experimental machine called the AMI was developed by Hiroshi Motoyama who claims it is able to measure the functions of the meridians and imbalances with the meridian systems. The AMI apparatus includes 28 electrodes that are attached to the terminal acupuncture points of each of the 12 meridians and 2 carrier vessels. After studying over 5,000 subjects, Motoyama identified

Qi as primarily an electromagnetic energy with accompanying infrared and infrasonic energy signatures. See Montoyama, H. (1981). *Theories of the chakra: Bridge to higher consciousness.* Wheaton, IL: Theosophical.

[8] See for example, The Energy Field, Journal and Newsletter for the Association for Comprehensive Energy Psychology, P.O. Box 910244, San Diego, CA 92121 or www.energypsych.org. Other sources for the voluminous publications in the field of energy psychology are listed in one of the classic overviews in the field, Gallo, F. (2002). *Energy psychology in psychotherapy.* New York: W. W. Norton. Also see Feinstein, D. (2004). *Energy psychology interactive.* Ashland, OR: Innersource.

[9] For more information on this survey, see Feinstein, D. (2004). Ibid, Chapter on "State of the Art."

[10] For an more extensive examination of research on the field of energy psychology see Dr. David Feinstein's article, *An Overview of Research in Energy Psychology,* at; http://www.innersource.net/energy_psych/epi_research.htm, For a broader view of references to Qigong research see index of this book, and Volume I (Mayer, 2004b, op. cit.).

[11] Updated reports can be found at www.eftupdate.com/ResearchonEFT.HTML

[12] Some references that relate to this material on brain research are Schore (2003), op. cit., and Ruden (2005), op. cit.

[13] I gleaned this information from a workshop by Dr. Jim Lane at a conference workshop sponsored by the Association for Comprehensive Energy Psychology in May of 2006. Dr. Lane's website is, www.weheal4u@cs.com

[14] I completed the 150-hour certification program at the Acupressure Institute of Berkeley, CA, and would recommend it as one source of training for psychotherapists or anyone who wants further training in these methods.

[15] Energy psychologists might take umbrage at saying there is a one-size-fits-all approach. And there is some truth to this in that there are different treatment protocols in some energy psychology approaches for phobias, trauma, hypertension, etc. However, the sophistication of Chinese medicine involves much more ideographic, patient-specific, time-tested diagnostic and treatment methods for any single disorder. In favor of the energy psychology tradition is that the power of point touching is enhanced by the power of the mind, and the life issue behind the disorder, as it is focused upon in energy psychotherapy. In later chapters I will show why in BMHP there is a focus on the unique meaning of a patient's healing solutions that are expressed in symbols, movements, and stances that derive from the depths of that person's unconscious (see Chapter 5). BMHP does not preclude, at appropriate times, the suggestion of holding or tapping places on the body that seem fitting with the patient's sensibilities. In this way, BMHP in general is more aligned with phenomenological and inner-directed, rather than prescriptive, solutions. Though from the more meta-systematic, medicine wheel perspective outlined in Chapter 2, whatever works is used.

[16] For a more complete review of the literature on muscle testing and applied kinesiology, see Feinstein, D. (2002). *Energy psychology interactive: Studies pertaining to energy checking (muscle testing).* Compiled by The International College of Applied Kinesiology, www.icakusa.com. For an excellent article on the subject of muscle testing involving a trialogue between three experienced clinicians examining the values and problems with muscle testing, see Durlacher, 2002, op.cit.

[17] See index of Volume I (Mayer, 2004b) regarding "the axis mundi" in cross-cultural traditions in general, and how Tai Chi cultivates this central axis.

[18] One of these scales is the Stanford Hypnotic Susceptibility Scale, see Wickramasekera, 1998, op. cit.

Chapter 4

[1] It is beyond the scope of this book to review all such traditions, some of which include: Dravidian folk dancing (Tomio, 1994), Indian dance, Tibetan dance, the health dance of the animals (Diepersloot, 1994; Mayer 2004b), the healing dance of the Kung tribesman (Mayer, 2004b). Some Native American tribes also have traditions of shape-shifting whereby a shaman imbibes the essence of a given animal for ritual healing purposes. One of the co-members of our integrative health clinic,

Phillip Scott, a Native American chief, did such healing rituals there (www.ancestralways.com). His taking on the movements and sounds of the bear makes the participant in the healing circle feel as if a bear is actually in the room. There are many sources for the importance of self-touch and massage and their roles in energy healing, too numerous to cite (Gach, 2004; Teeguarden, 1989).

[2] Gold, S. (2006, March 3). From temple Chochmat Halev's Berkeley, California, Shabbat service *Torah* reading. Written commentary on the *parsha* (part) of the *Torah*, called Terumah of the Old Testament for the week of March 3, from Rabbi Shefa Gold.

[3] Temple Chochmat Halev in Berkeley, California has a training program in Jewish Spirituality and Meditation. In this program and in their Friday night Shabbat services such songs are introduced, see www.chochmat.org

[4] The Taoist tradition actually contains both transcendent and immanent dimensions and practices. For example, the human being is seen as being comprised of a *Hun* (heavenly) soul and a *Po* (earthly) soul; it is believed that the *Hun* soul rises up to the heavens after death, and the *Po* soul descends back to the Earth. There are practices, such as Wuji Standing Meditation and various Taoist Alchemy practices, which are oriented to activate a path to the transcendent state of *wuji* (the mother of Qi, the void); and there are immanent practices — for example, the meditative focus on the belly (*Tan Tien*), and the practice of the animal forms of Qigong.

[5] Erickson, M. (1948/1980). *The collected papers of Milton Erickson on hypnosis IV*, (New York: Irvington), p. 38. See Rossi, E. (1986). *The psychobiology of mind/body healing*, op.cit, p. 67.

[6] Such esoteric traditions as alchemy, which uses metals and chemical processes as metaphors (Edinger, 1985), and astrological symbols, which use the celestial bodies as metaphors (Mayer, 1984), are examples, as are using the everyday metaphors of life to make a link to the wider whole of which we are a part (Gordon, 1978; Wallas, 1985).

[7] For example, Wilhelm Reich advocated a bio-energetic psychology, and was put in jail for advocating the use of orgone energy. It is true that, nowadays, forefront psychological educational institutions have somatic psychology training programs; and leading-edge thinkers are advocating the incorporation of the body in psychotherapeutic training. However, this is not mainstream psychotherapy quite yet.

[8] Papadakis, T. (1988). *Epidauros: The sanctuary of Asclepius*, (Verlag Schnell: Zurich), p. 6. Stories also say he "raised from the dead" the heroes Lycurgos and Tyndareos.

[9] See for example the teaching tale of the Gnostics called "The Hymn of the Pearl," discussed in Mayer, M. H. (1994). *Trials of the heart*, Berkeley, CA: Celestial Arts.

[10] See Bandler, R., & Grindler, J. (1975). *The structure of magic, II*, (Palo Alto, CA: Science and Behavior Books). Hypnotherapists have shown that different people have strengths and weaknesses in accessing a "trance" state through a given representational system — visual, kinesthetic, auditory, and olfactory. The art of hypnotherapy is in how to blend and cross over from one to the other to facilitate activating an individual's healing resources.

[11] There are numerous descriptions of *Microcosmic Orbit Breathing* in addition to the best-known sources (Wilhelm, 1931; Cleary, 1991). Huang, Wen-Shan, (1974). *Fundamentals of Tai Qi Chuan*, (Hong Kong, China: South Sky Book Company); Chia, M, (1986). *Iron shirt Qi Kung healing*, (Huntington, NY: Tao Books). The *Microcosmic Orbit Breath* method that is outlined here combines the classical methodology the *River of Life* method that I developed. The river merges into the "*Sea of Elixir*."

[12] Chan, L. (1995, October). A visit to an unique Qigong hospital. *T'ai Qi Magazine, 19*(5), 34-35.

[13] In a personal communication from Dr. Larry Stoler, psychologist, president of the Association for Comprehensive Energy Psychology, and one of Luke Chan's students, he said that Luke reported that on the day he videotaped this healing, 5 out of 7 people's tumors disappeared. Professor Feng Li Da of Beijing reports the ability of Qigong masters to increase or decrease bacteria cell growth in multiple laboratory settings by placing their hands over a cell culture of bacteria or cancer cells. See Eisenberg, D. (1985). *Encounters with Qi*, (W. W. Norton). Thermally sensitive film shows Qigong masters emitting energy down lines similar to classical acupuncture meridians. According to Eisenberg, D. (1990, Spring). *Energy medicine in China*, (Noetic Science Review). As cited in Lerner, M. (1994). *Choices in*

healing, (Cambridge, MA: MIT Press), p. 389. There is a need for replicating the scientific validity of these studies in order to investigate the reality of these reported effects. See also Sancier, K. (1996, January). Medical applications of Qigong. *Alternative Therapies, 2*(1). For more current research on this topic, Dr. Garret Yount, of the California Pacific Medical Center, and Beverly Rubik of The Institute of Frontier Science (brubik@earthlink.net) are two of the top researchers in this field. Right now, on the growing edge of research, it seems that such results do occur but not consistently; therefore scientific research questions whether such results are merely due to chance. The Qigong master's mental set needs to be considered as a confounding variable.

[14] See Achterberg, J. (1985). *Imagery and healing*, p. 199; and above cited study. Achterberg discusses the Basmajian study that provides evidence that human beings can learn to voluntarily control the electrical activity of a single cell (p. 198). Basmajian, J., (1963, August) Control and training of individual motor units, *Science Magazine*, 2, 440-441.

Chapter 5

[1] The methods in the last chapter, which combine breathing methods and symbolic process approaches, serve as an introduction to the Bodymind Healing Qigong (BMHQ) system. BMHQ combines ten systems of Qigong into an integrated method, which I synthesized from 30 years of training with some of the most respected Tai Chi and Qigong Masters. See Volume I (Mayer, 2004b), or the Bodymind Healing Qigong DVD (Mayer, 2000).

[2] The term, "transpersonal," in one of its earliest usages implied "beyond and through the person," thereby including both transcending and transmuting aspects in its definition. Dane Rudhyar (1975) said that the "transpersonal attitude may be one involving a reaching beyond the personal — an ascent of consciousness, to seek to attain greater heights and peak experience .... But it also implies a descent of spiritual power focusing itself through a person, as diffused solar light is focused through a clear lens" (p. 38). Dane Rudhyar used the term this way in a small magazine called *The Glass Hive* in 1930, and wrote about it in his 1948 book entitled, *Modern man's conflict: The creative challenge of a global society,* (New York: Philosophical Library). See his chapter entitled, "The Transpersonal Way and the New Manhood." I was honored to have been able to study, and meet privately, with Dane Rudhyar during my doctoral dissertation years in the 1970s. I still appreciate the deep influence he had on the development of my way of seeing the world.

[3] Hillman, J. (1979b). *Dreams and the underworld*; Gendlin, E. (1986). *Let your body interpret your dreams.*

[4] The idea of a "true self" is not a fixed concept in the Western mystery tradition. For example, the astrological meta-system includes the notion of a natal chart, which is a mandala for meditation through which a person reflects upon his or her beginning essential nature. As well there is a progressed chart whereby one reflects upon the self that has developed and progressed to a given moment in time. The symbols of the astrological mandala enable one to reflect upon his or her life's meaning and identity. For more information on this phenomenological meaning reorganization point of view (Fingarette, 1963), which transcends the issue regarding the objective correspondence between the celestial sphere and one's personality, see my book, *The mystery of personal identity* (Mayer, 1984). It was the first book to show how astrological symbols could function as a metaphorical tool in depth psychotherapy to help a patient come to terms with his or her life's meaning and identity.

[5] "It would be an interesting subject of research to examine the bio-chemical differences between just imagining, versus imagining with the use of *Microcosmic Orbit Breath*. For more on how this research has already begun, see Lascow (1998), and the discussion in Chapter 4 of this book.

[6] See Mayer, M. H. (2004b). *Secrets to living younger longer*, and Mayer, M. H. (2000). *Bodymind Healing Qigong DVD*, available from www.bodymindhealing.com

[7] See Gendlin's early research that showed from listening to psychotherapy tapes of many different types of therapy that this type of focusing is what made psychotherapy work regardless of which tradition was being used. Gendlin, E. (1962). *Experiencing and the creation of meaning*, (Free Press of Glencoe); and Gendlin, E. (1978). *Focusing*, (Bantam Books).

[8] Actually the state-specific state of consciousness of *White Crane Spreads Wings* is not just a transcendent state. One hand is up by the third-eye representing the crane's transcendent, rising above ability; however, a grounded dimension is also experienced in this posture as the practitioner places the other hand down by the belly, pressing down toward the earth, while the practitioner stands grounded on one leg. (For an illustration, see Volume I (Mayer, 2004b)).

[9] A recent article bears on this topic of scientific measurement of psychotherapy practice. Adam Phillips, psychoanalyst and author, says the following in this article:

> *Since at least the middle of the nineteenth century, Western societies have been divided between religious truth and scientific truth, but none of the new psychotherapies are trying to prove they are genuine religions. Nor is there much talk, outside of university literature departments, of psychotherapy trying to inhabit the middle ground of arts, in which truth and usefulness have traditionally been allowed a certain latitude (nobody measures Shakespeare or tries to prove his value)....*
>
> *It would clearly be naïve for psychotherapists to turn a blind eye to science, or to be 'against' scientific methodology. But the attempt to present psychotherapy as a hard science is merely an attempt to make it a convincing competitor in the marketplace. It is a sign, in other words, of a misguided wish to make psychotherapy both respectable and servile to the very consumerism it is supposed to help people deal with. In the so-called arts it has always been acknowledged that many of the things we value most — the gods and God, love and sexuality, mourning and amusement, character and inspiration, the past and the future — are neither measurable or predictable. Indeed, this may be one of the reasons they are so abidingly important to us. The things we value most, just like the things we most fear, tend to be those we have least control over. If psychotherapy has anything to offer, and this should always be in question, it should be something aside from the dominant trends in the culture. And this means now that its practitioners should not be committed either to making money, or to trivializing the past, or to finding a science of the soul...*

Phillips, A. (2006, February 26). A mind is a terrible thing to measure. *New York Times*.

[10] This is spoken of in terms of "from Qi (energy) to Yi (intention)," which refers to the ability to "first cultivate, then utilize, then manifest," as my Sifu Fong Ha says. Or, as the founding grandmaster of the *Yi Chuan* tradition says, "big circles are very good, small circles are even better, and no circles are best."

[11] Parallels between the ancient concept of underworld journeys and modern psychotherapy are discussed in Meier, 1967, op. cit., pp. 93-112; and Hillman, 1979b, op. cit., p. 21.

Chapter 6

[1] Los Angeles Times, (1995, April 24). *Billions spent on new hypertension drugs*, p. A-17. Prescriptions for just one class of anti-anxiety drugs, the benzodiazapines, are estimated as costing being between $100-800 million a year. A variety of questions have been raised as to whether the new drugs that are coming onto the market are really superior to the old ones. New drugs, including calcium antagonists and ACE inhibitors, add $10 billion to consumer costs over old diuretics and beta-blockers, with scanty evidence to prove that they are superior.

[2] Altrocchi, J. (1994). Non-drug treatment of anxiety. *American Family Physician*, 10, 161-6. He reports that 10 percent of adults have an anxiety disorder, yet only one-fourth receive treatment. Treatment is usually given in a general medical setting rather than through the mental health system. Most patients

with anxiety disorders are treated by non-psychiatrist physicians who are generally more familiar with pharmacological management of anxiety. However, non-drug treatment can be more effective and may be both more time-efficient and less risky.

[3] NIH (National Institute of Health) Technology Assessment Panel. (1996, July 24). Integration of behavioral and relaxation approaches into the treatment of chronic pain and insomnia. *Journal of the American Medical Association, 276*(4). See also Hilts, P. (1995, Winter). Spiritual side finds favor in medical field. *Qi: Journal of Trad. Eastern Health & Fitness, 5*(4), 45. Reprinted from the New York Times.

[4] For example, Elmer Green, in the Copper Wall Project at the Menninger Clinic, scientifically documented the energy activated by healers from a variety of traditions entering into a meditative altered state. See Green, E., et al. (1991). Anomalous electrostatic phenomena in exceptional subjects. *Subtle Energies, 2*(3), 69-94.

[5] See Mayer, M. H. (2004). *Secrets to living younger longer: The self-healing path of Qigong, standing meditation and Tai Chi*, (Berkeley, CA: The Bodymind Healing Center). Also see *Bodymind Healing Qigong DVD* (Mayer, 2000) available at www.bodymindhealing.com

[6] Bodymind Healing Psychotherapy's use of a holographic/energetic model to healing seemingly goes in a different direction from the managed care approach that wants brief, solution-oriented approaches. Managed cares' conservative, Newtonian, economically based viewpoint moves away from holistic approaches and seeks to legislate a narrower range of approaches to fix specific psychological issues, i.e. cognitive-behavioral therapy, drug therapy, etc. Further research needs to be done to compare the two approaches to explore whether — paradoxically — deeper, more integrative models are better in their ability to achieve long-lasting results, and more cost-effective over a long time span, than are "brief therapies."

[7] *Elevator Breathing* is a simple variation I developed to simplify the commonly used Taoist breathing practice *Microcosmic Orbit Breathing*. Whereas *Microcosmic Orbit Breathing* emphasizes circulating the breath up the Governing Vessel (*Du*, also called *Tu Mei* Channel) on the back on the inhalation, and down the front Conception Vessel (*Ren*, also called *Jen Mei* Channel) of the body on the exhalation, *Elevator Breathing* emphasizes the up and down of raising the spirit and sinking the Qi. The Taoists believe that by cultivating the breath in such a way, through focus on the center of the body at the *Tan Tien*, that one can become more centered, revitalized, and can enter into an experience of discovering the reservoir of universal Qi, which aids in healing and activates transcendental awareness. My preliminary clinical research with *Elevator Breathing* shows promising results as an adjunct to treatment with a wide variety of psychological issues, such as: over intellectualization, anxiety and panic disorders, borderline issues, obsessive traits, substance abuse issues, general stress reduction, and as part of hypnotherapy for trance induction. Further research is needed to validate these preliminary results. Two audio tapes are available from the following conferences where I presented: Mayer, M. H. (Speaker). (1987). *An integrated approach to anxiety and phobias*. (Cassette Recording). From the Eighth Annual Conference and Training Institute on Phobias and Related Anxiety Disorders, sponsored by Langley Porter Neuro-psychiatric Institute. San Francisco; and secondly, Mayer, M. H. (1997). *Psychotherapy & Qigong: Partners in healing anxiety*. (Cassette Recording). From the Second World Congress on Qigong. San Francisco: Conference Recording Services.

[8] There are some patient populations that have more difficulty feeling the sinking of Qi than others, such as those who suffer from severe dissociative conditions and some schizophrenic patients. The use and adaptation of this method to different clinical populations is refined through experience.

[9] Before doing this exercise and others like it, have yourself checked by a Western medical doctor to make sure there aren't any medical problems that could be exacerbated by pressing into your stomach. In particular, please check with a doctor first if you have high blood pressure, or if you have had a stroke, heart condition, circulation problems, detached retinas, aneurysm, diabetes, varicose veins, clotting or inflammation of a blood vessel. And, for comfort, it's best to practice this massage when your bladder is not full. For a more complete exposition of this technique, and contraindications and

cautions, see Chia, M. (1990). *Chi Nei Tsang: Internal organ massage.* (Huntington, NY: Healing Tao Books).

[10] See Gendlin, E. (1978). *Focusing.* (Bantam Books). It is best to learn this method from a trained Focusing teacher or guide, since there are many subtle intricacies to its steps. See www.focusing. org. This way of inner accessing won an award from the American Psychological Association. It is an invaluable technique to help find felt meaning, and has been used in a wide variety of settings such as the Simonton Cancer Clinic.

[11] The *Macrocosmic Orbit* comes down the front of the body down the *Ren* Channel and out the feet through the *Bubbling Well* points (Kidney-1). See Huang, W. S. (1974). *Fundamentals of Tai Chi Chuan,* (Hong Kong, China: South Sky Book Co.), p. 472.

[12] I suggested this idea about "clearing a space" to Dr. Gendlin when I was his Focusing Training Coordinator of the East Bay-San Francisco area in the late 1970s, and he liked the idea to add to his various methods. I wrote about this in a blurb about this integration of Focusing and Taoist breathing methods for the Transpersonal Psychology Association's newsletter in the early 1980s.

[13] Archetypes, as Carl Jung said, are "energy potentials." When internal representations of the people in our own lives are insufficient as healing images, our wider psyches can activate archetypally energized images from the wider whole of which we are a part to promote healing. I discuss this idea of moving from the personal to archetypal level as a therapeutic strategy in Chapter 23 using *Tai Chi Push Hands* movements as an initiatory analogy.

[14] An alternative is to place the whole hand over this area, which gives a more expansive but less focused feeling.

[15] For example, I presented this concept in my presentation, *An Integrated Approach to Anxiety and Phobias,* at the Eighth Annual Conference and Training Institute on Phobias and Related Anxiety Disorders, sponsored by Langley Porter Neuropsychiatric Institute, in San Francisco, in 1987.

[16] I learned two traditions of Standing Meditation in my three decades of Qigong practice. From my Sifu Fong Ha's kind introduction to three masters, I learned *Wuji Qigong* from Master Cai Song Fang of Canton, China; and I learned *Yi Chuan Standing,* also called, *Zhan Zhuang,* from Master Han Xiyuan, and from Master Sam Tam. I continued these practices with my sifu, Master Fong Ha. *Wuji* means the void or stillness from which movement and Tai Chi derives. Ken Cohen, author of *The Way of Qigong,* (Ballantine Books, 1997), to whom I taught these methods, says that they are the million-dollar secret of Qigong. For more information, see Mayer, M. H. (2004b). *Secrets to living younger longer,* op. cit. Also see Diepersloot, J. (1995). *Warriors of stillness,* (Walnut Creek, CA: Center for the Healing Arts).

[17] See Note 3 in Chapter 24 for some research on Standing Meditation regarding increasing coherence between left and right hemispheres of the brain and other positive health effects.

Chapter 7

[1] *The Pain and Absenteeism Report: A Study of Full Time Employees and Employee Benefit Managers.* (1996, June). Ortho McNeil Pharmaceutical and Louis Harris and Associates, Inc. For a copy of this report, fax 212-885-0570.

[2] The cost of $90 billion includes compensation claims, time off work, medication, disability allowance, and direct treatment. See Taylor, S. (1991). *Health psychology* (2nd Ed.), (New York: McGraw Hill). Quoted by Groth-Maarnat, G. (1996). Professional psychologists in general healthcare settings: A review of the financial efficacy of direct treatment interventions. *Professional Psychology: Research and Practice,* 27(2), 166. The statistic of $100 billion for pain remedies includes temporary pain relief from colds, headaches, chronic pain, etc. Taylor, S. (1991). *Health psychology* (2nd Ed.), New York: McGraw Hill. Quoted by Groth-Maarnat, G. (1996). Professional psychologists in general healthcare settings: A review of the financial efficacy of direct treatment interventions. *Professional Psychology: Research and Practice,* 27(2), 161-174.

[3] For a review of the literature on various relaxation and behavioral techniques for relieving chronic pain, see NIH (National Institute of Health) Technology Assessment Panel. (1996, July 24).

Notes

Integration of behavioral and relaxation approaches into the treatment of chronic pain and insomnia. *Journal of the American Medical Association, 276*(4). The NIH panel reviewed numerous well-designed studies of pain relief that used a variety of behavioral medicine approaches including: relaxation methods such as progressive relaxation (tightening and loosening various muscles of the body), meditation, hypnosis, autogenic training, biofeedback, and cognitive-behavioral therapy.

[4] One source for a wide review and discussion of the medical literature on pain medication is the Roxane Pain Institute, www.Roxane.com. In terms of medical devices there are a wide variety, such as electrical transcutaneous electrical nerve stimulation (T.E.N.S. units). These electrical stimulation devices give relief to many who suffer from sports-related and other kinds of pain. Some of the modern drugs that are used for pain relief are coumarin (a chemical compound found in many plants) which has collagen reducing effects, cortico-steroids, percodan, elavil and heparin. The most recent advertised "panacea" for severe pain are the long-acting opiates, such as morphine — now given in graduated doses to provide steady relief, but no euphoria. The idea behind this pharmacological advance is that graduated doses will lessen addiction to these drugs; and there is some evidence to prove this is the case. Addiction is composed of two factors: tolerance — the compulsive craving for increasing amounts of a drug over time, and dependence — the withdrawal symptoms that come from stopping a drug abruptly without tapering off. The evidence is still inconclusive, but research at this time seems to show that, when taken properly, long-acting opiates do not produce tolerance in most people; however, they can produce dependency. See Jetter, A. (1996, September). The end of pain. *Hippocrates*, p. 45.

[5] Side effects of various drugs need to be carefully weighed in the decision as to whether and when to use various medications. Speak to your physician about this and check for yourself such books as: the *Physicians Desk Reference, (PDR)*; *Worst pills, best pills II*, Public Citizens Health Research Group, 1993; Breggin, P., *Toxic psychiatry*, op. cit.

[6] Different points of view about taking medication are presented in, Jetter, A., *The end of pain*, op. cit. On the "critical of opiates" side of the debate is John Loeser, a neurosurgeon from the University of Washington School of Medicine in Seattle. On the pro-opiate side is Dr. James Campbell, who runs the pain clinic at John Hopkins Hospital. Also, Dr. Russell Portnoy, a neurologist at New York's Sloan Kettering Hospital reports that his cancer patients who took opiates did not develop tolerance (the compulsive craving for increased amounts of the drug).

Another area of caution involves contradictory scientific reports on the relationship between opiates and cognitive deficits. Jetter, A., (1996). Hippocrates, op cit. p. 48. Dr. Loeser says that the opiates dull patient's thinking in some cases, whereas a study at John Hopkins on 20 patients found no evidence of mental clouding after six months of use. Other studies support Loeser's view. Some areas of consideration that need to be taken into account when taking these drugs are the early side effects of sleepiness and nausea during the initial phase of taking it, and constipation often can be longer lasting. A potentially fatal risk factor involves the person who takes too much at once and doesn't listen to the advice of their physician — who usually advises carefully ratcheting up the dosage over a few weeks. Going against the advice of a doctor in this case can potentially have dire consequences — respiratory failure and death. Those who use morphine pumps to provide graduated doses often get infections at the point of insertion. On the other hand, many people in severe pain get the benefit of relief since long-acting opiates mimic the body's pain fighting endorphins by blanketing the spine's pain receptors, and preventing the message from arriving.

[7] Chopra, D. (1989). *Quantum healing*, (Bantam Books), pp. 62-63. Rossi (1986) says the placebo effect is responsible for about 55 percent of cure rates as determined by meta-analytic studies (p.16).

[8] Another very well-designed, double-blinded study by Wirth (1991) showed the effect of non-contact therapeutic touch (i.e. a form of external emission Qigong) on wound healing. Due to its focus on external emission rather than self-healing practices, it is outside the scope of this book

[9] Two sources for research on the beneficial results of using imagery in healing are: Achterberg, J. (1985). *Imagery in healing: Shamanism and modern medicine*, (New Science); and Rossi, E. (1988). *Mind-body therapy: Methods of ideodynamic healing in hypnosis*, (W. W. Norton).

[10] Check with an acupuncture chart to see the exact location of K-1, which is slightly forward of the bottom center of the foot.

[11] There is voluminous research which demonstrates that by imagining something to be real in the body, physiological changes take place. See for example Achterberg (1985), Chopra (1990), and Rossi (1998).

[12] In China there are a wide variety of reports that Qigong masters can emit energy from their hands and affect cell cultures, increasing or decreasing bacteria, and even killing cancer cells. See Sancier, K. (1991). Medical application of Qigong and emitted Qi on humans, animals, cell cultures, and plants: Review of selected scientific research. *American Journal of Acupuncture, 19*(4). Also see McGee & Chow, E. (1994). *Qigong: Miracle healing in China,* pp. 164-165, op. cit, for reports of Feng Li Da's controlled study whereby killing and inactivation of 31 percent of cancer cells occurred in the experimental group with emitted Qi. All cancer cells survived in the control group. Reported at the First Medical Conference for Medical Exchange of Medical Qigong, 1988. The line is difficult to draw between whether studies on Qi emission prove emission of Qi, or prove it is a function of hypnosis, some psychokinetic phenomenon, biochemical release of endorphins, or other neurotransmitters, etc. Also, there are often replicability issues with these studies — one problem seems to be the condition of the Qigong master on the day of the experiment. Research in this emerging field needs to be subjected to further research and analysis. In private correspondence Dr. Sancier reported that low frequency sound in the 3-12 hertz range has been measured from the Laogong points on the palms. There are those that have developed "Qi Machines" that attempt to replicate the vibratory rate of Qi, such as Richard Lee, China Healthways 1-800-743-5608. Further research needs to be done as to how these machines compare to Qigong practice, and what the positive and negative side effects of such machines may be.

[13] See Hilgard and Hilgard, (1983) *Hypnosis in the relief of pain,* (William Kaufman Inc.), pp. 241-250. Arlene Morgan and Josephine Hilgard standardized the scale.

[14] For example, one energy gate in the center of the palms is called the *Laogong* point or Pericardium-8. It can be found by making the fingers curl inward into a fist, where the middle finger presses into the inner palm between the extensions of the bones of the two inner middle fingers. These points are useful on a cold day to generate heat in the hands. Massage practitioners and healers that use Qigong use these points for emitting Qi to heal others.

[15] *Yi Chuan Qigong* ("yi" means "intention" in Chinese), also called *Zhan Zhuang* (Standing like a Tree), has been one of my main practices for thirty years. As discussed in the introduction, I introduced students to it at JFK University and at the California Institute of Integral Studies Doctoral Program. Masters Fong Ha and Han Xingyuan, the latter having studied with the originator of *Yi Chuan Qigong,* Wang Xiangzhai, introduced me to it. One person to whom I taught it, Taoist Scholar, Ken Cohen, describes this method as the million-dollar secret of Qigong in his *Way of Chi Gung Tapes* (Boulder, CO: Sounds True Catalogue). One written source for learning how to work with the ball of magnetic force between the hands in the *Zhan Zhuang* tradition is Chuen, L. (1991). *The way of energy,* (Gaia Books), p. 127. Also see Diepersloot, J. (1995). *Warriors of stillness,* (Walnut Creek, CA: Center for Healing and the Arts). Paul Dong (1990) in his book, *Chi Gong: The ancient Chinese way to health,* (New York: Marlowe & Co.), p. 127, reports that the *Zhan Zhuang* standing meditation practice began 2,000 years ago with Taoist philosopher Wang Chong-Yang. *Yi Chuan Qigong* is also used to embark upon the path toward developing the much talked about "empty force," (*kung jing),* whereby the practitioner supposedly discharges a fellow practitioner without touching them. For a realistic appraisal of this issue, see Ha, F. (1991, August). Is empty force real? *Tai Chi Magazine, 15*(4); also see Dong, P. (1990). *Chi Gong,* (New York: Marlowe and Co.), and his later book specifically on "*kong jing.*"

[16] The Qigong meditation posture in stillness is called *wuji,* translated as the void, stillness or reservoir from which Qi emerges.

[17] For more specific instructions see Ha, F. (1996), Diepersloot (1994), Mayer (2004b). The best way to learn these methods to assure proper posture and training is to study with a teacher of the *Yi Chuan.*

For example, when standing we can imagine four points in a straight line to activate our center-line — the points being: the point between the two feet, the *Huiyin* point between the anus and genitals, the center point between the *Tan Tien* and *Ming Men* right below the navel, and the *Baihui* point at the top of the head. Without postural corrections from a teacher, limitations or pitfalls in practice can arise.

[18] Taoists believed that this energy center, two or three finger-widths beneath the navel, was a key point for meditation.

[19] Some evidence to support the idea that Qi is emitted from the *Laogong* points, also called Pericardium-8, can be found in McGee, C., & Chow, E. (1994). *Qigong: Miracle healing from China*, (Medi-Press), pp. 37-38. Measures include Raman spectra, ultraviolet spectra, and infrasonic emission at low frequencies in the 1-12 hertz range, microwave emissions, magnetic field generation, and electrostatic field generation. Reports in this book say that Qigong Master Yan Xin could affect the decay rate of a radioactive compound. The studies reported in this book often were not footnoted, or subjected to Western scientific methodology standards, and need to be further documented and replicated. Scientists with whom I have dialogued in private correspondence have many doubts about some of the data, in particular on Raman spectra and the effects on radioactive compounds. These sources say reports on infrasonic emissions from the hands may be more likely to have validity. (See Qigong Database from the Qigong Institute of San Francisco, op.cit.). Another clinician and researcher, Dr. Leonard Lascow, (in a controlled study) reports measuring the ability of magnetic field emission from his hands to inhibit tumor cells 18 percent while practicing *Microcosmic Orbit Breathing*. See Lascow L. (1992). *Healing with love*, (Harper and Row), p. 306.

[20] Stone, J. (1996). *Tai Chi Chih*, (Beverly Hills, CA: Interarts Productions). *Tai Chi Ruler* can also be practiced without the technological devices of the ruler or balls by doing circular movements with the hands held apart like a ball.

[21] Jou, T. (1980). *The Tao of Tai Chi Chuan*. (Vermont: Charles, Tuttle), pp. 77- 78. He discusses the classic notion of how Tai Chi, the yin and yang of creation, derives from *wuji*, or nothingness. One of the feelings associated with *wuji* and Qi is of heaviness and lightness at the same time. For more about the *Wuji Qigong* tradition that I have studied with Masters Cai Songfang and Fong Ha, see Diepersloot (1995) and Mayer (2004b).

[22] It would be interesting to have further research studies to determine if the methods above enhance healing compared to a non-treated control group.

[23] Hall, C. (1996, October 10). Snail venom may zap pain, *S.F. Chronicle*, p. B1, B4. Final proof that SNX-111 is a long way off. Questions remain regarding side effects and dosage. However, its use appears promising in patients unable to tolerate conventional pain treatments including morphine. The drug blocks the calcium channel, which is the neurochemical pathway through which pain signals travel through the spinal cord to the brain.

[24] Quizhi, S. & Zhao, L. (1993). Clinical observation of Qigong as a therapeutic aid for advanced cancer patients. *Proceedings of the Second World Conference for Academic Exchange of Medical Qigong*, Beijing, China. See Sancier, K. (1996, January). Medical Applications of Qigong. *Alternative Therapies*, 2(1), 43.

[25] There is well-documented evidence of the use of Mindfulness Meditation in reducing pain at the Stress Reduction Clinic at the University of Massachusetts Medical Center. In one study there, meditators showed a 36 percent improvement in pain on the McGill-Melzack Pain Rating Index (PRI), while non-meditators showed no improvement; meditators showed a 87 percent improvement in mood, while the non-meditators showed only a 22 percent improvement; mediators showed a 77 percent improvement in psychological distress, non-meditators had an 11 percent improvement. Kabat-Zinn (1990) also reports that several laboratory experiments with acute pain have shown that "tuning into sensations is a more effective way of reducing the level of pain experienced when the pain is intense and prolonged than is distracting yourself" (p. 291).

²⁶ My ten years serving as Eugene Gendlin's Focusing training coordinator for the San Francisco East Bay area helped me develop some of the important groundwork of what was to become Bodymind Healing Psychotherapy.

²⁷ These results need to be subjected to a scientific research design, replicated by others, controlled for halo effects and positive transference in the self-reports of patients, etc.

Chapter 8

¹ Cognitive Restructuring Therapy was developed by Dr. Aaron Beck (1967), a psychologist who used cognitive restructuring therapy with his depressive patients. The method has now been adapted to treat a wider variety of psychological issues including anxiety, self-esteem issues, etc.

² Scientists such as David Bohm and F. David Peat (1997) subscribe to the theory that mind creates physical reality. "Bottom up" theories posit that consciousness is a by-product of molecules that create mind, while "top down" theories propose just the opposite — that consciousness is the creative force of the universe. This is a matter of ongoing debate (Tiller, 1997), but many mind-body clinicians use the term "bottom up" loosely, to speak about the need in certain psychological syndromes to emphasize the role of the body in creating new, more healthy cognitive and affective abilities. See also van der Kolk, 2002, p. 68. From a Taoist perspective, why dichotomize between the creative powers of above and below? From a cross-cultural mythological perspective there are creation myths of Gods of the earth and the heavens (see Von Franz, M. L. (1972). *Creation myths*. Zurich, Switzerland: Spring Publications.)

³ See Volume I (Mayer, 2004b) to hear about my experience of how the practice of Tai Chi helped in healing my early trauma experience.

Chapter 10

¹ Cooper, A. (2006, March 9). Asleep at the wheel. *CNN*. This information came from CNN anchor Anderson Cooper who reported cases of some people who "woke up" after driving in an erratic manner, and didn't remember getting in the car to drive to the store in the middle of the night.

² See Volume I for specific complementary movements for repetitive stress syndrome, such as *Commencement* in Tai Chi, and *Moving a Snake through your Joints*. First the Qi needs to be built up with practices such as *Wuji Standing or Sitting Meditation*.

Chapter 11

¹ See Chapter 24, note 3, on the study by Yang Sihuan (1993) 2nd World Conference for Academic Exchange on Medical Qigong, reported in the Qigong Database: Qigong Institute of San Francisco. This study analyzed the EEG patterns of young students and reported that Qigong training had affected coherence of EEGs between the two frontal regions, between the two occipital regions, and between the two temporal regions of the Qigong group student's brains while they meditated.

Chapter 12

¹ http://www.mercola.com/2004/dec/18/vioxx.htm
² Reuters. Retrieved May 16, 2005, from http://msnbc.msn.com/id/7876902.

Chapter 13

¹ Reuter's Health. (2005). *Tai Chi may lessen arthritis pain*. New York: Reuters. Retrieved January 6, 2005, from energeticsart@yahoogroups.com

² One respected source of knowledge on natural herbal remedies is herbologist Karen Sanders, who does the *Herbal Highway* show on KPFA radio 94.1 FM, Berkeley, CA.

³ This study is reported by Pelletier, 2000, op. cit., p. 144.

⁴ Pelletier, (2000) reports this 1991 study by Hanerdos on the efficacious treatment of fibromyalgia with hypnosis (p. 70).

Chapter 14

¹ The Tarasoff law allows an exception to confidentiality laws, and requires psychotherapists to report someone who is "dangerous to self or others" to the appropriate authorities. Additionally, it requires the therapist to let the intended victim know about the potential danger.

Chapter 15

¹ For more on dual relationship issues see Chapter 22 of this book, as well as checking the most recent ethical guidelines of the American Psychological Association.

Chapter 16

¹ Mayer, M. H. (1994). *Trials of the heart*. Berkeley, CA: Celestial Arts. In this book I suggested a method for constructive clearing of negative feelings for interpersonal relationships, which in part involves (1) Positive intention (2) Expressing feelings as "I feel" versus "you are" statements and (3) I want statements. See Chapter 19 for an illustration of this method.

Chapter 18

¹ Castelman, S. (1995, September). Beginners mind. *Spirit Rock Meditation Newsletter*, p. 14.

² Issues about dual relationships are addressed in Chapter 22. For more information see the APA Guidelines for Ethical Practice, www.apa.org

³ One victim of rape was working with another therapist, and was a Tai Chi student of mine for a year. One day a man approached her at a laundromat and put his hand on hers, coming on to her sexually. She adeptly and instinctively warded off his touch in such a way that fear came over his face. She told me that this was an important step in her re-empowerment and recovery.

Chapter 19

¹ For a good introduction to transpersonal psychology, see the many publications of Ken Wilber, or for a current overview of the field, see the Association for Transpersonal Psychology (www.atpweb.org). There you will see a list of members, information on receiving their journals, and information on their conferences.

² It should be noted that energy psychology does not just use single energy psychology interventions. From the perspective of energy psychology, this patient would be looked at as involved in a case of "psychological reversal;" and energy psychology has its methods for dealing with such imbedded patterns that stand in the way of patients finding a sense of love for themselves. See for example Feinstein, 2004, pp. 75-91.

Chapter 20

[1] From the frontpiece to the Association for Transpersonal Psychology's Second East Coast Conference, November, 1984.
[2] See Hillman, 1975, op. cit., and Bly, 1975, op. cit. Also see Gimbutas, M. (1982). *The goddesses and gods of old Europe*. University of California Press; Von Franz, M. L. (1982). *Individuation in fairy tales*. Spring Publications; Salant, N. S. (1989). *The borderline personality: Vision and healing*. Chiron Publications; Krippner, S., & Feinstein, D. (1988). *Personal mythology,* Tarcher Pub.
[3] For an excellent discussion of the use of "story" to enhance self-awareness, see Keen, S. (1973). *Telling your story.* New American Library.
[4] Edinger, E. (1972). *Ego and archetype.* Putnam.
[5] Gendlin, E, (1968). Focusing ability in psychotherapy, personality, and creativity. *Research in Psychotherapy,* 3.
[6] For a more complete discussion of the Focusing process, see Gendlin, 1978, op. cit.
[7] Several references to the journey to the underworld are in: Harner, M. (1980). *The way of the shaman.* Harper and Row; Eliade, M. (1972). *Shamanism.* Princeton University Press; Halifax, J. (1982). *Shaman: The wounded healer.* Crossroad Pub.; Meier, C. A. (1967). *Ancient incubation and modern psychotherapy.* Northwestern University Press; Campbell, J. (1978). *The mysteries.* Princeton University Press, .
[8] For a more complete understanding of this type of breathing meditation, see Huang, W.S. *Fundamentals of Tai Chi Chuan.* American Academy of Chinese Culture, 1973; Yu, l. K. (1972). *The secrets of Chinese meditation.* Samuel Weiser,; Jou, T.H. (1980). *The Tao of Tai Chi Chuan.* Charles Tuttle Pub. We also discuss this method in Chapter 4.
[9] See Gendlin's *Focusing* for a discussion of the distinction between a feeling and a "felt sense." A feeling is clear and well defined, whereas the felt sense is an unclear edge around the feeling that contains its wider felt meaning, i.e. what it's "all about." Gendlin gives an example of a woman whose husband spilled some milk after a job promotion. The feeling she had was anger; when she tuned into the felt sense she discovered that she was afraid of being left behind in life.
[10] I learned this particular way of getting in touch with the felt sense from shared Focusing sessions with Ann Weiser, when we were both district coordinators of Focusing in the San Francisco area.
[11] The person here was referring to the "Maiden of the Lake" in the story of King Arthur, who helped repair the sword that Arthur broke when he angrily struck Lancelot. The maiden appeared after Arthur repented and lamented that he did not deserve the sword for his violent use of it against such a pure knight.
[12] For more on the healing power of "the name," see Mayer, M. H. (1985). *The mystery of personal identity.* San Diego, CA: ACS Publications.

Chapter 21

[1] The psychological awareness that was present in pre-modern times may not have been the same as "psychological awareness" today. It is beyond the scope of this book to differentiate the similarities and differences between pre-modern and modern psycholological healing.
[2] Jacobson, E. (1964) defines "self representations," as "the unconscious preconscious and conscious endopsychic representations of the bodily and mental self in the system ego" (p. 19). I am proposing that the combination of somatically oriented psychotherapy, along the lines of BMHP, can help to transmute those dysfunctional identifications which the ego uses to represent his or her self.
[3] There are Qigong traditions, such as Taoist Alchemy, which are oriented to transcendence. However, for the most part, Qigong and Tai Chi foster greater bodily awareness and being in the present. It is true that psychotherapy is oriented more to being present in one's "emotional body," and for that

reason the blending of traditions is beneficial to incorporate both greater body awareness (which can develop from Qigong) and emotional self-awareness (which comes from Western psychotherapy).

[4] See Chapter 22 on "ethics," for discussions on dual relationships and how to introduce "experimental" new traditions into the psychotherapeutic setting. It is also important here to remind clinicians that BMHP uses non-movement methods of Qigong, and in extracting the essence of Qigong (breathing, visualization, and other methods) the psychotherapist can introduce many of its methods without ever mentioning a word about Qigong.

Chapter 22

[1] Summarized from APA Ethics Code 10.01(b), 2.01(d).
[2] http://www.apa.org/monitor/jan03/newcode.html
[3] Jansen, N., & Barron J. (1988, Winter). *Introduction and overview: Psychologist use of physical interventions in psychotherapy*, 25; Goodman, M., & Teicher, A. (1988, Winter). To touch or not to touch. *Psychotherapy*, 25(4).
[4] Training in Bodymind Healing Qigong and Bodymind Healing Psychotherapy are given in locations across the country. Please see www.bodymindhealing.com to find a training in a location near you, or to arrange training adapted to your needs.
[5] Standard 3.05(a) of the American Psychological Association's Ethics Code.
[6] Private communication from Dr. Fromm. See www.markfromm.com.

Chapter 23

[1] Some of these schools in the San Francisco Bay Area include: the California Institute of Integral Studies, John F. Kennedy University, Saybrook Institute, and the Transpersonal Psychology Institute.
[2] Many of the founders of the United States were reported to be Freemasons. At the center of Freemasonry was the study of, use of, and initiation into symbolic process traditions. Benjamin Franklin was a past grandmaster of the Pennsylvania Freemasons, George Washington was a Mason, and Paul Revere began his famous ride after an adjourned meeting of a Masonic lodge. In addition, according to Case (1976), Thomas Jefferson practiced astrology.
[3] The suggested readings here are meant to provide a broad overview, and thereby leave out a significant portion of the symbolic process traditions that could be useful for therapeutic training. Apologies to unmentioned authors who have contributed to this field.

Chapter 24

[1] Roger Jahnke, OMD, and "Getting Your Immune System in Shape." In *Boosting Immunity: Creating Wellness Naturally*, New World Library, 2002. From the web site of the Health Medicine Institute, 3799 Mount Diablo Blvd., Lafayette, CA 94549. Tel: 925-962-3799. http://www.healthmedicineinstitute.com/default.cfm.
[2] I want to express my great gratitude to my respected teachers and sources from whom and from which I have synthesized my Bodymind Healing Qigong system over three decades of practice and teaching. I am not making a representation that this system is a direct representation of my honored teachers' transmissions, I have adapted each of their teachings to fit with my own understanding, healing imagery methods, and experience with Western bodymind healing traditions.
I have trained in Standing Meditation for 30 years with my Sifu Master Fong Ha, with additional training from Masters Han Xingyuan, Cai Songfang, and Master Sam Tam. I learned the *Dispersing Stagnant Qi* exercises from my friend and colleague Ken Cohen as part of our sharing our traditions; I was the first person to teach the Taoist scholar Ken Cohen, *Yi Chuan Standing Meditation*. I learned *Tai Chi Ruler* from Sifu Master Ha. *Ocean Wave Breathing* I first learned in a workshop by Arnold

Tayam and Shoshanna Katzman at a National Qigong Association conference. *Moving a Snake through the Joints* I adapted and added to from trainings with various Qigong Masters. *Crane Walking and Flying* I learned from training with Sifu Dr. Alex Feng. *Yi Chuan Walking Meditation Qigong* I learned from training with Masters Ha, Xingyuan, and Tam

[3] Yang, S. (1993). *Second World Conference for Academic Exchange on Medical Qigong*. Reported in the Qigong Database: the Qigong Institute of S.F. This study analyzed the EEG patterns of young students, 17 to 20 years old, who had been practicing *Zhan Zhuang Qigong (Standing like a Tree)* for one year. Thirty-two persons in the Qigong group and thirty-five persons in the control group were involved in this experiment. During a one year period of observation, the subjects of the Qigong group practiced Qigong for 40 minutes every day. The EEGs of the Qigong group were analyzed every half-year in meditation, and the EEGs were also recorded before learning Qigong. The students in the control group did not take part in the Qigong training and their EEG s were investigated at rest twice within an interval of one year. In the test, eight channels of EEGs were simultaneously processed by a computer on line for 20 minutes. After one year of Qigong training, total coherence between the left and right frontal regions increased from 0. 84~0.07 to 0. 87~0.06 ($p < 0.05$). Before Qigong training, the total coherence between the left and right occipital areas was 0.68~0.14. After a half year of training, it increased to 0.79~0.10, and after one year of training it was 0.76~0.10, ($p < 0.001$). The total coherence between the left and right temporal areas before Qigong training was 0.48~0.17; half year after Qigong training it was 0.55~0.13, compared with that before Qigong training ($p < 0.05$). One year after Qigong training it was 0.64~0.12, compared with those before Qigong training and half year after Qigong training ($p < 0.001$). Qigong training had no significant influence on coherence between the left and right central regions and between adjacent anterior and posterior brain regions (F3-C3, F4-C4, C3-01, C4-O2). The data from the two tests of the control group showed that the total coherence did not change significantly between the left and right corresponding brain regions and between the anterior and posterior adjacent brain regions. The author of the study (Yang, 1993) summarized, "The results showed that Qigong training had affected coherence of EEGs between the two frontal regions, between two occipital regions and between two temporal regions of the Qigong group in meditation. The most significant is that, with the increase of training period, the total coherence value between the left and right temporal areas went up. It seems that there is certain dosage effect relationship." Another study on *Zhan Zhuang* is by Li, C. (1995). Preliminary Exploration on the Scientific Proof of Being Sober-Minded, Sharp-Eyed and Energetic after Practicing Zhan Zhuang. Reported at the *Fourth International Conference on Qigong, Vancouver*, 200-24. This study reports improvement in uric acid level after practice. See Qigong Database from the Qigong Institute of San Francisco.

Afterward

[i] See previous discussion in Chapter 5 about the "psyche," ("soul") being defined as our own unique composition of the elements of nature, and of the universe (Hillman, 1975; Rudhyar, 1970).

REFERENCES

Achterberg, J. (1985). *Imagery in healing: Shamanism and modern medicine.* Boston: New Science Library.

Achterberg, J., Dossey, B., & Kolkmeier, L. (1994). *Rituals of healing: Using imagery for health and wellness.* New York: Bantam Books.

Achterberg, J., Dosey, L., Gordon, J. S., Hegedus, C., Hermann, M. .W., & Nelson, R. (1992). Mind-body interventions in alternative medicine. *Expanding medical horizons: A report to the National Institute of Health on alternative medical systems and practices in the United States.* Washington, DC: USGPO.

Ader, R., & Felton, D. (1991). *Psychoneuroimmunology.* San Diego: Academic Press.

Alexander, C., Langer, E., Newman, T., Chandler, H., & Davies, J. (1989). Trancendental meditation, mindfulness, and longevity. *Journal of Personality and Social Psychology, 58,* 950-964.

Alexander, C., & Langer, E. (1990). *Higher stages of human development.* New York: Oxford University Press.

Alexander, C., Reinforth, M., & Gelderloos, P. (1991). Transcendental meditation, self-actualization and psychological health. *Journal of Social Behavior and Personality, 6,* 186-247.

Allen, J. J. B., Schnyer, R. N., & Hitt, S. K. (1998). The efficacy of acupuncture in the treatment of major depression in women. *Psychological Science, 9*(5), 397-401.

Almas, A. H. (1988). *The pearl beyond price.* Berkeley, CA: Diamond Books.

Alpert, R. (also known as Ram Dass) (1971). *Be here now.* San Cristobal, NM: Lama Foundation.

Altrocchi, J. (1994). Non-drug treatment of anxiety, *American Family Physician, 10,* 161-166.

American Psychiatric Association. (2000). *Diagnostic and statistical manual of mental disorders* (4th ed). Washington, DC: Author.

Anand, B. K., Chhina, G. S., & Singh, B. (1961). Some aspects of EEG studies in yogis. *Electroencephalography & Clinical Neurophysiology, 13,* 452-456.

Anderson, C. (2000). What's new in pain management? *Home Healthcare Nurse, 18*(10), 648-658.

Andrade, J., & Feinstein, D. (2003). Energy psychology: Theory, indications, evidence. In D. Feinstein, *Energy psychology interactive.* Ashland, OR: Innersource.

Andreson, J. (2000). Medicine meets behavioral medicine. *Journal of Consciousness Studies, 7,* 17-24.

Andreychuk, T., & Skriver, C. (1975). Hypnosis and biofeedback in the treatment of migraine headache. *International Journal of Clinical Experimental Hypnosis, 23,* 172-183.

Archart-Treichel, J. (2003). Efficacy evidence builds for vagus nerve procedure. *Psychiatric News, 38*(17), 26.

Arguelles, J. (1972). *Mandala.* Berkeley, CA: Shambhala.

Arkowitz, H., & Mannon, B. (2002). A cognitive-behavioral assimilative integration. In F. Lebow (Ed.), *Comprehensive handbook of psychotherapy, 4* (pp. 317-337). New York: Wiley.

Arthur, J. (2000). *Mushrooms and mankind: The impact of mushrooms on human consciousness and religion.* Escondido, CA: The Book Tree.

Asch, S. (1955). On the use of metaphor in the description of persons. In H. Werner (Ed.), *On expressive language.* Worcester, MA.: Clark University Press.

Assagioli, R. (1965). *Psychosynthesis.* New York: Viking Press.

Assagioli, R. (1991). *Transpersonal development: The dimension beyond psychosynthesis.* London: Crucible.

Astin, J. A., Berman, B. M., Bausell, B., Lee, W. L., Hochberg, M., & Forys, K. L. (2003, October). The efficacy of mindfulness meditation plus Qigong movement therapy in the treatment of fibromyalgia: A randomized controlled trial. *Journal of Rheumatology, 30*(10), 2257-62.

Astin, J. A., Shapiro, S. L., & Schwartz, G. E. (2000). Meditation. In D. Novey (Ed.) *Clinician's rapid access guide to complementary and alternative medicine.* St. Louis, MO: Mosby. {As cited in Pelletier K. (2004), p. 28.}

Ausubel, K. (2000). *When healing becomes a crime.* Rochester, VT: Healing Arts Press.

Baer, R. (2003). Mindfulness training as a clinical intervention. A conceptual and empirical review. *Clinical Psychology: Science and Practice, 10,* 125-143.

Baggott, A. (1999). *The encyclopedia of energy healing: A complete guide to using the major forms of healing for the body, mind and spirit.* New York: Godsfield Press.

Baker, A. H., & Carrington, P. (2005). *A comment on Waite and Holder's research supposedly invalidating EFT.* Retrieved from www.energypsych.org/research-critique-eft.htm

Baker, A. H., & Siegel, L. S. (2005). *Can a 45 minute session of EFT lead to reduction of intense fear of rats, spiders, and water bugs? A replication and extension of the Wells et al. (2003) laboratory study.* Manuscript in preparation.

Bandler, R., & Grinder, J. (1975). *The structure of magic.* Palo Alto, CA: Science and Behavior Books.

Bandler, R., & Grinder, J. (1979). *Frogs into princes: Neuro-linguistic programming.* Moab UT: Real People Press.

Bandler, R., & Grinder, J. (1981). *Trance-formations: Neurolinguistic programming and the structure of hypnosis.* Moab, UT: Real People Press.

Barber, T. (1978). Hypnosis, suggestion, and psychosomatic phenomena: A new look from the standpoint of recent experimental studies. *American Journal of Clinical Hypnosis, 21*(1), 13-27.

Barber, T., & Meyer, D. (1984). Changing unchangeable bodily processes by (hypnotic) suggestions: A new look at hypnosis, cognitions, imaging and the mind body problem. *Advances, 1*(2), 7-40.

Barcia, R. C. (1972). Effects of rupture of membranes on fetal heart rate pattern. *International Journal of Gynecology and Obstetrics, (19),* 169. In J. Robbins (1996), *Reclaiming our Health: Exploding the medical myth and embracing the source of true healing* (p. 47). Tiburon, CA: H.J. Kramer.

References

Barefoot, J. C., Dahlstrom, W. G., & Wiliams R. B. (1983). *Psychosomatic Medicine, 45*, 50-63.

Barnes, P. M., Powell-Griner, E., McFann, K., & Nahin R. L. (2004). Complementary and alternative medicine use among adults. United States: Centers for Disease Control and Prevention National Center for Health Statistics. Advance Data, No. 343, (2002, May 27).

Barring, A., & Cashford, C. (1991). *The myth of the goddess: Evolution of an image*. London: Viking Arkana.

Basmajian, J.V. (1963, August). Control and training of individual motor units, *Science*(2): 440-441.

Beck, A. T. (1979). *Cognitive therapy of depression*. New York: Guilford Press.

Becker, R. (1985). *The body electric: Electromagnetism and the foundation of life*. New York: William Morrow.

Becker, R. (1990). *Cross currents: The promise of electro medicine*. San Diego, CA: Jeremy Tarcher.

Becker, R., Spadao, J., Marino, A. (1977). Clinical experiences with low intensity direct current stimulation of bone growth. *Clinical Orthopedics and Related Research, 124*, 75-83.

Benor, K. J. (1992). *Healing research: Holistic energy medicine and spirituality* (Vol. 1). Munich, Germany: Helix Verlag.

Benson, H. (1975). *The maximum mind*. New York: Avon.

Benson, H. (1975b). *The relaxation response*. New York: Avon.

Benson, H. (1983). The relaxation response and norepinephrine: A new study illuminates mechanisms. *Integrative Psychiatry, 1*, 15-18.

Benson, H. (1983b, July). The relaxation response: Its subjective and objective historical precedents and physiology. *Trends in Neuroscience*, 281-284.

Benson, H. (1984). *Beyond the relaxation response*. New York: Avon.

Benson, H. (1975). *The maximum mind*. New York: Avon.

Benson, H. (1975b). *The relaxation response*. New York: Avon.

Benson, H., Rosner, B.A., & Marzetta, B.R. (1973). Decreased systolic BP in hypertensive subjects who practice meditation. *Journal of Clinical Investigation, 52*, 80.

Bettleheim, B. (1977). *The uses of enchantment*. New York: Vintage Press.

Black, A. (1994). The drugging of America's children. *Redbook*, December, 1994.

Blount, A. (Ed.). (1998). *Integrated primary care: The future of mental health collaboration,* New York: W. W. Norton.

Bly, R. (1975). *A little book on the human shadow*. San Francisco: Harper and Row.

Bly, R. (1990). *Iron John: A book about men*. New York: Addison Wesley.

Bogart, G. (1991). Meditation and psychotherapy: A review of the literature. *The American Journal of Psychotherapy, XLV*(3), 383.

Bowlby, J. (1969). *Attachment and loss, Vol. I: Attachment*. New York: Basic Books.

Braun, B. G. (1979) Hypnotherapy for Raynaud's disease. In Burrows, G. D., Collison, D. R., & Dennerstein, L. (Eds.), *Hypnosis* (pp. 141-156). Amsterdam: Elsevier/North-Holland Biomedical Press.

Breggin, P. (2001). *The anti-depressant fact book*. Cambridge, MA: Perseus Pub.

Breggin, P. (1991). *Toxic psychiatry*. New York: St. Martin's Press.

Brennan, B. (1990). *Hands of light*. New York: Bantam.

Briere, J. (1992) Theory and treatment of severe sexual abuse trauma. An overview. Presented at the Orange County CA Annual Child Abuse Conference, Anaheim, CA

Briere, J. (1997). *Psychological assessment of adult posttraumatic states*. Washington, DC: American Psychological Association.

Brown, J.W., Robertson, L.S., Kosa, J., & Alpert, J.J. (1971). A study of general practice in Massachusetts. *Journal of the American Medical Association, 216*, 301-306.

Bugental, J. G. (1978). *Psychotherapy and process: The fundamentals of an existential-humanistic approach*. Reading, MA: Addison-Wesley.

Burini, D., et al., (2006).A randomized controlled cross-over trial of aerobic training versus Qigong in advanced Parkinson's disease. *Eura Medicophys., September, 42* (3):231-8.

Burr, H.S. (1972). *The fields of life*. New York: Ballantine, 1972.

Burr, H.S., & Northrup, F.S. (1935). The electro-dynamic theroy of life. *Quarterly Review of Biology, 10*, 322-333.

Cahn, R., & Polich J. (2006). Meditation states and traits: EEG, ERP and neuroimaging studies. *Psychological Bulletin. 132,* 100-211.

Cai, S. F. (1986). *Wujishi breathing exercise*. Translated by M. Den. Revised by T. Shen. Hong Kong, China: Medicine & Health Publishing Co.

Callahan, R. (1985). *Five minute phobia cure*. Wilmington, DE: Enterprise.

Callahan, R. (2001). *Tapping the healer within*. Chicago, IL: Contemporary Books.

Campbell, J. (1978). *The mysteries: Papers from the eranos yearbooks* (Bolingen Series XXX). Princeton, NJ: Princeton University Press.

Campbell, J. (1988). *Historical atlas of world mythology: The way of the animal powers* (Vol. 1). New York: Perennial Library.

Cannon, W. (1914). The inter-relationship of emotions as suggested by recent physiologial research. *American Journal of Psychology, 25*, 256.

Canter, P., & Ernst, E. (2003). The cumulative effects of Transcendental Meditation on cognitive function: A systematic review of randomized controlled trials. *Wiener Klinische Wochenschrift, 115*, 758-766.

Capra, F. (1975). *The tao of physics*. Boulder, CO: Shambhala.

Carbonell, J. (1997). An experimental study of TFT and acrophobia. *The Thought Field, 2* (3), 1-6.

Carbonell, J. L., & Figley, C. (1999). A systematic clinical demonstration project of promising PTSD treatment approaches. *Traumatology, 5*(1), Article 4. Retrieved from www.fsu.edu/~trauma

Carey, B. (2005). Can brain scans see depression? *New York Times*, 2005, October 18. Retrieved from www.nytimes.com/2005/10/18/health/psychology

Carlson, L. E., Speca, M., Patl, K. D., & Goodey, E. (2003). Mindfulness based stress reduction in relation to quality of life, mood, symptoms of stress and immune parameters in breast and prostrate cancer outpatients. *Psychosomatic Medicine. 65,* 572-581.

Case, P. (1976). *The great seal of the United States: Its history, symbolism, and message for the new age*. Santa Barbara, CA: J. F. Rowny Press.

Cheek, D. (1969). Communication with the critically ill. *The American Journal of Clinical Hypnosis, 12*(2), 75-85.

Chen H.H., Yeh, M.L., Lee, F.Y. (2006). The effects of baguanjin Qigong in the prevention of bone loss for middle-aged women, *American Journal of Chinese Medicine*, Vol. 34 (5),: 741-7.

Chen, K., & Yeung, R. (2002). A review of Qigong therapy for cancer treatment. *Journal of International Society of Life Information Science* (ISLIS), Vol. 20(2), 532-542.

Cheney, R. (1996). *Akashic records: Past lives and new directions.* Upland, CA: Astara.

Chia, M. (1986). *Iron Shirt Chi Gung I.* Huntington, NY: Healing Tao Books.

Chia, M., & Chia, M. (1990). *Chi Nei Tsang.* Huntington, NY: Healing Tao Books.

Cho, Z. H., Chung, J. P., Jones, J. B., Park, H. J., Lee, H. J., Wong, E. K., & Min, B. I. (1998). New findings of the correlation between acu-points and corresponding brain cortices using functions MRI. *Proceedings of the National Academy of Science,* March 3, 95, 267-73.

Chuen, L. K. (1991). *The way of energy.* London: Gaia Books.

Chuen, L. K. (1999). *The way of healing: Chi kung.* New York: Broadway Books.

Cleary, T. (1991). *The secret of the golden flower.* San Francisco: Harper Collins.

Clinton, A. (2002). Seemorg matrix work. In F. Gallo (Ed.), *Energy psychology in psychotherapy: A comprehensive source book.* New York: W. W. Norton.

Cohen, K. (1997). *The way of Qigong.* New York: Ballentine Books.

Cohen, S., & Herbert, T. B. (1998). *Psychosomatic medicine.* Paper presented at the annual meeting of the American Heart Association. Published 1993, in Stress and immunity in humans: A meta-analytic review. *Psychosomatic Medicine, 55*(4), 364-379.

Colum, P. (1944). *The complete Grimm's fairy tales.* New York: Pantheon.

Conn, L., & Mott, T. (1984). Plethysmographic demonstration of rapid vasodilation by direct suggestion: A case of Raynaud's disease treated by hypnosis. *The American Journal of Clinical Hypnosis, 26*(3), 166-170.

Corbin, H., (2001). *History of Islamic philosophy.* New York: Kegan Paul.

Cortwright, B., (2007, in press). *Integral psychology.* New York: SUNY Press.

Craig, G., & Fowlie, A. (1995, 1997). *Emotional freedom techniques: The manual.* Sea Ranch, CA: Author.

Crasilneck, H. B., & Hall J. A. (1985). *Clinical Hypnosis: Principles and Applications.* Orlando, FL: Grune & Stratton.

Creamer, P., Singh, B. B., Hochberg, M. C., & Berman, B. M. (2000). Sustained improvement produced by nonpharmacologic intervention in fibromyalgia: Results of a pilot study. *Arthritis Care Research, 13*(4), 198-204.

Crown, D. P., & Marlow, D. (1960). A new scale of social desirability independent of psychopathology. *Journal of Consulting Psychology, 24,* 349-354.

Damasio, A. R. (1994). *Descartes error.* New York: Grosset/Putnam.

Danaos, D. (2002). *Nei Kung: Secret teachings of the warrior sages.* Rochester, VT: Inner Traditions.

Dao, D. M., (1990). *Scholar warrior: An introduction to the Tao of everyday life.* San Francisco: Harper Collins.

Darby, D. (2001). *The efficiency of thought field therapy as a treatment modality for individuals diagnosed with blood-injection-injury phobia.* Unpublished doctoral dissertation. Minneapolis, MN: Walden University.

Davidson, R., Kabat-Zinn, J., Schumacher, J., Rosenkranz, M., Muller, D., Santorelli, S. et al. (2003). Alterations in brain and immune function produced by mindfulness meditation, *Psychosomatic Medicine, 65,* 564-570.

Deadman, P., Al-Khafami, M., Baker, K. (1998). *A manual of acupuncture.* East Sussex, England: Journal of Chinese Medicine Publications.

Deatherage, G. (1975). The Clinical Use of Mindfulness Meditation Techniques in Short-term Psychotherapy. *Journal of Transpersonal Psychology, 7,* 133-43.

Deikman, A. (1982). *The observing self.* Boston, MA: Beacon Press.

Delmonte, M. M. (1984) Meditation: Similarities with Hypnoidal States and Hypnosis. *International Journal of Psychosomatics, 31*(3), 24-34.

Delmonte, M. M. (1985). Biochemical Indices Associated with Meditation Practice: A Literature Review. *Neuro-Science and Bio-Behavioral Review, 9,* 557-561.

Delmonte, M. M. (1987). Constructivist View of Meditation. *American Journal of Psychotherapy, 41,* 286-98.

Deri, S. (1990). Changing concepts of the ego in psychoanalytic theory. *Psychoanalytic Review, 77,* 512-58.

Devine, E. C., & Westlake, S. K. (1995). The effects of psycho-educational care provided to adults with cancer: Meta-analysis of 116 studies. *Oncology Nursing Forum, 22*(9), 1369-1381.

Diamond, J. (1979). *Behavioral kinesiology.* New York: Harper & Row.

Diepersloot, J. (1994). *Warriors of stillness.* Walnut Creek, CA: Center for Health and the Arts.

Diepold, J. H. (2000). Touch and breath: An alternative treatment approach with meridian based psychotherapies. *Electronic Journal of Traumatology, 6*(2). Retrieved from www.fsu.edu/trauma

Diepold, J. H., Jr., & Goldstein, D. (2000). *Thought field therapy and EEG changes in the treatment of trauma: A case study.* Moorestown, NJ: Author.

Don, N. S. (1977). The transformation of conscious experience and its EEG correlates. *Journal of Altered States of Consciousness, 3.*

Dossey, L. (1992). But is it energy? Reflections on consciousness, healing and the new paradigm. *Subtle Energies, 3*(3), 69–81.

Dossey, L. (1993). *Healing words: The power of prayer and the practice of medicine.* New York: Harper San Francisco.

Dossey, L. (1994). Healing Energy and consciousness: Into the future or a retreat to the past? *Subtle Energies, 5*(1).

Dreher, H. (1998). Mind-body interventions for surgery: Evidence and exigency. *Advances in Mind-Body Medicine, 14*(3), 207-222.

Dunn, A. L., Trivedi, M. H., Kampert, J. B., Clark, C. G., & Chambliss, H. O. (2005). Exercise treatment for depression: Efficacy and dose response. *American Journal of Preventive Medicine, 28*(1), 1-8.

Durlacher, J., & Scott, W. (2002). An energy psychobiology trialogue: The physican's perspective. In F. Gallo, (Ed.), *Energy psychology in psychotherapy: A comprehensive source book*. New York: W. W. Norton.

Dusseldorp, E., van Elderen, T., Maes, S., Meulman, J., & Draij, V. (1999). A meta-analysis of psychoeducational programs for coronary heart disease patients. *Health Psychology, 18*(5), 506-519.

Dychtwald, K. (1977). *Bodymind*. New York: Pantheon.

Eden, D. (1998). *Energy Medicine*. New York: Jeremy Tarcher.

Edinger, E. (1972). *Ego and archetype*. New York: Putnam.

Edinger, E. F. (1985). *Anatomy of the psyche: Alchemical symbolism in psychotherapy*. La Salle, IL: Open Court.

Eisenberg, D, (1995). *Encounters with Qi: Exploring Chinese medicine*. New York: W.W. Norton.

Eisenberg, D. M., Davis, R. B., Ettner, S. L., et al. (1998, November 11). Trends in alternative medicine use in the United States, 1990-1997. *Journal of the American Medical Association, 280*(18), 1569-1575.

Eisenberg, D. M., Kessler, R. C., Foster, C., Norlock, F. E., Calkins, D .R., & Delbanco, T. L. (1993). Unconventional medicine in the United States. Prevalence, costs, and patterns of use. *New England Journal of Medicine, 328*, 246–252.

Eliade, M. (1956). *The forge and the crucible: The origins and structures of alchemy*. Chicago: University of Chicago Press.

Eliade, M. (1958). *Rites and symbols of initiation*. New York: Harper Torchbooks

Eliade, M. (1959). *The sacred and the profane*. New York: Harcourt, Brace, & World.

Eliade, M. (1964). *Shamanism: Archaic techniques of ecstacy* (Bollingen Series). Princeton, NJ: Princeton University Press.

Eliade, M. (1965). *The two and the one*. New York: Harper & Row.

Eliade, M., & Trask, W. (1954). *The myth of the eternal return*. Princeton, NJ: Princeton University Press, Bollingen Foundation.

Engel, G. I. (1977). The need for a new medical model: A challenge for biomedicine. *Science, 196*, 129-136.

Engler, J. (1986). Therapeutic aims in psychotherapy and meditation. In K. Wilber, J. Engler, & D. Brown D. (Eds.), *Transformations of consciousness*. Boston: Shambhala.

Epstein, M., & Lieff, J. (1986). Psychiatric Complications of Meditation Practice. In K. Wilber, J. Engler, & D. P. Brown (Eds.), *Transformations of Consciousness*. Boston, Shambhala,.

Epstein, S. S. (1998). *The politics of cancer: Revisited*. Fremont Center, NY: East Ridge Press.

Erickson, M. (1948/1980). *The Collected papers of Milton Erickson on Hypnosis* (IV). New York: Irvington.

Feinstein, D. (2004). *Energy psychology interactive* (Book and CD). Ashland OR: Innersource.

Feinstein, D. (2004b). *State of the art*, from module in CD of *Energy psychology interactive*. ibid. Ashland, OR: Innersource.

Feinstein, D., Eden, E., & Craig G. (2005). *The promise of energy psychology*. New York: Jeremy Tarcher.

Feinstein, D. (2006, March-May.). *Energy psychology in disaster relief. Shift: At the Frontiers of Consciousness*. The Institute of Noetic Sciences.

Feinstein D. & Eden D., (2006b). *Six pillars of energy medicine: Clinical strengths of a complementary paradigm*, from www.energymedicineprinciples.com, currently in journal review process.

Feinstein, D. (2006c). *Energy psychology in disaster relief: New Applications for an Age-Old Paradigm*, (Draft version submitted for Journal Publication, Private communication to author.)

Feng, A. (2003). *The five animals play Qigong*. Oakland, CA: The Taoist Center.

Fingarette, H. (1963). *The self in transformation*. New York: Harper & Row.

Fitzgerald, P. B. et al. (2003). Low field magnetic stimulation in the treatment of depression: A double blind, placebo controlled trial. *Archives of General Psychiatry, 60*, 1002-1008.

Fleming, T. (1996). *Reduce traumatic stress in minutes: The tapas acupressure technique (TAT) workbook*. Torrance, CA: Author.

Fleming, T. (1999). *You can heal now: The tapas acupressure technique (TAT)*. Redondo Beach, CA: TAT International.

Fox, R. E. (2006). Economics, politics, and psychological practice. *The National Psychologist. January/February*, 13.

Francis, B. K. (1993). *Opening the energy gates of your body*. Berkeley, CA: North Atlantic Books.

Francis, B. K., (1998). *The power of internal martial arts*. Berkeley, CA: North Atlantic.

Frankl, V. (1967). *Psychotherapy and existentialism: Selected papers in logotherapy*. New York: Simon and Schuster.

Frenier, C., & Hogan, L. S. (n.d.). *Engaging the imaginal realm: Doorway to collective wisdom*. Retrieved July 5, 2006, from www. collectivewisdominitiative.org papers/frenier_imaginal. htm#imaginal

Frese, E., Brown, M., & Norton, B. J. (1987). Clinical reliability of manual muscle testing. *Physical Therapy, 67*, 1072-1076.

Freud, S. (1923). *The ego and the id*. London: Hopgarthe Press.

Freud, S. (1933,1990). *New introductory lectures on psychoanalysis*. New York: Norton.

Freud, S. (1899, 1965). *The interpretation of dreams*. New York: Avon Books.

Gach, M. (1990). *Acupressure potent points*. New York: Bantam.

Gach, M. (2004). *Emotional Healing with Acupressure*. New York: Bantam.

Gach, M., & Marco, C. (1981). *Acu-yoga: Self help techniques to relieve tension*. New York: Japan Publications, Inc.

Gagne, D., & Toye, R. (1994). The effects of therapetuic touch and relaxation techniques in reducing anxiety. *Archives of Psychiatric Nursing, 8*(3), 183-189.

Gallo, F. P. (2000). *Energy diagnostic and treatment methods*. New York: Norton.

Gallo, F. P. (2002). *Energy psychology in psychotherapy: A comprehensive source book*. New York: W. W. Norton.

Gallo, F. P. (2004). Research in energy psychology. Retrieved from: www.energypsych.com/Content/readings-num7.htm

Garber, J., & Seligman, M. E. (1980). *Human helplessness: Theory and applications.* New York: Academic Press.

Garlinkle, M. S., et al. (1998, November 11). Yoga-based interventional for carpal tunnel syndrome. *Journal of the American Medical Association, 280*(18), 1601-1603.

Gatchel, R. J., & Blanchard, E. B. (1993, 1998). *Psychophysiological disorders: Research and clinical applications.* Washington, DC: American Psychiatric Association.

Gendlin, E. (1962). *Experiencing and the Creation of Meaning.* Toronto, Ontario: Free Press of Glencoe.

Gendlin, E. (1978). *Focusing.* New York: Bantam Books.

Gendlin, E. (1986). *Let your body interpret your dreams.* Wilmette, IL: Chiron Publications.

Gerber, R. (1996). *Vibrational medicine.* Santa Fe, NM: Bear & Co.

Goleman, D. (1988). *The meditative mind.* New York: J. P. Tarcher.

Goleman, D. (2003). *Destructive emotions.* New York: Bantam Books.

Goodheart, G. (1964). *Applied kinesiology.* Detroit, MI: Author.

Goodman, F. D. (1990). *Where spirits ride the wind: Trance journeys and other ecstatic experiences.* Indianapolis: IN: University Press.

Goodman, M. (1988, Winter). To Touch or Not to Touch. *Psychotherapy, 25*(4), 492-500.

Gordon, D. (1978). *Therapeutic metaphors.* Cupertino, CA: Meta Publications

Gore, B., (1995). *Ecstatic body postures.* Santa Fe, NM: Bear & Co.

Gorman, D. (2002, August 5). Why Tai Chi is the perfect exercise. *Time.*

Gorton, B. (1957). The physiology of hypnosis. *Journal of the American Society of Psychosomatic Dentistry, 4*(3), 86-103.

Grauds, C., & Childers, D. (2005). *The energy prescription: Giving yourself abundant vitality.* New York: Bantam Books.

Grauds, D. (1994). *Jungle Medicine.* San Rafael, CA: Center for Spirited Medicine.

Graves, R. (1955). *The Greek myths, I and II.* New York: Penguin.

Green, M. M. (2002). Energy applications in medical settings. In F. Gallo (Ed.), op. cit., 2002.

Gross, L., & Ratner, H. (2002). The use of hypnosis and EMDR combined with energy therapies in the treatment of phobias and dissociative, posttraumatic stress, and eating disorders. In F. Gallo (Ed.), op. cit., 2002.

Grosskurth, P. (1986). *Melanie Klein: Her world and her work.* New York: Alfred A. Knopf, Inc.

Grotstein, J. (1984). Forgery of the soul. In C. Nelson & M. Eigen (Eds.), *Evil, self, and culture.* New York: Human Sciences Press.

Gruen, W. (1972). A successful application of systematic self-relaxation and self-suggestions about postoperative reactions in a case of cardiac surgery. *International Journal of Clinical and Experimental Hypnosis, 20,* 141-151.

Guthrie, E. (1998). Somatization is essentially a normal process. *Advances in Mind-Body Medicine, 14,* 103-105.

Ha, F. (1995). *Stillness in movement; the practice of Tai Chi Chuan* (Video/DVD). San Francisco, CA: Vision Arts.

Ha, F., & Olsen E. (1996). *Yiquan and the nature of energy.* Berkeley, CA: Summerhouse Publications.

Haddock, C. K., Rowan, A. B., Andrasik, R., Wilson, P. G., Talcotte, G. W., & Stein, R. J. (1997). Home-based behavioral treatments for chronic benign headache: a meta-analysis of controlled trials, *Cephalalgia,* 17(2), 113-118.

Hadhazy, V. A., Ezzo, J., Creanerm, C., & Berman, B. M. (in press). Mind-body therapies for the treatment of fibromyalgia: A systematic review. *Journal of Rheumatology.*

Hahn, R. A., Teutsch, S.M., Rothenberg R. B., & Marks, J. S. (1990). Excess deaths for nine chronic diseases in the United States. 1986. *Journal of the American Medical Association,* 264(20), 2654-2659.

Hall, M. (1988). *The secret teachings of all ages.* Los Angeles: The Philosophical Research Society.

Hamer, R. (1997). *Scientific chart of the new medicine.* Ontario, Canada: Quintessanz.

Hammer, L. (1990). *Dragon rises, red bird flies: Psychology and Chinese medicine.* New York: Station Hill Press,

Harner, M. (1990). *The way of the shaman.* New York: Harper & Row.

Harris, R., Porges, S., Clemenson-Carpenter, M., & Vincenz, L. (1993). Hypnotic susceptibility, mood state, and cardiovascular reactivity. *American Journal of Clinical Hypnosis,* 36, 15-25.

Hartman, C. A., Manos, T. M., Winter, C., Hartman, D. M., Li, B., & Smith, J. C. (2000, December). Effects of T'ai Chi training on function and quality of life indicators in older adults with osteoarthritis. *Journal of the American Geriatrics Society,* 48(12), 1553-1559.

Hartung, J. G., & Galvin, M. D. (2002). Combining eye movement desensitization and reprocessing (EMDR) and energy therapies. In F. Gallo (Ed.), *Energy psychology in psychotherapy,* op. cit., 2002.

Heinerman J. (1988). *Encyclopedia of Fruits, Vegetables and Herbs.* West Nyack, NY: Parker Publishing Company.

Hernandez-Reif, Field T., & Thimas, E. (2001, April). *Journal of Bodywork and Movement Therapies,* 5(2), 120-12.

Heuscher, J. (1974). *Myths and fairytales: Their origin, meaning and usefulness. A psychiatric study of fairytales.* Springfield, IL: Charles C. Thomas.

Hilgard, E. (1965). *Hypnotic susceptibility.* New York: Harcourt.

Hilgard, E., & Hilgard, J. (1983). *Hypnosis in the relief of pain.* Los Altos, CA: William Kaufman, Inc.

Hillman, J. (1972). *The myth of analysis.* Evanston, IL: Northwestern.

Hillman, J. (1975). *Revisioning psychology.* New York: Harper and Row.

Hillman, J. (1976, 1979a). Peaks and vales. In J. Needleman (Ed.), (1976). *On the Way to Self Knowledge* New York: A. A. Knopf. Also in Hillman, J. (Ed.), (1979). *Puer papers* (pp. 54-72). Irving, TX: Spring Publications.

Hillman, J. (1979b). *The dream and the underworld.* New York: Harper & Row.

Hilts, P. (1995, Winter). Spiritual side finds favor in medical field. *Qi: Journal of Trad. Eastern Health & Fitness,* 5(4), 45. Reprinted from the *New York Times.*

Hinds, M. W., et al. (1985, March 15). Neonatal outcome in planned vs. unplanned out of hospital births in Kentucky. *Journal of the American Medical Asoication,* 253(11).

Hoffman, E. (1981). *The way of splendor: Jewish mysticism and modern psychology.* Boulder, CO: Shambhala.

Hover-Kramer, D. (1996). *Healing touch: A resource for healthcare professionals.* Albany, NY: Delmar.

Hover-Kramer, D., & Murphy M. (2006). *Creating right relationships.* Albany, NY: Delmar.

Hover-Kramer, D., & Shames, K. H. (1997). *Energetic approaches to emotional healing.* Albany, NY: Delmar.

Horner, A. (1990). *The primacy of structure: Psychotherapy of underlying character pathology.* Northvale, NJ: Jason Aronson, Inc.

Houston, J. (1992). *The hero and the goddess: The odyssey as mystery and initiation.* New York: Ballentine Books.

Huang, W. S. (1974). *Fundamentals of Tai Chi Chuan.* Hong Kong, China: South Sky Book Co.

Hue, K. K. S., et al. (2000). Acupunture modulates the limbic system and subcortical gray structures of the human brain. Evidence from MRI studies in normal subjects. *Human Brain Mapping, 9*(1), 13-25.

Huxley, A. (1969). *Brave new world.* New York: Perennial Library.

Huxley, A. (1970). *The perennial philosophy.* New York: Harper Colophon.

Idel, M. (1988). *The mystical experience in Abraham Abulafia.* Albany, NY: State University of New York Press.

Ingerman, S. (1991). *Soul retrieval: Mending the fragmented self.* New York: Harper Collins.

Iwao, M., Kajiyama, S., Mori, H., & Oogakio, K. K. (1999). Effects of Qigong walking on diabetic patients. *Journal of Alternative and Complementary Medicine, 5*(40), 353-358.

Jacob, R. G., Chesney, M. A., Williams, D. M., Ding, Y., & Shapiro, A. P. (1991). Relaxation therapy for hypertension. Design effects and treatment effects. *Annals of Behavioral Medicine, 13,* 9-17.

Jacobson, A., Hackett, T., Surman, O., & Silverberg, E. (1973). Raynaud's phenomenon: Treatment with hypnotic and operant technique. *Journal of the American Medical Association, 225,* 739-740.

Jacobson, E. (1964). *The self and object world.* New York: International University Press.

Jahnke, R. (2002a). *The healing promise of Qi,* New York: McGraw Hill.

Jahnke, R. OMD (2002b). *Getting Your Immune System in Shape. Boosting Immunity: Creating Wellness Naturally.* Novato, CA: New World Library.

Jansen, N., & Barron, J. (1988, Winter). Introduction and Overview: Psychologist use of Physical Interventions. *Psychotherapy, 25.*

Jerosch, J., & Wustner, P. (2002). *Effect of a sensorimotor training program on patients with subacromial pain syndrome.* In German *Unfallchirurg* JID–8502736, *105*(1), 36-43. Also see *Time,* 2002. Aug 5, *160*(6), 68.

Jetter, A. (1996, Sept.). The end of pain, *Hippocrates Magazine.*

Jin, P. (1944). Theoretical perspectives on a form of physical and cognitive exercise: Tai Chi. In Davidson, G. (Ed.). (1994). Lessons-Oceania. Also see Sandlund, E., & Torsten, N. (2000). The effects of Tai Chi Chuan relaxation and exercise on stress responses and well-being: An overview of research. *International Journal of Stress Management, 7*(2).

Jing, G. (1988). Observations on the curative effects of Qigong self-adjustment therapy in hypertension. *Proceedings of the First World Conference for Academic Exchange of Medical Qigong, Beijing, China*, 115-117.

Johnson, J. (2000). *Chinese medical Qigong therapy: A comprehensive clinical text*. Pacific Grove, CA: The International Institute of Medical Qigong.

Johnston, M., & Vogele, D. (1993). Benefits of psychological preparation for surgery: A meta-analysis. *Annals of Behavioral Medicine, 15*, 245-256.

Joint National Committee on Detection, Evaluation, and Treatment of High BP (5th Report). (1993). *Archives of Internal Medicine, 153*, 154-183.

Jonas, W. B., & Levin, J. S. (2000). *Essentials of complementary and alternative medicine*. New York: Lippencott, Williams, & Wilkins.

Jonte-Pace, D. (1998). The swami and the Rorschach. In R. Forman (Ed.), *The innate capacity: Mysticism, psychology and philosophy*. New York: Oxford University Press.

Judith, A. (1990). *Wheels of life: A user's guide to the chakra system*. St. Paul, MN: Llewelyn.

Jung, C. G. (1936). *Yoga and the West* (Collected Works, Vol. 11). Princeton, NJ: Princeton University Press.

Jung, C. G. (1953). *Two essays on analytical psychology*. New York: World Publishing Company.

Jung, C. G. (1955). *Mysterium coniunctionis* (Collected Works, Vol. 14). Princeton, NJ: Princeton University Press.

Jung, C. G. (1957-1970). *The collected works of C. G. Jung* (Vols. 1-19, Bollingen Series). Princeton, NJ: Princeton University Press.

Jung, C. G. (1960). *The structure and dynamics of the psyche* (Bollingen Series XX). Princeton, NJ: Princeton University Press.

Jung, C. G. (1974). *Dreams* (Bollingen Series). Princeton, NJ: Princeton University Press.

Jung, E. (1974). *Animus and anima*. Zurich, Switerland: Spring Publications.

Kabat-Zinn, J. (1990). *Full catastrophe living: Using the wisdom of your body and mind to face stress, pain, and illness*. New York: Dell.

Kabat-Zinn, J. (2003). Mindfulness-based interventions in context: Past, present and further. *Clinical Psychology: Science and Practice, 10*, 144-156.

Kalsched, D. (1996). *The inner world of trauma: Archetypal defenses of the personal spirit*. London: Routledge.

Kaptchuk, T. (1983). *The web that has no weaver: Understanding Chinese medicine*. New York: Congdon & Weed.

Karasek, R., Baker, D., Marxer, F., Ahibom, A., & Theorell, T. (1981). Job decision latitude, job demands, and cardiovascular disease: A prospective study of Swedish men. *American Journal of Public Health, 71*, 694-705.

Kasamatsu, A., & Hirai, T. (1969). An electroencephalographic study on the Zen Meditation (Zazen). *Psychologia, 12*, 205-225.

Katie, B. (2002). *Loving what is*. New York: Harmony Books.

Kelleman, S. (1985). *Emotional anatomy*. Berkeley, CA: Center Press.

Kerenyi, C. (1951/1979). *The gods of the greeks*. London: Thames and Hudson.

Kerenyi, C. (1976). *Dionysos: Archetypal image of indestructible life* (Bollingen Series LXV-2). Princeton, NJ: Princeton University Press.

Kilburg, R. (1988, Winter). Psychologists and physical interventions: Ethics, standard, and legal implications. *Psychotherapy, 25*(4), 487-491.

Kingsley, P. (1999). *In the dark places of wisdom*. Inverness, CA: Golden Sufi Center.

Kirsteins, A. E., Dietz, F., & Hwang, S. M. (1991). Evaluating the safety and potential use of a weight-bearing exercise, Tai-Chi Chuan, for rheumatoid arthritis patients. *American Journal of Physical Medicine & Rehabilitation, 70*(3), 136-141.

Kober, A., Scheck, T., Greher, M., Lieba, F., Fleischhackl, R., Fleischhackl, S., Randunsky, F., & Hoerauf, K. (2002). Pre-hospital analgesia with acupressure in victims of minor trauma: A prospective, randomized, double-blinded trial. *Anesthesia & Analgesia, 95*(3), 723-727.

Kohn, L. (1989). *Taoist meditation and longevity techniques*. Ann Arbor, MI: Michigan University.

Kohn, L. (2001). *Daoism and Chinese culture*. Cambridge, MA: Three Pines Press.

Kohut, H. (1977). *The restoration of the self*. New York: International Universities Press.

Kohut, H. (1971). *The analysis of the self*. New York: International Press.

Kornfield, J. (1993). Even the best meditators have old wounds to heal: Combining meditation and psychotherapy. In R. Walsh & G. Vaughn (Eds.), *Paths beyond ego* (pp. 67-68). New York: Tarcher/Putnam.

Korte, D., & Scaer, R. (1992). *A good birth: A safe birth: choosing and having the childbirth experience you want*. Cambridge, MA: Harvard Common Press.

Kostis, J., Rosen, R., Holzer, B., Randolph, C., Taska, L., & Miller, M. (1990). CNS side effects of centrally-active anti-hypertensive agents: A prospective placebo-controlled study of sleep, mood state, and cognitive and sexual function in hypertensive males. *Psychopharmacology, 102*, 163-170.

Kramer, P. D. (1997). *Listening to Prozac*. New York: Penguin.

Krippner, S., & Conti, B. A. (2006). The furrows of reality: Scientific and spiritual implications of the reenchanted cosmos. In E. Laszlo (Ed.), *Science and the reenactment of the cosmos: The rise of the integral vision of reality*, (pp. 95-100). Rochester, VT: Inner Traditions.

Krippner, S., & Powers, S. M. (1997). *Broken images, broken selves: Dissociative narratives in clinical practice*. Washington, DC: Brunner/Mazel.

Kristof, N. (1991, April 14). China sets example in healthcare. *New York Times, Ann Arbor News*, A-6.

Krysal, H. (1978). Trauma and affects. *Psychoanalytic Study of the Child, 22*, 81-116.

Kuang, A., Wang, C., Xu, D., & Qian, Y. (1991). Research on the anti-aging effect of Qigong, *Journal of Traditional Chinese Medicine, 11*(2), 153-158; and *11*(3), 224-227.

Kuhn, T. (1996). *The structure of scientific revolutions*. Chicago, IL: University of Chicago Press.

Lam, K. C. (1999). *Chi Kung: The way of healing, Chinese exercises for quieting the mind and strengthening the body*. New York: Broadway Books.

Lammers, W. (2002). Inner child, inner parent resolution: Meridian-based treatment focused on archaic states and introjects. In F. Gallo (Ed.), op. cit., 2002.

Larson, S. (1990). *The mythic imagination: your quest for meaning through personal mythology.* New York: Bantam Books.

Lascow, L. (1998). *Healing with love.* San Francisco: Harper and Row.

Laszarus, D. (2005, March 1). Sleep: Can't get enough of it. *San Francisco Chronicle,* C4-5.

Laszlo, E. (2006). (Ed.). *Science and the reenchantment of the cosmos: The rise of the integral vision of reality.* Rochester, VT: Inner Traditions.

Laszlo E. (2004). *Science and the Akashic field: An integral theory of everything.* Rochester, Vermont, Inner traditions.

Lean, M., & Hankey, C. (2004). Aspartame and its effects on health. *British Medical Journal, 329,* 755-756.

LeDoux, J. (1986). *Mind and Brain: Dialogues in cognitive neuroscience.* New York: Cambridge University Press.

LeDoux, J. (1992). Emotion and memory: Anatomical systems underlying indelible neural traces. In S. A. Christianson (Ed.), *Handbook of emotion and memory* (pp. 269-288). Hillsdale, NJ: Eribaum.

Lee, M. S., Hwa, J., Jeong, H., Kim, B. G., Ryu, H., Lee, H., Kim, J., Taeg, H., & Chung, H. (2002). Effects of Qi-training on heart rate variability *The American Journal of Chinese Medicine, 30*(4), 463–470.

Lehrer, P. M., & Woolfolk, R. L. (Eds.). (1993). *Principles and practice of stress management* (2nd ed.). New York: Guilford.

Lerner, M. (1994). *Choices in healing.* Cambridge, MA: MIT Press.

LeShan, L. (1974). *How to meditate.* New York: Bantam Books.

Levine, P. A. (1997). *Waking the tiger: Healing trauma.* Berkeley, CA: North Atlantic.

Leveno, K. J., Cunningham, F. G., Nelson, S., Roark, M., Williams, M. L., Guzick, D., et al. (1986). A prospective comparison of selective and universal electronic fetal monitoring in 34,995 pregnancies. *New England Journal of Medicine, 315*(10). In J. Robbins, 1986, op. cit., p. 48.

Levy, B., et al. (1971, January). Reducing neonatal mortality rates with nurse-midwives. *American Journal of Obstetrics and Gynecology, 109.*

Liboff, A.R. (2004). Toward an electromagnetic paradigm for biology and medicine. *Journal of Alternative and Complimentary Medicine, 10*(1) 41-47.

Linden, W., & Chambers, L. (1994). Clinical effectiveness of non-drug treatment for hypertension: A meta-analysis. *Annals of Behavioral Medicine, 16,* 35-45.

Linden, W., Stossel, C., & Maurice, J. (1996). Psychosocial interventions for patients with coronary artery disease. *Archives of Internal Medicine, 156,* 745-752.

Lipton, F. (2005). *The biology of belief.* Santa Rosa, CA: Elite Books.

Lipton, F. (2006, May 4). From keynote address at Association for Comprehensive Energy Psychology Conference. Santa Clara, CA.

Little, P., Girling, G., Hasler, A., & Trafford, A. (1991). A controlled trial of low sodium, low fat, high fiber diet in treated hypertensive patients: Effect on anti-hypertensive drug requirement in clinical practice. *Journal of Human Hypertension, 5,* 175-181.

Lorig, K., Chastain, R., et al. (1989). Development and evaluation of a scale to measure perceived self-efficacy in people with arthritis. *Arthritis and Rheumatism, 32,* 37-44.

Lorig, K., Laurin, J., Gines, G. E. (1984). Arthritis self-management. A five year history of a patient education program. *Nursing Clinics of North America, 19*(4), 637-645.

Lorig, K., et al. (1993). Evidence suggesting that health education for self-management in patents with chronic arthritis has sustained health benefits while reducing health care costs. *Arthritis and Rheumatism, 36*(4), 430-53.

Lorish, C. D., Abraham, N., et al. (1991). Disease and psychosocial factors related to physical functioning in rheumatoid arthritis. *Journal of Rheumatology, 18,* 1150-1157.

Lowen, A. (1971). *The language of the body.* New York: Macmillan Books.

Lowen, A. (1975). *Bioenergetics.* New York: Penguin Books.

Luk, C. (1972). *The secrets of Chinese meditation.* New York: Samuel Weiser.

Luk, C. (1977). *Taoist yoga: Alchemy and immortality.* New York: Samuel Weiser.

Lynch, J. (1977). *The broken heart: Medical consequences of loneliness.* New York: Basic.

Lynn, S., & Rhue, J. (Eds.). (1991). *Theories of hypnosis: Current models and perspectives.* New York: Guilford.

Mahler, M. (1952). On child psychosis and schizophrenia. *Psychoanalytic study of the child, 7,* 286-305.

Mahler, M., Pine, F., & Bergman, S. (1975). *The psychological birth of the human infant.* New York: Basic Books.

Manga report: Executive summary. (1994, July). *Townsend letter for doctors* (p. 814).

Mannerkorpi, K. (2005, March). Exercise in fibromyalgia. *Current Opinions in Rheumatology, 17*(2), 190-194. Related articles, links.

Mannerkorpi, K., Arndorw, M. (2004, November). Efficacy and feasibility of a combination of body awareness therapy and Qigong in patients with fibromyalgia: A pilot study. *Journal Rehabilitation Medicine, 36*(6), 279-81.

Matthews, J., & Matthews, C. (1986). *The western way: A practical guide to the western mystery tradition. Volume II: The hermetic tradtion.* London: Arkana Paperbacks.

Mayer, M. H. (1977). *A holistic language of meaning and identity: Astrological metaphor as a language of personality in psychotherapy.* Doctoral dissertation. San Francisco: Saybrook Institute.

Mayer, M. H. (1982). The mythic journey process. *The Focusing Folio, 2*(2).

Mayer, M. H. (1984). *The mystery of personal identity.* San Diego, CA: ACS Publications.

Mayer, M. H. (1993). *Trials of the heart.* Berkeley, CA: Celestial Arts.

Mayer, M. H. (1996). Qigong and behavioral medicine: An integrated approach to chronic pain. Qi: *The Journal of Eastern Health and Fitness, 6*(4), 20-31.

Mayer, M. H. (1997a). *Psychotherapy and Qigong: Partners in healing anxiety.* Berkeley, CA: The Berkeley Psychotherapy & Healing Center.

Mayer, M. H. (1997b). Combining behavioral healthcare and Qigong with one chronic hypertensive adult. *Mt. Diablo Hospital-Health Medicine Forum.* Unpublished study. (Video available from Health Medicine Forum, Walnut Creek, CA)

Mayer, M. H. (1999). Qigong and hypertension: A critique of research. *Journal of Alternative and Complementary Medicine, 5*(4), 371-382. (Peer-reviewed)

Mayer, M. H. (2000). *Bodymind healing Qigong* (DVD). Orinda, CA: Bodymind Healing Center.

Mayer, M. H. (2001a). *Find your hidden reservoir of healing energy: A guided meditation on cancer* (Audio cassette). Orinda, CA: Bodymind Healing Publications.

Mayer, M. H. (2001b). *Find your hidden reservoir of healing energy: A guided meditation on chronic disease* (Audio cassette). Orinda, CA: Bodymind Healing Publications.

Mayer, M. H. (2003). Qigong clinical studies. In W. B. Jonas (Ed.), *Healing, intention, and energy medicine* (pp. 121-137). England: Churchill Livingston. (Peer-reviewed)

Mayer, M. H. (2004a). *Qigong: Ancient path to modern health* (DVD of keynote address to National Qigong Association). Orinda, CA: Bodymind Healing Publications.

Mayer, M. H. (2004b). *Secrets to living younger longer: The self-healing path of Qigong, standing meditation and Tai Chi.* Orinda, CA: Bodymind Healing Publications.

McClare, C. W. F. (1974). Resonance in Bioenergetics. *Annals of the New York Academy of Sciences, 227,* 74-97.

McDougall, W. (1911). *Body and Mind.* New York: Beacon Press.

McGinnis, J. M., & Foege, W. H. (1993). Actual causes of death in the United States. *Journal of the American Medical Association, 287*(20), 2711-2712.

McGee, D. & Chow, E., (1994). *Qigong: Miracle healing in China.* Coure d Alene, ID: Medipress.

McTaggart, L. (2003). *The field.* New York: Harper.

Meier, C. A. (1967). *Ancient incubation and modern psychotherapy.* Evanston, IL: Northwestern University Press.

Merck manual of medical information (Home ed.). (1997). Whitehouse Station, NJ: Merck Research Laboratories.

Meyer, T. J., & Mark, M. M. (1995). Effects of psychosocial interventions with adult cancer patients: A meta-analysis of randomized experiments. *Health Psychology, 14,* 101-108.

Michaud, G., McGlowan, J. L., van der Jagt, R., Wells, G., & Tugwell, P. (1998). Are therapeutic decisions supported by evidence from health care research? *Archives of Internal Medicine, 158*(15), 1665-1668.

Miller, J., Fletcher, K., Kabbat-Zinn, J. (1995). Three year follow up and clinical implications of a mindfulness-base intervention in the treatment of anxiety disorders. *General Hospital Psychiatry, 17,* 192-200.

Mindell, A. (1985). *Working with the dreaming body.* Boston: Routledge.

Mindell, A. (2000). *Quantum mind.* Portland, OR: Lao Tse.

Ming, Y. J. (1986). *Advanced yang style Tai Chi Chuan.* Jamaica Plains, NY: Yang's Martial Arts Association.

Minor, M. A. (1991). Physical activity and management of arthritis. *Annals of Behavioral Medicine, 13,* 117-124.

Mollon, P. (2001). *Releasing the self: The healing legacy of Heinz Kohut.* London: Whurr Publishers.

Moncrieff, J., & Kirsch, I. (2005, Jul 16). Efficacy of antidepressants in adults. *British Medical Journal, 331,* 155-157.

Monte, D. A., Sinnott, J., Marchese, M., Kunkel, E. J., & Greenson, J. (1999). Muscle test comparisons of congruent and incongruent self-referential statements. *Perceptual & Motor Skills, 88,* 1019-1028.

Moore, T. (1992). *Care of the soul: A guide for cultivating depth and sacredness in everyday life.* New York: Harper Collins.

Morin, C. M., Culbert, J. P., & Schwartz, S. M. (1999). Non-pharmacological interventions for insomnia. American Academy of Sleep Medicine review. *Sleep, 22*(8), 1134-1156.

Morin, C. M., Mimeault, V., Gagne, A. (1999). Non-pharmacological treatment of late-life insomnia. *Journal of Psychomatic Research, 46*(2), 103-116.

Morris, L. (2000, April). Tai Chi: Relieving a painful shoulder injury. *Positive Health, 51,* 21-23.

Morrison, A. L. (1999). *The anti-depression sourcebook.* New York: Doubleday.

Murphy, M. (1992). *The future of the body.* Los Angeles: Tarcher.

Murphy M., & Donovan S. (1997). *The physical and psychological affects of meditation* (2nd Ed.). Petaluma, CA: Institute of Noetic Sciences.

National Institute of Health Technology Panel (1996). Integration of behavioral and relaxation approaches into the treatment of chronic pain and insomnia. In *Journal of the American Medical Association, 276*(4), 313-318.

Needham, J. (1956). Science and civilization in China (Vol. 2). England: Cambridge University Press.

Nemiah, J. C. (1991). Dissociation, conversion and somatization. In A. Tasman & A. Goldfinger (Eds.), *American Psychiatric Press Review of Psychiatry* (Vol. 10, pp. 248-260). Washington, DC: American Psychiatric Press.

Nerem, R., Levesqu, M. J., Cornhill, J. F. (1980, June 27). Social environment as a factor in diet-induced artheriosclerosis. *Science, 208,* 1475-1476.

Neumann, E. (1954). *The origins and history of consciousness* (Bollingen Series). Princeton, NJ: Princeton University Press.

Neumann, E. (1956). *Amor and psyche.* Princeton, NJ: Princeton University Press.

Nims, L. P. (1998). *Be set free fast. Training manual.* Orange, CA: Author.

Noble, K. D. (1987). Psychological health and the experience of transcendence. *The Counseling Psychologist, 15,* 601-14.

Nordenstrom, B. E. (1983). *Biologically closed circuits: Experimental and theoretical evidence for an additional circulatory system.* Stockholm, Sweden: Nordic Medical Publications.

Nurse Healers-Professional Associates, Inc. (2000). *Compendium of therapeutic touch research to date.* Reson, VA. Retrieved from www.therapteutic touch.org (see here the Moreland, 1997 study).

O'brien, J. (2004). *Nei jia quan: Internal martial arts.* Berkeley, CA: North Atlantic Books.

O'Connell, P. J., Wang, X., Leon-Ponte, M., Griffiths, C., Pingle, S. C., Gerard, P., & Ahern, G. P. (2006, February). A novel form of immune signaling revealed by transmission of the inflammatory mediator serotonin between dendritic cells and T cells. *Blood, 107*(3), 1010-1017.

Odanjnyk, W. V. (1988). Gathering the light: A Jungian exploration of meditation. *Quadrant, 21,* 35-51.

Ornish, D., et al. (1993). Can lifestyle changes reverse coronary disease? *Lancet, 336,* 129-133.

Oschman, J. (2000). Energy medicine: The scientific basis. New York: Churchill Livingston.

Oxford English dictionary (Compact ed.). (1979). London: Oxford University Press.

Paske, B. (1982). *Rape and ritual.* Toronto, CA: Inner City Books.

Peat, F. D. (1997). *Infinite potential: The life and times of David Bohm.* New York: Addison-Wesley.

Pedraza, R. (1977). *Hermes and his children.* Zurich, Switzerland: Spring Publications.

Pelletier, K. R. (2000). *The best alternative medicine, What works? What does not?* New York: Simon & Schuster.

Pelletier, K.R. (2003, March 3). Conventional and integraive medicine — evidence based? Sorting fact from fiction. *Focus on Alternative and Complementary Therapies, 8*(1).

Pelletier, K. R. (2004). Mind-body medicine in ambulatory care: An evidence-based assessment. *Journal of Ambulatory Care Management, 27*(1), 25-42.

Pennebaker, J. W. (1993). Putting stress into words. Health, linguistic and therapeutic implications. *Behavior Research and Therapy, 31*(6), 539-548.

Perlman, O. L., & McCann, L. O. (1992). Constructivist self-develpment theory. In D. K. Sakheim & S. K. Devine (Eds.), *Out of darkness.* New York: Lexington.

Perot, C., Meldener, R., & Gouble, F. (1991). Objective measurement of proprioceptive technique consequences on muscular maximal voluntary contraction during manual muscle testing. *Agressologie, 32*(10), 471-474.

Pert, C. B. (1997). *Molecules of emotion: The science behind mind-body medicine.* New York: Touchstone.

Pert, C. B. (2004). *Forward to energy psychology interactive.* Ashland, OR : Inner Source.

Pollare, T., Lithell, H., Selinus, I., & Berne, C. (1989) A comparison of the effects of hydrochlorothiazide and captopril on glucose and lipid metabolism in patients with hypertension. *British Medical Journal, 321,* 868-873.

Pollare, T., Uthd, H., Sdinus, I., & Berne, C. (1989). Sensitivity to insulin during treatment with atenolol and metoprolol a randomized double blind study of effects on carbohydrate and lipoprotein metabolism in hypertensive patients. *New England Journal of Medicine, 321,* 868-873.

Popp, F. A., Li K., & Gu, Q. (Eds.). (1992). *Recent Advances in Biophoton Research.* Singapore: World Scientific

Propst, L. R. (1988). *Psychotherapy in a religious framework: Spirituality in the emotional healing process.* New York: Human Sciences Press.

Province, M., Hadley, E., Hornbrook, Lipsitz, A., Miller, P., Mulrow, C., Ory, M., Sattin, R.,Tinetti, & Wolf, S. (1995, May 3). The effects of exercise on falls in elderly patients: A pre-planned meta-analysis of the FICSIT trails. *Journal of the American Medical Association (JAMA), 272*(17), 1341-1347.

Pulos, L. (2002). Integrating energy psychology and hypnosis, In F. Gallo (Ed.), *Energy psychology in psychotherapy*, op.cit., pp. 167-178.

Quinn, J., & Stelkaudal, A. J. (1993). Psychoimmunologic effects of therapeutic touch on practitioners and recently bereaved recipients. *Advances in Nursing Science, 12*(4), 13-26.

Rael, L., & Rudhyar, D. (1980). *Astrological aspects.* New York: ASI Publishers.

Rama, S., Ballentine, T., & Weinstock, A. (1976). *Yoga and psychotherapy: the evolution of consciousnss.* Honesdale, PA: Himalayan Institute.

Rampton, S., & Stauber, J. (2001). *Trust us we're experts: How industry manipulates science and gambles with your future.* New York: Tarcher.

Rauch, S. L., van der Kolk, B. A., Fisler, R. E., et. al. (1996). A symptom provocation study of posttraumatic stress disorder using positron emission tomography and script-driven imagery. *Archives of General Psychiatry, 53*, 380-387.

Reich, W. (1970). *Character analysis.* New York: Farrar, Straus, & Giroux.

Rein, G. (1992). *Quantum biology.* Northpoint, NY: Quantum Biology Research Labs.

Reinhardt, E. (2004). *Journal of the American Medical Association, 202*(10), 1227-1230. From handout at professional seminar by Dr. Ken Pelletier, "Stress-Free for Good," slide on International Medical Expenditures.

Requena, Y. (1989). *Character and health: the relationship of acupuncture and psychology.* Brookline, MA: Paradigm Pub.

Reuther, I., & Laderidge, D. (1998). Qigong Yangsheng as a complementary therapy in the management of asthma. *The Journal of Alternative and Complementary Medicine, 4*(2), 173-183.

Rinpoche, S. (1993). *The Tibetan book of living and dying.* San Francisco: Harper Collins.

Robbins, J. (1996). *Reclaiming our Health: Exploding the medical myth and embracing the source of true healing.* Tiburon, CA: H. J. Kramer.

Roberts, S. J. (1994). Somatization in primary care: the common presentation of psychosocial problems through physical complaints. *Nurse-Practitioner, 19*(47), 50-56.

Rohan, M., et al. (2004). Low field magnetic stimulation in bipolar depression using an MRI based stimulator. *American Journal of Psychiatry, 161*, 93-98.

Rosch, E. (1999). Is wisdom in the brain? *Psychological Science. 10*, 222-224.

Rosen, M. (1989). *The cesarean myth.* New York: Viking.

Rosen, S. (1982). *My voice will go with you: The teaching tales of Milton H. Erickson.* New York: W. W. Norton.

Rossi, E. (1986). *The psychobiology of mind-body healing: New concepts of therapeutic hypnosis.* New York: Norton.

Rossi, E. (1990). Mind-molecular communication: Can we really talk to our genes? *Hypnosis, 17*(1), 3-14.

Rossi, E. (2002). *The psychobiology of gene expression: Neuroscience and neurogenesis in hypnosis and the healing arts.* New York: W. W. Norton & Co.

Rossi, E., & Cheek, D. (1988). *Mind-body therapy: Methods of ideodynamic healing in hypnosis.* New York: Norton.

Rowe, J. (2005, July). The effects of EFT on long term psychological symptoms. *Counseling and Psychology Journal, 2*(3), 104-111.

Rubik, B. (2002). The biofield hypothesis: It's biophysical basis and its role in medicine. *Journal of Alternative and Complementary Medicine, 8,* 703-717.

Ruden, R. A. (2005, Summer). Why tapping works: Speculations from the observable brain. *The Energy Field, 6*(2), 1-4.

Rudhyar D. (1970). *The astrology of personality.* New York: Doubleday.

Rudhyar D. (1975). *From humanistic to transpersonal astrology.* Palo Alto, CA: The Seed Center.

Salt, W. B., & Neimark, N. F. (2002). *Irritable Bowel syndrome and the mind-body-spirit connection.* Columbus, OH: Parkview.

Sancier, K. (1996a). Anti-aging benefits of Qigong. *Journal of the International Society of Life Information Science, 11*(1), 12-21.

Sancier, K. (1996b). Medical applications of Qigong. *Alternative Therapies, 2*(1), 40-46.

Sancier, K. M., & Holman, D. (2004). Multifaceted health benefits of medical Qigong. *Journal of Alternative and Complementary Medicine, 10*(1), 163-166.

Sapolsky, R. M. (1998). *Why zebras don't get ulcers: An updated guide to stress, stress-related diseases, and coping.* New York: W. H. Freeman & Company.

Schafer, E. (1977). *Pacing the void: T'ang approaches to the stars.* Berkeley, CA: University of California Press.

Schmitz-Hubsch, et al. (2005, October 14). Qigong exercise helps reduce the motor and non-motor symptoms of Parkinson's disease: A randomized controlled pilot study. *Movement Disorders.*

Schneider, R. H., Alexander, C. N., et al. (2005). A randomized controlled trial of stress reduction in African American treated for hypertension for over one year. *American Journal of Hypertension, 18,* 8-98.

Schneider, R. H., Staggers, F., Alexander, C. N., Sheppard, W., Rainforth, M., Kondwani, D., Smith, S., & King, C. G. (1995). A randomized controlled trial of stress reduction for hypertension in older African Americans. *American Heart Association, Hypertension, 226,* 820-827.

Scholem, G. (1969). *Jewish mysticism.* Jerusalem: Schocken Publishing House.

Schoninger, B. (2001). *Thought field therapy in the treatment of speaking anxiety.* Unpublished doctoral dissertation. Cincinnati, OH: Union Institute.

Schore, A. N. (2003). *Affect regulation and the repair of the self.* New York: W. W. Norton & Company

Schram, S. (2002, October). Tefillin: An ancient acupuncture point prescription for mental clarity. *Journal of Chinese Medicine, 70,* 5-8

Schure, E. (1977). *The great initiates.* New York: Steiner Books.

Seem, M. (1989). *Bodymind energetics: Toward a dynamic model of health.* Rochester, VT: Healing Arts Press.

Segall, S. G. (2003). *Encountering Buddhism: Western psychology and Buddhist teachings.* New York: SUNY Press.

Selfridge, N., & Peterson, F. (2001). *Freedom from Fibromyalgia: The five week program proven to conquer pain.* New York: Three Rivers Press.

Selye, H. (1975). Confusion and controversy in the stress field. *Journal of Human Stress, 1,* 37.

Sha, Z. G. (2003). *Power Healing: Four Keys to energizing your body, mind, and spirit.* San Francisco: Harper Collins

Shapiro, D., & Astin, J. (1998). *Control therapy.* New York: Wiley.

Shapiro, D. H., & Giber, D. (1978). Meditation and psychotherapeutic effects: Self-regulation strategy and altered states of consciousness. *Archives General Psychiatry, 35,* 294-302.

Shapiro, F. (1995). *Eye movement desensitization and reprocessing.* New York: Guilford Press.

Shapiro, R. (1997). *Minyan: Ten principles for living a life of integrity.* New York: Random House

Shearer, A. (1982). *The yoga sutras of patanjali.* New York: Random House.

Sheldrake, R. (1988). *The presence of the past: Morphic resonance and the habits of nature.*

Shepard, A. (2005). *Monkey: A superhero tale from China.* Skyhook Press.

Silver, L., & Wolfe, S. (1992). Unnecessary sections: How to cure a national epidemic. *Public Citizen Health Research Group,* Washington, DC. Quoted in D. Koret, *A good birth, a safe birth: Choosing and having the childbirth experience you want* (p. 135). Cambridge, MA: Harvard Common Press.

Smith, R. (1991). Where is the wisdom? The poverty of medical evidence. *British Medical Journal, 303,* 798-799.

Smith, R. W. (1972). Pa- kua: Chinese boxing for fitness and self-defense. New York: Harper & Row.

Smith, R.W. (2003). *Hsing-I: Chinese mind-body boxing.* Berkeley, CA: North Atlantic Books.

Smith, T. W., Peck, et al. (1988). Cognitive distortion in rheumatoid arthritis: Relationship to depression and disability. *Journal of Consulting and Clinical Psychology, 56,* 412-516.

Snell, B. (1969). *The discovery of mind.* New York: Harper & Row.

Sparks, T. (1993). *The wide open door: The twelve steps, spiritual tradition and the new psychology.* Center City, MI: Hazeldon.

Sperry, L. (2001). *Spirituality in clinical practice: Incorporating the spiritual dimension in psychotherapy.* Philidelphia, PA: Brunner-Routledge.

Starfield, B. (2000). Is U.S. health really the best in the world? *Journal of the American Medical Association, 209*(20), 2651-2662.

Stein, M. (1982). *Jungian analysis.* London: Open Court.

Stein, M., Wallston, K. A., et al. (1986). Correlates of a clinical classification schema for the arthritis helpless subscale. *Arthritis and Rheumatism, 31,* 876-881.

Steiner, R. (1973). *Mystery knowledge and mystery centres.* London: Rudolf Steiner Press.

Sternbach, R. (1986). Survey of pain in the United States: The Nuprim pain report. *The Clinical Journal of Pain, 1,* 49-53.

Stolorow, R. D., Brandchaft, F., & Atwood, G. E. (1987). *Psychoanalytic treatment: An intersubjective approach.* Hillsdale, NJ: The Analytic Press.

Stone, M. (1976). *When God was a woman.* New York: Harcourt, Brace, Jonovich.

Storm, H. (1972). *Seven arrows.* New York: Harper& Row.

Sturgis, L., & Coe, W. (1990). Psychological responsiveness during hypnosis. *International Journal of Clinical Hypnosis,* 38(3), 196-207.

Suares, C. (1973). *The cipher of genesis.* Berkeley, CA: Shambhala.

Suares, C. (1976). *The sepher yetsira.* Boulder, CO: Shambhala.

Swingel, P. (2000, May). *Effects of Emotional Freedom Techniques(EFT) method on seizure frequency in children diagnosed with epilepsy.* Paper presented at the annual meeting of the Association for Comprehensive Energy Psychology, Las Vegas, NV.

Swingle, P., Pulos, L., & Swingle, M. (2000). Neorophysiological correlates of successful EFT treatment of posttraumatic stress disorder. Manuscript submitted for publications. In F. Gallo (Ed.), 2002, op. cit., p. 172.

Taggart, H. M., Arslanian, C. L., Bae, S., & Singh, K. (2003, September-October). Effects of Tai Chi exercise on fibromyalgia symptoms and health-related quality of life. *Orthopedic Nursing,* 22(5), 353-60.

Tart, C. (1968). *Altered states of consciousness.* New York: John Wiley & Sons.

Taylor, R. (1988). *The Confucian way of contemplation.* University of South Carolina Press.

Taylor, S. (1991). *Health psychology* (2nd ed.). New York: Mcgraw Hill.

Teeguarden, I. M. (1978). *Acupressure way of health: Jin hin do.* Tokyo: Japan Publications.

Teeguarden, I. M. (1989). *The Joy of Feeling: Bodymind acupressure.* Tokyo: Japan Publications.

Tiller, W. A. (1997). *Science and human transformation: Subtle energies, intentionality, and consciousness.* Walnut Creek, CA: Pavior.

Tloczynski, J., & Tantriells, M. (1998). A comparison of the effects of Zen breath meditation on college adjustment. *Psychologia,* 41, 32-43.

Tomio, N. (1994). *The Bodhisattva warriors.* New York: Samuel Weiser.

Travis, F., Arenander, A., & Dubios, D. (2002). Psychological and physiological characteristics of a proposed object referral/self referral continuum of self awareness. *Consciousness and Cognition.* 13, 401- 420.

Trieschmann, R. B. (1999). Energy medicine for long-term disabilities. *Disability and Rehabilitation,* 21(5), 269-276.

Tsang, H.W., Mok, Y.T., Yeung A., Chan S. Y. (2003).The effect of Qigong on general and psychosocial health of elderly with chronic physical illnesses: A randomized clinical trial. *International Journal of Geriatric Psychiatry.* 18, (5), May, 441-449.

Tsang, H.W., Cheung, L., Lak D.C. (2002).Qigong as a psychosocial intervention for depressed elderly with chronic physical illnesses. *International Journal of Geriatric Psychiatry.* 17 (12), December, 1146-1154.

van der Kolk, B. A. (1987). *Psychological trauma.* Washington, DC: American Psychiatric Press.

van der Kolk, B. A. (1994). The body keeps the score: Memory and the evolving psychobiology of posttraumatic stress. *Harvard Review of Psychiatry,* 1, 253-265.

van der Kolk, B. A. (2002). Beyond the talking cure: Somatic experience and subcortical imprints in the treatment of trauma. In F. Shapiro (Ed.), *EMDR, Promises for a Paradigm Shift*, APA Press.

van der Kolk, B. A., & Fisler, R. E. (1995). Dissociation and the fragmentary nature of traumatic memories: Overview and exploratory study. *Journal of Traumatic Stress, 8*, 505-525.

van der Kolk, B. A., et. al. (1996). *Traumatic stress: The effects of overwhelming experience on mind, body, and society*. New York: Guilford Press.

van Deusen, J., & Harlowe, D. (1987). The efficacy of the ROM Dance Program for adults with rheumatoid arthritis. *American Journal of Occupational Therapy, 41*(2), 90-95.

van Tulder, M. J. W., Ostelo, R., Vlaeyen, J. W., Linton, S. J., Morley, S. J., & Assendelft, W. J. (2000). Behavioral treatment for chronic low back pain: A systematic review with the framework of the Cochrane back review group. *Spine, 25*(20), 2688-2699.

Wade, J. F. (1990). *The effects of the Callahan phobia treatment techniques on self concept*. Unpublished doctoral dissertation. San Diego, CA: The Professional School of Psychological Studies.

Wagner, M. (1993, Fall). An epidemic of unnecessary cesareans, *Mothering, Fall,* 72.

Wain, H., Amen, D., & Oetgen, W. (1984). Hypnotic intervention in cardiac arrhythmias. *The American Journal of Clinical Hypnosis, 27*(1), 70-75.

Waite, W. L., & Holder, M. D. (2003, Spring/Summer). Assessment of the Emotional Freedom Technique: An alternative treatment for fear. *The Scientific Review of Mental Health Practice, 2*(1), 20-26.

Wallas, L. W. (1985). *Stories for the third ear*. New York: W. W. Norton.

Walsh, R. (1999). *Essential spirituality: The seven central practices*. New York: Wiley.

Walsh, R., & Shapiro, S. (2006, April). The meeting of meditative disciplines and Western psychology. *American Psychologist, 61*(3), 227-239.

Walsh, R., & Vaughn, F. (1993). *Paths beyond ego*. Los Angeles: Jeremy Tarcher.

Wang, C., Xu, D., Qian, Y., Shi, W., Bao, Y., & Kuang, A. (1995). The beneficial effects of Qigong on the ventricular function and microcirculation of deficiency in heart energy hypertensive patients. *Chinese Journal of Internal Medicine, 1*, 21-23.

Warnke, G. (1987). *Gadamer: Hermeneutics, tradition and reason (key contemporary thinkers)*. Stanford, CA: Stanford University Press.

Watkins, M. (1984). *Waking dreams*. New York: Gordon & Breach.

Watts, A. W. (1961).*Psychotherapy east and west*. New York: Ballentine.

Weil, A. (1995). *Spontaneous healing*. New York: Alfred Knopf.

Weil, A. (2004, September). *Self-healing newsletter*.

Weinstein, E., & Au, P. (1991). Use of hypnosis before and after angioplasty. *American Journal of Clinical Hypnosis, 34*, 29-37.

Weintraub, M. I. (2001). Qigong and neurologic illness. *Alternative and Complementary Treatments in Neurologic Illness, 15*, 197-220. As reported on www.Qigonginstitute.org

Weizel, M. S., et al. (1998). Courses involving complementary and alternative medicine at U.S. medical schools. *Journal of the American Medical Association, 280*, 784-787.

Wells, S., Polglase, K., Andrews, H., Carrington, P., & Baker, A. H. (2003). Evaluation of a meridian-based intervention, Emotional Freedom Techniques (EFT) for reducing specific phobias of small animals. *Journal of Clinical Psychology, 59*(9), 943-966.

Wheeler, M. S. (2002). Integrating past and present: The early recollection techniques. In F. Gallo (Ed.), 2002, op. cit.

Wickramasekera, I. (1998). Secrets kept for the mind but not the body of behavior: The unsolved problems of identifying and treating somatization and psycho-physiological disease.*Advances, 14*, 81-132.

Wilbur, K. (1980). *The atman project*. Wheaton, IL: Quest Books.

Wilbur, K. (2000). *The eye of the spirit: An integral vision for a world gong slightly mad* (Vol. 7). *The collected works of Ken Wilber*. Boston: Shambhala.

Wilbur, K., Engler, J., & Brown, D. P. (Eds.). (1986). *Transformations of consciousness. Conventional and contemplative perspectives on development*. Boston: Shambhala/New Science Library.

Wilhelm, R. (1931, 1963). *The secret of the golden flower*. New York: Harcourt, Brace, & Jovovich.

Wirth, D. (1991). The effect of non–contact therapeutic touch on the healing rate of full thickness dermal wound. *Journal of Subtle Energies, I*(1), 1-20.

Wiseman, R., & Schliz, N. (1997). Experimenter effects and remote detection of staring. *The Journal of Parapsychology, 61*,201-207.

Wolf, E. S. (1988). *Treating the self*. New York: Guilford Press.

Wolf, S. L., Coogler, C., & Xu, T. (1997). Exploring the basis for Tai Chi Chuan as a therapeutic exercise approach. *Archives Physical Medical Rehabilitation, 78*, 886-890.

Wollam, G., & Hall, W. (Eds.). (1988). *Hypertension management: clinical practice and therapeutic dilemmas*. Chicago: Yearbook Publishers. Quoted by R. Rosen, E. Brondolo, & J. Kostis (1998). Non-pharmacological treatment of essential hypertension: Research and clinical applications. In R. Gatchel, & E. Blanchard (Eds.), *Psychophysiological disorders: Research and clinical applications* (pp. 63-100). Washington, DC: American Psychological Association.

Wolpe, J. (1958). *Psychotherapy by reciprocal inhibition*. Stanford, CA: Stanford University Press.

Wu, R., & Liu, Z. (1993). Study of Qigong on hypertension and reduction of hypotension. *Proceedings of Second World Conference for Academic Exchange of Medical Qigong*, Beijing, China, 125. From Sancier, Qigong Computerized Database, op. cit., record # 7970, full article provided by author translated into English.

Wu, W. H., Bandilla, E., Ciccone, D. S., Yang, J., Cheng, S., Carner, N., Wu, Y., & Shen, R. (1999, January). Effects of Qigong on late-stage complex regional pain syndrome. *Alternative Therapies, 5*(1). Peer reviewed.

Wuthnow, R. (1978). Peak experiences: Some empirical tests. *Journal of Humanistic Psychology, 18*(3), 59-75.

Yanovski, A. (1962). The feasibility of alteration of cardiovascular manifestations in hypnosis. *The American Journal of Clinical Hypnosis, 5*, 8-16.

References

Yapko, M. (1997). *Breaking the patterns of depression.* New York: Doubleday.

Young, L. D. (1993). Rheumatoid arthritis. In Gatchel (Ed.), *Psychophysiological disorders.* Washington, DC: American Psychological Association.

Zamara, J. W., Schneider, R. H., et al. (1996). Usefulness of the transcendental meditation program in the treatment of patients with coronary artery disease. *American Journal of Cardiology, 78,* 77-80.

Zautra, A. J., & Manne, S. E. (1992). Coping with rheumatoid arthritis: A review of a decade of research. *Annals of Behavioral Medicine, 14,* 31-39.

Zeig, J. K. (1985). *Ericksonian psychotherapy:* (Vol. I and II): *Clinical Applications.* New York: Brunner Mazel.

Zur, O. (2005, January/February). *The National Psychologist.*

INDEX

A

Activating the River of Life through Microcosmic Orbit Breathing 91–95
Acu-points. *See* Acupressure
Acu-yoga 117, 123, 151
Acupressure. *See also* Self-touch; Tapping
  and carpal tunnel syndrome 187
  Conception Vessel-17 128
  and EFT 54–55
  and hypertension 175
  and insomnia 165–166
  Karate Chop Point 54, 70, 211, 233
  meaning of points 70, 212
  and pain 139–140
  and self-soothing 128–130
  Tapas technique 53
  and Tefillin 77
Acupuncture. *See also* Acupressure
  research on 50, 59, 93
Addictions 153–161
Aesclepius 13, 44, 131, 201, 310
  staff of 85–89
Affect modulation 26, 209–212
  and Tai Chi 215–218, 220
  ten-point scale 222
  and trauma 147
Alchemy 107, 270, 293
  alchemical joining 265
Alphabet
  Tai Chi as healing alphabet 80, 300
Alternative Medicine. *See* Complementary and Alternative Medicine
Anchors/Anchoring 32, 61, 299
  and the five elements 233
  hypnotic anchors 76–77
    kinesthetic anchors 77
    Qigong as 79–80, 119–120, 180–182, 248
    songs as anchors 76, 182
Ancient sacred wisdom traditions 75, 76–79, 271, 294, 303
Animal Qigong movements XXXVII, 44, 81, 86, 149, 180, 303
  Animal Frolics 289
  Bear 80, 180, 182
  Crane 249, 288–289, 314
  and psychotherapy 274
  Tiger 180
Anima mundi 251
Anima personalis 251
Anxiety
  and BMHP 121–132
  and meditation 26, 121
  and Qigong 32, 94, 122, 132
  research on 55–56, 121, 134, 314
  and touch 50
Archetypes XXXVI, 79, 271, 293, 316
  archetypal psychology 240–241, 270
  psychoid nature of 88, 299, 303
Arm levitation 41, 100
Arteriosclerosis 27, 98
Arthritis 16, 183–186
Asthma 20, 27
Astrological metaphor 270, 293, 303, 309, 313
Attachment/attachment styles 147, 161, 257
Attention Deficit Hyperactivity Disorder 7–8, 8, 20
Autoimmune disorders 183
Axis mundi 36, 94, 278, 303, 309

B

Back pain/problems 4–5, 10, 16, 100, 142, 166
Bandler & Grinder. *See* Anchors/Anchoring
Bantering 220–223
Behavioral health 21–22
  and BMHP XL, 109, 116, 120, 297–299
  versus medication 179
  and Qigong 118, 133–143, 255–258
Binge eating 159
Bipolar disorder
  and energy medicine 50
Body-oriented therapies 38–46, 75, 88, 219, 312
  and psychoanalysis 42
  and trauma 145–147
Body energy/image dialectic. *See* Image/body energy dialectic
Body language. *See* Gestures
Bodymind
  the term XXXIII
Bodymind Healing Psychotherapy
  contributions to energy psychology 299–300
  contributions to psychotherapy and behavioral health 297–299
  contributions to Qigong/Tai Chi 300
  definition of XXXIII, 105
  and energy psychology 70–71
  outline of 105–120
  principles of

image/body energy dialectic 107–110
Life as a School 217
shape-shifting 110–112
transcending/transmuting dialectic 106–107
transcending methodologies 105
and Qigong 118–120
Ten Psychoenergetic Holographic Dimensions 117–118
Bodymind Healing Psychotherapy practices and techniques. *See also* Mythic Journey Process; River of Life practice
Activating the River of Life through Microcosmic Orbit Breathing 294–296
Circle, stop, and feel method 71
Energy Ball between Your Hands 96–97
Energy Hula-Hoop 137
Experiencing the Light of Qi: Using a Candle 95–96
Full Extension Breathing 95
Insomnia treatment protocol 164–166
Intention and the Direction of Your Qi 97–98
Sacrificial Object Method 157–158
Smoking Addiction treatment protocol 154–160
Yin-Yang Balancing Method 136–137, 139, 149, 187
Bodymind Healing Qigong 81, 109. *See also* Qigong
and hypertension 175
and insomnia 167
practices for activating healing energy 90–102
twenty-minute routine 278–292
Bone density 20
Bottom up theories 146, 320
Breath/Breathing methods. *See also* Elevator; Long-breath; Macrocosmic Orbit; Microcosmic Orbit; Ocean Wave;
reverse breathing 174
Buddha Opens the Heart to the Heavens 167, 176

C

Callahan, Roger 52, 67. *See also* Thought Field Therapy (TFT)
Campbell, Joseph 237
Cancer 195
and imagery 96
Qigong research on 20, 97, 141, 307, 312, 318
research on 16, 27, 50, 94
Cardiovascular problems/disease 16, 38–39
heart replacement surgery 50

Carpal tunnel syndrome XXXVIII–XXXIX, 186–187
Case illustrations
abandonment 241–242
The Absent Father and Karate Chop Point Patient 210–211, 216
affect modulation 209–212
and Tai Chi 216–218
The Art of Bantering 220–223, 224–225
Attacking Your Patients to Heal Them 224–225
binge eating 159
boundary setting 216–217
carpal tunnel syndrome XXXVIII–XL
centering at a court trial 147
chronic pain 133–140
codependence 161
A Critical Perfectionist's Mythic Journey Process 248–252
depression 181–182
The Desperately Grasping Parrot 250–251
Finding the "Right Man" 205–206, 250–252
flying phobia 231–232
hypertension 172, 173–174, 176–177
impulse control 203–204
insomnia 167–168
irritable bowel syndrome 194
lower back surgery 4–5
neediness 241–242
obsessive-compulsive disorder 220–223
panic disorder 123–131
The Passive Aggressive Ostrich 248–249
physical trauma 150–151
The Placating Professor and the Sword Mudra 212–213
Qigong psychosis 197–198
sacrificial object 160
Sexual Abuse and Fist under Elbow 209–210, 216
social phobia 201–202
trauma 244–245
The Wife of the Verbally Adept Salesman 224–225
withdrawal 248–249
writer's block 228–231
Catharsis 86
Chiltan Spirit Posture 129
Chi Nei Tsang (belly massage) 117, 123, 125–126, 165, 194, 256, 315
Chinese medicine 18, 51, 60, 101, 128, 130. *See also* Acupressure
treatment of various conditions 136, 159, 174–176, 186, 190, 311

Index

Chiron
  and chiropractic 86
Chronic diseases 12, 145, 195, 287
Chronic fatigue syndrome 32. *See also* Fibromyalgia
Chronic pain 32, 94, 133–143
  and medication 317
  research on 16, 20, 27, 133–135, 317, 319
  and self-touch. *See also* Self-touch
Chuan Fa 253
  esoteric meaning of Chuan 138, 253
Circle, stop, and feel method 71, 118, 165, 300
Circle that Arises from Stillness 184, 185, 191, 280
Codependence 161
Cognitive psychotherapy 46
  and arthritis 185
  cognitive restructuring 117, 123, 130–131, 146, 166. *See also* Emotional Freedom Technique; Eye Movement Desensitization and Reprocessing
  and depression 181
  and sleep/insomnia 163
Cohesiveness of self 32, 182, 257, 297
Commencement XXXIX, 41, 186
Communication. *See* Constructive communication
Complementary and Alternative Medicine 13–16
Comprehensive energy psychology 51, 52, 68. *See* Energy psychology
Constructive communication 321
  four-step process 211, 233–235, 303
Craig, Gary. *See* Emotional Freedom Technique (EFT)
Crohn's disease 193
Cultivating the Golden Ball 80

D

Daimons 294
Davening 293
Death/Dying 195
Depression 50, 179–182
  and energy medicine 50
  and exercise 179–180
  and medication 179
  and Qigong 32, 180
  research on 59, 179
Depth psychology 300
  definition of 78
  and trauma 149

Devas 294–296
Diabetes 20, 27, 191–192
Dipping Your Hands into the Waters of Life 185, 187, 286–287
Disaster relief
  and energy psychology 57–59
Dispersing Stagnant Qi 191, 278, 282, 283
Dossey, Larry 89
Dreams/Dream work 77–78, 86, 110–112, 131
Drug companies 3, 7, 163, 179, 305
  drug companies 314
Dual relationships XXXVIII, 262–265
Dying. *See* Death/Dying

E

Einsteinian medicine model 47, 51, 310
Elementals 294
Elements
  adept of the elements 272
  of constructive communication 233–235
  five elements 228, 253
  and healing 96, 141, 227–235, 289, 294
  and internal martial arts 233
  of the soul/self 96, 118–119
  and Tai Chi 272
  of touch 63, 187
Elevator breathing 124–125, 148, 315
Emotional Freedom Technique (EFT) 52, 54, 61
  and BMHP 118
  research on 68
Energy XXXIV, 42–43. *See also* Qi
  and healing 84, 89
  and intention 89, 97
  and overall health 74–75
  and psychoanalysis 42
  and symbols 88
Energy Ball between Your Hands 96–97
Energy Hula-Hoop 137
Energy medicine 47–49
  conditions treated by 49
Energy psychology 51–70
  and behavioral healthcare 53
  Callahan, Roger. *See* Thought Field Therapy (TFT)
  use in disaster relief 57–59
  meaning of points 70, 212
  methods 53–55, 60–64, 71
  origins of 52, 67, 74–89
  research on 54, 55–57
    research issues 68–69
  and touch 56

Erickson, Milton 45, 84. *See also* Hypnosis
Ethics of incorporating Qigong and psychotherapy 259–266
Exercise 12, 17
  and arthritis 184
  and depression 179–180
  Qigong as 33, 180
Exercises. *See* Qigong practices; Tai Chi, practices
Experiencing the Light of Qi: Using a Candle 95–96
Eye Movement Desensitization and Reprocessing (EMDR) 31, 37, 61, 117, 123, 146, 255

F

Fairy tales 83–84, 108, 110, 270
Falls amongst the elderly 20, 50, 289
False transcendence 24, 32, 33, 40, 63, 219
Fear response 61, 92, 100, 147, 285
Fibromyalgia 16, 20, 27, 32, 188–191
Fist under Elbow 150, 209, 210, 216
Focusing method 241
  and constructive communication of negative feelings 234
  and brain research 37
  clearing a space 37, 126, 316
  felt sense 322
  and insomnia 166
  and Microcosmic Orbit Breathing 37
  and Mythic Journey Process 240–243, 298
  and pain 142–143
  six-step process 36–37, 126–127
Full Extension Breathing 95

G

Gendlin, Eugene 36–37, 240–242. *See also* Focusing method
Gestures
  patient gestures 208–214
Grasping the Bird's Tail. *See* Ward Off
Greek mythology 22, 83, 107, 110, 254, 293
  Amor and Psyche 78
  Ariadne's thread 241, 251
  Chiron 86
  Heracles and the Hydra 5
  Hermes 240
  Odyssey 78
  Perseus and Medusa 238–239, 271

H

Headaches 16, 192–193
Healer
  healing the healer 277, 281, 299
  wounded healer 269
Healthcare crisis 3–11
  birthing industry 9–10
  corporatization of health 6–11, 304, 305
  drug companies 3–4, 7, 179, 305, 314
  medical errors 3, 305
  unnecessary surgical procedures 4–5, 305
Hillman, James XXXIII, 25, 237
Holding Golden Balls in the Waters of Life 281
Holding the Golden Ball of the Heart 167, 206, 208
Hormonal disorders 27
hormonal disorders 27
Horse Whipping Tail 187
Hypercholesterolemia 27
hypercholesterolemia 27
Hypertension 21, 38, 171–177
  and Qigong 50, 94, 171–173, 174–176, 283
  research on 16, 27, 171–172
Hypnosis 39–44, 270. *See also* Anchors/Anchoring; State-specific state of consciousness; Transpersonal hypnosis
  activity-passivity paradox 42, 256
  ameliorates alarm response 39
  and BMHP 298
  ideomotor signaling 138, 209, 298
  meditation 30
  and Qigong 32, 79–80, 138–139

I

Identification 95
Ideomotor signaling 138, 209, 298
Image/body energy dialectic 88–90, 107–110
Imagery 270. *See also* Imaginal processes
  and shape-shifting 84
  and healing 96
  imaginal realm 85, 213
  and Qigong 81
Imaginal
  defined 85
Imaginal processes 77, 83–85, 88. *See also* Mythic Journey Process; River of Life practice
  and Microcosmic Orbit Breathing 93
Immune system 38–39, 50, 74, 179, 307
  immune response 45
  and Qigong 17, 20, 184, 190

Individuation XXXIV, XXXIX
Insomnia 32, 50, 94, 163–169
  BMHP treatment protocol 164–166
  and BMHQ 167
  rebound insomnia 164, 169
  research on 16, 163–164
Integral psychotherapy approach 30–31, 67, 116, 203, 297
Integrative medicine 13–20
Integrative psychotherapy 116–117
Intentionality
  and energy 89
Intention and the Direction of Your Qi 97–98
Internal martial arts 89, 120, 122, 304
  and five elements 233
  and psychotherapy 208–213, 219–226
  and trauma 148
Irritable bowl syndrome 194
Isomorphism 308

J

Joint problems 32, 187–188, 287, 290
Jung, Carl XXXIV–XXXV, XXXVI, 25, 88, 299, 303

K

Kabbalah XXXVI, 79, 82, 112, 293
  and codependence 161
Karate Chop Point 54, 70, 210–211, 233
Katie, Byron 46
Klein, Melanie
  "depressive position" 206
Klesas 253, 294

L

Language
  astrological 293
  psychological 220
  verbal Tai Chi 220–223
Lascow, Leonard 94
Learned helplessness 182, 184, 186
Levine, Peter 37, 146, 309
Life stance 46, 132, 201–206
  and Tai Chi 225, 248, 300

Lipton, Bruce 145
Long-breath 91, 95, 124, 283
Longevity 20
Lowering the Qi with Heavenly Palms 175–176
Lumen naturae 149, 149–150

M

Macrocosmic Orbit Breathing 94, 135–136
Mandala, healing XXXVIII, 159.
    See Psychotherapeutic mandala
Medicine wheel 35, 140–141
Meditation 24, 27, 29, 32, 83
  and anxiety 26, 121
  benefits and problems 24–27
  effects on pain 319
  physiological benefits 27–28
  psychological benefits 25–27, 29
  psychotherapy and 24–26, 308
  Qigong as 29, 31–33
  research 27–29
  study on advanced meditators 27–28
  styles of 29
Meridian-based therapies 52, 67. *See also* Energy psychology
Metaphors 107, 220, 238, 312. *See also* Symbols/Symbolism
  and healing 41, 79, 126
  and shape-shifting 110–112
  symptoms as 193
Microcosmic Orbit Breathing XXXIX, 37, 135
  healing attributes 92–94
  and Lascow, Leonard 94
  outline of 91–95
  and River of Life practice 91–94, 113, 165
Mind-Body medicine 15–17
Movement disorders 290
Moving a Snake through the Joints 185, 187, 230, 278, 286–287
Multiple personality disorder 45
Muscle testing 53, 64–65
Mystery traditions, Eastern and Western XXVIII, 79, 201, 270, 297
Myth/Mythology 83, 108, 110, 237–242, 270. *See also* Greek mythology
Mythic Journey Process 109, 237–251, 298, 300
  case illustrations 244–251
  identifying your demons 238
  mythic dimension illustrated 243–247
  outline of 242–244

N

Native American 82, 294
  medicine names XXVII
  medicine wheel 35, 140
  shape-shifiting 311
  stories 44
Nature metaphors 111
New biology 145, 228
  nano-antennas 287
Numen 149

O

Object relations 24, 205
Obsessive-compulsive disorder 50, 220–223
Ocean Wave Breathing 139, 285
Opening the Golden Sphere of the Heart 205, 282
Opening the Shoulder Well 230
Opening Your Heart to the Heavens 185, 187, 286–287
Opus contra naturum 270, 273
Osteoarthritis 183, 184

P

Pain. *See* Chronic pain
Panic disorders 121–132. *See also* Anxiety
Paradoxical intention method 229
Parkinson's disease 20, 50, 290, 308
Pelletier, Kenneth 13, 16–17
Personification 244
Phobias 121–132. *See also* Anxiety
  public speaking 130
  research on 55–56, 59
  social phobia 201–202
Posttraumatic stress disorder 145–152. *See also* Trauma
  and energy psychology 57–59
Postural initiation XXXVIII, 33, 80, 206, 253–254, 294
Primordial psychotherapy 130, 160, 206
Primordial Self XXXV, 45, 120, 207–214, 220, 303
  primordial, the term XXXVI
Psoriasis 27
Psyche XXXIII, 51, 75, 78, 106–107, 270
  healing of 111, 116
  and myth 237–240

Psychoanalysis 35, 42–43, 78
Psychobiology 38–39
Psychodrama 44, 86
Psychodynamic psychotherapy
  aspects of BMHP 117–118, 127–128, 232
    and addiction 158
    and depression 181
    and insomnia 166
Psychoid XXXIV, 299, 303
Psychological language 220
Psychology
  origins of XXXIII, 129, 271, 293
Psychoneuroimmunology XXXVII, XL, 38–39, 45
Psychosynthesis 46, 203
Psychotherapeutic mandala 34–36, 269, 271
Psychotherapy
  contributions to Qigong XLIII, 253–255
  dual relationships 262–265
  ethics of incorporating Qigong and psychotherapy 260–266
  exploring resistance 273
  integrated with Qigong XXXVIII–XL, 271–276
  meditation and 24–26
  opus contra naturum 270, 273
  perspective on research of 314
  training 269–271

Q

Qi. *See also* Dispersing Stagnant Qi; Energy
  practices to experience Qi 95–98, 137–138
    Energy Ball between Your Hands 96–97
    Experiencng the Light of Qi: Using a Candle 95–96
    Intention and the Direction of Your Qi 97–98
  primordial Qi XXXVI
  research on 307, 311
  sinking the Qi 92, 148
Qigong. *See also* Animal Qigong Movements; Bodymind Healing Qigong; Standing Meditation; Tai Chi; Yi Chuan Qigong
  and anxiety 122, 132
  and behavioral health 118, 133–143, 255–258
  and BMHP 118–120, 297–299
  BMHQ twenty-minute routine 278–292
  and cancer research 97, 141, 307, 312, 318
  and carpal tunnel syndrome XXXVIII–XXXIX, 186–187
  and chronic pain 32, 133–143
  and codependence 161
  definition of XXXVII, 17, 81, 300, 306

Index

as exercise 20, 33, 180
healing benefits XXXVII, 31–34, 307–308
history of 18
and hypertension 171–173, 174–176
and hypnosis 32–33, 40, 79–80
as a form of meditation 29, 31–33
origins of 41, 306
and psychotherapy 253–258
  contributions to psychotherapy XLIII, 255–258
  ethics 259–266
  integrated with psychotherapy XXXVIII–XL, 31–34, 264–266, 271–276
research on 307–308, 324
  Laogong points 319
research on conditions treated 18–19, 50
and shape-shifting 80, 119, 272
soul-oriented 118–119, 300
static postures 33, 81, 95–97
and tapping 63–64
teachers XXIX, 323
and touch XXXVII, 63–64
and trauma 31–32
types of 18
Qigong practices. *See also* Microcosmic Orbit Breathing
  Buddha Opens the Heart to the Heavens 167
  Circle that Arises from Stillness 184, 185, 191, 280
  Crane Walking and Flying 288–289
  to cultivate Qi 137–138
  Cultivating the Golden Ball 80
  Dipping Your Hands into the Waters of Life 185, 187, 286–287
  Dispersing Stagnant Qi 191, 278, 282–283
  Energy Ball between Your Hands 96–97
  Energy Hula-Hoop 137
  Fist under Elbow 150, 209, 210, 216
  Holding Golden Balls in the Waters of Life 281
  Holding the Golden Ball of the Heart 167, 206
  Horse Whipping Tail 187
  Light of Qi 95–96
  Lowering the Qi with Heavenly Palms 175–176
  Moving a Snake through the Joints 185, 187, 230, 278, 286–287
  Ocean Wave Breathing 285
  Opening the Golden Sphere of the Heart 205, 282
  Opening the Shoulder Well 230
  Opening Your Heart to the Heavens 185, 187, 286–287
  Raising and Lowering the Qi XXXIX, 186
  Raising Qi to Heavens & Returning it to Earth 167
  Standing like a Tree 40, 80, 81, 132, 279
  to experience Qi 95–98
  Wild Goose Says Hello and Goodbye 282
  Yin-Yang Balancing Method 136–137, 187
Qigong psychosis 197–198
Qigong Walking
  and diabetes 191–192

R

Raising and Lowering the Qi XXXIX, 186
Raising Qi to Heavens & Returning it to Earth 167
Raynaud's syndrome 39, 193
Reciprocal inhibition 32, 61
  and Tai Chi 148
Reductionism 30, 74
Reframing 126
Relaxation methods 15–16
  meditation 25, 30
  Qigong 32
  use in psychotherapy 33
Relaxation response 38–39, 45, 255
River of Life practice 150–151, 299
  Activating the River of Life through Microcosmic Orbit Breathing 294–296
  and carpal tunnel syndrome 187
  and impulse control 203
  and insomnia 165, 166
  outline of the practice 112–113
  and smoking addictions 154–157
Roll Back 273
Rosetta stone
  Tai Chi as 80, 298
Rossi, Ernest 42, 68, 138, 310

S

Sacrificial Object Method 157–158
  sacrifice as tool for healing 160
Sapolsky, Robert 145
Schore, Allan 23
Self
  the term XXXIV–XXXV, 303
Self-care
  for the healer 277
Self-healing
  the term XXXIV

Self-soothing 117, 123, 128–130, 155, 165, 233, 255, 261, 273
  BMHP method 131, 159, 190
Self-touch. *See also* Acupressure; Circle, stop, and feel method; Touch
  aspects of BMHP 118, 128–130, 300
  and insomnia 165–166
Self psychology 43
Shamanism XL, 44, 75, 79, 85, 86, 96, 242, 289, 311
Shape-Shifting XL, 44–46, 46, 84–87, 98, 110–112, 201–206, 250, 294, 298, 311
  and cognitive psychotherapy 46
  and hypnosis 44–46
  and psychosynthesis 46
  and Qigong 80, 119, 272
Shingles
  and Tai Chi 20, 308
Sitting Meditation 138
Sleep disorders. *See* Insomnia
Smoking addiction
  BMHP treatment protocol 153–159
Somatic therapies. *See* Body-oriented therapies
Somatization (disorders) 39, 183, 189, 190, 193, 194, 217
Songs
  as hypnotic anchors 76, 182
  and healing 293
Soul XXXIII. *See also* Psyche
  distinguished from spirit 25
  and Qigong 118–120
Soul retrieval 96
Spirit versus soul 25
Splitting 206, 263
Standing like a Tree 40, 80, 81, 132, 279
Standing Meditation (Qigong) 80, 81, 132, 138, 279
  and hypertension 175
  research on brain coherence 324
State-dependent state of consciousness. *See* State-specific state of consciousness
State-specific state of consciousness 31, 45, 46, 76, 298, 310. *See also* Transpersonal state-specific state of consciousness
  and healing 98
Static Qigong postures 33, 81, 95–97
Stomach disorders 193–194
Storytelling 78, 82–85, 108
  and shape-shifting 84
Stress
  and healing 38–40, 50, 283

and autoimmune disorders 183
  research on 145–148
Strokes 6, 19, 20, 172
Subpersonalities 46, 126–127, 148, 298
Sung 31, 42, 147, 281
  and hypertension 175
Symbolic process traditions 78–79, 300, 303. *See also* Imaginal processes
  four dimensions 107–108
  training in 270–271
  used in BMHP's full-spectrum approach 108–110, 112, 298
Symbols/Symbolism 112. *See also* Imagery; Metaphors
  definition of symbol 109, 238
  and energy 88
Sympathetic nervous system overload 92, 146, 189, 258, 285. *See also* Fear response; Stress
Systematic desensitization 124, 148

T

Tai Chi. *See also* Qigong
  and affect modulation 215–218
  and arthritis 183–186
  as language/verbal Tai Chi 220–223, 274, 300
  practices
    Commencement XXXIX, 41, 186
    Roll Back 273
    Tai Chi Push Hands 149, 162, 202, 220, 223, 271–273
    Ward Off 215–218
  as rosetta stone 80, 298
Tai Chi Push Hands 149, 162, 202, 220, 223, 271–273
Tai Chi Ruler (Qigong) 99–100, 139, 147, 167, 184, 194, 230, 284–285
Taoist techniques/traditions 312. *See also* Chi Nei Tsang (belly massage)
  alchemical breathing method. *See* Microcosmic Orbit Breathing
  for cultivating Qi 137–138
  for relaxation 124–126
  Tao of re-parenting 128–130
  Yin-Yang Balancing Method 136–137
Tapas acupressure technique 53
Tapping 53, 59, 60–63, 117, 214, 311
Teaching stories
  Rabbi in the Woods 274
  The Shaman and the Shattered Crystal Ball 23
  Shape-shifting in the Cave of Life 44

The Stream and the Sands 73–74
The Taoist Initiate Who Sees the Sacred in Every-
     day Movements 207–208
Tefillin 77
Thought Field Therapy (TFT) 52, 60
Touch. *See also* Self-touch
  and cognitive restructuring 130
  elements of touch 63, 187
  and energy psychology 56, 71
  and healing 49, 98, 232
  and Qigong XXXVII, 63–64
Trance states 40, 82, 90, 306, 312. *See also* State-
     specific states, Transpersonal state-specific
     states of consciousness
  activation of 70, 94, 99, 135, 138–139, 299
Transcendent function 206
Transcending/transmuting dialectic XLI, 20,
     106–107, 299
  and River of Life practice 112–113
Transpersonal
  the term 298, 313
Transpersonal hypnosis 108, 109, 227–235, 228,
     231, 299. *See also* Hypnosis
Transpersonal psychology XL, 83, 227–228
  definition of 269
Transpersonal state-specific state of consciousness
     79–80, 298. *See also* State-specific state of
     consciousness
Trauma 145–152, 285, 309. *See also* Posttraumatic
     stress disorder
  and the body 145–147
  and EMDR 37, 146
  and Tai Chi Push Hands 149
Tsimtsum 161
Twelve Step programs 161

V

van der Kolk, Bessel 23–24, 145–147, 219
Vital, primordial Self. *See* Primordial Self

W

Walking Meditation Qigong 289–290
Walsh, Roger 30
Ward Off 215–218
  psychological meaning of 217

Western Medicine 12–13
Wild Goose Says Hello and Goodbye 282
Withdrawal 248
Wound healing 50, 317
Wuji Standing Meditation 185, 280, 291. *See*
     also Standing Meditation
  myth of the eternal return 291
Wuji state 35, 75, 97
  definition of 71

Y

Yi Chuan Qigong 42, 63, 89, 98, 137–138, 149,
     167, 192, 208, 253, 257, 278, 281, 290, 318
Yin-Yang Balancing Method 136–137, 187
  and touch 139
Yoga 29

Z

Zhan Zhuang. *See* Standing Meditation (Qigong)

Other Books, Articles, and Media Publications
by Michael Mayer

Secrets to Living Younger Longer:
The Self-Healing Path of Qigong, Standing Meditation and Tai Chi,
Bodymind Healing Publications, Orinda, CA, 2004.

Trials of the Heart: Healing the Wounds of Intimacy,
Celestial Arts, 1994.

The Mystery of Personal Identity
ACS, 1985.

Qigong Clinical Research,
Ed: Dr. Wayne Jonas, *Healing Intention and Energy Medicine,*
Elsevier Science Limited, U.K., 2003 (Peer reviewed).

Qigong and Hypertension: A Critique of Research,
Journal of Alternative and Complementary Medicine, Vol. 5 (4),
Aug., 1999 (Peer reviewed).

Qigong and Behavioral Medicine: An Integrated Approach to Chronic Pain,
Qi Magazine, Winter, 1997.

Psychotherapy and Qigong: Partners in Healing Anxiety,
The Psychotherapy & Healing Center, 1997.

The River of Life: A Guided Meditation for Bodymind Healing,
Bodymind Healing Publications, 2007.

Bodymind Healing Qigong, DVD (1 hour),
Bodymind Healing Center, 2004.

Find your Hidden Reservoir of Healing Energy:
A Guided Meditation for Cancer,
Audio Tape, 2002.

Find your Hidden Reservoir of Healing Energy:
A Guided Meditation for Chronic Disease,
Audio Tape, 2002.

Special Offer for Accompanying Products and Services
of The Tao of Bodymind Healing Series

Secrets to Living Younger Longer:
The Self-Healing Path of Qigong, Standing Meditation and Tai Chi

Benefit from learning health and longevity practices that Dr. Mayer synthesized from 30 years of training with some of the most respected Tai Chi and Qigong masters. You'll find here a unique blend: Qigong, Western psychological methods, and cross-cultural anthropological research. Discover how Qigong, Tai Chi, and Standing Meditation have roots in Shamanism and a lost, integrative Self-healing lineage. Dr. Wayne Jonas, Former Director, National Institute of Health, Office of Alternative Medicine says, *A wonderful guide for learning the ancient healing practices of Qigong. Full of clear and practical exercises.*

Bodymind Healing Qigong DVD (60 minutes)

Become initiated into the core Qigong and Tai Chi Chuan methods that Dr. Mayer learned from 30 years training with some of the most respected masters of these traditions. After 25 years of teaching, he synthesized this knowledge into a single form. Learn practices for: simultaneously relaxing and energizing your body; balancing energies of your internal organs, computer tension in the shoulders, activating your immune system, increasing balance, limbering joints, and more. Dr. Van der Kolk, Medical Director, Trauma Center, Boston University Medical School says, *I liked your Bodymind Healing Qigong DVD so much that in the course I taught we started with two or three sections of it every day.*

The River of Life:
A Guided Meditation for Bodymind Healing (30 minutes)

Originally published as an audiotape for Cancer and Chronic Diseases, many of Doctor Mayer's patients now use this CD to help the healing process for insomnia, hypertension, and general stress reduction. As discussed in the book Bodymind Healing Psychotherapy, the CD is an enhancement to this core method of BMHP practice. It is used in hospitals, and by mental health professionals and body workers to complement treatment.

See next page for a Triple Offer Coupon

This Triple-Offer Coupon Entitles the Bearer to:

- ❖ **DISCOUNTED PRODUCTS:** One copy of *Secrets to Living Younger Longer,* (usually $24.95), one copy of *Bodymind Healing Qigong DVD* (usually $24.95) and one copy of *The River of Life CD* (usually $14.95) for a total $ 55 (plus free shipping). And for a limited amount of time while they last I may also request to receive a free copy of one of the Audio Tapes, *Find Your Hidden Reservoir of Healing Energy: A Guided Meditation for Cancer* or for *Chronic Disease.*

- ❖ **FREE CONSULTATION:** For a limited time, with purchase of the above three products I can have a free 15 minute consultation (if long distance, I just pay the phone charges) about how the exercises in the *Secrets to Living Younger Longer* book, *The River of Life CD,* and the *Bodymind Healing Qigong DVD* can be tailored to my individual needs.

- ❖ **DISCOUNTED COACHING:** Discount on first session of Bodymind Health Coaching: For a limited time, after the free 15 minute, consultation mentioned above, I will receive a 50% discount on my first session of Bodymind Health Coaching. For more information on Bodymind Health Coaching see www.bodymindhealing.com.

Name: _____

Address: _____

Phone: _____

E-mail Address: _____

** **Please note:** Michael Mayer, Ph.D. is not a medical doctor and therefore any advice about Self-healing exercises is not medical advice, nor is it a substitute for your medical doctor's care.

Please make check out to Michael Mayer, Ph.D.
Send it to the following address:
Bodymind Healing Center
2029 Durant Ave.
Berkeley, CA 94704
510-849-2878,
or contact Dr. Mayer through his e-mail address: drmichael@bodymindhealing.com.
website: www.bodymindhealing.com

Michael Mayer, Ph.D., is a licensed psychologist, hypnotherapist, and Qigong/Tai Chi teacher who specializes in giving his patients self-healing methods for health problems. Dr. Mayer presents his approach to bodymind healing at professional conferences, national/international workshops, universities, and hospitals; and he is a keynote speaker. He was a co-founder of, and a practitioner at, The Health Medicine Institute, a multi-disciplinary medical clinic practicing integrative health-care. Dr. Mayer pioneered the integration of Qigong and psychotherapy, and was the first person in the United States to train doctoral psychology students in these methods. The World Institute for Self-Healing gave him an award for outstanding research and contribution to the advancement of mind-body medicine. He is the author of ten publications on bodymind healing including four books, audiotapes on cancer and chronic disease, and articles on chronic pain and anxiety. His peer reviewed article on Qigong and hypertension appeared in *The Journal of Alternative and Complementary Medicine*, and is updated in the book *Healing, Intention and Energy Medicine*, by Dr Wayne Jonas, past director of the National Institute of Health, Office of Alternative Medicine. Dr. Mayer has served as a peer reviewer for *The Journal of Alternative and Complementary Medicine, Complementary Therapies in Medicine,* and *Annals of Internal Medicine.* His Bodymind Healing Qigong DVD is currently being used in training of trauma therapists by Dr. Bessel van der Kolk, Medical Director, The Trauma Center, Boston University School of Medicine. Dr. Mayer's certification programs include Bodymind Healing Qigong for Qigong practitioners/teachers, and a Bodymind Health Practitioner's Certification Program for health professionals.